Algorithms on Strings

This book is intended for lectures on string processing and pattern matching in master's courses of computer science and software engineering curricula. The details of algorithms are given with correctness proofs and complexity analysis, which make them ready to implement. Algorithms are described in a C-like language.

This book is also a reference for students in computational linguistics or computational biology. It presents examples of questions related to the automatic processing of natural language, to the analysis of molecular sequences, and to the management of textual databases.

Professor MAXIME CROCHEMORE received his PhD in 1978 and his Doctorat d'état in 1983 from the University of Rouen. He was involved in the creation of the University of Marne-la-Vallée, where he is currently a professor. He also created the Computer Science Research Laboratory of this university in 1991. Professor Crochemore has been a senior research fellow at King's College London since 2002.

CHRISTOPHE HANCART received his PhD in Computer Science from the University Paris 7 in 1993. He is now an assistant professor in the Department of Computer Science at the University of Rouen.

THIERRY LECROQ received his PhD in Computer Science from the University of Orléans in 1992. He is now a professor in the Department of Computer Science at the University of Rouen.

Algorithms on Strings

MAXIME CROCHEMORE
Université de Marne-la-Vallée

CHRISTOPHE HANCART
Université de Rouen

THIERRY LECROQ
Université de Rouen

CAMBRIDGE UNIVERSITY PRESS
Cambridge, New York, Melbourne, Madrid, Cape Town, Singapore,
São Paulo, Delhi, Dubai, Tokyo, Mexico City

Cambridge University Press
32 Avenue of the Americas, New York, NY 10013-2473, USA

www.cambridge.org
Information on this title: www.cambridge.org/9780521848992

Originally published in French as
Algorithmique du texte by Maxime Crochemore, Christophe Hancart, Thierry Lecroq

English edition (a translation from the French-language edition) first published by Cambridge University Press

First published in this edition 2007
Reprinted 2009

A catalog record for this publication is available from the British Library

Library of Congress Cataloging in Publication data

Crochemore, Maxime, 1947–
Algorithms on strings / Maxime Crochemore, Christophe Hancart, Thierry Lecroq.
p. cm.
Includes bibliographical references and index.
ISBN-13: 978-0-521-84899-2 (hardback)
ISBN-10: 0-521-84899-7 (hbk.)
1. Computer algorithms. 2. Matching theory. 3. Computational biology.
I. Hancart, Christophe, 1964– II. Lecroq, Thierry. III. Title.
QA76.9.A43C757 2007
005.1–dc22 2006039263

ISBN 978-0-521-84899-2 Hardback

Contents

Preface

This book presents a broad panorama of the algorithmic methods used for processing texts. For this reason it is a book on algorithms, but whose object is focused on the handling of texts by computers. The idea of this publication results from the observation that the rare books entirely devoted to the subject are primarily monographs of research. This is surprising because the problems of the field have been known since the development of advanced operating systems, and the need for effective solutions becomes essential because the massive use of data processing in office automation is crucial in many sectors of the society. In 1985, Galil pointed out several unsolved questions in the field, called after him, Stringology (see [12]). Most of them are still open.

In a written or vocal form, text is the only reliable vehicle of abstract concepts. Therefore, it remains the privileged support of information systems, despite of significant efforts toward the use of other media (graphic interfaces, systems of virtual reality, synthesis movies, etc.). This aspect is still reinforced by the use of knowledge databases, legal, commercial, or others, which develop on the Internet. Thanks, in particular, to the Web services.

The contents of the book carry over into formal elements and technical bases required in the fields of information retrieval, of automatic indexing for search engines, and more generally of software systems, which includes the edition, the treatment, and the compression of texts. The methods that are described apply to the automatic processing of natural languages, to the treatment and analysis of genomic sequences, to the analysis of musical sequences, to problems of safety and security related to data flows, and to the management of the textual databases, to quote only some immediate applications.

The selected subjects address pattern matching, the indexing of textual data, the comparison of texts by alignment, and the search for local regularities. In addition to their practical interest, these subjects have theoretical and combinatorial aspects that provide astonishing examples of algorithmic solutions.

The goal of this work is principally educational. It is initially aimed at graduate and undergraduate students, but it can also be used by software designers.

We warmly thank the researchers who took time to read and comment on the preliminary outlines of this book. They are Saïd Abdeddaïm, Marie-Pierre Béal, Christian Charras, Raphaël Clifford, Christiane Frougny, Gregory Kucherov, Sabine Mercier, Laurent Mouchard, Johann Pelfrêne, Bruno Petazzoni, Mathieu Raffinot, Giuseppina Rindone, and Marie-France Sagot. Remaining flaws are ours.

Finally, extra elements to the contents of the book are accessible on the site `http://chl.univ-mlv.fr` or from the Web pages of the authors.

Maxime Crochemore
Christophe Hancart
Thierry Lecroq
Marne-la-Vallée, London, Rouen
June 2006

1

Tools

This chapter presents the algorithmic and combinatorial framework in which are developed the following chapters. It first specifies the concepts and notation used to work on strings, languages, and automata. The rest is mainly devoted to the introduction of chosen data structures for implementing automata, to the presentation of combinatorial results, and to the design of elementary pattern matching techniques. This organization is based on the observation that efficient algorithms for text processing rely on one or the other of these aspects.

Section 1.2 provides some combinatorial properties of strings that occur in numerous correctness proofs of algorithms or in their performance evaluation. They are mainly periodicity results.

The formalism for the description of algorithms is presented in Section 1.3, which is especially centered on the type of algorithm presented in the book, and introduces some standard objects related to queues and automata processing.

Section 1.4 details several methods to implement automata in memory, these techniques contribute, in particular, to results of Chapters 2, 5, and 6.

The first algorithms for locating strings in texts are presented in Section 1.5. The sliding window mechanism, the notions of search automaton and of bit vectors that are described in this section are also used and improved in Chapters 2, 3, and 8, in particular.

Section 1.6 is the algorithmic jewel of the chapter. It presents two fundamental algorithmic methods used for text processing. They are used to compute the border table and the prefix table of a string that constitute two essential tables for string processing. They synthesize a part of the combinatorial properties of a string. Their utilization and adaptation is considered in Chapters 2 and 3, and also punctually come back in other chapters.

Finally, we can note that intuition for combinatorial properties or algorithms sometimes relies on figures whose style is introduced in this chapter and kept thereafter.

1.1 Strings and automata

In this section, we introduce notation on strings, languages, and automata.

Alphabet and strings

An ***alphabet*** is a finite nonempty set whose elements are called ***letters***. A ***string*** on an alphabet A is a finite sequence of elements of A. The zero letter sequence is called the ***empty string*** and is denoted by ε. For the sake of simplification, delimiters, and separators usually employed in sequence notation are removed and a string is written as the simple juxtaposition of the letters that compose it. Thus, ε, a, b, and baba are strings on any alphabet that contains the two letters a and b. The set of all the strings on the alphabet A is denoted by A^*, and the set of all the strings on the alphabet A except the empty string ε is denoted by A^+.

The ***length*** of a string x is defined as the length of the sequence associated with the string x and is denoted by $|x|$. We denote by $x[i]$, for $i = 0, 1, \ldots, |x| - 1$, the letter at index i of x with the convention that indices begin with 0. When $x \neq \varepsilon$, we say more specifically that each index $i = 0, 1, \ldots, |x| - 1$ is a ***position* on** x. It follows that the ith letter of x is the letter at position $i - 1$ on x and that:

$$x = x[0]x[1]\ldots x[|x| - 1].$$

Thus an elementary definition of the identity between any two strings x and y is:

$$x = y$$

if and only if

$$|x| = |y| \text{ and } x[i] = y[i] \text{ for } i = 0, 1, \ldots, |x| - 1.$$

The set of letters that occur in the string x is denoted by $\text{alph}(x)$. For instance, if $x = \texttt{abaaab}$, we have $|x| = 6$ and $\text{alph}(x) = \{\texttt{a}, \texttt{b}\}$.

The ***product*** – we also say the ***concatenation*** – of two strings x and y is the string composed of the letters of x followed by the letters of y. It is denoted by xy or also $x \cdot y$ to show the decomposition of the resulting string. The neutral element for the product is ε. For every string x and every natural number n, we define the nth ***power*** of the string x, denoted by x^n, by $x^0 = \varepsilon$ and $x^k = x^{k-1}x$ for $k = 1, 2, \ldots, n$. We denote respectively by zy^{-1} and $x^{-1}z$ the strings x and y when $z = xy$. The ***reverse*** – or ***mirror image*** – of the string x is the string $x^\sim$ defined by:

$$x^\sim = x[|x| - 1]x[|x| - 2]\ldots x[0].$$

b	a	b	a	a	b	a	b	a

Figure 1.1. An occurrence of string aba in string babaababa at (left) position 1.

A string x is a ***factor*** of a string y if there exist two strings u and v such that $y = uxv$. When $u = \varepsilon$, x is a ***prefix*** of y; and when $v = \varepsilon$, x is a ***suffix*** of y. The string x is a ***subsequence***[1] of y if there exist $|x| + 1$ strings $w_0, w_1, \ldots, w_{|x|}$ such that $y = w_0x[0]w_1x[1]\ldots x[|x| - 1]w_{|x|}$; in a less formal way, x is a string obtained from y by deleting $|y| - |x|$ letters. A factor or a subsequence x of a string y is ***proper*** if $x \neq y$. We denote respectively by $x \preceq_{\text{fact}} y$, $x \prec_{\text{fact}} y$, $x \preceq_{\text{pref}} y$, $x \prec_{\text{pref}} y$, $x \preceq_{\text{suff}} y$, $x \prec_{\text{suff}} y$, $x \preceq_{\text{sseq}} y$, and $x \prec_{\text{sseq}} y$ when x is a factor, a proper factor, a prefix, a proper prefix, a suffix, a proper suffix, a subsequence, and a proper subsequence of y. One can verify that $\preceq_{\text{fact}}$, $\preceq_{\text{pref}}$, $\preceq_{\text{suff}}$, and $\preceq_{\text{sseq}}$ are orderings on A^*.

The ***lexicographic ordering***, denoted by $\leq$, is an ordering on strings induced by an ordering on the letters and denoted by the same symbol. It is defined as follows. For $x, y \in A^*$, $x \leq y$ if and only if, either $x \preceq_{\text{pref}} y$, or x and y can be decomposed as $x = uav$ and $y = ubw$ with $u, v, w \in A^*$, $a, b \in A$, and $a < b$. Thus, ababb < abba < abbaab assuming a < b.

Let x be a nonempty string and y be a string, we say that there is an ***occurrence*** of x in y, or, more simply, that x ***occurs* in** y, when x is a factor of y. Every occurrence, or every appearance, of x can be characterized by a position on y. Thus we say that an occurrence of x ***starts*** at the ***left position*** i on y when $y[i\,..\,i + |x| - 1] = x$ (see Figure 1.1). It is sometimes more suitable to consider the ***right position*** $i + |x| - 1$ at which this occurrence ***ends***. For instance, the left and right positions where the string $x =$ aba occurs in the string $y =$ babaababa are:

i	0	1	2	3	4	5	6	7	8
$y[i]$	b	a	b	a	a	b	a	b	a
left positions		1			4		6		
right positions				3			6		8

The ***position of the first occurrence*** $pos(x)$ of x in y is the minimal (left) position at which starts the occurrence of x in yA^*. With the notation on the languages recalled thereafter, we have:

$$pos(x) = \min\{|u| : uxA^* \cap yA^* \neq \emptyset\}.$$

[1] We avoid the common use of "subword" because it has two definitions in literature: one of them is factor and the other one is subsequence.

The square bracket notation for the letters of strings is extended to factors. We define the factor $x[i\,..\,j]$ of the string x by:

$$x[i\,..\,j] = x[i]x[i+1]\dots x[j]$$

for all integers i and j satisfying $0 \le i \le |x|, -1 \le j \le |x|-1$, and $i \le j+1$. When $i = j+1$, the string $x[i\,..\,j]$ is the empty string.

Languages

Any subset of A^* is a ***language*** on the alphabet A. The product defined on strings is extended to languages as follows:

$$XY = X \cdot Y = \{xy : (x, y) \in X \times Y\}$$

for every languages X and Y. We extend as well the notion of power as follows $X^0 = \{\varepsilon\}$ and $X^k = X^{k-1}X$ for $k \ge 1$. The ***star*** of X is the language:

$$X^* = \bigcup_{n \ge 0} X^n.$$

We denote by X^+ the language defined by

$$X^+ = \bigcup_{n \ge 1} X^n.$$

Note that these two latter notation are compatible with the notation A^* and A^+. In order not to overload the notation, a language that is reduced to a single string can be named by the string itself if it does not lead to any confusion. For instance, the expression A^*abaaab denotes the language of the strings in A^* having the string abaaab as suffix, assuming $\{\mathtt{a}, \mathtt{b}\} \subseteq A$.

The notion of length is extended to languages as follows:

$$|X| = \sum_{x \in X} |x|.$$

In the same way, we define alph(X) by

$$\text{alph}(X) = \bigcup_{x \in X} \text{alph}(x)$$

and $X^{\sim}$ by

$$X^{\sim} = \{x^{\sim} : x \in X\}.$$

The sets of factors, prefixes, suffixes, and subsequences of the strings of a language X are particular languages that are often considered in the rest of the book; they are respectively denoted by Fact(X), Pref(X), Suff(X), and Subs(X).

The ***right context*** of a string y relatively to a language X is the language:

$$y^{-1}X = \{y^{-1}x : x \in X\}.$$

The equivalence relation defined by the identity of right contexts is denoted by $\equiv_X$, or simply[2] $\equiv$. Thus

$$y \equiv z \text{ if and only if } y^{-1}X = z^{-1}X$$

for $y, z \in A^*$. For instance, when $A = \{\texttt{a}, \texttt{b}\}$ and $X = A^*\{\texttt{aba}\}$, the relation $\equiv$ admits four equivalence classes: $\{\varepsilon, \texttt{b}\} \cup A^*\{\texttt{bb}\}$, $\{\texttt{a}\} \cup A^*\{\texttt{aa}, \texttt{bba}\}$, $A^*\{\texttt{ab}\}$, and $A^*\{\texttt{aba}\}$. For every language X, the relation $\equiv$ is an equivalence relation that is compatible with the concatenation. It is called the ***right syntactic congruence*** associated with X.

Regular expressions and languages

The ***regular expressions*** on an alphabet A and the languages they describe, the ***regular languages***, are recursively defined as follows:

- $\texttt{0}$ and $\texttt{1}$ are regular expressions that respectively describe $\emptyset$ (the empty set) and $\{\varepsilon\}$,
- for every letter $a \in A$, $\boldsymbol{a}$ is a regular expression that describes the singleton $\{a\}$,
- if $\boldsymbol{x}$ and $\boldsymbol{y}$ are regular expressions respectively describing the regular languages X and Y, then $(\boldsymbol{x})\texttt{+}(\boldsymbol{y})$, $(\boldsymbol{x})\cdot(\boldsymbol{y})$, and $(\boldsymbol{x})\texttt{*}$ are regular expressions that respectively describe the regular languages $X \cup Y$, $X \cdot Y$, and X^*.

The priority order of operations on the regular expressions is $\texttt{*}$, $\cdot$, then $\texttt{+}$. Possible writing simplifications allow one to omit the symbol $\cdot$ and some parentheses pairs. The language described by a regular expression $\boldsymbol{x}$ is denoted by $\text{Lang}(\boldsymbol{x})$.

Automata

An ***automaton*** M on the alphabet A is composed of a finite set Q of ***states***, of an ***initial*** state[3] q_0, of a set $T \subseteq Q$ of ***terminal*** states, and of a set $F \subseteq Q \times A \times Q$

[2] As in all the rest of the book, the notation is indexed by the object to which they refer only when it could be ambiguous.

[3] The standard definition of automata considers a set of initial states rather than a single initial state as we do in the entire book. We leave the reader to convince himself that it is possible to build a correspondence between any automaton defined in the standard way and an automaton with a single initial state that recognizes the same language.

of ***arcs*** – or ***transitions***. We denote the automaton M by the quadruplet:

$$(Q, q_0, T, F).$$

We say of an arc (p, a, q) that it leaves the state p and that it enters the state q; state p is the ***source*** of the arc, letter a its ***label***, and state q its ***target***. The number of arcs outgoing a given state is called the ***outgoing degree*** of the state. The ***incoming degree*** of a state is defined in a dual way. By analogy with graphs, the state q is a ***successor*** by the letter a of the state p when $(p, a, q) \in F$; in the same case, we say that the pair (a, q) is a ***labeled successor*** of the state p.

A ***path*** of length n in the automaton $M = (Q, q_0, T, F)$ is a sequence of n consecutive arcs

$$\langle (p_0, a_0, p'_0), (p_1, a_1, p'_1), \ldots, (p_{n-1}, a_{n-1}, p'_{n-1}) \rangle,$$

that satisfies

$$p'_k = p_{k+1}$$

for $k = 0, 1, \ldots, n-2$. The ***label*** of the path is the string $a_0 a_1 \ldots a_{n-1}$, its ***origin*** the state p_0, its ***end*** the state p'_{n-1}. By convention, there exists for each state p a path of null length of origin and of end p; the label of such a path is ε, the empty string. A path in the automaton M is ***successful*** if its origin is the initial state q_0 and if its end is in T. A string is ***recognized*** – or ***accepted*** – by the automaton if it is the label of a successful path. The language composed of the strings recognized by the automaton M is denoted by $\text{Lang}(M)$.

Often, more than its formal notation, a diagram illustrates how an automaton works. We represent the states by circles and the arcs by directed arrows from source to target, labeled by the corresponding letter. When several arcs have the same source and the same target, we merge the arcs and the label of the resulting arc becomes an enumeration of the letters. The initial state is distinguished by a short incoming arrow and the terminal states are double circled. An example is shown in Figure 1.2.

A state p of an automaton $M = (Q, q_0, T, F)$ is ***accessible*** if there exists a path in M starting at q_0 and ending in p. A state p is ***co-accessible*** if there exists a path in M starting at p and ending in T.

An automaton $M = (Q, q_0, T, F)$ is ***deterministic*** if for every pair $(p, a) \in Q \times A$ there exists at most one state $q \in Q$ such that $(p, a, q) \in F$. In such a case, it is natural to consider the ***transition function***

$$\delta \colon Q \times A \to Q$$

of the automaton defined for every arc $(p, a, q) \in F$ by

$$\delta(p, a) = q$$

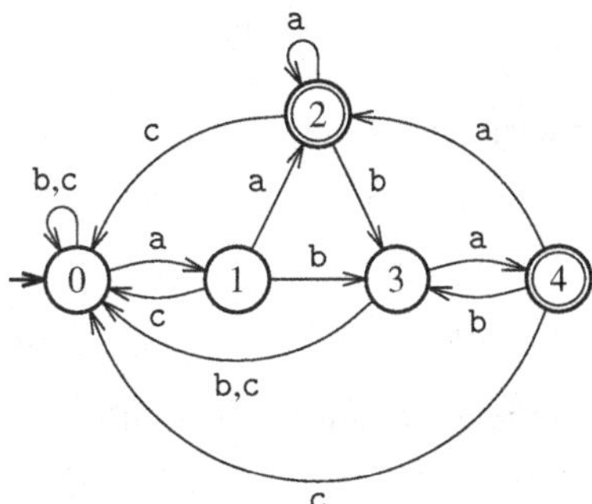

Figure 1.2. Representation of an automaton on the alphabet $A = \{\mathtt{a}, \mathtt{b}, \mathtt{c}\}$. The states of the automaton are numbered from 0 to 4, its initial state is 0, and its terminal states are 2 and 4. The automaton possesses $3 \times 5 = 15$ arcs. The language that it recognizes is described by the regular expression `(a+b+c)*(aa+aba)`, that is, the set of strings on the three letter alphabet `a`, `b`, and `c` ending by `aa` or `aba`.

and not defined elsewhere. The function δ is easily extended to strings. It is enough to consider its extension $\bar{\delta}: Q \times A^* \to Q$ recursively defined by $\bar{\delta}(p, \varepsilon) = p$ and $\bar{\delta}(p, wa) = \delta(\bar{\delta}(p, w), a)$ for $p \in Q$, $w \in A^*$, and $a \in A$. It follows that the string w is recognized by the automaton M if and only if $\bar{\delta}(q_0, w) \in T$. Generally, the function δ and its extension $\bar{\delta}$ are denoted in the same way.

The automaton $M = (Q, q_0, T, F)$ is ***complete*** when for every pair $(p, a) \in Q \times A$ there exists at least one state $q \in Q$ such that $(p, a, q) \in F$.

Proposition 1.1

For every automaton, there exists a deterministic and complete automaton that recognizes the same language. ■

To complete an automaton is not difficult: it is enough to add to the automaton a ***sink*** state, then to make it the target of all undefined transitions. It is a bit more difficult to ***determinize*** an automaton, that is, to transform an automaton $M = (Q, q_0, T, F)$ into a deterministic automaton recognizing the same language. One can use the so-called method of ***construction by subsets***: let M' be the automaton whose states are the subsets of Q, the initial state is the singleton $\{q_0\}$, the terminal states are the subsets of Q that intersect T, and the arcs are the triplets (U, a, V) where V is the set of successors by the letter a of the states p belonging to U; then M' is a deterministic automaton that recognizes the same language as M. In practical applications, we do not construct the automaton M' entirely, but only its accessible part from the initial state $\{q_0\}$.

A language X is ***recognizable*** if there exists an automaton M such that $X = \text{Lang}(M)$. The statement of a fundamental theorem of automata theory that establishes the link between recognizable languages and regular languages on a given alphabet follows.

Theorem 1.2 (Kleene's Theorem)
A language is recognizable if and only if it is regular. ∎

If X is a recognizable language, the ***minimal automaton*** of X, denoted by $\mathcal{M}(X)$, is determined by the right syntactic congruence associated with X. It is the automaton whose set of states is $\{w^{-1}X : w \in A^*\}$, the initial state is X, the set of terminal states is $\{w^{-1}X : w \in X\}$, and the set of arcs is $\{(w^{-1}X, a, (wa)^{-1}X) : (w, a) \in A^* \times A\}$.

Proposition 1.3
The minimal automaton $\mathcal{M}(X)$ of a language X is the automaton having the smallest number of states among the deterministic and complete automata that recognize the language X. The automaton $\mathcal{M}(X)$ is the homomorphic image of every automaton recognizing X. ∎

We often say of an automaton that it is minimal though it is not complete. Actually, this automaton is indeed minimal if one takes care to add a sink state.

Each state of an automaton, or even sometimes each arc, can be associated with an ***output***. It is a value or a set of values associated with the state or the arc.

1.2 Some combinatorics

We consider the notion of periodicity on strings for which we give the basic properties. We begin with presenting two families of strings that have interesting combinatorial properties with regard to questions of periodicities and repeats examined in several chapters.

Some specific strings

Fibonacci numbers are defined by the recurrence:

$$\begin{aligned} F_0 &= 0, \\ F_1 &= 1, \\ F_n &= F_{n-1} + F_{n-2} \quad \text{for } n \geq 2. \end{aligned}$$

These famous numbers satisfy properties all more remarkable than the others. Among those, we just give two:

- for every natural number $n \geq 2$, $\gcd(F_n, F_{n-1}) = 1$,
- for every natural number n, F_n is the nearest integer of $\Phi^n/\sqrt{5}$, where $\Phi = \frac{1}{2}(1 + \sqrt{5}) = 1{,}61803\ldots$ is the ***golden ratio***.

Fibonacci strings are defined on the alphabet $A = \{\mathtt{a}, \mathtt{b}\}$ by the following recurrence:

$$\begin{aligned} f_0 &= \varepsilon, \\ f_1 &= \mathtt{b}, \\ f_2 &= \mathtt{a}, \\ f_n &= f_{n-1} f_{n-2} \quad \text{for } n \geq 3. \end{aligned}$$

Note that the sequence of lengths of the strings is exactly the sequence of Fibonacci numbers, that is, $F_n = |f_n|$. Here are the first ten Fibonacci numbers and strings:

n	F_n	f_n
0	0	ε
1	1	b
2	1	a
3	2	ab
4	3	aba
5	5	abaab
6	8	abaababa
7	13	abaababaabaab
8	21	abaababaabaababaababa
9	34	abaababaabaababaababaabaababaabaab

The interest in Fibonacci strings is that they satisfy many combinatorial properties and they contain a large number of repeats.

The de Bruijn strings considered here are defined on the alphabet $A = \{\mathtt{a}, \mathtt{b}\}$ and are parameterized by a non-null natural number. A nonempty string $x \in A^+$ is a ***de Bruijn string*** of order k if each string on A of length k occurs once and only once in x. A first example: ab and ba are the only two de Bruijn strings of order 1. A second example: the string aaababbbaa is a de Bruijn string of order 3 since its factors of length 3 are the eight strings of A^3, that is, aaa, aab, aba, abb, baa, bab, bba, and bbb, and each of them occurs exactly once in it.

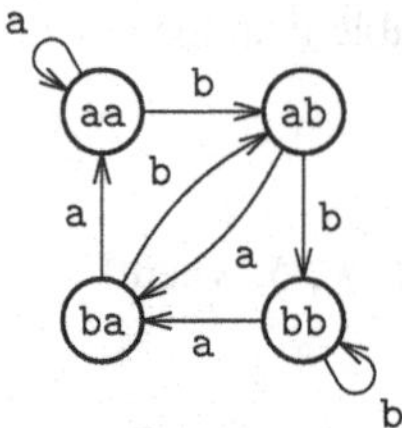

Figure 1.3. The order 3 de Bruijn automaton on the alphabet {a, b}. The initial state of the automaton is not specified.

The existence of a de Bruijn string of order $k \geq 2$ can be verified with the help of the ***automaton*** defined by

- states are the strings of the language A^{k-1},
- arcs are of the form (av, b, vb) with $a, b \in A$ and $v \in A^{k-2}$,

the initial state and the terminal states are not given (an illustration is shown in Figure 1.3). We note that exactly two arcs exit each of the states, one labeled by a, the other by b; and that exactly two arcs enter each of the states, both labeled by the same letter. The graph associated with the automaton thus satisfies the Euler condition: the outgoing degree and the incoming degree of each state are identical. It follows that there exists an Eulerian circuit in the graph. Now, let

$$\langle (u_0, a_0, u_1), (u_1, a_1, u_2), \ldots, (u_{n-1}, a_{n-1}, u_0) \rangle$$

be the corresponding path. The string $u_0 a_0 a_1 \ldots a_{n-1}$ is a de Bruijn string of order k, since each arc of the path is identified with a factor of length k. It follows in the same way that a de Bruijn string of order k has length $2^k + k - 1$ (thus $n = 2^k$ with the previous notation). It can also be verified that the number of de Bruijn strings of order k is exponential in k.

The de Bruijn strings are often used as examples of limit cases in the sense that they contain all the factors of a given length.

Periodicity and borders

Let x be a nonempty string. An integer p such that $0 < p \leq |x|$ is called a ***period*** of x if:

$$x[i] = x[i + p]$$

for $i = 0, 1, \ldots, |x| - p - 1$. Note that the length of a nonempty string is a period of this string, such that every nonempty string has at least one period. We define thus without any ambiguity ***the period*** of a nonempty string x as the smallest of its periods. It is denoted by per(x). For instance, 3, 6, 7, and 8 are periods of the string $x = \texttt{aabaabaa}$, and the period of x is per(x) $= 3$.

We note that if p is a period of x, its multiples kp are also periods of x when k is an integer satisfying $0 < k \leq \lfloor |x|/p \rfloor$.

Proposition 1.4
Let x be a nonempty string and p an integer such that $0 < p \leq |x|$. Then the five following properties are equivalent:

1. *The integer p is a period of x.*
2. *There exist two unique strings $u \in A^*$ and $v \in A^+$ and an integer $k > 0$ such that $x = (uv)^k u$ and $|uv| = p$.*
3. *There exist a string t and an integer $k > 0$ such that $x \preceq_{\text{pref}} t^k$ and $|t| = p$.*
4. *There exist three strings u, v, and w such that $x = uw = wv$ and $|u| = |v| = p$.*
5. *There exists a string t such that $x \preceq_{\text{pref}} tx$ and $|t| = p$.*

Proof $1 \Rightarrow 2$: if $v \neq \varepsilon$ and $k > 0$, then k is the quotient of the integer division of $|x|$ by p. Now, if the triplet (u', v', k') satisfies the same conditions than the triplet (u, v, k), we have $k' = k$ then, due to the equality of length, $|u'| = |u|$. It follows immediately that $u' = u$ and $v' = v$. This shows the uniqueness of the decomposition if it exists. Let k and r be respectively the quotient and the remainder of the Euclidean division of $|x|$ by p, then u and v be the two factors of x defined by $u = x[0\,..\,r-1]$ and $v = x[r\,..\,p-1]$. Thus $x = (uv)^k u$ and $|uv| = p$. This demonstrates the existence of the triplet (u, v, k) and ends the proof of the property.

$2 \Rightarrow 3$: it is enough to consider the string $t = uv$.

$3 \Rightarrow 4$: let w be the suffix of x defined by $w = t^{-1}x$. As $x \preceq_{\text{pref}} t^k$, w is also a prefix of x. Thus the existence of two strings u $(= t)$ and v such that $x = uw = wv$ and $|u| = |v| = |t| = p$.

$4 \Rightarrow 5$: since $uw \preceq_{\text{pref}} uwv$, we have $x \preceq_{\text{pref}} tx$ with $|t| = p$ by simply setting $t = u$.

$5 \Rightarrow 1$: let i be an integer such that $0 \leq i \leq |x| - p - 1$. Then:

$$\begin{aligned} x[i+p] &= (tx)[i+p] && (\text{since } x \preceq_{\text{pref}} tx) \\ &= x[i] && (\text{since } |t| = p). \end{aligned}$$

This shows that p is a period of x. ■

We note, in particular, that property 3 can be expressed in a more general way by replacing $\preceq_{\text{pref}}$ by $\preceq_{\text{fact}}$ (Exercise 1.4).

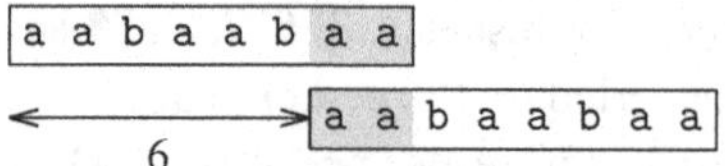

Figure 1.4. Duality between the notions of border and period. String aa is a border of string aabaabaa; it corresponds to period 6 = |aabaabaa| − |aa|.

A ***border*** of a nonempty string x is a proper factor of x that is both a prefix and a suffix of x. Thus, ε, a, aa, and aabaa are the borders of the string aabaabaa.

The notions of border and of period are dual as shown by property 4 of the previous proposition (see Figure 1.4). The proposition that follows expresses this duality in different terms.

We introduce the function Border: $A^* \to A^*$ defined for every nonempty string x by

$$\text{Border}(x) = \text{the longest border of } x.$$

We say of Border(x) that it is ***the border*** of x. For instance, the border of every string of length 1 is the empty string and the border of the string aabaabaa is aabaa. Also note that, when defined, the border of a border of a given string x is also a border of x.

Proposition 1.5
Let x be a nonempty string and n be the largest integer k for which $\text{Border}^k(x)$ *is defined (thus* $\text{Border}^n(x) = \varepsilon$*). Then*

$$\langle \text{Border}(x), \text{Border}^2(x), \ldots, \text{Border}^n(x) \rangle \tag{1.1}$$

is the sequence of borders of x in decreasing order of length, and

$$\langle |x| - |\text{Border}(x)|, |x| - |\text{Border}^2(x)|, \ldots, |x| - |\text{Border}^n(x)| \rangle \tag{1.2}$$

is the sequence of periods of x in increasing order.

Proof We proceed by recurrence on the length of strings. The statement of the proposition is valid when the length of the string x is equal to 1: the sequence of borders is reduced to $\langle \varepsilon \rangle$ and the sequence of periods to $\langle |x| \rangle$.

Let x be a string of length greater than 1. Then every border of x different from Border(x) is a border of Border(x), and conversely. It follows by recurrence hypothesis that the sequence (1.1) is exactly the sequence of borders of x. Now, if p is a period of x, Proposition 1.4 ensures the existence of three strings u, v, and w such that $x = uw = wv$ and $|u| = |v| = p$. Then w is a border of x

and $p = |x| - |w|$. It follows that the sequence (1.2) is the sequence of periods of x. ■

Lemma 1.6 (Periodicity Lemma)
If p and q are periods of a nonempty string x and satisfy

$$p + q - \mathrm{gcd}(p, q) \leq |x|,$$

then $\mathrm{gcd}(p, q)$ *is also a period of x.*

Proof By recurrence on $\max\{p, q\}$. The result is straightforward when $p = q = 1$ and, more generally when $p = q$. We can then assume in the rest that $p > q$.

From Proposition 1.4, the string x can be written both as uy with $|u| = p$ and y a border of x, and as vz with $|v| = q$ and z a border of x.

The quantity $p - q$ is a period of z. Indeed, since $p > q$, y is a border of x of length less than the length of the border z. Thus, y is a border of z. It follows that $|z| - |y|$ is a period of z. And $|z| - |y| = (|x| - q) - (|x| - p) = p - q$.

But q is also a period of z. Indeed, since $p > q$ and $\mathrm{gcd}(p, q) \leq p - q$, we have $q \leq p - \mathrm{gcd}(p, q)$. On the other hand we have $p - \mathrm{gcd}(p, q) = p + q - \mathrm{gcd}(p, q) - q \leq |x| - q = |z|$. It follows that $q \leq |z|$. This shows that the period q of x is also a period of its factor z.

Moreover, we have $(p - q) + q - \mathrm{gcd}(p - q, q) = p - \mathrm{gcd}(p, q)$, which, as can be seen above, is a quantity less than $|z|$.

We apply the recurrence hypothesis to $\max\{p - q, q\}$ relatively to the string z, and we obtain thus that $\mathrm{gcd}(p, q)$ is a period of z.

The conditions on p and q (those of the lemma and $\mathrm{gcd}(p, q) \leq p - q$) give $q \leq |x|/2$. And as $x = vz$ and z is a border of x, v is a prefix of z. It has moreover a length that is a multiple of $\mathrm{gcd}(p, q)$. Let t be the prefix of x of length $\mathrm{gcd}(p, q)$. Then v is a power of t and z is a prefix of a power of t. It follows then by Proposition 1.4 that x is a prefix of a power of t, and thus that $|t| = \mathrm{gcd}(p, q)$ is a period of x. Which ends the proof. ■

To illustrate the Periodicity Lemma, let us consider a string x that admits both 5 and 8 as periods. Then, if we assume moreover that x is composed of at least two distinct letters, $\mathrm{gcd}(5, 8) = 1$ is not a period of x, and, by application of the lemma, the length of x is less than $5 + 8 - \mathrm{gcd}(5, 8) = 12$. It is the case, for instance, for the four strings of length greater than 7 which are prefixes of the string abaababaaba of length 11. Another illustration of the result is proposed in Figure 1.5.

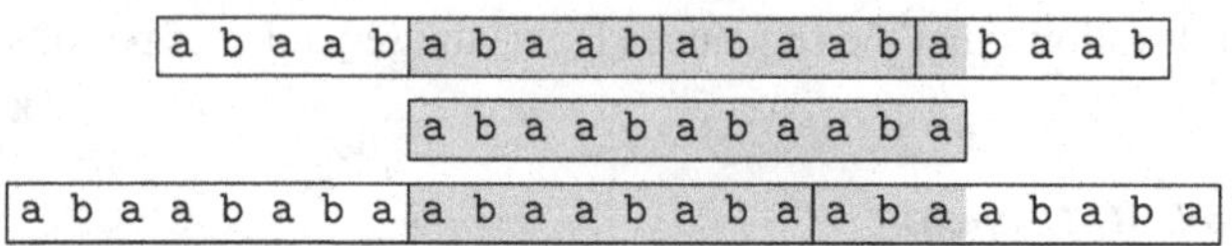

Figure 1.5. Application of the Periodicity Lemma. String abaababaaba of length 11 possesses 5 and 8 as periods. It is not possible to extend them to the left nor to the right while keeping these two periods. Indeed, if 5 and 8 are periods of some string, but 1, the greatest common divisor of 5 and 8, is not, then this string is of length less than $5 + 8 - \gcd(5, 8) = 12$.

We wish to show in what follows that one cannot weaken the condition required on the periods in the statement of the Periodicity Lemma. More precisely, we give examples of strings x that have two periods p and q such that $p + q - \gcd(p, q) = |x| + 1$ but which do not satisfy the conclusion of the lemma. (See also Exercise 1.5.)

Let β: $A^* \to A^*$ be the function defined by

$$\beta(uab) = uba$$

for every string $u \in A^*$ and every letters $a, b \in A$.

Lemma 1.7
For every natural number $n \geq 3$, $\beta(f_n) = f_{n-2}f_{n-1}$.

Proof By recurrence on n. The result is straightforward when $3 \leq n \leq 4$. If $n \geq 5$, we have:

$$\begin{aligned}
\beta(f_n) &= \beta(f_{n-1}f_{n-2}) && \text{(by definition of } f_n\text{)} \\
&= f_{n-1}\beta(f_{n-2}) && \text{(since } |f_{n-2}| = F_{n-2} \geq 2\text{)} \\
&= f_{n-1}f_{n-4}f_{n-3} && \text{(by recurrence hypothesis)} \\
&= f_{n-2}f_{n-3}f_{n-4}f_{n-3} && \text{(by definition of } f_{n-1}\text{)} \\
&= f_{n-2}f_{n-2}f_{n-3} && \text{(by definition of } f_{n-2}\text{)} \\
&= f_{n-2}f_{n-1} && \text{(by definition of } f_{n-1}\text{).}
\end{aligned}$$

■

For every natural number $n \geq 3$, we define the string g_n as the prefix of length $F_n - 2$ of f_n, that is, f_n with its last two letters chopped off.

Lemma 1.8
For every natural number $n \geq 6$, $g_n = {f_{n-2}}^2 g_{n-3}$.

Proof We have:

$$\begin{aligned} f_n &= f_{n-1} f_{n-2} && \text{(by definition of } f_n\text{)} \\ &= f_{n-2} f_{n-3} f_{n-2} && \text{(by definition of } f_{n-1}\text{)} \\ &= f_{n-2}\beta(f_{n-1}) && \text{(from Lemma 1.7)} \\ &= f_{n-2}\beta(f_{n-2} f_{n-3}) && \text{(by definition of } f_{n-1}\text{)} \\ &= {f_{n-2}}^2\beta(f_{n-3}) && \text{(since } |f_{n-3}| = F_{n-3} \geq 2\text{).} \end{aligned}$$

The stated result immediately follows. ■

Lemma 1.9
For every natural number $n \geq 3$, $g_n \preceq_{\text{pref}} {f_{n-1}}^2$ and $g_n \preceq_{\text{pref}} {f_{n-2}}^3$.

Proof We have:

$$\begin{aligned} g_n \preceq_{\text{pref}} & f_n f_{n-3} && \text{(since } g_n \preceq_{\text{pref}} f_n\text{)} \\ = \; & f_{n-1} f_{n-2} f_{n-3} && \text{(by definition of } f_n\text{)} \\ = \; & {f_{n-1}}^2 && \text{(by definition of } f_{n-1}\text{).} \end{aligned}$$

The second relation is valid when $3 \leq n \leq 5$. When $n \geq 6$, we have:

$$\begin{aligned} g_n \; = \; & {f_{n-2}}^2 g_{n-3} && \text{(from Lemma 1.8)} \\ \preceq_{\text{pref}} \; & {f_{n-2}}^2 f_{n-3} f_{n-4} && \text{(since } g_{n-3} \preceq_{\text{pref}} f_{n-3}\text{)} \\ = \; & {f_{n-2}}^3 && \text{(by definition of } f_{n-2}\text{).} \end{aligned}$$

■

Now, let n be a natural number, $n \geq 5$, so that the string g_n is both defined and of length greater than 2. It follows then:

$$\begin{aligned} |g_n| &= F_n - 2 && \text{(by definition of } g_n\text{)} \\ &= F_{n-1} + F_{n-2} - 2 && \text{(by definition of } F_n\text{)} \\ &\geq F_{n-1} && \text{(since } F_{n-2} \geq 2\text{).} \end{aligned}$$

It results from this inequality, from Lemma 1.9, and from Proposition 1.4 that F_{n-1} and F_{n-2} are two periods of g_n. In addition note that, since $\gcd(F_{n-1}, F_{n-2}) = 1$, we also have:

$$\begin{aligned} F_{n-1} + F_{n-2} - \gcd(F_{n-1}, F_{n-2}) &= F_n - 1 \\ &= |g_n| + 1. \end{aligned}$$

Thus, if the conclusion of the Periodicity Lemma applied to the string g_n and its two periods F_{n-1} and F_{n-2}, g_n would be the power of a string of length 1. But the first two letters of g_n are distinct. This indicates that the condition of the Periodicity Lemma is in some sense optimal.

Powers, primitivity, and conjugacy

Lemma 1.10
Let x and y be two strings. If there exist two positive integers m and n such that $x^m = y^n$, x and y are powers of some string z.

Proof It is enough to show the result in the nontrivial case where neither x nor y are empty strings. Two subcases can then be distinguished, whether $\min\{m, n\}$ is equal to 1 or not.

If $\min\{m, n\} = 1$, it is sufficient to consider the string $z = y$ if $m = 1$ and $z = x$ if $n = 1$.

Otherwise, $\min\{m, n\} \geq 2$. Then we note that $|x|$ and $|y|$ are periods of the string $t = x^m = y^n$ which satisfy the condition of the Periodicity Lemma: $|x| + |y| - \gcd(|x|, |y|) \leq |x| + |y| - 1 < |t|$. Thus it is sufficient to consider the string z defined as the prefix of t of length $\gcd(|x|, |y|)$ to get the stated result. ■

A nonempty string is ***primitive*** if it is not the power of any other string. In other words, a string $x \in A^+$ is primitive if and only if every decomposition of the form $x = u^n$ with $u \in A^*$ and $n \in \mathbf{N}$ implies $n = 1$, and then $u = x$. For instance, the string abaab is primitive, while the strings ε and $\mathtt{bababa} = (\mathtt{ba})^3$ are not.

Lemma 1.11 (Primitivity Lemma)
A nonempty string is primitive if and only if it is a factor of its square only as a prefix and as a suffix. In other words, for every nonempty string x,

$$x \text{ primitive}$$

if and only if

$$yx \preceq_{\text{pref}} x^2 \text{ implies } y = \varepsilon \text{ or } y = x.$$

An illustration of this result is proposed in Figure 1.6.

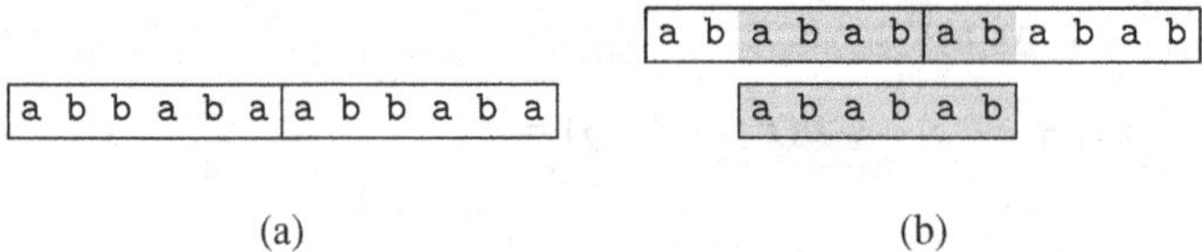

Figure 1.6. Application of the Primitivity Lemma. **(a)** String $x = \mathtt{abbaba}$ does not possess any "nontrivial" occurrence in its square x^2 – that is, neither a prefix nor a suffix of x^2 – since x is primitive. **(b)** String $x = \mathtt{ababab}$ possesses a "nontrivial" occurrence in its square x^2 since x is not primitive: $x = (\mathtt{ab})^3$.

Proof If x is a nonempty nonprimitive string, there exist $z \in A^+$ and $n \geq 2$ such that $x = z^n$. Since x^2 can be decomposed as $z \cdot z^n \cdot z^{n-1}$, the string x occurs at the position $|z|$ on x^2. This shows that every nonempty nonprimitive string is a factor of its square without being only a prefix and a suffix of it.

Conversely, let x be a nonempty string such that its square x^2 can be written as yxz with $y, z \in A^+$. Due to the length condition, it first follows that $|y| < |x|$. Then, and since $x \preceq_{\text{pref}} yx$, we obtain from Proposition 1.4 that $|y|$ is a period of x. Thus, $|x|$ and $|y|$ are periods of yx. From the Periodicity Lemma, we deduce that $p = \gcd(|x|, |y|)$ is also a period of yx. Now, as $p \leq |y| < |x|$, p is also a period of x. And as p divides $|x|$, we deduce that x is of the form t^n with $|t| = p$ and $n \geq 2$. This shows that the string x is not primitive. ■

Another way of stating the previous lemma is that the primitivity of x is equivalent to saying that $\text{per}(x^2) = |x|$.

Proposition 1.12
For every nonempty string, there exists one and only one primitive string which it is a power of.

Proof The proof of the existence comes from a trivial recurrence on the length of the strings. We now have to show the uniqueness.

Let x be a nonempty string. If we assume that $x = u^m = v^n$ for two primitive strings u and v and two positive integers m and n, then u and v are necessarily powers of a string $z \in A^+$ from Lemma 1.10. But their primitivity implies $z = u = v$, which shows the uniqueness and ends the proof. ■

If x is a nonempty string, we say of the primitive string z which x is the power of that it is the ***root*** of x, and of the natural number n such that $x = z^n$ that it is the ***exponent***[4] of x.

Two strings x and y are ***conjugate*** if there exist two strings u and v such that $x = uv$ and $y = vu$. For instance, the strings abaab and ababa are conjugate. It is clear that conjugacy is an equivalence relation. It is not compatible with the product.

Proposition 1.13
Two nonempty strings are conjugate if and only if their roots also are conjugate.

Proof The proof of the reciprocal is immediate.

For the proof of the direct implication, we consider two nonempty conjugate strings x and y, and we denote by z and t then m and n their roots and exponents

[4] More generally, the exponent of x is the quantity $|x|/\text{per}(x)$ which is not necessarily an integer (see Exercise 9.2).

respectively. Since x and y are conjugate, there exist $z', z'' \in A^+$ and $p, q \in \mathbf{N}$ such that $z = z'z''$, $x = z^p z' \cdot z'' z^q$, $y = z'' z^q \cdot z^p z'$, and $m = p + q + 1$. We deduce that $y = (z''z')^m$. Now, as t is primitive, Lemma 1.10 implies that $z''z'$ is a power of t. This shows the existence of a natural non-null number k such that $|z| = k|t|$. Symmetrically, there exists a natural non-null number ℓ such that $|t| = \ell|z|$. It follows that $k = \ell = 1$, that $|t| = |z|$, then that $t = z''z'$. This shows that the roots z and t are conjugate. ■

A consequence of Proposition 1.13 and of the Primitivity lemma is that, for any primitive string x, each of its conjugates occurs exactly once in xxA^{-1} (or $A^{-1}xx$).

Proposition 1.14
Two nonempty strings x and y are conjugate if and only if there exists a string z such that $xz = zy$.

Proof $\Rightarrow$: x and y can be decomposed as $x = uv$ and $y = vu$ with $u, v \in A^*$, then the string $z = u$ suits since $xz = uvu = zy$.

$\Leftarrow$: in the nontrivial case where $z \in A^+$, we obtain by an immediate recurrence that $x^k z = z y^k$ for every $k \in \mathbf{N}$. Let n be the (non-null) natural number such that $(n-1)|x| \leq |z| < n|x|$. There exist thus $u, v \in A^*$ such that $x = uv$, $z = x^{n-1}u$, and $vz = y^n$. It follows that $y^n = vx^{n-1}u = (vu)^n$. Finally, since $|y| = |x|$, we have $y = vu$, which shows that x and y are conjugate. ■

1.3 Algorithms and complexity

In this section, we present the algorithmic elements used in the rest of the book. They include the writing conventions, the evaluation of the algorithm complexity, and some standard objects.

Writing conventions of algorithms

The style of the algorithmic language used here is relatively close to real programming languages but at a higher abstraction level. We adopt the following conventions:

- Indentation means the structure of blocks inherent to compound instructions.
- Lines of code are numbered in order to be referenced in the text.
- The symbol ▷ introduces a comment.

- The access to a specific attribute of an object is signified by the name of the attribute followed by the identifier associated with the object between brackets.
- A variable that represents a given object (table, queue, tree, string, automaton) is a pointer to this object.
- The arguments given to procedures or to functions are managed by the "call by value" rule.
- Variables of procedures and of functions are local to them unless otherwise mentioned.
- The evaluation of boolean expressions is performed from left to right in a lazy way.

We consider, following the example of a language like the C language, the iterative instruction **do-while** – used instead of the traditional instruction **repeat-until** – and the instruction **break** which produces the termination of the most internal loop in which it is located.

Well adapted to the sequential processing of strings, we use the formulation:

```
for each letter a of u, sequentially do
        processing of a
```

for every string u. It means that the letters $u[i]$, $i = 0, 1, \ldots, |u| - 1$, composing u are processed one after the other in the body of the loop: first $u[0]$, then $u[1]$, and so on. It means that the length of the string u is not necessarily known in advance, the end of the loop can be detected by a marker that ends the string. In the case where the length of the string u is known, this formulation is equivalent to a formulation of the type:

```
for i ← 0 to |u| − 1 do
        a ← u[i]
        processing of a
```

where the integer variable i is free (its use does not produce any conflict with the environment).

Pattern matching algorithms

A ***pattern*** represents a nonempty language not containing the empty string. It can be described by a string, by a finite set of strings, or by other means. The ***pattern matching*** problem is to search for occurrences of strings of the language in other strings – or in ***texts*** to be less formal. The notions of occurrence, of appearance, and of position on the strings are extended to patterns.

According to the specified problem, the input of a pattern matching algorithm is a string x or a language X and a text y, together or not with their lengths.

The output can take several forms. Here are some of them:

- Boolean values: to implement an algorithm that tests whether the pattern occurs in the text or not, without specifying the positions of the possible occurrences, the output is simply the boolean value TRUE in the first situation and FALSE in the second.
- A string: during a sequential search, it is appropriate to produce a string $\bar{y}$ on the alphabet $\{0, 1\}$ that encodes the existence of the right positions of occurrences. The string $\bar{y}$ is such that $|\bar{y}| = |y|$ and $\bar{y}[i] = 1$ if and only if i is the right position of an occurrence of the pattern on y.
- A set of positions: the output can also take the form of a set P of left – or right – positions of occurrences of the pattern on y.

Let e be a predicate having value TRUE if and only if an occurrence has just been detected. A function corresponding to the first form and ending as soon as an occurrence is detected should integrate in its code an instruction:

```
if e then
        return TRUE
```

in the heart of its searching process, and return the value FALSE at the termination of this process. The second form needs to initialize the variable $\bar{y}$ with ε, the empty string, then to modify its value by an instruction:

```
if e then
        ȳ ← ȳ · 1
else ȳ ← ȳ · 0
```

then to return it at the termination. It is identical for the third form, where the set P is initially empty, then augmented by an instruction:

```
if e then
        P ← P ∪ {the current position on y}
```

and finally returned.

To present only one variant of the code for an algorithm, we consider the following special instruction:

OUTPUT-IF(e) means, at the location where it appears, an occurrence of the pattern at the current position on the text is detected when the predicate e has value TRUE.

Expression of complexity

The model of computation for the evaluation of the algorithm's complexity is the standard random access machine model.

In a general way, the algorithm complexity is an expression including the input size. This includes the length of the language represented by the pattern, the length of the string in which the search is performed, and the size of the alphabet. We assume that the letters of the alphabet are of size comparable to the machine word size, and, consequently, the comparison between two letters is an elementary operation that is performed in constant time.

We assume that every instruction OUTPUT-IF(e) is executed in constant time[5] once the predicate e has been evaluated.

We use the notation recommended by Knuth [78] to express the orders of magnitude. Let f and g be two functions from **N** to **N**. We write "$f(n)$ is $O(g(n))$" to mean that there exists a constant K and a natural number n_0 such that $f(n) \leq Kg(n)$ for every $n \geq n_0$. In a dual way, we write "$f(n)$ is $\Omega(g(n))$" if there exists a constant K and a natural number n_0 such that $f(n) \geq Kg(n)$ for every $n \geq n_0$. We finally write "$f(n)$ is $\Theta(g(n))$" to mean that f and g are of the same order, that is to say that $f(n)$ is both $O(g(n))$ and $\Omega(g(n))$.

The function $f: \mathbf{N} \rightarrow \mathbf{N}$ is ***linear*** if $f(n)$ is $\Theta(n)$, ***quadratic*** if $f(n)$ is $\Theta(n^2)$, ***cubic*** if $f(n)$ is $\Theta(n^3)$, ***logarithmic*** if $f(n)$ is $\Theta(\log n)$, ***exponential*** if there exists $a > 0$ for which $f(n)$ is $\Theta(a^n)$.

We say that a function with two parameters $f: \mathbf{N} \times \mathbf{N} \rightarrow \mathbf{N}$ is linear when $f(m, n)$ is $\Theta(m + n)$ and quadratic when $f(m, n)$ is $\Theta(m \times n)$.

Some standard objects

Queues, states, and automata are objects often used in the rest of the book. Without telling what their true implementations are – they can actually differ from one algorithm to the other – we indicate the minimal attributes and operations defined on these objects.

For queues, we only describe the basic operations.

EMPTY-QUEUE() creates then returns an empty queue.

QUEUE-IS-EMPTY(F) returns TRUE if the file F is empty, and FALSE otherwise.

[5] Actually we can always come down to it even though the language represented by the pattern is not reduced to a single string. For that, it is sufficient to only produce one descriptor – previously computed – of the set of strings that occur at the current position (instead for instance, of producing explicitly the set of strings). It then remains to use a tool that develops the information if necessary.

ENQUEUE(F, x) adds the element x to the tail of the queue F.
HEAD(F) returns the element located at the head of the queue F.
DEQUEUE(F) deletes the element located at the head of the queue F.
DEQUEUED(F) deletes the element located at the head of the queue F then returns it;
LENGTH(F) returns the length of the queue F.

States are objects that possess at least the two attributes *terminal* and *Succ*. The first attribute indicates if the state is terminal or not and the second is an implementation of the set of labeled successors of the state. The attribute corresponding to an output of a state is denoted by *output*. The two standard operations on the states are the functions NEW-STATE and TARGET. While the first creates then returns a nonterminal state with an empty set of labeled successors, the second returns the target of an arc given the source and the label of the arc, or the special value NIL if such an arc does not exist. The code for these two functions can be written in a few lines:

```
NEW-STATE()
    allocate an object p of type state
    terminal[p] ← FALSE
    Succ[p] ← ∅
    return p
```

```
TARGET(p, a)
    if there exists a state q such that (a, q) ∈ Succ[p] then
        return q
    else return NIL
```

The objects of the type automaton possess at least the attribute *initial* that specifies the initial state of the automaton. The function NEW-AUTOMATON creates then returns an automaton with a single state. It constitutes its initial state and has an empty set of labeled successors. The corresponding code is the following:

```
NEW-AUTOMATON()
    allocate an object M of type automaton
    q0 ← NEW-STATE()
    initial[M] ← q0
    return M
```

1.4 Implementation of automata

Some pattern matching algorithms rely on specific implementations of the deterministic automata they consider. This section details several methods, including the data structures and the algorithms, that can be used to implement these objects in memory.

Implementing a deterministic automaton (Q, q_0, T, F) consists in setting in memory, either the set F of its arcs, or the sets of the labeled successors of its states, or its transition function δ. Those are equivalent problems that fit in the general framework of representing ***partial functions*** (Exercise 1.15). We distinguish two families of implementations:

- the family of ***full*** implementations in which all the transitions are represented,
- the family of ***reduced*** implementations that use more or less elaborate techniques of compression in order to reduce the memory space of the representation.

The choice of the implementation influences the time necessary to compute a transition, that is to execute TARGET(p, a), for a state $p \in Q$ and a letter $a \in A$. This computation time is called the ***delay*** since it measures also the time necessary for going from the current letter of the input to the next letter. Typically, two models can be opposed:

- The ***branching model*** in which δ is implemented with a $Q \times A$ matrix and where the delay is constant (in the random access model).
- The ***comparisons model*** in which the elementary operation is the comparison of letters and where the delay is typically $O(\log \operatorname{card} A)$ when any two letters can be compared in one unit of time (general assumption formulated in Section 1.3).

We also consider in the next section an elementary technique known as the "bit-vector model" whose application scope is restricted: it is especially interesting when the size of the automaton is very small.

For each of the implementation families, we specify the orders of magnitude of the necessary memory space and of the delay. There is always a trade-off to be found between these two quantities.

Full implementations

The most simple method for implementing the function δ is to store its values in a $Q \times A$ matrix, known as the ***transition matrix*** (an illustration is given

	a	b	c
0	1	0	0
1	2	3	0
2	2	3	0
3	4	0	0
4	2	3	0

Figure 1.7. The transition matrix of the automaton of Figure 1.2.

in Figure 1.7) of the automaton. It is a method of choice for a deterministic complete automaton on an alphabet of relatively small size and when the letters can be identified with indices on a table. Computing a transition reduces to a mere table look-up.

Proposition 1.15
In an implementation by transition matrix, the necessary memory space is $O(\text{card } Q \times \text{card } A)$ *and the delay* $O(1)$. ■

In the case where the automaton is not complete, the representation remains correct except that the execution of the automaton on the text given as an input can now stop on an undefined transition. The matrix can be initialized in time $O(\text{card } F)$ only if we implement partial functions as proposed in Exercise 1.15. The above-stated complexities for the memory space as well as for the delay remain valid.

An automaton can be implemented by means of an adjacency matrix as it is classical to do for graphs. We associate then with each letter of the alphabet a boolean $Q \times Q$ matrix. This representation is in general not adapted for the applications developed in this book. It is, however, related to the method that follows.

The method by ***list of transitions*** consists in implementing a list of triplets (p, a, q) that are arcs of the automaton. The required space is only $O(\text{card } F)$. Having done this, we assume that this list is stored in a hash table in order to allow a fast computation of the transitions. The corresponding hash function is defined on the pairs $(p, a) \in Q \times A$. Given a pair (p, a), the access to the transition (p, a, q), if it is defined, is done in average constant time with the usual assumptions specific to this type of technique.

These first types of representations implicitly assume that the alphabet is fixed and known in advance, which opposes them to the representations in the comparison model considered by the method described below.

The method by ***sets of labeled successors*** consists in using a table t indexed on Q for which each element $t[p]$ gives access to an implementation of the set of the labeled successors of the state p. The required space is $O(\text{card } Q + \text{card } F)$.

This method is valuable even when the only authorized operation on the letters is the comparison. Denoting by s the maximal outgoing degree of the states, the delay is $O(\log s)$ if we use an efficient implementation of the sets of labeled successors.

Proposition 1.16

In an implementation by sets of labeled successors, the space requirement is $O(\text{card}\, Q + \text{card}\, F)$ *and the delay* $O(\log s)$ *where* s *is the maximal outgoing degree of states.* ■

Note that the delay is also $O(\log \text{card}\, A)$ in this case: indeed, since the automaton is assumed to be deterministic, the outgoing degree of each of the states at most than card A, thus $s \leq \text{card}\, A$ with the notation used above.

Reduced implementations

When the automaton is complete, the space complexity can, however, be reduced by considering a ***successor by default*** for the computation of the transitions from any given state – the state occurring the most often in a set of labeled successors is the best possible candidate for being the successor by default. The delay can also be reduced since the size of the sets of labeled successors becomes smaller. For pattern matching problems, the choice of the initial state as successor by default suits perfectly. Figure 1.8 shows an example where short gray arrows mean that the state possesses the initial state as successor by default.

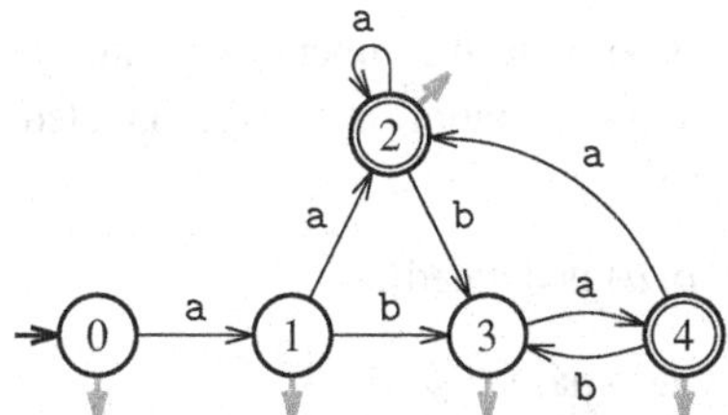

Figure 1.8. Reduced implementation by adjunction of successors by default. We consider the automaton of Figure 1.2 and we chose the initial state as unique successor by default (this choice perfectly suits for pattern matching problems). States that admit the initial state as successor by default (indeed all of them in this case) are indicated by a short gray arrow. For example, the target of the transition from state 3 by letter a is state 4, and by every other letter, here b or c, the target is the initial state 0.

Another method to reduce the implementation space consists in using a failure function. The idea is here to reduce the necessary space for implementing the automaton, by redirecting, in most cases, the computation of the transition from the current state to the one from another state but by the same letter. This technique serves to implement deterministic automata in the comparison model. Its principal advantage is generally to provide linear size representations and to simultaneously get a linear time computation of series of transitions even when the computation of a single transition cannot be done in constant time.

Formally, let

$$\gamma : Q \times A \to Q$$

and

$$f : Q \to Q$$

be two functions. We say that the pair (γ, f) represents the transition function δ of a complete automaton having δ as transition function if and only if γ is a subfunction of δ, f defines an ordering on elements of Q, and for every pair $(p, a) \in Q \times A$

$$\delta(p, a) = \begin{cases} \gamma(p, a) & \text{if } \gamma(p, a) \text{ is defined,} \\ \delta(f(p), a) & \text{otherwise.} \end{cases}$$

When it is defined, we say of the state $f(p)$ that it is the ***failure state*** of the state p. We say of the functions γ and f that they are respectively, and jointly, a ***subtransition*** and a ***failure function*** of δ.

We indicate the link state-failure state by a directed dash arrow in figures (see the example in Figure 1.9).

The space needed to represent the function δ by the functions γ and f is $O(\text{card } Q + \text{card } F')$ in the case of an implementation by sets of labeled successors where

$$F' = \{(p, a, q) \in F : \gamma(p, a) \text{ is defined}\}.$$

Note that γ is the transition function of the automaton (Q, q_0, T, F').

A complete example

The method presented here is a combination of the previous ones together with a fast computation of transitions and a compact representation of transitions due to the joint use of tables and of a failure function. It is known as "compression of transition table."

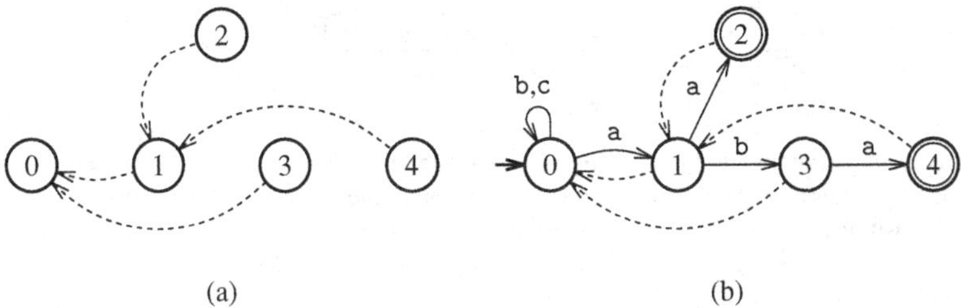

Figure 1.9. Reduced implementation by adjunction of a failure function. We take again the example of the automaton of Figure 1.2. **(a)** A failure function given under the form of a directed graph. As this graph does not possess any cycle, the function defines an ordering on the set of states. **(b)** The corresponding reduced automaton. Each link from a state to its failure state is indicated by a dashed arrow. The computation of the transition from state 4 by the letter c is transferred to state 1, then to state 0. State 0 is indeed the first among states 4, 1, and 0, in this order, to possess a transition defined by c. Finally, the target of the transition from state 4 by c is state 0.

Two extra attributes, *fail* and *base*, are added to states, the first has values in Q and the second in $\mathbf{N}$. We consider also two tables indexed by $\mathbf{N}$ and with values in Q: *target* and *control*. For each pair $(p, a) \in Q \times A$, $base[p] + rank[a]$ is an index on both *target* and *control*, denoting by *rank* the function that associates with every letter of A its rank in a fixed ordered sequence of letters of A.

The computation of the successor of a state $p \in Q$ by a letter $a \in A$ proceeds as follows:

1. If $control[base[p] + rank[a]] = p$, $target[base[p] + rank[a]]$ is the target of the arc of source p and labeled by a.
2. Otherwise the process is repeated recursively on the state $fail[p]$ and the letter a (assuming that *fail* is a failure function).

The (nonrecursive) code of the corresponding function follows.

```
TARGET-BY-COMPRESSION(p, a)
while control[base[p] + rank[a]] ≠ p do
        p ← fail[p]
return target[base[p] + rank[a]]
```

In the worst case, the space required by the implementation is $O(\text{card } Q \times \text{card } A)$ and the delay is $O(\text{card } Q)$. This method allows us to reduce the space in $O(\text{card } Q + \text{card } A)$ with a constant delay in the best case.

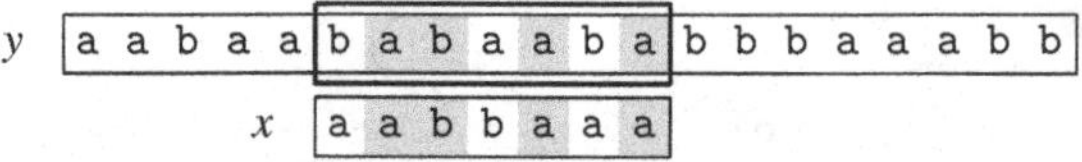

Figure 1.10. An attempt to locate string $x =$ aabbaaa in text $y =$ aabaababaababbbaaabb. The attempt takes place at position 5 on y. The content of the window and the string matches in four positions.

1.5 Basic pattern matching techniques

In this section, we present elementary approaches for the pattern matching problem. It includes the notion of sliding window common to many searching algorithms, the utilization of heuristics in order to reduce the computation time, the general method based on automata when the texts are to be processed in a sequential order, and the use of techniques that rely on the binary encoding of letters realized by machine words.

Notion of sliding window

When the pattern is a nonempty string x of length m, it is convenient to consider that the text y of length n in which the search is performed, is examined through a ***sliding window***. The window delimits a factor of the text, called the ***content of the window***, which has, in most cases, the length of the string x. It slides along the text from the beginning to the end, from left to right.

The window being at a given position j on the text, the algorithm tests whether the string x occurs or not at this position, by comparing some letters of the content of the window with aligned letters of the string. We speak of an ***attempt*** at the position j (see an example in Figure 1.10). If the comparison is successful, an occurrence is signaled. During this phase of test, the algorithm acquires some information on the text which can be exploited in two ways:

- to set up the length of the next ***shift*** of the window according to rules that are specific to the algorithm,
- to avoid comparisons during next attempts by memorizing a part of the collected information.

When the shift slides the window from the position j to the position $j + d$ ($d \geq 1$), we say that the shift is of ***length*** d. To answer to the given problem, a shift of length d for an attempt at the position j must be ***valid***, that is it must ensure that, when $d \geq 2$, there is no occurrence of the searched string x from positions $j + 1$ to $j + d - 1$ on the text y.

The naive algorithm

The simplest implementation of the sliding window mechanism is the so-called naive algorithm. The strategy consists here in considering a window of length m and in sliding it one position to the right after each attempt. This leads, if the comparison of the content of the window and of the string is correctly implemented, to an obviously correct algorithm.

We give below the code of the algorithm. The variable j corresponds to the left position of the window on the text. It is clear that the comparison of the strings in line 2 is supposed to be performed letter by letter according to a pre-established order.

NAIVE-SEARCH(x, m, y, n)
1 **for** $j \leftarrow 0$ **to** $n - m$ **do**
2   OUTPUT-IF$(y[j \mathinner{..} j + m - 1] = x)$

In the worst case, the algorithm NAIVE-SEARCH executes in time $\Theta(m \times n)$, as for instance when x and y are powers of the same letter. In the average case,[6] its behavior is rather good, as claimed by the following proposition.

Proposition 1.17
With the double assumption of an alphabet nonreduced to a single letter and of both a uniform and independent distribution of letters of the alphabet, the average number of comparisons of letters performed by the operation NAIVE-SEARCH(x, m, y, n) *is* $\Theta(n - m)$.

Proof Let c be the size of the alphabet. The number of comparisons of letters necessary to determine if two strings u and v of length m are identical on average is

$$1 + 1/c + \cdots + 1/c^{m-1},$$

independently of the permutation of positions considered for comparing letters of the strings. When $c \geq 2$, this quantity is less than $1/(1 - 1/c)$, which is itself no more than 2.

It follows that the average number of comparisons of letters counted during the execution of the operation is less than $2(n - m + 1)$. Thus the result holds since at least $n - m + 1$ comparisons are performed. ■

[6] Even when the patterns and the texts considered in practice have no reason to be random, the average cases express what one can expect of a given pattern matching algorithm.

Heuristics

Some elementary processes sensibly improve the global behavior of pattern matching algorithms. We detail here some of the most significant. They are described in connection with the naive algorithm. But most of the other algorithms can include them in their code, the adaptation being more or less easy. We speak of heuristics since we are not able to formally measure their contribution to the complexity of the algorithm.

When locating all the occurrences of the string x in the text y by the naive method, we can start by locating the occurrences of its first letter, $x[0]$, in the prefix $y[0\,..\,n-m+1]$ of y. It then remains to test, for each occurrence of $x[0]$ at a position j on y, the possible identity between the two strings $x[1\,..\,m-1]$ and $y[j+1\,..\,j+m-1]$. As the searching operation for the occurrence of a letter is generally a low level operation of operating systems, the reduction of the computation time is often noticeable in practice. This elementary search can still be improved in two ways:

- by positioning $x[0]$ as a sentinel at the end of the text y, in order to have to test less frequently the end of the text,
- by searching, non-necessarily $x[0]$, but the letter of x which has the smallest frequency of appearance in the texts of the family of y.

It should be noted that the first technique assumes that such an alteration of the memory is possible and that it can be performed in constant time. For the second, besides the necessity of having to know the frequency of letters, the choice of the position of the distinguished letter requires a precomputation on x.

A different process consists in applying a shift that takes into account only the value of the rightmost letter of the window. Let j be the right position of the window. Two antagonist cases can be envisaged whether or not the letter $y[j]$ occurs in $x[0\,..\,m-2]$:

- in the case where $y[j]$ does not occur in $x[0\,..\,m-2]$, the string x cannot occur at right positions $j+1$ to $j+m-1$ on y,
- in the other case, if k is the maximal position of an occurrence of the letter $y[j]$ on $x[0\,..\,m-2]$, the string x cannot occur at right positions $j+1$ to $j+m-1-k-1$ on y.

Thus the valid shifts to apply in the two cases have lengths: m for the first, and $m-1-k$ for the second. Note that they do not depend on the letter $y[j]$ and in no way on its position j on y.

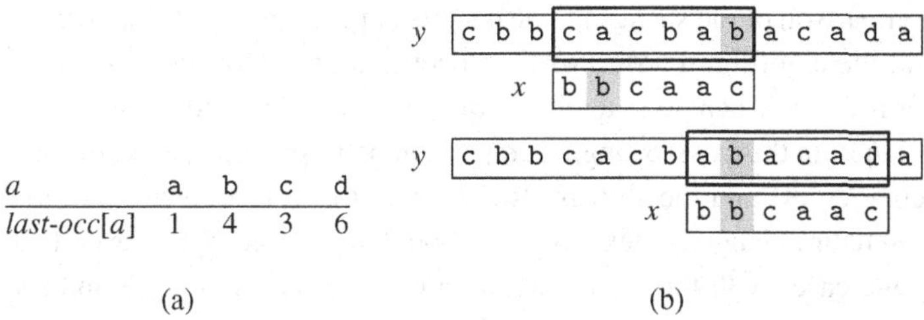

a	a	b	c	d
last-occ[a]	1	4	3	6

(a) (b)

Figure 1.11. Shift of the sliding window with the table of the last occurrence, *last-occ*, when $x =$ bbcaac. **(a)** The values of the table *last-occ* on the alphabet $A = \{$a, b, c, d$\}$. **(b)** The window on the text y is at right position 8. The letter at this position, $y[8] =$ b, occurs at the maximal position $k = 1$ on $x[0 \,..\, |x| - 2]$. A valid shift consists in sliding the window of $|x| - 1 - k = 4 =$ *last-occ*[b] positions to the right.

To formalize the previous observation, we introduce the table

$$\textit{last-occ}\colon A \to \{1, 2, \ldots, m\}$$

defined for every letter $a \in A$ by

$$\textit{last-occ}[a] = \min(\{m\} \cup \{m - 1 - k : 0 \le k \le m - 2 \text{ and } x[k] = a\}).$$

We call *last-occ* the ***table of the last occurrence***. It expresses a valid shift, *last-occ*[$y[j]$], to apply after the attempt at the right position j on y. An illustration is proposed in Figure 1.11. The code for the computation of *last-occ* follows. It executes in time $\Theta(m + \text{card } A)$.

```
LAST-OCCURRENCE(x, m)
for each letter a ∈ A do
        last-occ[a] ← m
for k ← 0 to m − 2 do
        last-occ[x[k]] ← m − 1 − k
return last-occ
```

We give now the complete code of the algorithm FAST-SEARCH obtained from the naive algorithm by adding the table *last-occ*.

```
FAST-SEARCH(x, m, y, n)
last-occ ← LAST-OCCURRENCE(x, m)
j ← m − 1
while j < n do
        OUTPUT-IF(y[j − m + 1 .. j] = x)
        j ← j + last-occ[y[j]]
```

If the comparison of the strings in line 4 starts at position $m-1$, the searching phase of the algorithm FAST-SEARCH executes in time $\Theta(n/m)$ in the best case. As for instance when no letter at positions congruent modulo m to $m-1$ on y occurs in x; in this case, a single comparison between letters is performed during each attempt[7] and the shift is always equal to m. The behavior of the algorithm on natural language texts is very good. One can show, however, that in the average case (with the double assumption of Proposition 1.17 and for a set of strings having the same length), the number of comparisons per text letter is asymptotically lower bounded by $1/\operatorname{card} A$. The bound is independent of the length of the pattern.

Search engine

Some automata can serve as a ***search engine*** for the online processing of texts. We describe in this part two algorithms based on an automaton for locating patterns. We assume the automata are given; Chapter 2 presents the construction of some of these automata. Section 6.6 considers another automation.

Let us consider a pattern $X \subseteq A^*$ and a deterministic automaton M that recognizes the language A^*X (Figure 1.12(a) displays an example). The automaton M recognizes the strings that have a string of X as a suffix. For locating the strings of X that occur in a text y, it is sufficient to run the automaton M on the text y. When the current state is terminal, this means that the current prefix of y – the part of y already parsed by the automaton – belongs to A^*X; or, in other words, that the current position on y is the right position of an occurrence of a string of X. This remark leads to the algorithm whose code follows. An illustration of how the algorithm works is presented in Figure 1.12(b).

```
DET-SEARCH(M, y)
r ← initial[M]
for each letter a of y, sequentially do
    r ← TARGET(r, a)
    OUTPUT-IF(terminal[r])
```

Proposition 1.18
When M is a deterministic automaton that recognizes the language A^*X for a pattern $X \subseteq A^*$, the operation DET-SEARCH(M, y) *locates all the occurrences of strings of X in the text $y \in A^*$.*

7 Note that it is the best case possible for an algorithm detecting a string of length m in a text of length n; at least $\lfloor n/m \rfloor$ letters of the text must be inspected before the nonappearance of the searched string can be determined.

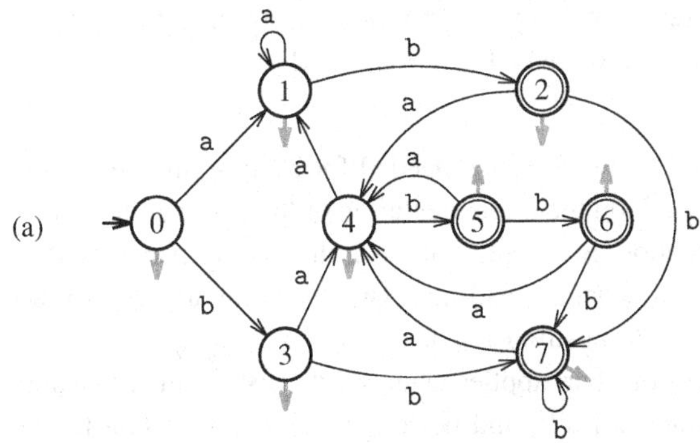

(b)

j	$y[j]$	state r	
		0	
0	c	0	
1	b	3	
2	a	4	
3	b	5	occurrence of ab
4	b	6	occurrences of babb and bb
5	a	4	

Figure 1.12. Search for occurrences of a pattern with a deterministic automaton (see also Figure 1.13). **(a)** With alphabet $A = \{\texttt{a}, \texttt{b}, \texttt{c}\}$ and pattern $X = \{\texttt{ab}, \texttt{babb}, \texttt{bb}\}$, the deterministic automaton represented above recognizes language A^*X. The gray arrows exiting each state stand for arcs having for source these same states, for target the initial state 0, and labeled by a letter that is not already present. To locate occurrences of strings of X in a text y, it is sufficient to operate the automaton on y and to signal an occurrence each time that a terminal state is reached. **(b)** Parsing example with $y = \texttt{cbabba}$. From the utilization of the automaton, it follows that there is at least one occurrence of a string of X at positions 3 and 4 on y, and none at other positions.

Proof Let δ be the transition function of the automaton M. As the automaton is deterministic, it follows immediately that

$$r = \delta(\mathit{initial}[M], u), \tag{1.3}$$

where u is the current prefix of y, is satisfied after the execution of each of the instructions of the algorithm.

If an occurrence of a string of X ends at the current position, the current prefix u belongs to A^*X. And thus, by definition of M and after property (1.3), the current state r is terminal. As the initial state is not terminal (since $\varepsilon \notin X$), it follows that the operation signals this occurrence.

Conversely, assume that an occurrence has just been signaled. The current state r is thus terminal, which, after property (1.3) and by definition of M, implies that the current prefix u belongs to A^*X. An occurrence of a string of X ends thus at the current position, which ends the proof. ■

The execution time and the extra space needed for running the algorithm DET-SEARCH uniquely depend on the implementation of the automaton M. For example, in an implementation by transition matrix, the time to parse the text is $\Theta(|y|)$, since the delay is constant, and the extra space, in addition to the matrix, is also constant (see Proposition 1.15).

The second algorithm of this part applies when we dispose of an automaton N recognizing the language X itself, and no longer A^*X. By adding to the automaton an arc from its initial state to itself and labeled by a, for each letter $a \in A$, we simply get an automaton N' that recognizes the language A^*X. But the automaton N' is not deterministic, and therefore the previous algorithm cannot be applied. Figure 1.13(a) presents an example of automaton N' for the same pattern X as the one of Figure 1.12(a).

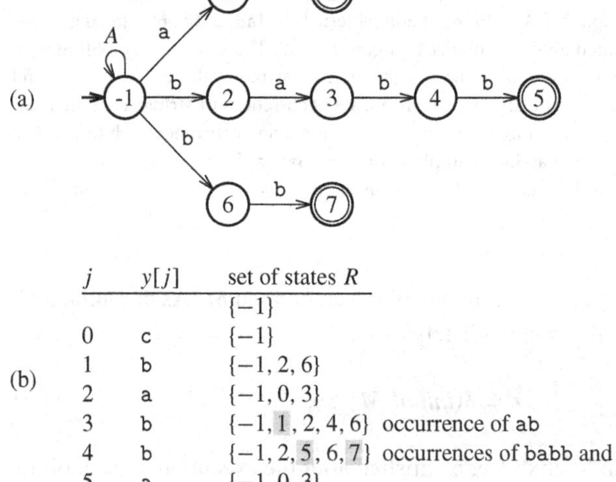

(b)

j	$y[j]$	set of states R	
		$\{-1\}$	
0	c	$\{-1\}$	
1	b	$\{-1, 2, 6\}$	
2	a	$\{-1, 0, 3\}$	
3	b	$\{-1, 1, 2, 4, 6\}$	occurrence of ab
4	b	$\{-1, 2, 5, 6, 7\}$	occurrences of babb and bb
5	a	$\{-1, 0, 3\}$	

Figure 1.13. Search for occurrences of a pattern with a nondeterministic automaton (see also Figure 1.12). **(a)** The nondeterministic automaton recognizes the language A^*X, with alphabet $A = \{\mathtt{a}, \mathtt{b}, \mathtt{c}\}$ and pattern $X = \{\mathtt{ab}, \mathtt{babb}, \mathtt{bb}\}$. To locate the occurrences of strings of X that occur in a text y, it is sufficient to operate the automaton on y and to signal an occurrence each time that a terminal state is reached. **(b)** Example when $y = \mathtt{cbabba}$. The computation amounts to simultaneously follow all possible paths. It results that the pattern occurs at right positions 3 and 4 on y and nowhere else.

In such a situation, the retained solution usually consists in simulating the automaton obtained by the determinization of N', following in parallel all the possible paths having a given label. Since only states that are the ends of paths may perform the occurrence test, we simply keep the set R of reached states. It is what realizes the algorithm NON-DET-SEARCH below. Actually, it is even not necessary to modify the automaton N since the loops on its initial state can also be simulated. This is realized in line 4 of the algorithm by adding systematically the initial state to the set of states. During the execution of the automaton on the input y, the automaton is not in a single state, but in a set of states, R. This subset of the set of states is recomputed after the analysis of the current letter of y. The algorithm calls the function TARGETS that performs a transition on a set of states, which function is an immediate extension of the function TARGET.

```
NON-DET-SEARCH(N, y)
1  q0 ← initial[N]
2  R ← {q0}
3  for each letter a of y, sequentially do
4      R ← TARGETS(R, a) ∪ {q0}
5      t ← FALSE
6      for each state p ∈ R do
7          if terminal[p] then
8              t ← TRUE
9      OUTPUT-IF(t)
```

```
TARGETS(R, a)
S ← ∅
for each state p ∈ R do
    for each state q such that (a, q) ∈ Succ[p] do
        S ← S ∪ {q}
return S
```

Lines 5–8 of the algorithm NON-DET-SEARCH give the value TRUE to the boolean variable t when the intersection between the set of states R and the set of terminal states is nonempty. An occurrence is then signaled, line 9, if the case arises. Figure 1.13(b) illustrates how the algorithm works.

Proposition 1.19

When N is an automaton that recognizes the language X for a pattern $X \subseteq A^*$, the operation NON-DET-SEARCH(N, y) *locates all the occurrences of strings of X in the text $y \in A^*$.*

Proof Let us denote by q_0 the initial state of the automaton N and, for every string $v \in A^*$, R_v the set of states defined by

$$R_v = \{q : q \text{ end of a path of origin } q_0 \text{ and of label } v\}.$$

One can verify, by recurrence on the length of the prefixes of y, that the assertion

$$R = \bigcup_{v \preceq_{\text{suff}} u} R_v, \tag{1.4}$$

where u is the current prefix of y, is satisfied after the execution of each of the instructions of the algorithm, except in line 1.

If an occurrence of a string of X ends at the current position, one of the suffixes v of the current prefix u belongs to X. Therefore, by the definition of N, one of the states $q \in R_v$ is terminal, and by property (1.4), one of the states of R is terminal. It follows that the operation signals this occurrence since no string of X is empty.

Conversely, if an occurrence has just been signaled, it means that one of the states $q \in R$ is terminal. Property (1.4) and the definition of N imply the existence of a suffix v of the current prefix u that belongs to X. It follows that an occurrence of a string of X ends at the current position. This ends the proof of the proposition. ■

The complexity of the algorithm NON-DET-SEARCH depends both on the implementation retained for the automaton N and the realization chosen for manipulating the sets of states. If, for instance, the automaton is deterministic, its transition function is implemented by a transition matrix, and the sets of states are implemented by boolean vectors which indices are states, the function TARGETS executes in time and space $O(\text{card } Q)$, where Q is the set of states. In this case, the analysis of the text y runs in time $O(|y| \times \text{card } Q)$ and utilizes $O(\text{card } Q)$ extra space.

In the following paragraphs, we consider an example of realization of the above simulation adapted to the case of a very small automaton that possesses a tree structure.

Bit-vector model

The ***bit-vector model*** refers to the possibility of using machine words for encoding the states of the automata. When the length of the language associated with the pattern is not larger than the size of a machine word counted in bits, this technique gives algorithms that are efficient and easy to implement. The technique is also used in Section 8.4.

Here, the principle is applied to the method that simulates a deterministic automaton and described in the previous paragraphs. It encodes the set of reached states into a bit vector, and executes a transition by a simple shift controlled by a mask associated with the considered letter.

Let us start with specifying the notation used in the rest for bit vectors. We identify a bit vector with a string on the alphabet $\{0, 1\}$. We denote respectively by $\vee$ and $\wedge$ the "or" and "and" bitwise operators. These are binary operations internal to the sets of bit vectors of identical lengths. The first operation, $\vee$, puts to 1 the bit of the result if one of the two bits at the same position of the two operands is equal to 1, and to 0 otherwise. The second operation, $\wedge$, puts to 1 the bits of the result if the two bits at the same position of the two operands are equal to 1, and to 0 otherwise. We denote by $\dashv$ the shift operation defined as follows: with a natural number k and a bit vector the result is the bit vector of same length obtained from the first one by shifting the bits to the right by k positions and by completing it to the left with k 0's. Thus, $1001 \vee 0011 = 1011$, $1001 \wedge 0011 = 0001$, and $2 \dashv 1101 = 0011$.

Let us consider a finite nonempty set X of nonempty strings. Let N be the automaton obtained from the card X elementary deterministic automata that recognizes the strings of X by merging their initial states into a single one, say q_0. Let N' be the automaton built on N by adding the arcs of the form (q_0, a, q_0), for each letter $a \in A$. The automaton N' recognizes the language A^*X. The search for the occurrences of strings of X in a text y is realized here as in the above paragraphs by simulating the deterministic automaton equivalent to N' by means of N (see Figure 1.13(a)).

Let us set $m = |X|$ and let us number the states of N from -1 to $m - 1$ using a depth-first traversal of the structure from the initial state q_0 – it is the numbering used in the example of Figure 1.13(a). Let us encode now each set of states $R \setminus \{-1\}$ by a vector r of m bits with the following convention:

$$p \in R \setminus \{-1\} \text{ if and only if } r[p] = 1.$$

Let r be the vector of m bits that encodes the current state of the search, $a \in A$ be the current letter of y, and s be the vector of m bits that encodes the next state. It is clear that the computation of s from r and a observes the following rule: $s[p] = 1$ if and only if there exists an arc of label a, either from the state -1 to the state p, or from the state $p - 1$ to the state p with $r[p - 1] = 1$. Let us consider *init* the vector of m bits defined by $init[p] = 1$ if and only if there exists an arc with state -1 as its source and state p as its target. Let us consider also the table *masq* indexed on A and with values in the set of vectors of m bits, defined for every letter $b \in A$ by $masq[b][p] = 1$ if and only if there exists an arc of label b and of target the state p. Then r, a, and s satisfy the identity:

$$s = (init \vee (1 \dashv r)) \wedge masq[a].$$

This latter expression translates the transition performed in line 4 of algorithm NON-DET-SEARCH in terms of bitwise operations, except for the initial state. The bit vector *init* encodes the potential transitions from the initial state, and one-bit right shift from reached states. The table *masq* validates the transitions labeled by the current letter.

It only remains to indicate how to test whether one of the states represented by a vector r of m bits that encodes the current state of the search is terminal or not. To this goal, let *term* be the vector of m bits defined by $term[p] = 1$ if and only if the state p is terminal. Then one of the states represented by r is terminal if and only if:

$$r \wedge term \neq 0^m.$$

The code of the function SMALL-AUTOMATON that computes the vectors *init* and *term*, and the table *masq* follows, then the code of the pattern matching algorithm is given.

```
SMALL-AUTOMATON(X, m)
init ← 0^m
term ← 0^m
for each letter a ∈ A do
        masq[a] ← 0^m
p ← −1
for each string x ∈ X do
        init[p + 1] ← 1
        for each letter a of x, sequentially do
                p ← p + 1
                masq[a][p] ← 1
        term[p] ← 1
return (init, term, masq)
```

```
SHORT-STRINGS-SEARCH(X, m, y)
(init, term, masq) ← SMALL-AUTOMATON(X, m)
r ← 0^m
for each letter a of y, sequentially do
        r ← (init ∨ (1 ⊣ r)) ∧ masq[a]
        OUTPUT-IF(r ∧ term ≠ 0^m)
```

(a)

k	0	1	2	3	4	5	6	7
init[k]	1	0	1	0	0	0	1	0
term[k]	0	1	0	0	0	1	0	1
masq[a][k]	1	0	0	1	0	0	0	0
masq[b][k]	0	1	1	0	1	1	1	1
masq[c][k]	0	0	0	0	0	0	0	0

(b)

j	$y[j]$	bit vector r	
		00000000	
0	c	00000000	
1	b	00100010	
2	a	10010000	
3	b	01101010	occurrence of ab
4	b	00100111	occurrences of babb and bb
5	a	10010000	

Figure 1.14. Using bit vectors to search for the occurrences of the pattern $X = \{$ab, babb, bb$\}$ (see Figure 1.13). **(a)** Vectors *init* and *term*, and table of vectors *masq* on the alphabet $A = \{$a, b, c$\}$. These vectors are of length 8 since $|X| = 8$. The first vector encodes the potential transitions from the initial state. The second encodes the terminal states. The vectors of the table *masq* encode the occurrences of letters of the alphabet in the strings of X. **(b)** Successive values of the vector r that encodes the current state of the search for strings of X in the text $y =$ cbabba. The gray area that marks some bits indicates that a terminal state has been reached.

An example of computation is treated in Figure 1.14.

Proposition 1.20
Running the operation SHORT-STRINGS-SEARCH(X, m, y) *takes a* $\Theta(m \times \text{card}\, A + m \times |y|)$ *time. The required extra memory space is* $\Theta(m \times \text{card}\, A)$.

Proof The time necessary for initializing the bit vectors *init*, *term*, and *masq*[a], for $a \in A$, is linear in their size, thus $\Theta(m \times \text{card}\, A)$. The instructions in lines 4 and 5 execute in $\Theta(m)$ time each. The stated complexities follow. ■

Once this is established, when the length m is no more than the number of bits of a machine word, every bit vector of m bits can be implemented with the help of a machine word whose first m bits only are significant. This gives the following result.

Corollary 1.21
When $m = |X|$ *is no more than the length of a machine word, the operation* SHORT-STRINGS-SEARCH(X, m, y) *executes in time* $\Theta(|y| + \text{card}\, A)$ *with an extra memory space* $\Theta(\text{card}\, A)$. ■

1.6 Borders and prefixes tables

In this section, we present two fundamental methods for locating efficiently patterns or for searching for regularities in strings. There are two tables, the table of borders and the table of prefixes, that both store occurrences of prefixes of a string that occur inside itself. The tables can be computed in linear time. The computation algorithms also provide methods for locating strings that are studied in details in Chapters 2 and 3 (a prelude is proposed in Exercise 1.24).

Table of borders

Let x be a string of length $m \geq 1$. We define the table

$$border: \{0, 1, \ldots, m-1\} \to \{0, 1, \ldots, m-1\}$$

by

$$border[k] = |\text{Border}(x[0\,..\,k])|$$

for $k = 0, 1, \ldots, m-1$. The table *border* is called the ***table of borders*** for the string x, meaning that they are borders of the nonempty prefixes of the string. Here is an example of the table of borders for the string $x = $ `abbabaabbabaaaabbabbaa`:

k	0	1	2	3	4	5	6	7	8	9	10	11
$x[k]$	a	b	b	a	b	a	a	b	b	a	b	a
$border[k]$	0	0	0	1	2	1	1	2	3	4	5	6

k	12	13	14	15	16	17	18	19	20	21
$x[k]$	a	a	a	b	b	a	b	b	a	a
$border[k]$	7	1	1	2	3	4	5	3	4	1

The following lemma provides the recurrence relation used by the function BORDERS, given thereafter, for computing the table *border*.

Lemma 1.22
For every $(u, a) \in A^+ \times A$, we have

$$\text{Border}(ua) = \begin{cases} \text{Border}(u)a & \text{if Border}(u)a \preceq_{\text{pref}} u, \\ \text{Border}(\text{Border}(u)a) & \text{otherwise.} \end{cases}$$

Proof We first note that if Border(ua) is a nonempty string, it is of the form wa where w is a border of u.

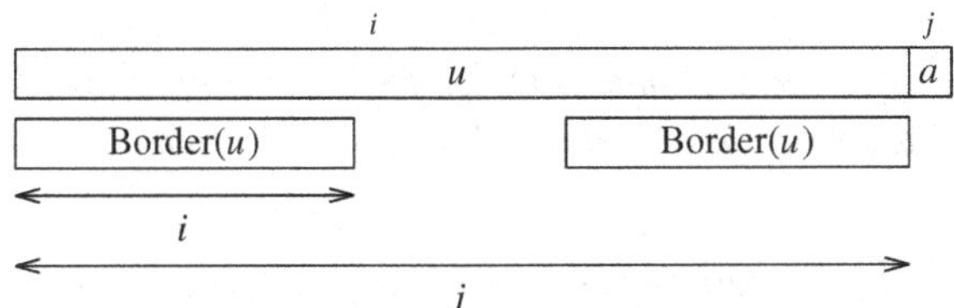

Figure 1.15. Schema showing the correspondence between variables i and j considered in line 3 of the function BORDERS and in Lemma 1.22.

If Border$(u)a \preceq_{\text{pref}} u$, the string Border$(u)a$ is then a border of ua, and the previous remark shows that it is the longest string of this kind. It follows that Border$(ua) =$ Border$(u)a$ in this case.

Otherwise, Border(ua) is both a prefix of Border(u) and a suffix of Border$(u)a$. As it is of maximal length with this property, it is indeed the string Border(Border$(u)a$). ■

Figure 1.15 schematizes the correspondence between the variables i and j of the function *Borders*, which code follows, and the statement of Lemma 1.22.

```
BORDERS(x, m)
 1  i ← 0
 2  for j ← 1 to m − 1 do
 3      border[j − 1] ← i
 4      while i ≥ 0 and x[j] ≠ x[i] do
 5          if i = 0 then
 6              i ← −1
 7          else i ← border[i − 1]
 8      i ← i + 1
 9  border[m − 1] ← i
10  return border
```

Proposition 1.23
The function BORDERS *applied to a string x and its length m produces the table of borders for x.*

Proof The table *border* is computed by the function BORDERS sequentially: it runs from the prefix of x of length 1 to x itself. During the execution of the **while** loop of lines 4–7, the sequence of borders of $x[0\,..\,j-1]$ is inspected following Proposition 1.5. When exiting this loop, we have $|\text{Border}(x[0\,..\,j])| = |x[0\,..\,i]| = i + 1$, in accordance with Lemma 1.22. The correctness of the code follows. ■

Proposition 1.24
The operation BORDERS(x, m) *executes in time* $\Theta(m)$. *The number of comparisons between letters of the string* x *is within* $m-1$ *and* $2m-3$ *when* $m \geq 2$. *These bounds are tight.*

We say, in the rest, that the comparison between two given letters is ***positive*** when these two letters are identical, and is ***negative*** otherwise.

Proof Let us note that the execution time is linear in the number of comparisons performed between the letters of x. It is thus sufficient to establish the bound on the number of comparisons.

The quantity $2j-i$ increases by at least one unit after each comparison of letters: the variables i and j are both incremented after a positive comparison; the value of i is decreased by at least one and the value of j remains unchanged after a negative comparison. When $m \geq 2$, this quantity is equal to 2 for the first comparison ($i=0$ and $j=1$) and at most $2m-2$ during the last ($i \geq 0$ and $j=m-1$). The overall number of comparisons is thus bounded by $2m-3$ as stated.

The lower bound of $m-1$ is tight and is reached for $x = ab^{m-1}$. The upper bound of $2m-3$ comparisons is tight: it is reached for every string x of the form $a^{m-1}b$ with $a, b \in A$ and $a \neq b$. This ends the proof. ∎

Another proof of the bound $2m-3$ is proposed in Exercise 1.22.

Table of prefixes

Let x be a string of length $m \geq 1$. We define the table

$$pref\colon \{0, 1, \ldots, m-1\} \to \{0, 1, \ldots, m-1\}$$

by

$$pref[k] = |lcp(x, x[k\,..\,m-1])|$$

for $k = 0, 1, \ldots, m-1$, where $lcp(u, v)$ is the ***longest common prefix*** of strings u and v.

The table *pref* is called the ***table of prefixes*** for the string x. It memorizes the prefixes of x that occur inside the string itself. We note that $pref[0] = |x|$. The following example shows the table of prefixes for the string $x =$ `abbabaabbabaaaabbabbaa`.

k	0	1	2	3	4	5	6	7	8	9	10	11
$x[k]$	a	b	b	a	b	a	a	b	b	a	b	a
$pref[k]$	22	0	0	2	0	1	7	0	0	2	0	1

k	12	13	14	15	16	17	18	19	20	21
$x[k]$	a	a	a	b	b	a	b	b	a	a
$pref[k]$	1	1	5	0	0	4	0	0	1	1

Some string matching algorithms (see Chapter 3) use the table *suff* which is nothing but the analogue of the table of prefixes obtained by considering the reverse of the string x.

The method for computing *pref* that is presented below proceeds by determining $pref[i]$ by increasing values of the position i on x. A naive method would consist in evaluating each value $pref[i]$ independently of the previous values by direct comparisons; but it would then lead to a quadratic-time computation, in the case where x is the power of a single letter, for example. The utilization of already computed values yields a linear-time algorithm. For that, we introduce, the index i being fixed, two values g and f that constitute the key elements of the method. They satisfy the relations

$$g = \max\{j + pref[j] : 0 < j < i\} \tag{1.5}$$

and

$$f \in \{j : 0 < j < i \text{ and } j + pref[j] = g\}. \tag{1.6}$$

We note that g and f are defined when $i > 1$. The string $x[f \,..\, g-1]$ is then a prefix of x, thus also a border of $x[0 \,..\, g-1]$. It is the empty string when $f = g$. We can note, moreover, that if $g < i$ we have then $g = i - 1$, and that on the contrary, by definition of f, we have $f < i \leq g$.

The following lemma provides the justification for the correctness of the function PREFIXES.

Lemma 1.25
If $i < g$, we have the relation

$$pref[i] = \begin{cases} pref[i-f] & \text{if } pref[i-f] < g-i, \\ g-i & \text{if } pref[i-f] > g-i, \\ g-i+\ell & \text{otherwise,} \end{cases}$$

where $\ell = |lcp(x[g-i \,..\, m-1], x[g \,..\, m-1])|$.

Proof Let us set $u = x[f \,..\, g-1]$. The string u is a prefix of x by the definition of f and g. Let us also set $k = pref[i-f]$. By the definition of *pref*, the string $x[i-f \,..\, i-f+k-1]$ is a prefix of x but $x[i-f \,..\, i-f+k]$ is not.

In the case where $pref[i-f] < g-i$, an occurrence of $x[i-f \,..\, i-f+k]$ starts at the position $i-f$ on u – thus also at the position i on x – which shows

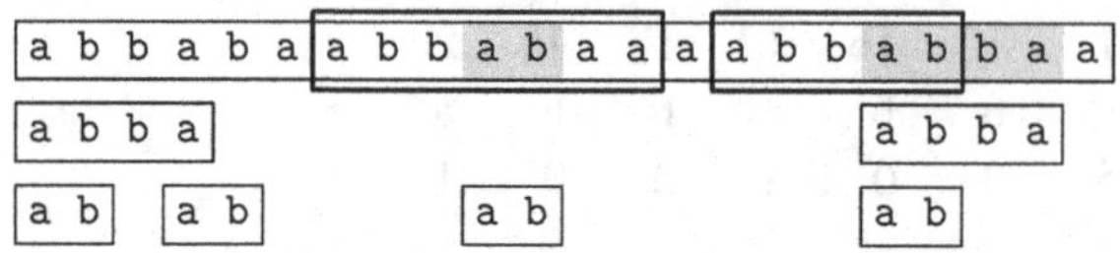

Figure 1.16. Illustration of the function PREFIXES. The framed factors $x[6\,..\,12]$ and $x[14\,..\,18]$, and the gray factors $x[9\,..\,10]$ and $x[17\,..\,20]$ are prefixes of string $x =$ abbabaabbabaaaabbabbaa. For $i = 9$, we have $f = 6$ and $g = 13$. The situation at this position is the same as at position $3 = 9 - 6$. We have $pref[9] = pref[3] = 2$ which means that ab, of length 2, is the longest factor at position 9 that is a prefix of x. For $i = 17$, we have $f = 14$ and $g = 19$. As $pref[17 - 14] = 2 = 19 - 17$, we deduce that string ab $= x[i\,..\,g - 1]$ is a prefix of x. Letters of x and $x[i\,..\,m - 1]$ have to be compared from respective positions 2 and g for determining $pref[i] = 4$.

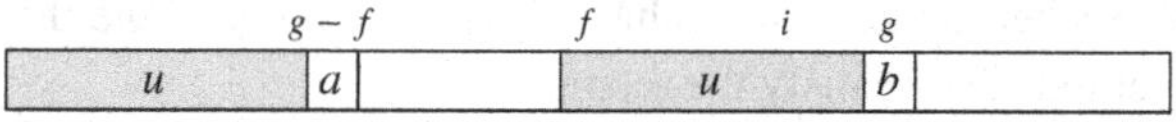

Figure 1.17. Variables i, f, and g of the function PREFIXES. The main loop has for invariants: $u = lcp(x, x[f\,..\,m - 1])$ and thus $a \neq b$ with $a, b \in A$, then $f < i$ when f is defined. The schema corresponds to the situation in which $i < g$.

that $x[i - f\,..\,i - f + k - 1]$ is the longest prefix of x starting at position i. Therefore, we get $pref[i] = k = pref[i - f]$.

In the case where $pref[i - f] > g - i$, $x[0\,..\,g - i - 1] = x[i - f\,..\,g - f - 1] = x[i\,..\,g - 1]$, and $x[g - i] = x[g - f] \neq x[g]$. We have thus $pref[i] = g - i$.

In the case where $pref[i - f] = g - i$, we have $x[g - i] \neq x[g - f]$ and $x[g - f] \neq x[g]$, therefore we cannot decide on the result of the comparison between $x[g - i]$ and $x[g]$. Extra letter comparisons are necessary and we conclude that $pref[i] = g - i + \ell$. ■

In the computation of $pref$, we initialize the variable g to 0 to simplify the writing of the code of the function PREFIXES, and we leave f initially undefined. The first step of the computation consists thus in determining $pref[1]$ by letter comparisons. The utility of the above statement comes for computing next values. An illustration of how the function works is given in Figure 1.16. A schema showing the correspondence between the variables of the function and the notation used in the statement of Lemma 1.25 and its proof is given in Figure 1.17.

```
Prefixes(x, m)
 1  pref[0] ← m
 2  g ← 0
 3  for i ← 1 to m − 1 do
 4      if i < g and pref[i − f] ≠ g − i then
 5          pref[i] ← min{pref[i − f], g − i}
 6      else (g, f) ← (max{g, i}, i)
 7          while g < m and x[g] = x[g − f] do
 8              g ← g + 1
 9          pref[i] ← g − f
10  return pref
```

Proposition 1.26
The function Prefixes *applied to a string x and to its length m produces the table of prefixes for x.*

Proof We can verify that the variables f and g satisfy the relations (1.5) and (1.6) at each step of the execution of the loop.

We note then that, for i fixed satisfying the condition $i < g$, the function applies the relation stated in Lemma 1.25, which produces a correct computation. It remains thus to check that the computation is correct when $i \geq g$. But in this situation, lines 6–8 compute $|lcp(x, x[i \mathinner{..} m-1])| = |x[f \mathinner{..} g-1]| = g - f$ which is, by definition, the value of $pref[i]$.

Therefore, the function produces the table $pref$. ■

Proposition 1.27
The execution of the operation Prefixes(x, m) *runs in time* $\Theta(m)$. *Less than* $2m$ *comparisons between letters of the string x are performed.*

Proof Comparisons between letters are performed in line 7. Every comparison between equal letters increments the variable g. As the value of g never decreases and that it varies from 0 to at most m, there are at most m positive comparisons. Each negative comparison leads to the next step of the loop. Then there are at most $m - 1$ of them. Thus less than $2m$ comparisons on the overall.

The previous argument also shows that the total time of all the executions of the loop of lines 7–8 is $\Theta(m)$. The other instructions of the loop 3–9 take a constant time for each value of i giving again a global time $\Theta(m)$ for their execution and that of the function. ■

The bound of $2m$ on the number of comparisons performed by the function Prefixes is relatively tight. For instance, we get $2m - 3$ comparisons for a

a	b	b	a	b	a	a	b	b	a	b	a	a	a	a	b	b	a	b	b	a	a

Figure 1.18. Relation between borders and prefixes. Considering the string $x =$ abbabaabbabaaaabbabbaa, we have the equality $\mathit{pref}[9] = 2$ but $\mathit{border}[9 + 2 - 1] = 5 \neq 2$. We also have both $\mathit{border}[15] = 2$ but $\mathit{pref}[15 - 2 + 1] = 5 \neq 2$.

string of the form $a^{m-1}b$ with $m \geq 2$, $a, b \in A$, and $a \neq b$. Indeed, it takes $m - 1$ comparisons to compute $\mathit{pref}[1]$, then one comparison for each of the $m - 2$ values $\mathit{pref}[i]$ with $1 < i < m$.

Relation between borders and prefixes

The tables *border* and *pref*, whose computation is described above, both memorize occurrences of prefixes of x. We explicit here a relation between these two tables.

The relation is not immediate for the reason that follows, which is illustrated in Figure 1.18. When $\mathit{pref}[i] = \ell$, the factor $u = x[i \mathinner{..} i + \ell - 1]$ is a prefix of x but it is not necessarily the border of $x[0 \mathinner{..} i + \ell - 1]$ because this border can be longer than u. In the same way, when $\mathit{border}[j] = \ell$, the factor $v = x[j - \ell + 1 \mathinner{..} j]$ is a prefix of x but it is not necessarily the *longest* prefix of x occurring at position $j - \ell + 1$.

The proposition that follows shows how the table *border* is expressed using the table *pref*. One can deduce from the statement an algorithm for computing the table *border* knowing the table *pref*.

Proposition 1.28
Let $x \in A^+$ and j be a position on x. Then:

$$\mathit{border}[j] = \begin{cases} 0 & \text{if } I = \emptyset, \\ j - \min I + 1 & \text{otherwise,} \end{cases}$$

where $I = \{i : 0 < i \leq j \text{ and } i + \mathit{pref}[i] - 1 \geq j\}$.

Proof We first note that, for $0 < i \leq j$, $i \in I$ if and only if $x[i \mathinner{..} j] \preceq_{\text{pref}} x$. Indeed, if $i \in I$, we have $x[i \mathinner{..} j] \preceq_{\text{pref}} x[i \mathinner{..} i + \mathit{pref}[i] - 1] \preceq_{\text{pref}} x$, thus $x[i \mathinner{..} j] \preceq_{\text{pref}} x$. Conversely, if $x[i \mathinner{..} j] \preceq_{\text{pref}} x$, we deduce, by definition of $\mathit{pref}[i]$, $\mathit{pref}[i] \geq j - i + 1$. And thus $i + \mathit{pref}[i] - 1 \geq j$. Which shows that $i \in I$. We also note that $\mathit{border}[j] = 0$ if and only if $I = \emptyset$.

It follows that if $\mathit{border}[j] \neq 0$ (thus $\mathit{border}[j] > 0$) and $k = j - \mathit{border}[j] + 1$, we have $k \leq j$ and $x[k \mathinner{..} j] \preceq_{\text{pref}} x$. No factor $x[i \mathinner{..} j]$, $i < k$, satisfies the relation $x[i \mathinner{..} j] \preceq_{\text{pref}} x$ by definition of $\mathit{border}[j]$. Thus $k = \min I$ by the first remark, and $\mathit{border}[j] = j - k + 1$ as stated. ■

The computation of the table *pref* from the table *border* can lead to an iteration, and does not seem to give a simple expression, comparable to the one of the previous statement (see Exercise 1.23).

Notes

The chapter contains the basic elements for a precise study of algorithms on strings. Most of the notions that are introduced here are dispersed in different books. We cite here those that are often considered as references in their domains.

The combinatorial aspects on strings are dealt with in the collective books of Lothaire [79–81]. One can refer to the book of Aho, Hopcroft, and Ullman [69] for algorithmic questions: expression of algorithms, data structures, and complexity evaluation. We were inspired by the book of Cormen, Leiserson, and Rivest [75] for the general presentation and the style of algorithms. Concerning automata and languages, one can refer to the book of Berstel [73] or the one of Pin [82]. The books of Berstel and Perrin [74] and of Béal [71] contain elements on the theory of codes (Exercises 1.10 and 1.11). Finally, the book of Aho, Sethi, and Ullman [70] describes methods for the implementation of automata.

Section 1.5 on basic techniques contains elements frequently selected for the final development of software using algorithms that process strings. They are, more specifically, heuristics and utilization of machine words. This last technique is also tackled in Chapter 8 for approximate pattern matching. This type of technique has been initiated by Baeza-Yates and Gonnet [99] and by Wu and Manber [218]. The algorithm Fast-search is from Horspool [156]. The search for a string by means of a hash function is analyzed by Karp and Rabin [166].

The treatment of notions in Section 1.6 is original. The computation of the table of borders is classical. It is inspired by an algorithm of Morris and Pratt of 1970 (see [10]) that is at the origin of the first string matching algorithm running in linear time. The table of prefixes synthesizes differently the same information on a string as the previous table. The dual notion of table of suffixes is used in Chapter 3. Gusfield [6] makes it a fundamental element of string matching methods. (His Z algorithm corresponds to the algorithm Suffixes of Chapter 3).

The inverse problem related to borders is to test whether an integer array is the border array of a string or not, and to exhibit a corresponding string if it is. This question is solved in linear time by Franěk, Gao, Lu, Ryan, Smyth, Sun, and Yang in [140] for an unbounded alphabet and by Duval, Lecroq, and Lefebvre [132] for a bounded alphabet.

Exercises

1.1 (Computation)

What is the number of prefixes, suffixes, factors, and subsequences of a given string? Discuss if necessary.

1.2 (Fibonacci morphism)

A ***morphism*** f on A^* is an application from A^* into itself that satisfies the rules:

$$f(\varepsilon) = \varepsilon,$$
$$f(x \cdot y) = f(x) \cdot f(y) \quad \text{for } x, y \in A^*.$$

For every natural number n and every string $x \in A^*$, we denote by $f^n(x)$ the string defined by $f^0(x) = x$ and $f^k(x) = f^{k-1}(f(x))$ for $k = 1, 2, \ldots, n$.

Let us consider the alphabet $A = \{\mathtt{a}, \mathtt{b}\}$. Let φ be the morphism on A^* defined by $\varphi(\mathtt{a}) = \mathtt{ab}$ and $\varphi(\mathtt{b}) = \mathtt{a}$. Show that the string $\varphi^n(\mathtt{a})$ is identical to f_{n+2}, the Fibonacci string of index $n + 2$.

1.3 (Permutation)

We call a permutation on the alphabet A a string u that satisfies the condition $\text{card alph}(u) = |u| = \text{card } A$. This is thus a string in which all the letters of the alphabet occur exactly once.

For $k = \text{card } A$, show that there exists a string of length less than $k^2 - 2k + 4$ that contains as subsequences all the permutations on A. Design a construction algorithm for such a string. (*Hint:* see Mohanty [187].)

1.4 (Period)

Show that the condition 3 of Proposition 1.4 can be replaced by the following condition: there exists a string t and an integer $k > 0$ such that $x \preceq_{\text{fact}} t^k$ and $|t| = p$.

1.5 (Limit case)

Show that the string $(\mathtt{ab})^k\mathtt{a}(\mathtt{ab})^k\mathtt{a}$ with $k \geq 1$ is the limit case for the Periodicity Lemma.

1.6 (Periods)

Let p be a period of x that is not a multiple of $\text{per}(x)$. Show that $p > |x| - \text{per}(x)$.

Let p and q be two periods of x such that $p < q$. Show that:

- $q - p$ is a period of $\mathit{first}_{|x|-p}(x)$ and of $(\mathit{first}_p(x))^{-1}x$,
- p and $q + p$ are periods of $\mathit{first}_q(x)x$.

(The definition of first_k is given in Section 4.4.)

Show that if $x = uvw$, uv, and vw have period p and $|v| \geq p$, then x has period p.

Let us assume that x has period p and contains a factor v of period r with r divisor of q. Show that r is also a period of x.

1.7 (Three periods)

On the triplets of sorted positive integers (p_1, p_2, p_3), $p_1 \leq p_2 \leq p_3$, we define the derivation by: the derivative of (p_1, p_2, p_3) is the triplet made of the integers $p_1, p_2 - p_1$, and $p_3 - p_1$. Let (q_1, q_2, q_3) be the first triplet obtained by iterating the derivation from (p_1, p_2, p_3) and such that $q_1 = 0$.

Show that if the string $x \in A^*$ has p_1, p_2, and p_3 as periods and that

$$|x| \geq \frac{1}{2}(p_1 + p_2 + p_3 - 2\gcd(p_1, p_2, p_3) + q_2 + q_3),$$

then it has also $\gcd(p_1, p_2, p_3)$ as period. (*Hint:* see Mignosi and Restivo [80], or Constantinescu and Ilie [117].)

1.8 (Three squares)

Let u, v, and w be three nonempty strings. Show that we have $2|u| < |w|$ if we assume that u is primitive and that $u^2 \prec_{\text{pref}} v^2 \prec_{\text{pref}} w^2$ (see Proposition 9.17 for a more precise consequence).

1.9 (Conjugates)

Show that two nonempty conjugate strings have the same exponent and conjugate roots.

Show that the conjugacy class of every nonempty string x contains $|x|/k$ elements where k is the exponent of x.

1.10 (Code)

A language $X \subseteq A^*$ is a ***code*** if every string of X^+ has a unique decomposition in strings of X.

Show that the ASCII codewords of characters on the alphabet $\{0, 1\}$ form a code according to this definition.

Show that the languages $\{a, b\}^*$, ab^*, $\{aa, ba, b\}$, $\{aa, baa, ba\}$, and $\{a, ba, bb\}$ are codes. Show that this is not the case of the languages $\{a, ab, ba\}$ and $\{a, abbba, babab, bb\}$.

A language $X \subseteq A^*$ is prefix if the condition

$$u \preceq_{\text{pref}} v \text{ implies } u = v$$

is satisfied for every strings $u, v \in X$. The notion of a suffix language is defined in a dual way.

Show that every prefix language is a code. Do the same for suffix languages.

1.11 (Default theorem)

Let $X \subseteq A^*$ be a finite set that is not a code. Let $Y \subseteq A^*$ be a code for which Y^* is the smallest set of this form that contains X^*. Show that card $Y <$ card X. (*Hint:* every string $x \in X$ can be written in the form $y_1 y_2 \ldots y_k$ with $y_i \in Y$ for $i = 1, 2, \ldots, k$; show that the function $\alpha: X \to Y$ defined by $\alpha(x) = y_1$ is surjective but is not injective; see [79].)

1.12 (Commutation)

Show by the default theorem (see Exercise 1.11), then by the Periodicity Lemma that, if $uv = vu$, for two strings $u, v \in A^*$, u and v are powers of a same string.

1.13 (nlogn)

Let $f: \mathbf{N} \to \mathbf{N}$ be a function defined by

$$\begin{aligned} f(1) &= a, \\ f(n) &= f(\lfloor n/2 \rfloor) + f(\lceil n/2 \rceil) + bn \quad \text{for } n \geq 2, \end{aligned}$$

with $a \in \mathbf{N}$ and $b \in \mathbf{N} \setminus \{0\}$. Show that $f(n)$ is $\Theta(n \log n)$.

1.14 (Filter)

We consider a code for which characters are encoded on 8 bits. We want to develop a pattern matching algorithm using an automaton for strings written on the alphabet {`A`, `C`, `G`, `T`}.

Describe data structures to realize the automaton with the help of a transition matrix of size $4 \times m$ (and not $256 \times m$), where m is the number of states of the automaton, possibly using an amount of extra space which is independent of m.

1.15 (Implementation of partial functions)

Let $f: E \to F$ be a partial function where E is a finite set. Describe an implementation of f able to perform each of the four following operations in constant time:

- initialize f, such that $f(x)$ is undefined for $x \in E$,
- set the value of $f(x)$ to $y \in F$, for $x \in E$,
- test whether $f(x)$ is defined or not, for $x \in E$,
- produce the value of $f(x)$, for $x \in E$.

One can use $O(\text{card } E)$ space. (*Hint:* simultaneously use a table indexed by E and a list of elements x for which $f(x)$ is defined, with cross-references between the table and the list.)

Deduce that the implementation of such a function can be done in linear time in the number of elements of E whose images by f are defined.

1.16 (Not so naive)

We consider here a slightly more elaborate implementation for the sliding window mechanism that the one described for the naive algorithm. Among the strings x of length $m \geq 2$, it distinguishes two classes: one for which the first two letters are identical (thus $x[0] = x[1]$), and the antagonist class (thus $x[0] \neq x[1]$). This elementary distinction allows us to shift the window by two positions to the right in the following cases: string x belongs to the first class and $y[j+1] \neq x[1]$; string x belongs to the second class and $y[j+1] = x[1]$. On the other hand, if the comparison of the string x with the content of the window is always performed letter by letter, it considers positions on x in the following order $1, 2, \ldots, m-1, 0$.

Give the code of an algorithm that applies this method.

Show that the number of comparisons between text letters is on the average less than 1 when the average is evaluated on the set of strings of same length, that this length is more than 2 and that the alphabet contains at least four letters. (*Hint:* see Hancart [148].)

1.17 (End of window)

Let us consider the method that, as the algorithm FAST-SEARCH using the rightmost letter in the window for performing a shift, uses the two rightmost letters in the window (assuming that the string is of length at least 2).

Give the code of an algorithm that applies this method.

In which cases does it seem efficient? (*Hint:* see Zhu and Takaoka [220] or Baeza-Yates [98].)

1.18 (After the window)

Same statement than the one of Exercise 1.17, but with using the letter located immediately to the right of the window (beware of the overflow at the right extremity of the text). (*Hint:* see Sunday [211].)

1.19 (Sentinel)

We come back again to the string matching problem: locating occurrences of a string x of length m in a text y of length n.

The sentinel technique can be used for searching the letter $x[m-1]$ by performing the shifts with the help of the table *last-occ*. Since the shifts can be of length m, we set $y[n\,..\,n+m-1]$ to $x[m-1]^m$. Give a code for this sentinel method.

To speed up the process and decrease the number of tests on letters, it is possible to chain several shifts without testing the letters of the text. For that, we back up the value of *last-occ*$[x[m-1]]$ in a variable, let say d, then we fix the value of *last-occ*$[x[m-1]]$ to 0. We can then chain shifts until one of them is of length 0. We then test the other letters of the window, signaling an occurrence when it arises, and we apply a shift of length d. Give a code for this method. (*Hint:* see Hume and Sunday [157].)

1.20 (In C)

Give an implementation in C language of the algorithm SHORT-STRINGS-SEARCH. The operators $\vee$, $\wedge$, and $\dashv$ are encoded by `|`, `&`, and `<<`. Extend the implementation so that it accepts any parameter m (possibly greater than the number of bits of a machine word).

Compare the obtained code to the source of the Unix command `agrep`.

1.21 (Short strings)

Describe a pattern matching algorithm for short strings in a similar way to the algorithm SHORT-STRINGS-SEARCH, but in which the binary values `0` and `1` are swapped.

1.22 (Bound)

Show that the number of positive comparisons and the number of negative comparisons performed during the operation BORDERS(x, m) are at most $m-1$. Prove again the bound $2m-3$ of Proposition 1.24.

1.23 (Table of prefixes)

Describe a linear time algorithm for the computation of the table *pref*, given the table *border* for the string x.

1.24 (Location by the borders or the prefixes)

Show that the table of borders for the string $x\$y$ can be directly used in order to locate all the occurrences of the string x in the string y, where $\$ \notin \text{alph}(xy)$.

Same question with the table of prefixes for the string xy.

1.25 (Cover)

A string u is a cover of a string x if for every position i on x, there exists a position j on x for which $0 \le j \le i < j + |u| \le |x|$ and $u = x[j \,..\, j + |u| - 1]$.

Design an algorithm for the computation of the shortest cover of a string. State its complexity.

1.26 (Long border)

Let u be a nonempty border of the string $x \in A^*$.

Let $v \in A^*$ be such that $|v| < |u|$. Show that v is a border of u if and only if it is a border of x.

Show that x has another nonempty border if u satisfies the inequality $|x| < 2|u|$. Show that x has no other border satisfying the same inequality if $\text{per}(x) > |x|/4$.

1.27 (Border free)

We say that a nonempty string u is border free if $\text{Border}(u) = \varepsilon$, or, equivalently, if $\text{per}(u) = |u|$.

Let $x \in A^*$. Show that $C = \{u : u \preceq_{\text{pref}} x \text{ and } u \text{ is border free}\}$ is a suffix code (see Exercise 1.10).

Show that x uniquely factorizes into $x_k x_{k-1} \ldots x_1$ according to the strings of C ($x_i \in C$ for $i = 1, 2, \ldots, k$). Show that x_1 is the shortest string of C that is a suffix of x and that x_k is the longest string of C that is a prefix of x.

Design a linear time algorithm for computing the factorization.

1.28 (Maximal suffix)

We denote by $MS(\le, u)$ the maximal suffix of $u \in A^+$ for the lexicographic ordering where, in this notation, $\le$ denotes the ordering on the alphabet. Let $x \in A^+$.

Show that $|x| - |MS(\le, x)| < \text{per}(x)$.

We assume that $MS(\le, x) = x$ and we denote by $w_1, w_2, \ldots, w_k$ the borders of x in decreasing order of length (we have $k > 0$ and $w_k = \varepsilon$). Let $a_1, a_2, \ldots, a_k \in A$ and $z_1, z_2, \ldots, z_k \in A^*$ be such that

$$x = w_1 a_1 z_1 = w_2 a_2 z_2 = \cdots = w_k a_k z_k.$$

Show that $a_1 \le a_2 \le \cdots \le a_k$.

Design a linear-time algorithm that computes the maximal suffix (for the lexicographic ordering) of a string $x \in A^+$. (*Hint:* use the algorithm that computes the borders of Section 1.6 or see Booth [108]; see also [4].)

1.29 (Local periods)

Let $x \in A^+$. For each position i on x, we denote by

$$rep(i) = \min\{|u| : u \in A^+,\ A^*u \cup A^*x[0\,..\,i-1] \neq \emptyset \text{ and } uA^* \cup x[i\,..\,|x|-1]A^* \neq \emptyset\}$$

the ***local period*** of x at position i. Design a linear-time algorithm for computing the table of local periods associated with *rep*. (*Hint:* see Duval, Kolpakov, Kucherov, Lecroq, and Lefebvre [133].)

1.30 (Critical factorization)

Let $x \in A^+$ and $w = MS(\leq, x)$ (*MS* is defined in Exercise 1.28). Assume that $|w| \leq |MS(\leq^{-1}, x)|$ and show that $rep(|x| - |w|) = \text{per}(x)$, where *rep* is defined in the previous exercise. (*Hint:* note that the intersection of the two orderings on strings induced by $\leq$ and $\leq^{-1}$ is the prefix ordering, and use Proposition 1.4; see Crochemore and Perrin [128] and Crochemore and Rytter [4].)

2

Pattern matching automata

In this chapter, we address the problem of searching for a pattern in a text when the pattern represents a finite set of strings. We present solutions based on the utilization of automata. Note first that the utilization of an automaton as solution of the problem is quite natural: given a finite language $X \subseteq A^*$, locating all the occurrences of strings belonging to X in a text $y \in A^*$ amounts to determine all the prefixes of y that ends with a string of X; this amounts to recognize the language A^*X; and as A^*X is a regular language, this can be realized by an automaton. We additionally note that such solutions particularly suit to cases where a pattern has to be located in data that have to be processed in an online way: data flow analysis, downloading, virus detection, etc.

The utilization of an automaton for locating a pattern has already been discussed in Section 1.5. We complete here the subject by specifying how to obtain the deterministic automata mentioned at the beginning of this section. Complexities of the methods exposed at the end of Section 1.5 and that are valid for nondeterministic automata are also compared with those presented in this chapter.

The plan is decomposed as follows. We exhibit a type of deterministic and complete automata recognizing the language A^*X. We consider two reduced implementations of this type of automata. The first utilizes a failure function and the second the initial state as successor by default (notions introduced in Section 1.4). Each of the two implementations possesses its own advantage: while the first realizes an implementation of size linear in the sum of the lengths of the strings of X, the second naturally ensures a detection in real time when the alphabet is considered as fixed. We consider the particular case where the set X is reduced to a single string and we show that the delay of the search algorithm is logarithmic in the length of the string for the two considered implementations.

2.1 Trie of a dictionary

Let $X \subseteq A^*$ be a ***dictionary*** (on A), that is, a finite nonempty language not containing the empty string ε, and let $y \in A^*$ be the text in which we want to locate all the occurrences of strings of X.

The methods described in the rest of the chapter are based on an automaton that recognizes X. We denote it by $\mathcal{T}(X)$. It is an automaton whose:

- set of states is $\text{Pref}(X)$,
- initial state is the empty string ε,
- set of terminal states is X,
- arcs are of the form (u, a, ua).

Proposition 2.1
The automaton $\mathcal{T}(X)$ is deterministic. It recognizes X.

Proof Immediate. ■

We call $\mathcal{T}(X)$ the ***trie*** of the dictionary X (we identify it with the tree whose distinguished vertex, the root, is the initial state of the automaton). Figure 2.1 illustrates the situation.

The function TRIE, whose code is given below, produces the trie of any dictionary X. It successively considers each string of X in the **for** loop of lines 2–10 and inserts them inside the structure letter by letter during the execution of the **for** loop of lines 4–9.

```
TRIE(X)
 1  M ← NEW-AUTOMATON()
 2  for each string x ∈ X do
 3        t ← initial[M]
 4        for each letter a of x, sequentially do
 5              p ← TARGET(t, a)
 6              if p = NIL then
 7                    p ← NEW-STATE()
 8                    Succ[t] ← Succ[t] ∪ {(a, p)}
 9              t ← p
10        terminal[t] ← TRUE
11  return M
```

Proposition 2.2
The operation TRIE(X) *produces the automaton* $\mathcal{T}(X)$. ■

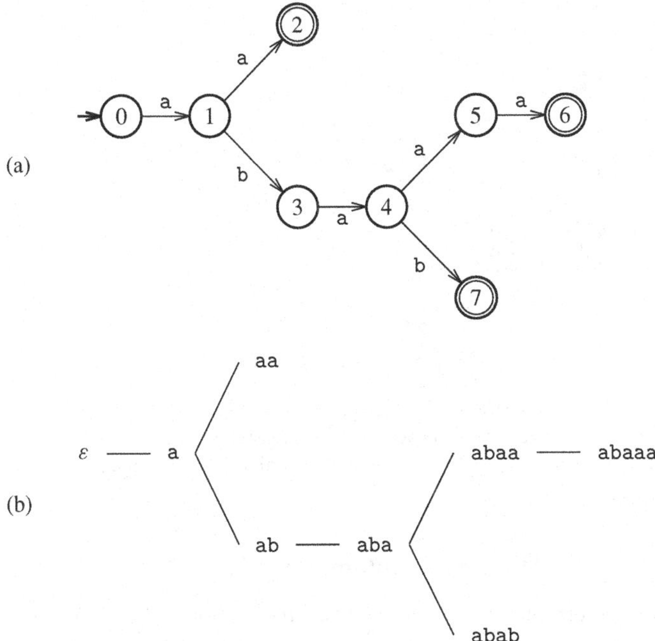

Figure 2.1. **(a)** The trie $\mathcal{T}(X)$ when $X = \{\texttt{aa}, \texttt{abaaa}, \texttt{abab}\}$. The language recognized by the automaton $\mathcal{T}(X)$ is X. The states are identified with the prefixes of strings in X. For instance, state 3 corresponds to the prefix of length 2 of abaaa and abab. **(b)** Tree representation of X.

2.2 Searching for several strings

In this section, we present a deterministic and complete automaton that recognizes the language A^*X. The particularity of this automaton is that its states are the prefixes of the strings of X: during a sequential parsing of the text, it is indeed sufficient, as we are going to see, to memorize only the longest suffix of the part of text already parsed that is a prefix of a string of X. The automaton that we consider is not minimal in the general case, but it is relatively simple to build. It is also at the basis of different constructions of the next sections. The automaton possesses the same states as $\mathcal{T}(X)$ and the same initial state. It contains the terminal states and the arcs of $\mathcal{T}(X)$.

In the rest, we indicate a construction of the automaton dissociated from the searching phase. One can also consider to build it in a "lazy" way, that is to say when needed during the search. This construction is left as an exercise (Exercise 2.4).

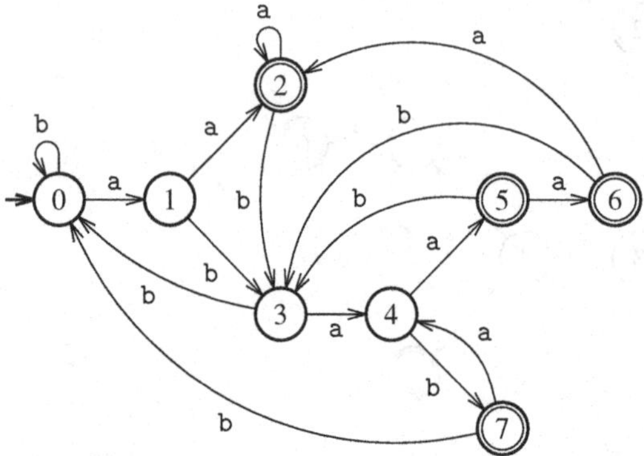

Figure 2.2. The dictionary automaton $\mathcal{D}(X)$ when $X = \{\texttt{aa}, \texttt{abaaa}, \texttt{abab}\}$ and $A = \{\texttt{a}, \texttt{b}\}$. The automaton $\mathcal{D}(X)$ recognizes the language A^*X. Compared to the trie of the same dictionary illustrated in Figure 2.1, we note that state 5 is terminal: it corresponds to abaa whose suffix aa belongs to X.

Dictionary automaton

To formalize the pattern matching automaton of the dictionary $X \subseteq A^*$, we introduce the function

$$h: A^* \to \text{Pref}(X)$$

defined by

$$h(u) = \text{the longest suffix of } u \text{ that belongs to Pref}(X)$$

for every string $u \in A^*$. Let $\mathcal{D}(X)$ be the automaton whose:

- set of states is $\text{Pref}(X)$,
- initial state is the empty string ε,
- set of terminal states is $\text{Pref}(X) \cap A^*X$,
- arcs are of the form $(u, a, h(ua))$.

The proof of the next proposition, that relies on Lemma 2.4, is postponed after the proof of this lemma.

Proposition 2.3
The automaton $\mathcal{D}(X)$ is deterministic and complete. It recognizes A^*X.

We call $\mathcal{D}(X)$ the ***dictionary automaton*** of X. An illustration is given in Figure 2.2. The proof of the proposition relies on the following result.

Lemma 2.4
The function h satisfies the following properties:

1. $u \in A^*X$ *if and only if* $h(u) \in A^*X$, *for every* $u \in A^*$.
2. $h(\varepsilon) = \varepsilon$.
3. $h(ua) = h(h(u)a)$, *for every* $(u, a) \in A^* \times A$.

Proof Let $u \in A^*$ and $a \in A$.

Let us assume that $u \in A^*X$. The string u then decomposes into vx with $v \in A^*$ and $x \in X$. Now, by definition of h, $x \preceq_{\text{suff}} h(u)$. It follows that $h(u) \in A^*X$. Conversely, let us assume that $h(u) \in A^*X$. As $h(u) \preceq_{\text{suff}} u$, $u \in A^*X$. This proves property 1.

Property 2 is clearly satisfied.

It remains to show property 3. Strings $h(ua)$ and $h(u)a$ being both suffixes of ua, one of these two strings is a suffix of the other. We consecutively consider the two possibilities.

First possibility: $h(u)a \prec_{\text{suff}} h(ua)$. Let v be the string defined by

$$v = h(ua)a^{-1}.$$

Then $h(u) \prec_{\text{suff}} v \preceq_{\text{suff}} u$. And as $h(ua) \in \text{Pref}(X)$, $v \in \text{Pref}(X)$. It follows that v is a string that contradicts the maximality of $h(u)$. This first possibility is thus impossible.

Second possibility: $h(ua) \preceq_{\text{suff}} h(u)a$. Then $h(ua) \preceq_{\text{suff}} h(h(u)a)$. And as $h(u)a \preceq_{\text{suff}} ua$, $h(h(u)a) \preceq_{\text{suff}} h(ua)$. Thus $h(ua) = h(h(u)a)$.

This establishes property 3 and ends the proof. ∎

Proof of Proposition 2.3 Let $z \in A^*$. After properties 2 and 3 of Lemma 2.4, it comes that the sequence of arcs of the form

$$(h(z[0\,.\,.\,i-1]), z[i], h(z[0\,.\,.\,i]))$$

for $i = 0, 1, \ldots, |z| - 1$ is a path in $\mathcal{D}(X)$ from state ε to $h(z)$ labeled by z. Then, as $h(z) \in \text{Pref}(X)$, it comes after Lemma 2.4 that $z \in A^*X$ if and only if $h(z) \in \text{Pref}(X) \cap A^*X$. This shows that $\mathcal{D}(X)$ recognizes the language A^*X and ends the proof. ∎

Construction of the dictionary automaton

The construction algorithm of the dictionary automaton $\mathcal{D}(X)$ from the trie $\mathcal{T}(X)$ proposed in the rest uses a breadth-first search of the trie. Together with the function h defined above, we introduce the function

$$f : A^* \to \text{Pref}(X)$$

defined by

$$f(u) = \text{the longest proper suffix of } u \text{ that belongs to } \mathrm{Pref}(X)$$

for every string $u \in A^+$ and not defined for ε.

The three results that follow show that it is sufficient to know the state $f(u)$ for each of the states $u \neq \varepsilon$ reached during the scan of the trie, in order to ensure a correct construction of $\mathcal{D}(X)$.

Lemma 2.5
For every $(u, a) \in A^* \times A$ we have

$$h(ua) = \begin{cases} ua & \text{if } ua \in \mathrm{Pref}(X), \\ h(f(u)a) & \text{if } u \neq \varepsilon \text{ and } ua \notin \mathrm{Pref}(X), \\ \varepsilon & \text{otherwise.} \end{cases}$$

Proof The identity is trivial when $ua \in \mathrm{Pref}(X)$ or when $u = \varepsilon$ and $ua \notin \mathrm{Pref}(X)$. It remains to examine the case where $u \neq \varepsilon$ and $ua \notin \mathrm{Pref}(X)$. If we assume the existence of a suffix v of ua for which $v \in \mathrm{Pref}(X)$ and $|v| > |f(u)a|$, it comes that va^{-1} is a proper suffix of u that belongs to $\mathrm{Pref}(X)$; this contradicts the maximality of $f(u)$. It follows that $h(f(u)a)$ is the longest suffix of ua that belongs to $\mathrm{Pref}(X)$, which validates the last identity that remained to establish and ends the proof. ■

Lemma 2.6
For every $(u, a) \in A^* \times A$ we have

$$f(ua) = \begin{cases} h(f(u)a) & \text{if } u \neq \varepsilon, \\ \varepsilon & \text{otherwise.} \end{cases}$$

Proof Let us examine the case where $u \in A^+$. If we assume the existence of a suffix v of ua such that $v \in \mathrm{Pref}(X)$ and $|v| > |f(u)a|$, it comes that va^{-1} is a proper suffix of u that belongs to $\mathrm{Pref}(X)$, which contradicts the maximality of $f(u)$. It follows that $f(ua)$, the longest proper suffix of ua that belongs to $\mathrm{Pref}(X)$, is a suffix of $f(u)a$. By the maximality of h, the mentioned suffix is also $h(f(u)a)$, which ends the proof. ■

Lemma 2.7
For every $u \in A^*$ we have:

$$u \in A^*X \text{ if and only if } u \in X \text{ or } (u \neq \varepsilon \text{ and } f(u) \in A^*X).$$

Proof It is clearly sufficient to show that

$$u \in (A^*X) \setminus X \text{ implies } f(u) \in A^*X,$$

since then $u \neq \varepsilon$ because $\varepsilon \notin X$. Thus, let $u \in (A^*X) \setminus X$. The string x is of the form vw where $v \in A^*$ and w is a proper suffix of u belonging to X. It follows that, by definition of f, w is a suffix of $f(u)$. Thus $f(u) \in A^*X$. This ends the proof. ■

The function DMA-COMPLETE, whose code follows, implements the construction algorithm of $\mathcal{D}(X)$. The first three letters of its identifier mean "Dictionary Matching Automaton." A running step of the function is illustrated in Figure 2.3.

```
DMA-COMPLETE(X)
 1  M ← TRIE(X)
 2  q0 ← initial[M]
 3  F ← EMPTY-QUEUE()
 4  for each letter a ∈ A do
 5        q ← TARGET(q0, a)
 6        if q = NIL then
 7              Succ[q0] ← Succ[q0] ∪ {(a, q0)}
 8        else ENQUEUE(F, (q, q0))
 9  while not QUEUE-IS-EMPTY(F) do
10        (p, r) ← DEQUEUED(F)
11        if terminal[r] then
12              terminal[p] ← TRUE
13        for each letter a ∈ A do
14              q ← TARGET(p, a)
15              s ← TARGET(r, a)
16              if q = NIL then
17                    Succ[p] ← Succ[p] ∪ {(a, s)}
18              else ENQUEUE(F, (q, s))
19  return M
```

The function DMA-COMPLETE proceeds as follows. It begins by building the automaton $\mathcal{T}(X)$ in line 1. It then initializes, from line 3 to line 8, the queue F with the pairs of states that correspond to pairs of the form (a, ε) with $a \in A \cap \text{Pref}(X)$. In the meantime, it adds to the initial state q_0 the arcs of the form (q_0, a, q_0) for $a \in A \setminus \text{Pref}(X)$. One can then assume that to each pair of states (p, r) in the queue F corresponds a pair of the form $(u, f(u))$ with $u \in \text{Pref}(X) \setminus \{\varepsilon\}$, that the set of the labeled successors of each of the already visited states is the set that it has in $\mathcal{D}(X)$, and that it is the set it has in $\mathcal{T}(X)$ for the others. This constitutes an invariant of the **while** loop of lines 9–18.

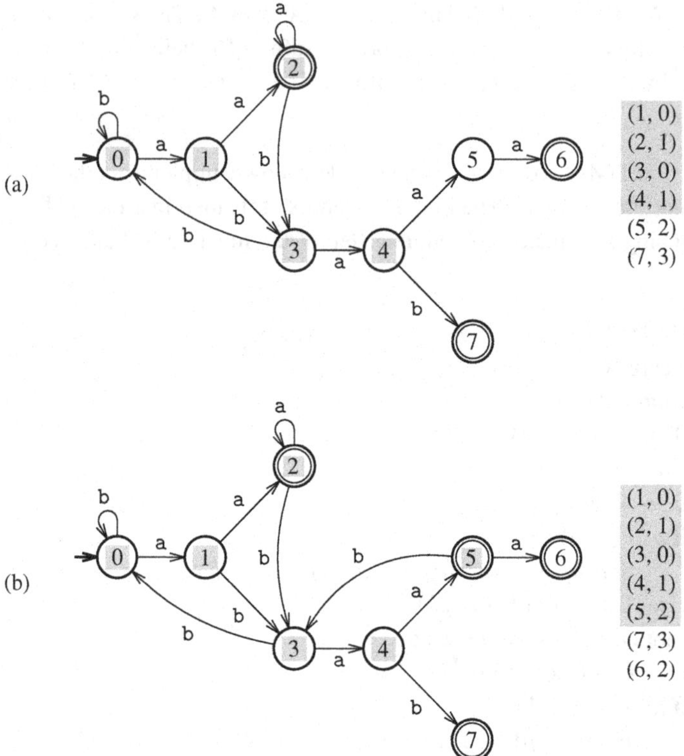

Figure 2.3. A step during the execution of the operation DMA-COMPLETE(X) with $X = \{\texttt{aa}, \texttt{abaaa}, \texttt{abab}\}$ and $A = \{\texttt{a}, \texttt{b}\}$. **(a)** States 0, 1, 2, 3, and 4 of the automaton have already been visited. The structure in construction matches with $\mathcal{D}(X)$ on these states, and with $\mathcal{T}(X)$ on those that are still to be visited. The queue contains two elements: pairs (5, 2) and (7, 3). **(b)** The step. The element (5, 2) is deleted from the queue. As state 2 is terminal, state 5 is made terminal. This corresponds to the fact that aa, that belongs to X, is a suffix of abaa, string associated with state 5. Function DMA-COMPLETE considers then the two arcs that exit state 2, arcs (2, a, 2) and (2, b, 3). For the first arc, and since there already exists a transition by the letter a from state 5 having target state 6, it adds pair (6, 2) to the queue. While for the second, it adds arc (5, b, 3) to the structure.

Indeed, to each of the card A arcs (r, a, s) considered in line 15 corresponds an arc of the form $(f(u), a, h(f(u)a))$. At this point, two cases can arise:

- If there is not already a transition defined with source p and label a in the structure, it means that $ua \notin \text{Pref}(X)$. Lemma 2.5 indicates then that $h(ua) = h(f(u)a)$. It is sufficient thus to add the arc (p, a, s) as realized in line 17.

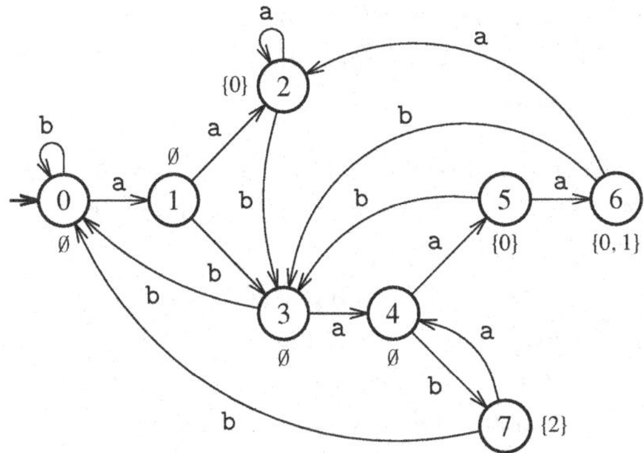

Figure 2.4. Version with outputs of the dictionary automaton of Figure 2.2 obtained by numbering the strings of the dictionary: 0 for aa, 1 for abaaa, and 2 for abab. The output of each state corresponds to the set of strings of X that are suffixes of the prefix associated with the state. The terminal states are those that possess a nonempty output.

- Otherwise $ua \in \text{Pref}(X)$, thus $h(ua) = ua$, string that corresponds to state q. The instruction in line 18 adds then the pair (q, s) to the queue F in order to be able to continue the breadth-first search. Besides, Lemma 2.6 indicates that $h(f(u)a) = f(ua)$. This shows that the pair (q, s) is of the expected form.

For the terminal states specific to $\mathcal{D}(X)$, they are marked by the conditional **if** of lines 11–12 in accordance with Lemma 2.7. This proves the following result.

Proposition 2.8
The operation DMA-COMPLETE(X) *produces the automaton* $\mathcal{D}(X)$. ■

Output of the occurrences

To operate the automaton $\mathcal{D}(X)$ on the text y, we can use the algorithm DET-SEARCH described in Section 1.5. This latter algorithm signals an occurrence each time an occurrence of one of the strings of X ends at the current position. The marking of terminal states can, however, be sharper in order to allow us to locate which are the strings of X that occur at a given position on the text. To do this, we associate an output with each state.

Let us denote by $x_0, x_1, \ldots, x_{k-1}$ the k (= card X) strings of X. We define the output of a state u of $\mathcal{D}(X)$ as the set of indices i for which x_i is a suffix of u (see the illustration given in Figure 2.4). Thus an occurrence of the string x_i of X ends at the current position on the text if and only if the index i is an element of the output of the current state. By noting that only terminal states have a nonempty output, the computation of the outputs – instead of the terminal states – can proceed as follows:

1. The instruction in line 2 of the function NEW-STATE is replaced by the assignment $output[p] \leftarrow \emptyset$ (function NEW-STATE is called in line 7 of function TRIE; its code is given in Section 1.3).
2. The instruction in line 10 of the function TRIE is replaced by the assignment $output[t] \leftarrow \{i\}$ where i is the index of the string of X dealt with during the execution of the **for** loop of lines 2–10.
3. The instruction in line 12 of the function DMA-COMPLETE is replaced by the assignment $output[p] \leftarrow output[p] \cup output[r]$.

The occurrence test in line 4 of algorithm DET-SEARCH becomes $output[r] \neq \emptyset$. In the case where this test happens to be positive, occurrences of strings of X can then be signaled (see Note 5, Chapter 1).

Implementation by transition matrix

The automaton $\mathcal{D}(X)$ being complete, it is natural to implement its transition function by a transition matrix.

Proposition 2.9
When the automaton $\mathcal{D}(X)$ is implemented with the help of a transition matrix, the size of the implementation is $O(|X| \times \text{card}\, A)$, and the time for building it by the function DMA-COMPLETE *is $O(|X| \times \text{card}\, A)$. The extra space required for the execution of the function* DMA-COMPLETE *is $O(\text{card}\, X)$.*

Proof The number of states of $\mathcal{D}(X)$ is equal to card $\text{Pref}(X)$, number itself no more than $|X| + 1$. On the other hand, the transition function being implemented by a matrix, each of the look-ups (function TARGET) or modifications (adds to the sets of labeled successors) takes a time $O(1)$. Finally, the queue – that constitutes the essential of the space required by the computation – contains always no more elements than branches in the tree, thus at most card X elements. The announced complexities follow. ∎

The algorithm DET-SEARCH of Section 1.5 can be used to operate the automaton $\mathcal{D}(X)$ on the text y. We have then the following result, which is an immediate consequence of Proposition 1.15.

Proposition 2.10
The detection of the occurrences of strings of X in a text y can be performed in time $O(|y|)$ if we utilize the automaton $\mathcal{D}(X)$ implemented with the help of a transition matrix. The delay and the extra memory space are constant. ∎

Note that, by comparison with the results of Section 1.5, using the automaton $\mathcal{D}(X)$ allows one to gain a factor $O(|X|)$ in the space and time complexities of the searching phase: if this latter is realized by the algorithm NON-DET-SEARCH applied with the automaton $\mathcal{T}(X)$ considered in the same model (the branching model, with implementation by transition matrix) and if the sets of states of $\mathcal{T}(X)$ are encoded with the help of boolean vectors, the time is indeed $O(|X| \times |y|)$, the delay and the extra memory space are $O(|X|)$.

The memory space and the time necessary to memorize and build the automaton can lead to disregard such an implementation when the size of the alphabet A is relatively large comparing to X. We show in the next two sections two methods that implement the automaton in time and in space independent of the alphabet in the comparison model.

2.3 Implementation with failure function

In this section, we present a reduced implementation of the automaton $\mathcal{D}(X)$ in the comparison model with the help of a failure function (see Section 1.4). This function is nothing but the function f, defined in Section 2.2, that associates with every nonempty string its longest proper suffix belonging to the set $\mathrm{Pref}(X)$.

We begin by specifying the implementation. We are interested then in its utilization for the detection of the occurrences of the strings of X in a text, then in its construction. Finally, we indicate a possible optimization of the failure function.

Definition of the implementation

Let

$$\gamma\colon \mathrm{Pref}(X) \times A \to \mathrm{Pref}(X)$$

be the function partially defined by

$$\gamma(u, a) = \begin{cases} ua & \text{if } ua \in \mathrm{Pref}(X), \\ \varepsilon & \text{if } u = \varepsilon \text{ and } a \notin \mathrm{Pref}(X). \end{cases}$$

Proposition 2.11
The functions γ and f are respectively a subtransition and a failure function of the transition function of $\mathcal{D}(X)$.

Proof For every nonempty prefix u of $\mathrm{Pref}(X)$, $f(u)$ is defined and we have $|f(u)| < |u|$. It follows that f defines an order on $\mathrm{Pref}(X)$, the set of the states of $\mathcal{D}(X)$. The function $\delta\colon \mathrm{Pref}(X) \times A \to \mathrm{Pref}(X)$ defined by $\delta(u, a) = h(ua)$

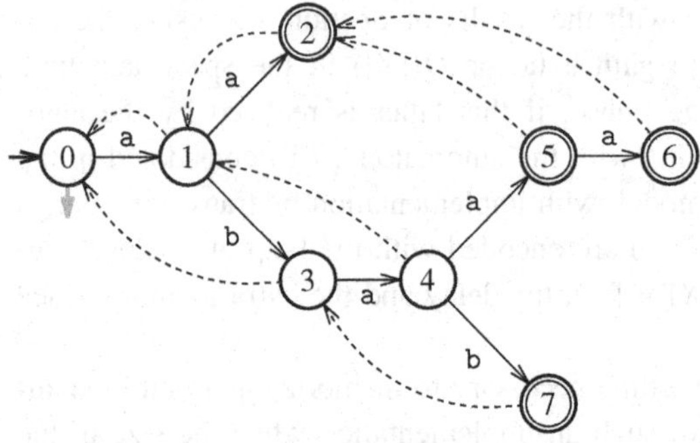

Figure 2.5. Implementation $\mathcal{D}_F(X)$ of the dictionary automaton $\mathcal{D}(X)$ when $X = \{\texttt{aa}, \texttt{abaaa}, \texttt{abab}\}$. (Refer to Figure 2.3 where the failure states, computed during the breadth-first search of the trie $\mathcal{T}(X)$, are also indicated in the margin.)

for every pair $(u, a) \in \text{Pref}(X) \times A$ is the transition function of the automaton. One can easily check with the help of Lemma 2.5 that:

$$\delta(u, a) = \begin{cases} \gamma(u, a) & \text{if } \gamma(u, a) \text{ is defined,} \\ \delta(f(u), a) & \text{otherwise.} \end{cases}$$

This shows that γ and f are indeed a subtransition and a failure function of δ as expected (see Section 1.4). ■

Let $\mathcal{D}_F(X)$ be the structure made of

- the automaton $\mathcal{T}(X)$ whose transition function is implemented by sets of labeled successors,
- the initial state of $\mathcal{T}(X)$ as successor by default of itself,
- the failure function f.

An illustration is given in Figure 2.5.

Theorem 2.12
Let X be a dictionary. Then $\mathcal{D}_F(X)$ is an implementation of the dictionary automaton $\mathcal{D}(X)$ of size $O(|X|)$.

Proof The fact that $\mathcal{D}_F(X)$ is an implementation of $\mathcal{D}(X)$ is a consequence of the definitions of $\mathcal{T}(X)$ and γ, and of Proposition 2.11. For the size of the implementation, it is linear in the number of states of $\mathcal{T}(X)$, which number is bounded by $|X| + 1$. ■

Searching phase

The detection of the occurrences of strings of X in a text y with the help of the implementation $\mathcal{D}_F(X)$ requires the simulation of the transitions of the automaton $\mathcal{D}(X)$ with the successor by default and the failure function. We consider the attribute *fail* added to each of the state objects. For the initial state of the automaton object M, we set

$$fail[initial[M]] = \text{NIL}$$

to signify that the failure state is not defined for this state. The code given below realizes the simulation. The object automaton M is global.

```
TARGET-BY-FAILURE(p, a)
1  while p ≠ NIL and TARGET(p, a) = NIL do
2       p ← fail[p]
3  if p = NIL then
4       return initial[M]
5  else return TARGET(p, a)
```

The **while** loop of lines 1–2 and the return of the function in lines 3–5 are correct since they agree with the notion of failure state.

We adapt the algorithm DET-SEARCH (Section 1.5) for locating the occurrences by modifying its code: the construction of the automaton is performed inside the algorithm by the function DMA-BY-FAILURE given further; line 3, that corresponds to line 4 in the code below, calls the function TARGET-BY-FAILURE instead of the function TARGET; this gives the following code.

```
DET-SEARCH-BY-FAILURE(X, y)
1  M ← DMA-BY-FAILURE(X)
2  r ← initial[M]
3  for each letter a of y, sequentially do
4       r ← TARGET-BY-FAILURE(r, a)
5       OUTPUT-IF(terminal[r])
```

Lemma 2.13
The number of tests TARGET$(p, a) =$ NIL *realized during the searching phase of the operation* DET-SEARCH-BY-FAILURE(X, y) *is at most* $2|y| - 1$.

Proof Let us denote by u the current prefix of y and by $|p|$ the level in $\mathcal{T}(X)$ of parameter p of the function TARGET-BY-FAILURE (by setting $|p| = -1$ when $p =$ NIL). Then, the quantity $2|u| - |p|$ increases by at least one unit after each of the mentioned tests. Indeed, the quantities $|p|$ and $|u|$ are incremented after a positive result of the test; the quantity $|p|$ is decreased by at least one unit and the quantity $|u|$ remains unchanged after a negative result of the test. Moreover, the quantity $2|u| - |p|$ is equal to $2 \times 0 - 0 = 0$ during the first test and at most $2 \times (|y| - 1) - 0 = 2|y| - 2$ during the last test. It follows that the number of tests is thus bounded by $2|y| - 1$ as stated. ■

Lemma 2.14
The maximal outgoing degree of the states of the automaton $\mathcal{T}(X)$ is at most $\min\{\text{card alph}(X), \text{card } X\}$.

Proof The automaton being deterministic, the outgoing arcs of any of its states are labeled by pairwise distinct letters that occur in the strings of X. Moreover, it possesses at most card X external states (nodes), thus each state possesses at most card X outgoing arcs. The bound follows. ■

Theorem 2.15
The running time of the searching phase for the occurrences of the strings of X in a text y with the algorithm DET-SEARCH-BY-FAILURE *is $O(|y| \times \log s)$ and the delay $O(\ell \times \log s)$ where*

$$s \leq \min\{\text{card alph}(X), \text{card } X\}$$

is the maximal outgoing degree of the states of the trie $\mathcal{T}(X)$ and ℓ the maximal length of the strings of X.

Proof As the cost of each test TARGET$(p, a) =$ NIL is $O(\log s)$ (Proposition 1.16), the number of these tests is linear in the length of y (Lemma 2.13), and the execution time of these tests is representative of the total time of the search, this latter is $O(|y| \times \log s)$.

During the execution of the operation TARGET-BY-FAILURE(p, a), the number of executions of the body of the **while** loop of lines 1–2 cannot exceed the level of the state in the trie, thus the bound of the delay follows, by application of Proposition 1.16.

It remains to add that the bound on s comes after Lemma 2.14. ■

We conclude the part devoted to the searching phase by showing that the bound of the number of tests given in Lemma 2.13 is optimal on every alphabet having at least two letters.

Proposition 2.16
When card $A \geq 2$, *there exists a dictionary X and a nonempty text y for which the number of tests* TARGET$(p, a) =$ NIL *realized during the detection of the occurrences of the strings of X in y by the algorithm* DET-SEARCH-BY-FAILURE *is equal to* $2|y| - 1$.

Proof Let a and b be any two distinct letters of A. Let us consider a dictionary X whose set $\mathrm{Pref}(X)$ contains the string ab but not the string aa. Let us assume, moreover, that $y \in \{a\}^*$. Then the mentioned test is executed once on the first letter of y, and twice on each of the next letters. The stated result follows. ■

Construction of the implementation

The implementation $\mathcal{D}_F(X)$ is built during a breadth-first search of the trie $\mathcal{T}(X)$. But the process is simpler than the one given for $\mathcal{D}(X)$ since:

- no arc needs to be added to the structure,
- there is no need to put in the queue the failure states.

The code of the function DMA-BY-FAILURE that produces the implementation $\mathcal{D}_F(X)$ follows.

```
DMA-BY-FAILURE(X)
 1  M ← TRIE(X)
 2  fail[initial[M]] ← NIL
 3  F ← EMPTY-QUEUE()
 4  ENQUEUE(F, initial[M])
 5  while not QUEUE-IS-EMPTY(F) do
 6        t ← DEQUEUED(F)
 7        for each pair (a, p) ∈ Succ[t] do
 8              r ← TARGET-BY-FAILURE(fail[t], a)
 9              fail[p] ← r
10              if terminal[r] then
11                    terminal[p] ← TRUE
12              ENQUEUE(F, p)
13  return M
```

The only delicate part of the code is located in lines 8–9 in the case where t is the initial state of the automaton. Note now that the function TARGET-BY-FAILURE produces the initial state when its input parameter state is NIL. It is then sufficient to show that the instructions in lines 8–9 agree with Lemma 2.6, which yields the following statement.

Proposition 2.17
The operation DMA-BY-FAILURE(X) *produces* $\mathcal{D}_F(X)$, *implementation of* $\mathcal{D}(X)$ *by failure function.* ■

Theorem 2.18
The running time for the operation DMA-BY-FAILURE(X) *is* $O(|X| \times \log \min\{\text{card alph}(X), \text{card } X\})$. *The extra memory space required for this operation is* $O(\text{card } X)$.

Proof Running time: let us rename by s the input state of the function TARGET-BY-FAILURE; we proceed in the same way as for the proof of Lemma 2.13, but by looking this time to values of the expression $2|t| - |s|$ considered along each of the different branches of the trie $\mathcal{T}(X)$; we then note that the sum of the lengths of the branches is bounded by $|X|$; then we use Lemma 2.14. Extra space: see proof of Proposition 2.9. ■

Optimization of the failure function

The searching phase can be sensibly improved if the useless calls to the failure function are eliminated.

Let us come back to the example given in Figure 2.5 and let us study two cases.

- Let us assume that state 6 is reached. Whatever the value of the current letter of the text is, the failure function is called twice in a row, before finally reaching state 1. It is thus preferable to choose 1 as failure state of 6.
- Let us assume now that state 4 is reached. If the current letter is neither a, nor b, it is useless to transit by states 1 then 0 for finally come back to the initial state 0 and proceed to the next letter. The computation here can also be done in a single step by considering the initial state as successor by default of state 4.

By following an analogue reasoning for each state, we get the optimized representation given in Figure 2.6.

Formally, the implementation $\mathcal{D}_{\text{F}}(X)$ of automaton $\mathcal{D}(X)$ can be optimized for the searching phase by considering another failure function than the function f. Let us denote by *Next*(u) the set defined for every string $u \in \text{Pref}(X)$ by

$$Next(u) = \{a : a \in A, ua \in \text{Pref}(X)\}.$$

Let now f' be the function from Pref(X) to itself defined by $f'(u) = f^k(u)$ for every string $u \in \text{Pref}(X) \setminus \{\varepsilon\}$ for which the natural number

$$k = \min\{\ell : Next(f^\ell(u)) \not\subseteq Next(u)\}$$

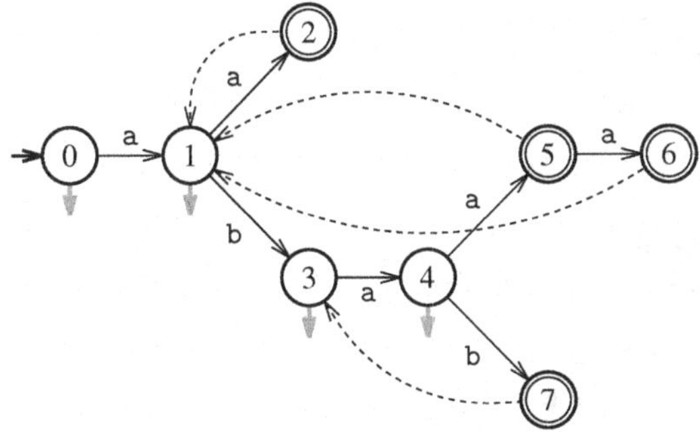

Figure 2.6. The optimized representation of the implementation $\mathcal{D}_F(X)$ when $X = \{\texttt{aa}, \texttt{abaaa}, \texttt{abab}\}$ (the original implementation is given in Figure 2.5).

is defined, and undefined everywhere else. Then the searching structure made of

- the automaton $\mathcal{T}(X)$, as for the implementation $\mathcal{D}_F(X)$,
- the initial state of $\mathcal{T}(X)$ as successor by default for each state whose image by f' is not defined,
- the failure function f',

is an implementation of the dictionary automaton $\mathcal{D}(X)$ in the comparison model.

Even though f' is substituted to f for the searching phase, the improvement is not quantifiable in term of the "O" notation. In particular, the delay remains proportional to the maximal length of the strings of the dictionary in the worst case. This is what shows the following example.

Let us assume that the alphabet A contains (at least) the three letters a, b, and c. Let $L(m)$ be the language defined for an integer m, $m \geq 1$, by

$$\begin{aligned} L(m) = &\{\texttt{a}^{m-1}\texttt{b}\} \\ &\cup \{\texttt{a}^{2k-1}\texttt{ba} : 1 \leq k < \lceil m/2 \rceil\} \\ &\cup \{\texttt{a}^{2k}\texttt{bb} : 0 \leq k < \lfloor m/2 \rfloor\}. \end{aligned}$$

For some integer $m \geq 1$, let us set $X = L(m)$. Then, if the string $\texttt{a}^{m-1}\texttt{bc}$ is a factor of the text, m calls to the failure function (line 2 of the function Target-by-failure) are performed when c is the current letter. And m is exactly the

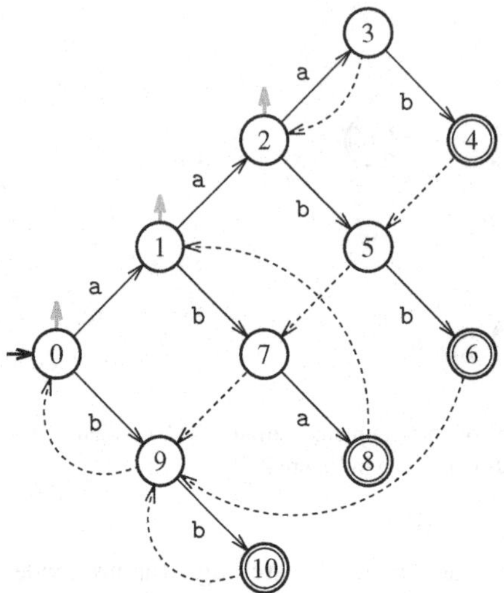

Figure 2.7. In the worst case, the delay of the algorithm DET-SEARCH-BY-FAILURE is proportional to the maximal length of the strings of the dictionary X. This remains true even if we consider the optimized version f' of the failure function f of the implementation $\mathcal{D}_F(X)$ of $\mathcal{D}(X)$. As for instance when $X = L(4) = \{$aaab, aabb, aba, bb$\}$ and that aaabc is a factor of the text: four successive calls to f' are performed, the current state taking successively the values 4, 5, 7, 9, then 0.

length of the string $\mathtt{a}^{m-1}\mathtt{b}$, one of the longest strings of X. (See the illustration proposed in Figure 2.7.)

2.4 Implementation with successor by default

In this section, we study the implementation $\mathcal{D}_D(X)$ obtained from the automaton $\mathcal{D}(X)$ by deleting any arc whose target is the initial state and by adding the initial state as successor by default (see the illustration proposed in Figure 2.8). This reduced implementation of $\mathcal{D}(X)$ in the comparison model turns out to be particularly interesting, regarding its initialization as well as its utilization, when the sets of labeled successors are sorted according to the alphabet.

The plan is the following: we start by showing that the size of the implementation $\mathcal{D}_D(X)$ is both reasonable and independent of the size of the alphabet; we are interested then in the construction of this particular implementation; then we express the complexities of the searching phase; we finally compare the different implementations of $\mathcal{D}(X)$ exposed in the first part of the chapter.

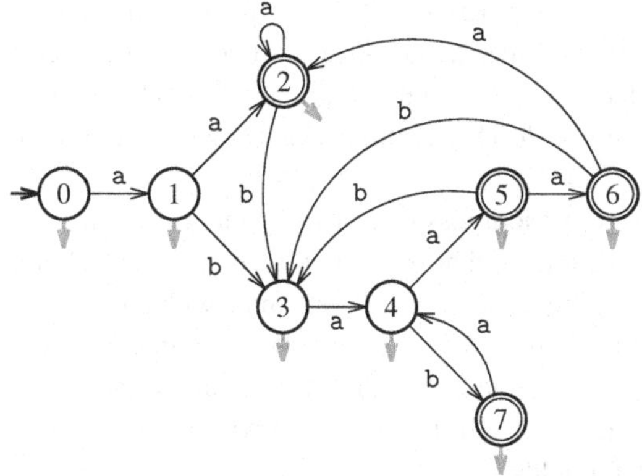

Figure 2.8. Implementation $\mathcal{D}_{\text{D}}(X)$ of the dictionary automaton $\mathcal{D}(X)$ when $X = \{\texttt{aa}, \texttt{abaaa}, \texttt{abab}\}$. Every state has the initial state as successor by default. This representation has to be compared with the one given in Figure 2.2.

Size of the implementation

In the implementation $\mathcal{D}_{\text{D}}(X)$, let us call ***forward arc*** an arc of the form (u, a, ua) – in other words an arc of the trie $\mathcal{T}(X)$ – and ***backward arc*** every other arc. The automaton represented in Figure 2.8 possesses thus seven forward arcs and six backward arcs. More generally now, we have the following result.

Proposition 2.19
The number of forward arcs in $\mathcal{D}_{\text{D}}(X)$ is at most $|X|$, and the number of backward arcs is at most $|X| \times \operatorname{card} X$.

The proof of this result will be established after the one of the following lemma. Before, let us call shift of an arc (u, a, u') in $\mathcal{D}_{\text{D}}(X)$ the integer $|ua| - |u'|$, and let us say of an arc that it is directed from $x \in X$ to $x' \in X$ if its source is a prefix of x and its target a prefix of x'.

Lemma 2.20
If x and x' are strings of X, then the shifts of distinct backward arcs directed from x to x' are distinct.

Proof By contradiction. Let us assume the existence of two distinct backward arcs (u, a, u') and (v, b, v') directed from x to x' and having identical shifts, that is, so that

$$|ua| - |u'| = |vb| - |v'|. \tag{2.1}$$

If we assume $u = v$, we get, after (2.1), $|u'| = |v'|$, then, as u' and v' are prefixes of x', $u' = v'$. On the other hand, since the two arcs are backward arcs, they do not enter the initial state; thus, $x'[|u'| - 1] = a$ and $x'[|v'| - 1] = b$. It follows that $a = b$. This contradicts the assumption of two distinct arcs.

We can from now on assume without loss of generality that $v \prec_{\text{pref}} u$. For questions of length, it comes after (2.1) that $|v'| < |u'|$, then, as u' and v' are prefixes of x', $v' \prec_{\text{pref}} u'$. Now, since $u' \preceq_{\text{suff}} ua$, we compute with the help of (2.1): $x'[|v'| - 1] = x[|v'| - 1 + |ua| - |u'|] = x[|v|]$. This is impossible: on one hand $x'[|v'| - 1] = b$, the arc (v, b, v') does not enter the initial state since it is a backward arc; on the other hand $x[|v|] \neq b$, or otherwise this arc would be a forward arc. Thus the result holds. ∎

Proof of Proposition 2.19 In $\mathcal{D}_{\text{D}}(X)$, each forward arc is identified by its target, which belongs to $\text{Pref}(X) \setminus \{\varepsilon\}$. The first stated bound follows.

If x and x' are two strings of X, the shifts of the possible backward arcs directed from x to x' are distinct after Lemma 2.20 and are within 1 and $|x|$. It follows that the number of backward arcs directed from x to x' is bounded by $|x|$. The total number of backward arcs of the implementation $\mathcal{D}_{\text{D}}(X)$ is thus bounded by $\sum_{x \in X} |x| \times \text{card}\, X$, this establishes the second bound. ∎

We just established the bounds on the total number of arcs in $\mathcal{D}_{\text{D}}(X)$. Let us now note that locally, in each of the states, we have the following result.

Lemma 2.21
The maximal outgoing degree of the states in $\mathcal{D}_{\text{D}}(X)$ is at most $\text{card}\,\text{alph}(X)$.

Proof This results from the fact that the arcs exiting from a same state are labeled by letters of $\text{alph}(X)$. ∎

Theorem 2.22
The implementation $\mathcal{D}_{\text{D}}(X)$ of the dictionary automaton $\mathcal{D}(X)$ is of size $O(|X| \times \min\{\text{card}\,\text{alph}(X), \text{card}\, X\})$.

Proof The total space necessary for memorizing the automaton $\mathcal{D}(X)$ under the form $\mathcal{D}_{\text{D}}(X)$ is linear in the number of states and the number of arcs in $\mathcal{D}_{\text{D}}(X)$. The first of these numbers is no more than $|X| + 1$. For the second, it is no more than $|X| \times (1 + \text{card}\, X)$ after Proposition 2.19. This yields the bound $O(|X| \times \text{card}\, X)$. For the bound $O(|X| \times \text{card}\,\text{alph}(X))$, it is an immediate consequence of Lemma 2.21. ∎

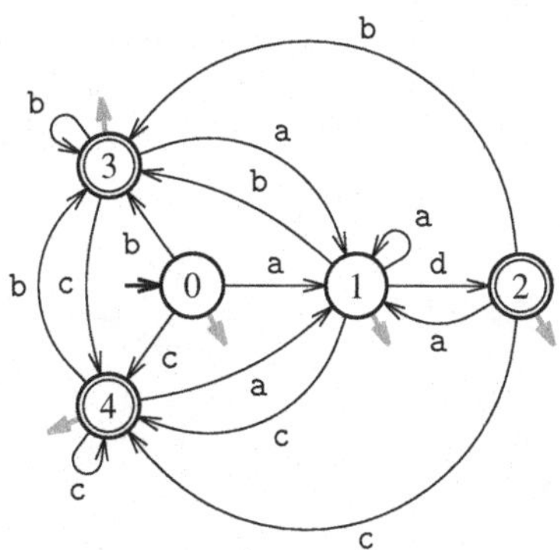

Figure 2.9. An implementation $\mathcal{D}_{\mathrm{D}}(X)$ with a maximal number of arcs with card X and $|X|$ fixed, thus with $(|X| \times (1 + \text{card } X) = 16$ arcs. Here $X = \{\texttt{ad}, \texttt{b}, \texttt{c}\}$.

When the number and the sum of the lengths of the strings of X are fixed, the bound of the number of arcs given in Proposition 2.19 can be reached. That is what suggests the example of Figure 2.9,

and this is what establishes the proposition that follows for the general case.

Proposition 2.23
For every non-null integer $k <$ card A, *for every integer* $m \geq k$, *there exists a dictionary* X *such that* card $X = k$ *and* $|X| = m$, *for which the number of arcs in* $\mathcal{D}_{\mathrm{D}}(X)$ *is equal to* $m \times (k + 1)$.

Proof Let us choose $k + 1$ pairwise distinct letters $a_0, a_1, \ldots, a_k$ in A. Then let us consider the dictionary X composed of the string $a_0 {a_k}^{m-k}$ on the one hand, and of the strings $a_1, a_2, \ldots, a_{k-1}$ on the other hand. In the implementation $\mathcal{D}_{\mathrm{D}}(X)$, exactly k backward arcs labeled each by one of the letters $a_0, a_1, \ldots, a_{k-1}$ go out from each of the m states different from the initial state. As the implementation possesses also m forward arcs, it possesses $k \times m + m = m \times (k + 1)$ arcs on the overall. ■

Construction of the implementation

To build the implementation $\mathcal{D}_{\mathrm{D}}(X)$, we take the code of function DMA-COMPLETE that produces the automaton $\mathcal{D}(X)$. We modify it (lines 4–8 and 17 correspond here to lines 4–5 and 14–15) in order not to generate the arcs of $\mathcal{D}(X)$ that have the initial state for target.

```
DMA-BY-DEFAULT(X)
 1  M ← TRIE(X)
 2  q0 ← initial[M]
 3  F ← EMPTY-QUEUE()
 4  for each pair (a, q) ∈ Succ[q0] do
 5        ENQUEUE(F, (q, q0))
 6  while not QUEUE-IS-EMPTY(F) do
 7        (p, r) ← DEQUEUED(F)
 8        if terminal[r] then
 9              terminal[p] ← TRUE
10        for each letter a ∈ A do
11              q ← TARGET(p, a)
12              s ← TARGET-BY-DEFAULT(r, a)
13              if q = NIL then
14                    if s ≠ q0 then
15                          Succ[p] ← Succ[p] ∪ {(a, s)}
16              else  ENQUEUE(F, (q, s))
17  return M
```

Line 12 calls function TARGET-BY-DEFAULT that simulates the transitions to the initial state in the part already built of the implementation. The code of this function is specified below. The object automaton M is assumed to be global.

```
TARGET-BY-DEFAULT(p, a)
1  if there exists a state q such that (a, q) ∈ Succ[p] then
2        return q
3  else  return initial[M]
```

Proposition 2.24
The operation DMA-BY-DEFAULT(X) *produces* $\mathcal{D}_{\mathrm{D}}(X)$*, implementation with successor by default of* $\mathcal{D}(X)$.

Proof Immediate after Proposition 2.8. ■

The theorem that follows establishes the complexities of function DMA-BY-DEFAULT. It specifies, in particular, that maintaining the sets of the labeled successors sorted according to the alphabet ensures an efficient execution.

Theorem 2.25
Assume that we consider sets of the labeled successors as lists sorted according to the alphabet during the execution of the operation DMA-BY-DEFAULT(X). *Then, the running time of this operation is of the same order as the size of*

the implementation $\mathcal{D}_D(X)$ *of the automaton* $\mathcal{D}(X)$ *that it produces, that is,* $O(|X| \times \min\{\text{card}\,\text{alph}(X), \text{card}\,X\})$. *The extra memory space necessary to the execution is* $O(\text{card}\,X)$.

Proof During the construction of the trie $\mathcal{T}(X)$, each call to the function TARGET and each addition in a list of labeled successors has a cost at most linear in the maximum of the outgoing degrees of the states. As the number of each of these two operations is at most equal to $|X|$, it follows after Lemma 2.14 that the total cost of the execution of line 1 is $O(|X| \times \min\{\text{card}\,\text{alph}(X), \text{card}\,X\})$.

Then, the lists of labeled successors of p (as in $\mathcal{T}(X)$) and of r (as in $\mathcal{D}_D(X)$) being sorted according to the alphabet, the **for** loop of lines 10–16 is implemented as a merge operation of the two lists (where only one copy of each element is kept). It is thus realized in linear time in the length of the list coming from p (as in $\mathcal{D}_D(X)$ now). It comes then, by application of Theorem 2.22, that the running time of the execution of lines 6–16 is also $O(|X| \times \min\{\text{card}\,\text{alph}(X), \text{card}\,X\})$.

The total running time of function DMA-BY-DEFAULT follows. For the justification of the size of the space necessary to the computation, it has already been given during the proof of Proposition 2.9. ■

Searching phase

To locate the occurrences of the strings of the dictionary X in the text y with the implementation $\mathcal{D}_D(X)$, we utilize, as for the automaton $\mathcal{D}(X)$, the algorithm DET-SEARCH. We, however, modify its code since we have here to simulate the transitions to the initial state. Line 3, that corresponds to line 4 in the code below, henceforth calls the function TARGET-BY-DEFAULT instead of the function TARGET. The code of the associated searching algorithm follows.

```
DET-SEARCH-BY-DEFAULT(X, y)
1  M ← DMA-BY-DEFAULT(X)
2  r ← initial[M]
3  for each letter a of y, sequentially do
4      r ← TARGET-BY-DEFAULT(r, a)
5      OUTPUT-IF(terminal[r])
```

Lemma 2.26
The number of comparisons between letters performed during the searching phase of operation DET-SEARCH-PAR-DEFAULT(X, y) *is at most* $(1 + \text{card}\,X) \times |y| - 1$ *when the text* y *is nonempty, whatever the order in which the elements of the sets of labeled successors are examined during the computation of the*

transitions (each of the elements being inspected at most once during one computation).

Proof During the computation of a transition, the result of a comparison between the current letter of the text and the letter of the current element in the current set of labeled successors is either positive or negative. In the latter case, the computation is pursued. It can stop in the first case, but this is not important regarding the result that we want to establish.

Let us note that since we want to get a bound, we always can assume – even if it means to extend the alphabet with one letter – that the last letter of y occurs in no string of X. The number of positive comparisons is bounded by $|y| - 1$ in such a case. We further show that the number of negative comparisons is bounded by card $X \times |y|$, this will end the proof.

Let us first note that if (a, u) is an element of the current set of the labeled successors inspected with a negative result at position i on the text y (thus $y[i] \neq a$), the value $i - |u| + 1$ is also a position on y, that is, it satisfies the double inequality

$$0 \leq i - |u| + 1 \leq |y| - 1, \tag{2.2}$$

since $u \neq \varepsilon$, $ua^{-1} \preceq_{\text{pref}} y[0\,..\,i-1]$, and $i < |y|$.

Let us now assume the existence of two elements (a, u) and (b, v) negatively inspected at respective positions i and j. Then, if we have

$$i - |u| + 1 = j - |v| + 1, \tag{2.3}$$

u and v are prefixes of two distinct strings of X. To prove this assertion, we successively consider the two possibilities $i = j$ and $i < j$ (the possibility $i > j$ being symmetrical to the second).

First possibility: $i = j$. From (2.3) it comes then that $|u| = |v|$. As a and b are the last letters of u and v, respectively, we necessarily have $a \neq b$. This shows that $u \neq v$, then that the assertion is satisfied in this case.

Second possibility: $i < j$. From (2.3) it follows that $|u| < |v|$. To show that the assertion is satisfied, it is sufficient to show that u is not a prefix of v. By contradiction, assume that $u \prec_{\text{pref}} v$. We then have:

$$\begin{aligned}
y[i] &= v[i - j + |v| - 1] && (\text{since } v[0\,..\,|v|-2] \preceq_{\text{suff}} y[0\,..\,j-1]) \\
&= v[|u| - 1] && (\text{after } (2.3)) \\
&= a && (\text{since } u \prec_{\text{pref}} v).
\end{aligned}$$

Thus there is a contradiction with the assumption of a negative comparison at i for the element (a, u), which ends the proof of the assertion.

In other words, for each string $x \in X$, the values of the expression $i - |u| + 1$ with $u \preceq_{\text{pref}} x$ that are associated with negative comparisons are pairwise distinct. It then comes, with the help of (2.2), that at most $|y|$ negative comparisons are associated with each string of X. Overall, the number of negative comparisons is thus bounded by $\text{card}\, X \times |y|$, as stated. ∎

Theorem 2.27
The operation DET-SEARCH-PAR-DEFAULT(X, y) *has a searching phase that executes in time* $O(|y| \times \min\{\log \text{card alph}(X), \text{card}\, X\})$ *and a delay that is* $O(\log \text{card alph}(X))$.

Proof The bound for the delay is a consequence of Lemma 2.21 and Proposition 1.16, because the sets of the labeled successors can be built and sorted according to the alphabet without extra cost. The bound $O(|y| \times \log \text{card alph}(X))$ for the searching time follows. The bound $O(|y| \times \text{card}\, X)$ comes from Lemma 2.26. ∎

To complete the result of Lemma 2.26, we show below that the bound of the number of comparisons is reached when $\text{card}\, X$ and $|y|$ are fixed.

Proposition 2.28
For every non-null integer $k < \text{card}\, A$, *for every non-null integer* n, *there exists a dictionary* X *of* k *strings and a text* y *of length* n *such that the number of comparisons between letters performed during the searching phase of the operation* DET-SEARCH-PAR-DEFAULT(X, y) *is equal to* $(k + 1) \times n - 1$, *the order in which the sets of the labeled successors are examined being irrelevant.*

Proof Let us choose an integer $m \geq k + 1$, let us consider the dictionary X defined in the proof of Proposition 2.23, then the text $y = a_0{}^n$. During the search, the first letter of y is compared with letters $a_0, a_1, \ldots, a_{k-1}$, which are the labels of the outgoing arcs of the initial state ε; and the other letters of y are compared with letters $a_0, a_1, \ldots, a_k$, labels of the outgoing arcs of state a_0. In the worst case, k comparisons are performed on the first letter of y and $k + 1$ on the next letters. Thus $(k + 1) \times n - 1$ comparisons on the overall. ∎

An example that illustrates the worst case that has just been mentioned in the proof: for $k = 3$ and $m = 4$, we take $X = \{\texttt{ad}, \texttt{b}, \texttt{c}\}$ and $y \in \{\texttt{a}\}^*$; the implementation $\mathcal{D}_{\text{D}}(X)$ is shown in Figure 2.9.

Challenge of implementations

The implementations $\mathcal{D}_{\text{F}}(X)$ and $\mathcal{D}_{\text{D}}(X)$ are two concurrent implementations of the dictionary automaton $\mathcal{D}(X)$ in the comparison model. The results established in this section and in the previous section plead rather in favor of the first: smaller size of the implementation, faster construction, and faster searching phase (Theorems 2.12, 2.18, and 2.15 vs. Theorems 2.22, 2.25, and 2.27). Only the order of the delay of the searching phase is smaller for the second implementation (Theorems 2.15 and 2.27 once again). It is however possible, by giving up this result on the delay, to improve the implementation $\mathcal{D}_{D}(X)$ in such a way that never more comparisons between letters are performed during the searching phase than with $\mathcal{D}_{F}(X)$ (original version or optimized version), and without increasing the order of the other complexities. This is what express the next paragraph and Figure 2.10.

The drawback with the implementation $\mathcal{D}_{D}(X)$, is that, for computing a transition during the searching phase, the set of successors of the source state may have to be considered entirely. Whereas if it is considered by parts (disjoint of course, in order not to do twice the same comparison), the part with the targets of larger level first, the one with the targets of immediately inferior level then, and so on, the considered parts are all of cardinal at most equal to their homologous in the implementation $\mathcal{D}_{F}(X)$. It follows that with this particular scanning of the sets of successors, the number of comparisons between letters for $\mathcal{D}_{D}(X)$ is at most equal to the number of comparisons between letters for $\mathcal{D}_{F}(X)$. To build the partition in the same time and with the same space that the one required for the original version of $\mathcal{D}_{D}(X)$, it is sufficient, for instance, to maintain for each state p the following elements: a list of labeled successors, let us say $S_0(p)$, sorted according to the alphabet; a partition of labeled successors, let us say $S_1(p)$, sorted by decreasing levels; the pointers of each element of $S_0(p)$ to its correspondent in $S_1(p)$. The pointers allow us to delete in constant time doubles in a copy of $S_1(r)$ during the fusion of $S_0(r)$ and $S_0(p)$ (to give $S_0(p)$, see lines 10–16 of function DMA-BY-DEFAULT). The partition $S_1(p)$ is then obtained by appending to the sequence of its original value (the set of labeled successors of p in $\mathcal{T}(X)$) the possibly modified copy of $S_1(r)$ (the elements of $S_1(r)$ being of strictly inferior levels to the one of the previous).

For the two implementations now, and comparing with a search of nondeterministic type using the trie of the dictionary (or from an even more rudimentary automaton that recognizes also X, as the one mentioned in Section 1.5), the factor of the time complexity that multiplies the length of the text is linked to the number of strings in the dictionary, while it presents at least a factor linked to the sum of the lengths of the strings of the dictionary in the second case (because of the management of the sets of states); this shows the interest of the two reduced implementations when $|X|$ is large.

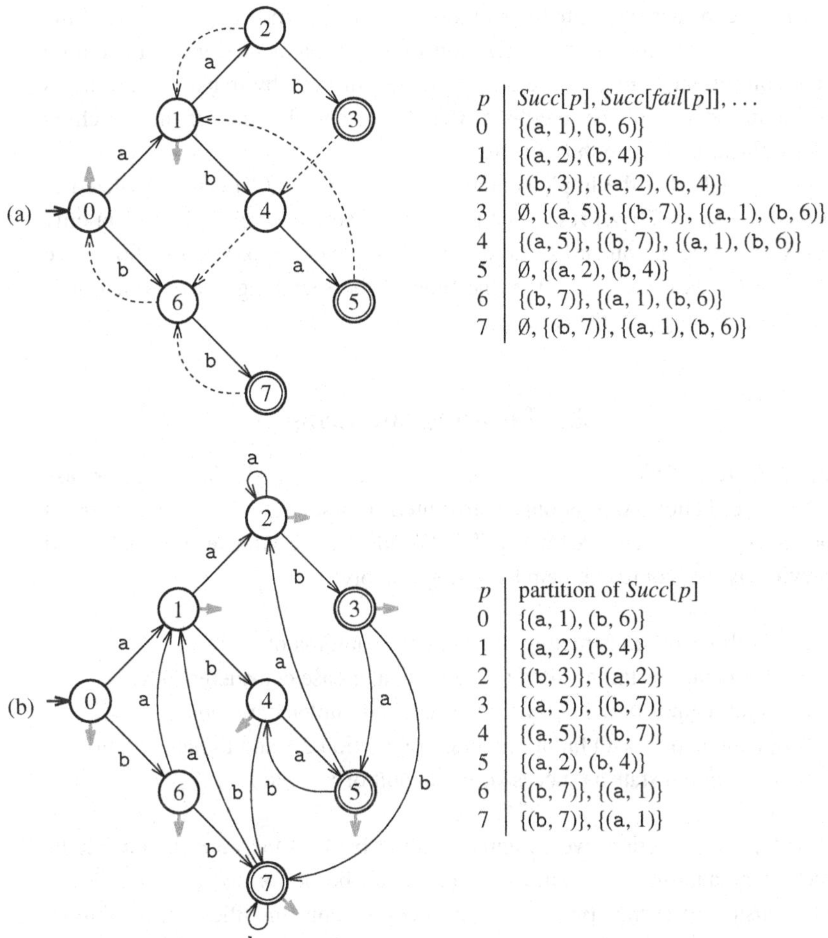

(a)

p	$Succ[p], Succ[fail[p]], \ldots$
0	{(a, 1), (b, 6)}
1	{(a, 2), (b, 4)}
2	{(b, 3)}, {(a, 2), (b, 4)}
3	∅, {(a, 5)}, {(b, 7)}, {(a, 1), (b, 6)}
4	{(a, 5)}, {(b, 7)}, {(a, 1), (b, 6)}
5	∅, {(a, 2), (b, 4)}
6	{(b, 7)}, {(a, 1), (b, 6)}
7	∅, {(b, 7)}, {(a, 1), (b, 6)}

(b)

p	partition of $Succ[p]$
0	{(a, 1), (b, 6)}
1	{(a, 2), (b, 4)}
2	{(b, 3)}, {(a, 2)}
3	{(a, 5)}, {(b, 7)}
4	{(a, 5)}, {(b, 7)}
5	{(a, 2), (b, 4)}
6	{(b, 7)}, {(a, 1)}
7	{(b, 7)}, {(a, 1)}

Figure 2.10. Two optimizations for the implementations $\mathcal{D}_F(X)$ and $\mathcal{D}_D(X)$ of the dictionary automaton $\mathcal{D}(X)$. Here with $X = \{\texttt{aab}, \texttt{aba}, \texttt{bb}\}$ (or $X = L(3)$ with the notation of the end of Section 2.3). **(a)** Implementation $\mathcal{D}_F(X)$ with the optimized version f' of failure function f. On the right, the sequences of sets of labeled successors that can be scanned for the computation of a transition from the state current. The scanning ends as soon as the current letter occurs in one of the elements belonging to the current set or when the list is empty. **(b)** In order to never perform more comparisons than with the implementation $\mathcal{D}_F(X)$, the implementation $\mathcal{D}_D(X)$ can consider sequences of sets of labeled successors as follows: for each state, the partition of the set of its labeled successors are obtained by sorting the labeled successors in decreasing order of their levels in the trie $\mathcal{T}(X)$ (the states with the same level are located on a same vertical line on the picture). Such an optimization can be obtained without altering the order of magnitude of the complexities for the construction of the implementation.

If we consider the alphabet as fixed, the time of the construction and the space necessary for the memorization of the implementations (with failure function, initial state as successor by default or even by transition matrix) is linear in the sum of the lengths of the strings and the time of the searching phase linear in the length of the text.

Let us add that the implementations $\mathcal{D}_F(X)$ and $\mathcal{D}_D(X)$ can be realized in a memory space $O(|X| \times \text{card } A)$ but with construction times dependent only on X by using a standard technique for implementing partial functions (see Section 1.4 and Exercise 1.15); the time of the searching phase is then also linear in the length of the text.

2.5 Locating one string

In all the rest of the chapter (Sections 2.5 to 2.7), we study the particular case where the dictionary X is only constituted of a single string. We consider a nonempty string x, and we set $X = \{x\}$. We adapt some of the results established previously. We complete them by giving notably:

- the methods for constructing the dictionary automaton and its implementations more suited to the particular case considered here,
- the tight bounds of the delay for the reduced implementations (implementation with failure function of Section 2.6 and implementation with the initial state as successor by default of Section 2.7).

In the present section, we essentially come back to the construction of the dictionary automaton by showing that it can be performed sequentially on the considered string. Besides, it produces without modification a minimal automaton.

Let us start by rewriting the functions h and f with the notion of border. For every pair $(u, a) \in A^* \times A$ we have:

$$h(ua) = \begin{cases} ua & \text{if } ua \preceq_{\text{pref}} x, \\ \text{Border}(ua) & \text{otherwise.} \end{cases}$$

And for every string $u \in A^+$, we have:

$$f(u) = \text{Border}(u).$$

For the equality concerning the function f, it is a consequence of its definition and of that of Border. For the equality concerning the function h, it is a consequence of Lemmas 2.5 and 2.6, and of the rewriting of f. The automaton $\mathcal{D}(\{x\})$ of Section 2.2 is defined by

$$\mathcal{D}(\{x\}) = (\text{Pref}(x), \varepsilon, \{x\}, F_x) \tag{2.4}$$

with

$$\begin{aligned} F_x = \ &\{(u, a, ua) : u \in A^*, a \in A, ua \preceq_{\text{pref}} x\} \cup \\ &\{(u, a, \text{Border}(ua)) : u \in A^*, u \preceq_{\text{pref}} x, a \in A, ua \not\preceq_{\text{pref}} x\}. \end{aligned}$$

Let us note—we need it to simply establish some of the results that follow—that the Identity (2.4) can be extended to the empty string, the automaton $(\text{Pref}(\varepsilon), \varepsilon, \{\varepsilon\}, F_\varepsilon)$ recognizing the empty string.

The construction of the automaton $\mathcal{D}(\{x\})$ can be done in a sequential way on x, this means that it requires neither the preliminary construction of the automaton $\mathcal{T}(\{x\})$ as in Section 2.2, nor of the function Border. This is suggested by the next result.

Proposition 2.29
We have $F_\varepsilon = \{(\varepsilon, b, \varepsilon) : b \in A\}$. *Moreover, for every pair* $(u, a) \in A^* \times A$, *we have* $F_{ua} = F' \cup F''$ *with*

$$F' = (F_u \setminus \{(u, a, \text{Border}(ua))\}) \cup \{(u, a, ua)\}$$

and

$$F'' = \{(ua, b, v) : (\text{Border}(ua), b, v) \in F'\}.$$

Proof The property is clearly satisfied for F_ε. Then, let u, a, F', and F'' be as in the statement of the proposition.

Each arc in F_{ua} that exits a state of length at most $|u|$ is in F'. The converse is also true.

It remains to show that every arc in F_{ua} exiting the state ua belongs to F'', and conversely. This amounts to show that, for every letter $b \in A$, the targets v and v' of the arcs (ua, b, v) and $(\text{Border}(ua), b, v')$ are identical. Now, by definition of $\mathcal{D}(\{ua\})$, we have $v = \text{Border}(uab)$; and if $\text{Border}(ua)b \preceq_{\text{pref}} ua$, $v' = \text{Border}(ua)b$, and $v' = \text{Border}(\text{Border}(ua)b)$ otherwise. Thus we deduce, by application of Lemma 1.22, that $v = v'$, which ends the proof. ∎

It is nice to "visually" interpret the previous result: we get $\mathcal{D}(\{ua\})$ from $\mathcal{D}(\{u\})$ by "unwinding" the arc of source u and of label a; the target is duplicated with its outgoing arcs. An illustration is proposed in Figure 2.11.

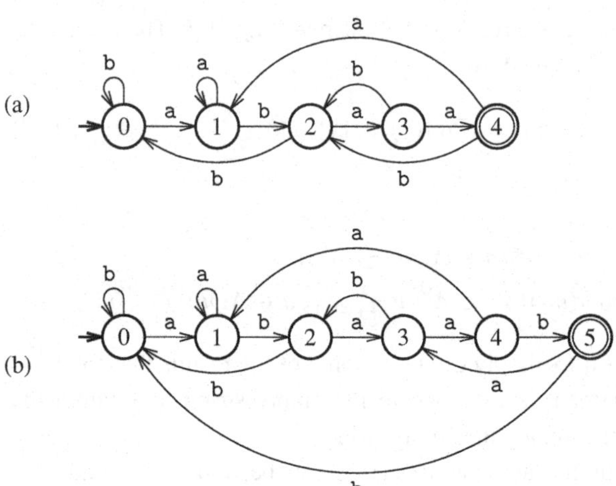

Figure 2.11. The automaton $\mathcal{D}(\{ua\})$, for $u \in A^*$ and $a \in A$, can be obtained from the automaton $\mathcal{D}(\{u\})$ by "unwinding" the arc $(u, a, \text{Border}(ua))$ in this latter automaton. For instance, from the automaton $\mathcal{D}(\{\texttt{abaa}\})$ (a), we get the automaton $\mathcal{D}(\{\texttt{abaab}\})$ (b) by creating a new state, 5, by "redirecting" the arc $(4, \texttt{b}, 2)$ to state 5, then by giving to state 5 the same set of labeled successors that the one of state 2 once the operation is performed. The order of execution of these operations matters.

The code of function SMA-COMPLETE that constructs then returns the automaton $\mathcal{D}(\{x\})$ follows. The first three letters of the identifier of the function means "String Matching Automaton."

```
SMA-COMPLETE(x)
M ← NEW-AUTOMATON()
q0 ← initial[M]
for each letter b ∈ A do
        Succ[q0] ← Succ[q0] ∪ {(b, q0)}
t ← q0
for each letter a of x, sequentially do
        p ← NEW-STATE()
        r ← TARGET(t, a)
        Succ[t] ← Succ[t] \ {(a, r)}
        Succ[t] ← Succ[t] ∪ {(a, p)}
        Succ[p] ← Succ[r]
        t ← p
terminal[t] ← TRUE
return M
```

An invariant property of the **for** loop of lines 6–12 is that the structure already built coincides with the string matching automaton of the current prefix of the string x, except in what concerns the terminal state. This detail is fixed in line 13.

Proposition 2.30
The operation SMA-COMPLETE(x) *produces* $\mathcal{D}(\{x\})$.

Proof It is sufficient to check that the code correctly applies Proposition 2.29. ■

2.6 Locating one string and failure function

We study the implementations of the dictionary automaton $\mathcal{D}(\{x\})$ with the failure function f and its optimized version f' introduced in Section 2.3. We start by establishing some properties satisfied by f'. These properties show that the function f' can directly be used during the construction phase of the implementation $\mathcal{D}_F(\{x\})$, though it is deduced from the function f in the general case of any dictionary. We then tackle precisely the construction phase, to finally come to the analysis of the searching phase. In this last subdivision, we show, in particular, that the delay is logarithmic in the length of the searched string when the failure function f' is used.

Properties of the optimized failure function

The function f': Pref(x) $\rightarrow$ Pref(x) – as done above for functions h and f – can be more simply rewritten with the notion of border. It can be reformulated in

$$f'(x) = \text{Border}(x)$$

for x, then in

$$f'(u) = v$$

for every $u \prec_{\text{pref}} x$ for which there exists a string v such that

$$v = \text{the longest border of } u \text{ with } x[|u|] \neq x[|v|],$$

and it is not defined everywhere else.

From this reformulation, we deduce the two properties that follow.

Lemma 2.31
For every string $u \prec_{\text{pref}} x$ *for which* $f'(u)$ *is defined, we have:*

$$f'(u) = \begin{cases} \text{Border}(u) & \text{if } x[|u|] \neq x[|\text{Border}(u)|], \\ f'(\text{Border}(u)) & \text{otherwise.} \end{cases}$$

Proof The string $f'(u)$ is a border of u. If the longest border of u does not suit, that is, when $x[|u|] = x[|\text{Border}(u)|]$, $f'(u)$ is exactly $f'(\text{Border}(u))$, which string ensures that the two letters $x[|f'(\text{Border}(u))|]$ and $x[|\text{Border}(u)|]$ are distinct. Thus, the equality holds. ∎

Lemma 2.32
Let $ua \preceq_{\text{pref}} x$ with $u \neq \varepsilon$ and $a \in A$. If $a \neq x[|\text{Border}(u)|]$, then Border($ua$) *is, either the longest of the strings of the form $x[0\,..\,|f'^k(\text{Border}(u))|]$, with $k \geq 1$, satisfying $x[|f'^k(\text{Border}(u))|] = a$, or ε when no natural k suits.*

Proof Analogous to the second part of the proof of Lemma 1.22. ∎

Implementation of the failure functions with tables

We choose for all the rest a data structure particularly well adapted to the studied case, in which each state in the trie $\mathcal{T}(\{x\})$ is represented by its level. It is thus sufficient for representing $\mathcal{T}(\{x\})$, its terminal state and one of the failure functions (f or f') to store:

- the string x,
- its length $m = |x|$,
- a table indexed from 0 to m having values in $\{-1, 0, \ldots, m-1\}$,

the value NIL for the states being replaced, by convention, by the integer value -1. The tables corresponding respectively to failure functions f and f' are denoted by *good-pref* and *best-pref*. The first is called the ***table of good prefixes***, the second the ***table of best prefixes***. They are thus defined by

$$\textit{good-pref}[i] = \begin{cases} |\text{Border}(x[0\,..\,i-1])| & \text{if } i \neq 0, \\ -1 & \text{otherwise,} \end{cases}$$

and

$$\textit{best-pref}[i] = \begin{cases} |f'(x[0\,..\,i-1])| & \text{if } f'(x[0\,..\,i-1]) \text{ is defined,} \\ -1 & \text{otherwise,} \end{cases}$$

for $i = 0, 1, \ldots, m$. We note that

$$\textit{good-pref}[i] = \textit{border}[i-1]$$

for $i = 1, 2, \ldots, m$ (the table *border* is introduced in Section 1.6). An example is shown in Figure 2.12.

The two following codes produce the table *good-pref* and the table *best-pref* respectively. The first code is an adaptation of the code of the function BORDERS

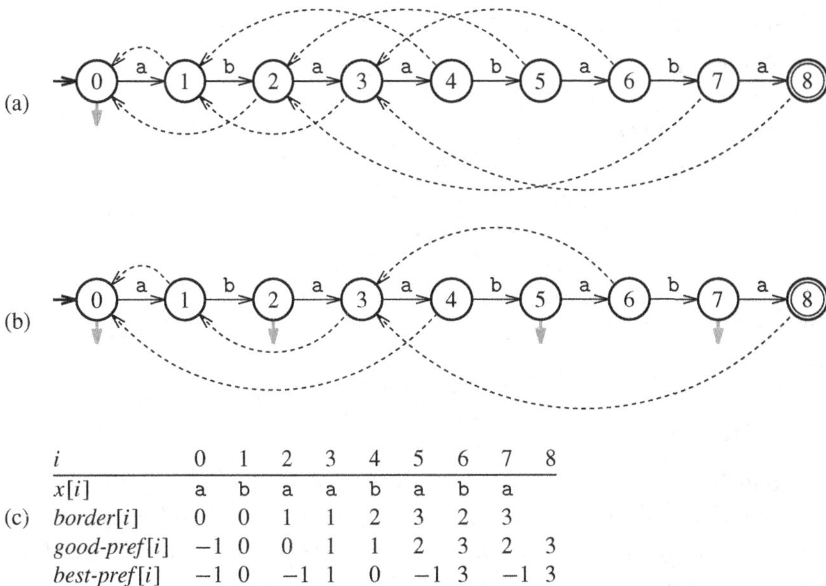

	i	0	1	2	3	4	5	6	7	8
	$x[i]$	a	b	a	a	b	a	b	a	
(c)	*border*$[i]$	0	0	1	1	2	3	2	3	
	good-pref$[i]$	−1	0	0	1	1	2	3	2	3
	best-pref$[i]$	−1	0	−1	1	0	−1	3	−1	3

Figure 2.12. Table representation of the failure functions f and f' for the implementation $\mathcal{D}_F(\{x\})$ of the dictionary automaton $\mathcal{D}(\{x\})$ when $x = $ abaababa. **(a)** The implementation $\mathcal{D}_F(\{x\})$ and its failure function f (this is nothing else but the function Border). **(b)** The implementation $\mathcal{D}_F(\{x\})$ and its optimized failure function f'. **(c)** Tables *border*, *good-pref*, and *best-pref*. The second corresponds to f, and the third to f'.

that produces the table *border*. The “shift” of one unit on the indices allows a more simple algorithmic formulation, notably at the level of the loop of lines 6–7 on the borders of the prefix $x[0\,..\,j-1]$. We follow the same schema for the second function, by applying the results of Lemmas 2.31 and 2.32.

```
GOOD-PREFIX(x, m)
 1  good-pref[0] ← −1
 2  i ← 0
 3  for j ← 1 to m − 1 do
 4      ▷ Here, x[0 . . i − 1] = Border(x[0 . . j − 1])
 5      good-pref[j] ← i
 6      while i ≥ 0 and x[j] ≠ x[i] do
 7          i ← good-pref[i]
 8      i ← i + 1
 9  good-pref[m] ← i
10  return good-pref
```

```
BEST-PREFIX(x, m)
best-pref[0] ← −1
i ← 0
for j ← 1 to m − 1 do
      ▷ Here, x[0 . . i − 1] = Border(x[0 . . j − 1])
      if x[j] = x[i] then
            best-pref[j] ← best-pref[i]
      else best-pref[j] ← i
            do   i ← best-pref[i]
            while i ≥ 0 and x[j] ≠ x[i]
      i ← i + 1
best-pref[m] ← i
return best-pref
```

Theorem 2.33
The operations GOOD-PREFIX(x, m) *and* BEST-PREFIX(x, m) *produce respectively the table of good prefixes and the table of best prefixes of the string x of non-null length m.*

Proof This is a consequence of the definitions of tables *good-pref* and *best-pref*, of Proposition 1.23, and of Lemmas 2.31 and 2.32. ■

Theorem 2.34
The execution of the operation GOOD-PREFIX(x, m) *takes a time $\Theta(m)$ and requires at most $2m - 3$ comparisons between letters of the string x. Same result for the operation* BEST-PREFIX(x, m).

Proof See proof of Proposition 1.24. ■

Let us recall that the bound of $2m - 3$ comparisons has been established by reasoning on the local variables of function BORDERS (i and j) and not by a combinatorial study on the strings of length m. We showed that it is reached in the case of the computation of the table *border*. So it is for *good-pref*. But it is not that tight for *best-pref*. One can indeed show that it is never reached when $m \geq 3$, and that only strings of the form aba^{m-2} or $aba^{m-3}c$ with $a, b, c \in A$ and $a \neq b \neq c \neq a$ require $2m - 4$ comparisons. Establishing this tight bound is proposed as an exercise (Exercise 2.8).

Searching phase

The code of the algorithm that realizes the search for the nonempty string x of length m with the help of one of the two tables *good-pref* or *best-pref* in a text

y is given below. The parameter π represents any one of the two tables. The conditional instruction[1] in lines 4–5 remains to set $x[0\,.\,.\,i-1]$ as the longest proper prefix of the string x that is also a suffix of the scanned part of y; as an occurrence of x has just been located, this prefix is the border of x.

```
PREFIX-SEARCH(x, m, π, y)
1  i ← 0
2  for each letter a of y, sequentially do
3        ▷ Here, x[0..i − 1] is the longest prefix of x
         ▷    which is also a suffix of y
4        if i = m then
5              i ← π[m]
6        while i ≥ 0 and a ≠ x[i] do
7              i ← π[i]
8        i ← i + 1
9        OUTPUT-IF(i = m)
```

Theorem 2.35
Whether the parameter π represents the table good-pref or the table best-pref, the operation PREFIX-SEARCH(x, m, π, y) *executes in time $\Theta(|y|)$ and the number of comparisons performed between letters of x and letters of y never exceeds $2|y|-1$.*

Proof The bound of the number of comparisons can be established by considering the quantity $2|u| - i$ where u is the current prefix of y (refer to the proof of Lemma 2.13). The linearity in $|y|$ for the time complexity follows. ■

As indicated in the proof of Proposition 2.16, the worst case of $2|y| - 1$ comparisons is reached when, for $a, b \in A$ with $a \neq b$, ab is a prefix of x while y is only composed of a's.

If it does not translate on the bound of the worst case of the number of comparisons, the utilization of the optimized failure function is qualitatively appreciable: a letter of the text y is never compared to two identical letters of the string x consecutively. An example is given in Figure 2.13. We use this illustration to show that the search for a string with an automaton (or of one of its implementations) can very well be interpreted with the help of the sliding window mechanism. In the present case, the assignment $i \leftarrow \pi[i]$ in line 7 of PREFIX-SEARCH corresponds to a shift of the window by $i - \pi[i]$ positions to

[1] Note that this instruction can be deleted if we can put a letter that does not occur in y at the end of x, at the index m.

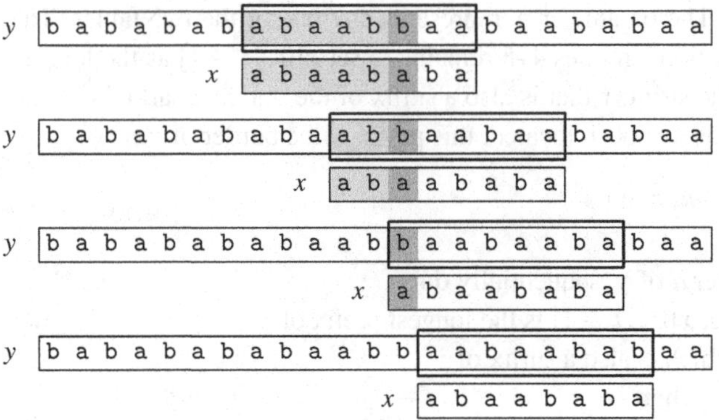

Figure 2.13. Local behaviors for the implementation $\mathcal{D}_F(\{x\})$ whether the failure function f is used or its optimized version f' is, with $x =$ abaababa. (Refer to Figure 2.12 to see the values of the two corresponding tables *good-pref* and *best-pref*.) The illustration uses artifacts used elsewhere for string matching algorithms using a sliding window. The suffix of length 5 of the current prefix of the text (its already scanned portion, top line of the picture) and the prefix of length 5 of x are identical (light gray areas). The comparison of the letters at the next positions is negative (dark gray areas). With the failure function f, the window is shifted by $5 - \textit{good-pref}[5] = \text{per}(\texttt{abaab}) = 3$ positions; the next two comparisons being still negative, the window is shifted by $2 - \textit{good-pref}[2] = \text{per}(\texttt{ab}) = 2$ positions, then by $0 - \textit{good-pref}[0] = 1$ position. Thus, 3 comparisons overall on the same letter of the text, for an eventual shift by 6 positions. On the contrary, if the optimized version f' is used, the window is directly shifted by $5 - \textit{best-pref}[5] = 6$ positions, after only one comparison.

the right; and the assignment $i \leftarrow \pi[m]$ in line 5, corresponds to a shift by the period of the string x.

More generally now, if the number of comparisons on a same letter of the text can reach m with the failure function f (when $x = a^m$ with $a \in A$ and a different letter of a is aligned with the last letter of x), it is no more than $\log_\Phi(m+1)$ with the failure function f'. This is what indicates Corollary 2.38, established after Lemma 2.36 and Theorem 2.37.

Lemma 2.36
We have

$$f'^2(u) \text{ defined implies } |u| \geq |f'(u)| + |f'^2(u)| + 2$$

for every $u \prec_{\text{pref}} x$.

Proof Since the strings $f'(u)$ and $f'^2(u)$ are borders of u, the integers $p = |u| - |f'(u)|$ and $q = |u| - |f'^2(u)|$ are periods of u. By contradiction, if we assume that $|u| \le |f'(u)| + |f'^2(u)| + 1$, we have also $(|u| - |f'(u)|) + (|u| - |f'^2(u)|) - 1 \le |u|$, thus $p + q - 1 \le |u|$. The Periodicity Lemma indicates then that $q - p$ is a period of u. As a consequence the two letters $x[|f'^2(u)|]$ and $x[|f'(u)|]$ of u are identical since they are located at distance $q - p$, which contradicts the definition of $f'^2(u)$ and ends the proof. ∎

Theorem 2.37

During the operation Prefix-search$(x, m, \textit{best-pref}, y)$, *the number of consecutive comparisons performed on a same letter of the text* y *is no more than the largest integer* k *that satisfies the inequality* $|x| + 1 \ge F_{k+2}$.

Proof Let k be the largest integer associated with the sequences

$$\langle u, f'(u), f'^2(u), \ldots, f'^{k-1}(u)\rangle$$

where $u \prec_{\text{pref}} x$ and $f'^k(u)$ is not defined. This integer k bounds the number of comparisons considered in the statement of the theorem. We now show by recurrence on k that:

$$|u| \ge F_{k+2} - 2. \tag{2.5}$$

Inequality (2.5) is satisfied when $k = 1$ (since $F_3 - 2 = 0$) and $k = 2$ (since $F_4 - 2 = 1$, and it is necessary that u is nonempty in order that $f'(u)$ is defined). Let us assume for the rest $k \ge 3$. In this case, $f'(u)$ and $f'^2(u)$ exist, and the recurrence applies to these two strings. It follows thus that:

$$\begin{aligned} |u| &\ge |f'(u)| + |f'^2(u)| + 2 && \text{(after Lemma 2.36)} \\ &\ge (F_{k+1} - 2) + (F_k - 2) + 2 && \text{(recurrence)} \\ &= F_{k+2} - 2. \end{aligned}$$

This ends the proof by recurrence of Inequality (2.5).

Finally, since $u \prec_{\text{pref}} x$, it follows that $|x| + 1 \ge |u| + 2 \ge F_{k+2}$, which is the stated result. ∎

Corollary 2.38

During the operation Prefix-search$(x, m, \textit{best-pref}, y)$, *the number of consecutive comparisons performed on a same letter of the text* y *is no more than* $\log_\Phi(|x| + 1)$. *The delay of the operation is* $O(\log |x|)$.

Proof If k is the maximal number of consecutive comparisons performed on a same letter of the text, we have, after Theorem 2.37:

$$|x| + 1 \ge F_{k+2}.$$

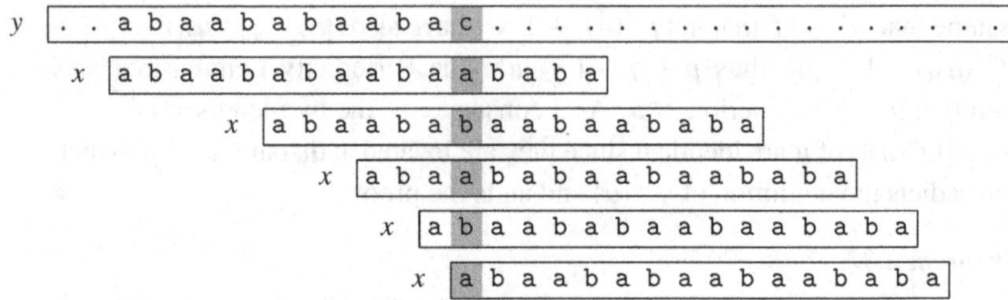

Figure 2.14. When the string x is a prefix of a Fibonacci string and k is the integer such that $F_{k+2} \leq |x| + 1 < F_{k+3}$, the number of consecutive comparisons performed on one letter of the text y during a search with the implementation $\mathcal{D}_{\mathrm{F}}(\{x\})$ can be equal to k. Here, $x =$ abaababaabaababa. It is a prefix of f_8; $F_7 = 13$, $|x| + 1 = 17$, $F_8 = 21$, thus $k = 5$; and five comparisons are effectively performed on the letter c of y.

From the classical inequality

$$F_{n+2} \geq \Phi^n,$$

it comes $|x| + 1 \geq \Phi^k$, which leads to $\log_\Phi(|x| + 1) \geq k$. The stated results follow. ■

The bound on the length of x given in the statement of Theorem 2.37 is very tight: it is reached when x is a prefix of a Fibonacci string. An example is given in Figure 2.14.

2.7 Locating one string and successor by default

We again consider the implementation of the dictionary automaton with the initial state as successor by default (see Section 2.4) by applying it in the particular case of a dictionary composed of a single nonempty string x. We show that, contrary to the general case, it is not necessary to maintain the sets of labeled successors sorted according to the alphabet in order to ensure the linearity of the construction of the implementation $\mathcal{D}_{\mathrm{D}}(\{x\})$ according to the length of the string x to locate. We also show that the delay is logarithmic in the length of the searched string, independently of a possible order in the sets of labeled successors.

Construction of the implementation

The following result comes directly from the definition of $\mathcal{D}(\{x\})$ and from Propositions 2.19 and 2.23.

Theorem 2.39
The size of $\mathcal{D}_D(\{x\})$ *is* $O(|x|)$. *More precisely,* $\mathcal{D}_D(\{x\})$ *possesses* $|x| + 1$ *states,* $|x|$ *forward arcs, and at most* $|x|$ *backward arcs.* ∎

The construction method of the implementation follows the one developed for the complete automaton (Section 2.2). It consists here in not generating the arcs of $\mathcal{D}(\{x\})$ that enter the initial state. To this aim, we adapt the code of function SMA-COMPLETE by deleting the **for** loop of lines 3–4 and by inserting, after line 8, instructions for simulating the return to the initial state of some arcs. We get the code that follows:

```
SMA-BY-DEFAULT(x)
 1  M ← NEW-AUTOMATON()
 2  q0 ← initial[M]
 3  t ← q0
 4  for each letter a of x, sequentially do
 5      p ← NEW-STATE()
 6      r ← TARGET(t, a)
 7      if r = NIL then
 8          r ← q0
 9      else Succ[t] ← Succ[t] \ {(a, r)}
10      Succ[t] ← Succ[t] ∪ {(a, p)}
11      Succ[p] ← Succ[r]
12      t ← p
13  terminal[t] ← TRUE
14  return M
```

Proposition 2.40
The operation SMA-BY-DEFAULT(x) *produces* $\mathcal{D}_D(\{x\})$, *implementation of the automaton* $\mathcal{D}(\{x\})$ *by successor by default.* ∎

We establish now a result on the construction of the implementation that is more than an immediate adaptation of Theorem 2.25.

Theorem 2.41
The operation SMA-BY-DEFAULT(x) *runs in time* $O(|x|)$ *using a constant extra space, whether the sets of labeled successors is sorted according to the alphabet or not.*

Proof The operations on the set of labeled successors of a state that is neither the initial state, nor the terminal state of the automaton are those of lines 11, 5, 6, possibly 9, then 10 of function SMA-BY-DEFAULT. Each of them is realized in time at most linear in the final size of the set. It is clear that it is the same for the initial state and the terminal state. Overall, it comes that the construction time is at most linear in the sum of the cardinals of the sets of labeled successors, which is $O(|x|)$ after Theorem 2.39. ■

Searching phase

The next theorem directly follows after Lemma 2.26 and Proposition 2.28.

Theorem 2.42
For the operation DET-SEARCH-BY-DEFAULT($\{x\}$, y), *the searching phase executes in time* $O(|y|)$. *More precisely, the number of comparisons performed between letters of* x *and of* y *is at most equal to* $2|y| - 1$ *when* $y \neq \varepsilon$, *whatever the order in which the elements of the sets of labeled successors are examined is.* ■

It remains to specify the order of magnitude of the delay. Let us recall that it depends directly on the maximal outgoing degree of the states of the implementation $\mathcal{D}_{\mathrm{D}}(\{x\})$. Furthermore, we denote by deg_u the function that associates with every state v in $\mathcal{D}_{\mathrm{D}}(\{u\})$ its outgoing degree. Lemmas 2.43 and 2.44 express the recurrence relations on the outgoing degrees.

Lemma 2.43
Let $(u, a) \in A^* \times A$. *Then, for every* $w \preceq_{\text{pref}} ua$, *we have:*

$$deg_{ua}(w) = \begin{cases} deg_u(\text{Border}(ua)) & \text{if } w = ua, \\ deg_u(u) + 1 & \text{if } w = u \text{ and Border}(ua) = \varepsilon, \\ deg_u(w) & \text{otherwise.} \end{cases}$$

Proof This is a direct consequence of Proposition 2.29. ■

Lemma 2.44
We have:

$$deg_x(x) = deg_x(\text{Border}(x)).$$

Moreover, for every $va \preceq_{\text{pref}} x$, *with* $v \prec_{\text{pref}} x$ *and* $a \in A$, *we have:*

$$deg_x(v) = \begin{cases} deg_x(\text{Border}(v)) + 1 & \text{if } v \neq \varepsilon \text{ and Border}(va) = \varepsilon, \\ deg_x(\text{Border}(v)) & \text{if } v \neq \varepsilon \text{ and Border}(va) \neq \varepsilon, \\ 1 & \text{if } v = \varepsilon. \end{cases}$$

Proof This is a direct consequence of Lemma 2.43. ■

The result that follows is the "cornerstone" of the proof of the logarithmic bound that will be given in Lemma 2.46.

Lemma 2.45
For every nonempty prefix u of x, we have:

$$2|\text{Border}(u)| \geq |u| \textit{ implies } deg_x(\text{Border}(u)) = deg_x(\text{Border}^2(u)).$$

Proof Let us set $k = 2|\text{Border}(u)| - |u|$, then $w = u[0\,.\,.\,k-1]$ and $a = w[k]$. Let us note that, since wa is a border of $\text{Border}(u)a$, the border of $\text{Border}(u)a$ is not empty. We apply then Lemma 2.44 to the prefix $va = \text{Border}(u)a$ of x and we get the result. ∎

Lemma 2.46
For every $u \preceq_{\text{pref}} x$, we have:

$$deg_x(u) \leq \lfloor \log_2(|u| + 1) \rfloor + 1.$$

Proof We show the property by recurrence on the length $|u|$ of the proper prefixes u of x. If $|u| = 0$, the property holds since $deg_x(\varepsilon) = 1$. For the recurrence step, $|u| \geq 1$, let us set that the property holds for all the prefixes of x of length at most $|u|$. Let $i \in \mathbf{N}$ be such that

$$2^i \leq |u| + 1 < 2^{i+1}, \tag{2.6}$$

and let $j \in \mathbf{N}$ be such that

$$|\text{Border}^{j+1}(u)| + 1 < 2^i \leq |\text{Border}^j(u)| + 1. \tag{2.7}$$

For $k = 0, 1, \ldots, j-1$, we have

$$\begin{aligned} 2|\text{Border}^{k+1}(u)| &\geq 2^{i+1} - 2 && \text{(after Inequality (2.7))} \\ &\geq |u| && \text{(after Inequality (2.6))} \\ &\geq |\text{Border}^k(u)|. \end{aligned}$$

It follows then, by applying Lemma 2.45, that:

$$deg_x(|\text{Border}^{k+1}(u)|) = deg_x(|\text{Border}^{k+2}(u)|)$$

for $k = 0, 1, \ldots, j-1$. This leads to

$$deg_x(|\text{Border}(u)|) = deg_x(|\text{Border}^{j+1}(u)|). \tag{2.8}$$

As a consequence, we have:

$$\begin{aligned} deg_x(u) &\leq deg_x(\text{Border}(u)) + 1 && \text{(after Lemma 2.44)} \\ &= deg_x(\text{Border}^{j+1}(u)) + 1 && \text{(after Equality (2.8))} \\ &\leq \lfloor \log_2(|\text{Border}^{j+1}(u)| + 1) \rfloor + 2 && \text{(recurrence),} \\ &\leq i + 1 && \text{(by definition of } j) \\ &= \lfloor \log_2(|u| + 1) \rfloor + 1 && \text{(by definition of } i). \end{aligned}$$

The property is thus true for every string of length $|u|$, which ends the proof by recurrence. ■

Theorem 2.47
The degree of any state of the implementation $\mathcal{D}_\mathrm{D}(\{x\})$ is no more than $\min\{\text{card alph}(x), 1 + \lfloor \log_2 |x| \rfloor\}$.

Proof The bound that depends on the alphabet of the string results from Proposition 2.21. For the bound that depends on the length of the string, this is a direct consequence of Lemmas 2.44 (for the state x) and 2.46 (for the other states). ■

A consequence of Theorem 2.47 is the following corollary.

Corollary 2.48
For the operation DET-SEARCH-BY-DEFAULT($\{x\}$, y), *the delay is* $O(s)$ *where*

$$s = \min\{\text{card alph}(x), 1 + \lfloor \log_2 |x| \rfloor\}$$

whatever the order in which the elements of the sets of labeled successors are examined is. When these sets are sorted according to the alphabet, the delay becomes $O(\log s)$. ■

The bound on the degree given in Theorem 2.47 is optimal for $|x|$ fixed (and by taking the alphabet into account). Let us consider the function on strings

$$\xi : A^* \to A^*$$

defined by the recurrence

$$\xi(\varepsilon) = \varepsilon$$
$$\xi(ua) = \xi(u) \cdot a \cdot \xi(u) \quad \text{for } (u, a) \in A^* \times A.$$

Then, when the string $\xi(a_1 a_2 \ldots a_{k-1})a_k$ is a prefix of the string x with $k = \min\{\text{card } A, 1 + \lfloor \log_2 |x| \rfloor\}$ and $a_1, a_2, \ldots, a_k$ are pairwise distinct letters, the outgoing degree of the state $\xi(a_1 a_2 \ldots a_{k-1})$ is exactly k. An example is shown in Figure 2.15 on an alphabet containing at least the letters a, b, c, and d, and with $x = \xi(\texttt{abc})\texttt{d}$.

Challenge of implementations for searching for one string

The observations made at the end of Section 2.4 concerning the two implementations with failure function and with successor by default have to be partially

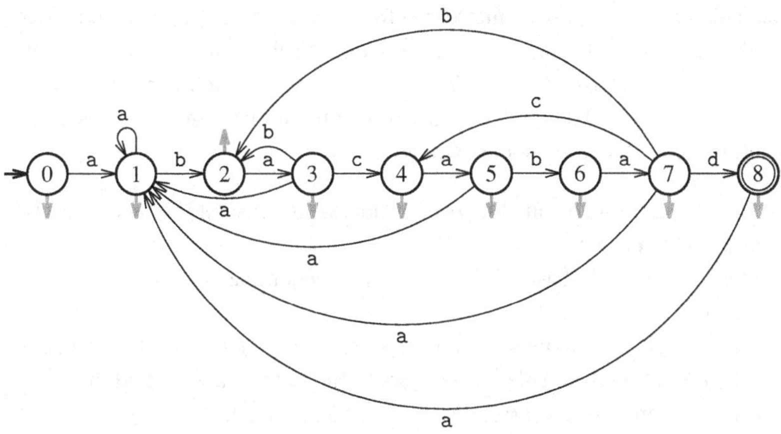

Figure 2.15. The implementation $\mathcal{D}_D(\{x\})$ when $x =$ abacabad. The maximal outgoing degree of states is equal to 4 (state 7), this is the maximum possible for a string that, as x, has a length within 2^3 and $2^4 - 1$, and is formed of at least four distinct letters.

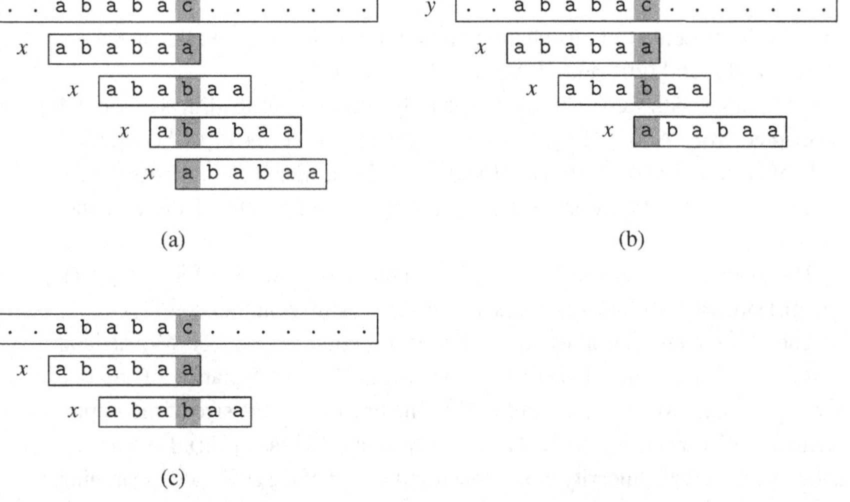

Figure 2.16. Behavior of three sequential string matching algorithms when the last letter of the pattern $x =$ ababaa is aligned with the letter c that occurs in the text y. **(a)** Implementation $\mathcal{D}_F(\{x\})$ with failure function f; 4 comparisons between the letters of x and the current letter of y, with 2 redundant comparisons. **(b)** Its version with f'; 3 comparisons, the last one being redundant. **(c)** Implementation $\mathcal{D}_D(\{x\})$ when the elements of the sets of labeled successors are scanned in order of decreasing level; 2 comparisons only, and it cannot be done better.

amended here. In the case of the search for a single string, the time and space complexities are all linear, either in the length of the string to locate for the structures to memorize, or in the length of the text in which is performed the search of the string. The implementation with the initial state as successor by default presents, however, some extra advantages:

1. It runs in real time on an alphabet considered as constant (i.e., the delay is bounded by a constant).
2. It has a logarithmic-based 2 delay, which is better than a logarithmic-based Φ delay.
3. It makes a smaller number of comparisons between letters of the string and of the text when the labeled successors of the states are inspected in decreasing order of level (see the example in Figure 2.16).
4. The order of inspection of the successors is modifiable, without any consequence on the linearity of the complexities.

Notes

The results presented in this chapter come initially from the works of Knuth, Morris, and Pratt [170], and of Aho and Corasick [87].

The search with failure function for a dictionary described in Section 2.3 is adapted from Aho and Corasick [87]. Based on the result of Section 4.5 and other techniques, Dori and Landau [131] designed a linear-time preprocessing of the dictionary automaton that is independent of the alphabet size.

The treatment of Section 2.4 is original; it pursues the works of Simon [207], and of Hancart [149] for locating a single string with an automaton.

The search algorithm by the prefixes (Section 2.6) is of Morris and Pratt [188]. Its optimized version (same section) is an adaptation of the one given by Knuth, Morris, and Pratt [170]. The linearity of the size of the implementation $\mathcal{D}_{\mathrm{D}}(\{x\})$ (Section 2.7) is due to Simon [207] (see [32]). He simultaneously showed the linearity of the construction and of the associated searching phase. The fact that the order of inspection does not modify the linearity of the construction and of the searching phases is due to Hancart [149]. He gave the exact bound on the delay. The exact bound on the number of comparisons for the sequential search for a string in the comparison model was then given by Hancart [149] (see Exercise 2.10) and, for a close problem, by Breslauer, Colussi, and Toniolo [110] (see Exercise 2.14).

Exercises

2.1 (Regular)

Compare the complexities of the algorithms searching for the occurrences of the strings of a dictionary described in this chapter with the standard algorithms having a regular expression describing the dictionary as input.

2.2 (Determinization)

Show that if we consider the construction by subset to determinize the automaton $\mathcal{T}(X)$ augmented with a loop on the initial state, the states of the deterministic automaton are of the form

$$\{u, f(u), f^2(u), \ldots, \varepsilon\}$$

with $u \in \mathrm{Pref}(X)$.

2.3 (Failure)

Show that the function f can be expressed independently of function h, that is, it satisfies for every $(u, a) \in A^* \times A$ the relation:

$$f(ua) = \begin{cases} f(u)a & \text{if } u \neq \varepsilon \text{ and } f(u)a \in \mathrm{Pref}(X), \\ f(f(u)a) & \text{if } u \neq \varepsilon \text{ and } f(u)a \notin \mathrm{Pref}(X), \\ \varepsilon & \text{otherwise.} \end{cases}$$

2.4 (Laziness)

Design for each of the pattern matching algorithms of the chapter a lazy version that constructs the associated automaton, or one of its particular implementations, when needed during the search.

2.5 (Fast loop)

Code the implementation of $\mathcal{D}_{\mathrm{F}}(X)$ with a fast loop on the initial state with the help of a table on the alphabet. (*Hint:* it actually consists of the original algorithm of Aho and Corasick [87].)

2.6 (Truly linear)

Algorithms of the chapter that are meant for the construction of dictionary automata have a running time that depends on the alphabet size. Show that it is possible to get a linear-time algorithm on a bounded integer alphabet by using the suffix array construction of Section 4.5 to build the tree, and the suffix tree of reverse strings of the dictionary to set up the failure function. (*Hint:* see Dori and Landau [131].)

2.7 (Blindly ahead)

We consider that the sets of labeled successors of the implementation $\mathcal{D}_{\text{D}}(X)$ are lists. We apply to these lists the technique of autoadaptative search which, for each successful search of a particular element in a list, reorganizes the list by putting the found element at the head. What is the complexity of the construction of this implementation? What is the complexity of the searching phase (including the updating of the lists)?

2.8 (Bound)

Show that $2m - 4$ is the exact bound of the maximal number of comparisons between letters performed during the computation of the table of best prefixes of strings x of length $m \geq 3$ during the operation Best-prefix(x, m). (*Hint:* possibly show that the bound of $2m - 3$ comparisons is only reached for strings of the form $a^{m-1}b$ with $m \geq 2, a, b \in A$ and $a \neq b$ during the operation Good-prefix(x, m). Show then that only strings of the form aba^{m-2} or $aba^{m-3}c$ with $m \geq 3, a, b, c \in A$, and $a \neq b \neq c \neq a$ require $2m - 4$ comparisons.)

2.9 (The worst case unveiled)

Show that some prefixes of the Fibonacci strings reach the bound on the number of consecutive comparisons of Corollary 2.38.

2.10 (The first at the end)

Show that the number of comparisons performed during the search for every string x of non-null length m in a text of length n is at most $(2 - 1/m)n$ if we utilize the implementation $\mathcal{D}_{\text{D}}\{x\}$ by inspecting the forward arc at the end during the computation of each transition.

Show that the bound $(2 - 1/m)n$ is a lower bound of the worst case of the sequential search in the comparison model. (*Hint:* see Hancart [149].)

2.11 (Real time)

Show that the search for a string or for several strings can be performed in real time when the letters of the alphabet are binary encoded.

2.12 (Conjugates)

Give an algorithm that tests if two strings u and v are conjugate of each others and that runs in time $O(|u| + |v|)$.

2.13 (Palindromes)

We denote by P the set of palindromes of even length. Show that we can test if a string x belongs or not to P^* – called *palstars*, for *even palindromes starred* – in time and in space $O(|x|)$. (*Hint:* see Knuth, Morris, and Pratt [170].)

2.14 (Prefix-matching)

The problem of *prefix-matching* consists, for a given string x and a given text y, in determining at each of the positions on the text the longest prefix of x whose occurrence ends here. Show that this problem admits solutions and bounds (see Exercise 2.10) identical to the sequential search for a string in a text in the comparison model. (*Hint:* see Breslauer, Colussi, and Toniolo [110].)

2.15 (Codicity test)

We consider a dictionary $X \subset A^*$ and the associated graph $\mathcal{G} = (Q, F)$ in which $Q = \text{Pref}(X) \setminus \{\varepsilon\}$ and F is the set of pairs (u, v) of strings of Q such that $uv \in X$ (crossing arc) or, both, $v \notin X$ and $uz = v$ for a string $z \in X$ (forward arc).

Show that X is a code (see Exercise 1.10) if and only if the graph $\mathcal{G}$ has no path that links two elements of X.

Write a construction algorithm of $\mathcal{G}$ that uses the dictionary automaton associated with X.

Complete the algorithm to get a codicity test of X.

What is the complexity of the algorithm? (*Hint:* see Sardinas and Patterson [204].)

3

String searching with a sliding window

In this chapter, we consider the problem of searching for all the occurrences of a fixed string in a text. The methods described here are based on combinatorial properties. They apply when the string and the text are in central memory or when only a part of the text is in a memory buffer. Contrary to the solutions presented in the previous chapter, the search does not process the text in a strictly sequential way.

The algorithms of the chapter scan the text through a window having the same length as the pattern length. The process that consists in determining if the content of the window matches the string is called an attempt, following the sliding window mechanism described in Section 1.5. After the end of each attempt the window is shifted toward the end of the text. The executions of these algorithms are thus successions of attempts followed by shifts.

We consider algorithms that, during each attempt, perform the comparisons between letters of the string and of the window from right to left, that is to say, in the opposite direction of the usual reading direction. These algorithms match thus suffixes of the string inside the text. The interest of this technique is that during an attempt the algorithm accumulates information on the text that is possibly processed later on.

We present three more and more efficient versions in terms of number of letter comparisons performed by the algorithms. The first memorizes no information, the second memorizes the match of the previous attempt, and the third keeps track of all the matches of previous attempts. The number of comparisons is an indicator used to evaluate the obtained gains. In the last section, we consider a method that generalizes the process for searching a text for strings of a dictionary.

3.1 Searching without memory

Let x be a string of length m that we want to search for all the occurrences in a text y of length n. In the rest, we say of x that it is ***periodic*** when $\text{per}(x) \leq m/2$.

We first present a method that realizes the search by mean of the principle recalled in the introduction. When the string x is nonperiodic, it performs less than $3n$ comparisons between letters. One of the characteristics of this algorithm is that it keeps no memory of the previous attempts.

This section contains, moreover, a weak version of the method, which analysis is given thereafter. The preprocessing phase of this version, that executes in time and in space $O(m)$, is more simple; it is developed in Section 3.3. The preprocessing of the initial version, based on an automaton, is described in Section 3.4.

In this chapter, we consider that when an attempt takes place at position j on the text y, the window contains the factor $y[j-m+1 \,..\, j]$ of the text y. The index j is thus the right position of the factor. The ***longest common suffix*** of two strings u and v being denoted by

$$lcsuff(u, v),$$

for an attempt T at position j on the text y, we set

$$z = lcsuff(y[0 \,..\, j], x),$$

and d the length of the shift applied just after the attempt T.

The general situation at the end of the attempt T is the following: the suffix z of x has been identified in the text y and, if $|z| < |x|$, a negative comparison occurred between the letter $a = x[m-|z|-1]$ of the string and the letter $b = y[j-|z|]$ of the text. In other words, by setting $i = m-|z|-1$, we have $z = x[i+1 \,..\, m-1] = y[j-m+i+2 \,..\, j]$ and, either $i = -1$, or $i \geq 0$ with $a = x[i]$, $b = y[j-m+i+1]$ and $a \neq b$ (see Figure 3.1).

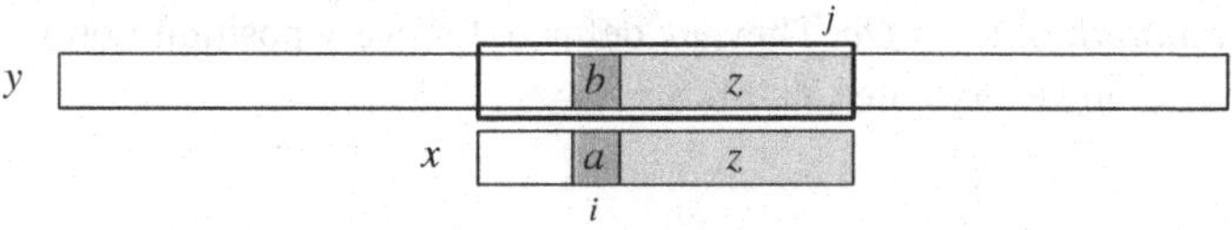

Figure 3.1. General situation at the end of an attempt at position j. The comparison of the content of the window $y[j-m+1 \,..\, j]$ with the string x proceeds by letter comparisons, from right to left. The string z is the longest common suffix of $y[0 \,..\, j]$ and x (positive comparison area, indicated in light gray). When this suffix of the string x is not x itself, the position i on x in which occurs a negative comparison (in dark gray) satisfies $i = m-|z|-1$.

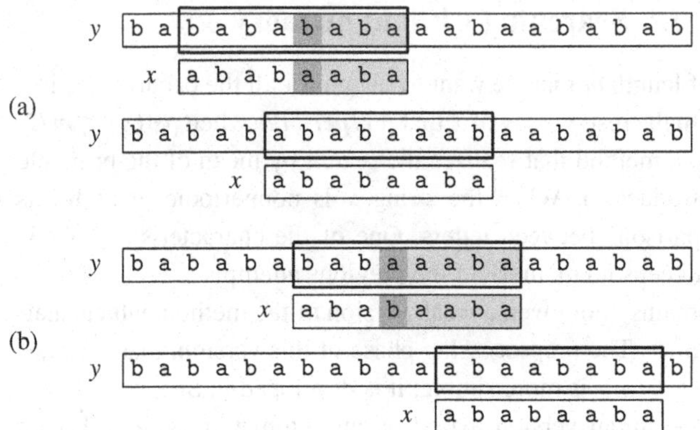

Figure 3.2. Shifts following attempts. (**a**) During the attempt at position 9, the suffix aba of the string is detected in the text. A negative comparison occurs between $x[4] = \texttt{a}$ and $y[6] = \texttt{b}$. The shift to apply consists in aligning the factor baba of the text with its (rightmost) occurrence in x. We apply here a shift of length 3. (**b**) During the attempt at position 13, the suffix aaba of the string matches the text. A negative comparison occurs between $x[3] = \texttt{b}$ and $y[9] = \texttt{a}$. The factor aaaba does not occur in x; the shift to apply consists in aligning a longest prefix of the string matching with a suffix of the factor aaaba of the text. Here, this prefix is aba and the length of the shift is 5.

Taking into account the information collected on the text y during the attempt, the natural shift to apply consists in aligning the factor bz of the text with its rightmost occurrence in x. If bz is not a factor of x, we must then perform the alignment (to the right) considering the longest prefix of x that is also a suffix of z. These two cases are illustrated in Figure 3.2.

In the two situations that have just been examined, the computation of the shift following T is rather independent of the text. It can be previously computed for each position of the string and for each letter of the alphabet. To this aim, we define two conditions that correspond to the case where the string z is the suffix $x[i+1\,..\,m-1]$ of x. They are the ***suffix condition*** Sc and the ***occurrence condition*** of letter Oc. They are defined, for every position i on x, every shift d of x, and every letter $b \in A$, by

$$Sc(i,d) = \begin{cases} 0 < d \leq i+1 \text{ and } x[i-d+1\,..\,m-d-1] \preceq_{\text{suff}} x \\ \text{or} \\ i+1 < d \text{ and } x[0\,..\,m-d-1] \preceq_{\text{suff}} x \end{cases}$$

and

$$Oc(b, i, d) = \begin{cases} 0 < d \leq i \text{ and } x[i - d] = b \\ \text{or} \\ i < d. \end{cases}$$

Then, the ***function of the best factor***, denoted by *best-fact*, is defined in the following way: for every position i on x and every letter $b \in A$,

$$\textit{best-fact}(i, b) = \min\{d : Sc(i, d) \text{ and } Oc(b, i, d) \text{ hold}\}.$$

We note that *best-fact*(i, b) is always defined since the conditions are satisfied for $d = m$.

A direct implementation of the function of the best factor requires a memory space $O(m \times \text{card } A)$. Actually, a finer solution based on an automaton only requires a space $O(m)$. It is presented in Section 3.4. We further introduce a weak version of the function for which the space linearity of the implementation is immediate.

Searching phase

During an attempt at position j on the text y, and when a negative comparison is performed between the letter $x[i]$ of the string and the letter $y[j - m + 1 + i]$ of the text, we apply a shift of length

$$d = \textit{best-fact}(i, y[j - m + 1 + i]).$$

Once the shift is performed, the first condition, $Sc(i, d)$, ensures that the factor $y[j - m + 2 + i \,..\, j]$ of the text and the factor (or prefix) of the string with which it is aligned are identical. Whereas the second condition $Oc(y[j - m + 1 + i], i, d)$ ensures that if a letter of the string is aligned with $y[j - m + 1 + i]$ then it matches this one.

We note that, if during an attempt, an occurrence of the string is discovered in the text (which corresponds to $i = -1$), the shift to apply is of length $\text{per}(x)$. We moreover note that

$$\textit{best-fact}(0, b) = \text{per}(x)$$

for every letter $b \in A$.

The algorithm MEMORYLESS-SUFFIX-SEARCH, whose code is given below, implements the method that has just been described.

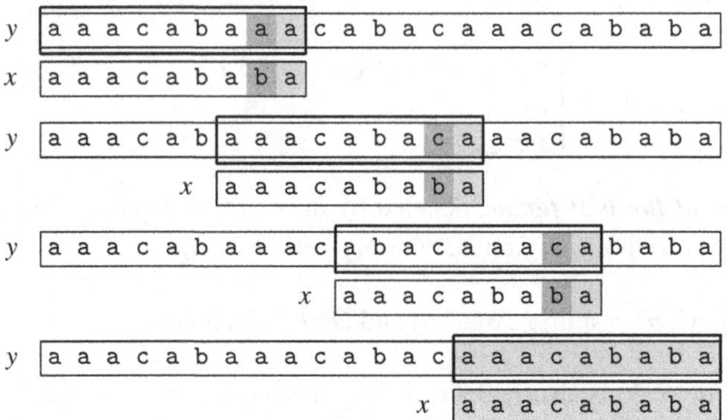

Figure 3.3. Running example of algorithm MEMORYLESS-SUFFIX-SEARCH. In this case, 15 comparisons between letters of the string and letters of the text are performed.

```
MEMORYLESS-SUFFIX-SEARCH(x, m, y, n)
j ← m − 1
while j < n do
    i ← m − 1
    while i ≥ 0 and x[i] = y[j − m + 1 + i] do
        i ← i − 1
    OUTPUT-IF(i < 0)
    if i < 0 then
        j ← j + per(x)
    else j ← j + best-fact(i, y[j − m + 1 + i])
```

An example of execution is given in Figure 3.3. The values of the strings x and y considered in this example will be used again thereafter. They serve to illustrate the difference of behavior of the diverse searching algorithms presented in the chapter.

Theorem 3.1
The algorithm MEMORYLESS-SUFFIX-SEARCH *finds all the occurrences of the string x in the text y.*

Proof By definition of the functions *best-fact* and per, all the shifts applied by the algorithm MEMORYLESS-SUFFIX-SEARCH are valid. The algorithm cannot thus miss any occurrence of x in y. ■

We easily find cases for which the behavior of the algorithm MEMORYLESS-SUFFIX-SEARCH is quadratic, $O(m \times n)$, for instance when $x = \mathrm{a}^m$ and $y = \mathrm{a}^n$.

Weak version

It is possible to approximate the function of the best factor in order to avoid the requirement of having to use an automaton, which simplifies the realization of the whole algorithm. The approximation is given by a function called good suffix implemented by a table. It is traditional to add to it the table *last-occ* introduced in Section 1.5.

We define the new weak-occurrence condition *WOc* by

$$WOc(i, d) = \begin{cases} 0 < d \leq i \text{ and } x[i-d] \neq x[i] \\ \text{or} \\ i < d. \end{cases}$$

The ***table of the good suffix*** is then defined, for a position i on x, by

$$\textit{good-suff}[i] = \min\{d : Sc(i, d) \text{ and } WOc(i, d) \text{ are satisfied}\}.$$

The condition $WOc(i, d)$ ensures that if a letter c of the string is aligned with the letter $b = y[j - m + 1 + i]$ after the shift, then c is different from the letter $a = x[i]$ which was aligned with b just before the shift and caused a mismatch. This weakens the condition $Oc(b, i, d)$ that imposes the identity of the letters c and b (line 9 of algorithm MEMORYLESS-SUFFIX-SEARCH). We note that in the case of a binary alphabet the utilization of the table of the good suffix in the searching algorithm is equivalent to using the function of the best factor because the two functions are identical.

The preprocessing phase of the algorithm W-MEMORYLESS-SUFFIX-SEARCH thus comes down to the computation of the table *good-suff* only. It is presented in Section 3.3. As previously, we note that *good-suff* [0] has for value per(x).

In the code that follows, we only utilize the table *good-suff*, the addition of the heuristic *last-occ* being an immediate variant. An example of execution of the algorithm is shown in Figure 3.4.

```
W-MEMORYLESS-SUFFIX-SEARCH(x, m, good-suff, y, n)
j ← m − 1
while j < n do
    i ← m − 1
    while i ≥ 0 and x[i] = y[j − m + 1 + i] do
        i ← i − 1
    OUTPUT-IF(i < 0)
    if i < 0 then
        j ← j + per(x)
    else j ← j + good-suff[i]
```

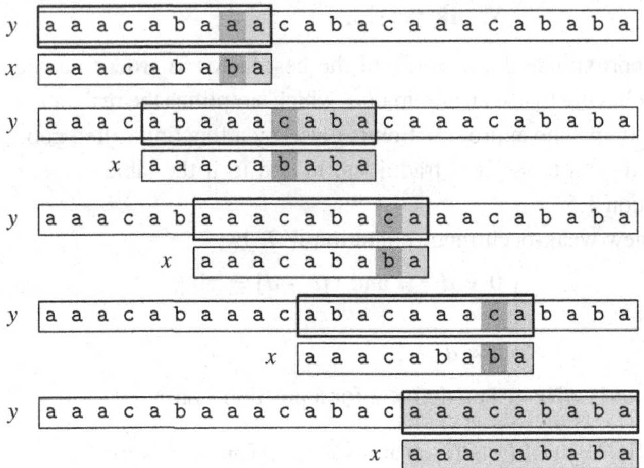

Figure 3.4. Execution, on the example of Figure 3.3, of the algorithm W-MEMORYLESS-SUFFIX-SEARCH that uses the good suffix table. With this algorithm, 19 comparisons between letters of the string and of the text are performed.

Theorem 3.2
The algorithm W-MEMORYLESS-SUFFIX-SEARCH *finds all the occurrences of the string x in the text y.*

Proof By definition of the table *good-suff* and of the function per, all the shifts applied by the algorithm W-MEMORYLESS-SUFFIX-SEARCH are valid. The algorithm cannot thus miss any occurrence of the string x in the text y. ∎

3.2 Searching time

We show, in this part, that the algorithm W-MEMORYLESS-SUFFIX-SEARCH performs at most $4n$ comparisons between letters of the string and letters of the text when it is used for searching a text of length n for a string x that satisfies the condition $\text{per}(x) > m/3$. We start by showing three technical results that serve as a basis for the proof of the result.

The first statement is illustrated in Figure 3.5.

Lemma 3.3
Let x be a string, y be a text, v be a primitive string, and k be an integer such that $v^2 \preceq_{\text{suff}} x$, $y = v^k$, and $k \geq 2$. During the execution of the operation W-MEMORYLESS-SUFFIX-SEARCH($x, m, \textit{good-suff}, y, n$), *if there exists an attempt T_0 at a position j_0 on y that is not of the form $\ell|v| - 1$ ($\ell \in \mathbf{N}$), this attempt is*

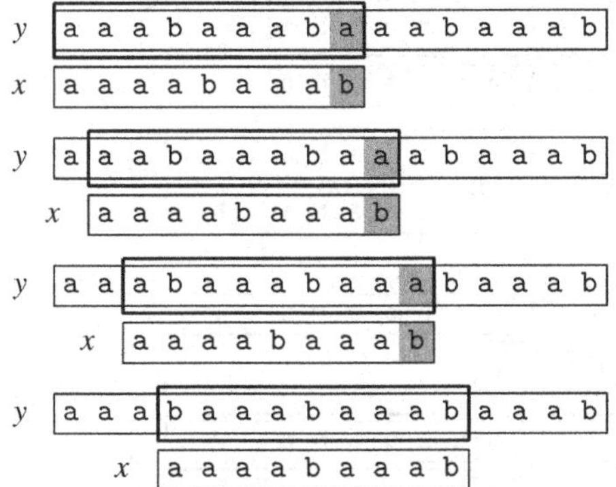

Figure 3.5. Example in support of Lemma 3.3. We search for $x = \mathtt{a}(\mathtt{aaab})^2$ in $y = (\mathtt{aaab})^4$. After the attempt at the (right) position 8, 3 shifts (each of length 1) happen, and the window reaches position 11 that corresponds to a right position of a factor aaab in y. This adjusts the search according to the period of y.

followed, immediately or not, by an attempt at the position

$$j = \min\{h : h = \ell|v| - 1, h > j_0, \ell \in \mathbf{N}\}.$$

Proof Since v is primitive, from the Primitivity Lemma, it comes that at most $|v|$ comparisons are performed during the attempt T_0. Let $a = x[i]$ be the letter of the string that caused the mismatch ($b = y[j_0 - m + 1 + i]$ and $a \neq b$). Let $d_0 = j - j_0$. The condition $Sc(i, d_0)$ is satisfied: $d_0 \leq i$ and $x[i - d_0 + 1 \,..\, m - d_0 - 1] \preceq_{\text{suff}} x$. Same for $WOc(i, d_0)$: $d_0 \leq i$ and $b = x[i - d_0] \neq x[i] = a$. It follows that $\textit{good-suff}[i] \leq d_0$.

If $\textit{good-suff}[i] < d_0$, let j_1 be the (right) position of the window during the attempt T_1 that immediately follows T_0. We have $0 < d_1 = j - j_1 < d_0$. The argument applied to the attempt T_0 also applies to the attempt T_1. Therefore, a finite sequence of such attempts leads eventually to the attempt at position j. ■

Let T be an attempt at position j on y. We assume that the following properties hold: $bz \preceq_{\text{suff}} y[0 \,..\, j]$, $az \preceq_{\text{suff}} x$, $a \neq b$, $z = wv^k$, $w \prec_{\text{suff}} v$, $aw \preceq_{\text{suff}} x$, $k \geq 2$, and v primitive. These properties are assumptions of the next two lemmas and also of their corollary. Figure 3.6 illustrates the following statement.

Lemma 3.4
Under the above assumptions there is no attempt at positions $j - \ell|v|$, $1 \leq \ell \leq k - 1$, before the attempt T.

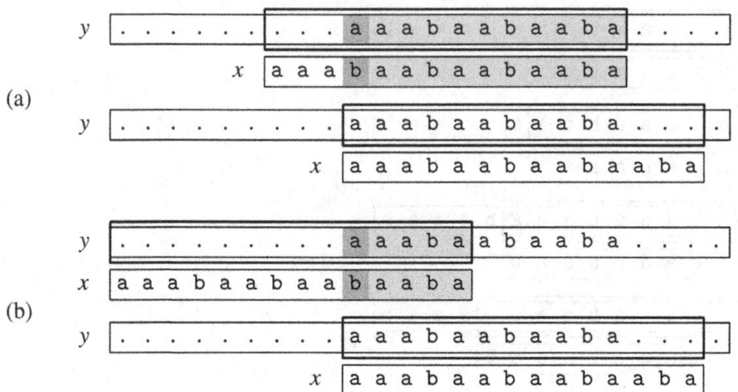

Figure 3.6. Illustration of Lemma 3.4. **(a)** Let j be the position on y of the current attempt. We detect the suffix $\mathtt{a(aba)}^3$ of x in y. A negative comparison occurs between the letters b and a that precede this factor in the string and the text respectively. The shift to apply is of length 3. **(b)** If the attempt described here would have existed previously, it would have led to the same final situation that the one of part (a). This would contradict the existence of the attempt at position j.

Proof Let us assume, by contradiction, that there has been an attempt at a position $j_0 = j - \ell_0|v|$ for some ℓ_0 such that $1 \leq \ell_0 \leq k - 1$. We would have $bwv^{k-\ell_0} \preceq_{\text{suff}} y[0 \mathinner{.\,.} j_0]$ and $awv^{k-\ell_0} \preceq_{\text{suff}} x$. For i_0 defined by $i_0 = m - |w| - (k - \ell_0)|v|$, we have then $d_0 = \textit{good-suff}\,[i_0] > \ell_0|v|$.

The existence of any shift having a smaller length nonmultiple of $|v|$ would contradict the fact that v is primitive. Any shift having a smaller length multiple of $|v|$ would align a letter a of the string with the letter b of the text. It follows that the shift applied after an attempt at position $j_0 = j - \ell_0|v|$ has a length greater than ℓ_0. Thus the contradiction. ∎

Lemma 3.5

Under the above assumptions, before the attempt T, there is no attempt at positions ℓ such that $j - |z| + |v| \leq \ell \leq j - |v|$.

Proof From Lemma 3.4, we deduce that there cannot exist an attempt at positions $j - \ell|v|$ for $1 \leq \ell \leq k - 1$. And from Lemma 3.3, we deduce that every attempt at another position between $j - |z| + |v|$ and $j - |v|$ is followed (immediately or not) by an attempt at a position $j - \ell|v|$ with $1 \leq \ell \leq k - 1$. This gives the result. ∎

Corollary 3.6
Under the above assumptions, before the attempt T, at most $3|v| - 3$ letters of the factor z of y have been compared to letters of x.

Proof After Lemma 3.5, the attempts preceding the attempt T and in which the letters of z have been compared could only have taken place at positions in the intervals $[j - |z| + 1, j - |z| + |v| - 1]$ on one hand, and $[j - |v| + 1, j - 1]$ on the other hand. For the first interval, the prefix of z submitted to comparisons is of maximal length $|v| - 1$. For the second that contains $|v| - 1$ positions, the factor of z possibly submitted to comparisons is $z[|z| - 2|v| + 1 \,.\,.\, |z| - 2]$. Indeed, the number of comparisons performed during an attempt at a position in the interval $[j - |v| + 1, j - 1]$ is less than $|v|$ since v is primitive. The number of occurrences of letters compared is thus bounded by the sum of the lengths of the two considered factors of z, that is to say $3(|v| - 1)$. This is what we wanted to prove. ■

Theorem 3.7
During the localization of a string x of length m satisfying $\text{per}(x) > m/3$ *in a text y of length n, the algorithm* W-MEMORYLESS-SUFFIX-SEARCH *performs less than $4n$ comparisons between letters of x and letters of y.*

Proof For an attempt T at position j, we denote by t the number of occurrences of letters compared for the first time during this attempt, and by d the length of the shift that follows. We are to bound the number of comparisons performed during attempt T by $3d + t$.

Let us set $z = \mathit{lcsuff}(x, y[0 \,.\,.\, j])$.

If $|z| \leq 3d$, the number of comparisons performed during the attempt T is at most $|z| + 1$ and the letter $y[j]$ had not been compared before the attempt T. Thus $|z| + 1 \leq 3d + 1$.

If $|z| > 3d$, this implies the conditions $z = wv^k$, $bz \preceq_{\text{suff}} y[0 \,.\,.\, j]$, $az \preceq_{\text{suff}} x$, $a \neq b$, $k \geq 1$, $w \prec_{\text{suff}} v$, and v primitive, due to the assumption $\text{per}(x) > m/3$. Moreover $k \geq 2$, $aw \prec_{\text{suff}} v$, and $d \geq |v|$. Thus, by Corollary 3.6, at most $3|v| - 3$ letters of z have been compared before the attempt T. It follows that $t \geq |z| - 3|v| + 3 \geq |z| - 3d + 3$. The number of comparisons performed during attempt T, $|z| + 1$, which is less than $3d + |z| - 3d + 3 = |z| + 3$, is thus less than $3d + t$.

Since the sum of the lengths of all the shifts is less than n and that the number of letters that can be compared for the first time is less than n, the result follows. ■

The $4n$ bound of the previous theorem is not optimal. Actually, we can show the following result that we state without proof.

Theorem 3.8

During the search for a nonperiodic string x of length m (i.e., a string for which $\text{per}(x) > m/2$*) in a text y of length n, the algorithm* W-MEMORYLESS-SUFFIX-SEARCH *performs at most $3n$ comparisons between letters of x and letters of y.* ■

The theorem does not apply to the case where the string x is periodic. For these strings, it is sufficient to slightly modify the algorithm W-MEMORYLESS-SUFFIX-SEARCH in order to get a linear-time algorithm. Indeed, the index i can continue to run from $m-1$ to 0 except when an occurrence has just been signaled in which case it rather runs from $m-1$ to $m-\text{per}(x)$. The algorithm WL-MEMORYLESS-SUFFIX-SEARCH below implements this technique, called "prefix memorization."

```
WL-MEMORYLESS-SUFFIX-SEARCH(x, m, good-suff, y, n)
ℓ ← 0
j ← m − 1
while j < n do
      i ← m − 1
      while i ≥ ℓ and x[i] = y[j − m + 1 + i] do
            i ← i − 1
      OUTPUT-IF(i < ℓ)
      if i < ℓ then
            ℓ ← m − per(x)
            j ← j + per(x)
      else ℓ ← 0
            j ← j + good-suff[i]
```

The bound given in Theorem 3.8 is quasi optimal as shows the following example. Let $x = \mathtt{a}^{k-1}\mathtt{b}\mathtt{a}^{k-1}$ and $y = \mathtt{a}^{k-1}(\mathtt{aba}^{k-1})^{\ell}$ with $k \geq 2$ (we then have $m = 2k-1$ and $n = \ell(k+1)+(k-1)$). On each of the first $\ell - 1$ factors $\mathtt{aba}^{k-1}$ (of length $k+1$) of y, the number of comparisons performed by the algorithm W-MEMORYLESS-SUFFIX-SEARCH is $(k-1)+(k+1)+(k-2) = 3k-2$. On the rightmost factor of this kind, $(k-1)+(k+1) = 2k$ comparisons are done. And on the prefix of length $k-1$ of y, $k-2$ comparisons are executed. On the overall, the algorithm W-MEMORYLESS-SUFFIX-SEARCH performs

$$\frac{3k-2}{k+1}(n-k+1) = \left(n - \frac{m-1}{2}\right)\left(3 - \frac{10}{m+3}\right)$$

comparisons. Figure 3.7 illustrates the bound with the values $k = 5$ and $\ell = 4$.

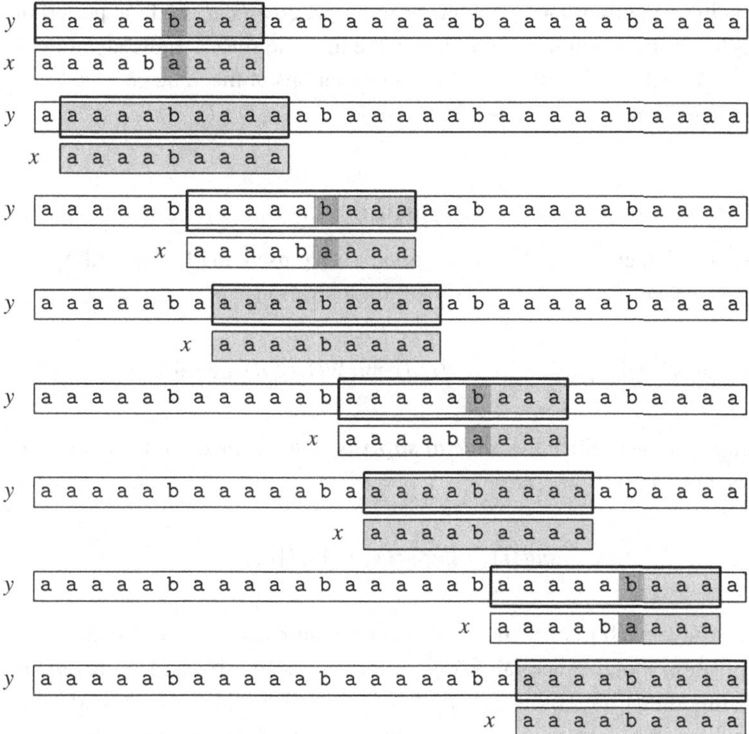

Figure 3.7. Illustration of the bound of Theorem 3.8 with $x = \mathtt{a}^4\mathtt{b}\mathtt{a}^4$ and $y = \mathtt{a}^4(\mathtt{aba}^4)^4$. The string x is of length 9, the text y of length 28, and 52 comparisons are performed. For each factor abaaaa (of length 6) of the text, 13 comparisons are performed.

Corollary 3.9

The algorithm W-MEMORYLESS-SUFFIX-SEARCH *finds the first occurrence of a string of length m in a text of length n in time $O(n)$ and in space $O(m)$.*

Proof The result is a consequence of Theorem 3.2 and of Theorem 3.7 (or of Theorem 3.8). ∎

3.3 Computing the good suffix table

In this section, we consider the preprocessing on the pattern that is required by the searching algorithm W-MEMORYLESS-SUFFIX-SEARCH. The preprocessing consists in computing both the good suffix table, *good-suff*, and the period of x. This latter computation is contained in the first one since we already noticed that per(x) = *good-suff*[0]. Two other computations of the table *good-suff* are proposed as exercises (Exercises 3.10 and 3.11).

Algorithm

Let us recall that the table of the good suffix used in the algorithm W-MEMORYLESS-SUFFIX-SEARCH is defined, for a position i on x, by

$$\textit{good-suff}[i] = \min\{d : Sc(i,d) \text{ and } WOc(i,d) \text{ are satisfied}\}.$$

To compute it, we utilize the ***table of suffixes***, *suff*, defined on the string x as follows. For $i = 0, 1, \ldots, m-1$,

$$\textit{suff}[i] = |\textit{lcsuff}(x, x[0\,..\,i])|,$$

that is to say, *suff*[i] is the maximal length of suffixes of x that occur at the right position i on x. The table *suff* is the analogue, obtained by reversing the reading direction, of the table *pref* of Section 1.6. This latter provides the maximal lengths of prefixes of x beginning at each of its positions. Figure 3.8 gives the two tables *suff* and *good-suff* for the string x = aaacababa.

The computation of table *suff* is performed by the algorithm SUFFIXES below that is directly adapted from algorithm PREFIXES computing the table *pref* (see Section 1.6).

(a)

i	0	1	2	3	4	5	6	7	8
$x[i]$	a	a	a	c	a	b	a	b	a
suff[i]	1	1	1	0	1	0	3	0	9
good-suff[i]	8	8	8	8	8	2	8	4	1

(b)

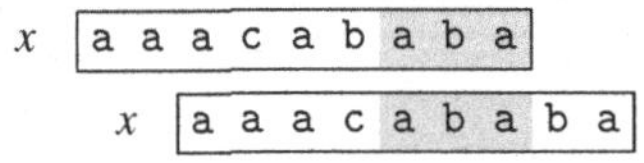

```
x  a a a c a b a b a
     x  a a a c a b a b a
```

Figure 3.8. We consider the string x = aaacababa. (**a**) Values of tables *suff* and *good-suff*. (**b**) We have *suff*[6] = 3. This indicates that the longest suffix of x ending at position 6 is aba, string that has length 3. As *suff*[6] = 3, we have *good-suff*[$9-1-3$] = $9-1-6=2$, value that is computed in line 8 of Algorithm GOOD-SUFFIX.

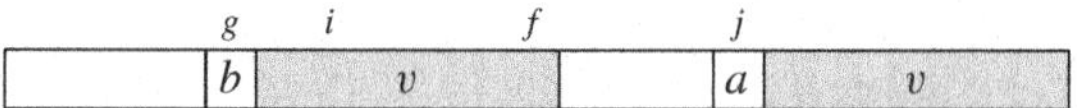

Figure 3.9. Variables i, j, f, and g of Algorithm SUFFIXES. The main loop admits for invariants: $v = lcsuff(x, x[0\,..\,f])$ and thus $a \neq b$ $(a, b \in A)$, $j = g + m - 1 - f$, and $i < f$. The schema corresponds to the situation in which $g < i$.

```
SUFFIXES(x, m)
  g ← m − 1
  suff[m − 1] ← m
  for i ← m − 2 downto 0 do
      if i > g and suff[i + m − 1 − f] ≠ i − g then
          suff[i] ← min{suff[i + m − 1 − f], i − g}
      else g ← min{g, i}
          f ← i
          while g ≥ 0 and x[g] = x[g + m − 1 − f] do
              g ← g − 1
          suff[i] ← f − g
  return suff
```

The schema of Figure 3.9 describes the variables of algorithm SUFFIXES and the invariants of its main loop. The correctness proof of the algorithm is similar to the one of PREFIXES (see Section 1.6).

Now, we can describe the algorithm GOOD-SUFFIX that computes the table *good-suff* by means of the table *suff*.

```
GOOD-SUFFIX(x, m, suff)
  j ← 0
  for i ← m − 2 downto −1 do
      if i = −1 or suff[i] = i + 1 then
          while j < m − 1 − i do
              good-suff[j] ← m − 1 − i
              j ← j + 1
  for i ← 0 to m − 2 do
      good-suff[m − 1 − suff[i]] ← m − 1 − i
  return good-suff
```

The schema of Figure 3.10 presents the invariants of the second loop of GOOD-SUFFIX. We show that this algorithm computes the table *good-suff*. For that, we start by stating two intermediate lemmas.

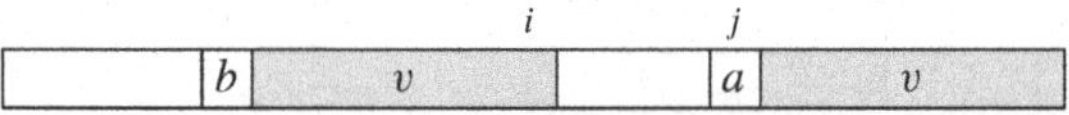

Figure 3.10. Variables i and j of the algorithm Good-suffix. Situation where $suff[i] < i+1$. The loop of lines 7–8 admits the following invariants: $v = lcsuff(x, x[0\,.\,.\,i])$ and thus $a \neq b$ $(a, b \in A)$, and $suff[i] = |v|$. We deduce $good\text{-}suff[j] \leq m-1-i$ with $j = m-1-suff[i]$.

Lemma 3.10

For $0 \leq i \leq m-2$, if $suff[i] = i+1$ then, for $0 \leq j < m-1-i$, $good\text{-}suff[j] \leq m-1-i$.

Proof The assumption $suff[i] = i+1$ is equivalent to $x[0\,.\,.\,i] \preceq_{\rm suff} x$. Thus $m - suff[i] = m-1-i$ is a period of x. Let j be an index that satisfies $0 \leq j < m-1-i$. The condition $Sc(j, m-1-i)$ is satisfied since $m-1-i > j$ and $x[0\,.\,.\,m-(m-1-i)-1] = x[0\,.\,.\,i] \preceq_{\rm suff} x$. It is the same for the condition $WOc(j, m-1-i)$ since $m-1-i > j$. This shows, by definition of *good-suff*, that $good\text{-}suff[j] \leq m-1-i$ as stated. ■

Lemma 3.11

For $0 \leq i \leq m-2$, we have $good\text{-}suff[m-1-suff[i]] \leq m-1-i$.

Proof If $suff[i] < i+1$, the condition $Sc(m-1-suff[i], m-1-i)$ is satisfied since we have on one hand $m-1-i \leq m-1-suff[i]$ and on the other hand $x[i-suff[i]+1\,.\,.\,i] = x[m-1-suff[i]+1\,.\,.\,m-1]$. Moreover, the condition $WOc(m-1-suff[i], m-1-i)$ is also satisfied since $x[i-suff[i]] \neq x[m-1-suff[i]]$ by definition of *suff*. Thus $good\text{-}suff[m-1-suff[i]] \leq m-1-i$.

Now, if $suff[i] = i+1$, by Lemma 3.10, we have in particular, for $j = m-1-suff[i] = m-i-2$, the inequality $good\text{-}suff[j] \leq m-1-i$. This ends the proof. ■

Proposition 3.12

The algorithm Good-suffix *computes the table good-suff of the string x by means of the table suff of the same string.*

Proof We have to show, for each index j, $0 \leq j < m$, that the final value d assigned to $good\text{-}suff[j]$ by Good-suffix is the minimal value that satisfies the conditions $Sc(j, d)$ and $WOc(j, d)$.

Let us first assume that d results from an assignment during the execution of the loop of lines 2–6. Thus the first part of the condition Sc is not satisfied.

We check then using Lemma 3.10 that d is the minimal value that satisfies the second part of condition $Sc(j, d)$. In this case, $d = m - 1 - i$ for a value i that both satisfies $suff[i] = i + 1$ and $j < m - 1 - i$. This last inequality shows that the condition $WOc(j, d)$ is also satisfied. This proves the result in this situation, that is to say, $d = good\text{-}suff[j]$.

Let us now assume that d results from an assignment during the execution of the loop of lines 7–8. We thus have $j = m - 1 - suff[i]$ and $d = m - 1 - i$, and, after Lemma 3.11, $good\text{-}suff[j] \leq d$. We also have $0 < d \leq i$, this shows that the second parts of conditions $Sc(j, d)$ and $WOc(j, d)$ cannot be satisfied. As the quantity $m - 1 - i$ decreases during the execution of the loop, d is the smallest value of $m - 1 - i$ for which $j = m - 1 - suff[i]$. We thus have $d = good\text{-}suff[j]$. This ends the proof. ■

Complexity of the computation

The preparation time of the table *good-suff*, used by the algorithm W-MEMORYLESS-SUFFIX-SEARCH, is linear. We can note that this time does not depend on the size of the alphabet.

Proposition 3.13
The algorithm SUFFIXES *applied to a string of length m executes in time $O(m)$ and requires a constant extra space.*

Proof The proof comes from the one that concerns algorithm PREFIXES in Section 1.6. Let us recall that all the executions of the loop of lines 8–9 takes a time $O(m)$ since the values of g always decreases. The execution of the other instructions takes a constant time for each value of i, thus globally $O(m)$.

The algorithm needs an extra space only for some integer variables, thus a constant space. ■

Proposition 3.14
The algorithm GOOD-SUFFIX *applied to a string of length m executes in time $O(m)$ (even if the computation time of the intermediate table suff is included) and requires an extra space $O(m)$.*

Proof The space necessary for the computation (in addition to the string x and the table *suff*) is composed of the table *good-suff* and of some integer variables. Thus a space $O(m)$.

The execution of the loop in lines 2–6 takes a time $O(m)$ since each operation executes in constant time for each value of i and for each value of j, and since these variables take $m + 1$ distinct values.

The loop of lines 7–8 executes also in time $O(m)$, which shows the result. Including the computation time of table *suff* gives the same conclusion after Proposition 3.13. ■

3.4 Automaton of the best factor

In this section, we show that the shift function of the best factor – function used in the string searching algorithm MEMORYLESS-SUFFIX-SEARCH presented in Section 3.1 – can be implemented in space $O(m)$. The implementation uses an automaton. Beyond the theoretical complement, we do not show any saving on the asymptotic complexities.

We call ***automaton of the best factor*** of the string x the automaton whose

- states are the empty string ε and the factors of x of the form cz with $c \in A$ and $z \prec_{\text{suff}} x$,
- initial state is the empty string ε,
- terminal state is x,
- arcs are of the form (z, c, cz).

Moreover, each state is provided with an output that corresponds to the length of a shift of the window to be applied during the search for x. The definition of the output is given below. It differs whether the state is a suffix of x or not:

1. The output of a state z with $z \preceq_{\text{suff}} x$ is the length of the shortest nonempty suffix z' of x for which $x \preceq_{\text{suff}} zz'$.
2. The output of a state of the form cz, $c \in A$, and $z \preceq_{\text{suff}} x$, with $cz \not\preceq_{\text{suff}} x$, is the length of the shortest suffix z' of x for which $czz' \preceq_{\text{suff}} x$.

An example of automaton of the best factor is shown in Figure 3.11.

With the notation of Section 3.1 in the case of a negative comparison for an attempt at a position j on the text, that is, by denoting i the current position on x ($i \geq 0$), $b = y[j - m + 1 + i]$ ($b \neq x[i]$), $z = x[i + 1 \,..\, m - 1]$, and by calling δ the transition function of the automaton, we have:

$$best\text{-}fact(i, b) = \begin{cases} \text{output of } \delta(z, b) & \text{if } \delta(z, b) \text{ is defined,} \\ \text{output of } z & \text{otherwise.} \end{cases}$$

The searching algorithm that utilizes the automaton can be written as follows.

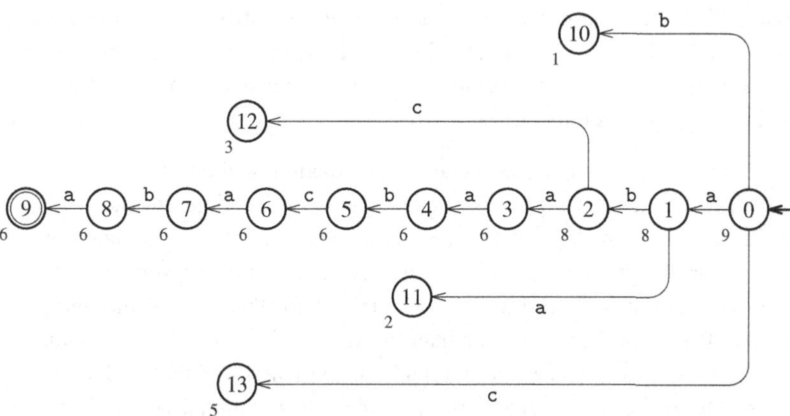

Figure 3.11. The automaton of the best factor for $x =$ abacbaaba. The outputs of the states indicate the length of the shift to apply to the window either when the state does not possess any successor or when no outgoing transition of the current state has an identical label to the current letter of the window.

```
BEST-FACT-SEARCH(x, m, y, n)
let M be the automaton of the best factor of x
j ← m − 1
while j < n do
      p ← initial[M]
      k ← m − 1
      while Succ[p] ≠ ∅
         and TARGET(p, y[j − m + 1 + k]) ≠ NIL do
            p ← TARGET(p, y[j − m + 1 + k])
            k ← k − 1
      OUTPUT-IF(terminal[p])
      j ← j + output[p]
```

The advantage of the automaton of the best factor is triple: it perfectly synthesizes attempts and shifts; its size is linear, $O(m)$; its construction can be realized in time $O(m)$. For the size, we can directly show that the number of states of the automaton that are not suffixes of x (or, equivalently, arcs that enter these states, since the incoming degree of all the states, except of the initial state, are equal to 1) is at most equal to $m - 1$ (see Exercise 3.5). Another proof of this bound is included in the proof of Theorem 3.16.

Theorem 3.15
The size of the automaton of the best factor of any string x of length m is $O(m)$.

Proof The automaton has $m+1$ states that are suffixes of x and at most $m-1$ states that are not (see Exercise 3.5). It also has m arcs that enter states that are suffixes of x and at most $m-1$ arcs that enter states that are not suffixes of x. Its total size is thus $O(m)$. ■

In the next paragraphs, we detail a construction method of the automaton for which we show that it can be implemented to run in time $O(m)$.

Let us denote by M_x the structure that corresponds to the automaton of the best factor of x but in which the output of any state z that is a suffix of x (state of type 1) is not defined. Let us now note that for these states, the output is the smallest period of x greater than or equal to $|x|-|z|$. It follows that if we have M_x and, for instance, the table of the lengths of the borders of the nonempty suffixes (analogue to the table of borders of prefixes of Section 1.6), the computation of the outputs of states of type 1 can be done in time $O(m)$. It thus remains to build M_x.

The construction of M_x can be done in a sequential way on x, by processing the suffixes by increasing length. The structure M_ε reduces to the state ε, that is both an initial and terminal state. Let at be a suffix of x with $a \in A$ and $t \prec_{\text{suff}} x$, and assume that M_t is built. The structure M_{at} contains

- the states and the arcs of M_t, the state t not bearing the mark of terminal states,
- the terminal state at, of type 1, and the arc (t, a, at),
- every state of type 2 of the form az, with $z \prec_{\text{suff}} t$, whose output is $|t|-|z|$, and the associated arcs of the form (z, a, az).

Let us focus on the computation of objects of the last point. The state az being of type 2, z is a border of t. Moreover, the length of z is necessarily not less than the length of the string Border(at). Indeed, in the contrary case, the output of az would be of length no more than $|\text{Border}(at)|-1-|z|$, quantity less than $|t|-|z|$; which is contrary to the assumption. Now, among all the borders z of t of length not less than $|\text{Border}(at)|$, only those for which the state az is not already in the structure are to be inserted in this one, with $|t|-|z|$ as output, the associated arcs (z, a, az) being inserted in the same way. Let us note that testing the presence of such states in M_{at} comes down to test if there exits a transition labeled by a from z. Let us also add that the access to the borders of t is immediate as soon as, in parallel to the construction of M_{at}, the table of border lengths of the suffixes of x is computed.

Theorem 3.16
The construction of the automaton of the best factor of any string x of length m can be realized in time $O(m)$ if we use an extra space $O(m + \text{card}\, A)$.

Proof The construction of the automaton proposed above utilizes the table of border lengths of the suffixes of x. This table is computed in parallel to the construction. The extra space used to store it is $O(m)$.

With the previous notation, the only borders z of t that are kept as candidates for a possible insertion of the state az in the structure M_{at} are the suffixes of t that are preceded by a letter distinct from a. They correspond thus to the negative comparisons between letters performed during the computation of the table; we know that their number is at most equal to $m - 1$ (see Exercise 1.22). This confirms the bounds given above for the number of states that are not suffixes of x, and for the number of arcs that enter these states.

In the comparison model, a test prior to each insertion, and, if necessary, the insertion itself take $O(\log m)$ time; but this would give a time complexity $O(m \times \log m)$. We can, on the contrary, add states and arcs without test in a first step: the overstructure of M_x thus obtained is always of size $O(m)$ after the previous result. Then, with the help of a table on the alphabet, we prune the structure by removing the undesirable arcs (for a given letter, only the arc with minimal output is kept). This is performed in time $O(m)$.

Finally, as mentioned above, the computation of the outputs of states that are suffixes of x can be done in time $O(m)$ with the table of border lengths of the suffixes of x. This ends the proof. ∎

The effective construction of the function *best-fact* by means of the automaton of the best factor of x is left as an exercise (Exercise 3.9). We deduce from the above proof another computation of the table of the good suffix than the one presented in Section 3.3 (see Exercise 3.10).

3.5 Searching with one memory

This section presents a less "oblivious" algorithm than the one of Section 3.1. During the search, it remembers at least one information on the previous matches: the last suffix of the string met in the text. It is a technique named "factor memorization" that extends the technique of prefix memorization implemented by the algorithm WL-MEMORYLESS-SUFFIX-SEARCH. It requires a constant extra space with respect to the algorithm MEMORYLESS-SUFFIX-SEARCH. The behavior of the algorithm is not quadratic anymore and no more than $2n$ comparisons are performed in order to search for all the occurrences of a string in a text of length n. Besides, the preprocessing phase of this algorithm is the same as the one of the algorithm MEMORYLESS-SUFFIX-SEARCH or of its version W-MEMORYLESS-SUFFIX-SEARCH.

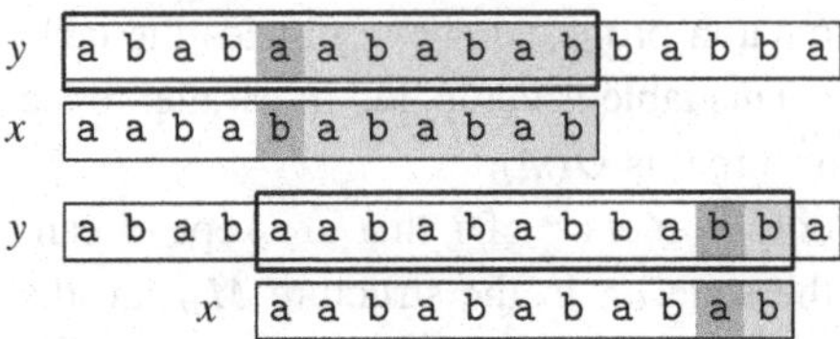

Figure 3.12. Conditions of a turbo-shift. During the attempt at position 10, we recognize the suffix ababab of the string. We shift by 4 positions as would the algorithm MEMORYLESS-SUFFIX-SEARCH do (we note that the suffix abababab of the string has period 4). Thus the factor aababab of y matches the factor of x aligned with it. During the next attempt, we recognize the suffix b. The letters $y[9] = \texttt{a}$ and $y[13] = \texttt{b}$ show that this portion of the text does not have 4 as period. Thus the suffix abababab of the string, that admits 4 as period, cannot be simultaneously aligned with $y[9]$ and $y[13]$. This leads to a shift of length $|\texttt{ababab}| - |\texttt{b}| = 5$.

Searching phase

After each of its shifts, the algorithm MEMORYLESS-SUFFIX-SEARCH wastes all the information gathered during previous attempts. We improve the behavior of this algorithm by taking into account the last occurrence of a suffix of the string x recognized in the text y. The memorization of this factor of the text recognized during the previous attempt presents two advantages for the current attempt:

- it possibly allows to perform a "jump" above this factor,
- it possibly allows to lengthen the next shift.

These possibilities are partially exploited in the algorithm of this section. The memorization of a single factor is performed in a precise case and the lengthening of the shift is realized by what we call a ***turbo-shift***.

We describe more precisely the technique. The general situation during an attempt T of the searching phase of algorithm TURBO-SUFFIX-SEARCH is illustrated in Figure 3.12. During the previous attempt T', at position j', a suffix z' of the string has been recognized in the text and a shift of length $d' = \mathit{best\text{-}fact}(m - 1 - |z'|, y[j' - |z'|])$ has been applied.

During the current attempt T at position $j = j' + d'$, a jump above the factor z' of y can be done if the suffix of the string of length d' is recognized in y at this position. In this case, it is useless to compare the factors z' of the string and of the text since, by the definition of the shift, it is sure that they match. A turbo-shift can be applied if the suffix z recognized during the current attempt is shorter than z'. The length of the turbo-shift is $|z'| - |z|$.

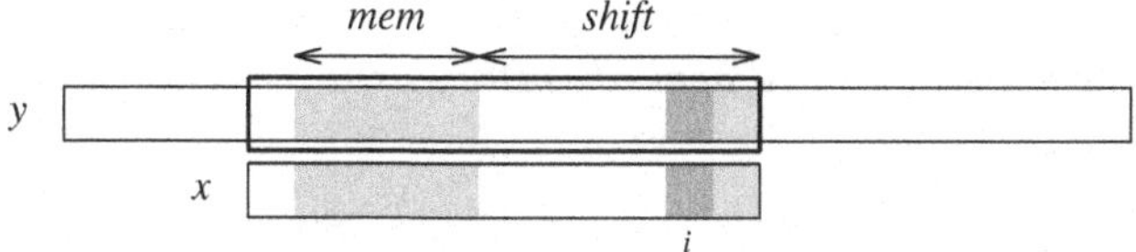

Figure 3.13. Variables i, *mem*, and *shift* when executing the instruction in line 10 of the algorithm TURBO-SUFFIX-SEARCH. The light gray areas refer to matches, while the dark gray area refers to a mismatch.

In the case where the value of the turbo-shift is greater than $\textit{best-fact}(m - |z|, y[j - |z|])$, we note that the shift to apply after the current attempt can, moreover, be longer than $|z|$. The memorization of a factor can only be done after a shift given by *best-fact*, the correctness of the method being based on periodicity arguments.

We now give the code of algorithm TURBO-SUFFIX-SEARCH. The code makes reference to the function *best-fact* of Section 3.4. But it is also possible to use the table *good-suff* for computing the lengths of shifts.

```
TURBO-SUFFIX-SEARCH(x, m, y, n)
 1  shift ← 0
 2  mem ← 0
 3  j ← m − 1
 4  while j < n do
 5       i ← m − 1
 6       while i ≥ 0 and x[i] = y[j − m + 1 + i] do
 7            if i = m − shift then
 8                 i ← i − mem − 1      ▷ Jump
 9            else i ← i − 1
10       OUTPUT-IF(i < 0)
11       if i < 0 then
12            shift ← per(x)
13            mem ← m − shift
14       else turbo ← mem − m + 1 + i
15            if turbo ≤ best-fact(i, y[j − m + 1 + i]) then
16                 shift ← best-fact(i, y[j − m + 1 + i])
17                 mem ← min{m − shift, m − i}
18            else shift ← max{turbo, m − 1 − i}
19                 mem ← 0
20       j ← j + shift                  ▷ Shift
```

The schema of Figure 3.13 gives an indication on the meaning of variables.

Theorem 3.17
The algorithm TURBO-SUFFIX-SEARCH *applied to strings x and y finds all the occurrences of x in y.*

Proof The differences between the algorithms MEMORYLESS-SUFFIX-SEARCH and TURBO-SUFFIX-SEARCH concern essentially the computation of shifts since the correctness of jumps comes from the above discussion. Thus, it is sufficient to show that the shift computed in line 18 is valid. We first show that the turbo-shift of length *turbo* is valid. We then show that the shift of length $m - 1 - i$ is also valid. Note that the instruction in line 18 is executed when we have $turbo > best\text{-}fact(i, y[j - m + 1 + i])$, which implies $turbo > 1$.

The value of the variable *mem* is the length of the suffix z' recognized during the previous attempt T'. The length of the suffix $z = x[i + 1 \,..\, m - 1]$ recognized during the current attempt T is $m - 1 - i$. The value of the variable *turbo* is $|z'| - |z|$. Let $a = x[i]$ be the letter that precedes the suffix z in the string and let $b = y[j - m + 1 + i]$ be the letter that precedes the corresponding occurrence of z in the text. Let $u = x[m - d \,..\, i]$ (we have $z'uz \preceq_{\text{suff}} x$). Since z is shorter than z', az is a suffix of z'. It follows that the letters a and b occur at a distance $d = |uz|$ in the text. But as the suffix $z'uz$ of the string has a period $d = |uz|$ (because z' is a border of $z'uz$), the shifts of length less than $|z'| - |z| = turbo$ lead to mismatches. Thus the shift of length *turbo* is valid (see Figure 3.12).

We now show that a shift of length $|z| = m - 1 - i$ is valid. Indeed, let us set $\ell = best\text{-}fact(i, b)$. By definition of *best-fact*, we have $x[i - \ell] \neq x[i]$. As the integer ℓ is a period of z, the two letters $x[i - \ell]$ and $x[i]$ cannot both be aligned with letters of the occurrence of z in y. We thus deduce that the shift of length $|z| = m - 1 - i$ is valid.

In conclusion of the above two points, the shift of line 18 whose length is the maximum of the lengths of two valid shifts, is itself also valid. This ends the proof. ■

Two examples of execution of the algorithm TURBO-SUFFIX-SEARCH, one using the function *best-fact*, the other the table *good-suff*, are shown in Figure 3.14.

Running time of the searching phase

We show that the algorithm TURBO-SUFFIX-SEARCH has a linear behavior in the worst case.

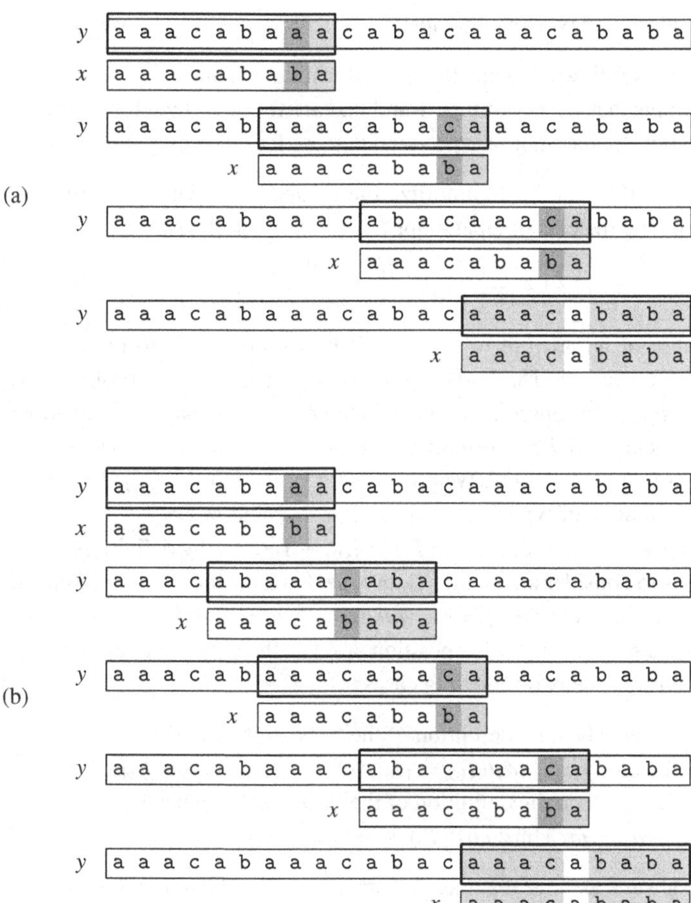

Figure 3.14. Examples of two runs of the algorithm TURBO-SUFFIX-SEARCH. **(a)** Using function *best-fact*. In this case, 14 letter comparisons are performed. **(b)** Using table *good-suff*. In this case, 18 letter comparisons are performed.

Theorem 3.18

During the search for all the occurrences of a string x of length m in a text y of length n the algorithm TURBO-SUFFIX-SEARCH *performs at most* $2n$ *comparisons of letters.*

Proof Using the notation of the proof of Theorem 3.17, we say that the shift of length d applied after the attempt T, is short if $2d < |z| + 1$, and long otherwise.

We consider three types of attempts:

1. The attempts followed by an attempt performing a "jump."
2. The attempts that are not of type 1 and that are followed by a long shift.
3. The attempts that are not of type 1 and that are followed by a short shift.

The idea of the proof is to amortize the comparisons with the shifts. For that, let us define the cost of an attempt T, $cost(T)$, as follows:

$$cost(T) = \begin{cases} 1 & \text{if } T \text{ is of type 1,} \\ 1 + |z| & \text{if } T \text{ is of type 2 or 3.} \end{cases}$$

In the case of an attempt of type 1, the cost corresponds to the test that produces the mismatch. The costs of the other comparisons are postponed to the next attempt. As a consequence, the total number of comparisons performed during the execution of the algorithm TURBO-SUFFIX-SEARCH is equal to the sum of the costs of all the attempts. We prove that $\sum_T cost(T) \leq 2 \sum_T d \leq 2n$.

For an attempt T_0 of type 1: $cost(T_0) = 1 < 2d_0$ since $d_0 \geq 1$.

For an attempt T_0 of type 2: $cost(T_0) = |z_0| + 1 \leq 2d_0$ by definition.

It remains to consider an attempt T_0 of type 3 at a position j_0 on y. Since in this case $d_0 < |z_0|$, we have $d_0 = best\text{-}fact(m - |z_0|, y[j_0 - |z_0|])$. This means that during the next attempt T_1 at position j_1 on y, there can be a turbo-shift.

Let us consider the two following cases:

a. $|z_0| + d_0 \leq m$. Then, by definition of the turbo-shift, we have:
$d_1 \geq |z_0| - |z_1|$. Thus: $cost(T_0) = |z_0| + 1 \leq |z_1| + d_1 + 1 \leq d_0 + d_1$.

b. $|z_0| + d_0 > m$. Then, by definition of the turbo-shift, we have:
$|z_1| + d_0 + d_1 \geq m$. Thus: $cost(T_0) \leq m \leq 2d_0 - 1 + d_1$.

We can always assume that case b happens during the attempt T_1 since it gives a larger bound on the value of $cost(T_0)$.

When the attempt T_1 is of type 1, we have $cost(T_1) = 1$ and $cost(T_0) + cost(T_1) \leq 2d_0 + d_1$. Which is better than the expected result.

When the attempt T_1 is of type 2 or when $|z_1| \leq d_1$, we have $cost(T_0) + cost(T_1) \leq 2d_0 + 2d_1$.

It remains to consider the case where both the attempt T_1 is of type 3 and $|z_1| > d_1$. This means that, as after the attempt T_0, we have $d_1 = best\text{-}fact(m - |z_1|, y[j_1 - |z_1|])$. The argument applied to the attempt T_1 applies also to the next attempt T_2. The case a only can happen during the attempt T_2. It results that $cost(T_1) \leq d_1 + d_2$. Finally, $cost(T_0) + cost(T_1) \leq 2d_0 + 2d_1 + d_2$.

This last argument gives the step of a proof by induction: if all the attempts $T_0, T_1, \ldots, T_k$ are of type 3 with $|z_j| > d_j$ for $j = 0, 1, \ldots, k$, then

$$cost(T_0) + cost(T_1) + \cdots + cost(T_k) \leq 2d_0 + 2d_1 + \cdots + 2d_k + d_{k+1}.$$

Let $T_{k'}$ be the first attempt after the attempt T_0 such that $|z_{k'}| \leq d_{k'}$. This attempt exists since, in the contrary case, this would mean that there exists an infinite sequence of attempts leading to shorter and shorter shifts, which is impossible. Therefore, $cost(T_0) + cost(T_1) + \cdots + cost(T_{k'}) \leq 2d_0 + 2d_1 + \cdots + 2d_{k'}$ and $\sum_T cost(T) < 2 \sum_T d_T \leq 2n$ as stated. ■

The bound of $2n$ comparisons of Theorem 3.18 is quasi optimal, as shows the following example. Let us set $x = \mathtt{a}^k\mathtt{b}\mathtt{a}^k$ and $y = (\mathtt{a}^{k+1}\mathtt{b})^\ell$ with $k \geq 1$. We have $m = 2k + 1$ and $n = \ell(k + 2)$. Except on the first and the last occurrence of $\mathtt{a}^{k+1}\mathtt{b}$ (of length $k + 2$) in y, the algorithm TURBO-SUFFIX-SEARCH performs $2k + 2$ comparisons. On the first, it performs $k + 2$ comparisons and on the last it performs k comparisons. We thus get the overall

$$(\ell - 1)(2k + 2) = 2n \left(\frac{m + 1}{m + 3}\right) - m - 1$$

number of letter comparisons. Figure 3.15 illustrates this example with the values $k = 3$ and $\ell = 6$.

Corollary 3.19
The algorithm TURBO-SUFFIX-SEARCH *finds all the occurrences of a string in a text of length n in time $O(n)$ with a constant extra space with respect to the algorithm* MEMORYLESS-SUFFIX-SEARCH.

Proof This is a direct consequence of Theorems 3.17 and 3.18. ■

3.6 Searching with several memories

In this section, we consider an algorithm of the same type as the previous ones but that works by memorizing more information. It requires an extra workspace $O(m)$ with respect to the algorithm MEMORYLESS-SUFFIX-SEARCH, but this leads to a reduction of the number of letter comparisons that drops down to $1.5n$ (vs. $3n$ and $2n$ respectively for the algorithms MEMORYLESS-SUFFIX-SEARCH and TURBO-SUFFIX-SEARCH).

The algorithm of this section, called MEMORY-SUFFIX-SEARCH, stores all the occurrences of suffixes of the string found in the text during the attempts. It uses this information, together with the table *suff* (Section 3.3), to perform "jumps," in the same way as algorithm TURBO-SUFFIX-SEARCH does, and for increasing the length of some shifts. Those shifts are computed by means of the function of the best factor, *best-fact*, but they can also be determined with the help of the table of the good suffix (see Section 3.1).

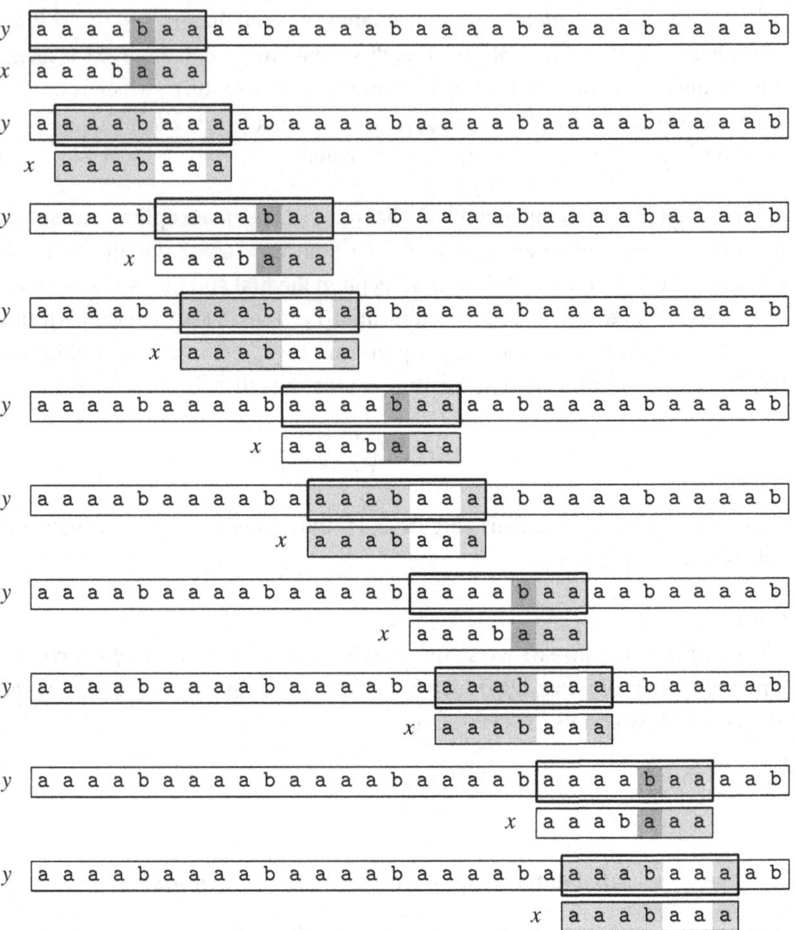

Figure 3.15. Worst case example for the algorithm TURBO-SUFFIX-SEARCH. Illustration of the bound of Theorem 3.18 with strings $x =$ aaabaaa and $y =$ (aaaab)^6. The string x is of length 7, the text y of length 30, and 40 comparisons are performed. For each of the four consecutive central factors aaaab of length 5 of the text, eight letter comparisons are performed.

Searching phase

We describe the essential elements of the method. After each attempt at a position j' on the text y, the length of the longest suffix of x recognized at the right position j', $|z'|$, is stored in the table denoted by S ($S[j'] = |z'|$). During the current attempt at the position j on the text y, if we have to

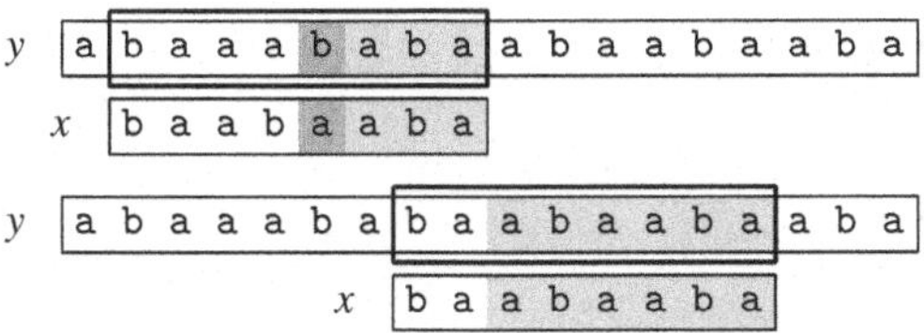

Figure 3.16. During the attempt at position 14, we recognize, by letter to letter comparisons, the suffix abaaba of length 6 of the string. We arrive at position 8 on y where we know (with the help of the attempt at position 8) that the longest suffix of x that ends at this position is of length 3. Besides, we know that the longest suffix of x ending at position 1 on x is of length 2. The assumptions of Lemma 3.20 hold. An occurrence of the string is thus detected at position 14, without comparing $y[7\,..\,8]$ again.

examine the position j', $j' < j$, (we have $y[j'+1\,..\,j] \prec_{\text{suff}} x$) for which the value $k = S[j']$ is defined, we know that $y[j'-k+1\,..\,j'] \preceq_{\text{suff}} x$. Let $i = m - 1 - j + j'$. It is then sufficient to know the length $s = \mathit{suff}[i]$, of the longest suffix of x ending at position i on x, to conclude the attempt in most situations.

Four cases can arise. We detail them in Lemmas 3.20 to 3.23 associated with Figures 3.16 to 3.19.

Lemma 3.20

When $s \leq k$ and $s = i + 1$, an occurrence of x occurs at right position j on the text y. We have $S[j] = m$ and the shift of length per(x) *is valid.*

Proof If $s = i + 1$ and $s \leq k$ (see Figure 3.16), $y[j'-k+1\,..\,j']$ and $x[0\,..\,i]$ are suffixes of x, and $x[0\,..\,i]$ is of length s. As $s \leq k$, we deduce that $x[0\,..\,i] \preceq_{\text{suff}} y[j'-k+1\,..\,j']$ and thus $y[j'-s+1\,..\,j'] = x[0\,..\,i]$. Thus, $y[j-m+1\,..\,j] = x$ as announced. The value of $S[j]$ is then m and the shift of length per(x) is valid. ■

Lemma 3.21

When $s \leq i$ and $s < k$, we have $S[j] = m - 1 - i + s$ and, by setting $j' = j - m + 1 + i$, the shift of length best-fact($i - s$, $y[j' - s]$) is valid.

Proof If $s \leq i$ and $s < k$ (see Figure 3.17), we have $x[i-s+1\,..\,i] \preceq_{\text{suff}} x$ and $x[i-s\,..\,i] \not\preceq_{\text{suff}} x$, and thus $x[i-s] \neq y[j'-s]$. The value of $S[j]$ is then $m - 1 - i + s$ (since $x[i-s+1\,..\,m-1] = y[j'-s+1\,..\,j]$ and $x[i-s] \neq y[j'-s]$) and the shift of length *best-fact*($i - s$, $y[j' - s]$) is valid. ■

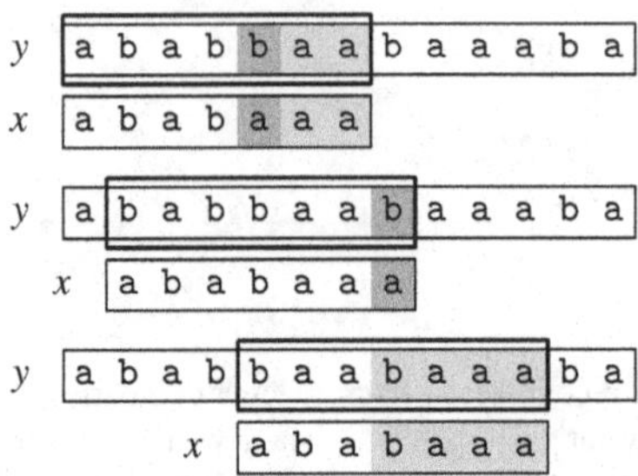

Figure 3.17. During the attempt at position 10, we recognize the suffix baaa of length 4 of the string. We arrive at position 6 on y, where we know (with the help of the attempt at position 6) that the longest suffix of x that ends at this position is of length 2. Besides, we know that the longest suffix of x ending at position 2 on x is of length 1. Thus, without comparing $y[4\,..\,6]$ again, we know that there is a mismatch between $x[1] =$ b and $y[5] =$ a.

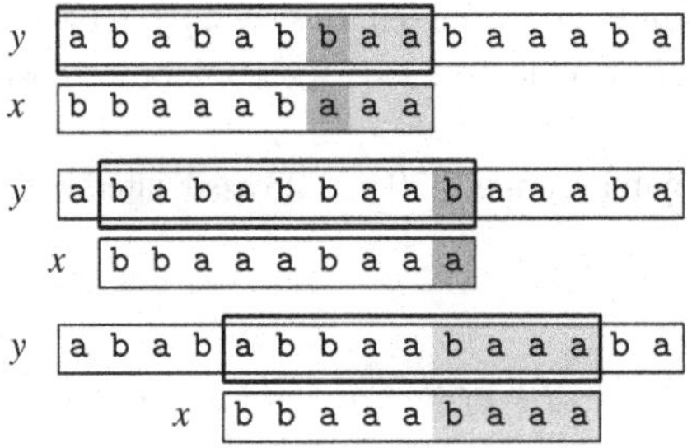

Figure 3.18. During the attempt at position 12, we recognize the suffix of length 4 of the string, and we arrive at position 8, where we know (with the help of the attempt at position 8) that the longest suffix of the string that ends at this position is of length 2. Besides, we know that the longest suffix of the string ending at position 4 on the string is of length 4. Thus, without any letter comparison, we know that there is a mismatch between $x[2] =$ a and $y[6] =$ b.

Lemma 3.22

When $k < s$, we have $S[j] = m - 1 - i + k$ and, by setting $j' = j - m + 1 + i$, the shift of length best-fact($i - k$, $y[j' - k]$) is valid.

Proof If $k < s$ (see Figure 3.18), we have $x[i - k + 1\,..\,i] \preceq_{\text{suff}} x$ and $x[i - k\,..\,i] \not\preceq_{\text{suff}} x$, and thus $x[i - k] \neq y[j' - k]$. The value of $S[j]$ is then $m - 1 - i + k$ (since $x[i - k + 1\,..\,m - 1] = y[j' - k + 1\,..\,j]$ and $x[i - k] \neq y[j' - k]$) and the shift of length *best-fact*($i - k$, $y[j' - k]$) is valid. ■

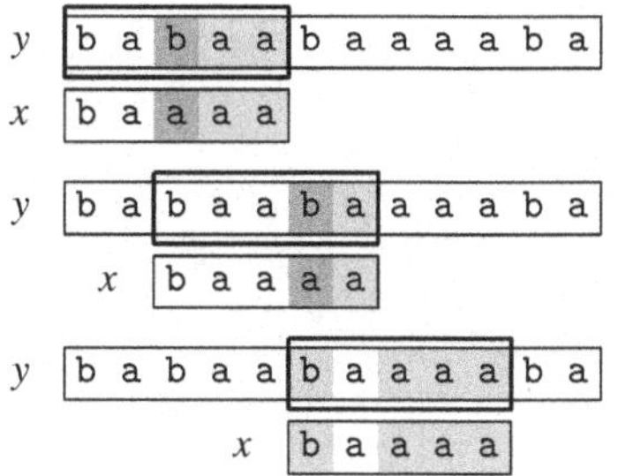

Figure 3.19. During the attempt at position 9, we recognize the suffix of length 3 of the string, and we arrive at position 6, where we know (with the help of the attempt at position 6) that the longest suffix of the string that ends at this position is of length 1. Besides, we know that the longest suffix of the string ending at position 1 on the string is also of length 1. We can thus perform a "jump" above $y[6]$, and resume the comparisons between $x[0]$ and $y[5]$.

Lemma 3.23
When $k = s$*, we have* $x[i - s + 1 \,..\, m - 1] = y[j' - s + 1 \,..\, j]$ *and*

$$S[j] = m - 1 - i + s + |lcsuff(x[0 \,..\, i - s], y[j - m + 1 \,..\, j' - s])| \quad (3.1)$$

with $j' = j - m + 1 + i$.

Proof If $k = s$ (see Figure 3.19), the two strings $x[i - s + 1 \,..\, i]$ and $y[j' - s + 1 \,..\, j']$ of same length are suffixes of x. We have thus $x[i - s + 1 \,..\, i] = y[j' - s + 1 \,..\, j']$. And since we assume that we have $x[i + 1 \,..\, m - 1] = y[j' + 1 \,..\, j]$, it follows $x[i - s + 1 \,..\, m - 1] = y[j' - s + 1 \,..\, j]$.

In the case where $s = i + 1$, we have $S[j] = m - 1 - i + s$ on one hand, and $lcsuff(x[0 \,..\, i - s], y[j - m + 1 \,..\, j' - s]) = \varepsilon$ on the other hand.

When $s \leq i$ now, we moreover know that $x[i - s] \neq x[m - 1 - s]$ and $y[j' - s] \neq x[m - 1 - s]$, this does not allow to conclude on the comparison between $x[i - s]$ and $y[j' - s]$. Equality (3.1) is a direct consequence of the previous inequality. ■

The code of the algorithm MEMORY-SUFFIX-SEARCH is given thereafter. It utilizes the function *best-fact* of Section 3.4 and the table *suff* of Section 3.3.

The memorization of suffixes of x that occur in the text is performed by the table S. The values of this table are initialized to 0 prior to the searching phase.

```
MEMORY-SUFFIX-SEARCH(x, m, y, n)
for j ← 0 to n − 1 do
    S[j] ← 0
j ← m − 1
while j < n do
    i ← m − 1
    while i ≥ 0 do
        if S[j − m + 1 + i] > 0 then
            k ← S[j − m + 1 + i]
            s ← suff[i]
            if s ≠ k then
                i ← i − min{s, k}
                break
            else i ← i − k ▷ Jump
        elseif x[i] = y[j − m + 1 + i] then
            i ← i − 1
        else break
    OUTPUT-IF(i < 0)
    if i < 0 then
        S[j] ← m
        j ← j + per(x)
    else S[j] ← m − 1 − i
        j ← j + best-fact(i, y[j − m + 1 + i])
```

Theorem 3.24
The algorithm MEMORY-SUFFIX-SEARCH *finds all the occurrences of a string x in a text y.*

Proof The proof is essentially a consequence of Lemmas 3.20 to 3.23. ∎

Two examples of execution of the algorithm MEMORY-SUFFIX-SEARCH are shown in Figure 3.20. The first utilizes the function of the best factor, and the second the table of the good suffix instead.

Complexity of the searching phase

We successively examine the space complexity then the running time of the algorithm MEMORY-SUFFIX-SEARCH.

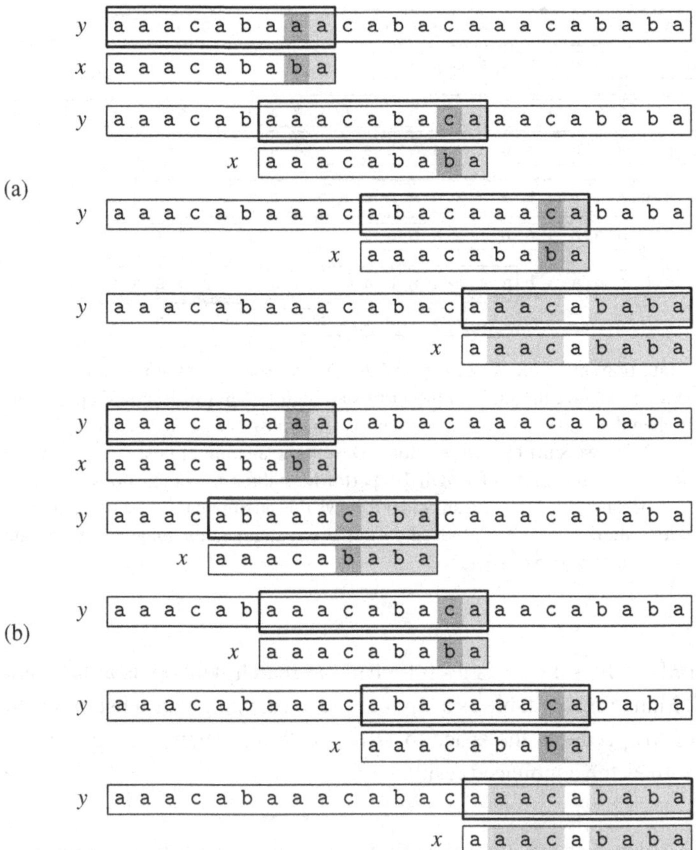

Figure 3.20. Two runs of the algorithm MEMORY-SUFFIX-SEARCH. **(a)** With the function *best-fact*. In this case, 13 comparisons between letters of the string and of the text are performed. **(b)** With the table *good-suff*. In this case, 17 letter comparisons are performed.

Proposition 3.25

To locate a string x of length m in a text, the algorithm MEMORY-SUFFIX-SEARCH *can be implemented in space $O(m)$.*

Proof The workspace is used for memorizing the table *suff*, for implementing the function *best-fact* or the table *good-suff*, and for storing the table S in addition to some other variables. The first three elements occupy a space $O(m)$ (see Section 3.4 for the function *best-fact*). For the table S, we note that only

Figure 3.21. Intuition of the proof of Lemma 3.26. During the attempt at position j on the text (top line), we recognize the suffix of the string of length 1, then we shift by six positions. We recognize then the suffix of length 3, we shift by four positions. Then we recognize the suffix of length 2 and we shift by five positions. During the attempt at position $j + 15$, we recognize the suffix of the string of length 19, performing three re-comparisons on letters $y[j + 8]$, $y[j + 3]$, and $y[j - 1]$. The shift that follows this attempt cannot be of length less than or equal to 3 after Lemma 3.26. Indeed the suffix aabaaabaaaabaaaaaa of the string cannot have a period less than or equal to 3.

its portion $S[j - m + 1 \mathinner{..} j]$ is useful when the search window is at the right position j. Managing the table as a circular list or realizing it as a list of useful elements of $S[\ell]$ reduces the space to $O(m)$ (without penalizing the running time). This gives the announced result. ■

We then show that the algorithm Memory-suffix-search has a running time $O(n)$. It performs at most $1.5n$ comparisons of letters for finding all the occurrences of x in y.

Let us first note that, if during the searching phase, an occurrence of a letter of the text is compared positively, then this letter will never be compared again in the rest of the execution of the algorithm. Therefore there are at most n comparisons of this kind (it is for instance the case when we search a^n for a^m, $a \in A$). The only letters that are possibly re-compared are thus those that have previously been involved in a mismatch with a letter of the pattern.

Figure 3.21 illustrates the next lemma.

Lemma 3.26

During an attempt of the algorithm Memory-suffix-search, *if k positive comparisons are done on letters of the text that have already been compared, the shift that follows this attempt is of length at least k.*

Proof Let T be an attempt of the algorithm MEMORY-SUFFIX-SEARCH during which k letters of the text having already been compared are compared again positively. According to the remark done before the statement, these letters have been compared negatively during k previous attempts. Let us denote by

$$b_0 v_0 b_1 u_1 v_1 b_2 u_2 v_2 \dots b_k u_k v_k$$

the factor of the text examined during the attempt T with

- b_0 is the letter that causes a mismatch during the attempt T,
- $v_0 b_1 u_1 v_1 b_2 u_2 v_2 \dots b_k u_k v_k$ is a suffix of the string x,
- the letters b_ℓ, $1 \leq \ell \leq k$, are the k letters that are compared again positively during the attempt T,
- the factors u_ℓ, $1 \leq \ell \leq k$, are the suffixes (possibly empty) of the string that have been recognized during those k attempts during which the b_ℓ's have been compared negatively. These factors are "jumped over" during attempt T,
- the factors v_ℓ, $1 \leq \ell \leq k$, are the factors of the text that are positively compared (for the first time) during attempt T.

By their definition, the strings $b_\ell u_\ell$, $1 \leq \ell \leq k$, are not suffixes of the string x.

The proof is by contradiction. Assume that the shift d applied just after attempt T is of length less than k. Let w be the suffix of x of length d. By definition, the string

$$v_0 b_1 u_1 v_1 b_2 u_2 v_2 \dots b_k u_k v_k w$$

is a suffix of x and has period $d = |w|$.

For two different indices $\ell' \neq \ell''$, $u_{\ell'}$ and $u_{\ell''}$ are aligned with the same position on a factor w, since there are at most $k - 1$ possible positions. This implies that $b_{\ell'} u_{\ell'} = b_{\ell''} u_{\ell''}$. The shifts applied after the two attempts where $b_{\ell'}$ and $b_{\ell''}$ have been compared are of same length. This implies that $b_{\ell'+1} u_{\ell'+1} = b_{\ell''+1} u_{\ell''+1}$. Thus there exists an index $\ell < k$ such that $b_\ell u_\ell = b_k u_k$, which contradicts the fact that the string x would have been previously aligned as during the attempt T.

It follows that the length of the shift applied after the attempt T is at least k. ■

Lemma 3.27
The algorithm MEMORY-SUFFIX-SEARCH *performs no more than $n/2$ comparisons concerning letters of the text having already been compared.*

Proof We group the attempts into packets, two attempts being in the same packet when they perform comparisons on common letters of the text. A packet

p of attempts that perform k positive re-comparisons of letters of the text contains at least $k+1$ attempts. Among these attempts at least k apply a shift of length at least 1 and one applies a shift of length at least k after Lemma 3.26. Thus, the total length of all the shifts of the attempts of the packet p is at least equal to $2k$.

The total sum of all the shifts applied during the algorithm MEMORY-SUFFIX-SEARCH is no more than n. The total number of re-comparisons is thus no more than $n/2$. ■

Theorem 3.28
During the search for all the occurrences of a string in a text y of length n, the algorithm MEMORY-SUFFIX-SEARCH *performs at most* $1.5n$ *comparisons between string and text letters.*

Proof The result directly comes from Lemma 3.27 and from the fact that there are at most n positive comparisons. ■

Corollary 3.29
The algorithm MEMORY-SUFFIX-SEARCH *performs the search for all the occurrences of a string of length m in a text of length n in time $O(n)$ with an extra space $O(m)$ with respect to the algorithm* MEMORYLESS-SUFFIX-SEARCH.

Proof It is a consequence of Theorem 3.24, by noting that the running time is asymptotically equivalent to the number of comparisons, and of Theorem 3.28. ■

The bound of $1.5n$ letter comparisons of Theorem 3.28 is almost reached when searching for the string $x = \mathtt{a}^{k-1}\mathtt{b}\mathtt{a}^k\mathtt{b}$ in the text $y = (\mathtt{a}^{k-1}\mathtt{b}\mathtt{a}^k\mathtt{b})^\ell$, with $k \geq 1$. The algorithm then performs exactly

$$2k + 1 + (3k+1)(\ell - 1) = \frac{3k+1}{2k+1}n - k$$

comparisons between letters of the string and of the text. Figure 3.22 illustrates this bound with the values $k = 3$ and $\ell = 4$.

3.7 Dictionary searching

With the sliding window technique, it is possible to efficiently solve the problem of the search for all the occurrences of strings belonging to a dictionary of k strings $X = \{x_0, x_1, \ldots, x_{k-1}\}$ in a text y. In this section, we denote respectively by m' and m'' the length of the shortest string and of the longest string of X.

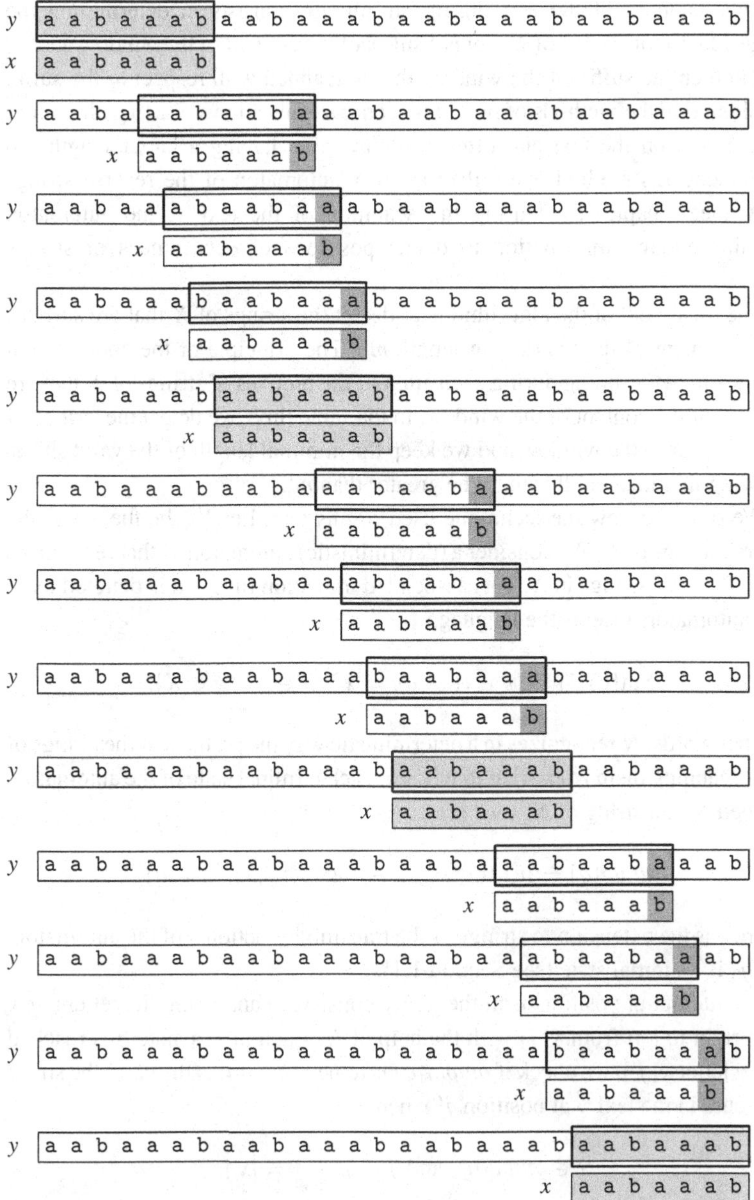

Figure 3.22. Illustration of the bound of Theorem 3.28 with $x =$ aabaaab and $y =$ (aabaaab)^4. The string is of length 7, the text of length 28, and 37 letter comparisons are performed. For each of the last three occurrences of the factor aabaaab of length 7 of y, the algorithm MEMORY-SUFFIX-SEARCH performs 10 comparisons.

The scanning of the text during an attempt consists in determining the longest factor of strings of X that is a suffix of the content of the window. Doing so lengthen the suffix of the window that is scanned with respect to the suffix considered in the methods of previous sections. This allows one to gather more information on the text and often leads to shifts having a larger length. To implement this method, we utilize a suffix automaton of the reverse strings of X (see Chapter 5). During the scanning of the text y, the automaton contains enough information to detect positions of occurrences of strings of X.

The local goal of the algorithm is to detect the strings of X that are suffixes of the content of the window of length m''. The principle of the computation consists in determining during each attempt the prefixes of strings of X that are suffixes of the content of the window. In the same time, we detect the strings of X that occur in the window and we keep the minimal length of the valid shifts, knowing that this length cannot be greater than m'.

We describe now the technique used to this aim. Let $X^{\sim}$ be the set of the reverse strings of X. We consider a (deterministic) automaton N that recognizes the suffixes of strings in $X^{\sim}$. Its associated transition function is denoted by δ. The automaton accepts the language

$$\text{Suff}(X^{\sim}) = \{v \in A^* : uv = x^{\sim}, u \in A^*, x \in X\}.$$

In other words, N recognizes in a deterministic way the prefixes of the strings of X by scanning them from right to left. For each terminal state of the automaton, reached with a string of $X^{\sim}$, we set

$$output[q] = \{i : 0 \leq i \leq k-1 \text{ and } \bar{\delta}(q_0, x_i{}^{\sim}) = q\},$$

where $\bar{\delta}$ is the extension to strings of the transition function δ of the automaton, and q_0 is its initial state (see Section 1.1).

An attempt at position j on the text y consists in analyzing the letters of y from right to left from $y[j]$ with the help of N. Each time a state q is reached with a letter $y[j']$, we check if $output[q]$ is nonempty; if it is the case, the string x_i occurs in the text y at position j' when

$$i \in output[q] \text{ and } j - j' + 1 = |x_i|.$$

Besides, if the state q is a terminal state, no valid shift can be of length greater than $m' - (j - j' + 1)$ when this quantity is positive. We can thus compute meanwhile the minimal length d of valid shifts. Finally, the attempt ends when there exists no more transition defined for the current letter from the current state. An example of search is shown in Figure 3.23. The algorithm that follows implements this method.

```
MULTIPLE-SUFFIX-SEARCH(X, m', y, n)
 1  let N be a (deterministic) automaton accepting the suffixes of the reverse
      strings of X
 2  j ← m' − 1
 3  while j ≤ n do
 4      q ← initial[N]
 5      j' ← j
 6      d ← m'
 7      while j' ≥ 0 and TARGET(q, y[j']) ≠ NIL do
 8          q ← TARGET(q, y[j'])
 9          if terminal[q] then
10              for each i ∈ output[q] do
11                  OUTPUT-IF(|x_i| = j − j' + 1)
12              if m' − j + j' − 1 > 0 then
13                  d ← min{d, m' − j + j' − 1}
14              else d ← 1
15          j' ← j' − 1
16      j ← j + d
```

Theorem 3.30
The algorithm MULTIPLE-SUFFIX-SEARCH *locates all the occurrences of the strings of a dictionary X in a text y.*

Proof Let us note that the algorithm detects only occurrences of strings of X (lines 10–11). Let us check that it does not forget any.

Let ℓ be the right position on y of an occurrence of a string $x_i \in X$. Let j be the right position of the window. We show in the rest that if $j \leq \ell$, the occurrence of x_i is detected. Let us note that we can, moreover, assume $\ell < j + m'$ since, the length of shifts being bounded by m', the variable j takes a value that satisfies the two conditions. We prove it by recurrence on the quantity $\ell - j$.

If $j = \ell$, the automaton N recognizing the prefixes of the strings of X, it accepts x_i. At position $j' = j - |x_i| + 1$, the current state is terminal, its output contains i, and the condition $|x_i| = j - j' + 1$ in line 11 holds, thus the occurrence is signaled.

Let us now assume that $j < \ell$, and let $x_i = uv$ where v is of length $\ell - j$. In this situation, u is a suffix of the content of the window. At position

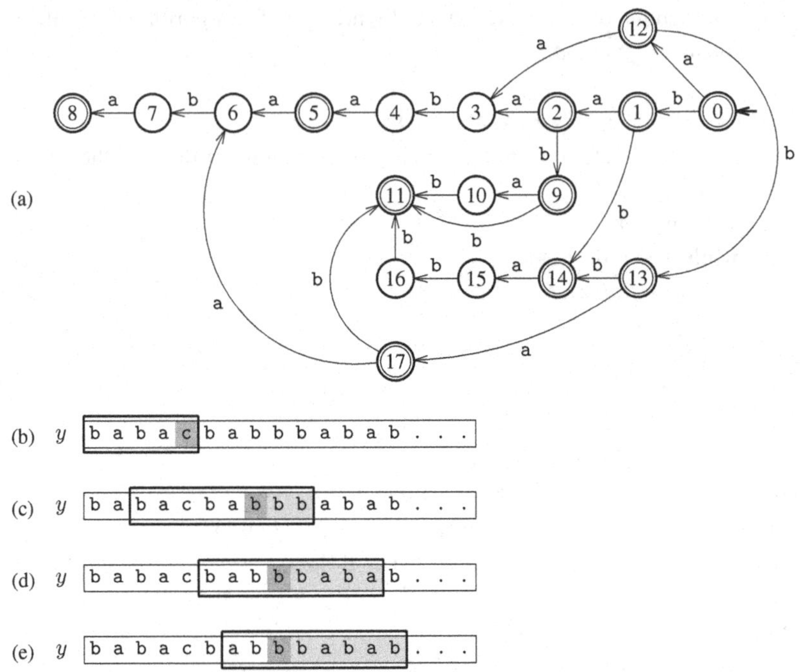

Figure 3.23. A run of the algorithm Multiple-suffix-search in the case where $X = \{\texttt{abaabaab}, \texttt{babab}, \texttt{bbabba}\}$ and y starts with babacbabbbabab. We have $m' = 5$. **(a)** An automaton that recognizes the prefixes of $X^{\sim}$. **(b)** First attempt. The length of the window is equal to the length of the longest string of X, thus 8, but the first attempt must start adjusted on the smallest string of X, thus $y[0\,..\,4]$. The scanning starts in the initial state 0. There is no transition defined from state 0 with the letter $y[4] = \texttt{c}$, thus the attempt ends and a shift of length 5 is applied. **(c)** Second attempt. The window of length 8 is positioned on the factor of the text $y[2\,..\,9] = \texttt{bacbabbb}$. From the initial state 0, we reach the terminal state 14 after parsing string bb. There is no transition defined from this state with the letter $y[7] = \texttt{b}$, thus the attempt ends and a shift of length $m' - |\texttt{bb}| = 3$ is applied. **(d)** Third attempt. We transit by states 0, 12, 13, 17, and 11. A shift of length $m' - |\texttt{baba}| = 1$ is applied. **(e)** Fourth attempt. We transit by states 0, 1, 2, 9, 10, and 11. An occurrence is signaled and a shift of length 1 is applied.

$j' = j - |u| + 1$, the current state is terminal, since u is a prefix of x_i, and the condition $j - j' + 1 \le m'$ holds. This limits the length of the shift to $m' - j + j' - 1 \le |v|$. The next value of j, let us say j'', will be thus such that $j'' \le \ell$ with $\ell - j'' < \ell - j$. The recurrence hypothesis leads to conclude that the occurrence of x_i is detected, which ends the recurrence.

Finally, we note that initially we have $j \le \ell$ for every right position of a string of X since j is initialized to $m' - 1$. Therefore, every occurrence of a string of X is signaled. ■

Though the algorithm MULTIPLE-SUFFIX-SEARCH has a very good behavior on common texts and patterns, its running time is $O(k \times m'' \times n)$ in the worst case. Indeed, instructions of the **while** loop in lines 3–16 may be executed n times (at most), those in lines 7–15 m'' times, and those of the **for** loop of lines 10–11 k times. Its running time can, however, be made linear by application of standard techniques.

Notes

The algorithm MEMORYLESS-SUFFIX-SEARCH has been first proposed by Boyer and Moore [109]. Theorems 3.7 and 3.8 have been established by Cole [114].

The idea of searching for the occurrences of a string using a window of length equal to the period of the string was exposed by Galil [142]. Hancart [148] designed the computation of the automaton of the best factor and the computation of the function of the best factor as reported in Section 3.4.

The algorithm TURBO-SUFFIX-SEARCH, also known as *Turbo-BM*, is from Crochemore, Czumaj, Gąsieniec, Jarominek, Lecroq, Plandowski, and Rytter [121].

Apostolico and Giancarlo [95] presented the idea of the algorithm MEMORY-SUFFIX-SEARCH. The version that is given here, and the proof of Theorem 3.28, were given by Crochemore and Lecroq [125].

The algorithm MULTIPLE-SUFFIX-SEARCH of the last section is from Crochemore et al. [122]. These authors also proposed a linear-time version of it. Raffinot [198] described a variant of this last algorithm implemented by the command `vfgrep` under the UNIX system.

The Boyer-Moore automata (see Exercise 3.6) were introduced by Knuth, Morris, and Pratt [170]. It is still unknown if the size of these automata is polynomial.

Precise lower bounds on the number of letter comparisons for locating a string in a text are established by Cole, Hariharan, Paterson, and Zwick in [116]. The expected running time of string matching algorithms is analyzed by Yao in [219] (see Exercise 3.7).

An animation of exact string matching algorithms (including those of this chapter) is proposed on the site [51], developed by Charras and Lecroq.

Exercises

3.1 (Implementation)

Write the algorithm MEMORYLESS-SUFFIX-SEARCH using two variables that have for values those of i and of $j - m + 1 + i$ in the code of Section 3.1. Redefine *best-fact* accordingly. Do the same for the other versions of the algorithm.

3.2 (Period)

Give the code of an algorithm that finds all the occurrences of x in y using a window of length $\text{per}(x)$ and that performs less than $3n$ comparisons between letters of the string and of the text. (*Hint:* see Galil [142].)

3.3 (Better)

Give an example of a string and of a text for which the algorithm MEMORYLESS-SUFFIX-SEARCH performs less comparisons when using the table *good-suff* than when using the function *best-fact*.

3.4 (Worse)

Give examples of strings and of texts for which all the algorithms of this chapter perform more comparisons than the algorithm FAST-SEARCH of Section 1.5.

3.5 (Number of arcs)

Show with a direct argument – that is to say without using a construction method – that the number of arcs of the automaton of the best factor of any nonempty string x that enter a state that is not a suffix of x is at most equal to $|x| - 1$. (*Hint:* as for the proof of Proposition 2.19, show that the outputs of these states are pairwise distinct and are between 1 and $|x| - 1$.)

3.6 (Boyer–Moore automaton)

The Boyer-Moore automaton is a deterministic automaton of the configurations of the window encountered during the execution of the algorithm MEMORYLESS-SUFFIX-SEARCH. The states bear the information on the content of the window collected during the previous comparisons.

We denote by B the automaton associated with the string $x \in A^+$ of length m. Its set of states is denoted by Q, its set of arcs by F. It possesses a shift function d that gives the length of the shift to execute, and a boolean output function s that signals an occurrence of x, both defined on F.

The states are defined as follows:

- Q is the part of $(A \cup \{\#\})^m$ accessible from the initial state. The letter # that does not belong to the alphabet A represents the absence of information on the corresponding letter of the window.
- The initial state is the string $\#^m$.

The set of arcs F and the functions d and s are defined as follows, for $u \in (A \cup \{\#\})^*$, $v \prec_{\text{suff}} x$, $w' \in \{\#\}^*$ and $a \in A$:

- $f = (u\#v, a, uav) \in F$ if $av \prec_{\text{suff}} x$ and $uav \neq x$; we have $d(f) = 0$ and $s(f) = \text{FALSE}$.

- $f = (u\#v, a, \text{Border}(x)w') \in F$ if $uav = x$; we have $d(f) = |w'| = \text{per}(x)$ and $s(f) = \text{TRUE}$.
- the triplet $f = (u\#v, a, ww') \in F$ if $av \not\prec_{\text{suff}} x$ and w is the longest string for which $w \prec_{\text{suff}} uav$ and, for $i = 0, 1, \ldots, |w| - 1$, $w[i] = x[i]$ or $w[i] = \#$; we have $d(f) = |w'|$ and $s(f) = \text{FALSE}$.

For $q \in Q$, $q[i] = \#$ means that the letter of the text aligned with $x[i]$ has never been inspected. The strategy used to compare the letters is similar to that of the searching algorithms of the chapter: scanning from right to left, but starting with the first noninspected letter.

Give the Boyer–Moore automaton of the string $x = \texttt{aabbabb}$. Design an algorithm searching for x with the automaton B. Design an algorithm that builds the automaton B. Give a tight bound of the size of B.

3.7 (Optimal)

Design a string matching algorithm (for a string of length m and a text of length n) using shifts based on $O(\log n)$ letters of the pattern and running in average time $O(n \log n/m)$. Show that the algorithm is time optimal. (*Hint:* see Yao [219].)

3.8 (Proof!)

Adapt the complexity proof of the algorithm W-MEMORYLESS-SUFFIX-SEARCH to the algorithm MEMORYLESS-SUFFIX-SEARCH.

3.9 (Best factor)

Deduce from Section 3.4 an implementation of the function *best-fact*. Design an algorithm that constructs the automaton of the best factor of every string x in time and space $O(|x|)$.

3.10 (Good suffix)

Design an algorithm that computes the table *good-suff* only with the help of the table *rbord* (and of m) defined for x by

$$rbord[i] = |\text{Border}(x[i\,..\,m-1])|,$$

for every position i on x.

3.11 (Bis)

Let GOOD-SUFFIX-BIS be the algorithm whose code follows.

```
GOOD-SUFFIX-BIS(x, m)
for i ← 0 to m − 1 do
    good-suff[i] ← 0
f[m − 1] ← m
j ← m − 1
for i ← m − 2 downto 0 do
    f[i] ← j
    while j < m and x[i] ≠ x[j] do
        if good-suff[j] = 0 then
            good-suff[j] ← j − i
        j ← f[j]
    j ← j − 1
for i ← 0 to m − 1 do
    if good-suff[i] = 0 then
        good-suff[i] ← j + 1
    if i = j then
        j ← f[j]
return good-suff
```

Show that we have $f[i] = m - 1 - rbord[i + 1]$ for every position i on x at the end of the execution of the algorithm (table *rbord* is defined in Exercise 3.10).

Show that the algorithm effectively computes the table *good-suff*. What is its running time?

3.12 (Quadratic)

Modify the algorithm GOOD-SUFFIX(x, m, *suff*) in order to obtain, for a string x of length m, an algorithm that runs in time and space $O(m \times \text{card}\, A)$, and that computes the table *best-fact-quad* of size $O(m \times \text{card}\, A)$ defined by

$$\textit{best-fact-quad}[i, a] = \textit{best-fact}(i, a)$$

for $0 \leq i \leq m - 1$ and $a \in A$.

3.13 (Witnesses)

Let $y \in A^+$ and w be a proper prefix of $x \in A^+$. We assume that w is periodic, that is to say

$$|w| \geq 2\text{per}(w).$$

Show that the string

$$w[0 \,.\,.\, 2\text{per}(w) - 2]$$

is not periodic.

Let $p = |w| - \text{per}(w)$ and $q = |w|$, and assume that $x[p] \neq x[q]$ (the integers p and q are witnesses of nonperiodicity $q - p$ of x). Show that if simultaneously $y[j + p] = x[p]$ and $y[j + q] = x[q]$ then the string x possesses no occurrence at positions $j + 1, j + 2, \ldots, j + p$ on y.

From the previous property, deduce an algorithm for locating the occurrences of x in y that performs at most $2|y|$ comparisons between letters of x and of y during the search and that uses only a constant extra space. (*Hint:* distinguish the three cases: no prefix of x is periodic; w is the longest periodic prefix of x and x is not periodic; x is periodic. See also Gąsieniec, Plandowski, and Rytter [145].)

3.14 (Heuristic)

Show that, in the algorithm TURBO-SUFFIX-SEARCH, if we utilize the heuristic *last-occ* and the table *good-suff*, and if the shift is given by the heuristic, then the length of the shift must be at least $|z|$ (the string z is the suffix of the string recognized during the attempt).

Give the complete code of the algorithm modified by incorporating the heuristic and using the above property.

3.15 (Lonely)

Adapt the algorithm MULTIPLE-SUFFIX-SEARCH to the case of the search of a single string. (*Hint:* see Crochemore, Czumaj, Gąsieniec, Jarominek, Lecroq, Plandowski, and Rytter [121].)

3.16 (Linear)

Combine the techniques of the search for a dictionary presented in Chapter 2 with those implemented in algorithm MULTIPLE-SUFFIX-SEARCH in order to get a searching algorithm working in linear time. (*Hint:* see Crochemore, Czumaj, Gąsieniec, Lecroq, Plandowski, and Rytter [122].)

4
Suffix arrays

This chapter addresses the problem of searching a fixed text. The associated data structure described here is known as the Suffix Array of the text. The searching procedure is presented first for a list of strings in Sections 4.1 and 4.2, and then adapted to a fixed text in the remaining sections.

The first three sections consider the question of searching a list of strings memorized in a table. The table is supposed to be fixed and can thus be preprocessed to speed up later accesses to it. The search for a string in a lexicon or a dictionary that can be stored in central memory of a computer is an application of this question.

We describe how to lexicographically sort the strings of the list (in maximal time proportional to the total length of the strings) in order to be able to apply a binary search algorithm. Actually, the sorting is not entirely sufficient to get an efficient search. The precomputation and the utilization of the longest common prefixes between the strings of the list are extra elements that make the technique very efficient. Searching for a string of length m in a list of n strings takes $O(m + \log n)$ time.

The suffix array of a text is a data structure that applies the previous technique to the n (nonempty) suffixes of a text of length n. It allows to determine all the occurrences of a factor of the text, in time $O(m + \log n)$ as above, and provides a solution complementary to the ones described in Chapters 2 and 3. The text is fixed and its preprocessing provides an efficient access to its suffixes. In this case, the preparation of the text, lexicographic sorting of its suffixes and computation of their common prefixes, can be adapted to run respectively in time $O(n \times \log n)$ and in time $O(n)$ though the sum of suffix lengths is quadratic.

In Section 4.5, we consider that the alphabet is a bounded segment of integers, as it can be considered in most real applications. Having this condition it is not necessary to sort individual letters of the text before sorting its suffixes.

This eliminates the bottleneck of the $O(n \times \log n)$ running time. Indeed, under this condition, the suffixes can be sorted in linear time.

Globally, the chapter presents an algorithmic solution to the problem of searching for a string in a fixed list and in the factors of a fixed text. Chapter 5 completes the study by proposing a solution based on data structures adapted to the memorization of the text suffixes. Finally, Chapter 9 presents an alternative solution to the preparation of a suffix array.

The interest to consider the suffixes of a string resides essentially in the applications to pattern matching and to index implementation that are described in Chapter 6. Indeed, the technique for searching a list allows one to compute the interval of strings of the list that possess a given prefix, and this is the reason why it adapts to pattern matching.

All this assumes the existence of an ordering on the alphabet. But this is not a constraint in practice because the data stored in a computer memory are encoded in binary and consequently we can use the lexicographic ordering of binary sequences.

4.1 Searching a list of strings

We consider a list L of n strings of A^* assumed to be stored in a table: $L_0, L_1, \ldots, L_{n-1}$. In this section and the next one, we assume that the strings are in increasing lexicographic order, $L_0 \leq L_1 \leq \cdots \leq L_{n-1}$. Sorting the list is studied in Section 4.3.

The basic problem considered in the chapter is the search for a string $x \in A^*$ in the list. In the applications, it is often more interesting to answer a more precise question that takes into account the structure of the elements of the list, that is to say, determine what are the strings of the list having x as a prefix. This problem is at the origin of an index implementation presented in Chapter 6 and it yields an efficient solution for string searching in a fixed text. We state formally the two problems considered in the section.

Interval problem

Let $n \geq 0$ and $L_0, L_1, \ldots, L_{n-1} \in A^*$, satisfying the condition $L_0 \leq L_1 \leq \cdots \leq L_{n-1}$. For $x \in A^*$, compute the indices d and f, $-1 \leq d < f \leq n$, for which: $d < i < f$ if and only if $x \preceq_{\text{pref}} L_i$.

The choice of the bounds -1 and n in the statement simplifies the algorithm (algorithm Interval of Section 4.2). We proceed as if the list is preceded by a string smaller (in the lexicographic order) than every other, and as if it is followed by a string larger that every other.

We can state the membership test of x in the list L in terms that simplify the previous problem and make the design of algorithm more direct. Besides, in addition to membership, solutions of the problem are able to locate x with respect to the sorted elements of the list even if does not belong to it.

Membership problem

Let $n \geq 0$ and $L_0, L_1, \ldots, L_{n-1} \in A^*$, satisfying the condition $L_0 \leq L_1 \leq \cdots \leq L_{n-1}$. For $x \in A^*$, compute an index i, $-1 < i < n$, for which $x = L_i$ if x occurs in the list L, or otherwise indices d and f, $-1 \leq d < f \leq n$, for which $d + 1 = f$ and $L_d < x < L_f$.

The search for x in the list L can be done in a sequential way without any preparation of the list, without even requiring that it is sorted. The execution time is then the sorting time $O(m \times n)$. By applying this method, we do not get any gain from the fact that the list is sorted and that it can be prepared before the search. A second solution consists in applying a binary search as it is classical to do on sorted tables of elements. The searching algorithm can easily be written as below. It provides a rather efficient answer to the membership problem, solution that is improved in the next section. The code of the algorithm calls the function *lcp* that is defined, for $u, v \in A^*$, by

$$lcp(u, v) = \text{the longest prefix common to } u \text{ and } v.$$

In the code below, we note that $L_i[\ell]$ is the letter at position ℓ on the string having index i in the list L. We also note that the initialization of d and f amounts to consider, as we already mentioned, that the list possesses two extra strings L_{-1} and L_n of length 1, the string L_{-1} consists of a letter smaller than all the letters of the strings $x, L_0, L_1, \ldots, L_{n-1}$, and the string L_n consists of a letter greater than all of them.

```
SIMPLE-SEARCH(L, n, x, m)
d ← −1
f ← n
while d + 1 < f do
    ▷ Invariant: L_d < x < L_f
    i ← ⌊(d + f)/2⌋
    ℓ ← |lcp(x, L_i)|
    if ℓ = m and ℓ = |L_i| then
        return i
    elseif (ℓ = |L_i|) or (ℓ ≠ m and L_i[ℓ] < x[ℓ]) then
        d ← i
    else f ← i
return (d, f)
```

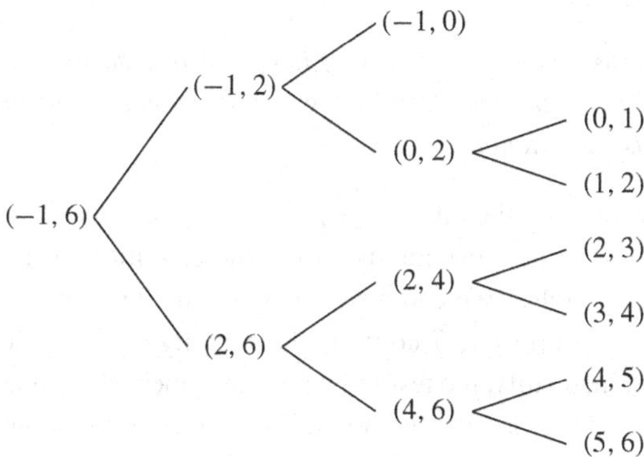

Figure 4.1. Tree of the binary search inside a list of six elements. The tree possesses $2 \times 6 + 1 = 13$ nodes, 6 are internal and 7 are external.

The algorithm Simple-search considers a set of pairs of integers (d, f) that is structured as a tree, the binary search tree. The execution of the algorithm corresponds to a scan along a branch of the tree, from the root $(-1, n)$. The scan stops on an external node of the tree when the string x does not belong to the list, otherwise it stops before. Figure 4.1 shows the tree of the binary search when $n = 6$.

The set N of nodes of the tree is inductively defined by the conditions:

- $(-1, n) \in N$;
- if $(d, f) \in N$ and $d + 1 < f$, then both $(d, \lfloor (d + f)/2 \rfloor) \in N$ and $(\lfloor (d + f)/2 \rfloor, f) \in N$.

The external nodes of the tree are all the pairs (d, f), $-1 \leq d < f \leq n$, for which $d + 1 = f$. An internal node (d, f), $-1 \leq d + 1 < f \leq n$, of the tree possesses two children: $(d, \lfloor (d + f)/2 \rfloor)$ and $(\lfloor (d + f)/2 \rfloor, f)$.

Lemma 4.1

The binary search tree associated with a list of n elements possesses $2n + 1$ *nodes.*

Proof The tree of the binary search possesses the $n + 1$ external nodes $(-1, 0), (0, 1), \ldots, (n - 1, n)$. Since the tree is binary and complete, the number of internal nodes is one unit less than the number of external nodes (simple proof by recurrence on the number of nodes). There are thus n internal nodes, which gives the result. ■

Proposition 4.2
The algorithm SIMPLE-SEARCH *locates a string x of length m in a sorted list of size n (membership problem) in time $O(m \times \log n)$ with a maximum of $m \times \lceil \log_2(n+1) \rceil$ comparisons of letters.*

Proof The algorithm stops because the difference $f - d$ decreases strictly at each execution of lines 5 to 11, which eventually makes the condition of the loop, the inequality $d + 1 < f$, false. We can also verify that the property of line 4 is invariant. Indeed, the test in line 7 controls the equality of strings x and L_i. And in the case of an inequality, the test in line 9 determines which one of the two strings is greater in the lexicographic order. We then deduce that the algorithm solves correctly the membership problem.

Each comparison of strings requires at most m letter comparisons counting the comparisons done for computing $|lcp(x, L_i)|$. The length of the interval of integers (d, f) goes from $n + 1$ to at most 1. This length (minus one unit) is divided by two at each step, thus there are at most $\lceil \log_2(n+1) \rceil$ steps. We deduce the result on the number of comparisons that is representative of the execution time.

The example below shows that the bound on the number of comparisons is tight, which ends the proof. ■

The result of the proposition is not surprising and the bound on the execution time is tight when x is not longer than the elements of the list. Indeed, the maximal number of comparisons is reached with the following example. We choose for list of n strings

$$L = \langle \mathtt{a}^{m-1}\mathtt{b}, \mathtt{a}^{m-1}\mathtt{c}, \mathtt{a}^{m-1}\mathtt{d}, \ldots \rangle$$

and for string $x = \mathtt{a}^m$. We assume the usual order on the letters: $\mathtt{a} < \mathtt{b}$, $\mathtt{b} < \mathtt{c}$, etc. The result of the algorithm SIMPLE-SEARCH is the pair $(-1, 0)$, which indicates that x is smaller than all the strings of L. If the comparisons between strings are done by letter comparisons from left to right (by increasing positions), exactly m letter comparisons are performed at each step; as their number is $\lceil \log_2(n+1) \rceil$, this gives the bound of the proposition.

When x is longer than the elements of L, a more suited expression of the execution time is $O(\ell \times \log n)$, where ℓ is the maximal length of the strings of L.

4.2 Searching with the longest common prefixes

The binary method of the previous section can be completed in order to speed up the search for x in the list L. This is done with the help of an extra information on the strings of the list: their longest common prefixes. The searching time goes from $O(m \times \log n)$ (algorithm SIMPLE-SEARCH of the previous section) down to $O(m + \log n)$ for the algorithm SEARCH below. The storage of the lengths of common prefixes requires an extra memory space $O(n)$.

The idea of the improvement is contained in Proposition 4.3 which is a remark on the common prefixes. In the statement of the proposition, the values ℓ_d and ℓ_f and those of the associated variables in the algorithm SEARCH are defined by

$$\ell_d = |lcp(x, L_d)|$$

and

$$\ell_f = |lcp(x, L_f)|.$$

The proposition focuses on two situations met during the execution of the algorithm SEARCH and that are illustrated by Figure 4.2. A third case is described

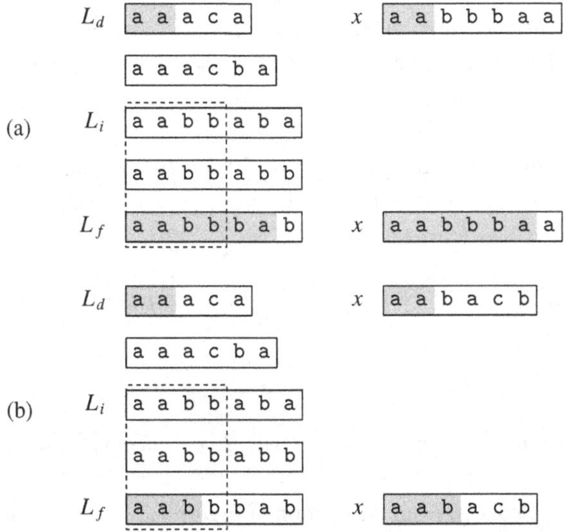

Figure 4.2. Illustration for the proof of Proposition 4.3 in the case $\ell_d \le \ell_f$. **(a)** Let $u = lcp(L_i, L_f)$ and a, b be the distinct letters for which $ua \preceq_{\text{pref}} L_i$ and $ub \preceq_{\text{pref}} L_f$. The list being ordered, we have $a < b$. Then, if $|u| = |lcp(L_i, L_f)| < \ell_f$, ub is also a prefix of x, thus $L_i < x$ and $|lcp(x, L_i)| = |lcp(L_i, L_f)|$. Here, we have $u = \texttt{aabb} = lcp(\texttt{aabbaba}, \texttt{aabbbab}) = lcp(\texttt{aabbbaa}, \texttt{aabbaba})$. The argument adapts to the case where $u = L_i$ and gives the same result. **(b)** Let $v = lcp(x, L_f)$ and a, b be the distinct letters for which $va \preceq_{\text{pref}} x$ and $vb \preceq_{\text{pref}} L_f$. As $x < L_f$, we have $a < b$. Then, if $|lcp(L_i, L_f)| > \ell_f = |v|$, vb is also a prefix of L_i, thus $x < L_i$ and $|lcp(x, L_i)| = |lcp(x, L_f)|$. Here, we have $v = \texttt{aab} = lcp(\texttt{aabacb}, \texttt{aabbbab}) = lcp(\texttt{aabacb}, \texttt{aabbaba})$. The argument adapts to the case where $v = x$ and gives the same result.

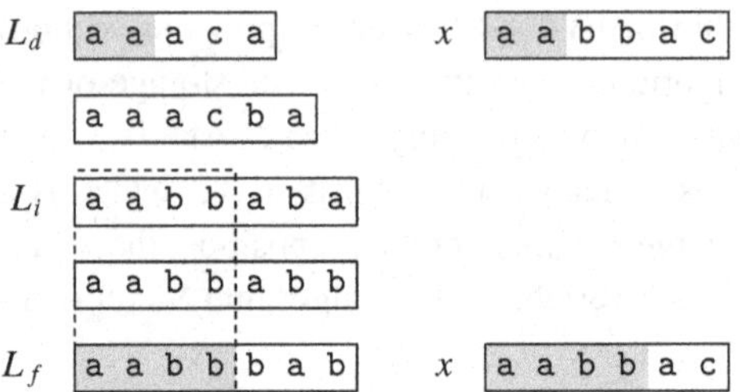

Figure 4.3. Illustration of how the algorithm SEARCH works for a complementary case to those of Proposition 4.3. We still consider that the condition $\ell_d \leq \ell_f$ holds. Let $u = lcp(L_i, L_f)$ and a, b be the distinct letters for which $ua \preceq_{\text{pref}} L_i$ and $ub \preceq_{\text{pref}} L_f$. The list being ordered, we deduce $a < b$. If $|u| = \ell_f$, ua' is a prefix of x for a letter a', $a' < b$. In this situation, we have to compare letters of x and L_i in order to locate x in the list. The letter comparisons, performed from left to right, are only necessary from position ℓ_f, where the letters a and a' occur in their respective strings. The algorithm takes into account the possibilities $u = x$ and $u = L_i$.

in Figure 4.3; it is the one for which more letter comparisons are necessary. Three other symmetrical cases are to be considered when we assume $\ell_d > \ell_f$.

Proposition 4.3
Let d, f, i be three integers, $0 \leq d < i < f < n$. Under the assumptions $L_d \leq L_{d+1} \leq \cdots \leq L_f$ and $L_d < x < L_f$, let $\ell_d = |lcp(x, L_d)|$ and $\ell_f = |lcp(x, L_f)|$ satisfying $\ell_d \leq \ell_f$. Then we have:

$$|lcp(L_i, L_f)| < \ell_f \text{ implies } L_i < x < L_f \text{ and } |lcp(x, L_i)| = |lcp(L_i, L_f)|,$$

and

$$|lcp(L_i, L_f)| > \ell_f \text{ implies } L_d < x < L_i \text{ and } |lcp(x, L_i)| = |lcp(x, L_f)|.$$

Proof The proof can be deduced from the caption of Figure 4.2. ■

The code of the algorithm that exploits Proposition 4.3 is given below. It calls the function *Lcp* defined as follows. For (d, f), $-1 \leq d < f \leq n$, pair of indices of the binary search tree, we denote by

$$Lcp(d, f) = |lcp(L_d, L_f)|$$

the maximal length of the prefixes common to L_d and L_f.

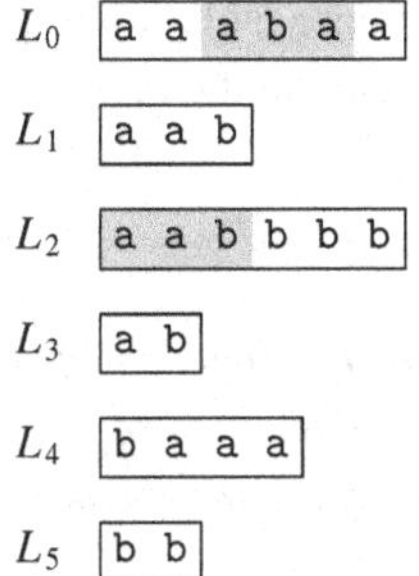

Figure 4.4. When searching for the string $x =$ aaabb in the list, the algorithm Search performs six comparisons of letters (gray letters). The output is the pair (0, 1), which indicates that $L_0 < x < L_1$.

```
Search(L, n, Lcp, x, m)
(d, ℓ_d) ← (−1, 0)
(f, ℓ_f) ← (n, 0)
while d + 1 < f do
      ▷ Invariant: L_d < x < L_f
      i ← ⌊(d + f)/2⌋
      if ℓ_d ≤ Lcp(i, f) and Lcp(i, f) < ℓ_f then
            (d, ℓ_d) ← (i, Lcp(i, f))      ▷ Figure 4.2(a)
      elseif ℓ_d ≤ ℓ_f and ℓ_f < Lcp(i, f) then
            f ← i                           ▷ Figure 4.2(b)
      elseif ℓ_f ≤ Lcp(d, i) and Lcp(d, i) < ℓ_d then
            (f, ℓ_f) ← (i, Lcp(d, i))
      elseif ℓ_f ≤ ℓ_d and ℓ_d < Lcp(d, i) then
            d ← i
      else  ℓ ← max{ℓ_d, ℓ_f}               ▷ Figure 4.3
            ℓ ← ℓ + |lcp(x[ℓ . . m − 1], L_i[ℓ . . |L_i| − 1])|
            if ℓ = m and ℓ = |L_i| then
                  return i
            elseif (ℓ = |L_i|) or (ℓ ≠ m and L_i[ℓ] < x[ℓ]) then
                  (d, ℓ_d) ← (i, ℓ)
            else  (f, ℓ_f) ← (i, ℓ)
return (d, f)
```

An example of how the algorithm works is given in Figure 4.4.

We evaluate the complexity of the algorithm Search under the assumption that sorting the list and computing the longest common prefixes are performed beforehand. This preparation is studied in the next section and it results that the computation of *Lcp*(r, s) $(-1 \leq r < s \leq n)$ amounts to a mere table look-up and can thus be executed in constant time, property that is used in the proof of the next proposition.

Proposition 4.4
The algorithm SEARCH *locates a string x of length m in a sorted list of n strings (membership problem) in time $O(m + \log n)$ with a maximum of $m + \lceil \log_2(n + 1) \rceil$ letter comparisons. The algorithm requires an extra memory space $O(n)$.*

Proof The code of the algorithm SEARCH is a modification of the code of the algorithm SIMPLE-SEARCH. It takes into account the result of Proposition 4.3. The correctness of the algorithm results essentially from Propositions 4.2 and 4.3, and from the caption of Figure 4.3.

For the evaluation of the execution time, we note that each positive letter comparison strictly increases the value of $\max\{\ell_d, \ell_f\}$ that goes from 0 to m at most. There are thus at most m comparisons of this kind. Besides, each letter mismatch leads to divide by two the quantity $f - d - 1$. The comparisons between ℓ_d, ℓ_f, and the precomputed *Lcp* values have the same effect when they do not lead to comparisons of letters. There are thus at most $\lceil \log_2(n + 1) \rceil$ comparisons of this kind. Therefore, we get the announced result on the execution time when the computation of *Lcp*(r, s), $-1 \leq r < s \leq n$, executes in constant time. This condition is realized by the implementation described in the next section.

The extra memory space is used to store the information on the ordering of the list and on the common prefixes necessary to the computations of the *Lcp*(r, s), $-1 \leq r < s \leq n$. The implementation described in the next section shows that a space $O(n)$ is sufficient, result that essentially comes from the fact that only $2n + 1$ pairs (r, s) come up in the binary search after Lemma 4.1. ∎

The algorithm SEARCH provides a solution to the membership problem. It easily transforms into a solution to the interval problem: the algorithm INTERVAL. Since we search now the strings of the list for which x is a prefix, we have to detect the case where $x \preceq_{\text{pref}} L_i$. It can be done by changing the test in line 16. This being done, it remains to determine the bounds of the wanted interval. We proceed by dichotomy before (resp. after) the string L_i for which x is a prefix, by determining the largest index $j < i$ (resp. smallest index $j > i$) for which *Lcp*$(i, j) < |x|$. The principle of the computation relies on Lemma 4.6 of Section 4.3.

The algorithm INTERVAL is obtained by replacing lines 16–17 of the algorithm SEARCH by the lines that follow.

```
▷ The following lines replace lines 16–17 of SEARCH
if ℓ = m then
        e ← i
        while d + 1 < e do
                j ← ⌊(d + e)/2⌋
                if Lcp(j, e) < m then
                        d ← j
                else  e ← j
        if Lcp(d, e) ≥ m then
                d ← max{d − 1, −1}
        e ← i
        while e + 1 < f do
                j ← ⌊(e + f)/2⌋
                if Lcp(e, j) < m then
                        f ← j
                else  e ← j
        if Lcp(e, f) ≥ m then
                f ← min{f + 1, n}
        return (d, f)
```

The letter comparisons performed by the algorithm INTERVAL are also done by the algorithm SEARCH. The asymptotic bound of the execution time is not modified by the above change. We thus get the following result.

Proposition 4.5
The algorithm INTERVAL *solves the interval problem for a string of length m and a sorted list of n strings in time $O(m + \log n)$ with a maximum of $m + \lceil \log_2(n + 1) \rceil$ letter comparisons. The algorithm requires an extra memory space $O(n)$.* ■

It is obvious that the time complexity of the algorithms SEARCH and INTERVAL is also $O(\ell + \log n)$ with $\ell = \max\{|L_i| : i = 0, 1, \ldots, n - 1\}$. This bound is a better expression when x is longer than the strings of the list.

4.3 Preprocessing the list

The algorithm SEARCH (as well as the algorithm INTERVAL) of the previous section works on a list of strings L lexicographically sorted and for which we

f	0	1	2	3	4	5	6	7	8	9	10	11	12
$LCP[f]$	0	2	3	1	0	1	0	0	2	0	0	0	0

Figure 4.5. Table LCP associated with the list of strings in Figure 4.4, $L = \{\texttt{aaabaa}, \texttt{aab}, \texttt{aabbbb}, \texttt{ab}, \texttt{baaa}, \texttt{bb}\}$ of length 6. For example, $LCP[2] = |lcp(L_1, L_2)| = |lcp(\texttt{aab}, \texttt{aabbbb})| = |\texttt{aab}| = 3$. And $LCP[8] = |lcp(L_0, L_2)| = |lcp(\texttt{aaabaa}, \texttt{aabbbb})| = |\texttt{aa}| = 2$ because $8 = 6 + 1 + \lfloor (0 + 2)/2 \rfloor$.

know their longest common prefixes. We show, in this section, how to perform these operations on the list.

Sorting such a list is usually realized by means of a series of radix sorting (bucket sort) analogue to the method used by the algorithm SORT of the next section. Doing so, the sorting executes in time $O(|L|)$, where $|L|$ is the sum of the lengths of the strings of the list.

We describe an implementation of the lengths of the common prefixes that is needed for the algorithm SEARCH. The implementation is realized by memorizing the values in a table. The algorithm SEARCH accesses the table through calls to the function Lcp below. We denote by

$$LCP: \{0, 1, \ldots, 2n\} \rightarrow \mathbf{N}$$

the table used for storing the lengths of the longest common prefixes. It is defined by:

- $LCP[f] = |lcp(L_{f-1}, L_f)|$, for $0 \leq f \leq n$,
- $LCP[n + 1 + i] = |lcp(L_d, L_f)|$, for $i = \lfloor (d + f)/2 \rfloor$ middle of a pair (d, f), $0 \leq d + 1 < f \leq n$, of the binary search tree,

assuming that $lcp(L_r, L_s) = \varepsilon$ when $r = -1$ or $s = n$. The representation of the values in the table LCP does not cause any ambiguity since each index i on the table only refers to one pair (d, f) coming up from the binary search. An example of LCP table is shown in Figure 4.5.

The equality that follows establishes the link between the table LCP and the function Lcp.

$$Lcp(d, f) = \begin{cases} LCP[f] & \text{if } d + 1 = f, \\ LCP[n + 1 + \lfloor (d + f)/2 \rfloor] & \text{otherwise.} \end{cases}$$

We deduce an implementation of the function Lcp that executes in constant time. This result is an assumption used in the previous section to evaluate the execution time of the algorithm SEARCH.

```
LCP(d, f)
if d + 1 = f then
        return LCP[f]
else return LCP[n + 1 + ⌊(d + f)/2⌋]
```

Computing the table *LCP* is done by scanning the list L in increasing order of the strings. The computation of $LCP[f]$ for $0 \le f \le n$ results from mere letter comparisons. The following lemma provides a property that serves to compute the other values.

Lemma 4.6
We assume that $L_0 \le L_1 \le \cdots \le L_{n-1}$. Let d, i, and f be integers such that $-1 < d < i < f < n$. Then

$$|lcp(L_d, L_f)| = \min\{|lcp(L_d, L_i)|, |lcp(L_i, L_f)|\}.$$

Proof Let $u = lcp(L_d, L_i)$ and $v = lcp(L_i, L_f)$. Without loss of generality, we assume $|u| \le |v|$ because the other case is analogue. The strings u and v being prefixes of L_i, we have then $u \preceq_{\text{pref}} v$ and $u \preceq_{\text{pref}} L_f$.

If $u = L_d$, we get $u = lcp(L_d, L_f)$, which gives the stated equality.

Otherwise, there exist three letters a, b, c such that $ua \preceq_{\text{pref}} L_d$, $ub \preceq_{\text{pref}} L_i$, and $uc \preceq_{\text{pref}} L_f$. We have $a \ne b$ by definition of u, and even $a < b$ since the sequence is in increasing order. If moreover $b = c$, we get $u = lcp(L_d, L_f)$, which gives the conclusion. If on the other hand $b \ne c$, the sequence being in increasing order, we have $b < c$, which gives again the same conclusion and ends the proof. ■

The algorithm LCP-TABLE implements the computation of the table *LCP*. The execution starts by the call LCP-TABLE$(-1, n)$, for $n \ge 0$, which has for effect to compute all the inputs of the table. The resulting table corresponds to its above definition, and the computation uses the previous lemma in line 8.

```
LCP-TABLE(d, f)
1  ▷ We have d < f
2  if d + 1 = f then
3          if d = −1 or f = n then
4                  LCP[f] ← 0
5          else LCP[f] ← |lcp(L_d, L_f)|
6          return LCP[f]
7  else i ← ⌊(d + f)/2⌋
8          LCP[n + 1 + i] ← min{LCP-TABLE(d, i), LCP-TABLE(i, f)}
9          return LCP[n + 1 + i]
```

We can check that the execution time of LCP-TABLE$(-1, n)$ is $O(|L|)$ as a consequence of Lemma 4.1. The proposition that follows sums up the elements discussed in the section.

Proposition 4.7
Preprocessing the list L for the algorithms SEARCH *and* INTERVAL, *that is, sorting it and computing its LCP table, takes $O(|L|)$ time.* ■

4.4 Sorting suffixes

The technique of the previous sections can be applied to the list of the suffixes of a string and it is the basis of an index implementation described in Chapter 6. The interval problem and its solution, the algorithm INTERVAL, are particularly interesting in this type of application to which they adapt without any modification.

In this section, we show how to sort in lexicographic order the suffixes of a string y of length n, preliminary condition for executing the algorithm INTERVAL on the list of the suffixes of y. In the next section, we complete the preparation of the string y by showing how to efficiently compute the longest prefixes common to the suffixes of y. The permutation that results from the sorting and the table of the longest common prefixes make up the ***suffix array*** of the string that is to index.

The goal of the sorting is to compute a permutation p of the indices on y that satisfies the condition

$$y[p[0]\,..\,n-1] < y[p[1]\,..\,n-1] < \cdots < y[p[n-1]\,..\,n-1]. \qquad (4.1)$$

We note that the inequalities are strict since two suffixes occurring at distinct positions cannot be identical.

The implementation of a standard lexicographic sorting method, as the one that is suggested in Section 4.3, leads to an algorithm whose running time is $O(n^2)$ because the sum of the lengths of the suffixes of y is quadratic. The sorting method that we use here relies on a technique of partial identification of the suffixes of y by means of their first k letters. The values of k increase in an exponential way, which produces a sorting in $\lceil \log_2 n \rceil$ steps. Each step is realized in linear time with the help of a lexicographic sort on pairs of integers of limited size, sorting that can be realized by radix sort.

Let k be an integer, $k > 0$. We denote, for $u \in A^*$:

$$first_k(u) = \begin{cases} u & \text{if } |u| \le k, \\ u[0\,..\,k-1] & \text{otherwise,} \end{cases}$$

a	b	a	a	b	b	a	b	b	a	a	a	b	b	a	b	b	b	a

Figure 4.6. Doubling. The rank of the factor aabbab, $R_6[2]$, is determined by the ranks $R_3[2]$ and $R_3[5]$ of aab and bab respectively. In particular, aabbab occurs at positions 2 and 10 since aab occurs at positions 2 and 10, and bab occurs at positions 5 ($= 2 + 3$) and 13 ($= 10 + 3$).

the beginning of order k of the string u. We define, for the positions $0, 1, \ldots, n - 1$ on y, a sequence of rank functions, denoted by R_k, in the following way. The value $R_k[i]$ is the rank (counted from 0) of $\mathit{first}_k(y[i \,..\, n-1])$ in the sorted list of the strings of the set $\{\mathit{first}_k(u) : u \preceq_{\text{suff}} y \text{ and } u \neq \varepsilon\}$. This set contains in general less than n elements for small values of k, which implies that different positions can be assigned the same value according to R_k. The function R_k induces an equivalence relation among the positions on y. It is denoted by $\equiv_k$, and defined by

$$i \equiv_k j$$

if and only if

$$R_k[i] = R_k[j].$$

When $k = 1$, the equivalence $\equiv_1$ amounts to identify the letters of y. For any $k \in \mathbf{N}$, two suffixes of length at least k are equivalent for $\equiv_k$ if their prefixes of length k are equal. When $k \geq n$, the equivalence $\equiv_k$ is discrete: each suffix is only equivalent to itself.

To simplify the statement of the property that is at the origin of the sorting algorithm SUFFIX-SORT thereafter, we extend the definition of R_k by setting $R_k[i] = -1$ for $i \geq n$. The property is illustrated in Figure 4.6

Lemma 4.8 (Doubling Lemma)
For two integers k and i with $k \geq 0$ and $0 \leq i < n$, $R_{2k}[i]$ is the rank of the pair $(R_k[i], R_k[i+k])$ in the lexicographically increasing list of all these pairs.

Proof Setting $R_k[i] = -1$ for an integer $i \geq n$ amounts to consider the infinite string ya^∞, where a is a letter smaller than all those that occur in y. Thus, when $i \geq n$, the factor of length k occurring at position i, a^k, is smaller than all the other strings of the same length occurring at a position on y. Its rank is thus less than the other ranks, which is compatible with the agreement to give it the value -1.

By definition, $R_{2k}[i]$ is the rank of $\mathit{first}_{2k}(y[i\,..\,i+2k-1])$ in the sorted list of the factors of length $2k$ of the string ya^∞. Let

$$u(i) = \mathit{first}_k(y[i\,..\,i+k-1])$$

and

$$v(i) = \mathit{first}_k(y[i+k\,..\,i+2k-1]).$$

From the equality

$$\mathit{first}_{2k}(y[i\,..\,i+2k-1]) = u(i)\cdot v(i)$$

we deduce, for $0 \le i \ne j < n$, that the inequality

$$\mathit{first}_{2k}(y[i\,..\,i+2k-1]) < \mathit{first}_{2k}(y[j\,..\,j+2k-1])$$

is equivalent to

$$(u(i), v(i)) < (u(j), v(j))$$

that is itself equivalent to

$$(R_k[i], R_k[i+k]) < (R_k[j], R_k[j+k])$$

by definition of R_k. Thus, the rank $R_{2k}[i]$ of $\mathit{first}_{2k}(y[i\,..\,i+2k-1])$ is equal to the rank of $(R_k[i], R_k[i+k])$ in the increasing sequence of these pairs, which ends the proof. ■

Relatively to the parameter k, we finally denote by p_k a permutation of the positions on y that satisfies, for $0 \le r < s < n$,

$$R_k[p_k(r)] \le R_k[p_k(s)].$$

The permutation is associated with the sorted sequence of the beginning of length k of the suffixes of y. When $k \ge n$, the strings $\mathit{first}_k(u)$ (where u is a nonempty suffix of y) being pairwise distinct, the previous inequality becomes strict. We get then a unique permutation satisfying the condition, it is the permutation defined by the table p and used in Section 6.1 for searching the string y. The algorithm Suffix-sort computes this permutation by means of the tables R_k.

```
Suffix-sort(y, n)
for r ← 0 to n − 1 do
        p[r] ← r
k ← 1
for i ← 0 to n − 1 do
        R_1[i] ← rank of y[i] in the sorted list of letters of alph(y)
p ← Sort(p, n, R_1, 0)
i ← card alph(y) − 1
while i < n − 1 do
        p ← Sort(p, n, R_k, k)
        p ← Sort(p, n, R_k, 0)
        i ← 0
        R_2k[p[0]] ← i
        for r ← 1 to n − 1 do
                if R_k[p[r]] ≠ R_k[p[r − 1]]
                   or R_k[p[r] + k] ≠ R_k[p[r − 1] + k] then
                        i ← i + 1
                R_2k[p[r]] ← i
        k ← 2k
return p
```

An illustration of how the algorithm Suffix-sort works is given in Figure 4.7.

The algorithm uses the property stated in Lemma 4.8 by calling the sorting algorithm Sort described below. The algorithm Sort has for inputs: p is a permutation of the integers $0, 1, \ldots, n-1$, R is a table on these integers with values in the set $\{-1, 0, \ldots, n-1\}$, and k is an integer. The algorithm Sort sorts the sequence of integers

$$p[0]+k, p[1]+k, \ldots, p[n-1]+k$$

in increasing order of their key R. This is to say that the value p' produced by Sort(p, n, R, k) is a permutation of $\{0, 1, \ldots, n-1\}$ that satisfies the inequalities

$$R[p'[0]+k] \leq R[p'[1]+k] \leq \cdots \leq R[p'[n-1]+k].$$

Moreover, Sort satisfies a stability condition that makes it appropriate to lexicographic sorting: the algorithm does not modify the relative position in the list of two elements that possess the same key. In other words, if r and t,

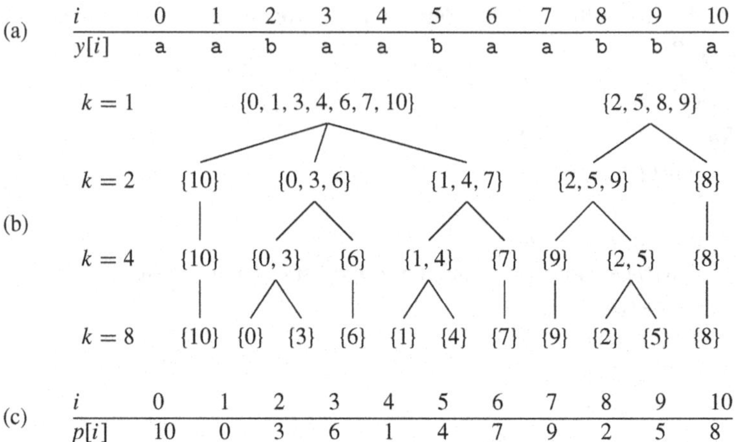

(a)

i	0	1	2	3	4	5	6	7	8	9	10
$y[i]$	a	a	b	a	a	b	a	a	b	b	a

(c)

i	0	1	2	3	4	5	6	7	8	9	10
$p[i]$	10	0	3	6	1	4	7	9	2	5	8

Figure 4.7. Computation by doubling of the partitions associated with equivalences $\equiv_k$ on the string $y =$ aabaabaabba. **(a)** The positions on the string y. **(b)** The classes of positions according to $\equiv_k$ are given from left to right in increasing order of the common rank of their elements. Thus, line $k = 2$, $R_2[10] = 0$, $R_2[0] = R_2[3] = R_2[6] = 1$, $R_2[1] = R_2[4] = R_2[7] = 2$, etc. For $k = 8$, the sequence of positions provides the suffixes in increasing order. **(c)** Permutation p corresponding to the sorted suffixes of y.

$0 \le r \ne t < n$, are two integers for which $R[p[r] + k] = R[p[t] + k]$, we have $p[r] < p[t]$ if and only if $p'[r] < p'[t]$. The implementation below satisfies the required properties.

```
SORT(p, n, R, k)
for i ← −1 to n − 1 do
        Bucket[i] ← EMPTY-QUEUE()
for r ← 0 to n − 1 do
        if p[r] + k < n then
                i ← R[p[r] + k]
        else  i ← −1
        ENQUEUE(Bucket[i], p[r])
r ← −1
for i ← −1 to n − 1 do
        while not QUEUE-IS-EMPTY(Bucket[i]) do
                j ← DEQUEUED(Bucket[i])
                r ← r + 1
                p'[r] ← j
return p'
```

Proposition 4.9
The algorithm SUFFIX-SORT *applied to the string* y *sorts its suffixes in lexicographic increasing order.*

Proof The instructions of the **while** loop serve to sort the integers $p[0], p[1], \ldots, p[n-1]$ on one hand, then to define the new ranks that are associated with them, on the other hand. This second part is done by the internal **for** loop and can be easily checked. The main part is the sorting phase.

We show below that the condition

$$\langle \mathit{first}_k(y[p[r]\,..\,n-1]) : r = 0, 1, \ldots, n-1\rangle \text{ is increasing} \tag{4.2}$$

is invariant by the **while** loop.

Let $p' = \text{SORT}(p, n, R_k, k)$ and $p'' = \text{SORT}(p', n, R_k, 0)$ during an execution of instructions of the **while** loop. The stability condition imposed to SORT leads to the consequence, for $0 \le r < n$ and $0 \le t < n$, that

$$p''[r] < p''[t]$$

implies

$$(R_k[p[r]], R_k[p[r]+k]) \le (R_k[p[t]], R_k[p[t]+k]).$$

Thus, after Lemma 4.8, the rank attributed to $p''[r]$, $0 \le r < n$, is $R_{2k}[p[r]]$. This means that just before the execution of the instruction of line 17 we have: $\langle \mathit{first}_{2k}(y[p''[r]\,..\,n-1]) : r = 0, 1, \ldots, n-1\rangle$ is increasing. Just after the execution of the instruction of line 17 the Condition (4.2) thus holds, which proves its invariance.

It can be directly checked that the Condition (4.2) is satisfied before the execution of the **while** loop thanks to the instruction of line 6. Thus, it still holds after the execution of this loop (for the termination, see the proof of Proposition 4.10). We then have $i \ge n-1$ and, more exactly, $i = n-1$, since the final value of i is the maximal rank of the factors $\mathit{first}_k(u)$, for u a nonempty suffix of y, that cannot be greater than $n-1$.

We show that the suffixes are in increasing order relatively to the permutation p after the execution of the **while** loop. Let u, w be two nonempty suffixes of y ($u \neq w$) of respective positions $p[r]$ and $p[t]$, $p[r] < p[t]$. By the Condition (4.2) we get the inequality $R_k[p[r]] \le R_k[p[t]]$. But the ranks being pairwise distinct, we even deduce $R_k[p[r]] < R_k[p[t]]$, which is equivalent to $\mathit{first}_k(u) < \mathit{first}_k(w)$. This inequality means that, either $\mathit{first}_k(u)$ is a proper prefix of $\mathit{first}_k(w)$, or $\mathit{first}_k(u) = vau'$ and $\mathit{first}_k(w) = vbw'$ with $v, u', w' \in A^*$,

$a, b \in A$, and $a < b$. In the first case, we have necessarily $first_k(u) = u$, which is thus a proper prefix of $first_k(w)$, and therefore of w. Then $u < w$. In the second case, we have $u = vau''$ and $w = vbw''$ for two strings u'' and w'', which shows that we still have $u < w$.

The permutation p that is produced by the algorithm SUFFIX-SORT satisfies the Condition (4.1) and corresponds therefore to the increasing sequence of the suffixes of y. ■

Proposition 4.10

The running time of the algorithm SUFFIX-SORT *applied to a string y of length n is* $O(n \times \log n)$. *The algorithm works in space* $O(n \times \log n)$ *when the tables* R_k *have to be stored, and in space* $O(n)$ *otherwise.*

Proof Lines 4–5 that refer implicitly to an ordering on the set of letters of y execute in time $O(n \times \log n)$. The other instructions located before the **while** loop, internal to this loop, and after this loop execute in time $O(n)$. The global execution time thus depends on the number of iterations of this loop.

As for $k \geq n$ the strings $first_k(u)$ (u a nonempty suffix of y) are pairwise distinct, their maximal rank is exactly $n - 1$, which is the condition that stops the **while** loop. The successive values of k are $2^0, 2^1, 2^2, \ldots$, until $2^{\lceil \log_2(n-1) \rceil}$ at most, which limits the number of iterations of the loop to $\lceil \log_2(n - 1) \rceil$. Thus the bound on the running time of SUFFIX-SORT holds.

Another consequence is that the number of tables R_k used by the algorithm is bounded by $\lceil \log_2(n - 1) \rceil + 1$ (a new table for each iteration). Which requires a space $O(n \times \log n)$ if they must all be stored. In the contrary case, we notice that a single table R is sufficient to the computation, thus an extra space $O(n)$ for this table. The same quantity is necessary to implement the buckets used by the algorithm SORT. ■

The suffix sorting described in this section heavily uses the bucket sort technique implemented by the algorithm SORT. But the global algorithm cannot be improved because of instructions in lines 4–5 of the algorithm SUFFIX-SORT that sort the letters. In the next section, we consider that this step is already done, or equivalently that the string is drawn from a bounded integer alphabet, leaving some space for improvement.

4.5 Sorting suffixes on bounded integer alphabets

In this section, we consider that the alphabet is a bounded segment of integers, as it can be considered in most real applications. The bound may depend on the length of the string y, and a common hypothesis is that the alphabet is included in an interval of integers of the form $[0, |y|^c[$, where c is a constant. Having this condition the alphabet can be sorted in $O(n)$ time. This eliminates the bottleneck of the $O(n \times \log n)$ running time that appears in the algorithm of the previous section. Indeed with such an alphabet the suffixes can be sorted in linear time by using techniques different from those presented in the previous section. In the rest of the section, we assume that the letters of the string are already sorted.

For the fixed text y of length n we consider the sets of positions P_{01} and P_2 defined by
if n is a multiple of 3

$$P_{01} = \{i : 0 \le i \le n \text{ and } (i \bmod 3 = 0 \text{ or } i \bmod 3 = 1)\}$$

but if n is not a multiple of 3

$$P_{01} = \{i : 0 \le i < n \text{ and } (i \bmod 3 = 0 \text{ or } i \bmod 3 = 1)\},$$

and

$$P_2 = \{i : 0 \le i < n \text{ and } i \bmod 3 = 2\}.$$

Note that $n \in P_{01}$ only when n is a multiple of 3. Also, note that the size of P_{01} is $\lfloor 2n/3 \rfloor + 1$ and that card $P_{01} \cap \{i : i \bmod 3 = 0\} = \lfloor n/3 \rfloor + 1$.

The present algorithm for sorting the suffixes of y proceeds in four steps as follows.

Step 1: Positions i of P_{01} are sorted according to $\mathit{first}_3(y[i \mathinner{..} n-1])$.
Let $t[i]$ be the rank of i in the sorted list.

Step 2: Suffixes of the 2/3-shorter string

$$z = t[0]t[3] \cdots t[3k] \cdots t[1]t[4] \cdots t[3k+1] \cdots$$

are recursively sorted. Let $s[i]$ be the rank of the suffix at position i on y in the sorted list of them ($i \in P_{01}$) derived from the sorted list of suffixes of z.

Step 3: Suffixes $y[j \mathinner{..} n-1]$, for $j \in P_2$, are sorted using the table s.

Step 4: The final step consists in merging the sorted lists obtained after the second and third steps.

A careful implementation of the algorithm leads to a linear running time. It is based on the following elements. The first step can be executed in linear time by using three radix sort (see the algorithm Sort of Section 4.4). Since the rank of suffixes $y[j+1\,..\,n-1]$ is already known from s, the third step can be done in linear time by just radix sorting pairs $(y[j], s[j+1])$. Comparing suffixes at positions i ($i \in P_{01}$) and j ($j \in P_2$) remains to compare pairs of the form $(y[i], s[i+1])$ and $(y[j], s[j+1])$ if $i = 3k$, or to compare pairs of the form $(\mathit{first}_2(y[i\,..\,n-1]), s[i+2])$ and $(\mathit{first}_2(y[j\,..\,n-1]), s[j+2])$ if $i = 3k+1$. This is done in constant time and the merge at the fourth step can thus be realized in linear time. Two examples are shown in Figures 4.8. and 4.9.

The next algorithm describes the method presented above in a more precise way. To shorten the presentation of the algorithm, we extend the definition of s (see line 11) to positions n and $n+1$ that are considered in lines 12 and 13 (call to COMP).

```
SKEW-SUFFIX-SORT(y, n)
 1  if n ≤ 3 then
 2        return permutation of the sorted suffixes of y
 3  else  P01 ← {i : 0 ≤ i < n and (i mod 3 = 0 or i mod 3 = 1)}
 4        if n mod 3 = 0 then
 5              P01 ← P01 ∪ {n}
 6        t ← table of ranks of positions i in P01 according to
              first3(y[i . . n − 1])
 7        z ← t[0]t[3] · · · t[3k] · · · t[1]t[4] · · · t[3k + 1] · · ·
 8        q ← SKEW-SUFFIX-SORT(z, ⌊2n/3⌋ + 1)
 9        L01 ← (3q[j] if 0 ≤ q[j] ≤ ⌊n/3⌋ + 1, 3q[j] + 1 otherwise
              with j = 0, 1, . . . , |z| − 1)
10        s ← table of ranks of positions in L01
11        (s[n], s[n + 1]) ← (−1, −1)
12        L2 ← list of positions j, 0 ≤ j < n and j mod 3 = 2,
              sorted according to (y[j], s[j + 1])
13        L ← merge of L01 (without n) and L2 using COMP()
14        return permutation of positions on y corresponding to L
```

```
COMP(i, j)
if i mod 3 = 0 then
      if (y[i], s[i + 1]) < (y[j], s[j + 1]) then
            return −1
      else return 1
else  u ← first2(y[i . . n − 1])
      v ← first2(y[j . . n − 1])
      if (u, s[i + 2]) < (v, s[j + 2]) then
            return −1
      else return 1
```

i	0	1	2	3	4	5	6	7	8	9	10
$y[i]$	a	a	b	a	a	b	a	a	b	b	a

$P_{01} = \{0, 1, 3, 4, 6, 7, 9, 10\}$
$P_2 = \{2, 5, 8\}$

	$i \bmod 3 = 0$				$i \bmod 3 = 1$			
i	0	3	6	9	1	4	7	10
$first_3(y[i \mathinner{..} n-1])$	aab	aab	aab	ba	aba	aba	abb	a
$t[i]$	1	1	1	4	2	2	3	0

$z = 1\,1\,1\,4\,2\,2\,3\,0$ and $L_{01} = (10, 0, 3, 6, 1, 4, 7, 9)$

$s[i]$	1	2	3	7	4	5	6	0

	$i \bmod 3 = 2$		
j	2	5	8
$(y[j], s[j+1])$	(b, 2)	(b, 3)	(b, 7)

$L_2 = (2, 5, 8)$

	$i \bmod 3 = 0$ or $i \bmod 3 = 1$								$i \bmod 3 = 2$		
i	10	0	3	6	1	4	7	9	2	5	8
$(u, s[i+2])$	(a, −1)				(ab, 2)	(ab, 3)	(ab, 7)		(ba, 5)		
$(y[i], s[i+1])$		(a, 4)	(a, 5)	(a, 6)				(b, 0)	(b, 2)		

i	0	1	2	3	4	5	6	7	8	9	10
$p[i]$	10	0	3	6	1	4	7	9	2	5	8

Figure 4.8. **(a)** String $y =$ aabaabaabba (see Figure 4.7) and its two sets of positions P_{01} and P_2. **(b)** Step 1. Strings $first_3(y[i \mathinner{..} n-1])$ for $i \in P_{01}$ and their ranks: $t[i]$ is the rank of i in the sorted list. Note that the rank 4 of position 9 is unique. **(c)** Step 2. Positions in P_{01} sorted according to their associated suffixes in z, resulting in L_{01} and the table of ranks s. **(d)** Step 3. Positions j in P_2 sorted according to pairs $(y[j], s[j+1])$ resulting in L_2. **(e)** Step 4. Pairs used for comparing positions when merging the sorted lists L_{01} and L_2 (u is $first_2(y[i \mathinner{..} n-1])$). Here, position 2 is compared to all positions in P_{01}; positions 5 and 8 are not compared to any. **(f)** Permutation p corresponding to the sorted suffixes of y.

Proposition 4.11
The algorithm SKEW-SUFFIX-SORT *applied to a string of length n runs in time* $O(n)$.

Proof The recursion of the algorithm (line 8) yields the recurrence relation $T(n) = T(2n/3) + O(n)$ with $T(n) = O(1)$ for $n \leq 3$ because all other lines

(a)

i	0	1	2	3	4	5	6	7	8
$y[i]$	a	b	a	a	a	a	a	a	a

$P_{01} = \{0, 1, 3, 4, 6, 7, 9\}$
$P_2 = \{2, 5, 8\}$

(b)

	$i \bmod 3 = 0$				$i \bmod 3 = 1$		
i	0	3	6	9	1	4	7
$\mathit{first}_3(y[i\,..\,n-1])$	aba	aaa	aaa	ε	baa	aaa	aa
$t[i]$	3	2	2	0	4	2	1

(c)

$z = 3\,2\,2\,0\,4\,2\,1$ and $L_{01} = (9, 7, 6, 4, 3, 0, 1)$

$s[i]$	5	4	2	0	6	3	1

(d)

	$i \bmod 3 = 2$		
j	2	5	8
$(y[j], s[j+1])$	(a, 4)	(a, 2)	(a, 0)

$L_2 = (8, 5, 2)$

(e)

	$i \bmod 3 = 0$ or $i \bmod 3 = 1$						$i \bmod 3 = 2$		
i	7	6	4	3	0	1	8	5	2
$(u, s[i+2])$	(aa, 0)		(aa, 2)				(a, −1)	(aa, 1)	
$(y[i], s[i+1])$		(a, 1)		(a, 3)	(a, 6)			(a, 2)	(a, 4)

(f)

i	0	1	2	3	4	5	6	7	8
$p[i]$	8	7	6	5	4	3	2	0	1

Figure 4.9. **(a)** String $y =$ abaaaaaaa and its two sets of positions P_{01} and P_2. Position 9 is in P_{01} because $|y|$ is a multiple of 3. **(b)** Step 1. Strings $\mathit{first}_3(y[i\,..\,n-1])$ for $i \in P_{01}$ and their ranks: $t[i]$ is the rank of i in the sorted list. Note that the rank 0 of position 9 is unique. Without position 9 this condition would not hold for position 6. **(c)** Step 2. Positions in P_{01} sorted according to their associated suffixes in z, resulting in L_{01} and the table of ranks s. **(d)** Step 3. Positions j in P_2 sorted according to pairs $(y[j], s[j+1])$ resulting in L_2. **(e)** Step 4. Pairs used for comparing positions when merging the sorted lists L_{01} and L_2 (u is $\mathit{first}_2(y[i\,..\,n-1])$). **(f)** Permutation p corresponding to the sorted suffixes of y.

execute in constant time or in $O(n)$ time. The recurrence has solution $T(n) = O(n)$, which gives the result. ■

The crucial point in the correctness proof of the algorithm is to show that the sorted list of suffixes of z transposes to a sorted list of the corresponding suffixes of y. This is the subject of the next lemma.

Lemma 4.12

Using the notation of the algorithm, let z_0 and z_1 be such that $z = z_0 z_1$ with $z_0 = t[0]t[3]\cdots t[3k]\cdots$ and $z_1 = t[1]t[4]\cdots t[3k+1]\cdots$. Let i'_0 and i'_1 be two positions on z. Let

$$i_0 = \begin{cases} 3 \times i'_0 & \text{if } i'_0 < \lfloor n/3 \rfloor + 1, \\ 3 \times i'_0 + 1 & \text{otherwise,} \end{cases}$$

and let

$$i_1 = \begin{cases} 3 \times i'_1 & \text{if } i'_1 < \lfloor n/3 \rfloor + 1, \\ 3 \times i'_1 + 1 & \text{otherwise.} \end{cases}$$

If $z[i'_0 \mathinner{..} |z|-1] < z[i'_1 \mathinner{..} |z|-1]$ then $y[i_0 \mathinner{..} n-1] < y[i_1 \mathinner{..} n-1]$.

Proof Let us recall that $|z_0| = \text{card}\, P_{01} \cap \{i : i \bmod 3 = 0\} = \lfloor n/3 \rfloor + 1$. First, note that the last letter of z_0, $z[\lfloor n/3 \rfloor]$, is unique because it corresponds to a unique factor of length 1 or 2 of y when $n \bmod 3 \neq 0$, and to the empty string otherwise due to line 5.

We assume that $z[i'_0 \mathinner{..} |z|-1] < z[i'_1 \mathinner{..} |z|-1]$ and we consider the length ℓ of their longest common prefix. The uniqueness of $z[\lfloor n/3 \rfloor]$ implies that this letter can appear in only one of the two words $z[i'_0 \mathinner{..} i'_0+\ell]$ and $z[i'_1 \mathinner{..} i'_1+\ell]$, and only as the last letter of it. Then each string is a factor of either z_0 or z_1 (none of them overlap the frontier between z_0 and z_1 in z). Therefore, as letters of z_0 and of z_1 are associated with consecutive factors of length 3 of y, they both correspond to factors of y at respective positions i_0 and i_1. The assumption implies the inequality $z[i'_0 \mathinner{..} i'_0+\ell] < z[i'_1 \mathinner{..} i'_1+\ell]$, which transfers to their corresponding factors in y and eventually to the suffixes $y[i_0 \mathinner{..} n-1] < y[i_1 \mathinner{..} n-1]$. Which proves the lemma. ■

Theorem 4.13

The algorithm Skew-suffix-sort *sorts the suffixes of a string of length n in time $O(n)$.*

Proof The correctness of the algorithm is essentially a consequence of Lemma 4.12. The bound of the running time comes from Proposition 4.11. ■

4.6 Common prefixes of the suffixes

In this section, we describe the second element that constitutes a suffix array of a text: the table of lengths of the longest common prefixes of its suffixes. These data complete the permutation of suffixes studied in the two previous sections, and allow the utilization of algorithms Search and Interval of Section 4.2.

(a)

i	0	1	2	3	4	5	6	7	8	9	10	11
$y[i]$	a	a	b	a	a	b	a	a	b	b	a	
$p[i]$	10	0	3	6	1	4	7	9	2	5	8	
$LCP[i]$	0	1	6	3	1	5	2	0	2	4	1	0

(b)

i	12	13	14	15	16	17	18	19	20	21	22
$LCP[i]$	0	1	0	1	1	0	0	0	0	0	0

Figure 4.10. Suffix array of the string $y = \texttt{aabaabaabba}$ composed of tables p and LCP. **(a)** Table p gives the list of suffixes in increasing lexicographic order: the first suffix starts at position 10, the second at position 0, etc. Table LCP contains the lengths of the longest common prefixes. For example, $LCP[6] = 2$ because $p[6] = 7$, $p[5] = 4$, and $|lcp(y[7\,..\,10], y[4\,..\,10])| = |\texttt{ab}| = 2$. **(b)** Other values of the LCP table corresponding to pairs of nonconsecutive positions of the binary search. For example, $LCP[15] = 1$ because $15 = 12 + \lfloor(2+5)/2\rfloor$, $p[2] = 3$, $p[5] = 4$, and $|lcp(y[3\,..\,10], y[4\,..\,10])| = |\texttt{a}| = 1$.

The computation of the longest common prefixes goes over the method of Section 4.3, realized by the algorithm LCP-TABLE, adapting it however to reduce its execution time. The algorithm LCP-TABLE applies to a sorted list of strings. The list L that we consider here is the sorted list of the suffixes of y, that is to say,

$$y[p[0]\,..\,n-1],\ y[p[1]\,..\,n-1],\ \ldots,\ y[p[n-1]\,..\,n-1],$$

where p is the permutation computed by the algorithm SUFFIX-SORT or the algorithm SKEW-SUFFIX-SORT and that satisfies Condition (4.1):

$$y[p[0]\,..\,n-1] < y[p[1]\,..\,n-1] < \cdots < y[p[n-1]\,..\,n-1].$$

The definition of the LCP table adapted to the sorted list of suffixes of y is

- $LCP[i] = |lcp(y[p[i]\,..\,n-1], y[p[i-1]\,..\,n-1])|$, for $0 \le i \le n$,
- $LCP[n+1+i] = |lcp(y[p[d]\,..\,n-1], y[p[f]\,..\,n-1])|$, for $i = \lfloor(d+f)/2\rfloor$ middle of a segment (d, f), $0 \le d+1 < f \le n$, of the binary search tree.

The goal of this section is to show how we can compute the table LCP associated with the list L as in Section 4.3. Figure 4.10 illustrates the expected result for the string aabaabaabba.

The direct utilization of LCP-TABLE (Section 4.3) to perform the computation leads to an execution time $O(n^2)$ since the sum of the suffix lengths is quadratic. We describe an algorithm, LCP-TABLE-SUFF, that do it in linear time. The modification of LCP-TABLE lies in an optimization of the computation of the longest common prefix of two suffixes that are consecutive in the lexicographic order. In LCP-TABLE (line 5) the computation is supposed to

```
(a)  2   b a a b a a b b a
     9   b a

(b)  3     a a b a a b b a
     0     a a b a a b a a b b a

(c)  4       a b a a b b a
     1       a b a a b a a b b a
```

Figure 4.11. Illustration of Lemma 4.14 on the string $y = \texttt{aabaabaabba}$ of Figure 4.10. We consider the longest common prefixes between the suffixes at positions 2, 3, and 4 and their predecessors in the lexicographic order. **(a)** $p[8] = 2$, $p[7] = 9$, and $LCP[8] = |lcp(y[2\,..\,10], y[9\,..\,10])| = 2$. **(b)** With the notation of the lemma, choosing $j = 3$ we get $i = 2$ since $p[2] = 3$, and $i' = 8$ since $p[8] = 3 - 1 = 2$. In this case $LCP[2] = |lcp(y[3\,..\,10], y[0\,..\,10])| = 6$, quantity that is greater than $LCP[8] - 1 = 1$. **(c)** Choosing $j = 4$ we get $i = 5$ since $p[5] = 4$, and $i' = 2$ since $p[2] = 4 - 1 = 3$. We have $LCP[5] = |lcp(y[4\,..\,10], y[1\,..\,10])| = 5$. In this case, we have the equality $LCP[5] = LCP[2] - 1$.

be done by straight letter comparisons that start from scratch for each pair of strings. Besides, it is difficult to proceed in another way without other information on the strings of the list. The situation is different for the suffixes of y since they are not independent of each others. The dependence allows to reduce the computation time by means of a quite simple algorithm, based on the following lemma illustrated by Figure 4.11.

Lemma 4.14
Let i, i', j be positions on y for which $p[i'] = j - 1$ and $p[i] = j$. Then $LCP[i'] - 1 \leq LCP[i]$.

Proof Let u be the longest common prefix between $y[j - 1\,..\,n - 1]$ and its predecessor in the lexicographic order, let us say $y[k\,..\,n - 1]$. We have $LCP[i'] = |u|$ by the definition of i'.

If u is the empty string the result is satisfied since $LCP[i] \geq 0$. Otherwise, u can be written cv where $c = y[j - 1]$ and $v \in A^*$. The string $y[j - 1\,..\,n - 1]$ admits then for prefix cvb for some letter b, and its predecessor admits for prefix cva for some letter a such that $a < b$, unless the predecessor is equal to cv.

Therefore, v is a common prefix between $y[j\,..\,n - 1]$ and $y[k + 1\,..\,n - 1]$. Moreover, $y[k + 1\,..\,n - 1]$, that starts by va or is equal to v, is smaller than $y[j\,..\,n - 1]$ that starts by vb. Thus $LCP[i]$, which is the maximal length of the prefixes common to $y[j\,..\,n - 1]$ and its predecessor in the lexicographic order cannot be less than $|u|$ (consequence of Lemma 4.6). We thus have $LCP[i] \geq |v| = |u| - 1 = LCP[i'] - 1$, which gives the result also when u is nonempty. ∎

Using the previous lemma, in order to compute $LCP[i]$ when $0 < i \leq n$, that is to say, to compute $|lcp(y[p[i]\,..\,n-1], y[p[i-1]\,..\,n-1])|$, we can start the letter comparisons exactly at the position where the previous computation stopped, position $LCP[i']$. Proceeding that way, it is sufficient to consider the suffixes from the longest to the shortest, and not in the lexicographic order despite this seems more natural. This is what is realized by the algorithm DEF-HALF-LCP that computes the values $LCP[i]$ for $0 \leq i \leq n$. Other values of the table may be determined with the algorithm LCP-TABLE-SUFF thereafter. Note that to determine the position i associated with position j, the algorithm DEF-HALF-LCP utilizes the inverse of the permutation p which is computed in a first step (lines 1–2). This function is represented by the table denoted by R. Indeed, it indicates the rank of each suffix in the sorted list of suffixes of y. The second step of the algorithm applies Lemma 4.14.

```
DEF-HALF-LCP(y, n, p)
 1  for i ← 0 to n − 1 do
 2       R[p[i]] ← i
 3  ℓ ← 0
 4  for j ← 0 to n − 1 do
 5       ℓ ← max{0, ℓ − 1}
 6       i ← R[j]
 7       if i ≠ 0 then
 8            j′ ← p[i − 1]
 9            while j + ℓ < n and j′ + ℓ < n
                 and y[j + ℓ] = y[j′ + ℓ] do
10                 ℓ ← ℓ + 1
11       else ℓ ← 0      ▷ optional instruction
12       LCP[i] ← ℓ
13  LCP[n] ← 0
```

Proposition 4.15
Applied to string y of length n and to the permutation p of its suffixes, the algorithm DEF-HALF-LCP *computes $LCP[i]$ for all positions i, $0 \leq i \leq n$, in time $O(n)$.*

Proof Let us first consider the execution of instructions in lines 5–12 for $j = 0$. If $i = 0$ in line 7, the value of ℓ is null and it is by definition the one of $LCP[i]$ since y is its own minimal suffix. Otherwise, as $\ell = 0$ before the execution of the **while** loop, just after, we have $\ell = |lcp(y[0\,..\,n-1], y[j'\,..\,n-1])|$. After the computation of the table R performed in lines 1–2, and as p is bijective, we have $p[i] = 0$. And after line 8, we have also $j' = p[i-1]$.

Thus, the value of ℓ is indeed the one of $LCP[i]$, that is, $|lcp(y[p[i]\,..\,n-1], y[p[i-1]\,..\,n-1])|$.

Let us consider then a position j, $0 < j < n$. If $i = 0$, the argument used previously is also valid here since $y[j\,..\,n-1]$ is then the minimal suffix of y. Let us assume now that $i = R[j]$ is non-null, thus, $i > 0$. By definition $LCP[i] = |lcp(y[p[i]\,..\,n-1], y[p[i-1]\,..\,n-1])|$ and thus, after the equality $j = p[i]$ and the value of j' computed in line 8, $LCP[i] = |lcp(y[j\,..\,n-1], y[j'\,..\,n-1])|$. The comparisons performed during the execution of the **while** loop computes thus the maximal length of the prefixes common to $y[j\,..\,n-1]$ and $y[j'\,..\,n-1]$ from the position ℓ on $y[j\,..\,n-1]$ (i.e., from position $j+\ell$ on y) by application of Lemma 4.14. The result is correct provided that the initial value of ℓ at this step is equal to $LCP[i']$ for the position i' such that $p[i'] = j-1$. But this comes from an iterative argument that starts with the validity of the computation for $j = 0$ that is shown above.

Finally, the value of $LCP[n]$ is correctly computed in line 13 since this one is null by definition.

Most of the instructions of the algorithm execute once for each of the n values of i or of j. It remains to check that the execution time of the **while** loop is also $O(n)$. This comes from the fact that each positive comparison of letters in line 9 increases by one unit the value of $j+\ell$ that never decreases afterwards, and that these values run from 0 to at most n. This ends the proof. ■

Let us note that the instruction of line 11 of the algorithm DEF-HALF-LCP is optional. We can prove this remark by an argument analogue to the one used in the proof of Lemma 4.14 and by noting that $y[j\,..\,n-1]$ is the minimal suffix of y in this situation.

The algorithm LCP-TABLE-SUFF below completes the computation of the table LCP (values $LCP[i]$ for $n+1 \le i \le 2n$). It applies to the table LCP partially computed by the previous algorithm. With respect to the algorithm LCP-TABLE, lines 3–5 are deleted since the considered value of $LCP[f]$ is already known. For lightening the writing of the algorithm, the permutation p is extended by setting $p[-1] = -1$ and $p[n] = n$.

```
LCP-TABLE-SUFF(d, f)
  ▷ We have d < f
  if d + 1 = f then
        return LCP[f]          ▷ already computed by DEF-HALF-LCP
  else i ← ⌊(d + f)/2⌋
        LCP[n + 1 + i] ← min { LCP-TABLE-SUFF(d, i)
                              { LCP-TABLE-SUFF(i, f)
        return LCP[n + 1 + i]
```

Proposition 4.16
The successive executions of DEF-HALF-LPC(y, n, p) *and of* LCP-TABLE-SUFF$(-1, n)$ *applied to the increasing list of suffixes of the string* y *of length* n *produce the table of their common prefixes, LCP, in time* $O(n)$.

Proof The correctness of the computation relies on the validity of DEF-HALF-LCP (Proposition 4.15) and on the validity of LCP-TABLE-SUFF (Lemma 4.6).

The running time of DEF-HALF-LPC(y, n, p) is linear after Proposition 4.15. Except for the recursive calls, the execution of LCP-TABLE-SUFF(d, f) takes a constant time for each pair (d, f). As there are $2n + 1$ pairs of this kind (Lemma 4.1) we still get a linear time for the total execution, which gives the announced result. ∎

With this section ends the presentation of algorithms for building a suffix array, data structure that is a basis for implementing a text index (see Chapter 6).

Notes

The suffix array of a string, as well as the associated searching algorithm based on the knowledge of the longest common prefixes (Section 4.2), is from Manber and Myers [182]. It gives a method for the realization of indexes (see Chapter 6) which, without being optimal, is rather light to implement and memory space economical compared to the structures of Chapter 5.

The suffix sorting presented in Section 4.4 is a variation on a process introduced by Karp, Miller, and Rosenberg [165]. This technique, called naming, that essentially includes the utilization of the rank functions and the Doubling Lemma, was one of the first efficient methods for computing repeats and for matching patterns in textual data. The naming adapts also to nonsequential data, like images and trees.

The algorithm SKEW-SUFFIX-SORT of Section 4.5 is from Kärkkäinen and Sanders [164]. Two other sorting methods having the same performance are from Kim, Sim, Park, and Park [169], and from Ko and Aluru [171].

The method used in Section 4.6 to compute the common prefixes to the sorted suffixes is from Kasai, Lee, Arimura, Arikawa, and Park [167]. Chapter 9 presents another procedure for preparing a suffix array that is closer to the method originally proposed by Manber and Myers.

The inverse problem related to the sorted suffixes of a string is to construct a string on the smallest possible alphabet, whose permutation of suffixes p is a given permutation of the integer $0, 1, \ldots, n-1$. A linear-time solution is given by Bannai, Inenaga, Shinohara, and Takeda in [100].

Of course, it is possible to build a suffix array by using one of the data structures developed in the next chapter. But doing so we lose a part of the advantages of the method since the structures have more greedy memory requirements. Besides, the suffix array can also be viewed as a particular implementation of the suffix tree of the next chapter.

Exercises

4.1 (All the common prefixes)

Let L be a sorted list of n strings, $L_0 \leq L_1 \leq \cdots \leq L_{n-1}$, of common length n. Describe an algorithm for computing the values $|lcp(L_i, L_j)|$, $0 \leq i, j < n$ and $i \neq j$, that runs in (optimal) time $O(n^2)$.

4.2 (Save memory)

Study the possibility of reducing the space necessary for storing the table *LCP* without changing the running time bounds of the algorithms that use or compute the table.

4.3 (Cheat)

Describe the computation of tables p and *LCP* by means of one of the automaton structures of the next chapter, suffix tree or suffix automaton. What are the time and space complexities of your algorithm? What become these values when the alphabet is fixed? Show that, in particular in this latter situation, the construction of the tables can be done in linear time.

4.4 (Tst !)

Let $X = \langle x_0, x_1, \ldots, x_{k-1} \rangle$ be a sequence of k pairwise distinct strings on the alphabet A, provided with an ordering. Denoting by $a = x_0[0]$ the first letter of x_0, we define L as the subsequence of strings of X that start with a letter smaller than a, and R as the subsequence of strings that start with a letter greater than a. Moreover, we denote by $C = \langle u_0, u_1, \ldots, u_{\ell-1} \rangle$ the sequence for which $\langle au_0, au_1, \ldots, au_{\ell-1} \rangle$ is the subsequence of all the strings of X that start with the letter a.

The ternary search tree associated with X and denoted by $\mathcal{A}(X)$ is the structure T defined as follows:

$$T = \begin{cases} \text{empty} & \text{if } k = 0, \\ \langle t \rangle & \text{if } k = 1, \\ \langle t, \ell(T), (a, c(T)), r(R) \rangle & \text{otherwise,} \end{cases}$$

where t is the root of T; $\ell(T)$, its left subtree, is $\mathcal{A}(L)$; $c(T)$, its central subtree, is $\mathcal{A}(C)$; and $r(T)$, its right subtree, is $\mathcal{A}(R)$. The leaves of the tree are labeled by strings: in the previous definition, if $k = 1$, the tree consists of a single leaf t whose label is the string x_0. We note that $T = \mathcal{A}(X)$ is a ternary tree, and that the link between its root and the root of its central subtree bears the label $a = x_0[0]$, first letter of the first string of X.

Design algorithms for the management of ternary search trees (search, insertion, deletion, ...). Evaluate the complexity of the operations. (*Hint:* see the *Ternary Search Trees* of Bentley and Sedgewick [103, 104].)

4.5 (On average)

Show that the mean length of the longest prefixes common to the suffixes of a string y is $O(\log |y|)$. What can we deduce on the average time of the search for x in y with the suffix array of y? What can we deduce on the average times for sorting the suffixes and for computing the common prefixes by the algorithms of Sections 4.4 and 4.6?

4.6 (Doubling of images)

Adapt the function $first_k$ on images (matrices of letters) and prove a corresponding Doubling Lemma.

4.7 (Image suffixes)

Introduce an ordering on images that enables to use the methodology presented in this chapter.

4.8 (Small difference, big consequence)

Run the example of Figure 4.9 with the algorithm SKEW-SUFFIX-SORT but without executing line 5. Do you get the correct answer?

4.9 (Optional)

Show that the instruction of line 11 of the algorithm DEF-HALF-LCP can be deleted without altering neither the algorithm correctness nor its execution time.

4.10 (LCP)

Let y be a nonempty string of length n, and let $y[j \mathinner{..} n-1]$ be its lexicographically minimal nonempty suffix. Let k be an integer and assume that $0 < k \le j$. Let i be such $p[i] = j - k$.

Show that $LCP[i] \le k$. In addition, show that if $LCP[i] = k$ then both $y[j-k \mathinner{..} j-1] = y[n-k \mathinner{..} n-1]$ and $y[n-k \mathinner{..} n-1]$ immediately precedes $y[j-k \mathinner{..} n-1]$ in the sorted list of suffixes.

5
Structures for indexes

In this chapter, we present data structures for storing the suffixes of a text. These structures are conceived for providing a direct and fast access to the factors of the text. They allow to work on the factors of the string in almost the same way as the suffix array of Chapter 4 does, but the more important part of the technique is put on the structuring of data rather than on algorithms to search the text.

The main application of these techniques is to provide the basis of an index implementation as described in Chapter 6. The direct access to the factors of a string allows a large number of other applications. In particular, the structures can be used for matching patterns by considering them as search machines (see Chapter 6).

Two types of objects are considered in this chapter, trees and automata, together with their compact versions. Trees have for effect to factorize the prefixes of the strings in the set. Automata additionally factorize their common suffixes. The structures are presented in decreasing order of size.

The representation of the suffixes of a string by a trie (Section 5.1) has the advantage to be simple but can lead to a quadratic memory space according to the length of the considered string. The (compact) suffix tree (Section 5.2) avoids this drawback and admits a linear memory space implementation.

The minimization (in the sense of automata) of the suffix trie gives the minimal suffix automaton described in Section 5.4. Compaction and minimization together give the compact suffix automaton of Section 5.5.

Most of the construction algorithms presented in this chapter run in time $O(n \times \log \operatorname{card} A)$ on a text of length n assuming that the alphabet is provided with an ordering relation. Their running time is thus linear when the alphabet is finite and fixed.

5.1 Suffix trie

The ***suffix trie*** of a string is the deterministic automaton that recognizes the set of suffixes of the string and in which two different paths of same source always have distinct ends. Thus, the underlying graph structure of the automaton is a tree whose arcs are labeled by letters. The methods of Section 1.4 can be used for the implementation of these automata. However, the tree structure allows a simplified representation.

Considering a tree implies that the terminal states of the tree are in one-to-one correspondence with the strings of the recognized language. The tree is thus finite only if its language is. As a consequence, the explicit representation of such a tree has an algorithmic interest only for finite languages.

Sometimes one imposes trees to only have terminal states on external nodes of the tree (leaves). With this constraint, a language L is representable by a tree only if no proper prefix of a string of L is in L. It results from this remark that if y is a nonempty string, only $\text{Suff}(y) \setminus \{\varepsilon\}$ is representable by a tree possessing this property, and this only happens when the last letter of y occurs only once in y. This is the reason why one sometimes adds a special letter at the end of the string. We prefer to assign an output to nodes of the trie, which fits better with the notion of automaton. Only nodes whose output is defined are considered as terminal nodes. Besides, there are just a few differences between the implementations of the two structures.

The suffix trie of a string y is the tree $\mathcal{T}(\text{Suff}(y))$ with the notation of Section 2.1. Its nodes are the factors of y, ε is the initial state, and the suffixes of y are the terminal states. The transition function δ of $\mathcal{T}(\text{Suff}(y))$ is defined by $\delta(u, a) = ua$ if ua is a factor of y and $a \in A$. The output of a terminal state, which is then a suffix, is the position of this suffix in y. By convention, the initial state (the root) is assigned the length of the string as output. An example of automaton is presented in Figure 5.1.

The construction of $\mathcal{T}(\text{Suff}(y))$ is generally performed by successively adding the suffixes of y in the tree, starting from the longest suffix, y itself, to the shortest one, the empty string.

The current situation consists in inserting the suffix at position i, $y[i\,..\,n-1]$, in the structure that already contains all the longer suffixes. We call ***head*** of the current suffix its longest prefix common to a suffix occurring at a smaller position. It is also the longest prefix of $y[i\,..\,n-1]$ which is the label of a path of the automaton exiting the initial state. The end state of this path is called a fork (two paths diverge from this state). If $y[i\,..\,k-1]$ is the

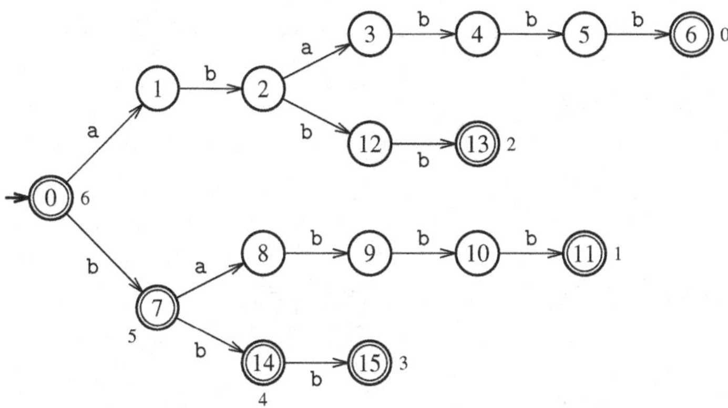

Figure 5.1. Suffix trie of the string ababbb, $\mathcal{T}$(Suff(ababbb)). With each terminal state – double circled – is associated an output which is the position of the suffix in the string ababbb.

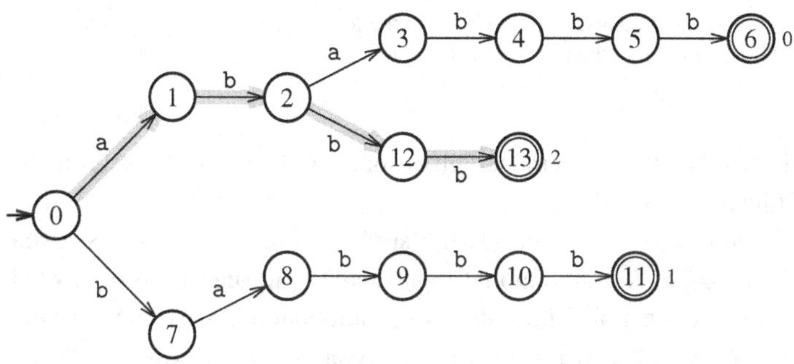

Figure 5.2. The trie $\mathcal{T}$(Suff(ababbb)) (see Figure 5.1) during its construction, just after the insertion of the suffix abbb. The fork, state 2, corresponds to the head ab of this suffix. It is the longest prefix of abbb occurring before the position of the current suffix. The tail of the suffix is bb, label of the path grafted from the fork at this step of the construction.

head of the suffix at position i, the string $y[k \,..\, n-1]$ is called the ***tail*** of the suffix. Figure 5.2 illustrates these notions.

More precisely, we call ***fork*** of the automaton every state that is of (outgoing) degree at least 2, or that is both of degree 1 and a terminal state. A fork corresponds to at least one of the longest common prefixes of the suffix array of

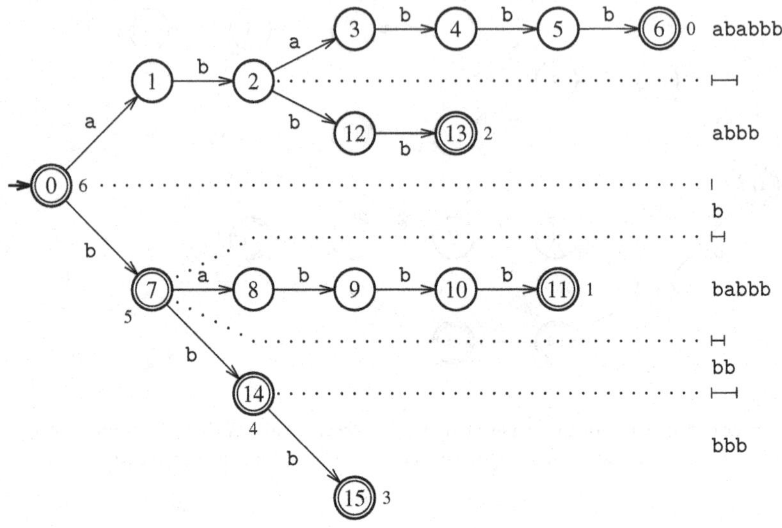

Figure 5.3. Correspondence between the forks of the suffix trie $\mathcal{T}$(Suff(ababbb)) and the longest prefixes common to consecutive suffixes in the lexicographic order. The number of forks is 4, and it is always less than n for a string of length n.

the string. Its depth in the trie is the length of some or several common prefixes. Figure 5.3 illustrates the relation.

The algorithm SUFFIX-TRIE builds the suffix trie of y. Its code is given below. We assume that the automaton is represented by means of sets of labeled successors (see Section 1.4). The states of the automaton possess the attribute *output* which value, when it is defined, is a position on the string y. When the function NEW-STATE() creates a new state, the value of the attribute is undefined. Only the output of a terminal state is defined by the algorithm. The insertion of the current suffix $y[i \, . \, . \, n-1]$ in the automaton, denoted by M, starts by the determination of its head $y[i \, . \, . \, k-1]$, and of the associated fork $p = \delta(\mathit{initial}[M], y[i \, . \, . \, k-1])$, from which we have to connect the tail of the suffix (δ is the transition function of M). The value returned by the function SLOW-FIND-ONE applied to the pair $(\mathit{initial}[M], i)$ is precisely the searched pair (p, k). Creating the path of origin p and of label $y[k \, . \, . \, n-1]$ together with the definition of the output of its end is realized in lines 5–9 of the code.

The end of the execution of the algorithm, that is to say the insertion of the empty suffix, consists just in defining the output of the initial state, whose value is $n = |y|$ by definition (line 10).

```
SUFFIX-TRIE(y, n)
 1  M ← NEW-AUTOMATON()
 2  for i ← 0 to n − 1 do
 3      (fork, k) ← SLOW-FIND-ONE(initial[M], i)
 4      p ← fork
 5      for j ← k to n − 1 do
 6          q ← NEW-STATE()
 7          Succ[p] ← Succ[p] ∪ {(y[j], q)}
 8          p ← q
 9      output[p] ← i
10  output[initial[M]] ← n
11  return M
```

```
SLOW-FIND-ONE(p, k)
 1  while k < n and TARGET(p, y[k]) ≠ NIL do
 2      (p, k) ← (TARGET(p, y[k]), k + 1)
 3  return (p, k)
```

Proposition 5.1
The algorithm SUFFIX-TRIE *builds the suffix trie of a string of length n in time* $\Omega(n^2)$.

Proof The correctness proof can be easily checked on the code of the algorithm.

For the evaluation of the running time, let us consider step i. Let us assume that $y[i\,..\,n-1]$ has for head $y[i\,..\,k-1]$ and for tail $y[k\,..\,n-1]$. We can check that the call to SLOW-FIND-ONE (line 3) executes $k-i$ operations and that the **for** loop of lines 5–8 executes $n-k$ operations, thus a total of $n-i$ operations. Thus the **for** loop of lines 2–9 indexed by i executes $n+(n-1)+\cdots+1$ operations, which gives a total running time $\Omega(n^2)$. ∎

Suffix links

It is possible to speed up the previous construction by improving the search for the forks. The technique described here is taken up in the next section where it leads to a gain in the running time, measurable by the asymptotic bound.

Let av be a suffix of y that has a nonempty head az with $a \in A$. The prefix z of v occurs thus in y before the considered occurrence. This implies that z is a prefix of the head of the suffix v. The search for this head, and for the corresponding fork, can thus be done from the state z instead of systematically starting from the initial state as it is done in the previous algorithm. However,

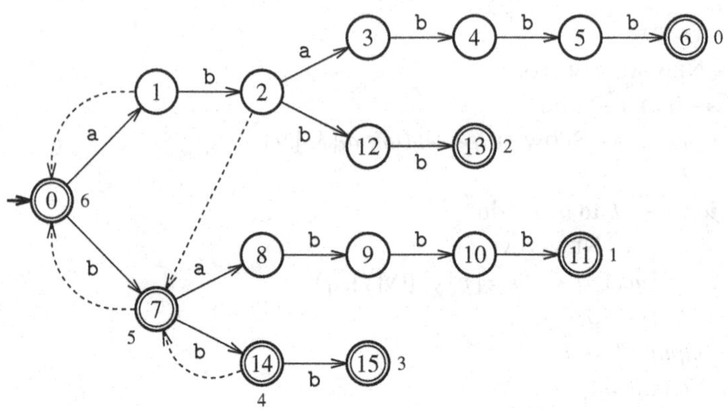

Figure 5.4. The automaton $\mathcal{T}$(Suff(`ababbb`)) with suffix links of the forks and of their ancestors indicated by dashed arrows.

this assumes that, given the state az, we have a fast access to the state z. For this, we introduce a function on the states of the automaton, called ***suffix link***. It is denoted by s and defined by $s(az) = z$ for each state az ($a \in A$, $z \in A^*$). The state $s(az)$ is called the ***suffix target*** of az. Figure 5.4 shows the suffix links of the trie of Figure 5.1.

The algorithm Suffix-trie-bis whose code follows implements and utilizes the suffix link for the computation of the suffix trie of y. The link is realized by means of an attribute, denoted by $s\ell$, for each state; the attribute is supposed to be initially given the value NIL. The suffix targets are effectively computed by the algorithm Slow-find-one-bis below only for the forks and their ancestors (except for the initial state) since the targets of the other nodes are not useful for the construction. The code is a mere adaptation of the algorithm Slow-find-one integrating the definition of the suffix targets.

```
SLOW-FIND-ONE-BIS(p, k)
while k < n and TARGET(p, y[k]) ≠ NIL do
    q ← TARGET(p, y[k])
    (e, f) ← (p, q)
    while e ≠ initial[M] and sℓ[f] = NIL do
        sℓ[f] ← TARGET(sℓ[e], y[k])
        (e, f) ← (sℓ[e], sℓ[f])
    if sℓ[f] = NIL then
        sℓ[f] ← initial[M]
    (p, k) ← (q, k + 1)
return (p, k)
```

```
SUFFIX-TRIE-BIS(y, n)
 1  M ← NEW-AUTOMATON()
 2  sℓ[initial[M]] ← initial[M]
 3  (fork, k) ← (initial[M], 0)
 4  for i ← 0 to n − 1 do
 5      k ← max{k, i}
 6      (fork, k) ← SLOW-FIND-ONE-BIS(sℓ[fork], k)
 7      p ← fork
 8      for j ← k to n − 1 do
 9          q ← NEW-STATE()
10          Succ[p] ← Succ[p] ∪ {(y[j], q)}
11          p ← q
12      output[p] ← i
13  output[initial[M]] ← n
14  return M
```

Proposition 5.2
The algorithm SUFFIX-TRIE-BIS *builds the suffix trie of y in time $\Omega(\text{card } Q)$, where Q is the set of states of $\mathcal{T}(\text{Suff}(y))$.*

Proof The operations of the main loop, except for line 6 and for the **for** loop of lines 8–11, execute in constant time, this gives a time $O(|y|)$ for their global execution.

Each operation of the internal loop of the algorithm SLOW-FIND-ONE-BIS that is called in line 6 has for effect to create a suffix target. The total number of targets being bounded by card Q, the cumulated time of all the executions of line 6 is $O(\text{card } Q)$.

The running time of the loop of lines 8–11 is proportional to the number of states that it creates. The cumulated time of all the executions of lines 8–11 is thus again $O(\text{card } Q)$.

Finally, as $|y| < \text{card } Q$ and card Q states are effectively created, the total time of the construction is $\Omega(\text{card } Q)$ as announced. ∎

The size of $\mathcal{T}(\text{Suff}(y))$ can be quadratic. It is, for instance, the case for a string whose letters are pairwise distinct. For this category of strings the algorithm SUFFIX-TRIE-BIS is actually not faster than SUFFIX-TRIE.

For some strings, it is sufficient to prune the dropping branches (below the forks) of $\mathcal{T}(\text{Suff}(y))$ to get a structure whose size is linear. This kind of pruning gives the position tree of y (an example is shown in Figure 5.5), which represents the shortest factors occurring at a single position in y and the suffixes that identify the other positions. However, the consideration of the position tree

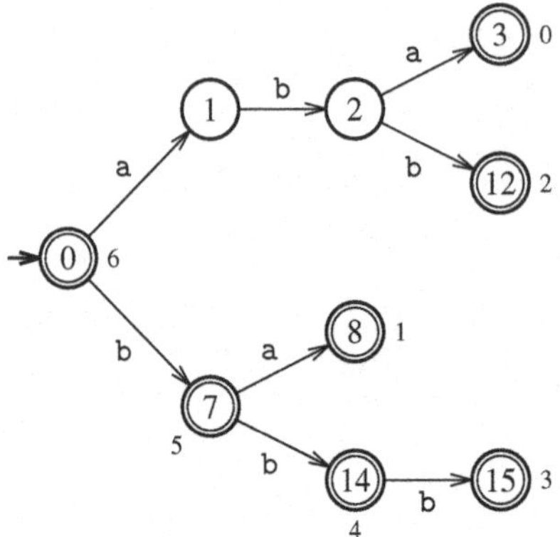

Figure 5.5. Position tree of the string ababbb. It recognizes the shortest factors or suffixes that identify uniquely the positions of the string.

does not totally solves the memory space drawback since this structure can also have a quadratic size. We notice, for instance, that the string $\mathtt{a}^k\mathtt{b}^k\mathtt{a}^k\mathtt{b}^k$ ($k \in \mathbf{N}$) of length $4k$ possesses a pruned suffix trie that contains more than k^2 nodes.

The compact tree of the next section is a solution for obtaining a structure of linear size. The automata of Sections 5.4 and 5.5 provide another type of solution.

5.2 Suffix tree

The ***suffix tree*** of y, denoted by $\mathcal{T}_C(y)$, is obtained by deleting the nodes of degree 1 that are not terminal in its suffix trie $\mathcal{T}(\mathrm{Suff}(y))$. It is what we call the ***compaction*** of the trie. The tree only keeps the forks and the terminal nodes of the suffix trie (note that external nodes are terminal nodes as well). The labels of arcs become then strings of variable positive length. We note that if two arcs exiting a same node are labeled by strings u and v, then their first letters are distinct, that is to say $u[0] \neq v[0]$. This comes from the fact that the suffix trie is a deterministic automaton.

Figure 5.6 shows the suffix tree obtained by compaction of the suffix trie of Figure 5.1. Figure 5.7 presents a suffix tree adapted to the case where the string ends with a special letter.

Proposition 5.3
The suffix tree of a string of length $n > 0$ possesses between $n + 1$ and $2n$ nodes. Its number of forks is between 1 and n.

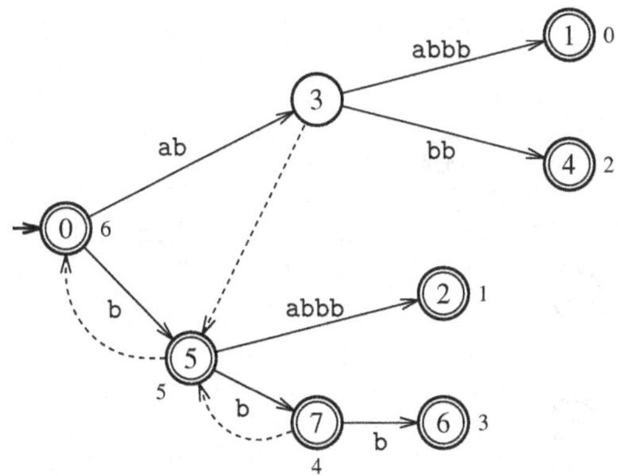

Figure 5.6. The suffix tree $\mathcal{T}_C$(ababbb) with its suffix links.

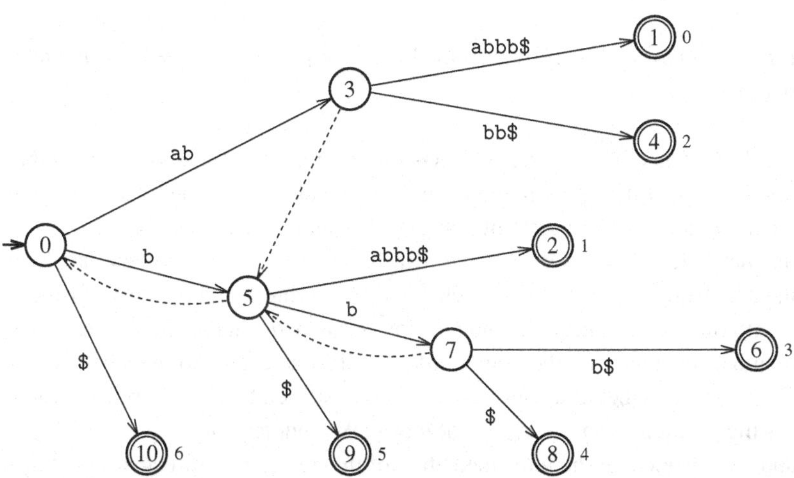

Figure 5.7. Adaptation of the suffix tree for the string ababbb of Figure 5.1 right-end marked with a special letter. Only external nodes are terminal states. They correspond to all the suffixes of the string (without the marker).

Proof The tree contains $n + 1$ distinct terminal nodes corresponding to the $n + 1$ suffixes that it represents. This gives the lower bound.

Each fork of the tree that is not terminal possesses at least two children. For a fixed number of external nodes, the maximal number of these forks is obtained when each of these nodes possesses exactly two children. In this case, we get at most n (terminal or not) forks. As for $n > 0$ the initial state is both a

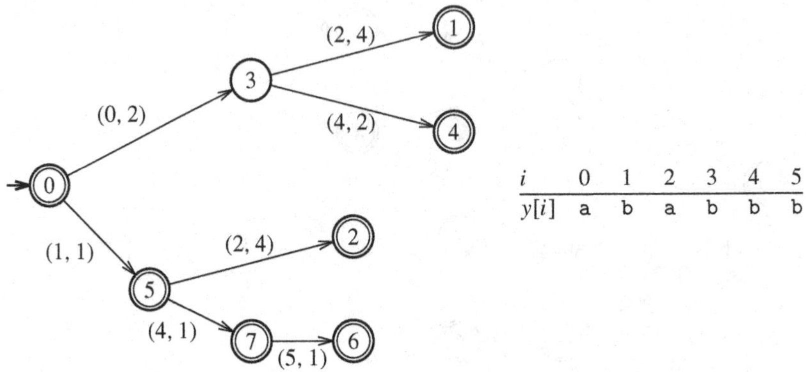

Figure 5.8. Representation of the labels in the suffix tree $\mathcal{T}_C$(ababbb) (see Figure 5.6). For example, the label (2, 4) of the arc (3, 1) represents the factor of length 4 and occurring at position 2 on y, that is, the string abbb.

fork and a terminal node, we get the bound $(n+1)+n-1=2n$ of the total number of nodes. ∎

The fact that the suffix tree of y has a linear number of nodes does not imply the linearity of its representation, since it depends also on the total size of the labels of arcs. The example of a string of length n that possesses n pairwise distinct letters shows that this size can be quadratic. However, the labels of the arcs being all factors of y, each one can be represented by a pair position-length (or also start position-end position), provided that the string y resides in memory together with the tree in order to allow an access to the labels. If the string u is the label of an arc (p, q), it is represented by the pair $(i, |u|)$ where i is the position of an occurrence of u in y. We denote by $label(p, q) = (i, |u|)$ and we assume that the implementation of the tree gives a direct access to this label (in constant time). This representation of labels is illustrated in Figure 5.8 for the tree of Figure 5.6.

Proposition 5.4
When labels of arcs are represented by pairs of integers, the total size of the suffix tree of a string is linear in its length, that is, $O(|y|)$.

Proof The number of nodes of $\mathcal{T}_C(y)$ is $O(|y|)$ after Proposition 5.3. The number of arcs of $\mathcal{T}_C(y)$ is one unit less than the number of nodes. The assumption on the representation of the arcs has for consequence that each arc requires a constant space, which gives the result. ∎

The suffix link introduced in the previous section finds its actual usefulness in the construction of the suffix tree. It allows a fast construction when, in addition, the slow find algorithm of the previous section is replaced by the fast find algorithm thereafter that has an analogue role. The possibility of keeping only the forks of the suffix trie in addition to the terminal states relies on the following lemma. It implies that the suffix links are unchanged by the compaction process.

Proposition 5.5

In the suffix trie of a string, the suffix target of a (nonempty) fork is a fork.

Proof For a nonempty fork, there are two cases to consider whether the fork, let us say au ($a \in A$, $u \in A^*$) is of degree at least 2, or simultaneously of degree 1 and terminal.

Let us assume first that the degree of au is at least 2. For two distinct letters, b and c, aub and auc are factors of y. The same property holds also for $u = s(au)$ that is then of degree at least 2 and is thus a fork.

Now, if the fork au is of degree 1 and is a terminal state, for some letter b the string aub is a factor of y and simultaneously au is a suffix of y. Thus, ub is a factor of y and u is a suffix of y, which shows that $u = s(au)$ is also a fork. ∎

The following property serves as a basis to the computation of the suffix targets in the construction algorithm of the suffix tree, SUFFIX-TREE. We denote by δ the transition function of $\mathcal{T}_C(y)$.

Lemma 5.6

Let (p, q) be an arc of $\mathcal{T}_C(y)$ and $y[j \,..\, k-1]$, $j < k$, its label. When q is a fork of the tree:

$$s(q) = \begin{cases} \delta(p, y[j+1 \,..\, k-1]) & \textit{if } p \textit{ is the initial state,} \\ \delta(s(p), y[j \,..\, k-1]) & \textit{otherwise.} \end{cases}$$

Proof As q is a fork, $s(q)$ is defined after Proposition 5.5. If p is the initial state of the tree, that is to say if $p = \varepsilon$, we have $s(q) = \delta(\varepsilon, y[j+1 \,..\, k-1])$ by definition of s.

In the contrary case, there exists a unique path from the initial state to the state p since $\mathcal{T}_C(y)$ is a tree. Let av be the nonempty label of this path with $a \in A$ and $v \in A^*$ (i.e., $p = av$). We thus have $\delta(\varepsilon, v) = s(p)$ and $\delta(\varepsilon, v \cdot y[j \,..\, k-1]) = s(q)$. It follows that $s(q) = \delta(s(p), y[j \,..\, k-1])$ since the automaton is deterministic, as announced. ∎

The strategy for building the suffix tree of y consists in successively inserting the suffixes of y in the structure, from the longest to the shortest, as done for the construction of the suffix trie in the previous section. As for the algorithm

SUFFIX-TRIE-BIS, the insertion of the tail of the current suffix is done after a slow find process from the suffix target of the current fork.

```
SUFFIX-TREE(y, n)
 1  M ← NEW-AUTOMATON()
 2  sℓ[initial[M]] ← initial[M]
 3  (fork, k) ← (initial[M], 0)
 4  for i ← 0 to n − 1 do
 5      k ← max{k, i}
 6      if sℓ[fork] = NIL then
 7          t ← parent of fork
 8          (j, ℓ) ← label(t, fork)
 9          if t = initial[M] then
10              ℓ ← ℓ − 1
11          sℓ[fork] ← FAST-FIND(sℓ[t], k − ℓ, k)
12      (fork, k) ← SLOW-FIND(sℓ[fork], k)
13      if k < n then
14          q ← NEW-STATE()
15          Succ[fork] ← Succ[fork] ∪ {((k, n − k), q)}
16      else q ← fork
17      output[q] ← i
18  output[initial[M]] ← n
19  return M
```

When this link does not exist, it is created (lines 6–11) using the property of the previous statement. The computation is realized by the algorithm FAST-FIND, that satisfies

$$\text{FAST-FIND}(r, j, k) = \delta(r, y[j\,..\,k-1])$$

for a state r of the tree and positions j, k on y for which

$$r \cdot y[j\,..\,k-1] \preceq_{\text{fact}} y.$$

Line 7, the access to the parent of *fork* must be understood as making explicit the value of t. This one can be recovered by means of a chaining to parent nodes. But we prefer a permanent memorization of the parent of the fork (this can lead to consider an artificial node, parent of the initial state). The schema for the insertion of a suffix inside the tree is presented in Figure 5.9.

The code of the slow find algorithm is adapted with respect to the algorithm SLOW-FIND-ONE for taking into account the fact that labels of arcs are strings. When the searched target falls in the middle of an arc, this arc must be cut. Let us note that TARGET(p, a), if it exists, is the state q for which a is the first

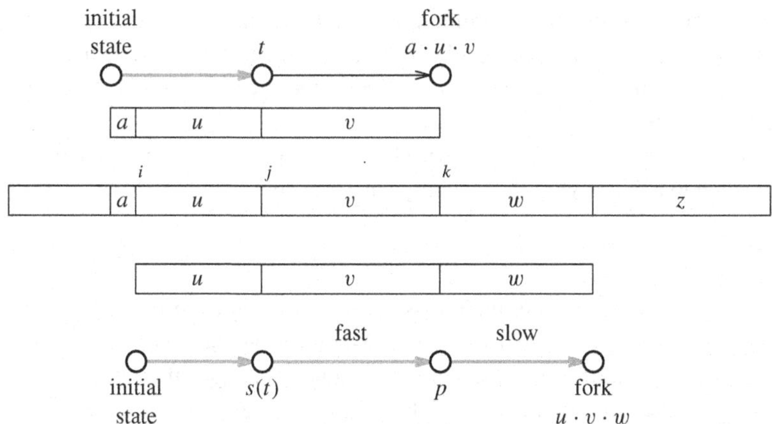

Figure 5.9. Schema for the insertion of the suffix $y[i\,..\,n-1] = u \cdot v \cdot w \cdot z$ in the suffix tree of y during its construction when the suffix link of the fork $a \cdot u \cdot v$ is not defined. Let t be the parent of this fork and v be the label of the associated arc. We first compute $p = \delta(s(t), v)$ by fast find, then the fork of the suffix by slow find as in Section 5.1.

letter of the label of the arc (p, q). Labels can be strings of length greater than 1, therefore we do not have in general $\text{Target}(p, a) = \delta(p, a)$.

```
SLOW-FIND(p, k)
while k < n and TARGET(p, y[k]) ≠ NIL do
      q ← TARGET(p, y[k])
      (j, ℓ) ← label(p, q)
      i ← j
      do   i ← i + 1
           k ← k + 1
      while i < j + ℓ and k < n and y[i] = y[k]
      if i < j + ℓ then
           Succ[p] ← Succ[p] \ {((j, ℓ), q)}
           r ← NEW-STATE()
           Succ[p] ← Succ[p] ∪ {((j, i − j), r)}
           Succ[r] ← Succ[r] ∪ {((i, ℓ − i + j), q)}
           return (r, k)
      p ← q
return (p, k)
```

The improvement on the running time of the computation of a suffix tree by the algorithm SUFFIX-TREE relies, in addition to the compaction of the data structure, on an extra algorithmic element: the implementation of FAST-FIND. The utilization of this particular algorithm described by the code below is essential for obtaining the linear running time of the tree construction algorithm in Theorem 5.9.

The algorithm FAST-FIND is used while computing a fork. It applies to a state r and to a factor $y[j\,..\,k-1]$ only when the condition

$$r \cdot y[j\,..\,k-1] \prec_{\text{fact}} y$$

is satisfied. In this situation, there exists a path starting from the state r and whose label has $y[j\,..\,k-1]$ for prefix. Moreover, as the automaton is deterministic, the shortest of these paths is unique. The algorithm utilizes this property for determining the arcs of the path by a single scan of the first letter of their label. The code below, or at least its main part, implements the recurrence relation given in the proof of Lemma 5.7.

The algorithm FAST-FIND serves more precisely for the evaluation of $\delta(r, y[j \cdot k-1])$ (or $\delta(r, v)$ using the notation of Lemma 5.7). When the end of the scanned path is not the searched state, a new state p is created and takes place between the last two encountered states.

```
FAST-FIND(r, j, k)
 ▷ Computation of δ(r, y[j..k − 1])
 if j ≥ k then
         return r
 else q ← TARGET(r, y[j])
         (j', ℓ) ← label(r, q)
         if j + ℓ ≤ k then
                 return FAST-FIND(q, j + ℓ, k)
         else Succ[r] ← Succ[r] \ {((j', ℓ), q)}
                 p ← NEW-STATE()
                 Succ[r] ← Succ[r] ∪ {((j', k − j), p)}
                 Succ[p] ← Succ[p] ∪ {((j' + k − j, ℓ − k + j), q)}
                 return p
```

Figure 5.10 illustrates how the slow find and fast find algorithms work.

The lemma that follows serves for the evaluation of the running time of FAST-FIND(r, j, k). It is an element of the proof of Theorem 5.9. It indicates that the computation time is proportional (with a multiplicative coefficient that comes from the computation time of transitions) to the number of nodes of the scanned path and not to the length of the label of the path. We would get this result immediately by applying the algorithm SLOW-FIND-ONE (Section 5.1).

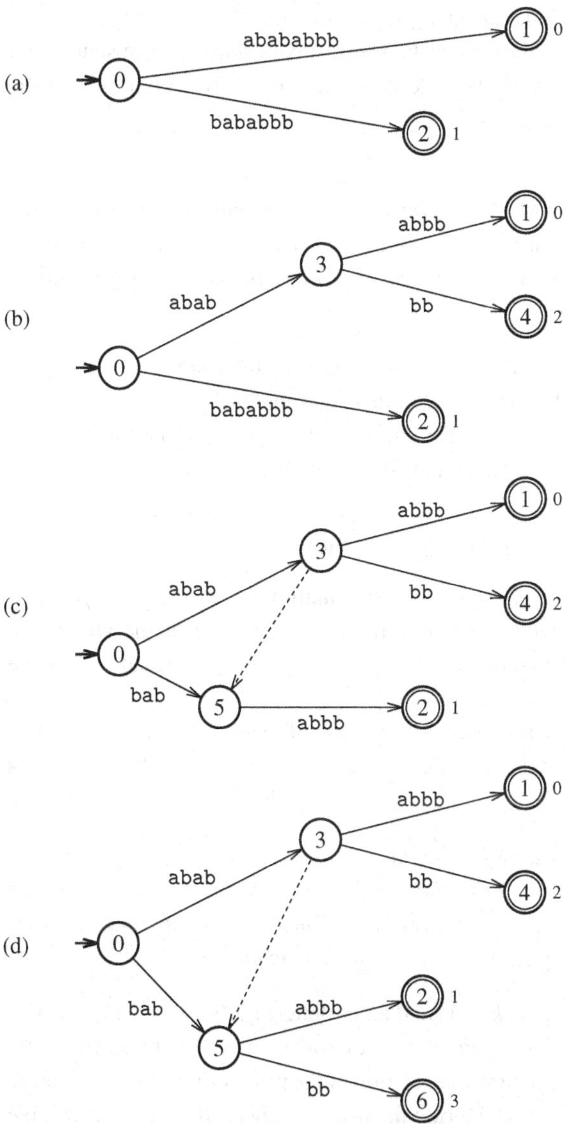

Figure 5.10. During the construction of $\mathcal{T}_{\text{C}}$(`abababbb`), insertion of the suffixes `ababbb` and `babbb`. **(a)** Automaton obtained after the insertion of the suffixes `abababbb` and `bababbb`. The current fork is the initial state 0. **(b)** We add the suffix `ababbb` by straight letter comparisons (slow find) from state 0. This leads to create fork 3. The suffix target of 3 is not yet defined. **(c)** The first step of the insertion of the suffix `babbb` starts with the definition of the suffix target of state 3 that is state 5. We proceed by fast find from state 0 with the string `bab`. **(d)** The second step of the insertion of `babbb` leads to the creation of state 6. State 5, that is the fork of the suffix `babbb`, becomes the current fork for the rest of the insertion.

For a state r of $\mathcal{T}_c(y)$ and a string $v \preceq_{\text{fact}} y$ satisfying the inequality $r \cdot v \preceq_{\text{fact}} y$, we denote by *end*$(r, v)$ the end of the shortest path starting from state r and whose label is prefixed by v. We note that *end*$(r, v) = \delta(r, v)$ only if v is the label of the path.

Lemma 5.7
Let r be a node of $\mathcal{T}_c(y)$ and v be a string for which $r \cdot v \preceq_{\text{fact}} y$. Let $\langle r, r_1, \ldots, r_\ell \rangle$ be the path starting from state r and ending at state $r_\ell = end(r, v)$ in $\mathcal{T}_c(y)$. The computation of end(r, v) can be realized in time $O(\ell \times \log \operatorname{card} A)$ in the comparison model.

Proof We note that the path $\langle r, r_1, \ldots, r_\ell \rangle$ exists by the condition $r \cdot v \preceq_{\text{fact}} y$ and is unique since the tree is a deterministic automaton.

If $v = \varepsilon$, we have *end*$(r, v) = r$. Otherwise, we have $r_1 = \text{TARGET}(r, v[0])$ and let v' be the label of the arc (r, r_1). We notice that

$$end(r, v) = \begin{cases} r_1 & \text{if } |v| \leq |v'| \ (i.e.\ v \preceq_{\text{pref}} v'), \\ end(r_1, v'^{-1}v) & \text{otherwise.} \end{cases}$$

This relation shows that each step of the computation takes a time $\alpha + \beta$ where α is a constant, that includes the time to access the label of the arc (r, r_1), and β is the computation time of $\text{TARGET}(r, v[0])$. It is $O(\log \operatorname{card} A)$ in the comparison model.

The computation of r_ℓ that includes the scan of the path $\langle r, r_1, \ldots, r_\ell \rangle$ thus takes a time $O(\ell \times \log \operatorname{card} A)$ as announced. ■

Corollary 5.8
Let r be a node of $\mathcal{T}_c(y)$ and j, k be the two positions on y, $j < k$, such that $r \cdot y[j\,..\,k-1] \preceq_{\text{fact}} y$. Let ℓ be the number of states of the tree inspected during the computation of FAST-FIND(r, j, k). *Then the running time of* FAST-FIND(r, j, k) *is $O(\ell \times \log \operatorname{card} A)$ in the comparison model.*

Proof Let us set $v = y[j\,..\,k-1]$ and let us denote by $\langle r, r_1, \ldots, r_\ell \rangle$ the path whose end is *end*(r, v). The computation of *end*(r, v) is performed by FAST-FIND that implements the recurrence relation of the proof of Lemma 5.7. It takes thus a time $O(\ell \times \log \operatorname{card} A)$. During the last recursive call, there is a possible creation of the state p and modification of the arcs. This operation takes again the time $O(\log \operatorname{card} A)$, which gives the global time $O(\ell \times \log \operatorname{card} A)$ of the statement. ■

Theorem 5.9
The operation SUFFIX-TREE(y, n), *that produces $\mathcal{T}_c(y)$, takes a time $O(n \times \log \operatorname{card} A)$ in the comparison model.*

Proof The fact that the operation SUFFIX-TREE(y, n) produces the automaton $\mathcal{T}_C(y)$ relies essentially on Lemma 5.6 by checking that the algorithm uses the elementary technique of Section 5.1.

The evaluation of the running time relies on the following observations (see Figure 5.9):

- each step of the computation performed by FAST-FIND, except maybe the last one, leads to the scan of a state and increases strictly the value of $k - \ell$ (j on the figure),
- each step of the computation performed by SLOW-FIND, except maybe the last one, increases strictly the value of k,
- each other instruction of the **for** loop leads to an incrementation of the value of i.

Since the values of the three above-mentioned expressions never decrease, the number of steps executed by FAST-FIND is thus bounded by n, which gives a total $O(n \times \log \operatorname{card} A)$ time for these steps after Corollary 5.8. The same argument holds for the number of steps executed by SLOW-FIND and for the other steps, giving again a time $O(n \times \log \operatorname{card} A)$.

Therefore, we get a total running time $O(n \times \log \operatorname{card} A)$. ■

5.3 Contexts of factors

In this section, we present the formal basis of the construction of the minimal automaton that accepts the suffixes of a string. Some properties go into the proof of the automaton construction (Theorems 5.19 and 5.28 further).

The (minimal) suffix automaton of a string y is denoted by $\mathcal{S}(y)$. Its states are the classes of the syntactic equivalence (or congruence) associated with the set Suff(y), that is to say of the sets of factors of y having the same right context inside y (see Section 1.1). These states are in bijection with the (right) contexts of the factors of y in y itself. Let us recall that the (right) context of a string u relatively to the suffixes of y is $u^{-1}\text{Suff}(y)$. We denote by $\equiv_{\mathit{Suff}(y)}$ the equivalence (syntactic congruence) that is defined, for $u, v \in A^*$, by

$$u \equiv_{\mathit{Suff}(y)} v$$

if and only if

$$u^{-1}\text{Suff}(y) = v^{-1}\text{Suff}(y).$$

We can also identify the states of $\mathcal{S}(y)$ to the sets of indices on y that are right positions of occurrences of equivalent factors.

The right contexts satisfy some properties stated below and that are used in the rest. The first remark concerns the link between the relation $\preceq_{\text{suff}}$ and the inclusion of contexts. For every factor u of y, we denote by

$$rpos(u) = \min\{|w| - 1 : w \preceq_{\text{pref}} y \text{ and } u \preceq_{\text{suff}} w\},$$

the right position of the first occurrence of u in y.

Lemma 5.10
Let $u, v \preceq_{\text{fact}} y$ with $|u| \leq |v|$. Then

$$u \preceq_{\text{suff}} v \textit{ implies } v^{-1}\text{Suff}(y) \subseteq u^{-1}\text{Suff}(y)$$

and

$$v^{-1}\text{Suff}(y) = u^{-1}\text{Suff}(y) \textit{ implies both } rpos(u) = rpos(v) \textit{ and } u \preceq_{\text{suff}} v.$$

Proof Let us assume $u \preceq_{\text{suff}} v$. Let $z \in v^{-1}\text{Suff}(y)$. By definition, $vz \preceq_{\text{suff}} y$ and, as $u \preceq_{\text{suff}} v$, we have also $uz \preceq_{\text{suff}} y$. Thus, $z \in u^{-1}\text{Suff}(y)$, this proves the first implication.

Let us assume now $v^{-1}\text{Suff}(y) = u^{-1}\text{Suff}(y)$. Let w, z be such that $y = w \cdot z$ with $|w| = rpos(u) + 1$. By definition of *rpos*, u is a suffix of w and z is the longest string of $u^{-1}\text{Suff}(y)$. The assumption implies that z is also the longest string of $v^{-1}\text{Suff}(y)$, this leads to $|w| = rpos(v) + 1$ and $rpos(u) = rpos(v)$. The strings u and v are thus both suffixes of w, and as u is shorter than v, we get $u \preceq_{\text{suff}} v$. This ends the proof of the second implication. ■

Another very useful property of the congruence is that it partitions the suffixes of a factor of y in intervals relatively to their length.

Lemma 5.11
Let $u, v, w \preceq_{\text{fact}} y$. If $u \preceq_{\text{suff}} v$, $v \preceq_{\text{suff}} w$, and $u \equiv_{Suff(y)} w$, then $u \equiv_{Suff(y)} v$ and $v \equiv_{Suff(y)} w$.

Proof By Lemma 5.10, the assumption implies:

$$w^{-1}\text{Suff}(y) \subseteq v^{-1}\text{Suff}(y) \subseteq u^{-1}\text{Suff}(y).$$

Then, the equivalence $u \equiv_{Suff(y)} w$ that means $u^{-1}\text{Suff}(y) = w^{-1}\text{Suff}(y)$ leads to the conclusion. ■

The following property has for consequence that the inclusion induces a tree structure on the right contexts. In this tree, the parent link consists of the proper set inclusion. This important link for the fast construction of the automaton corresponds to the suffix function defined then.

Corollary 5.12
Let $u, v \in A^*$. The contexts of u and v are comparable for the inclusion or disjoint, that is to say one at least of the three following conditions holds:

1. $u^{-1}\text{Suff}(y) \subseteq v^{-1}\text{Suff}(y)$,
2. $v^{-1}\text{Suff}(y) \subseteq u^{-1}\text{Suff}(y)$,
3. $u^{-1}\text{Suff}(y) \cap v^{-1}\text{Suff}(y) = \emptyset$.

Proof We prove the property by showing that the condition

$$u^{-1}\text{Suff}(y) \cap v^{-1}\text{Suff}(y) \neq \emptyset$$

implies

$$u^{-1}\text{Suff}(y) \subseteq v^{-1}\text{Suff}(y) \text{ or } v^{-1}\text{Suff}(y) \subseteq u^{-1}\text{Suff}(y).$$

Let $z \in u^{-1}\text{Suff}(y) \cap v^{-1}\text{Suff}(y)$. Then the strings uz and vz are suffixes of y, and thus u and v are suffixes of yz^{-1}. As a consequence one of the two strings u or v is a suffix of the other. We finally get the conclusion by Lemma 5.10. ■

Suffix function

On the set Fact(y), we consider the function denoted by[1] s, called ***suffix function*** relatively to y. It is defined, for every $v \in \text{Fact}(y) \setminus \{\varepsilon\}$, by

$$s(v) = \text{the longest string } u \prec_{\text{suff}} v \text{ for which } u \not\equiv_{\mathit{Suff}(y)} v.$$

After Lemma 5.10, we deduce the equivalent definition:

$$s(v) = \text{the longest string } u \prec_{\text{suff}} v \text{ for which } v^{-1}\text{Suff}(y) \subset u^{-1}\text{Suff}(y).$$

We note that, by definition, $s(v)$ is a proper suffix of v (that is to say, $|s(v)| < |v|$). The lemma that follows shows that the suffix function s induces a failure function (see Section 1.4) on the states of $\mathcal{S}(y)$.

Lemma 5.13
Let $u, v \in \text{Fact}(y) \setminus \{\varepsilon\}$. If $u \equiv_{\mathit{Suff}(y)} v$, then $s(u) = s(v)$.

Proof By Lemma 5.10 we can assume without loss of generality that $u \preceq_{\text{suff}} v$. Thus, u and $s(v)$ are suffixes of v, and then one is a suffix of the other. The string u cannot be a suffix of $s(v)$ since Lemma 5.11 would imply $s(v) \equiv_{\mathit{Suff}(y)} v$, which contradicts the definition of $s(v)$. As a consequence, $s(v)$ is a suffix of u.

[1] Though we use the same notation, the definition of the suffix function is syntactic in the sense that it uses the language of reference, while the one of the suffix link of Section 5.1 is only of algorithmic nature.

Since, by definition, $s(v)$ is the longest suffix of v that is not equivalent to v and since it is not equivalent to u, it is also $s(u)$. Therefore, $s(u) = s(v)$. ■

Lemma 5.14

Let $y \in A^+$. The string $s(y)$ is the longest suffix of y that occurs at least twice in y itself.

Proof The context $y^{-1}\mathrm{Suff}(y)$ is $\{\varepsilon\}$. As y and $s(y)$ are not equivalent, $s(y)^{-1}\mathrm{Suff}(y)$ contains a nonempty string z. Then, $s(y)z$ and $s(y)$ are suffixes of y, this shows that $s(y)$ occurs at least twice in y.

Every suffix w of y, longer that $s(y)$, is equivalent to y by definition of $s(y)$. It satisfies then $w^{-1}\mathrm{Suff}(y) = y^{-1}\mathrm{Suff}(y) = \{\varepsilon\}$. Which shows that w occurs only once in y as a suffix and that $s(y)$ is the longest suffix occurring at least twice. ■

The next lemma shows that the image of a factor of y by the suffix function is a string of maximal length in its equivalence class.

Lemma 5.15

Let $u \in \mathrm{Fact}(y) \setminus \{\varepsilon\}$. Then, every string equivalent to $s(u)$ is a suffix of $s(u)$.

Proof We denote by $w = s(u)$ and let $v \equiv_{Suff(y)} w$. The string w is a proper suffix of u. If the conclusion of the statement is wrong, we get $w \prec_{\mathrm{suff}} v$ after Lemma 5.10. Let then $z \in u^{-1}\mathrm{Suff}(y)$. As w is a suffix of u equivalent to v, we have $z \in w^{-1}\mathrm{Suff}(y) = v^{-1}\mathrm{Suff}(y)$. Then, u and v are suffixes of yz^{-1}, this implies that one is a suffix of the other. But this contradicts either the definition of $w = s(u)$ or the conclusion of Lemma 5.11, which proves that v is necessarily a suffix of $w = s(u)$. ■

The previous property is used in Section 6.6 where the automaton is used for pattern matching. We can check that the property of s is not satisfied in general on the minimal automaton that accepts the factors (and not only the suffixes) of a string, or, more exactly, is not satisfied by the similar function defined from the congruence $\equiv_{Fact(y)}$.

Evolution of the congruence

The online aspect of the suffix automaton construction of Section 5.4 relies on relations between $\equiv_{Suff(wa)}$ and $\equiv_{Suff(w)}$ that we examine here. By doing this, we consider that the generic string y is equal to wa for some letter a. The stated properties yield tight bounds on the size of the automaton in the next section.

The first relation (Lemma 5.16) states that $\equiv_{Suff(wa)}$ is a refinement of $\equiv_{Suff(w)}$.

Lemma 5.16
Let $w \in A^*$ and $a \in A$. The congruence $\equiv_{\mathit{Suff}(wa)}$ is a refinement of $\equiv_{\mathit{Suff}(w)}$, that is to say, for every strings $u, v \in A^*$, $u \equiv_{\mathit{Suff}(wa)} v$ implies $u \equiv_{\mathit{Suff}(w)} v$.

Proof Let us assume $u \equiv_{\mathit{Suff}(wa)} v$, that is, $u^{-1}\mathrm{Suff}(wa) = v^{-1}\mathrm{Suff}(wa)$, and let us show $u \equiv_{\mathit{Suff}(w)} v$, that is, $u^{-1}\mathrm{Suff}(w) = v^{-1}\mathrm{Suff}(w)$. We only show that $u^{-1}\mathrm{Suff}(w) \subseteq v^{-1}\mathrm{Suff}(w)$ since the opposite inclusion can be deduced by symmetry.

If the set $u^{-1}\mathrm{Suff}(w)$ is empty, the inclusion is trivial. Otherwise, let $z \in u^{-1}\mathrm{Suff}(w)$. We then have $uz \preceq_{\mathrm{suff}} w$, which implies $uza \preceq_{\mathrm{suff}} wa$. The assumption gives $vza \preceq_{\mathrm{suff}} wa$, and thus $vz \preceq_{\mathrm{suff}} w$ or $z \in v^{-1}\mathrm{Suff}(w)$, which ends the proof. ■

The congruence $\equiv_{\mathit{Suff}(w)}$ partitions A^* into equivalence classes. The Lemma 5.16 amounts to say that these classes are unions of classes relatively to $\equiv_{\mathit{Suff}(wa)}$ $(a \in A)$. It turns out that only one or two classes relatively to $\equiv_{\mathit{Suff}(w)}$ split into two subclasses to produce the partition induced by $\equiv_{\mathit{Suff}(wa)}$. One of these two classes is the one that comes from strings that do not occur in w. It contains the string wa itself that produces a new class and a new state of the suffix automaton (see Lemma 5.17). Theorem 5.19 and its corollaries give conditions for the splitting of another class and indicate how this one splits.

Lemma 5.17
Let $w \in A^*$ and $a \in A$. Let z be the longest suffix of wa that occurs in w. If u is a suffix of wa longer than z, the equivalence $u \equiv_{\mathit{Suff}(wa)} wa$ holds.

Proof It is a direct consequence of Lemma 5.14 since z occurs at least twice in wa. ■

Before stating the main theorem we give another relation concerning right contexts.

Lemma 5.18
Let $w \in A^*$ and $a \in A$. Then, for each string $u \in A^*$:

$$u^{-1}\mathrm{Suff}(wa) = \begin{cases} \{\varepsilon\} \cup u^{-1}\mathrm{Suff}(w)a & \text{if } u \preceq_{\mathrm{suff}} wa, \\ u^{-1}\mathrm{Suff}(w)a & \text{otherwise.} \end{cases}$$

Proof We first note that $\varepsilon \in u^{-1}\mathrm{Suff}(wa)$ is equivalent to $u \preceq_{\mathrm{suff}} wa$. It is sufficient thus to show $u^{-1}\mathrm{Suff}(wa) \setminus \{\varepsilon\} = u^{-1}\mathrm{Suff}(w)a$.

Let z be a nonempty string of $u^{-1}\mathrm{Suff}(wa)$. We have $uz \preceq_{\mathrm{suff}} wa$. The string uz can be written $uz'a$ with $uz' \preceq_{\mathrm{suff}} w$. Then, $z' \in u^{-1}\mathrm{Suff}(w)$, and thus $z \in u^{-1}\mathrm{Suff}(w)a$.

Conversely, let z be a (nonempty) string of $u^{-1}\text{Suff}(w)a$. It can be written $z'a$ for $z' \in u^{-1}\text{Suff}(w)$. Thus, $uz' \preceq_{\text{suff}} w$. This implies $uz = uz'a \preceq_{\text{suff}} wa$, that is, $z \in u^{-1}\text{Suff}(wa)$, which proves the reciprocity and ends the proof. ∎

Theorem 5.19
Let $w \in A^*$ and $a \in A$. Let z be the longest suffix of wa that occurs in w. Let z' be the longest factor of w for which $z' \equiv_{Suff(w)} z$. Then, for each u, $v \preceq_{\text{fact}} w$,

$$u \equiv_{Suff(w)} v \text{ and } u \not\equiv_{Suff(w)} z \text{ imply } u \equiv_{Suff(wa)} v.$$

Moreover, for each u such that $u \equiv_{Suff(w)} z$,

$$u \equiv_{Suff(wa)} \begin{cases} z & \text{if } |u| \leq |z|, \\ z' & \text{otherwise.} \end{cases}$$

Proof Let $u, v \preceq_{\text{fact}} w$ be such that $u \equiv_{Suff(w)} v$. By definition of the equivalence, we have $u^{-1}\text{Suff}(w) = v^{-1}\text{Suff}(w)$. We first assume $u \not\equiv_{Suff(w)} z$ and we show $u^{-1}\text{Suff}(wa) = v^{-1}\text{Suff}(wa)$, which gives the equivalence $u \equiv_{Suff(wa)} v$.

After Lemma 5.18, we simply have to show that $u \preceq_{\text{suff}} wa$ is equivalent to $v \preceq_{\text{suff}} wa$. Actually, it is sufficient to show that $u \preceq_{\text{suff}} wa$ implies $v \preceq_{\text{suff}} wa$ since the opposite implication can be deduced by symmetry.

Let us assume thus $u \preceq_{\text{suff}} wa$. We deduce from $u \preceq_{\text{fact}} w$ and from the definition of z that u is a suffix of z. We can, thus, consider the largest index $j \geq 0$ for which $|u| \leq |s_w{}^j(z)|$. Let us note that $s_w{}^j(z)$ is a suffix of wa (in the same way as z is), and that Lemma 5.11 ensures that $u \equiv_{Suff(w)} s_w{}^j(z)$. Thus, $v \equiv_{Suff(w)} s_w{}^j(z)$ by transitivity.

As $u \not\equiv_{Suff(w)} z$, we have $j > 0$. Lemma 5.15 implies that v is a suffix of $s_w{}^j(z)$, and then also of wa as wanted. This shows the first part of the statement.

Let us consider now a string u such that $u \equiv_{Suff(w)} z$.

When $|u| \leq |z|$, in order to show $u \equiv_{Suff(wa)} z$ using the above argument, we only have to check that $u \preceq_{\text{suff}} wa$ since $z \preceq_{\text{suff}} wa$. This is actually a simple consequence of Lemma 5.10.

Let us assume $|u| > |z|$. The existence of such a string u implies $z' \neq z$ and $|z'| > |z|$ ($z \prec_{\text{suff}} z'$). Consequently, by the definition of z, u and z' are not suffixes of wa. Using again the above argument, this proves $u \equiv_{Suff(wa)} z'$ and ends the proof. ∎

The two corollaries of the previous theorem stated below refer to simple situations to manage during the construction of the suffix automaton.

Corollary 5.20
Let $w \in A^*$ and $a \in A$. Let z be the longest suffix of wa that occurs in w. Let z' be the longest string such that $z' \equiv_{Suff(w)} z$. Let us assume $z' = z$. Then, for each $u, v \preceq_{\text{fact}} w$,

$$u \equiv_{Suff(w)} v \textit{ implies } u \equiv_{Suff(wa)} v.$$

Proof Let $u, v \preceq_{\text{fact}} w$ be such that $u \equiv_{Suff(w)} v$. We show the equivalence $u \equiv_{Suff(wa)} v$. The conclusion comes directly after Theorem 5.19 if $u \not\equiv_{Suff(w)} z$. Otherwise, $u \equiv_{Suff(w)} z$; by the assumption done on z and Lemma 5.10, we get $|u| \leq |z|$. Finally, Theorem 5.19 gives the same conclusion. ∎

Corollary 5.21
Let $w \in A^*$ and $a \in A$. If the letter a does not occur in w, for each $u, v \preceq_{\text{fact}} w$,

$$u \equiv_{Suff(w)} v \textit{ implies } u \equiv_{Suff(wa)} v.$$

Proof As a does not occur in w, the string z of Corollary 5.20 is the empty string. It is of course the longest of its class, which allows to apply Corollary 5.20 and gives the same conclusion. ∎

5.4 Suffix automaton

The ***suffix automaton*** of a string y, denoted by $\mathcal{S}(y)$, is the minimal automaton that accepts the set of suffixes of y. The structure is intended to be used as an index on the string but constitutes also a machine to search for factors of y inside another text (see Chapter 6). The most surprising property of this automaton is that its size is linear in the length of y though the number of factors of y can be quadratic. The construction of the automaton takes also a linear time on a fixed alphabet. Figure 5.11 shows an example of such automaton.

As we do not force the automaton to be complete, the class of strings that do not occur in y, whose right context is empty, is not a state of $\mathcal{S}(y)$.

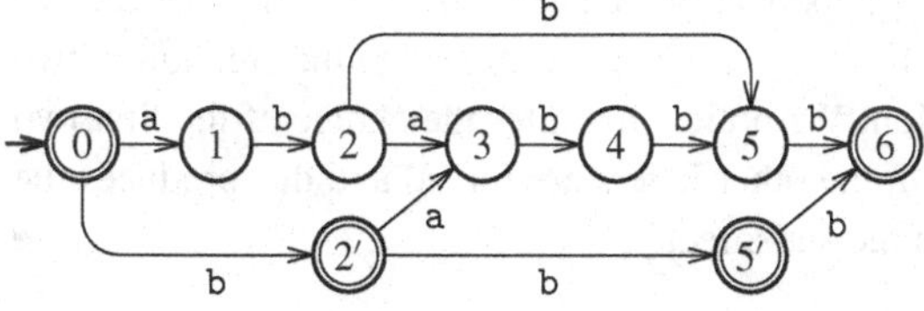

Figure 5.11. The suffix automaton $\mathcal{S}$(ababbb), minimal automaton accepting the suffixes of the string ababbb.

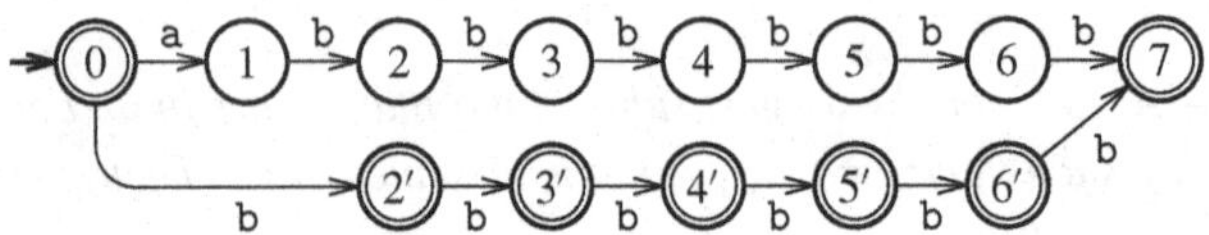

Figure 5.12. A suffix automaton with the maximal number of states for a string of length 7.

Size of the automaton

The size of an automaton is expressed both by the number of its states and by the number of its arcs. We show that $\mathcal{S}(y)$ possesses less than $2|y|$ states and less than $3|y|$ arcs, for a total size $O(|y|)$. This result is a consequence of Theorem 5.19 of the previous section. Figure 5.12 shows an automaton that possesses the maximal number of states for a string of length 7.

Proposition 5.22
Let $y \in A^*$ be a string of length n and $e(y)$ be the number of states of $\mathcal{S}(y)$. For $n = 0$, we have $e(y) = 1$; for $n = 1$, we have $e(y) = 2$; for $n > 1$ finally, we have

$$n + 1 \leq e(y) \leq 2n - 1,$$

and the upper bound is met if and only if y is of the form ab^{n-1}, for two distinct letters a, b.

Proof The equalities concerning the short strings can be checked directly. Let us assume that $n > 1$ for the rest. The minimal number of states of $\mathcal{S}(y)$ is obviously $n + 1$ (otherwise the path having label y would contain a cycle leading to an infinite number of strings recognized by the automaton), minimum that is reached with $y = a^n$ $(a \in A)$.

Let us show the upper bound. By Theorem 5.19, each letter $y[i]$, $2 \leq i \leq n - 1$, increases by at most two the number of states of $\mathcal{S}(y[0\,..\,i-1])$. As the number of states of $\mathcal{S}(y[0]y[1])$ is 3, it follows that $e(y) \leq 3 + 2(n-2) = 2n - 1$, as announced.

The construction of a string of length n whose suffix automaton possesses $2n - 1$ states is again a simple application of Theorem 5.19 noting that each of the letters $y[2], y[3], \ldots, y[n-1]$ must effectively lead to the creation of two states during the construction. We notice that after the choice of the first two letters that must be different, the other letters are forced and this produces the only possible form given in the statement. ■

Lemma 5.23
Let $y \in A^+$ and $f(y)$ be the number of arcs of $\mathcal{S}(y)$. Then

$$f(y) \leq e(y) + |y| - 2.$$

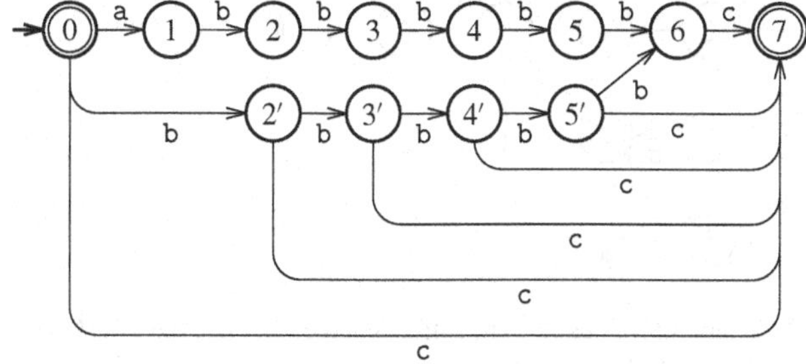

Figure 5.13. A suffix automaton with the maximal number of arcs for a string of length 7.

Proof Let us denote by q_0 the initial state of $\mathcal{S}(y)$, and let us consider the spanning tree of the longest paths having origin q_0 in $\mathcal{S}(y)$. The tree contains $e(y) - 1$ arcs of $\mathcal{S}(y)$ since exactly one arc enters each state except the initial state q_0.

With each other arc (p, a, q) of the automaton, we associate the suffix uav of y defined as follows: u is the label of the path of the tree starting from q_0 and ending in p; v is the label of the longest path from q and ending in a terminal state. In this way, we get an injection of the set of the mentioned arcs into the set of suffixes of y. The suffixes y and ε are not considered since they are labels of paths of the spanning tree. This shows that there are at most $|y| - 1$ arcs of the automaton that are not in the spanning tree.

Thus a total of $e(y) + |y| - 2$ arcs at most. ∎

Figure 5.13 shows an automaton that possesses the maximal number of arcs for a string of length 7, as the next proposition shows.

Proposition 5.24
Let $y \in A^*$ of length n and $f(y)$ be the number of arcs of $\mathcal{S}(y)$. For $n = 0$, we have $f(y) = 0$; for $n = 1$, we have $f(y) = 1$; for $n = 2$, we have $f(y) = 2$ or $f(y) = 3$; for $n > 2$ finally, we have

$$n \leq f(y) \leq 3n - 4,$$

and the upper bound is met when y is of the form $ab^{n-2}c$, where a, b, and c are three pairwise distinct letters.

Proof We can directly check the results for short strings. Let us consider that $n > 2$. The lower bound is immediate and met for the string $y = a^n$ $(a \in A)$.

Let us examine the upper bound. By Proposition 5.22 and Lemma 5.23, we get $f(y) \leq (2n - 1) + n - 2 = 3n - 3$. The quantity $2n - 1$ is the maximal number of states obtained only if $y = ab^{n-1}$ $(a, b \in A,\ a \neq b)$. But for this string the number of arcs is only $2n - 1$. Thus, $f(y) \leq 3n - 4$.

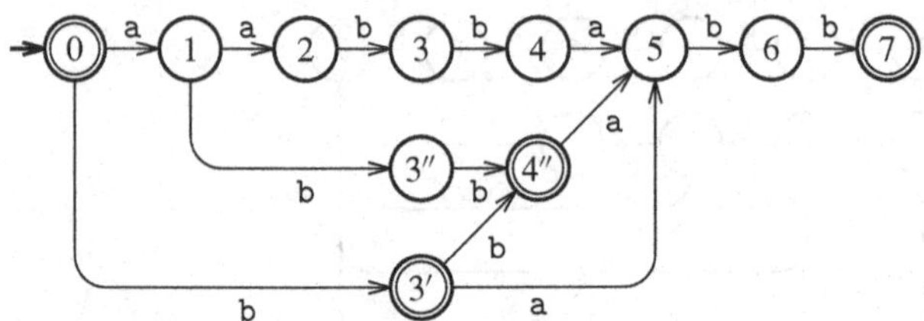

Figure 5.14. The suffix automaton $\mathcal{S}(\texttt{aabbabb})$. The suffix targets of the states are: $F[1] = 0$, $F[2] = 1$, $F[3] = 3''$, $F[3''] = 3'$, $F[3'] = 0$, $F[4] = 4''$, $F[4''] = 3'$, $F[5] = 1$, $F[6] = 3''$, $F[7] = 4''$, where F is the table implementing the suffix function f. The suffix path of 7 is $\langle 7, 4'', 3', 0\rangle$, it contains all the terminal states of the automaton and only them (see Corollary 5.27).

We can check that the automaton $\mathcal{S}(ab^{n-2}c)$ ($a, b, c \in A$, $\text{card}\{a, b, c\} = 3$) possesses $2n - 2$ states and $3n - 4$ arcs. ■

The statement that follows is an immediate consequence of Propositions 5.22 and 5.24.

Theorem 5.25
The total size of the suffix automaton of a string is linear in the length of the string. ■

Suffix link and suffix paths

Theorem 5.19 and its two corollaries provide the framework for the online construction of the suffix automaton $\mathcal{S}(y)$. The algorithm controls the conditions that occur in these statements by means of a function defined on the states of the automaton, the suffix link, and of a classification of the arcs in solid arcs and non-solid arcs. We define these two notions thereafter.

Let p be a state of $\mathcal{S}(y)$, different from the initial state. The state p is a class of factors of y equivalent with respect to the equivalence $\equiv_{\mathit{Suff}(y)}$. Let u be any string of the class ($u \neq \varepsilon$ since p is not the initial state). We define the ***suffix target*** of p, denoted by $f(p)$, as the equivalence class of $s(u)$. The function f is called the ***suffix link*** of the automaton. Lemma 5.13 shows that the value of $s(u)$ is independent of the string u chosen in the class p, which makes the definition of f consistent. The suffix link is a failure function in the sense of Section 1.4, that is, $f(p)$ is the failure state of p. The link is used with this meaning in Section 6.6. An example is given in Figure 5.14.

For a state p of $\mathcal{S}(y)$, we denote by $lg(p)$ the maximal length of strings u in the equivalence class p. It is also the length of the longest path from the initial state reaching p, path that is labeled by u. The longest paths from the initial state form a spanning tree of $\mathcal{S}(y)$ (consequence of Lemma 5.10). The arcs that belong to this tree are qualified as ***solid***. In a equivalent way,

$$\text{the arc } (p, a, q) \text{ is solid}$$

if and only if

$$lg(q) = lg(p) + 1.$$

This notion of solidity of arcs is used in the construction of the automaton for testing the condition of Theorem 5.19.

The suffix targets induce by iteration suffix paths in $\mathcal{S}(y)$ (see Figure 5.14). We can note that

$$q = f(p) \text{ implies } lg(q) < lg(p).$$

Thus, the sequence

$$\langle p, f(p), f^2(p), \ldots \rangle$$

is finite and ends with the initial state (that has no suffix target). It is called the ***suffix path*** of p in $\mathcal{S}(y)$, and denoted by $SP(p)$.

Let *last* be the state of $\mathcal{S}(y)$ that is the class of y itself. This state is characterized by the fact that it is the origin of no arc (otherwise $\mathcal{S}(y)$ would accept strings longer than y). The suffix path of *last*,

$$\langle last, f(last), f^2(last), \ldots, f^{k-1}(last) = q_0 \rangle,$$

where q_0 is the initial state of the automaton, plays an important role in the sequential construction algorithm. It is used for testing efficiently the conditions of Theorem 5.19 and of its corollaries. In the next proposition, δ is the transition function of $\mathcal{S}(y)$.

Proposition 5.26
Let $u \in \text{Fact}(y) \setminus \{\varepsilon\}$ and $p = \delta(q_0, u)$. Then, for each integer $j \geq 0$ for which $s^j(u)$ is defined, we have

$$f^j(p) = \delta(q_0, s^j(u)).$$

Proof We prove the result by recurrence on j. If $j = 0$, $f^j(p) = p$, and $s^j(u) = u$, thus the equality is satisfied by assumption. Let then $j > 0$ such that $s^j(u)$ is defined and assume by the recurrence assumption that $f^{j-1}(p) = \delta(i, s^{j-1}(u))$. By definition of f, $f(f^{j-1}(p))$ is the equivalence class of the string $s(s^{j-1}(u))$. Consequently, $f^j(p) = \delta(q_0, s^j(u))$, which ends the recurrence and the proof. ■

Corollary 5.27
The terminal states of $\mathcal{S}(y)$ are the states of the suffix path of the state last, SP(last).

Proof We first show that the states of the suffix path are terminal. Let p be a state of the suffix path of *last*. We have $p = f^j(\mathit{last})$ for an integer $j \geq 0$. As $\mathit{last} = \delta(q_0, y)$, Proposition 5.26 implies $p = \delta(q_0, s^j(y))$. And as $s^j(y)$ is a suffix of y, p is a terminal state.

Conversely, let p be a terminal state of $\mathcal{S}(y)$. Let then $u \preceq_{\text{suff}} y$ be such that $p = \delta(q_0, u)$. As $u \preceq_{\text{suff}} y$, we can consider the largest integer $j \geq 0$ for which $|u| \leq |s^j(y)|$. By Lemma 5.11, we get $u \equiv_{\mathit{Suff}(y)} s^j(y)$. Thus, $p = \delta(q_0, s^j(y))$ by definition of $\mathcal{S}(y)$. Thus, Proposition 5.26 applied to y implies $p = f^j(\mathit{last})$, which proves that p occurs in *SP*(*last*). This ends the proof. ∎

Online construction

It is possible to build the suffix automaton of y by application of standard minimization algorithms applied to the suffix trie of Section 5.1. But since the suffix trie can be of quadratic size, this gives a procedure having the same space complexity to the best. We present a sequential construction algorithm that avoids this problem, runs in time $O(|y| \times \log \operatorname{card} A)$, and requires only a linear memory space.

The algorithm processes the prefixes of y from the shortest, ε, to the longest, y itself. At each step, just after having processed the prefix w, we have the following information:

- the suffix automaton $\mathcal{S}(w)$ with its transition function δ,
- the attribute F, defined on the states of $\mathcal{S}(w)$, that implements the suffix function f_w,
- the attribute L, defined on the states of $\mathcal{S}(w)$, that implements the function of length lg_w,
- the state *last*.

The terminal states of $\mathcal{S}(w)$ are not explicitly marked, they are implicitly given by the suffix path of *last* (Corollary 5.27). The implementation of $\mathcal{S}(w)$ with these extra elements is discussed below just before the complexity analysis of the computation.

The construction algorithm SUFFIX-AUTO is based on the utilization of the procedure EXTENSION given further. This procedure processes the current letter a of the string y. It transforms the suffix automaton $\mathcal{S}(w)$ already built into the suffix automaton $\mathcal{S}(wa)$ ($wa \preceq_{\text{pref}} y$, $a \in A$). An example of how it works is given in Figure 5.15.

```
SUFFIX-AUTO(y, n)
M ← NEW-AUTOMATON()
L[initial[M]] ← 0
F[initial[M]] ← NIL
last[M] ← initial[M]
for each letter a of y, sequentially do
      ▷ Extension of M by the letter a
      EXTENSION(a)
p ← last[M]
do    terminal[p] ← TRUE
      p ← F[p]
while p ≠ NIL
return M
```

```
EXTENSION(a)
new ← NEW-STATE()
L[new] ← L[last[M]] + 1
p ← last[M]
do    Succ[p] ← Succ[p] ∪ {(a, new)}
      p ← F[p]
while p ≠ NIL and TARGET(p, a) = NIL
if p = NIL then
      F[new] ← initial[M]
else  q ← TARGET(p, a)
      if (p, a, q) is solid, i.e. L[p] + 1 = L[q] then
            F[new] ← q
      else  clone ← NEW-STATE()
            L[clone] ← L[p] + 1
            for each pair (b, q') ∈ Succ[q] do
                  Succ[clone] ← Succ[clone] ∪ {(b, q')}
            F[new] ← clone
            F[clone] ← F[q]
            F[q] ← clone
            do    Succ[p] ← Succ[p] \ {(a, q)}
                  Succ[p] ← Succ[p] ∪ {(a, clone)}
                  p ← F[p]
            while p ≠ NIL and TARGET(p, a) = q
last[M] ← new
```

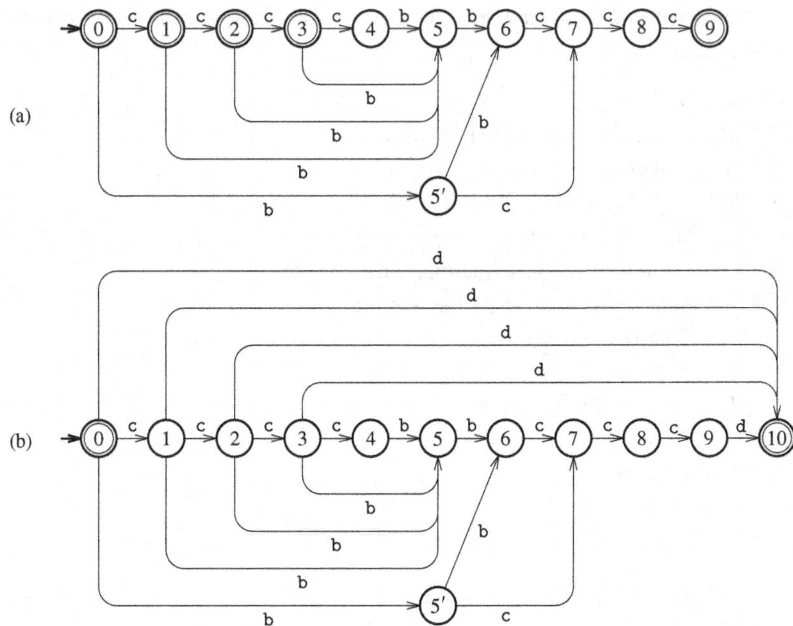

Figure 5.15. Illustration of how the procedure EXTENSION(a) works on the suffix automaton $\mathcal{S}$(ccccbbccc) according to three cases. **(a)** The automaton $\mathcal{S}$(ccccbbccc). **(b)** Case where $a =$ d. During the execution of the first loop of the procedure, the state p goes over the suffix path $\langle 9, 3, 2, 1, 0 \rangle$. In the same time, arcs labeled by the letter d are created, exiting these states and arriving on 10, the last created state. The loop stops on the initial state. This situation corresponds to Corollary 5.21. **(c)** Case where $a =$ c. The first loop of the procedure stops on state $3 = F[9]$ because an arc labeled by c exits this state. Moreover, the arc (3, c, 4) is solid. We directly get the suffix target of the newly created state: $F[10] = \delta(3, \texttt{c}) = 4$. There is nothing more to do according to Corollary 5.20. **(d)** Case where $a =$ b. The first loop of the procedure stops on state $3 = F[9]$ because an arc labeled by b exits this state. In the automaton $\mathcal{S}$(ccccbbccc), the arc (3, b, 5) is not solid. The string cccb is suffix of ccccbbcccb but ccccb is not, though these two strings lead, in $\mathcal{S}$(ccccbbccc), to state 5. In order to get $\mathcal{S}$(ccccbbcccb), this state is duplicated into the terminal state $5''$ that is the class of factors cccb, ccb, and cb. The arcs (3, b, 5), (2, b, 5), and (1, b, 5) of $\mathcal{S}$(ccccbbccc) are redirected to $5''$ in accordance with Theorem 5.19. And $F[10] = 5''$, $F[5] = 5''$, $F[5''] = 5'$.

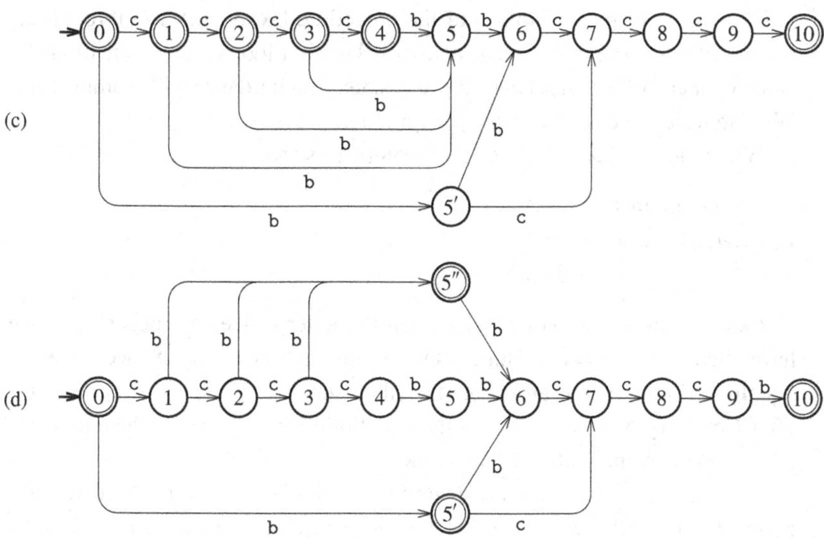

Figure 5.15. *(Continued)*

Theorem 5.28

The algorithm Suffix-auto *builds a suffix automaton, that is to say that the operation* Suffix-auto(y, n) *produces the automaton* $\mathcal{S}(y)$, *for* $y \in A^*$.

Proof We show by recurrence on $|y|$ that the automaton is correctly computed and that the attributes L and F and the variable *last* also are. We show at the end of the proof that the terminal states are correctly computed. If $|y| = 0$, the algorithm builds an automaton with a single state that is both initial and terminal. No transition is defined. The automaton recognizes the language $\{\varepsilon\}$, which is $\text{Suff}(y)$. The elements F, L, and *last* are also correctly computed.

We consider now that $|y| > 0$, and let $y = wa$, for $a \in A$ and $w \in A^*$. We assume, by recurrence, that the current automaton M is $\mathcal{S}(w)$ with its transition function δ_w, that $q_0 = initial[M]$, $last = \delta_w(q_0, w)$, that the attribute L satisfies $L[p] = lg_w(p)$ for every state p, and that the attribute F satisfies $F[p] = f_w(p)$ for every state p different from the initial state.

We first show that the procedure Extension correctly performs the transformation of the automaton M, of the variable *last*, and of the attributes L and F.

The values of the variable p of the procedure EXTENSION run through the states of the suffix path *SP*(*last*) of $\mathcal{S}(w)$. The first loop creates transitions labeled by a and of the target *new*, the new state, in accordance with Lemma 5.17. We also have the equality $L[new] = lg(new)$.

When the first loop stops, three disjoint cases arise:

1. p is not defined.
2. (p, a, q) is a solid arc.
3. (p, a, q) is a non-solid arc.

Case 1. This situation happens when the letter a does not occur in w; we have then $f_y(new) = q_0$. Thus, after the instruction of line 8, we have the equality $F[new] = f_y(new)$. For the other states r, we have $f_w(r) = f_y(r)$ after Corollary 5.21, which gives the equalities $F[r] = f_y(r)$ at the end of the execution of the procedure EXTENSION.

Case 2. Let u be the longest string for which $\delta_w(q_0, u) = p$. By recurrence and by Lemma 5.15, we have $|u| = lg_w(p) = L[p]$. The string ua is the longest suffix of y that is a factor of w. Thus, $f_y(new) = q$, this shows $F[new] = f_y(new)$ after the instruction of line 11.

As the arc (p, a, q) is solid, by recurrence again, we have $|ua| = L[q] = lg(q)$, this shows that the strings equivalent to ua according to $\equiv_{Suff(w)}$ are not longer than ua. Corollary 5.20 applies with $z = ua$. And as in Case 1, $F[r] = f_y(r)$ for every states different from the state *new*.

Case 3. Let u be the longest string for which $\delta_w(q_0, u) = p$. The string ua is the longest suffix of y that is a factor of w. As the arc (p, a, q) is not solid, ua is not the longest string of its equivalence class according to $\equiv_{Suff(w)}$. Theorem 5.19 applies with $z = ua$, and z' the longest string for which $\delta_w(q_0, z') = q$. The class of ua according to $\equiv_{Suff(w)}$ splits into two subclasses according to $\equiv_{Suff(y)}$ corresponding to states q and *clone*.

The strings v shorter than ua and such that $v \equiv_{Suff(w)} ua$ are of the form $v'a$ with $v' \preceq_{\rm suff} u$ (consequence of Lemma 5.10). Before the execution of the last loop, all these strings v satisfy $q = \delta_w(q_0, v)$. Consequently, after the execution of the loop, they satisfy $clone = \delta_y(q_0, v)$, as indicated by Theorem 5.19. The strings v longer than ua and such that $v \equiv_{Suff(w)} ua$ satisfy $q = \delta_y(q_0, v)$ after the execution of the loop as indicated by Theorem 5.19 again. We can check that the attribute F is updated correctly.

In each of the three cases, we can check that the value of *last* is correctly computed at the end of the execution of the procedure EXTENSION.

Finally, the recurrence shows that the automaton M, the state *last*, as well as the attributes L and F are correct after the execution of the procedure EXTENSION.

It remains to check that the terminal states are correctly marked during the execution of the last loop of the algorithm SUFFIX-AUTO. But this is a consequence of Corollary 5.27 since the values of the variable p are the elements of the suffix path of the state *last*. ■

Complexity

To analyze the complexity of the algorithm SUFFIX-AUTO, we start by describing a possible implementation of the elements required by the construction.

We assume that the automaton is represented by sets of labeled successors. By doing this, the operations add, access, and update concerning an arc execute in time $O(\log \text{card} A)$ with an efficient implementation of the sets in the comparison model (see Section 1.4). The function f is realized by the attribute F that gives access to $f(p)$ in constant time.

To implement the solidity of the arcs, we utilize the attribute L, representing the function lg, as suggests the description of the procedure EXTENSION (line 10). Another way of doing it consists in using a boolean value per arc of the automaton. This leads to a slight modification of the algorithm that can be described as follows: each first arc created during the execution of loops of lines 4–6 and of lines 19–22 must be marked as solid, the other created arcs are marked as being non-solid. This type of implementation does not require the utilization of the attribute L that can then be deleted; this saves some memory space. However, the attribute L finds its usefulness in applications as those of the Chapter 6. But we note that any chosen implementation provide a constant time access to the quality of an arc (solid or non-solid).

Theorem 5.29

The algorithm SUFFIX-AUTO *can be implemented in such a way that the construction of* $\mathcal{S}(y)$ *runs in time* $O(|y| \times \log \text{card} A)$ *with a memory space* $O(|y|)$.

Proof We choose an implementation of the transition function by sets of labeled successors. The states of $\mathcal{S}(y)$ and the attributes F and L require a space $O(e(y))$, the sets of labeled successors a space $O(f(y))$. Thus, the complete implementation takes a space $O(|y|)$, as a consequence of Propositions 5.22 and 5.24.

Another consequence of these propositions is that all the operations executed once per state or once per arc of the final automaton take a total time $O(|y| \times \log \text{card} A)$. The same result holds for the operations that are executed once per letter of y. It remains to show that the time spent for the execution of the two loops of lines 4–6 and 19–22 of the procedure EXTENSION is of the same order, that is to say $O(|y| \times \log \text{card} A)$.

We first examine the case of the loop of lines 4–6. Let us consider the execution of the procedure EXTENSION during the transformation of $\mathcal{S}(w)$ into $\mathcal{S}(wa)$ ($wa \preceq_{\text{pref}} y$, $a \in A$). Let u be the longest string of the state p during the test in line 6. The initial value of u is $s_w(w)$, and its final value satisfies $ua = s_{wa}(wa)$ (if p is defined). Let $k = |w| - |u|$, be the position of the suffix occurrence of u in w. Then, each test strictly increases the value of k during a call to the procedure. Moreover, the initial value of k at the beginning of the execution of the next call is not smaller than its final value reached at the end of the execution of the current call. Thus, the tests and instructions of this loop are executed at most $|y|$ times during all the calls to EXTENSION.

A similar argument holds for the second loop of lines 19–22 of the procedure EXTENSION. Let v be the longest string of the state p during the test of the loop. The initial value of v is $s_w{}^j(w)$, for $j \geq 2$, and its final value satisfies $va = s_{wa}{}^2(wa)$ (if p is defined). Then, the position of v as a suffix of w increases strictly at each test during successive calls of the procedure. Again, tests and instructions of the loop are executed at most $|y|$ times.

Consequently, the cumulated time of the executions of the two loops is $O(|y| \times \log \operatorname{card} A)$, which ends the proof. ∎

On a small alphabet, we can choose an implementation of the automaton by transition table that is even more efficient than by sets of labeled successors. It is sufficient then to manage the table as a sparse matrix. But the memory space requirement becomes larger. With this particular management, the operations on the arcs execute in constant time, which leads to the following result.

Theorem 5.30
In the branching model, the construction of $\mathcal{S}(y)$ by the algorithm SUFFIX-AUTO *takes a time $O(|y|)$.*

Proof To implement the transition matrix, we can use the technique for representing sparse matrices that gives a direct access to each of its inputs but avoids to completely initialize each of them (see Exercise 1.15). ∎

5.5 Compact suffix automaton

In this section, we succinctly describe a method for building a ***compact suffix automaton***, denoted by $\mathcal{S}_{\mathrm{C}}(y)$ for $y \in A^*$. This automaton can be viewed as the compact version of the suffix automaton of the previous section, that is to say, obtained from it by deletion of states that possess only one successor and

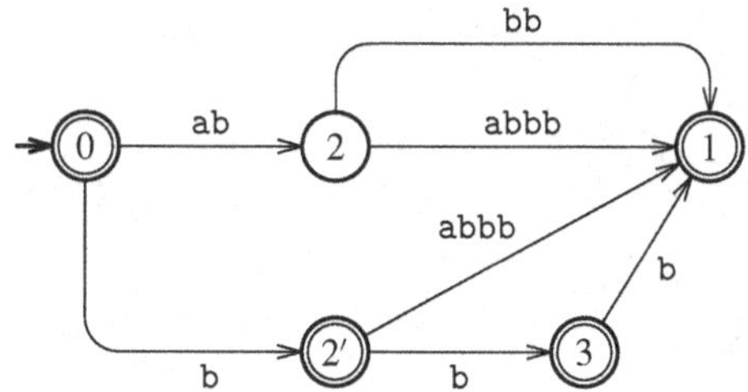

Figure 5.16. The compact suffix automaton $\mathcal{S}_C$(ababbb).

are not terminal. This is the process that is used on the suffix trie of Section 5.2 for getting a structure of linear size.

The compact suffix automaton is also the minimized version, in the sense of the automata, of the suffix tree. It is obtained by identifying the subtrees that recognize the same strings.

Figure 5.16 presents the compact suffix automaton of ababbb that can be compared to the tree of Figure 5.6 and to the automaton of Figure 5.11.

Exactly as for the trie $\mathcal{T}(\text{Suff}(y))$, we call ***fork*** in the automaton $\mathcal{S}(y)$ every state that is of (outgoing) degree at least 2, or that is both of degree 1 and terminal. The forks of the suffix automaton satisfy the same property as that of forks of the suffix tree. This property allows the compaction of the automaton. The proof of the proposition that follows is an immediate adaptation of the proof of Proposition 5.5 and is left to the reader.

Proposition 5.31

In the suffix automaton of a string, the suffix target of a fork (different from the initial state) is a fork. ■

When we delete the states that have an outgoing degree of 1 and that are not terminal, the arcs of the automaton must be labeled by (nonempty) strings and not only by letters. To get a structure of size linear in the length of y, it is necessary to store these labels in an implicit form. We proceed as for the suffix tree by representing them in constant space by means of pairs of integers. If the string u is the label of the arc (p, q), it is represented by the pair $(i, |u|)$ for which i is the position of an occurrence of u in y. We denote the pair by *label*(p, q) and we assume that the implementation of the automaton gives a direct access to this label. This imposes to store the string y with the structure. Figure 5.17 indicates how are represented the labels of the compact suffix automaton of ababbb.

The size of the compact suffix automaton can be evaluated quite directly from those of the suffix tree and of the suffix automaton.

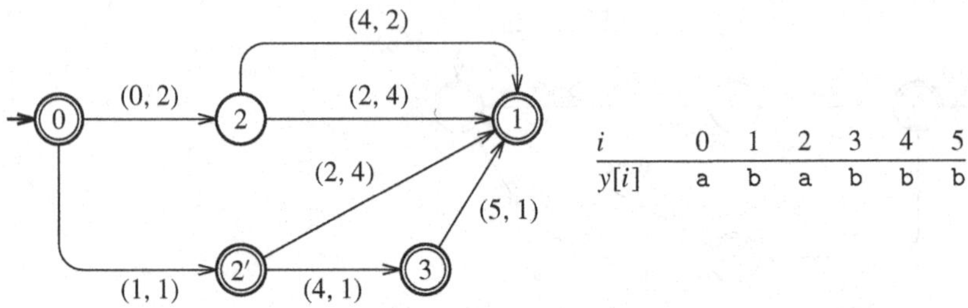

i	0	1	2	3	4	5
$y[i]$	a	b	a	b	b	b

Figure 5.17. Representation of labels of arcs in the compact suffix automaton $\mathcal{S}_{\mathrm{C}}$(ababbb) (see Figure 5.16 for explicit labels).

Proposition 5.32
Let $y \in A^*$ of length n and $e_{\mathrm{C}}(y)$ be the number of states of $\mathcal{S}_{\mathrm{C}}(y)$. For $n = 0$, we have $e_{\mathrm{C}}(y) = 1$; for $n > 0$, we have

$$2 \leq e_{\mathrm{C}}(y) \leq n + 1,$$

and the upper bound is reached for $y = a^n$, $a \in A$.

Proof The result can be directly verified for the empty string.

Let us assume $n > 0$. Let \$ be a special letter, $\$ \notin \mathrm{alph}(y)$, and let us consider the tree $\mathcal{T}_{\mathrm{C}}(y\$)$. This tree possesses exactly $n + 1$ external nodes and on each of them arrives an arc whose label ends precisely by the letter \$. It possesses at most n internal nodes since those nodes are of degree at least 2. When we minimize the tree in order to get a compact automaton, all the external nodes are identified in a single state, which reduces the number of states to $n + 1$ at most. The deletion of the letter \$ does not increase this value and thus we get the upper bound on $e_{\mathrm{C}}(y)$. It is immediate to check that $\mathcal{S}_{\mathrm{C}}(a^n)$ possesses exactly $n + 1$ states and that the obvious lower bound is reached when the alphabet of y is of size n, card $\mathrm{alph}(y) = n$, for $n > 0$. ■

Proposition 5.33
Let $y \in A^*$ be of length n and $f_{\mathrm{C}}(y)$ be the number of arcs of $\mathcal{S}_{\mathrm{C}}(y)$. For $n = 0$, we have $f_{\mathrm{C}}(y) = 0$; for $n = 1$, we have $f_{\mathrm{C}}(y) = 1$; for $n > 1$ finally, we have

$$f_{\mathrm{C}}(y) \leq 2(n - 1),$$

and the upper bound is reached for $y = a^{n-1}b$, a, b being two distinct letters.

Proof After verification of the results for the short strings, we note that if y is of the form a^n, $n > 1$, we have $f_{\mathrm{C}}(y) = n - 1$, whose quantity is no more than $2(n - 1)$.

Let us assume now that card alph(y) ≥ 2. We go on the proof of the previous lemma by considering the string $y\$$, $\$ \notin$ alph(y). Its compact tree possesses at most $2n$ nodes, its root being of degree at least 3. It possesses thus at most $2n - 1$ arcs which after compaction give $2n - 2$ arcs since the arc that is labeled by \$ and that starts from the initial state disappears. This gives the announced bound. Finally, we can directly check that the automaton $\mathcal{S}_{\mathrm{C}}(a^{n-1}b)$ possesses exactly n states and $2n - 2$ arcs. ■

The construction of $\mathcal{S}_{\mathrm{C}}(y)$ can be performed from the tree $\mathcal{T}_{\mathrm{C}}(y)$ or from the automaton $\mathcal{S}(y)$ (see Exercises 5.15 and 5.16). However, for saving the memory space during the construction, we rather use a direct construction. It is the schema of this construction that we describe here.

The construction borrows elements from algorithms SUFFIX-TREE and SUFFIX-AUTO. Thus, the arcs of the automaton are marked as solid or non-solid. The created arcs to new leaves of the tree become arcs to the state *last*. We use also the notions of slow find and fast find from the construction of the suffix tree. It is on these two procedures that the changes are essential and that we find the duplications of states and the redirections of arcs during the construction of the suffix automaton.

During the execution of a slow find, the attempt to traverse a non-solid arc leads to the cloning of its target, that is to say, to a duplication of it analogue to the one that happens during the execution of the procedure EXTENSION in lines 12–22. We can note that some arcs can be redirected by this process.

The second important point in the adaptation of the algorithms of the previous sections focuses on the fast find procedure. The algorithm uses the definition of a suffix target as the algorithm SUFFIX-TREE does. The difference happens here during the creation of the suffix target of a newly created fork (see lines 8–11 in the procedure FAST-FIND). If the new state must be created by cutting a solid arc, the same process applies. On the other hand, if the arc is non-solid, in a first time, there is a redirection of the arc to the fork, with an update of its label. This leaves undefined the suffix target and leads to an iteration of the same process.

The phenomena that are just described occur in any online construction of this type of automaton. Their taking into account is necessary for the correctness of the algorithm of the sequential computation of $\mathcal{S}_{\mathrm{C}}(y)$. They are present in the construction of $\mathcal{S}_{\mathrm{C}}(\texttt{ababbb})$ (see Figure 5.16) for which three steps are detailed in Figure 5.18.

As a conclusion of this section, we state the result on the direct construction of the compact suffix automaton. The description and the formal proof of the algorithm are left to the reader.

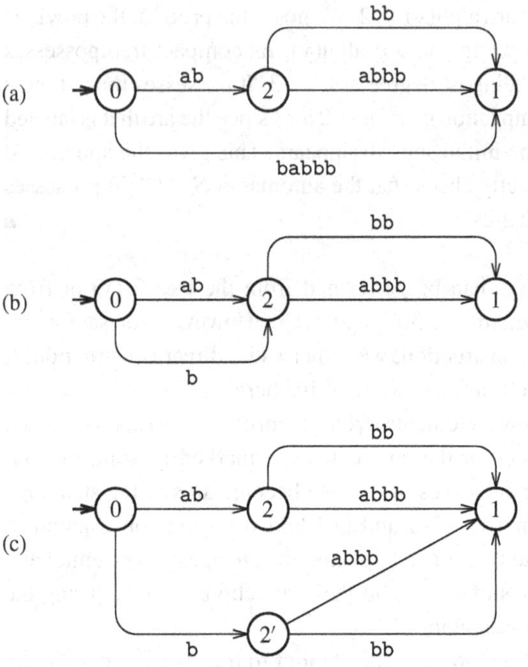

Figure 5.18. Three steps of the construction of $\mathcal{S}_C$(ababbb). **(a)** The automaton just after the insertion of the three longest suffixes of the string ababbb. The suffix link on the state 2 has still to be defined. **(b)** The computation by fast find of the suffix link of the state 2 leads to transform the arc (0, babbb, 1) in (0, b, 2). Meanwhile the suffix bbb has been inserted. **(c)** The insertion of the next suffix, bb, is done by slow find from state 0. The arc (0, b, 2) being non-solid, its target, state 2, is duplicated into 2′ that possesses the same transitions than 2. For ending the insertion of the suffix bb, it remains to cut the arc (2′, bb, 1) in order to create state 3. Finally, the rest of the construction consists in determining the terminal states, and we get the automaton of Figure 5.16.

Proposition 5.34

The computation of the compact suffix automaton $\mathcal{S}_C(y)$ can be realized in time $O(|y| \times \log \text{card}\, A)$ in a space $O(|y|)$. In the branching model, the computation executes in time $O(|y|)$. ■

Notes

The notion of position tree is from Weiner [216] who presented a computation algorithm of its compact version. The algorithm of Section 5.2 is from McCreight [184]. A strictly sequential version of the construction of the suffix tree was described by Ukkonen [214].

Apostolico in [93] describes the many applications of suffix trees, which are also valid for suffix automata after possible adaptations.

Among the many variants of suffix tree representations, let us quote the use of binary search trees by Irving and Love [162], or the notion of ternary search tree by Bentley and Sedgewick [103] (see Exercise 4.4).

As far as space requirements are concerned, there exist succinct representation of trees in which the structure is encoded with a linear number of bits without loosing much efficiency for searching a string. The reader can refer to Munro, Raman, and Rao [189] for its adaptation to suffix trees. See also Sadakane and Grossi [202] and references therein.

Kurtz [173] describes implementations of suffix trees that are tuned for reducing the memory space usage.

In situation where suffix links are not realizable, Cole and Hariharan [115] designed a randomized algorithm constructing a suffix tree in linear time with high probability.

For questions related to formal languages, as the notions of syntactic congruences and of minimal automata, we refer to the books of Berstel [73] and of Pin [82].

The suffix automaton of a text is also known under the name of *DAWG* that stands for *Directed Acyclic Word Graph*. Its linearity was discovered by Blumer et al. (see [105]), who gave a linear-time construction (on a fixed alphabet). The minimality of the structure as an automaton is from Crochemore [119] who showed how to build with the same complexity the factor automaton of a text (see Exercises 5.12, 5.13, and 5.14).

A compaction algorithm of the suffix automaton and a direct construction algorithm of the compact suffix automaton were presented by Crochemore and Vérin [130].

For the average analysis of the size of the different structures presented in the chapter, we refer to the articles of Blumer, Ehrenfeucht, and Haussler [107] and of Raffinot [198], that use methods described in the book of Sedgewick and Flajolet [83].

When the alphabet is potentially infinite, the construction algorithms of the suffix tree and of the suffix automaton are optimal since they imply a sorting on the letters of the alphabet. On particular integer alphabets, Farach-Colton [134] showed that the construction can be done in linear time. This result is also a consequence of the linear-time construction of a suffix array (Section 4.5) that further produces a suffix tree (see Exercise 5.4).

Besides, Allauzen, Crochemore, and Raffinot [88], introduced a reduced structure, called "suffix oracle," that has applications close to those of suffix automata.

Exercises

5.1 (Guess)

We consider the suffix tree built by the algorithm SUFFIX-TREE. Let (p, q) be an arc of the tree and $(i, \ell) = label(p, q)$ be its label. Does the equality $pos(y[i \mathinner{..} i + \ell - 1]) = i$ always hold?

5.2 (Time)

Check that the execution of SUFFIX-TREE(a^n) $(a \in A)$ takes a time $\Omega(n)$. Check that the one of SUFFIX-TREE(y) is done in time $\Omega(n \log n)$ when card alph$(y) = |y| = n$.

5.3 (In particular)

How many nodes are there in the suffix tree of a de Bruijn string and in the one of a Fibonacci string? Same question for their compact and noncompact suffix automata.

5.4 (Array to tree)

Design an algorithm that transforms the suffix array of a string into its suffix tree and that runs in linear time independently of the alphabet size.

5.5 (Common factor)

Give a computation algorithm of $LCF(x, y)$ $(x, y \in A^*)$, maximal length of the common factors to x and y, knowing the tree $\mathcal{T}_C(x \cdot c \cdot y)$, where $c \in A$ and $c \notin$ alph$(x \cdot y)$. What are the time and space complexities of the computation (see another solution in Section 6.6)?

5.6 (Cubes)

Give a tight bound of the number of cubes of primitive strings that can occur in a string of length n. Same question for squares. (*Hint:* use the suffix tree of the string.)

5.7 (Merge)

Design an algorithm for merging two suffix trees, both compact, or both noncompact. Same question for suffix automata.

5.8 (Several strings)

Describe a linear time and space algorithm (on a fixed alphabet) for the construction of the suffix tree of a finite set of strings. Show that the strings can be incorporated one after the other in the structure.

5.9 (Compaction)
Describe a compact version of the digital search tree $\mathcal{A}(X)$ associated with a finite set of strings X (see Exercise 4.4). Adapt the search, insertion, and deletion operations to the new structure.

5.10 (Sparse suffixes)
Given two integers k and p, $0 \le k < p$, and a string y, we consider the set $X = \{u : u \preceq_{\text{suff}} y \text{ and } pos_y(u) = k \bmod p\}$. Design a linear-time algorithm (on a finite and fixed alphabet) that builds the minimal (deterministic) automaton accepting X. (*Hint:* see Béal, Crochemore, and Fici [101].)

5.11 (Ternary)
Describe an implementation of suffix automata using the technique considered for ternary search trees in Exercise 4.4. Design the corresponding algorithms for building the structure and for searching it. (*Hint:* see Miyamoto, Inenaga, Takeda, and Shinohara [186].)

5.12 (Factor automaton)
Let y be a string in which the last letter occurs nowhere else. Show that $\mathcal{F}(y)$, the minimal deterministic automaton that recognizes the factors of y, possesses the same states and the same arcs as $\mathcal{S}(y)$ (only the terminal states differ).

5.13 (Bounds)
Give tight bounds on the number of states and on the number of arcs of the factor automaton $\mathcal{F}(y)$.

5.14 (Construction)
Design a sequential algorithm running in linear time and space (on a finite and fixed alphabet) for the construction of the factor automaton $\mathcal{F}(y)$.

5.15 (Other)
Describe a construction algorithm of $\mathcal{S}_{\text{c}}(y)$ from $\mathcal{T}_{\text{c}}(y)$.

5.16 (Again)
Describe a construction algorithm of $\mathcal{S}_{\text{c}}(y)$ from $\mathcal{S}(y)$.

5.17 (Program)
Write the detailed code of the direct construction of the compact suffix automaton $\mathcal{S}_{\text{c}}(y)$, informally described in Section 5.5.

Design an on-line construction of the automaton. (*Hint:* see Inenaga, Hoshino, Shinohara, Takeda, Arikawa, Mauri, and Pavesi [161].)

5.18 (Several strings, again)

Describe a linear time and space algorithm (on a fixed alphabet) for the construction of the suffix automaton of a set finite of strings. (*Hint:* see Blumer, Blumer, Haussler, McConnell, and Ehrenfeucht [106].)

5.19 (Bounded factors)

Let $\mathcal{T}_{\rm C}(y, k, \ell)$ be the compact tree that accepts the factors of the string y that have a length between k and ℓ (k, ℓ integers, $0 \le k \le \ell \le |y|$). Describe a construction algorithm of $\mathcal{T}_{\rm C}(y, k, \ell)$ that uses a memory space proportional to the size of the tree (and not $O(|y|)$) and that executes in the same asymptotic time as the construction of the suffix tree of y.

6
Indexes

The techniques introduced in the two previous chapters find immediate applications for the realization of the index of a text. The utility of considering the suffixes of a text for this kind of application comes from the obvious remark that every factor of a string can be extended in a suffix of the text (see Figure 6.1). By storing efficiently the suffixes, we get a kind of direct access to all the factors of the text or of a language, and this is certainly the main interest of these techniques. From this property comes quite directly an implementation of the notion of index on a text or on a family of texts, with efficient algorithms for the basic operations (Section 6.2) such as the membership problem and the computation of the positions of occurrences of a pattern. Section 6.3 gives a solution under the form of a transducer. We deduce also quite directly solutions for the detection of repetitions (Section 6.4) and for the computation of forbidden strings (Section 6.5). Section 6.6 presents an inverted application of the previous techniques by using the index of a pattern in order to help searching fro itself. This method is extended in a particularly efficient way to the search for the conjugates (or rotations) of a string.

6.1 Implementing an index

The aim of an index is to provide efficient procedures for answering questions related to the content of a fixed text. This text is denoted by y ($y \in A^*$) and its length by n ($n \in \mathbf{N}$). An ***index*** on y can be considered as an abstract data type whose basic set is the set of factors of y, $\mathrm{Fact}(y)$, and that possesses operations giving access to information relative to these factors. The notion is analogue to the notion of index of a book that refers to the text from selected keywords. We rather consider what is called a generalized index in which all the factors of the text are present. We are interested in the index of a single string,

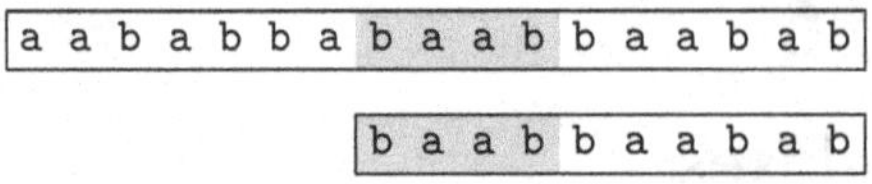

a	a	b	a	b	b	a	b	a	a	b	b	a	a	b	a	b

b	a	a	b	b	a	a	b	a	b

Figure 6.1. Every factor of a text is the prefix of a suffix of the text.

but the extension to a finite set of strings does not pose extra difficulties in general.

We consider four main operations on the index of a text. They concern a string x that we search for inside y: membership, position, number of occurrences, and list of positions. This list is generally extended in real applications, according to the nature of the data represented by y, in order to produce documentary search systems. But the four mentioned operations constitute the technical basis from which can be developed larger query systems.

We choose to present two main implementation methods that lead to efficient if not optimal algorithms. The first method utilizes the suffix array of the string y, the second relies on a data structure for representing the suffixes of y. The choice of the structure produces variants of the second method. In this section, we recall for each of these implementations the elements that must be available for realizing the operations of the index and that are described in Chapters 4 and 5. The operations themselves are considered in the next section.

The technique of suffix array (Chapter 4) is the first considered method. It focuses on a binary search in the set of suffixes of y. It provides a solution to the interval problem, which is extended in a method for locating patterns. To get it, it is necessary to sort the suffixes in lexicographic order and to compute their corresponding *LCP* table. Though card Fact(y) is $O(n^2)$, sorting the suffixes and computing *LCP*'s can be realized in time and space $O(n \log n)$ or even $O(n)$ on bounded integer alphabets (see Sections 4.4 to 4.6).

The permutation of suffixes of y that provides their lexicographic order is a table denoted by p and defined, for $r = 0, 1, \ldots, n-1$, by

$$p[r] = i$$

if and only if

$$y[i \,..\, n-1] \text{ is the } r\text{th smaller nonempty suffix of } y$$

for the lexicographic ordering. In other words, r is the rank of the suffix $y[i \,..\, n-1]$ in L, sorted list of the nonempty suffixes of y. The search for patterns inside y is based on the following remark: the suffixes of y starting with a same string u are consecutive in the list L.

The data structures for using the suffix array of the string y are made up of

- the string y itself, stored in a table,
- the table p: $\{0, 1, \ldots, n-1\} \rightarrow \{0, 1, \ldots, n-1\}$ that provides the indices of the suffixes in the increasing lexicographic order of these strings,
- the table LCP: $\{0, 1, \ldots, 2n\} \rightarrow \{0, 1, \ldots, n-1\}$ that gives the maximal length of the prefixes common to some suffixes, as indicated in Sections 4.3 and 4.6.

The computation of the tables p and LCP is presented in Sections 4.4 to 4.6.

The second method for the implementation of an index relies on the structures of suffix automata (Chapter 5). Thus, the suffix tree of y, $\mathcal{T}_c(y)$, provides a basis for the realization of an index. Let us recall that the data structures necessary for its utilization are composed of

- the string y itself stored in a table,
- an implementation of the automaton under the form of a transition matrix or of a set of labeled successors for representing the transition function δ, the access to the initial state, and a marking of the terminal states, for instance,
- the attribute $s\ell$, defined on the states, that realizes the suffix link of the tree.

We note that the string must be stored in memory because the labeling of arcs refers to it (see Section 5.2). The suffix link is only used for some applications, it can, of course, be deleted when the implemented operations do not use it.

We can also use the suffix automaton of y, $\mathcal{S}(y)$, that produces in a natural way an index on the factors of the text. The structure contains

- an implementation of the automaton as for the above tree,
- the attribute F that realizes the failure function defined on the states,
- the attribute L that indicates for each state the maximal length of the strings that lead to this state.

For this automaton, it is not necessary to memorize the string y. It is contained in the automaton as the label of the longest path starting from the initial state. The attributes F and L can be omitted if they are not useful for the considered operations.

Finally, the compact version of the suffix automaton can be used in order to save even more of the memory space necessary to store the structure. Its implementation uses in a standard way the same elements as the suffix automaton does (in a noncompact version) but with additionally the string y for the access to labels of arcs, as for the suffix tree. We get a noticeable gain in storage space when using this structure rather that the previous ones.

In the section that follows, we examine several types of solutions for the realization of the basic operations on the index.

6.2 Basic operations

In this section, we consider four operations relative to the factors of a text y: the membership (to Fact(y)), the first position, the number of occurrences, and the list of positions. The corresponding algorithms are presented after the global description of these four operations.

The first operation on an index is the membership of a string x to the index, that is to say the question to know whether x is a factor of y or not. This question can be specified in two complementary ways whether we expect to find an occurrence of x in y or not. If x does not occur in y, it is often interesting in applications to compute the longest beginning of x that is a factor of y. This is the type of usual answer necessary for the sequential search tools found for instance in a text editor.

Problem of the membership to the index: given $x \in A^*$, find the longest prefix of x that belongs to Fact(y).

In the contrary case ($x \preceq_{\text{fact}} y$), the methods produce without much modification the position of an occurrence of x, and even the position of the first or last occurrences of x in y.

Problem of the position: given $x \preceq_{\text{fact}} y$, find the (left) position of its first (respectively last) occurrence in y.

Knowing that x is in the index, another relevant information is the number of times x occurs in y. This information can differently direct the further searches.

Problem of the number of occurrences: given $x \preceq_{\text{fact}} y$, find how many times x occurs in y.

Finally, with the same assumption than previously, a complete information on the location of x in y is supplied by the list of positions of its occurrences.

Problem of the list of positions: given $x \preceq_{\text{fact}} y$, produce the list of positions of the occurrences of x in y.

The suffix array of a string presented in Chapter 4 provides a simple and elegant solution for the realization of the above operations. The suffix array of y consists of the pair of tables p and LCP as recalled in the previous section.

Proposition 6.1
By means of the suffix array of y (pair of tables p and LCP) that occupies a memory space $O(|y|)$ we can compute the longest prefix u of a string $x \in A^*$ for which $u \preceq_{\text{fact}} y$ in time $O(|u| + \log |y|)$.

When $x \preceq_{\text{fact}} y$, we can compute the position of the first occurrence of x in y and its number of occurrences in time $O(|x| + \log |y|)$, and produce all the positions of the occurrences in extra time proportional to their number.

Proof The algorithm can be obtained from the algorithm INTERVAL (Section 4.6). Let (d, f) be the result of this algorithm applied to the sorted list of suffixes of y (order provided by p) and using the table LCP. By construction of the algorithm (problem of the interval and Proposition 4.5), if $d + 1 < f$ the string x possesses $f - d - 1$ occurrences in y; they are at positions $p[d+1], p[d+2], \ldots, p[f-1]$. On the other hand, if $d + 1 = f$, the string x does not occur in y and we notice by a simple look at the proof of Proposition 4.4 that the search time is $O(|u| + \log |y|)$.

To produce the positions $p[d+1], p[d+2], \ldots, p[f-1]$, it takes a time proportional to their number, $f - d - 1$. This ends the proof. ■

We tackle then the solutions obtained by using the data structures of Chapter 5. The memory space occupied by the trees or automata is a bit larger than that necessary for the suffix array, although still $O(|y|)$. It can also be noted that the structures require sometimes to be enlarged to guarantee an optimal execution of the algorithms. However, the running times of the operations are different, and the structures allow other applications that are the subject of the next sections. The solutions use the basic algorithms designed below.

Proposition 6.2
Whether it is by means of $\mathcal{T}_{\text{C}}(y)$, $\mathcal{S}(y)$, or $\mathcal{S}_{\text{C}}(y)$, the computation of the longest prefix u of x that is factor of y ($u \preceq_{\text{fact}} y$) can be realized in time $O(|u| \times \log \text{card}\, A)$ in a memory space $O(|y|)$.

Proof By means of $\mathcal{S}(y)$, in order of determine the string u, it is sufficient to follow a path of label x from the initial state of the automaton. We stop the scan when a transition misses or when x is exhausted. This produces the longest prefix of x that is also prefix of the label of a path from the initial state, that is to say that occurs in y since all the factors of y are labels of the considered paths. Overall, we perform thus $|u|$ successful transitions and possibly one unsuccessful transition (when $u \prec_{\text{pref}} x$) at the end of the test. As each transition requires a time $O(\log \text{card}\, A)$ for an implementation in space $O(|y|)$ (Section 1.4), we get a global time $O(|u| \times \log \text{card}\, A)$.

The same process works with $\mathcal{T}_C(y)$ and $\mathcal{S}_C(y)$. ■

When taking into account the representation of the compact structures, some transitions are done by mere letter comparisons. This somehow speeds up the execution of the considered operation even if this does not modify its asymptotic bound.

Position

We examine now the operations for which it is assumed that x is a factor of y. The membership test that can be realized separately as in the previous proposition, can also be integrated to solutions to the other problems that we are interested in here. The utilization of transducers, which extend suffix automata, for this type of problem is tackled in the next section.

The computation of the position of the first occurrence of x in y, $pos(x)$, amounts to find its right position $rpos(x)$ (see Section 5.3) since

$$pos(x) = rpos(x) - |x| + 1.$$

Moreover, this is also equivalent to computing the maximal length of the right contexts of x in y,

$$lc(x) = \max\{|z| : z \in x^{-1}\mathrm{Suff}(y)\},$$

since

$$pos(x) = |y| - lc(x) - |x|.$$

In a symmetrical way, the search for the position $lpos(x)$ of the last occurrence of x in y amounts to compute the minimal length $sc(x)$ of its right contexts since

$$lpos(x) = |y| - sc(x) - |x|.$$

To quickly answer to queries on the first or the last positions of factors of y, the index structures alone are not sufficient, at least if we want to get optimal running times. Therefore, we precompute two attributes on the states of the automaton, which represent the functions lc and sc. We thus get the result that follows.

Proposition 6.3
The automata $\mathcal{T}_C(y)$, $\mathcal{S}(y)$, and $\mathcal{S}_C(y)$ can be processed in time $O(|y|)$ so that the first (or last) position in y of a string $x \preceq_{\mathrm{fact}} y$, and also the number of occurrences of x, can be computed in time $O(|x| \times \log \mathrm{card}\, A)$ in memory space $O(|y|)$.

Proof Let us denote by M the chosen automaton, by δ its transition function, by E its set of arcs (or edges), by q_0 its initial state, and by T the set of its terminal states.

Let us first consider the computation of $pos(x)$. The preprocessing of the automaton focuses on the computation of an attribute LC (longest context) defined on the states of M for representing the function lc. For a state p and a string $u \in A^*$ with $p = \delta(q_0, u)$, we set

$$LC[p] = lc(u),$$

this quantity is independent of the string u that leads to the state p (see Lemma 5.10). This value is also the maximal length of the paths starting from p and ending in a terminal state in the automaton $\mathcal{S}(y)$. For $\mathcal{T}_c(y)$ and $\mathcal{S}_c(y)$ this remark still holds if the length of an arc is defined as the length of its label.

The attribute LC satisfies the recurrence relation:

$$LC[p] = \begin{cases} 0 & \text{if } deg(p) = 0, \\ \max\{\ell + LC[q] : (p, v, q) \in E \text{ and } |v| = \ell\} & \text{otherwise.} \end{cases}$$

The relation shows that the computation of the values $LC[p]$, for all the states of the automaton M, is done during a simple depth-first traversal of the graph of the structure. As its number of nodes and its number of arcs are linear (see Sections 5.2, 5.4, and 5.5) and as the access to the length of the label of an arc can be done in constant time after the representation described in Section 5.2, the computation of the attribute takes a time $O(|y|)$ (independent of the alphabet).

Once the computation of the attribute LC is performed, the computation of $pos(x)$ is done by the search for $p = \delta(q_0, x)$, then by the computation of $|y| - LC[p] - |x|$. We get then the same asymptotic execution time as for the membership problem, that is, $O(|x| \times \log \operatorname{card} A)$. Let us note that if

$$end(q_0, x) = \delta(q_0, xw)$$

with w nonempty, the value of $pos(x)$ is then $|y| - LC[p] - |xw|$, which does not modify the asymptotic evaluation of the execution time.

The computation of the position of the last occurrence of x in y solves in an analogue way by considering the attribute SC (shortest context) defined by

$$SC[p] = sc(u),$$

with the above notation. The relation

$$SC[p] = \begin{cases} 0 & \text{if } p \in T, \\ \min\{\ell + SC[q] : (p, v, q) \in E \text{ and } |v| = \ell\} & \text{otherwise,} \end{cases}$$

shows that the preprocessing of SC requires a time $O(|y|)$, and that the computation of $lpos(x)$ requires then the time $O(|x| \times \log \operatorname{card} A)$.

Finally, for the access to the number of occurrences of x we precompute an attribute NB defined by

$$NB[p] = \operatorname{card}\{z \in A^* : \delta(p, z) \in T\},$$

that is precisely the searched quantity when $p = end(q_0, x)$. The linear precomputation can be deduced from the relation

$$NB[p] = \begin{cases} 1 + \sum_{(p,v,q)\in E} NB[q] & \text{if } p \in T, \\ \sum_{(p,v,q)\in E} NB[q] & \text{otherwise.} \end{cases}$$

Then, the number of occurrences of x is obtained by computing the state $p = end(q_0, x)$ and accessing $NB[p]$, which can be done in the same time as for the above operations.

This ends the proof. ■

Number of factors

A similar argument to the last element of the previous proof allows an efficient computation of the number of factors of y, that is to say of the size of $\operatorname{Fact}(y)$. To do this we evaluate the quantity $CS[p]$, for all the states p of the automaton, using the relation:

$$CS[p] = \begin{cases} 1 & \text{if } deg(p) = 0, \\ 1 + \sum_{(p,v,q)\in F}(|v| - 1 + CS[q]) & \text{otherwise.} \end{cases}$$

If $p = \delta(q_0, u)$ for a factor u of y, $CS[p]$ is the number of factors of y starting by u. This gives a linear computation of $\operatorname{card}\operatorname{Fact}(y) = CS[q_0]$, that is to say in time $O(|y|)$ independently of the alphabet A, the automaton being given.

List of positions

Proposition 6.4
By means of either the tree $\mathcal{T}_C(y)$, or the automaton $\mathcal{S}_C(y)$, the list L of positions on y of the occurrences of a string $x \preceq_{\text{fact}} y$ can be computed in time $O(|x| \times \log \operatorname{card} A + k)$ in a memory space $O(|y|)$, where k is the number of elements of L.

Proof We consider the tree $\mathcal{T}_C(y)$ which we denote by q_0 the initial state. Let us recall from Section 5.1 that a state q of the tree is a factor of y, and that, if it is terminal, it possesses an output that is the position of the suffix occurrence of q in y (we have in this case $q \preceq_{\text{suff}} y$ and $output[q] = pos(q) = |y| - |q|$). The positions of the occurrences of x in y are those of the suffixes prefixed by x. Therefore, we get these positions by searching the terminal states of the subtree rooted at $p = end(q_0, x)$ (see Section 5.2). The scan of this subtree takes a time proportional to its size or also to its number of terminal nodes since each nonterminal node possesses at least two children by definition of the tree. Finally, the number of terminal nodes is precisely the number k of elements of the list L.

To summarize, the computation of L requires the computation of p, then the scan of the subtree. The first phase executes in time $O(|x| \times \log \text{card}\, A)$, the second in time $O(k)$, this gives the announced result for the utilization of $\mathcal{T}_{\text{C}}(y)$.

An analogue argument holds for $\mathcal{S}_{\text{C}}(y)$. From state $p = end(q_0, x)$, we perform a depth-first scan of the automaton while memorizing the length of the current path (the length of an arc is the length of its label). A terminal state q to which we access by a path of length ℓ corresponds to a suffix of length ℓ that is thus at position $|y| - \ell$. This quantity is then the position of an occurrence of x in y. The complete scan takes a time $O(k)$ since it is equivalent to the scan of the subtree of $\mathcal{T}_{\text{C}}(y)$ described above. We thus get the same result as with the suffix tree. ■

Let us note that the result on the computation of the lists of positions is obtained without preprocessing of the automata. On the other hand, the utilization of the (noncompact) suffix automaton of y requires a preprocessing that consists in creating short-cuts for superimposing to it the structure of $\mathcal{S}_{\text{C}}(y)$ if we wish to obtain a computation having the same complexity.

6.3 Transducer of positions

Some of the problems related to the locations of factors inside the string y can be described by means of transducers, that is to say, automata in which the arcs possess an output in addition to the output of terminal states. For example, the function *pos* can be realized by the transducer of positions of y, denoted by $T(y)$. Figure 6.2 illustrates the transducer $T(\texttt{aabbabb})$.

The transducer $T(y)$ is defined from $\mathcal{S}(y)$ by adding outputs to the arcs and by changing the outputs associated with terminal states. The arcs of $T(y)$ are of the form $(p, (a, s), q)$ where p and q are states, and (a, s) the label of the

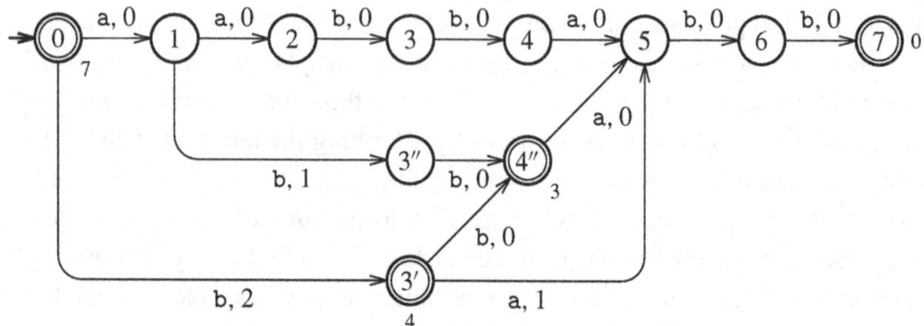

Figure 6.2. Transducer of positions $T(\texttt{aabbabb})$ that realizes in a sequential way the function *pos* of $y = \texttt{aabbabb}$. Each arc is labeled by a pair (a, s), where a is the input of the arc and s its output. When reading abb, the transducer produces the integer 1 $(= 0 + 1 + 0)$ that is the position of the first occurrence of abb in y. The target state having the output 3, we deduce that abb is a suffix at position 4 $(= 1 + 3)$ of y.

arc. The letter $a \in A$ is the ***input*** of the arc and the integer $s \in \mathbf{N}$ is its ***output***. The path

$$(p_0, (a_0, s_0), p_1), (p_1, (a_1, s_1), p_2), \ldots, (p_{k-1}, (a_{k-1}, s_{k-1}), p_k)$$

of the transducer has for input label the string $a_0a_1 \ldots a_{k-1}$, concatenation of the inputs of the labels of the arcs of the path, and for output the sum $s_0 + s_1 + \cdots + s_{k-1}$.

The transducer of positions $T(y)$ has for basis the automaton $\mathcal{S}(y)$. The transformation of $\mathcal{S}(y)$ into $T(y)$ is done as follows. When (p, a, q) is an arc of $\mathcal{S}(y)$ it becomes the arc $(p, (a, s), q)$ of $T(y)$ with output

$$s = rpos(v) - rpos(u) - 1,$$

where $u \in p$ and $v \in q$ (or equivalently $\delta(q_0, u) = p$ and $\delta(q_0, v) = q$), value that is also

$$LC[p] - LC[q] - 1$$

with the notation LC (that stands for Longest Context) used in the proof of Proposition 6.3. The output associated with a terminal state p is defined as $LC[p]$.

Proposition 6.5
Let v be the input label of a path from the initial state in the transducer $T(y)$. Then, the output label of the path is $pos(v)$.

Moreover, if the end of the path is a terminal state having output t, v is a suffix of y and the position of this occurrence of v is $pos(v) + t$.

Proof We prove the statement by recurrence on the length of v. The seed of the recurrence, for $v = \varepsilon$, is immediate. Let us assume $v = ua$ with $u \in A^*$ and $a \in A$. The output label of the path of input label ua is $r + s$ where r and s are respectively the output labels corresponding to the inputs u and a. By recurrence hypothesis, we have $r = pos(v)$. By definition of the labels in $T(y)$, we have

$$s = rpos(v) - rpos(u) - 1.$$

Thus the output associated with v is

$$pos(u) + rpos(v) - rpos(u) - 1$$

and since $rpos(w) = pos(w) + |w| - 1$,

$$pos(v) + |v| - |u| - 1$$

which is $pos(v)$ as expected. This ends the proof of the first part of the statement.

If the end of the considered path is a terminal state, its output t is, by definition, $LC[u]$ which is $|y| - rpos(u) - 1$ or also $|y| - pos(u) - |u|$. Thus $pos(u) + t = |y| - |u|$, which is indeed the position of the suffix u as announced. ■

We have seen in the proof of Proposition 6.3 how to compute the attribute LC that serves to the definition of the transducer $T(y)$. We deduce from that a computation of the outputs associated with the arcs and with the terminal states of the transducer. As a result, the transformation is performed in linear time.

Proposition 6.6
The computation of the transducer of positions $T(y)$ from the suffix automaton $\mathcal{S}(y)$ can be realized in linear time, $O(|y|)$. ■

The existence of the transducer of the positions described above shows that the position of a factor of y can be computed sequentially as the factor is read. The computation can even be done in real time when the transitions are executed in constant time.

6.4 Repetitions

In this section, we examine two problems concerning the repetitions of factors inside the text y. There are two dual problems that can be solved efficiently by the utilization of a suffix array or of a suffix automaton:

- compute a longest repeated factor of y,
- find a shortest factor of y that occurs only once in y.

We can also generalize the problem by searching factors that occur at least k times in y, for a given integer $k > 0$.

Problem of the longest repetition: find a longest string possessing at least two occurrences in y.

The suffix array of y being given (pair of tables p and *LCP*), a longest repetition is also a string that is the longest prefix common to two distinct suffixes. Two of these suffixes are then consecutive in the lexicographic order as a consequence of Lemma 4.6. Recalling that $LCP[f] = |lcp(y[p[f-1]\,..\,n-1], y[p[f]\,..\,n-1])|$, for $0 < f < n$, the length of the longest repetition is thus

$$\max\{LCP[f] : f = 1, 2, \ldots, n-1\}.$$

Let r be this value and f an index for which $LCP[f] = r$. We deduce

$$y[p[f-1]\,..\,p[f-1]+r-1] = y[p[f]\,..\,p[f]+r-1],$$

and that this string is a longest repetition in y.

Let us consider now the utilization of a suffix automaton, $\mathcal{S}(y)$ for instance. If the table *NB* defined in the proof of Proposition 6.3 is available, the problem of the longest repetition reduces to find a state p of $\mathcal{S}(y)$ that is the deepest in the automaton, and for which $NB[p] > 1$. The label of the longest path from the initial state to p is then a solution to the problem. Actually, the problem can be solved without the help to the attribute *NB* in the following way. We simply search a state, the deepest possible, that satisfies one of the two conditions:

- at least two arcs leave p,
- one arc leaves p and p is terminal.

The state p is then a fork and its search can be done by a simple traversal of the automaton. Proceeding in this way, no preprocessing of $\mathcal{S}(y)$ is necessary and we keep nevertheless a linear computation time. We can note that the running time does not depend on the branching time in the automaton since no transition is performed, the search only uses existing arcs.

The two above descriptions are summarized in the next proposition.

Proposition 6.7
By means of the suffix array of y or of the automata $\mathcal{T}_C(y)$, $\mathcal{S}(y)$ or $\mathcal{S}_C(y)$, the computation of a longest repeated factor of y can be realized in time $O(|y|)$. ■

The second problem dealt with, in this section, is the search for a marker. Such a factor is called a marker because it marks a precise position on y.

Problem of the marker: find a shortest string occurring exactly once in y.

The utilization of the suffix automaton provides a solution to the problem of the same kind as the search for a repetition. It consists in searching the automaton for a state, the least deep possible, and that is the origin of a single path to a terminal state. Again, a simple traversal of the automaton solves the question, which gives the following result.

Proposition 6.8
By means of the suffix automaton $\mathcal{S}(y)$, the computation of a marker, a shortest string occurring only once in y, can be realized in time and space $O(|y|)$. ■

6.5 Forbidden strings

The search for forbidden strings is complementary to the problems of the previous section. The notion is used, in particular, in the description of some text compression algorithms.

A string $u \in A^*$ is said to be ***forbidden*** in the string $y \in A^*$ if it is not a factor of y. And the string u is said to be ***minimal forbidden*** if, in addition, all its proper factors are factors of y. In other words, the minimality is relative to the ordering relation $\preceq_{\text{fact}}$. This notion is actually more relevant than the previous one. We denote by $I(y)$ the set of minimal forbidden strings in y.

We can note that, if u is a string of length k,

$$u \in I(y)$$

if and only if

$$u[1\,..\,k-1] \preceq_{\text{fact}} y,\ u[0\,..\,k-2] \preceq_{\text{fact}} y,\ \text{and } u \npreceq_{\text{fact}} y,$$

which translates into

$$I(y) = (A \cdot \text{Fact}(y)) \cap (\text{Fact}(y) \cdot A) \cap (A^* \setminus \text{Fact}(y)).$$

The identity shows, in particular, that the language $I(y)$ is finite. It is thus possible to represent $I(y)$ by a (finite) trie in which only the external nodes are terminal nodes because of the minimality condition of the strings.

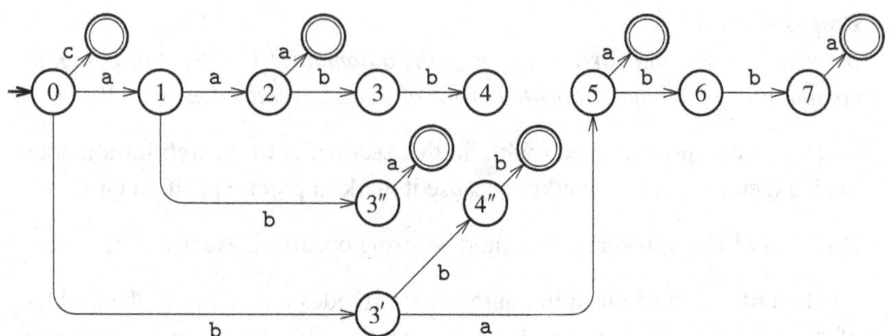

Figure 6.3. Trie of the minimal forbidden strings of the string aabbabb on the alphabet {a, b, c} as it is built by algorithm FORBIDDEN. The states that are not terminal are those of the automaton $\mathcal{S}$(aabbabb) of Figure 5.14. We note that states 3 and 4 and the arcs that enter them can be deleted. The string babba recognized by the trie is forbidden because it does not occur in aabbabb, and it is minimal because babb and abba are factors of aabbabb.

The algorithm FORBIDDEN, whose code is given below, builds the trie accepting $I(y)$ from the automaton $\mathcal{S}(y)$.

```
FORBIDDEN(S(y))
M ← NEW-AUTOMATON()
L ← EMPTY-QUEUE()
ENQUEUE(L, (initial[S(y)], initial[M]))
while not QUEUE-IS-EMPTY(L) do
      (p, p′) ← DEQUEUED(L)
      for each letter a ∈ A do
            if TARGET(p, a) = NIL and
               (p = initial[S(y)] or TARGET(F[p], a) ≠ NIL) then
                  q′ ← NEW-STATE()
                  terminal[q′] ← TRUE
                  Succ[p′] ← Succ[p′] ∪ {(a, q′)}
            elseif TARGET(p, a) ≠ NIL
               and TARGET(p, a) not yet reached then
                  q′ ← NEW-STATE()
                  Succ[p′] ← Succ[p′] ∪ {(a, q′)}
                  ENQUEUE(L, (TARGET(p, a), q′))
return M
```

In the algorithm, the queue L is used to traverse the automaton $\mathcal{S}(y)$ in a width-first manner. Figure 6.3 presents the example of the trie of strings forbidden in the string aabbabb that is obtained from the automaton of Figure 5.14.

Proposition 6.9
For $y \in A^*$, the algorithm FORBIDDEN *produces, from the automaton $\mathcal{S}(y)$, a trie that accepts the language $I(y)$. The execution can be realized in time $O(|y| \times \log \text{card}\, A)$.*

Proof We note that the arcs created in line 13 duplicate the arcs of the spanning tree of the shortest paths of the graph of $\mathcal{S}(y)$, since the traversal of the automaton is performed in increasing order of levels (the queue L is used to this aim). The other arcs are created in line 10 and are of the form (p', a, q') with $q' \in T'$, denoting by T' the set of terminal states of M. Let us denote by δ' the transition function associated with the arcs of M computed by the algorithm. By construction, the string u for which $\delta'(\mathit{initial}[M], u) = p'$ is the shortest string that leads to the state $p = \delta(\mathit{initial}[\mathcal{S}(y)], u)$ in $\mathcal{S}(y)$.

We start by showing that every string recognized by the trie produced by the algorithm is a minimal forbidden string. Let ua be such a string that cannot be the empty string ($u \in A^*$, $a \in A$). By assumption, the arc (p', a, q') has been created in line 10 and $q' \in T'$. If $u = \varepsilon$, we have $p' = \mathit{initial}[M]$ and we note that, by construction, $a \notin \text{alph}(y)$ thus ua is indeed minimal forbidden. If $u \neq \varepsilon$, let us denote it by bv with $b \in A$ and $v \in A^*$. We have

$$s = \delta(\mathit{initial}[\mathcal{S}(y)], v)$$

and $s \neq p$ because $|v| < |u|$ and, by construction, u is the shortest string that satisfies $p = \delta(\mathit{initial}[M], u)$. Thus $F[p] = s$, by definition of the suffix link. Then, again by construction, $\delta(s, a)$ is defined, which implies $va \preceq_{\text{fact}} y$. The string $ua = bva$ is thus minimal forbidden, since $bv, va \preceq_{\text{fact}} y$ and $ua \not\preceq_{\text{fact}} y$.

Conversely, we show that every forbidden string is recognized by the trie built by the algorithm. Let ua be such a string that cannot be the empty string ($u \in \text{Fact}(y)$, $a \in A$). If $u = \varepsilon$, the letter a does not occur in y, and thus $\delta(\mathit{initial}[\mathcal{S}(y)], a)$ is not defined. The condition in line 7 is satisfied and has for effect to create an arc that leads to the recognition of the string ua by the automaton M. If $u \neq \varepsilon$, let us write it bv with $b \in A$ and $v \in A^*$. Let

$$p = \delta(\mathit{initial}[\mathcal{S}(y)], u).$$

As $v \prec_{\text{suff}} u$ and $va \preceq_{\text{fact}} y$ while $ua \not\preceq_{\text{fact}} y$, if we let

$$s = \delta(\mathit{initial}[\mathcal{S}(y)], v),$$

we have necessarily $p \neq s$ and thus $s = F[p]$ by definition of the suffix link. The condition in line 7 is thus still satisfied in this case and has the same effect as above. As a conclusion, ua is recognized by the trie created by the algorithm, which ends the second part and the proof. ∎

We note that $y \in \{\mathtt{a}, \mathtt{b}\}^*$ possesses at most $|y|$ minimal forbidden strings (essentially because for every prefix za of y, there exists at most one minimal forbidden string of the form ub with $u \preceq_{\text{suff}} z$ and $a \neq b$). A noticeable and unexpected consequence of the existence of the trie of forbidden strings, given by the previous construction, is a bound on the number of minimal forbidden strings of a string on any alphabet. If the alphabet is reduced to two letters, the bound is $|y| + 1$ essentially because forbidden strings are associated with positions on y.

Proposition 6.10
A string $y \in A^*$ of length $|y| \geq 2$ possesses no more than $\text{card}\, A + (2|y| - 3) \times (\text{card}\, \text{alph}(y) - 1)$ *minimal forbidden strings. It possesses* $\text{card}\, A$ *of them if* $|y| < 2$.

Proof After the previous proposition, the number of minimal forbidden strings in y is equal to the number of terminal states of the trie recognizing $I(y)$, which is also the number of incoming arcs in these states.

There are exactly $\text{card}\, A - \alpha$ such outgoing arcs from the initial state, by denoting $\alpha = \text{card}\, \text{alph}(y)$. There are at most α outgoing arcs from the state corresponding to the unique state of $\mathcal{S}(y)$ that has no successor. From the other states there exit at most $\alpha - 1$ arcs. Since, for $|y| \geq 2$, $\mathcal{S}(y)$ possesses at most $2|y| - 1$ states (Proposition 5.22), we get

$$\text{card}\, I(y) \leq (\text{card}\, A - \alpha) + \alpha + (2|y| - 3) \times (\alpha - 1),$$

thus

$$\text{card}\, I(y) \leq \text{card}\, A + (2|y| - 3) \times (\alpha - 1),$$

as announced.

Finally, we have $I(\varepsilon) = A$ and, for $a \in A$, $I(a) = (A \setminus \{a\}) \cup \{aa\}$. Thus $\text{card}\, I(y) = \text{card}\, A$ when $|y| < 2$. ∎

6.6 Search machine

A suffix automaton can be used as a search machine for locating occurrences of patterns. We consider, in this section, the automaton $\mathcal{S}(x)$ in order to search for x in a string y. The other structures, the compact tree $\mathcal{T}_C(x)$ and the compact automaton $\mathcal{S}_C(x)$, can be used as well.

The algorithm relies on the consideration of a transducer represented by a failure function (Section 1.4). The transducer computes sequentially the lengths ℓ_i defined below. It is based on the automaton $\mathcal{S}(x)$, and the failure function is nothing else but the suffix link f defined on the states of the automaton. The searching method works as described in Section 1.4 and used in the string searching algorithms of Sections 2.3 and 2.6. The search is executed sequentially along the string y. The adaptation and the analysis of the algorithm to the tree $\mathcal{T}_C(x)$ are not totally immediate since the suffix link of this structure is not a failure function with the precise sense of this notion.

The advantage that brings the algorithm on the algorithms of Section 2.6 resides in a reduced processing time for each letter of y and a more direct analysis of the complexity of the process. The price for this improvement is a more important need of memory space used to store the automaton instead of a simple table.

Lengths of the common factors

The search for the string x is based on a computation of the lengths of factors of x occurring at every position of y. More accurately, the algorithm computes, at every position i on y, the length

$$\ell_i = \max\{|u| : u \in \text{Fact}(x) \cap \text{Suff}(y[0 \,.\,. i])\}$$

of the longest factor of x ending at this position. The detection of the occurrences of x follows then the remark:

$$x \text{ occurs at position } i - |x| + 1 \text{ in } y$$

if and only if

$$\ell_i = |x|.$$

The algorithm that computes the lengths $\ell_0, \ell_1, \ldots, \ell_{|y|-1}$ is given below. It uses the attributes F and L defined on the states of the automaton (Section 5.4). The attribute F is used to reset the current length of the recognized factor, after the computation of a suffix target (line 8). The correctness of this instruction is a consequence of Lemma 5.15.

i	0	1	2	3	4	5	6	7	8	9	10	11	12	13	14	15	16
$y[i]$	a	a	a	b	b	b	a	b	b	a	a	b	b	a	b	b	b
ℓ_i	1	2	2	3	4	2	3	4	5	4	2	3	4	5	6	7	2
p_i	1	2	2	3	4	4″	5	6	7	5	2	3	4	5	6	7	4″

Figure 6.4. With the automaton $\mathcal{S}$(aabbabb) (refer to Figure 5.14), the algorithm FACT-LENGTHS determines the common factors between aabbabb and y. Values ℓ_i and p_i are the respective values, relative to position i, of the variables ℓ and p of the algorithm. At position 8 for instance, we have $\ell_8 = 5$, which indicates that the longest factor of aabbabb ending there is of length 5; it is bbabb; the current state is 7. We detect an occurrence of the pattern when $\ell_i = 7 = |$aabbabb$|$, as in position 15.

```
FACT-LENGTHS(S(x), y, n)
(ℓ, p) ← (0, initial[S(x)])
for i ← 0 to n − 1 do
    if TARGET(p, y[i]) ≠ NIL then
        (ℓ, p) ← (ℓ + 1, TARGET(p, y[i]))
    else do  p ← F[p]
        while p ≠ NIL and TARGET(p, y[i]) = NIL
        if p ≠ NIL then
            (ℓ, p) ← (L[p] + 1, TARGET(p, y[i]))
        else (ℓ, p) ← (0, initial[S(x)])
    output ℓ
```

A simulation of the algorithm is shown in Figure 6.4.

Theorem 6.11
The algorithm FACT-LENGTHS *applied to the automaton* $\mathcal{S}(x)$ *and to the string* y $(x, y \in A^*)$ *produces the lengths* $\ell_0, \ell_1, \ldots, \ell_{|y|-1}$.

It performs less than $2|y|$ *transitions in* $\mathcal{S}(x)$ *and executes in time* $O(|y| \times \log \operatorname{card} A)$ *in space* $O(|x|)$.

Proof The correctness of the algorithm is proved by recurrence on the length of the prefixes of y. We show more exactly that the equalities

$$\ell = \ell_i$$

and

$$p = \delta(\mathit{initial}[\mathcal{S}(x)], y[i - \ell + 1 \,..\, i])$$

are invariants of the **for** loop, by letting δ be the transition function of $\mathcal{S}(x)$.

Let $i \geq 0$. The prefix already processed is of length i and the current letter is $y[i]$. We assume that the condition is satisfied for $i-1$. Thus, $u = y[i-\ell\,..\,i-1]$ is the longest factor of x ending at position $i-1$.

Let w be the suffix of $y[0\,..\,i]$ of length ℓ_i. Let us first assume $w \neq \varepsilon$; thus w can be written $v \cdot y[i]$ for $v \in A^*$. We note that v cannot be longer than u since this would contradict the definition of u. Therefore v is a suffix of u.

If $v = u$, $\delta(p, y[i])$ is defined and provides the next value of p. Moreover, $\ell_i = \ell + 1$. These two points correspond to the update of the pair (ℓ, p) performed in line 4, which shows that the condition is satisfied for i in this situation.

When $v \prec_{\text{suff}} u$, we consider the largest integer k, $k > 0$, for which $v \preceq_{\text{suff}} s_x{}^k(u)$ where s_x is the suffix function relatively to x (Section 5.3). Lemma 5.15 has for consequence that $v = s_x{}^k(u)$ and that the length of this string is $lg_x(q)$ where $q = \delta(\mathit{initial}[\mathcal{S}(x)], v)$. The new value of p is thus $\delta(q, y[i])$, and the new value of ℓ is $lg_x(q) + 1$. This is the result of the instruction in line 8 because F and L implement respectively the suffix function and the function of length of the automaton, and after Proposition 5.26 that makes the link with the function s_x.

When $w = \varepsilon$, this means that the letter $y[i] \notin \text{alph}(x)$. We should thus reset the pair (ℓ, p), which is done in line 9.

Finally, we note that the proof holds also for the processing of the first letter of y, this ends the proof of the invariance of the condition which proves the correctness of the algorithm.

For the complexity of the algorithm, we note that each computation of transition, successful or unsuccessful, leads to an incrementation of i or to a strict increasing of the value of $i - \ell$. As each of these two expressions varies from 0 to $|y|$, we deduced that the number of transitions performed by the algorithm is not larger than $2|y|$. Moreover, as the execution time of the transitions is representative of the total execution time, this one is $O(|y| \times \log \text{card } A)$.

The memory space required for running the algorithm is principally used for the automaton $\mathcal{S}(x)$ that has a size $O(|x|)$ after Theorem 5.25. This gives the last stated result and ends the proof. ■

The algorithm FACT-LENGTHS allows, for instance, an efficient computation of $LCF(x, y)$, the maximal length of the common factors to strings x and y. This quantity occurs, for instance, in the definition of the distance, known as factor distance:

$$d(x, y) = |x| + |y| - 2LCF(x, y).$$

Corollary 6.12
The computation of the longest common factor to two strings x and y such that $|x| \leq |y|$ *can be realized in time* $O((|x| + |y|) \times \log \operatorname{card} \operatorname{alph}(x))$ *in a space* $O(|x|)$*, or in time* $O(|x| + |y|)$ *in a space* $O(|x| \times \operatorname{card} A)$.

Proof We perform the computation in two steps. The first step produces $\mathcal{S}(x)$, the suffix automaton of x. In the second step, we execute the operation FACT-LENGTHS on $\mathcal{S}(x)$ and y memorizing during the computation the largest value of the variable ℓ and the corresponding position on y. The execution provides thus a longest common factor between x and y, after the previous theorem. Its (left) position is deduced from its length and its right position.

The complexity of the computation results from the computation of the automaton $\mathcal{S}(x)$ (Theorems 5.29 and 5.30) and from the computation of the lengths (Theorem 6.11), noting for this latter execution that, if the automaton is implemented by a transition matrix, the running time is $O(|x| + |y|)$ in a space $O(|x| \times \operatorname{card} A)$. ∎

Optimization of the suffix link

When we want to compute the delay of the algorithm FACT-LENGTHS that works in a sequential way, we quickly figure out that it is possible to modify the suffix function in order to reduce this delay. We follow a method close to the method applied in Section 2.3.

The optimization is based on the sets of letters, labels of the outgoing arcs of a state. We define, for p state of $\mathcal{S}(x)$, the set

$$Next(p) = \{a : a \in A \text{ and } \delta(p, a) \text{ is defined}\}.$$

Then, the new suffix link F' is defined, for a state p of $\mathcal{S}(x)$, by the relation:

$$F'[p] = \begin{cases} F[p] & \text{if } Next(p) \subset Next(F[p]), \\ F'[F[p]] & \text{otherwise, if this value is defined.} \end{cases}$$

The relation can leave $F'[p]$ undefined (in which case we can give to it the value NIL). The idea of this definition is similar to what is done for the optimization realized on the failure function of the dictionary automaton of a single string (Section 2.3).

We note that in the automaton $\mathcal{S}(x)$ we always have

$$Next(p) \subseteq Next(F[p]).$$

We can then reformulate the definition of F' in

$$F'[p] = \begin{cases} F[p] & \text{if } deg(p) \neq deg(F[p]), \\ F'[F[p]] & \text{otherwise, if this value is defined.} \end{cases}$$

The computation of F' can thus be realized in linear time by a simple consideration of the outgoing degrees (*deg*) of the states of the automaton.

The optimization of the suffix link leads to a reduction of the delay of the algorithm FACT-LENGTHS. The delay can be evaluated by the number of executions of the instruction in line 5. We get the next result that shows that the algorithm processes the letters of y in a time independent of the length of x and even in real time when the alphabet is fixed.

Proposition 6.13
For the algorithm FACT-LENGTHS *using the suffix link F', instead of F, the processing of a letter of y takes a time* $O(\text{card alph}(x))$.

Proof The result is an immediate consequence of the inclusions

$$Next(p) \subset Next(F'[p]) \subseteq A$$

for each state p for which $F'[p]$ is defined. ■

6.7 Searching for conjugates

The sequence of the lengths $\ell_0, \ell_1, \ldots, \ell_{|y|-1}$ of the previous section is a very rich information on the resemblances between the strings x and y. It can be exploited in various ways by string comparison algorithms.

We are interested here in the search for a conjugate of a string inside a text. The solution presented in this section is another consequence of the computation of the lengths of the factors common to two strings. We recall that a conjugate of the string x is a string of the form $v \cdot u$ where u and v satisfy $x = u \cdot v$.

Problem of searching for a conjugate: let $x \in A^*$. Find all the occurrences of conjugates of x that occur in a string y.

A first solution consists in applying the search algorithm for a finite set of strings (Section 2.3) after having built the dictionary of conjugates of x. The search time is then proportional to $|y|$ (depending also on the branching time), but the dictionary can have a quadratic size, $O(|x|^2)$, as can be the size of the suffix trie of x.

The solution based on the utilization of a suffix automaton does not have this drawback while conserving an equivalent execution time. The technique derives from the computation of the lengths of the previous section. We consider the suffix automaton of the string x^2, noting that every conjugate of x is factor of x^2. We could even consider the string $x \cdot wA^{-1}$ where w is the primitive root of x, but that does not change the following statement.

Proposition 6.14
Let $x, y \in A^*$. The search for the conjugates of x in y can be performed in time $O(|y| \times \log \text{card}\, A)$ within space $O(|x|)$.

Proof We consider a variant of the algorithm FACT-LENGTHS that produces the positions of the occurrences of factors having a length not smaller than a given integer k. The transformation is immediate since at each step of the algorithm the length of the current factor is memorized in the variable ℓ.

The modified algorithm is applied to the automaton $\mathcal{S}(x^2)$ and to the string y with $k = |x|$ for parameter. The algorithm determines thus the factors of length $|x|$ of x^2 that occur in y. The conclusion follows by noting that the set of factors of length $|x|$ of x^2 is exactly the set of conjugates of x. ∎

Notes

The notion of index is very useful in information retrieval. We refer to the book of Frakes and Baeza-Yates [58] or to the book of Baeza-Yates and Ribeiro-Neto [56] in order to initiate to this subject, or also to the book of Salton [65].

The individual indexing systems or the search robots on the Web often use more simple techniques such as the elaboration of lexicons containing manually selected strings, rare strings, or q-grams (factors of length q) with q relatively small.

Most of the subjects treated in this chapter are classical. The book of Gusfield [6] contains a long list of problems whose algorithmic solutions rely on the utilization of an index structure.

The notion of repetition considered in Section 6.4 is close to the notion of "special factor": such a factor can be extended in at least two different ways in the text. The special factors occur in combinatorial questions on strings.

The forbidden strings of Section 6.5 are used in the text compression algorithm DCA by Crochemore, Mignosi, Restivo, and Salemi [127].

The utilization of the suffix automaton as a search machine is from Crochemore [120]. The use of the suffix tree produces an immediate but less efficient solution (see Exercise 6.9).

For the implementation of index structures in external memory, we refer to Ferragina and Grossi [136].

Combining indexing and text compression, Grossi and Vitter [147] designed a text index based upon compressed representations of suffix arrays and suffix trees. For any constant c, $0 < c \leq 1$, their data structure achieves $O(m/\log_{\text{card}\, A} n + \log^c_{\text{card}\, A} n)$ search time and uses at most $(c^{-1} + O(1))n$ log card A bits of storage.

In the same vein, Ferragina and Manzini developed a compressed full-text index data structure called FM-Index based on the methods described in the previous sections as well as on text compression techniques (see for example [137] and references therein).

Exercises

6.1 (Several occurrences)

Let k be an integer, $k > 0$. Implement an algorithm, based on the suffix array of $y \in A^*$, that determines the factors occurring at least k times in y.

6.2 (Idem)

Let k be an integer, $k > 0$. Implement an algorithm, based on a suffix automaton of $y \in A^*$, that determines the factors occurring at least k times in y.

6.3 (Overlap free)

For $y \in A^*$, write an algorithm for computing the maximal length of factors of y that possess two nonoverlapping occurrences (that is to say, if u is a such factor, it occurs in y at two positions, i and j, such that $i + |u| \leq j$).

6.4 (Marker)

Design an algorithm for computing a marker for $y \in A^*$ and based on the suffix array of y.

6.5 (Forbidden code)

Show that $I(y)$, $y \in A^*$, is a code (see Exercise 1.10).

6.6 (Avoid)

We say that a language $M \subseteq A^*$ avoids a string $u \in A^*$ if u is not a factor of any string of M. Let L be the language that avoids all the strings of a finite set $I \subseteq A^*$. Show that L is recognized by an automaton. Give a construction algorithm of an automaton that accepts L from the trie of the strings of I. (*Hint:* follow the computation of the failure function given in Section 2.3.)

6.7 (Factor automaton)

Design an algorithm for the construction of the automaton $\mathcal{F}(y)$ (deterministic and minimal automaton that recognizes the factors of y) from the trie of forbidden strings $I(y)$. (*Hint:* see Crochemore, Mignosi, and Restivo [126].)

6.8 (Delay)

Give a tight bound of the delay of the algorithm FACT-LENGTHS using the nonoptimized suffix link F on the suffix automaton.

6.9 (Length of the factors)

Describe an algorithm, based on the utilization of the suffix tree, that computes the lengths of the factors common to two strings as done by the algorithm FACT-LENGTHS of Section 6.6. Analyze the computation time and the delay of this algorithm. Indicate how to optimize the suffix link and analyze the complexity of the algorithm using this new link.

6.10 (Distance)

Show that the function d introduced in Section 6.6 is a distance on A^* (the notion of distance on strings is defined in Section 7.1).

6.11 (Document mining)

Consider a set of d documents (texts), $y_0, y_1, \ldots, y_{d-1}$ on a fixed finite alphabet. The aim of the problem is to answer efficiently queries of the form: list the documents (their set of indices) containing a given string x.

Show that each query can be answered in time $O(|x| + doc)$, where doc is the size of the set of indices, output of the query, after preprocessing the texts in time and space $O(|y_0| + |y_1| + \cdots + |y_{d-1}|)$.

Adapt your method for listing all documents that contain at least k occurrences of the pattern x.

Adapt your method for listing all documents that contain two occurrences of x at positions i and j for which $|j - i| \leq k$. (*Hint:* store the texts in a common suffix tree and use colored-range queries data structures on the list of leaves of the tree, see Muthukrishnan [190].)

6.12 (Large dictionary)

Give an infinite family of strings for which each string possesses a dictionary automaton of its conjugates that is of quadratic size in the length of the string.

6.13 (Conjugate)

Design an algorithm for locating the conjugates of x in y (with $x, y \in A^*$), given the tree $\mathcal{T}_C(x \cdot x \cdot c \cdot y)$, where $c \in A$ and $c \notin \text{alph}(x \cdot y)$. What are the time and space complexities of the computation?

7
Alignments

Alignments constitute one of the processes commonly used to compare strings. They allow to visualize the resemblance between strings. This chapter deals with several methods that perform the comparison of two strings in this sense. The extension to comparison methods of more than two strings is delicate, leads to algorithms whose execution time is at least exponential, and is not treated here.

Alignments are based on notions of distance or of similarity between strings. The computations are usually realized by dynamic programming. A typical example used for the design of efficient methods is the computation of the longest subsequence common to two strings. It shows the algorithmic techniques that are to implement in order to obtain an efficient computation and to extend possibly to general alignments. In particular, the reduction of the memory space obtained by one of the algorithms is a strategy that can often be applied in the solutions to close problems.

After the presentation of some distances defined on strings, notions of alignment and of edit graph, Section 7.2 describes the basic techniques for the computation of the edit (or alignment) distance and the production of the associated alignments. The chosen method highlights a global resemblance between two strings using assumptions that simplify the computation. The method is extended in Section 7.4 to a close problem. The search for local similarities between two strings is examined in Section 7.5.

The possible reduction of the memory space required by the computations is presented in Section 7.3 concerning the computation of the longest common subsequences. Finally, Section 7.6 presents a method that is at the basis of one of the most commonly used software (Blast) for comparing biological sequences and searching data banks of sequences. This approximate method contains heuristics that speed up the execution on real data, since exact methods are often too slow for searching analogies in large data banks.

7.1 Comparison of strings

In this section, we introduce the notions of distance on strings, of edit operations, of alignment, and of edit graph.

Edit distance and edit operation

We are interested in the notion of resemblance or of similarity between two strings x and y of respective lengths m and n, or in a dual way, to the distance between these two strings.

We say that a function $d: A^* \times A^* \rightarrow \mathbf{R}$ is a ***distance*** on A^* if the four following properties are satisfied for every $u, v \in A^*$:

Positivity: $d(u, v) \geq 0$.
Separation: $d(u, v) = 0$ if and only if $u = v$.
Symmetry: $d(u, v) = d(v, u)$.
Triangle inequality: $d(u, v) \leq d(u, w) + d(w, v)$ for every $w \in A^*$.

Several distances on strings can be considered following factorizations of strings. These are the prefix, suffix, and factor distances. Their interest is essentially theoretical.

Prefix distance: defined, for every $u, v \in A^*$, by

$$d_{pref}(u, v) = |u| + |v| - 2 \times |lcp(u, v)|,$$

where $lcp(u, v)$ is the longest prefix common to u and v.

Suffix distance: distance defined symmetrically to the prefix distance, for every $u, v \in A^*$, by

$$d_{suff}(u, v) = |u| + |v| - 2 \times |lcsuff(u, v)|,$$

where $lcsuff(u, v)$ is the longest suffix common to u and v.

Factor distance: distance defined in a way analogue to the two previous distances (see also Section 6.6), for every $u, v \in A^*$, by

$$d_{fact}(u, v) = |u| + |v| - 2 \times LCF(u, v),$$

where $LCF(u, v)$ is the maximal length of factors common to u and v.

The ***Hamming distance*** provides a simple although not always relevant mean for comparing two strings. It is defined for two strings of same length as the number of positions in which the two strings possess different letters (see also Chapter 8).

Operation	Resulting string	Cost
replace A by A	A C G A	0
replace C by T	A T G A	1
replace G by G	A T G A	0
insert C	A T G C A	1
insert T	A T G C T A	1
replace A by A	A T G C T A	0

Figure 7.1. Notion of edit distance. Sequence of elementary operations for changing string ACGA into string ATGCTA. If, for all letters $a, b \in A$, we have the costs $Sub(a, a) = 0$, $Sub(a, b) = 1$ when $a \neq b$, and $Del(a) = Ins(a) = 1$, the total cost of the sequence of edit operations is $0 + 1 + 0 + 1 + 1 + 0 = 3$. We easily check that we cannot do better with such costs. In other words, the edit distance between the strings, Lev(ACGA, ATGCTA), is equal to 3.

The distances that are dealt with in the rest of the chapter are defined from operations that transform x into y. Three types of elementary operations are considered. They are called the ***edit operations***:

- ***substitution*** for a letter of x at a given position by a letter of y,
- ***deletion*** of a letter of x at a given position,
- ***insertion*** of a letter of y in x at a given position.

A cost (having a positive integer value) is associated with each of the operations. For $a, b \in A$, we denote by

- $Sub(a, b)$ the cost of substituting the letter b for the letter a,
- $Del(a)$ the cost of deleting the letter a,
- $Ins(b)$ the cost of inserting the letter b.

We implicitly assume that these costs are independent of the positions at which the operations are realized. A different assumption is examined in Section 7.4. From the elementary costs, we set

$$Lev(x, y) = \min\{\text{cost of } \sigma : \sigma \in \Sigma_{x,y}\},$$

where $\Sigma_{x,y}$ is the set of sequences of elementary edit operations that transform x into y, and the cost of an element $\sigma \in \Sigma_{x,y}$ is the sum of the costs of the edit operations of the sequence σ. In the rest of the chapter, we assume that the conditions stated in the proposition that follows are satisfied. The function Lev is then a distance on A^*, it is called the ***edit distance*** or ***alignment distance***. Figure 7.1 illustrates the notions that have just been introduced.

The Hamming distance mentioned above is a particular case of edit distance for which only the operation of substitution is considered. This amounts to set $Del(a) = Ins(a) = +\infty$, for each letter a of the alphabet, recalling that for this distance, the two strings are assumed to be of the same length.

Proposition 7.1

The function Lev is a distance on A^* if and only if Sub is a distance on A and $Del(a) = Ins(a) > 0$ for every $a \in A$.

Proof $\Rightarrow$: we assume that *Lev* is a distance and show the assumptions on the elementary operations. As $Lev(a, b) = Sub(a, b)$ for $a, b \in A$, we notice that *Sub* satisfies the conditions for being a distance on the alphabet. And, from the fact that $Del(a) = Lev(a, \varepsilon) = Lev(\varepsilon, a) = Ins(a)$, we get $Del(a) = Ins(a) > 0$, for $a \in A$, which shows the direct implication.

$\Leftarrow$: we show that the four properties of positivity, separation, symmetry, and triangle inequality are satisfied with the assumptions made on the elementary operations.

Positivity. The elementary costs of the operations of substitution, deletion, and insertion being all nonnegative, the cost of every sequence of edit operations is nonnegative. It follows that $Lev(u, v)$ is itself nonnegative.

Separation. It is clear that if $u = v$, then $Lev(u, v) = 0$, the substitution of a letter by itself having a null cost since *Sub* is a distance on A. Conversely, if $Lev(u, v) = 0$, then $u = v$, since the only edit operation of null cost is the substitution of a letter by itself.

Symmetry. As *Sub* is symmetrical and the costs of deletion and of insertion of any given letter are identical, the function *Lev* is also symmetrical (the sequence of minimal cost of the operations that transform v into u is the sequence obtained from the sequence of minimal cost of the operations that transform u into v by reversing it and exchanging operations of deletion by insertion.

Triangle inequality. By contradiction, assume the existence of $w \in A^*$ such that $Lev(u, w) + Lev(w, v) < Lev(u, v)$. Then the sequence obtained by concatenating the two sequences of minimal cost of edit operations transforming u into w and w into v, in this order, has a cost strictly less than the cost of every sequence of operations transforming u into v, which contradicts the definition of $Lev(u, v)$.

This ends the converse part and the proof. ■

The problem of computing $Lev(x, y)$ consists in determining a sequence of edit operations for transforming x into y that minimizes the total cost of the used operations. Computing the resemblance between x and y amounts generally also to maximize some notion of similarity between these two strings. Any solution, that is not necessarily unique, can be stated as a sequence of elementary operations of substitution, deletion, and insertion. It can also be represented in a similar way under the form of an alignment.

Operation	Aligned pair	Cost
replace A by A	(A, A)	0
replace C by T	(C, T)	1
replace G by G	(G, G)	0
insert C	(-, C)	1
insert T	(-, T)	1
replace A by A	(A, A)	0

Figure 7.2. Example of Figure 7.1 followed. The aligned pairs are indicated above. The corresponding alignment is:

$$\begin{pmatrix} \mathtt{A} & \mathtt{C} & \mathtt{G} & \mathtt{-} & \mathtt{-} & \mathtt{A} \\ \mathtt{A} & \mathtt{T} & \mathtt{G} & \mathtt{C} & \mathtt{T} & \mathtt{A} \end{pmatrix}.$$

This alignment is optimal since its cost, $0 + 1 + 0 + 1 + 1 + 0 = 3$, is the edit distance between the two strings.

Alignments

An ***alignment*** between two strings $x, y \in A^*$, whose respective lengths are m and n, is a way to visualize their similarities. An illustration is given in Figure 7.2. Formally an alignment between x and y is a string z on the alphabet of pairs of letters, more accurately on

$$(A \cup \{\varepsilon\}) \times (A \cup \{\varepsilon\}) \setminus \{(\varepsilon, \varepsilon)\},$$

whose projection on the first component is x and the projection on the second component is y. Thus, if z is an alignment of length p between x and y, we have

$$\begin{aligned} z &= (\bar{x}_0, \bar{y}_0)(\bar{x}_1, \bar{y}_1) \ldots (\bar{x}_{p-1}, \bar{y}_{p-1}), \\ x &= \bar{x}_0\bar{x}_1 \ldots \bar{x}_{p-1}, \\ y &= \bar{y}_0\bar{y}_1 \ldots \bar{y}_{p-1}, \end{aligned}$$

with $\bar{x}_i \in A \cup \{\varepsilon\}$ and $\bar{y}_i \in A \cup \{\varepsilon\}$ for $i = 0, 1, \ldots, p - 1$. An alignment

$$(\bar{x}_0, \bar{y}_0)(\bar{x}_1, \bar{y}_1) \ldots (\bar{x}_{p-1}, \bar{y}_{p-1})$$

of length p is also denoted by

$$\begin{pmatrix} \bar{x}_0 \\ \bar{y}_0 \end{pmatrix} \begin{pmatrix} \bar{x}_1 \\ \bar{y}_1 \end{pmatrix} \cdots \begin{pmatrix} \bar{x}_{p-1} \\ \bar{y}_{p-1} \end{pmatrix},$$

or by

$$\begin{pmatrix} \bar{x}_0 & \bar{x}_1 & \ldots & \bar{x}_{p-1} \\ \bar{y}_0 & \bar{y}_1 & \ldots & \bar{y}_{p-1} \end{pmatrix}.$$

An ***aligned pair*** of type (a, b) with $a, b \in A$ denotes the substitution of the letter b for the letter a. An aligned pair of type (a, ε) with $a \in A$ denotes the deletion of the letter a. Finally, an aligned pair of type (ε, b) with $b \in A$ denotes the insertion of the letter b. In the alignments or the aligned pairs, the symbol "-" is often substituted for the symbol ε, it is called a ***hole***.

We define the cost of an aligned pair by

$$\begin{aligned} cost(a, b) &= Sub(a, b), \\ cost(a, \varepsilon) &= Del(a), \\ cost(\varepsilon, b) &= Ins(b), \end{aligned}$$

for $a, b \in A$. The cost of an alignment is then defined as the sum of the costs associated with each of its aligned pairs.

The number of alignments between two strings is exponential. The following proposition specifies this quantity for a particular type of alignments and gives thus a lower bound on the total number of alignments.

Proposition 7.2
Let $x, y \in A$ of respective lengths m and n with $m \leq n$. The number of alignments between x and y that contain no consecutive deletions of letters of x is $\binom{2n+1}{m}$.

Proof We can check that each alignment of the considered type is uniquely characterized by the places of the substitutions at the n positions on y and by the ones of the deletions between the letters of y. There are exactly $n + 1$ places of this second category counting one possible deletion before $y[0]$ and one after $y[n - 1]$.

The alignment is thus characterized by the choice of the m substitutions or deletions at the $2n + 1$ possible places, this gives the announced result. ■

Edit graph

An alignment translates in terms of graph. For this, we introduce the ***edit graph*** $G(x, y)$ of two strings $x, y \in A^*$ of respective lengths m and n as follows. Figure 7.3 illustrates the notion.

We denote by Q the set of vertices of $G(x, y)$ and F its set of arcs. Arcs are labeled by the function *label*, whose values are aligned pairs, and valued by the cost of these pairs.

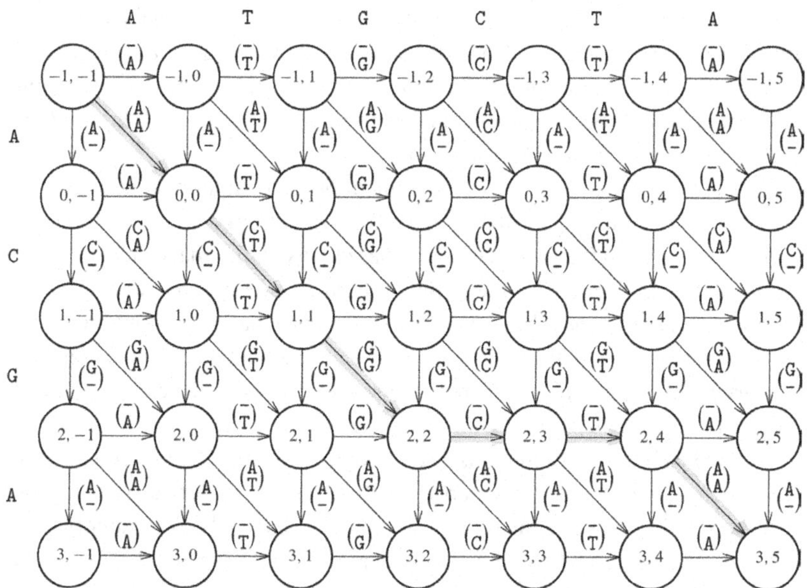

Figure 7.3. Sequel of the example of Figures 7.1 and 7.2. We show here the edit graph $G(\texttt{ACGA}, \texttt{ATGCTA})$ without the costs. Every path from vertex $(-1, -1)$ to vertex $(3, 5)$ corresponds to an alignment between ACGA and ATGCTA. The path in gray corresponds to the optimal alignment of Figure 7.2.

The set Q of vertices is

$$Q = \{-1, 0, \ldots, m-1\} \times \{-1, 0, \ldots, n-1\},$$

the set F of arcs is

$$\begin{aligned} F = \{&((i-1, j-1), (i, j)) : (i, j) \in Q \text{ and } i \neq -1 \text{ and } j \neq -1\} \\ \cup \{&((i-1, j), (i, j)) : (i, j) \in Q \text{ and } i \neq -1\} \\ \cup \{&((i, j-1), (i, j)) : (i, j) \in Q \text{ and } j \neq -1\}, \end{aligned}$$

and the function

$$\textit{label}: F \to (A \cup \{\varepsilon\}) \times (A \cup \{\varepsilon\}) \setminus \{(\varepsilon, \varepsilon)\}$$

is defined by

$$\begin{aligned} \textit{label}((i-1, j-1), (i, j)) &= (x[i], y[j]), \\ \textit{label}((i-1, j), (i, j)) &= (x[i], \varepsilon), \\ \textit{label}((i, j-1), (i, j)) &= (\varepsilon, y[j]). \end{aligned}$$

Every path of origin $(-1, -1)$ and of end $(m-1, n-1)$ is labeled by an alignment between x and y. Thus, by choosing $(-1, -1)$ for initial state and $(m-1, n-1)$ for terminal state, the edit graph $G(x, y)$ becomes an automaton that recognizes all the alignments between x and y. The cost of an arc f of $G(x, y)$ is the one of its label, that is to say, $cost(label(f))$.

The computation of an optimal alignment or the computation of $Lev(x, y)$ amounts to determine a path of minimal cost starting from $(-1, -1)$ and ending in $(m-1, n-1)$ in the graph $G(x, y)$. These paths of minimal cost are in one-to-one correspondence with the optimal alignments between x and y. Since the graph $G(x, y)$ is acyclic, it is possible to find a path of minimal cost by considering once and only once each vertex. It is sufficient for this to consider the vertices of G according to a topological order. Such an order can be obtained by considering the vertices column by column from left to right, and from top to bottom inside each column. It is also possible to get the result by considering the vertices line by line from top to bottom, and from left to right inside each line, or by scanning them according the antidiagonals, for example. The problem can be solved by dynamic programming as explained in the next section.

Dotplot

There exists a very simple method to highlight the similarities between two strings x and y of respective lengths m and n. We define for this a table Dot of size $m \times n$, called the ***dotplot*** between x and y. The values of the table Dot are defined for every position i on x and every position j on y by

$$Dot[i, j] = \begin{cases} \text{TRUE} & \text{if } x[i] = y[j], \\ \text{FALSE} & \text{otherwise.} \end{cases}$$

To visualize the dotplot, we put tokens on a grid to signify the value TRUE (an example is given in Figure 7.4). The areas of similarities between the two strings appear then as sequences of tokens on the diagonals of the grid.

It is possible to deduce a global alignment between the two strings, from a dotplot, by linking sequences of tokens. Diagonal links correspond to substitutions, horizontal links correspond to insertions and vertical links correspond to deletions. The global alignments correspond then to paths starting close to the upper left corner and ending close to the lower right corner.

It is worth to note that when we utilize this technique with $x = y$, the borders of x appear as diagonals of tokens starting and ending on the frames of the grid. Figure 7.5 illustrates this.

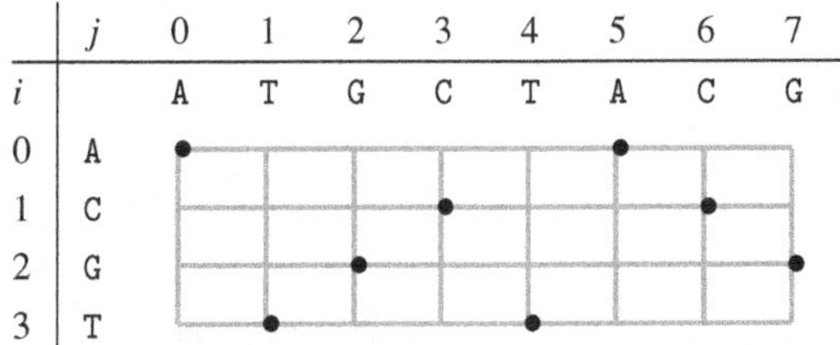

Figure 7.4. Dotplot between $x =$ ACGT and $y =$ ATGCTACG. A (black) token occurs in (i, j) if and only if $x[i] = y[j]$. The table highlights diagonals of tokens that signal similarities. Thus, the diagonal $\langle(0, 5), (1, 6), (2, 7)\rangle$ indicates that prefix ACG of x is a suffix of y. The antidiagonal $\langle(3, 1), (2, 2), (1, 3)\rangle$ shows that the factor CGT of x occurs in reverse order in y.

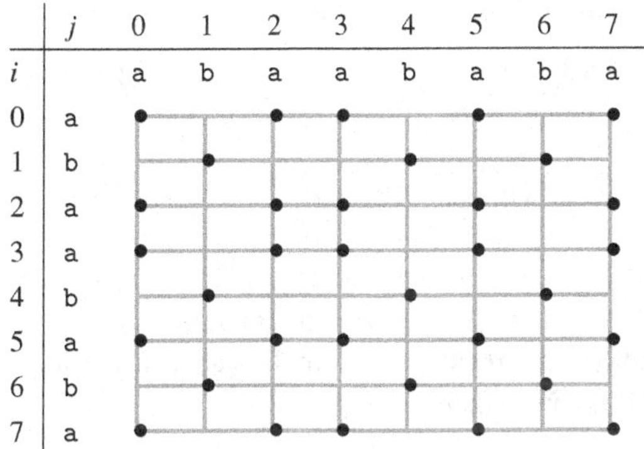

Figure 7.5. Dotplot of the string abaababa against itself. Among other elements occur the borders of the string: they correspond to the diagonals of tokens going from the top of the grid to its right border (except for the main diagonal). We distinguish the nonempty borders a and aba. The antidiagonals centered on the main diagonal indicate factors of x that are palindromes: the antidiagonal $\langle(7, 3), (6, 4), (5, 5), (4, 6), (3, 7)\rangle$ corresponds to palindrome ababa.

7.2 Optimal alignment

In this section, we present the method at the basis of the computation of an optimal alignment between two strings. The process utilizes a very simple technique called dynamic programming. It consists in memorizing the results of intermediate computations in order to avoid to have to recompute them. The production of an alignment between two strings x and y is based on the computation of the edit distance between the two strings. We start thus by

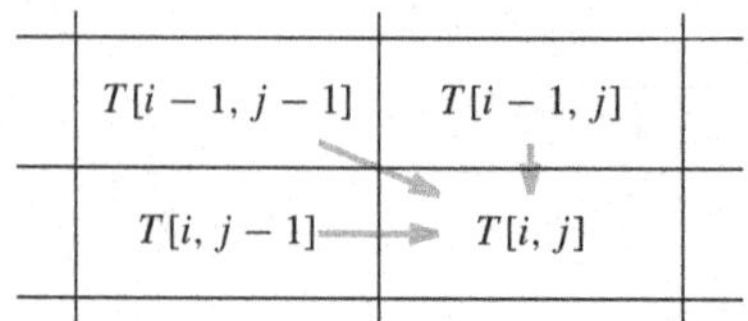

Figure 7.6. The value $T[i, j]$ only depends on the values at the three neighbor positions: $T[i-1, j-1]$, $T[i-1, j]$, and $T[i, j-1]$ (when $i, j \geq 0$).

explaining how to perform this computation. We then describe how to determine the associated optimal alignments.

Computation of the edit distance

For the two strings $x, y \in A^*$ of respective lengths m and n, we define the table T having $m+1$ lines and $n+1$ columns by

$$T[i, j] = Lev(x[0 \,..\, i], y[0 \,..\, j])$$

for $i = -1, 0, \ldots, m-1$ and $j = -1, 0, \ldots, n-1$. Thus, $T[i, j]$ is also the minimal cost of a path from $(-1, -1)$ to (i, j) in the edit graph $G(x, y)$.

To compute $T[i, j]$, we utilize the recurrence formula stated in the next proposition and whose proof is given further.

Proposition 7.3
For $i = 0, 1, \ldots, m-1$ and $j = 0, 1, \ldots, n-1$, we have

$$\begin{aligned}
T[-1, -1] &= 0, \\
T[i, -1] &= T[i-1, -1] + Del(x[i]), \\
T[-1, j] &= T[-1, j-1] + Ins(y[j]), \\
T[i, j] &= \min \begin{cases} T[i-1, j-1] + Sub(x[i], y[j]), \\ T[i-1, j] + Del(x[i]), \\ T[i, j-1] + Ins(y[j]). \end{cases}
\end{aligned}$$

The value at position $[i, j]$ in the table T, with $i, j \geq 0$, does only depend on the values at positions $[i-1, j-1]$, $[i-1, j]$, and $[i, j-1]$ (see Figure 7.6). An illustration of the computation is presented in Figure 7.7.

The algorithm Generic-DP, whose code is given below, performs the computation of the edit distance using the table T. The searched value is $T[m-1, n-1] = Lev(x, y)$ (Corollary 7.5).

(a)

Sub	A	C	D	E	G	K	L	P	Q	R	W	Y
A	0	3	3	3	3	3	3	3	3	3	3	3
C	3	0	3	3	3	3	3	3	3	3	3	3
D	3	3	0	3	3	3	3	3	3	3	3	3
E	3	3	3	0	3	3	3	3	3	3	3	3
G	3	3	3	3	0	3	3	3	3	3	3	3
K	3	3	3	3	3	0	3	3	3	3	3	3
L	3	3	3	3	3	3	0	3	3	3	3	3
P	3	3	3	3	3	3	3	0	3	3	3	3
Q	3	3	3	3	3	3	3	3	0	3	3	3
R	3	3	3	3	3	3	3	3	3	0	3	3
W	3	3	3	3	3	3	3	3	3	3	0	3
Y	3	3	3	3	3	3	3	3	3	3	3	0

	Del	*Ins*
A	1	1
C	1	1
D	1	1
E	1	1
G	1	1
K	1	1
L	1	1
P	1	1
Q	1	1
R	1	1
W	1	1
Y	1	1

(b)

T	j	-1	0	1	2	3	4	5	6	7	8	9	10	11
i		$y[j]$	E	R	D	A	W	C	Q	P	G	K	W	Y
-1	$x[i]$	0	1	2	3	4	5	6	7	8	9	10	11	12
0	E	1	0	1	2	3	4	5	6	7	8	9	10	11
1	A	2	1	2	3	2	3	4	5	6	7	8	9	10
2	W	3	2	3	4	3	2	3	4	5	6	7	8	9
3	A	4	3	4	5	4	3	4	5	6	7	8	9	10
4	C	5	4	5	6	5	4	3	4	5	6	7	8	9
5	Q	6	5	6	7	6	5	4	3	4	5	6	7	8
6	G	7	6	7	8	7	6	5	4	5	4	5	6	7
7	K	8	7	8	9	8	7	6	5	6	5	4	5	6
8	L	9	8	9	10	9	8	7	6	7	6	5	6	7

(c)

```
(E - - A W A C Q - G K - - L)
(E R D A W - C Q P G K W Y -)

(E - - A W A C Q - G K - L -)
(E R D A W - C Q P G K W - Y)

(E - - A W A C Q - G K L - -)
(E R D A W - C Q P G K - W Y)
```

Figure 7.7. Computation of the edit distance between the strings EAWACQGKL and ERDAWCQPGKWY, and the corresponding alignments. **(a)** Substitution matrix: values of the costs of the edit operations that are $Sub(a, b) = 3$ for $a \neq b$ and $Del(a) = Ins(a) = 1$. **(b)** Table T, computed by the algorithm GENERIC-DP. We get $Lev(\texttt{EAWACQGKL}, \texttt{ERDAWCQPGKWY}) = T[8, 11] = 7$. The three paths of minimal cost between positions $[-1, -1]$ and $[8, 11]$ are also given on the table. They can be computed by the algorithm ALIGNMENTS. **(c)** The three associated optimal alignments. We note that they highlight the subsequence EAWCQGK common to the two strings that is actually of maximal length as a common subsequence. We notice moreover that the above distance is also $|\texttt{EAWACQGKL}| + |\texttt{ERDAWCQPGKWY}| - 2 \times |\texttt{EAWCQGK}| = 7$ (see Section 7.3).

```
GENERIC-DP(x, m, y, n)
T[-1, -1] ← 0
for i ← 0 to m - 1 do
    T[i, -1] ← T[i - 1, -1] + Del(x[i])
for j ← 0 to n - 1 do
    T[-1, j] ← T[-1, j - 1] + Ins(y[j])
    for i ← 0 to m - 1 do
                         ⎧ T[i - 1, j - 1] + Sub(x[i], y[j])
        T[i, j] ← min    ⎨ T[i - 1, j] + Del(x[i])
                         ⎩ T[i, j - 1] + Ins(y[j])
return T[m - 1, n - 1]
```

We will now prove the validity of the computation process by first stating an intermediate result.

Lemma 7.4
For every $a, b \in A$, $u, v \in A^*$, we have

$$\begin{aligned} Lev(ua, \varepsilon) &= Lev(u, \varepsilon) + Del(a), \\ Lev(\varepsilon, vb) &= Lev(\varepsilon, v) + Ins(b), \\ Lev(ua, vb) &= \min \begin{cases} Lev(u, v) + Sub(a, b), \\ Lev(u, vb) + Del(a), \\ Lev(ua, v) + Ins(b). \end{cases} \end{aligned}$$

Proof The sequence of edit operations that transforms the string ua into the empty string can be arranged in such a way that it ends with the deletion of the letter a. The rest of the sequence transforms the string u into the empty string. We thus have

$$\begin{aligned} Lev(ua, \varepsilon) &= \min\{\text{cost of } \sigma : \sigma \in \Sigma_{ua,\varepsilon}\} \\ &= \min\{\text{cost of } \sigma' \cdot (a, \varepsilon) : \sigma' \in \Sigma_{u,\varepsilon}\} \\ &= \min\{\text{cost of } \sigma' : \sigma' \in \Sigma_{u,\varepsilon}\} + Del(a) \\ &= Lev(u, \varepsilon) + Del(a). \end{aligned}$$

Thus the first identity holds. The validity of the second identity can be established according to the same schema. For the third, it is sufficient to distinguish the case where the last edit operation is a substitution, a deletion, or an insertion. ∎

Proof of Proposition 7.3 It is a direct consequence of the equality $Lev(\varepsilon, \varepsilon) = 0$ and of Lemma 7.4 by setting $a = x[i]$, $b = y[j]$, $u = x[0\,.\,.\,i - 1]$, and $v = y[0\,.\,.\,j - 1]$. ∎

Corollary 7.5
The algorithm GENERIC-DP *produces the edit distance between x and y.*

Proof It is a consequence of Proposition 7.3: the computation performed by the algorithm applies the stated recurrence relation. ■

While a direct programming of the recurrence formula of Proposition 7.3 leads to an algorithm of exponential running time, we immediately see that the execution time of the operation GENERIC-DP(x, m, y, n) is quadratic.

Proposition 7.6
The algorithm GENERIC-DP, *applied to two strings of length m and n, executes in time $O(m \times n)$ in a space $O(\min\{m, n\})$.*

Proof The computation of the value at each position of the table T only depends on the three neighbor positions and this computation executes in constant time. There are $m \times n$ values computed in this way in the table T, after an initialization in time $O(m + n)$, which gives the result on the execution time. For the space, it is sufficient to note that only a space for two columns (or two lines) of the table T is sufficient for realizing the computation. ■

We get a result analogue to the statement of the proposition by performing the computation of the values of the table T according to the antidiagonals. It is sufficient in this case to memorize only three consecutive antidiagonals to correctly perform the computation.

Computation of an optimal alignment

The algorithm GENERIC-DP only computes the cost of the transformation of x into y. To get a sequence of edit operations that transforms x into y, or the corresponding alignment, we can perform the computation by tracing back the table T from the position $[m-1, n-1]$ to the position $[-1, -1]$. From a position $[i, j]$, we visit, among the three neighbor positions $[i-1, j-1]$, $[i-1, j]$, and $[i, j-1]$, the position whose associated value produces $T[i, j]$. The algorithm ONE-ALIGNMENT, whose code is given further, implements this method that produces an optimal alignment.

The validity of the process can be explained by means of the notion of ***active arc*** in the edit graph $G(x, y)$. They are the arcs that are considered for getting an optimal alignment. With the example of Figures 7.1 and 7.2, the algorithm GENERIC-DP computes the table T that is given in Figure 7.8. The associated edit graph is presented in Figure 7.3, and Figure 7.9 displays the subgraph of the active arcs that is deduced from the table. Formally, we say that the arc

T	j	-1	0	1	2	3	4	5
i		$y[j]$	A	T	G	C	T	A
-1	$x[i]$	0	1	2	3	4	5	6
0	A	1	0	1	2	3	4	5
1	C	2	1	1	2	2	3	4
2	G	3	2	2	1	2	3	4
3	A	4	3	3	2	2	3	3

(a)

(b) $\begin{pmatrix} \texttt{A} & \texttt{-} & \texttt{-} & \texttt{C} & \texttt{G} & \texttt{A} \\ \texttt{A} & \texttt{T} & \texttt{G} & \texttt{C} & \texttt{T} & \texttt{A} \end{pmatrix}$ $\begin{pmatrix} \texttt{A} & \texttt{C} & \texttt{G} & \texttt{-} & \texttt{-} & \texttt{A} \\ \texttt{A} & \texttt{T} & \texttt{G} & \texttt{C} & \texttt{T} & \texttt{A} \end{pmatrix}$

Figure 7.8. Example of Figure 7.3 followed. Computation of the edit distance between the two strings ACGA and ATGCTA and corresponding alignments. **(a)** Table T, as computed during the execution of the algorithm GENERIC-DP with the elementary costs $Sub(a, b) = 1$ for $a \neq b$ and $Del(a) = Ins(a) = 1$. We get $Lev(\texttt{ACGA}, \texttt{ATGCTA}) = T[3, 5] = 3$. The two paths of minimal cost between positions $[-1, -1]$ and $[3, 5]$ are also given. **(b)** The two associated optimal alignments.

$((i', j'), (i, j))$ of label (a, b) is active when

$$\begin{aligned} T[i, j] &= T[i', j'] + Sub(a, b) \text{ if } i - i' = j - j' = 1, \\ T[i, j] &= T[i', j'] + Del(a) \text{ if } i - i' = 1 \text{ and } j = j', \\ T[i, j] &= T[i', j'] + Ins(b) \text{ if } i = i' \text{ and } j - j' = 1, \end{aligned}$$

with $i, i' \in \{-1, 0, \ldots, m-1\}$, $j, j' \in \{-1, 0, \ldots, n-1\}$, and $a, b \in A$.

Lemma 7.7
The label of a path (not reduced to a single vertex) of $G(x, y)$ linking (k, ℓ) to (i, j) is an optimal alignment between $x[k \,..\, i]$ and $y[\ell \,..\, j]$ if and only if all its arcs are active. We have

$$Lev(x[k \,..\, i], y[\ell \,..\, j]) = T[i, j] - T[k, \ell].$$

Proof We note that the alignment is optimal, by definition, if the cost of the path is minimal. Moreover, we have in this case

$$Lev(x[k \,..\, i], y[\ell \,..\, j]) = T[i, j] - T[k, \ell].$$

Let us show the equivalence by recurrence on the positive length of the path (counted in number of arcs). Let (i', j') be the vertex that precedes (i, j) along the path.

Let us first consider that the path has length 1, that is, $(k, \ell) = (i', j')$. If the cost of the path is minimal, its value is

$$Lev(x[k \,..\, i], y[\ell \,..\, j]) = T[i, j] - T[k, \ell],$$

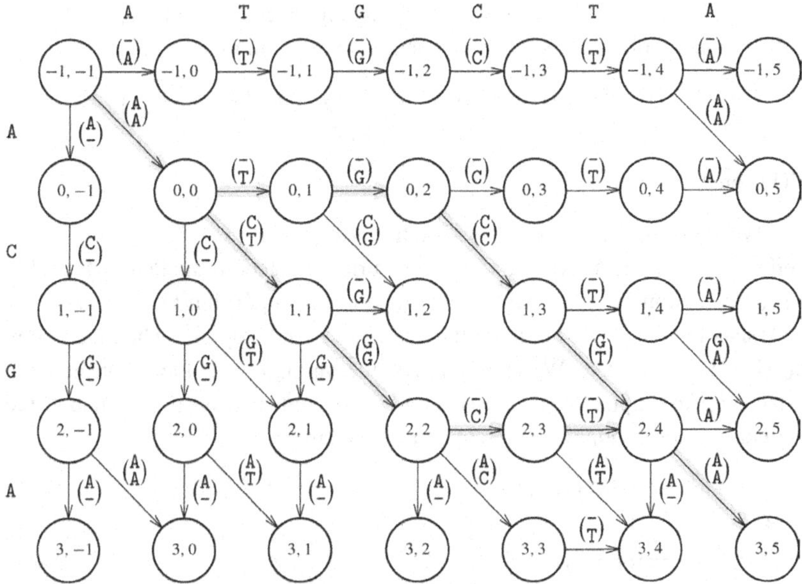

Figure 7.9. Active arcs of the edit graph of Figure 7.3. The gray paths link vertices $(-1, -1)$ and $(3, 5)$; they correspond to optimal alignments (see Figure 7.8). The arcs of these paths and their corresponding vertices constitute the automaton of optimal alignments.

and, as this cost is also $Sub(x[i], y[j])$, $Del(x[i])$ or $Ins(y[j])$ depending on the considered case, we deduce that the arc is active, by definition.

Conversely, if the arc of the path is active we have by definition either $T[i, j] - T[k, \ell] = Sub(x[i], y[j])$, $T[i, j] - T[k, \ell] = Del(x[i])$, or $T[i, j] - T[k, \ell] = Ins(y[j])$, according to the considered case. But these values are also the distance between the two strings that are of length no more than 1. Thus the path is of minimal cost.

Let us assume then that the path is of length greater than 1.

If the path is of minimal cost, it is the same for its segment linking (k, ℓ) to (i', j') and of the arc $((i', j'), (i, j))$. The recurrence hypothesis applied to the first segment indicates then that it consists of active arcs. The minimality of the cost of the last arc amounts also to say that it is an active arc (see Proposition 7.3).

Conversely, assume that the arcs of the path are all active. By applying the recurrence hypothesis to the segment of the path linking (k, ℓ) to (i', j'), we deduce that this one is of minimal cost and

$$T[i', j'] - T[k, \ell] = Lev(x[k \,..\, i'], y[\ell \,..\, j']).$$

As the last arc is active, its cost is minimal and is equal to $T[i, j] - T[i', j']$ after Proposition 7.3. The complete path is thus of minimal cost:

$$\begin{aligned} Lev(x[k \mathinner{..} i], y[\ell \mathinner{..} j]) &= (T[i, j] - T[i', j']) + (T[i', j'] - T[k, \ell]) \\ &= T[i, j] - T[k, \ell]. \end{aligned}$$

This ends the proof. ∎

We note that for every vertex of the edit graph, except for $(-1, -1)$, it enters at least one active arc after the recurrence relation satisfied by the table T (Proposition 7.3). The work performed by the algorithm ONE-ALIGNMENT consists thus in going up along the active arcs, and stopping when the vertex $(-1, -1)$ is reached. We consider that the variable z of the algorithm is a string on the alphabet $(A \cup \{\varepsilon\}) \times (A \cup \{\varepsilon\})$, and that, on this alphabet, the concatenation is done component by component.

```
ONE-ALIGNMENT(x, m, y, n)
 1  z ← (ε, ε)
 2  (i, j) ← (m − 1, n − 1)
 3  while i ≠ −1 and j ≠ −1 do
 4      if T[i, j] = T[i − 1, j − 1] + Sub(x[i], y[j]) then
 5          z ← (x[i], y[j]) · z
 6          (i, j) ← (i − 1, j − 1)
 7      elseif T[i, j] = T[i − 1, j] + Del(x[i]) then
 8          z ← (x[i], ε) · z
 9          i ← i − 1
10      else z ← (ε, y[j]) · z
11          j ← j − 1
12  while i ≠ −1 do
13      z ← (x[i], ε) · z
14      i ← i − 1
15  while j ≠ −1 do
16      z ← (ε, y[j]) · z
17      j ← j − 1
18  return z
```

Proposition 7.8
The execution of ONE-ALIGNMENT(x, m, y, n) *produces an optimal alignment between x and y, that is to say an alignment of cost* $Lev(x, y)$. *The computation executes in time and extra space* $O(m + n)$.

Proof The formal proof relies on Lemma 7.7. We notice that the conditions in lines 4 and 7 test the activity of arcs of the edit graph associated with the computation. The third case treated in lines 10–11 corresponds to the third condition of the definition of an active arc, since it always enters at least one active arc for each vertex different from $(-1, -1)$ of the graph. The complete computation produces thus the label of a path of origin $(-1, -1)$ and of end $(m-1, n-1)$ consisting uniquely of active arcs. After Lemma 7.7, this label is an optimal alignment between x and y.

Each operation significant of the execution time of the algorithm leads to decrease the value of i or the value of j that vary from $m-1$ and $n-1$, respectively, to -1. This gives the time $O(m+n)$. The extra space is used for storing the string z that is of maximal length $m+n$. This achieves the proof. ∎

We note that the validity tests of the three arcs coming in the vertex (i, j) of the edit graph can be performed in any order. There exist thus $3! = 6$ possible writings of lines 4–11. The one that is presented favors a path containing diagonal arcs. For instance, we get the highest path (relatively to the drawing of the edit graph as in Figure 7.9) by swapping lines 4–6 with lines 7–9. We can also program the computation in a way to get a random alignment among the optimal alignments.

To compute an alignment, it is also possible to store the active arcs under the form of "return arcs" in an extra table during the computation of the values of the table T. The computation of an alignment amounts then to follow these arcs from position $[m-1, n-1]$ to position $[-1, -1]$ in the table of return arcs. This requires a space $O(m \times n)$ like the space occupied by the table T. It should be noted that it is sufficient to store, for each position, one return direction among the three possible, which can be encoded with only two bits.

The process presented in this section to compute an optimal alignment uses the table T and requires thus a quadratic space. It is, however, possible to find an optimal alignment in linear space using the divide-and-conquer method described in Section 7.3.

Computation of all the optimal alignments

If all the optimal alignments between x and y must be exhibited, we can use the algorithm Alignments whose code is given thereafter. It calls the recursive procedure Al whose code is given just after and for which the variables x, y, and T are assumed to be global. It is based on the notion of active arc, as for the previous algorithm.

```
ALIGNMENTS(x, m, y, n)
AL(m − 1, n − 1, (ε, ε))
```

```
AL(i, j, z)
1  if i ≠ −1 and j ≠ −1
       and T[i, j] = T[i − 1, j − 1] + Sub(x[i], y[j]) then
2          AL(i − 1, j − 1, (x[i], y[j]) · z)
3  if i ≠ −1
       and T[i, j] = T[i − 1, j] + Del(x[i]) then
4          AL(i − 1, j, (x[i], ε) · z)
5  if j ≠ −1
       and T[i, j] = T[i, j − 1] + Ins(y[j]) then
6          AL(i, j − 1, (ε, y[j]) · z)
7  if i = −1 and j = −1 then
8          signal that z is an alignment
```

Proposition 7.9
The algorithm ALIGNMENTS *produces all the optimal alignments between its input strings. Its execution time is proportional to the sum of the lengths of all the produced alignments.*

Proof We notice that the tests in lines 1, 3, and 5 are used for checking the activity of an arc. The test in line 7 produces the current alignment when it is complete. The rest of the proof is similar to the proof of the algorithm ONE-ALIGNMENT.

The execution time of each test is constant. Moreover, each test leads to increase one pair of the current alignment. Thus the result on the total execution time holds. ■

The memorization of return arcs mentioned above can also be used for the computation of all the alignments. It is nevertheless necessary here to store three arcs at most by position, which can be encoded with three bits.

Producing all the alignments is not sound if there are too many of them (see Proposition 7.2). It is more pertinent to produce a graph containing all the information, graph that can then be queried later on.

Automaton of the optimal alignments

The optimal alignments between the string x and the string y are represented in the graph of alignment by the paths having origin $(-1, -1)$ and ending in $(m-1, n-1)$ that are made up of active arcs. The graph of the active arcs occurring on these paths and their associated vertices form a subgraph of $G(x, y)$. When we choose $(-1, -1)$ for initial state and $(m-1, n-1)$ for terminal state, it becomes an automaton that recognizes the optimal alignments between x and y (see Figure 7.9).

The construction of the automaton of optimal alignments is given by the algorithm whose code follows. The computation amounts to determine the co-accessible part (from vertex $(m-1, n-1)$) of the graph of the active arcs. The table E used in the algorithm provides a direct access to the state associated with each position on the table T considered during the execution of the algorithm.

```
Opt-align-aut(x, m, y, n, T)
  M ← New-automaton()
  initialize E
  E[−1, −1] ← initial[M]
  E[m − 1, n − 1] ← New-state()
  terminal[E[m − 1, n − 1]] ← TRUE
  Aa(m − 1, n − 1)
  return M
```

```
Aa(i, j)
  if i ≠ −1 and j ≠ −1
     and T[i, j] = T[i − 1, j − 1] + Sub(x[i], y[j]) then
       if E[i − 1, j − 1] = NIL then
           E[i − 1, j − 1] ← New-state()
           Aa(i − 1, j − 1)
       Succ[E[i − 1, j − 1]] ←
         Succ[E[i − 1, j − 1]] ∪ {((x[i], y[j]), E[i, j])}
  if i ≠ −1
     and T[i, j] = T[i − 1, j] + Del(x[i]) then
       if E[i − 1, j] = NIL then
           E[i − 1, j] ← New-state()
           Aa(i − 1, j)
       Succ[E[i − 1, j]] ← Succ[E[i − 1, j]] ∪ {((x[i], ε), E[i, j])}
  if j ≠ −1
     and T[i, j] = T[i, j − 1] + Ins(y[j]) then
       if E[i, j − 1] = NIL then
           E[i, j − 1] ← New-state()
           Aa(i, j − 1)
       Succ[E[i, j − 1]] ← Succ[E[i, j − 1]] ∪ {((ε, y[j]), E[i, j])}
```

The arguments for proving the validity of the process are identical to those used for the algorithms producing optimal alignments. We note the utilization of the table E of size $O(m \times n)$ that allows to process each vertex of $G(x, y)$ only once (it is possible to replace it by a table of linear size, see Exercise 7.5).

Proposition 7.10
Let e be the number of states of the automaton of the optimal alignments between x and y, and let f be its number of arcs. The operation Opt-align-aut(x, m, y, n, T) *builds the automaton by means of the table T in time* $O(e + f)$.

Proof The three tests performed in the procedure Aa serve to check the activity of arcs. It is sufficient then to check that the arcs of the automaton correspond to the active arcs of $G(x, y)$ which are on a path from $(-1, -1)$ to $(m - 1, n - 1)$.

Concerning the execution time, the only delicate point is the time for the initialization of the table E (line 2). This can be $\Omega(m \times n)$ if it is performed without care. But using a technique for implementing the partial functions (see Exercise 1.15) the table is initialized in constant time. ■

We note that the automaton of the optimal alignments can be of linear size $O(m + n)$, in the case where the optimal alignments are in small number for instance. In this situation the algorithm Opt-align-aut produces them all in linear time. We also note that the execution time of the algorithm is $O(m \times n)$ in contrast to the execution time of the algorithm Alignments.

7.3 Longest common subsequence

In this section, we are interested in the computation of a longest subsequence common to two strings. This problem is a specialization of the notion of edit distance in which we do not consider the operation of substitution. Two strings x and y can have several longest common subsequences. The set of these strings is denoted by $Lcs(x, y)$. The (unique) length of the strings of $Lcs(x, y)$ is denoted by $lcs(x, y)$.

If we set

$$Sub(a, a) = 0$$

and

$$Del(a) = Ins(a) = 1$$

for $a \in A$, and if we assume

$$Sub(a, b) > Del(a) + Ins(b) = 2$$

for $a, b \in A$ and $a \neq b$, the value $T[m - 1, n - 1]$ (see Section 7.2) represents what we call the ***subsequence distance*** between x and y denoted by $d_{subs}(x, y)$. The computation of this distance is a dual problem of the computation of the length of the ***longest common subsequences*** between x and y due to the next proposition (see Figure 7.7). This is why we consider the computation of the longest common subsequences.

Proposition 7.11
The subsequence distance satisfies the equality

$$d_{subs}(x, y) = |x| + |y| - 2 \times lcs(x, y). \tag{7.1}$$

Proof By definition, $d_{subs}(x, y)$ is the minimal cost of the alignments between the two strings, counted from elementary costs *Sub*, *Del*, and *Ins* that satisfy the above assumptions. Let z be an alignment having cost $d_{subs}(x, y)$. The inequality

$$Sub(a, b) > Del(a) + Ins(b)$$

means that z does not contain any substitution of two different letters since a deletion of a and an insertion of b costs less than a substitution of b for a when $a \neq b$. As $Del(a) = Ins(a) = 1$, the value $d_{subs}(x, y)$ is the number of insertions and of deletions contained in z. The other aligned pairs of z correspond to matches, their number is $lcs(x, y)$ (it cannot be smaller otherwise we would get a contradiction with the definition of $d_{subs}(x, y)$). If each of these pairs is replaced by an insertion followed by a deletion of the same letter, we get an alignment that contains only insertions and deletions; it is then of length $|x| + |y|$. The cost of z is thus $|x| + |y| - 2 \times lcs(x, y)$, which gives the equality of the statement. ■

A naive method for computing $lcs(x, y)$ consists in considering all the subsequences of x, in checking if they are subsequences of y and in keeping the longest ones. As the string x of length m can possess 2^m distinct subsequences, this method by enumeration is inapplicable for large values of m.

Computation by dynamic programming

Using the dynamic programming method, in a way analogue to the process of Section 7.2, it is possible to compute $Lcs(x, y)$ and $lcs(x, y)$ in time and space $O(m \times n)$. The method naturally leads to compute the lengths of the longest common subsequences between longer and longer prefixes of the two strings x and y.

For this, we consider the two-dimensional table S having $m + 1$ lines and $n + 1$ columns and defined, for $i = -1, 0, \ldots, m - 1$ and $j = -1, 0, \ldots, n - 1$, by

$$S[i, j] = \begin{cases} 0 & \text{if } i = -1 \text{ or } j = -1, \\ lcs(x[0 \,..\, i], y[0 \,..\, j]) & \text{otherwise.} \end{cases}$$

Computing

$$lcs(x, y) = S[m-1, n-1]$$

relies on a simple observation that leads to the recurrence relation of the next statement (see also Figure 7.7).

Proposition 7.12
For $i = 0, 1, \ldots, m-1$ *and* $j = 0, 1, \ldots, n-1$, *we have*

$$S[i, j] = \begin{cases} S[i-1, j-1] + 1 & \textit{if } x[i] = y[j], \\ \max\{S[i-1, j], S[i, j-1]\} & \textit{otherwise.} \end{cases}$$

Proof Let $ua = x[0\,.\,.\,i]$ and $vb = y[0\,.\,.\,j]$ ($u, v \in A^*$, $a, b \in A$). If $a = b$, a longest common subsequence between ua and vb ends necessarily with a (otherwise we could extend it by a, which would contradict the maximality of its length). It results that it is of the form wa where w is a longest subsequence common between u and v. Thus, $S[i, j] = S[i-1, j-1] + 1$ in this case.

If $a \neq b$ and if ua and vb possess a longest common subsequence that does not end with a, we have $S[i, j] = S[i-1, j]$. In a symmetrical way, if it does not end with b, we have $S[i, j] = S[i, j-1]$. That is to say $S[i, j] = \max\{S[i-1, j], S[i, j-1]\}$ as stated. ■

The equality given in the previous statement is used by the algorithm LCS-SIMPLE in order to compute all the values of the table S and to produce $lcs(x, y) = S[m-1, n-1]$.

```
LCS-SIMPLE(x, m, y, n)
for i ← −1 to m − 1 do
    S[i, −1] ← 0
for j ← 0 to n − 1 do
    S[−1, j] ← 0
    for i ← 0 to m − 1 do
        if x[i] = y[j] then
            S[i, j] ← S[i − 1, j − 1] + 1
        else S[i, j] ← max{S[i − 1, j], S[i, j − 1]}
return S[m − 1, n − 1]
```

Figure 7.10 shows how the algorithm works.

Proposition 7.13
The algorithm LCS-SIMPLE *computes the maximal length of subsequences common to* x *and* y. *It executes in time and space* $O(m \times n)$.

(a)

S	j	-1	0	1	2	3	4	5	6	7	8	9
i	$y[j]$		C	A	G	A	T	C	A	G	A	G
-1	$x[i]$	0	0	0	0	0	0	0	0	0	0	0
0	A	0	0	1	1	1	1	1	1	1	1	1
1	G	0	0	1	2	2	2	2	2	2	2	2
2	C	0	1	1	2	2	2	3	3	3	3	3
3	T	0	1	1	2	2	3	3	3	3	3	3
4	G	0	1	1	2	2	3	3	3	4	4	4
5	A	0	1	2	2	3	3	3	4	4	5	5

(b)

$$\begin{pmatrix} \text{-} & \text{A} & \text{G} & \text{C} & \text{-} & \text{T} & \text{-} & \text{-} & \text{G} & \text{A} & \text{-} \\ \text{C} & \text{A} & \text{G} & \text{-} & \text{A} & \text{T} & \text{C} & \text{A} & \text{G} & \text{A} & \text{G} \end{pmatrix} \quad \begin{pmatrix} \text{-} & \text{A} & \text{G} & \text{-} & \text{-} & \text{C} & \text{T} & \text{-} & \text{G} & \text{A} & \text{-} \\ \text{C} & \text{A} & \text{G} & \text{A} & \text{T} & \text{C} & \text{-} & \text{A} & \text{G} & \text{A} & \text{G} \end{pmatrix}$$

$$\begin{pmatrix} \text{-} & \text{A} & \text{G} & \text{-} & \text{C} & \text{T} & \text{-} & \text{-} & \text{G} & \text{A} & \text{-} \\ \text{C} & \text{A} & \text{G} & \text{A} & \text{-} & \text{T} & \text{C} & \text{A} & \text{G} & \text{A} & \text{G} \end{pmatrix} \quad \begin{pmatrix} \text{-} & \text{A} & \text{G} & \text{-} & \text{-} & \text{C} & \text{-} & \text{T} & \text{G} & \text{A} & \text{-} \\ \text{C} & \text{A} & \text{G} & \text{A} & \text{T} & \text{C} & \text{-} & \text{-} & \text{G} & \text{A} & \text{G} \end{pmatrix}$$

Figure 7.10. Computation of the longest common subsequences between strings $x =$ AGCTGA and $y =$ CAGATCAGAG. **(a)** Table S and paths of maximal cost between positions $[-1, -1]$ and $[5, 9]$ on the table. **(b)** The four associated alignments. It results that the strings AGCGA and AGTGA are the longest common subsequences between x and y.

Proof The algorithm correctness results from the recurrence relation of Proposition 7.12.

It is immediate that the computation time and the memory space are both $O(m \times n)$. ■

It is possible, after the computation of the table S, to find a longest common subsequence between x and y by tracing back the table S from position $[m - 1, n - 1]$ (see Figure 7.10), as done in Section 7.2. The code that follows performs this computation in the same way as the algorithm One-alignment does.

```
One-LCS(x, m, y, n, S)
z ← ε
(i, j) ← (m − 1, n − 1)
while i ≠ −1 and j ≠ −1 do
    if x[i] = y[j] then
        z ← x[i] · z
        (i, j) ← (i − 1, j − 1)
    elseif S[i − 1, j] > S[i, j − 1] then
        i ← i − 1
    else j ← j − 1
return z
```

It is of course possible to compute, as done in Section 7.2, all the longest subsequences common to x and y by extending the technique used in the previous algorithm.

Computation of the length in linear space

If only the length of the longest common subsequences is desired, it is easy to see that the memorization of two columns (or two lines) of the table S are sufficient for performing the computation (it is even possible to only use one single column or one single line for performing this computation; see Exercise 7.3). It is precisely what realizes the algorithm LCS-COLUMN whose code appears thereafter.

```
LCS-COLUMN(x, m, y, n)
 1  for i ← −1 to m − 1 do
 2      C1[i] ← 0
 3  for j ← 0 to n − 1 do
 4      C2[−1] ← 0
 5      for i ← 0 to m − 1 do
 6          if x[i] = y[j] then
 7              C2[i] ← C1[i − 1] + 1
 8          else C2[i] ← max{C1[i], C2[i − 1]}
 9      C1 ← C2
10  return C1
```

Proposition 7.14
The operation LCS-COLUMN(x, m, y, n) *produces a table* C *whose value* $C[i]$, *for* $i = -1, 0, \ldots, m-1$, *is equal to* $lcs(x[0\,..\,i], y)$. *The computation is realized in time* $O(m \times n)$ *and in space* $O(m)$.

Proof The table produced by the algorithm is the table C_1. We get the stated result by showing, by recurrence on the value of j, that $C_1[i] = S[i, j]$, for $i = -1, 0, \ldots, m-1$. Indeed, when $j = n-1$ at the end of the execution of the algorithm, we get $C_1[i] = S[i, n-1] = lcs(x[0\,..\,i], y)$, for $i = -1, 0, \ldots, m-1$, by definition of the table S, which is stated.

Just before the execution of the loop of lines 3–9, what precedes can be identified with the processing of the case $j = -1$; we have $C_1[i] = 0$ for each value of i. We also have $S[i, -1] = 0$, this proves that the relation holds for $j = -1$.

Let us now assume that j has a positive value. The corresponding value of the table C_1 is computed in lines 4–9 of the algorithm. After the instruction in line 9, it is sufficient to show that the table C_2 satisfies the above relation when, by recurrence hypothesis, C_1 satisfies it for the value $j-1$. We assume thus that $C_1[i] = S[i, j-1]$ for $i = -1, 0, \ldots, m-1$ and we show that after the execution of lines 4–8, we have $C_2[i] = S[i, j]$ for $i = -1, 0, \ldots, m-1$.

The proof is done by recurrence on the value of i. For $i = -1$, this corresponds to the initialization of the table C_2 in line 4 and we have $C_2[-1] = 0 = S[-1, j]$. When $i \geq 0$, two cases are considered. If $x[i] = y[j]$, the associated instruction leads to set $C_2[i] = C_1[i-1] + 1$, which is equal to $S[i-1, j-1] + 1$ by application of the recurrence hypothesis on j. This value is also $S[i, j]$ after Proposition 7.12, which gives finally $C_2[i] = S[i, j]$. If $x[i] \neq y[j]$, the instruction in line 8 gives $C_2[i] = \max\{C_1[i], C_2[i-1]\}$. It is equal to $\max\{S[i, j-1], C_2[i-1]\}$, after the recurrence hypothesis on j, then to $\max\{S[i, j-1], S[i-1, j]\}$ after the recurrence hypothesis on i. We finally get the searched result, $C_2[i] = S[i, j]$, again by Proposition 7.12.

This ends the recurrences on i and j, and gives the result. ■

The utilization of the algorithm LCS-COLUMN for computing the maximal length of the subsequences common to x and y does not in a simple way allow to produce a longest common subsequence as previously described (because the table S is not completely memorized). But the algorithm is used in an intermediate computation of the method that follows.

Computation of a longest subsequence in linear space

We now show how to exhibit a longest common subsequence by an approach of the type divide-and-conquer. The method executes entirely in linear space. The idea of the computation can be described on the associated edit graph of x and y. It consists in determining a vertex of the form $(k-1, \lfloor n/2 \rfloor - 1)$, with $0 \leq k \leq m$, through which goes a path of maximal cost from $(-1, -1)$ to $(m-1, n-1)$ in the graph $G(x, y)$. Once this vertex is known, it only remains to compute the two segments of the path, from $(-1, -1)$ to $(k-1, \lfloor n/2 \rfloor - 1)$, and from $(k-1, \lfloor n/2 \rfloor - 1)$ to $(m-1, n-1)$. This amounts to find a longest subsequence u common to $x[0 \,.\,.\, k-1]$ and $y[0 \,.\,.\, \lfloor n/2 \rfloor - 1]$ on the one hand, and a longest subsequence v common to $x[k \,.\,.\, m-1]$ and $y[\lfloor n/2 \rfloor \,.\,.\, n-1]$ on the other hand. These two computations are performed by recursively applying the same method (see Figure 7.11). The string $z = u \cdot v$ is then a longest common subsequence between x and y. Recursive calls stop when one of the two strings is empty or reduced to a single letter. In this case, a simple test allows to conclude.

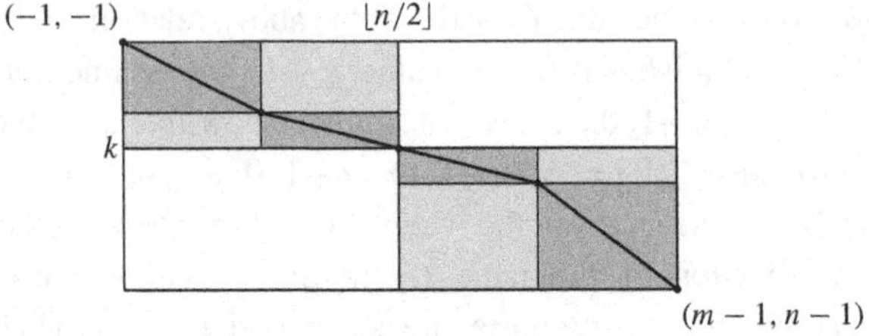

Figure 7.11. Schema of the divide-and-conquer method used to compute a longest common subsequence between two strings in linear space. The computation time of each step is proportional to the surface of the considered rectangles. As this surface is divided by two at each level of the recurrence, we get a total time $O(m \times n)$.

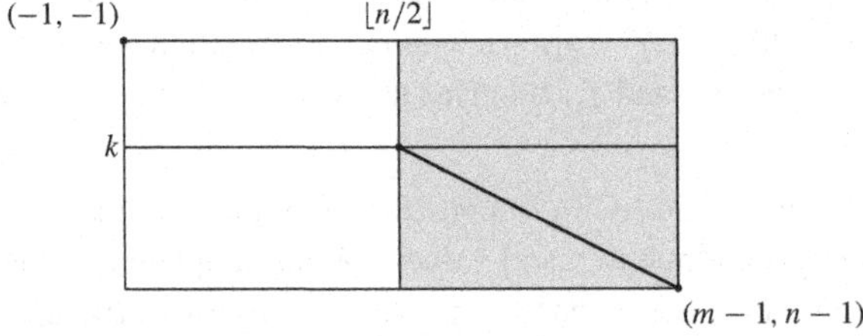

Figure 7.12. During the computation of the second half of the table (gray area), we memorize for each position (i, j) a position on the middle column through which goes a path of maximal cost from $(-1, -1)$ to (i, j). Only the pointer from $(m-1, n-1)$ is used for the rest of the computation.

It remains to describe how to get the index k that identifies the searched vertex $(k-1, \lfloor n/2 \rfloor - 1)$. The integer k is, by definition, an index within 0 and m for which the quantity

$$\begin{aligned} & lcs(x[0\,..\,k-1], y[0\,..\,\lfloor n/2 \rfloor - 1]) \\ & \qquad + lcs(x[k\,..\,m-1], y[\lfloor n/2 \rfloor\,..\,n-1]) \end{aligned}$$

is maximum (Figure 7.12). To find it, the algorithm LCS whose code is given further, starts by computing the column of index $\lfloor n/2 \rfloor - 1$ of the table S by calling (line 7) LCS-COLUMN$(x, m, y, \lfloor n/2 \rfloor)$. For the rest of the computation of this step (lines 8–18), and before the recursive calls, the algorithm processes the second half of the table S as the algorithm LCS-COLUMN does on the first half, but storing, in addition, pointers to the middle column. The computation utilizes two tables C_1 and C_2 in order to compute the values of S, and also two extra tables P_1 and P_2 to store the pointers.

These last two tables implement the table P defined, for $j = \lfloor n/2 \rfloor - 1, \lfloor n/2 \rfloor, \ldots, n-1$ and $i = -1, 0, \ldots, m-1$, by

$$P[i, j] = k$$

if and only if

$$0 \leq k \leq i + 1$$

and

$$\begin{aligned} lcs(x[0\,.\,.\,i], y[0\,.\,.\,j]) = \\ & lcs(x[0\,.\,.\,k-1], y[0\,.\,.\,\lfloor n/2 \rfloor - 1]) \\ & + lcs(x[k\,.\,.\,i], y[\lfloor n/2 \rfloor\,.\,.\,j]). \end{aligned} \tag{7.2}$$

The proposition that follows provides the mean used by the algorithm LCS, for computing the values of the table P. We notice that the stated recurrence allows a computation column by column as for the computation of the table S performed by LCS-COLUMN. This is partly this property that leads to a computation of a longest common subsequence in linear space. We show in Figure 7.13 an example of execution of the method.

Proposition 7.15
The table P satisfies the following recurrence relations:

$$P[i, \lfloor n/2 \rfloor - 1] = i + 1$$

for $i = -1, 0, \ldots, m-1$,

$$P[-1, j] = 0$$

for $j \geq \lfloor n/2 \rfloor$, and

$$P[i, j] = \begin{cases} P[i-1, j-1] & \textit{if } x[i] = y[j], \\ P[i-1, j] & \textit{if } x[i] \neq y[j] \textit{ and } S[i-1, j] > S[i, j-1], \\ P[i, j-1] & \textit{otherwise}, \end{cases}$$

for $i = 0, 1, \ldots, m-1$ and $j = \lfloor n/2 \rfloor, \lfloor n/2 \rfloor + 1, \ldots, n-1$.

Proof We show the property by recurrence on the pair (i, j) (using the lexicographically ordering of pairs).

If $j = \lfloor n/2 \rfloor - 1$, by definition of P, $k = i + 1$ since the second term of the sum in Equation (7.2) is null from the fact that $y[\lfloor n/2 \rfloor\,.\,.\,j]$ is the empty string. The initialization of the recurrence is thus correct.

Let us consider now that $j \geq \lfloor n/2 \rfloor$. If $i = -1$, by definition of P, $k = 0$ and Equation (7.2) is trivially satisfied since the considered factors of x are empty.

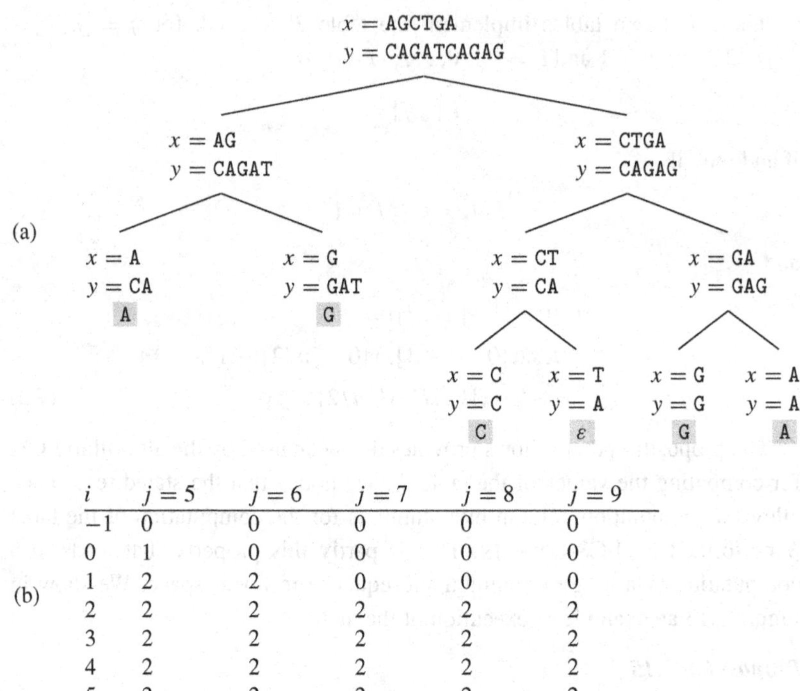

i	$j = 5$	$j = 6$	$j = 7$	$j = 8$	$j = 9$
−1	0	0	0	0	0
0	1	0	0	0	0
1	2	2	0	0	0
2	2	2	2	2	2
3	2	2	2	2	2
4	2	2	2	2	2
5	2	2	2	2	2

Figure 7.13. Illustration of the execution of algorithm LCS with strings AGCTGA and CAGATCAGAG. **(a)** Tree of the recursive calls. The longest common subsequence, AGCGA, produced by the algorithm is obtained by concatenating the results obtained on the leaves of the tree visited from left to right. **(b)** Values of the table P_1 of pointers after each of the iterations of the **for** loop of lines 10–18 during the initial call. The value of k computed during this call is $P_1[5] = 2$ obtained after the processing of $j = 9$, this corresponds to the decomposition $lcs(\texttt{AGCTGA}, \texttt{CAGATCAGAG}) = lcs(\texttt{AG}, \texttt{CAGAT}) + lcs(\texttt{CTGA}, \texttt{CAGAG})$.

It remains to deal with the general case $j \geq \lfloor n/2 \rfloor$ and $i \geq 0$. Let us assume that we have $x[i] = y[j]$. There exists then in the edit graph a path of maximal cost, from $(-1, -1)$ to (i, j), going through $(i - 1, j - 1)$. Thus there exists a path of maximal cost going through $(k - 1, \lfloor n/2 \rfloor - 1)$ where $k = P[i - 1, j - 1]$. In other words, we have after Proposition 7.12 $lcs(x[0 \,.\,.\, i], y[0 \,.\,.\, j]) = lcs(x[0 \,.\,.\, i - 1], y[0 \,.\,.\, j - 1]) + 1$, and by recurrence, $lcs(x[0 \,.\,.\, i - 1], y[0 \,.\,.\, j - 1]) = lcs(x[0 \,.\,.\, k - 1], y[0 \,.\,.\, \lfloor n/2 \rfloor - 1]) + lcs(x[k \,.\,.\, i - 1], y[\lfloor n/2 \rfloor \,.\,.\, j - 1])$. The assumption $x[i] = y[j]$ implying also $lcs(x[k \,.\,.\, i], y[\lfloor n/2 \rfloor \,.\,.\, j]) = lcs(x[k \,.\,.\, i - 1], y[\lfloor n/2 \rfloor \,.\,.\, j - 1]) + 1$, we deduce $lcs(x[0 \,.\,.\, i], y[0 \,.\,.\, j]) = lcs(x[0 \,.\,.\, k - 1], y[0 \,.\,.\, \lfloor n/2 \rfloor - 1]) +$

$lcs(x[k\,..\,i], y[\lfloor n/2 \rfloor\,..\,j])$, this gives, by definition of P, $P[i, j] = k = P[i-1, j-1]$, as indicated in the statement.

The last two cases are handled in a similar way. ■

The code of the algorithm LCS is given below in the form of a recursive function.

```
LCS(x, m, y, n)
if m = 1 and x[0] ∈ alph(y) then
        return x[0]
elseif n = 1 and y[0] ∈ alph(x) then
        return y[0]
elseif m = 0 or m = 1 or n = 0 or n = 1 then
        return ε
C1 ← LCS-COLUMN(x, m, y, ⌊n/2⌋)
for i ← −1 to m − 1 do
        P1[i] ← i + 1
for j ← ⌊n/2⌋ to n − 1 do
        (C2[−1], P2[−1]) ← (0, 0)
        for i ← 0 to m − 1 do
                if x[i] = y[j] then
                        (C2[i], P2[i]) ← (C1[i − 1] + 1, P1[i − 1])
                elseif C1[i] > C2[i − 1] then
                        (C2[i], P2[i]) ← (C1[i], P1[i])
                else (C2[i], P2[i]) ← (C2[i − 1], P2[i − 1])
        (C1, P1) ← (C2, P2)
k ← P1[m − 1]
u ← LCS(x[0 . . k − 1], k, y[0 . . ⌊n/2⌋ − 1], ⌊n/2⌋)
v ← LCS(x[k . . m − 1], m − k, y[⌊n/2⌋ . . n − 1], n − ⌊n/2⌋)
return u · v
```

Proposition 7.16
The operation LCS(x, m, y, n) *produces a longest subsequence common to strings x and y of respective lengths m and n.*

Proof The proof is done by recurrence on the length n of the string y. It consists in a simple verification when $n = 0$ or $n = 1$.

Let us consider then that $n > 1$. If $m = 0$ or $m = 1$, we simply check that the operation provides indeed a longest common subsequence to x and y. We can thus assume now that $m > 1$.

We notice that the instructions in lines 10–18 carry on the computation of the table C_1 started by the call to the algorithm LCS-COLUMN in line 7 by applying the same recurrence relation. We, moreover, notice that the table P_1 that implements the table P is computed by means of the recurrence relations of Proposition 7.15, which results from the correct computation of the table C_1. We thus have immediately after the execution of line 19 the equality $k = P_1[m-1] = P[m-1, n-1]$, this means that $lcs(x, y) = lcs(x[0\,..\,k-1], y[0\,..\,\lfloor n/2 \rfloor - 1]) + lcs(x[k\,..\,m-1], y[\lfloor n/2 \rfloor\,..\,n-1])$ by definition of P. As, by recurrence hypothesis, the calls to the algorithm in lines 20 and 21 provide a longest common subsequence to their input strings (that are correctly chosen), their concatenation is a longest common subsequence to x and y.

This ends the recurrence and the proof of the proposition. ■

Proposition 7.17
The operation LCS(x, m, y, n) *executes in time* $\Theta(m \times n)$. *It can be realized in space* $\Theta(m)$.

Proof During the initial call to the algorithm, the instructions in lines 1–19 execute in time $\Theta(m \times n)$.

The instructions in the same lines during immediate successive calls of lines 20 and 21 take respectively times proportional to $k \times \lfloor n/2 \rfloor$ and to $(m-k) \times (n - \lfloor n/2 \rfloor)$, thus globally $(m \times n)/2$ (see Figure 7.11).

It follows that the global execution time is $O(m \times n)$ since $\sum_i (m \times n)/2^i \leq 2m \times n$. But it is also $\Omega(m \times n)$ because of the first step, which gives the first result of the statement.

The memory space is used by the algorithm LCS for storing the tables C_1, C_2, P_1, and P_2, plus some variables that occupy a constant space. Altogether they occupy a space $O(m)$. And as the recursive calls to the algorithm do not require to keep the information stored in the tables, their space can be reused for the rest of the computation. Thus the result holds. ■

The following theorem provides the conclusion of the section.

Theorem 7.18
It is possible to compute a longest common subsequence between two strings of lengths m and n in time $O(m \times n)$ and space $O(\min\{m, n\})$.

Proof It is a direct consequence of Propositions 7.16 and 7.17 choosing for string x the shortest of the two input strings of the algorithm LCS. ■

7.4 Alignment with gaps

A ***gap*** is a consecutive sequence of holes in an alignment. The utilization of alignments on genetic sequences shows that it is sometimes desirable to penalize globally the formation of long gaps, in the computation of an alignment, instead of penalizing individually the deletion or the insertion of letters. Doing so, holes are not accounted for independently of their position. But no information external to the strings is used in the definition of the question.

In this context, the minimal cost of a sequence of edit operations is a distance under conditions analogue to those of Proposition 7.1, essentially since the symmetry between deletion and insertion is respected. We introduce the function

$$gap\colon \mathbf{N} \to \mathbf{R},$$

whose value $gap(k)$ indicates the cost of a gap of length k. The algorithm GENERIC-DP of Section 7.2 does not directly apply to the computation of a distance taking into account the above assumption, but its adaptation is relatively immediate.

To compute an optimal alignment in this situation, we utilize three tables: D, I, and T. The value $D[i, j]$ indicates the cost of an optimal alignment between $x[0\,..\,i]$ and $y[0\,..\,j]$ ending with deletions of letters of x. The value $I[i, j]$ indicates the cost of an optimal alignment between $x[0\,..\,i]$ and $y[0\,..\,j]$ ending with insertions of letters of y. Finally, the value $T[i, j]$ gives the cost of an optimal alignment between $x[0\,..\,i]$ and $y[0\,..\,j]$. The tables are linked by the recurrence relations of the proposition that follows.

Proposition 7.19
The cost $T[i, j]$ of an optimal alignment between $x[0\,..\,i]$ and $y[0\,..\,j]$ is given by the following recurrence relations:

$$\begin{aligned} D[-1,-1] &= D[i,-1] = D[-1,j] = \infty, \\ I[-1,-1] &= I[i,-1] = I[-1,j] = \infty, \end{aligned}$$

and

$$\begin{aligned} T[-1,-1] &= 0, \\ T[i,-1] &= gap(i+1), \\ T[-1,j] &= gap(j+1), \\ D[i,j] &= \min\{T[\ell,j] + gap(i-\ell) : \ell = 0,1,\ldots,i-1\}, \\ I[i,j] &= \min\{T[i,k] + gap(j-k) : k = 0,1,\ldots,j-1\}, \\ T[i,j] &= \min\{T[i-1,j-1] + Sub(x[i],y[j]), D[i,j], I[i,j]\}, \end{aligned}$$

for $i = 0, 1, \ldots, m-1$ and $j = 0, 1, \ldots, n-1$.

Proof The proof can be obtained using arguments similar to those of Proposition 7.3. It decomposes then in three cases, since an optimal alignment between $x[0\,..\,i]$ and $y[0\,..\,j]$ can only end in three different ways: either by a substitution of $y[j]$ for $x[i]$; or by the deletion of ℓ letters at the end of x; or by the insertion of k letters at the end of y with $0 \leq \ell < i$ and $0 \leq k < j$. ∎

If no restriction is done on the function *gap*, we can check that the problem of the computation of an optimal alignment between x and y solves in time $O(m \times n \times (m+n))$. On the other hand, we show that the problem solves in time $O(m \times n)$ if the function *gap* is an affine function, that is to say, is of the form

$$gap(k) = g + h \times (k-1)$$

with g and h two positive integer constants (in previous sections, $g = h$, and the function is linear in the number of holes). This type of function amounts to penalize the opening of a gap by a quantity g and to penalize differently the extension of a gap by a quantity h. In real applications, we usually choose the two constants so that $h < g$. The recurrence relations of the above proposition becomes:

$$\begin{aligned} D[i,j] &= \min\{D[i-1,j]+h, T[i-1,j]+g\}, \\ I[i,j] &= \min\{I[i,j-1]+h, T[i,j-1]+g\}, \\ T[i,j] &= \min\{T[i-1,j-1]+Sub(x[i],y[j]), D[i,j], I[i,j]\}, \end{aligned}$$

for $i = 0, 1, \ldots, m-1$ and $j = 0, 1, \ldots, n-1$. We moreover set

$$\begin{aligned} D[-1,-1] &= D[i,-1] = D[-1,j] = \infty, \\ I[-1,-1] &= \ I[i,-1] = \ I[-1,j] = \infty, \end{aligned}$$

for $i = 0, 1, \ldots, m-1$ and $j = 0, 1, \ldots, n-1$, and

$$\begin{aligned} T[-1,-1] &= 0, \\ T[0,-1] &= g, \\ T[-1,0] &= g, \\ T[i,-1] &= T[i-1,-1]+h, \\ T[-1,j] &= T[-1,j-1]+h, \end{aligned}$$

for $i = 1, 2, \ldots, m-1$ and $j = 1, 2, \ldots, n-1$.

The algorithm GAP, whose code follows, utilizes these recurrence relations. The tables D, I, and T considered in the code are of dimension $(m+1) \times (n+1)$. An example of execution of the algorithm is shown in Figure 7.14.

(a)

D	j	-1	0	1	2	3	4	5	6	7	8	9	10	11
i		$y[j]$	E	R	D	A	W	C	Q	P	G	K	W	Y
-1	$x[i]$	∞	∞	∞	∞	∞	∞	∞	∞	∞	∞	∞	∞	∞
0	E	∞	6	7	8	9	10	11	12	13	14	15	16	17
1	A	∞	3	6	7	8	9	10	11	12	13	14	15	16
2	W	∞	4	6	8	7	10	11	12	13	14	15	16	17
3	A	∞	5	7	9	8	7	10	11	12	13	14	15	16
4	C	∞	6	8	10	9	8	10	12	13	14	15	16	17
5	Q	∞	7	9	11	10	9	10	13	14	15	16	17	18
6	G	∞	8	10	12	11	10	11	10	13	14	15	16	17
7	K	∞	9	11	13	12	11	12	11	13	13	16	17	18
8	L	∞	10	12	14	13	12	13	12	14	14	13	16	17

(b)

I	j	-1	0	1	2	3	4	5	6	7	8	9	10	11
i		$y[j]$	E	R	D	A	W	C	Q	P	G	K	W	Y
-1	$x[i]$	∞	∞	∞	∞	∞	∞	∞	∞	∞	∞	∞	∞	∞
0	E	∞	6	3	4	5	6	7	8	9	10	11	12	13
1	A	∞	7	6	6	7	7	8	9	10	11	12	13	14
2	W	∞	8	7	8	9	10	7	8	9	10	11	12	13
3	A	∞	9	8	9	10	9	10	10	11	12	13	14	15
4	C	∞	10	9	10	11	12	11	10	11	12	13	14	15
5	Q	∞	11	10	11	12	13	12	13	10	11	12	13	14
6	G	∞	12	11	12	13	14	13	14	13	13	13	14	15
7	K	∞	13	12	13	14	15	14	15	14	15	16	13	14
8	L	∞	14	13	14	15	16	15	16	15	16	17	16	16

(c)

T	j	-1	0	1	2	3	4	5	6	7	8	9	10	11
i		$y[j]$	E	R	D	A	W	C	Q	P	G	K	W	Y
-1	$x[i]$	0	3	4	5	6	7	8	9	10	11	12	13	14
0	E	3	0	3	4	5	6	7	8	9	10	11	12	13
1	A	4	3	3	6	4	7	8	9	10	11	12	13	14
2	W	5	4	6	6	7	4	7	8	9	10	11	12	13
3	A	6	5	7	9	6	7	7	10	11	12	13	14	15
4	C	7	6	8	10	9	8	7	10	11	12	13	14	15
5	Q	8	7	9	11	10	9	10	7	10	11	12	13	14
6	G	9	8	10	12	11	10	11	10	10	10	13	14	15
7	K	10	9	11	13	12	11	12	11	13	13	10	13	14
8	L	11	10	12	14	13	12	13	12	14	14	13	13	16

(d)

$$\begin{pmatrix} \texttt{E} & \texttt{-} & \texttt{-} & \texttt{A} & \texttt{W} & \texttt{A} & \texttt{C} & \texttt{Q} & \texttt{-} & \texttt{G} & \texttt{K} & \texttt{-} & \texttt{L} \\ \texttt{E} & \texttt{R} & \texttt{D} & \texttt{A} & \texttt{W} & \texttt{-} & \texttt{C} & \texttt{Q} & \texttt{P} & \texttt{G} & \texttt{K} & \texttt{W} & \texttt{Y} \end{pmatrix}$$

$$\begin{pmatrix} \texttt{E} & \texttt{-} & \texttt{-} & \texttt{A} & \texttt{W} & \texttt{A} & \texttt{C} & \texttt{Q} & \texttt{-} & \texttt{G} & \texttt{K} & \texttt{L} & \texttt{-} \\ \texttt{E} & \texttt{R} & \texttt{D} & \texttt{A} & \texttt{W} & \texttt{-} & \texttt{C} & \texttt{Q} & \texttt{P} & \texttt{G} & \texttt{K} & \texttt{W} & \texttt{Y} \end{pmatrix}$$

Figure 7.14. Computation performed with the algorithm GAP on the strings of Figure 7.7, `EAWACQGKL` and `ERDAWCQPGKWY`. We consider the values $g = 3$, $h = 1$, $Sub(a, a) = 0$, and $Sub(a, b) = 3$ for all letters $a, b \in A$ such that $a \neq b$. **(a)–(c)** Tables D, I, and T. **(d)** The two optimal alignments obtained with a method similar to that of the algorithm ALIGNMENTS.

```
Gap(x, m, y, n)
for i ← −1 to m − 1 do
    (D[i, −1], I[i, −1]) ← (∞, ∞)
T[−1, −1] ← 0
T[0, −1] ← g
for i ← 1 to m − 1 do
    T[i, −1] ← T[i − 1, −1] + h
T[−1, 0] ← g
for j ← 1 to n − 1 do
    T[−1, j] ← T[−1, j − 1] + h
for j ← 0 to n − 1 do
    (D[−1, j], I[−1, j]) ← (∞, ∞)
    for i ← 0 to m − 1 do
        D[i, j] ← min{D[i − 1, j] + h, T[i − 1, j] + g}
        I[i, j] ← min{I[i, j − 1] + h, T[i, j − 1] + g}
        t ← T[i − 1, j − 1] + Sub(x[i], y[j])
        T[i, j] ← min{t, D[i, j], I[i, j]}
return T[m − 1, n − 1]
```

The tables D, I, and T used in the algorithm can be reduced to occupy a linear space by adapting the technique of Section 7.3. The statement that follows summarizes the result of the section.

Proposition 7.20
With an affine cost function of gaps, the optimal alignment of strings of lengths m and n can be computed in time $O(m \times n)$ and space $O(\min\{m, n\})$. ■

7.5 Local alignment

Instead of considering a global alignment between x and y, it is often more relevant to determine a best alignment between a factor of x and a factor of y. The notion of distance is not appropriate for stating this question. Indeed, when we try to minimize a distance, the factors that lead to the smallest values are the factors that occur simultaneously in the two strings x and y, factors that may be reduced to just a few letters. We thus rather utilize a notion of similarity between strings, for which equalities between letters are positively valued, and inequalities, insertions, and deletions are negatively valued. The search for a similar factor consists then in maximizing a quantity representative of the similarity between the strings.

Similarity

To measure the degree of similarity between two strings x and y, we utilize a ***score function***. This function, denoted by Sub_S, measures the degree of resemblance between two letters of the alphabet. The larger the value $Sub_S(a, b)$ is, the more similar the two letters a and b are. We assume that the function satisfies

$$Sub_S(a, a) > 0$$

for $a \in A$ and

$$Sub_S(a, b) < 0$$

for $a, b \in A$ with $a \neq b$. The function Sub_S is symmetrical. But it is not a distance since it does not satisfy the conditions of positivity, neither of separation, nor even of the triangle inequality. Indeed, we can attribute different scores to several equalities of letters: we can have $Sub_S(a, a) \neq Sub_S(b, b)$. This allows a better control of the equalities that are more greatly desired. The insertion and deletion functions must also be negatively valued (their values are integers):

$$Ins_S(a) < 0$$

and

$$Del_S(a) < 0$$

for $a \in A$.

We define then the ***similarity*** $sim(u, v)$ between the strings u and v by

$$sim(u, v) = \max\{\text{score of } \sigma : \sigma \in \Sigma_{u,v}\},$$

where $\Sigma_{u,v}$ is the set of sequences of edit operations transforming u into v. The score of an element $\sigma \in \Sigma_{u,v}$ is the sum of the scores of the edit operations of σ.

We can show the following property that establishes the relation between the notions of distance and of similarity (see notes).

Proposition 7.21

Given Sub, a distance on the letters, Ins, and Del, two functions on the letters, a constant value g, and a constant ℓ, we define a system of score in the following way:

$$Sub_S(a, b) = \ell - Sub(a, b)$$

and

$$Ins_s(a) = Del_s(a) = -g + \frac{\ell}{2}$$

for all the letters $a, b \in A$. *Then we have*

$$Lev(u, v) + sim(u, v) = \frac{\ell}{2}(|u| + |v|)$$

for every strings $u, v \in A^*$. ■

Computation of an optimal local alignment

An optimal local alignment between the strings x and y is a pair of strings (u, v) for which $u \preceq_{\text{fact}} x$, $v \preceq_{\text{fact}} y$, and $sim(u, v)$ is maximum. For performing its computation by a process analogue to what is done in Section 7.2, we consider a table S defined, for $i = -1, 0, \ldots, m - 1$ and $j = -1, 0, \ldots, n - 1$, by $S[i, j]$ is the maximum similarity between a suffix of $x[0 \,..\, i]$ and a suffix of $y[0 \,..\, j]$. Or also

$$S[i, j] = \max\{sim(x[\ell \,..\, i], y[k \,..\, j]) : 0 \le \ell \le i \text{ and } 0 \le k \le j\} \cup \{0\},$$

is the score of the local alignment in $[i, j]$. An optimal local alignment itself is then computed by tracing back the table from a maximal value.

Proposition 7.22
The table S satisfies the recurrence relations:

$$S[i, j] = \max \begin{cases} 0, \\ S[i-1, j-1] + Sub_s(x[i], y[j]), \\ S[i-1, j] + Del_s(x[i]), \\ S[i, j-1] + Ins_s(y[j]), \end{cases}$$

and

$$S[-1, -1] = S[i, -1] = S[-1, j] = 0$$

for $i = 0, 1, \ldots, m - 1$ *and* $j = 0, 1, \ldots, n - 1$.

Proof The proof is analogue to the proof of Proposition 7.3. ■

The following algorithm Local-alignment implements directly the recurrence relation of the previous proposition.

```
LOCAL-ALIGNMENT(x, m, y, n)
for i ← −1 to m − 1 do
    S[i, −1] ← 0
for j ← 0 to n − 1 do
    S[−1, j] ← 0
    for i ← 0 to m − 1 do
                       ⎧ 0
        S[i, j] ← max  ⎨ S[i − 1, j − 1] + Sub_S(x[i], y[j])
                       ⎪ S[i − 1, j] + Del_S(x[i])
                       ⎩ S[i, j − 1] + Ins_S(y[j])
return S
```

Proposition 7.23
The algorithm LOCAL-ALIGNMENT *computes the scores of all the local alignments between x and y.*

Proof This is an immediate application of Proposition 7.22, since the algorithm utilizes the relations of this proposition. ■

For finding an optimal local alignment, it is sufficient to locate a larger value in the table S. We trace back then the path from the position of this value by going up in the table (see Section 7.2). We stop the scan, in general, on a null value. An example is displayed in Figure 7.15.

7.6 Heuristic for local alignment

The alignment methods are often used for comparing selected strings. But they are also invaluable to search for resemblance between a chosen string (query) and strings of a data bank. In this case, we want to search for the similarities between a string $x \in A^*$ and each of the strings of a finite set $Y \subset A^*$. It is essential to perform each alignment in a reasonable time, since the process must be repeated on every strings $y \in Y$. We thus have to find faster solutions than those provided by the dynamic programming method. The usual solutions generally use heuristics and are approximate methods: they can miss some good answers to the given problem and can also give some erroneous answers. But they have a satisfactory behavior on real examples.

The method described here finds a good local alignment between a factor of x and a factor of y without allowing insertions nor deletions. This assumption simplifies the problem. The comparison is iterated on each strings y of the bank Y.

(a)

S	j	-1	0	1	2	3	4	5	6	7	8	9	10	11
i		$y[j]$	E	R	D	A	W	C	Q	P	G	K	W	Y
-1	$x[i]$	0	0	0	0	0	0	0	0	0	0	0	0	0
0	E	0	1	0	0	0	0	0	0	0	0	0	0	0
1	A	0	0	0	0	1	0	0	0	0	0	0	0	0
2	W	0	0	0	0	0	2	1	0	0	0	0	1	0
3	A	0	0	0	0	1	1	0	0	0	0	0	0	0
4	C	0	0	0	0	0	0	2	1	0	0	0	0	0
5	Q	0	0	0	0	0	0	1	3	2	1	0	0	0
6	G	0	0	0	0	0	0	0	2	1	3	2	1	0
7	K	0	0	0	0	0	0	0	1	0	2	4	3	2
8	L	0	0	0	0	0	0	0	0	0	1	3	2	1

(b) $\begin{pmatrix} \texttt{A} & \texttt{W} & \texttt{A} & \texttt{C} & \texttt{Q} & \texttt{-} & \texttt{G} & \texttt{K} \\ \texttt{A} & \texttt{W} & \texttt{-} & \texttt{C} & \texttt{Q} & \texttt{P} & \texttt{G} & \texttt{K} \end{pmatrix}$

Figure 7.15. Computation of an optimal local alignment between the strings EAWACQGKL and ERDAWCQPGKWY when $Sub_S(a, a) = 1$, $Sub_S(a, b) = -3$, and $Del_S(a) = Ins_S(a) = -1$ for $a, b \in A$, $a \neq b$. **(a)** Table S of the costs of all the local alignments, and the path ending on the position containing the largest value. **(b)** The corresponding optimal local alignment.

For two given integers ℓ and k, we consider the set of strings of length ℓ that are at distance at most k of a factor of length ℓ of the string x. We consider here a generalization of the Hamming distance that takes into account the cost of a substitution. The strings thus defined from all the factors of length ℓ of x are called the ***frequentable neighbors*** of the factors of length ℓ of x.

The analysis of the text y consists in locating in it the longest sequence of occurrences of frequentable neighbors; it produces a factor of y that is likely to be similar to a factor of x. To locate the factor of y, we utilize an automaton that recognizes the set of the frequentable neighbors. The construction of the automaton is an important element of the method.

We consider the distance d defined by

$$d(u, v) = \sum_{i=0}^{|u|-1} Sub(u[i], v[i])$$

for two strings u and v of the same length (we assume that Sub is a distance on the alphabet). For every natural integer ℓ, we denote by $\text{Fact}_\ell(x)$ the set of factors of length ℓ, called the ℓ-grams of the string x, and $V_k(\text{Fact}_\ell(x))$ its set of frequentable neighbors:

$$V_k(\text{Fact}_\ell(x)) = \{z \in A^\ell : d(w, z) \leq k \text{ for } w \in \text{Fact}_\ell(x)\}.$$

(a)

a	$L[a,0]$	$L[a,1]$	$L[a,2]$	$L[a,3]$	$L[a,4]$	$L[a,5]$
A	(A, 0)	(D, 2)	(E, 2)	(G, 3)	(K, 3)	(Q, 3)
C	(C, 0)	(Y, 2)	(A, 4)	(D, 5)	(E, 5)	(G, 5)
E	(E, 0)	(A, 2)	(D, 2)	(G, 3)	(K, 3)	(Q, 3)
G	(G, 0)	(A, 3)	(D, 3)	(E, 3)	(Q, 3)	(K, 4)
K	(K, 0)	(D, 2)	(A, 3)	(E, 3)	(Q, 3)	(R, 3)
L	(L, 0)	(Y, 3)	(A, 4)	(Q, 4)	(W, 4)	(D, 5)
Q	(Q, 0)	(D, 2)	(A, 3)	(E, 3)	(G, 3)	(K, 3)
W	(W, 0)	(R, 2)	(Y, 3)	(L, 4)	(K, 5)	(Q, 5)

a	$L[a,6]$	$L[a,7]$	$L[a,8]$	$L[a,9]$	$L[a,10]$
A	(C, 4)	(L, 4)	(R, 4)	(Y, 5)	(W, 6)
C	(K, 5)	(Q, 5)	(R, 5)	(L, 6)	(W, 7)
E	(R, 3)	(C, 5)	(L, 5)	(Y, 5)	(W, 6)
G	(C, 5)	(L, 5)	(R, 5)	(Y, 5)	(W, 6)
K	(G, 4)	(C, 5)	(L, 5)	(W, 5)	(Y, 5)
L	(E, 5)	(G, 5)	(K, 5)	(R, 5)	(C, 6)
Q	(R, 3)	(L, 4)	(C, 5)	(W, 5)	(Y, 5)
W	(A, 6)	(D, 6)	(E, 6)	(G, 6)	(C, 7)

(b)

factor	frequentable neighbors
EAW	EAW, EAR, EDW, EEW, AAW, DAW
AWA	AWA, AWD, AWE, ARA, DWA, EWA
WAC	WAC, WAY, WDC, WEC, RAC
ACQ	ACQ, ACD, AYQ, DCQ, ECQ
CQG	CQG, CDG, YQG
QGK	QGK, QGD, DGK
GKL	GKL, GDL

Figure 7.16. Illustration of the heuristic method for local alignment. **(a)** Table L that implements, for each letter a, the lists of pairs of the form $(b, Sub(a, b))$, for $b \in A$, sorted according to the second component of the pair. The alphabet is composed of the letters of the strings $x =$ EAWACQGKL and $y =$ ERDAWCQPGKWY. **(b)** The frequentable neighbors at maximal distance $k = 2$ of the 3-grams of x.

For building the set $V_k(\mathrm{Fact}_\ell(x))$ in time $O(\mathrm{card}\, V_k(\mathrm{Fact}_\ell(x)))$, we assume that we have, for each letter $a \in A$, the list of letters of the alphabet sorted in increasing order of the cost of their substitution to a. The elements of these lists are pairs of the form $(b, Sub(a, b))$. We access to the first element of such objects by the attribute *letter*, and to the second element by the attribute *cost*. These lists are stored in a two-dimensional table, denoted by L. For $a \in A$ and $i = 0, 1, \ldots, \mathrm{card}\, A - 1$, the object $L[a, i]$ is the pair corresponding to the $(i + 1)$th nearest letter of the letter a. An example is given in Figure 7.16.

The algorithm Generate-neighbors produces the set $V_t(\mathrm{Fact}_k(x))$. It calls the recursive procedure Gn. The call Gn$(i, \varepsilon, 0, 0, 0)$ (line 6 of the algorithm) computes all the frequentable neighbors of $x[i \mathinner{..} i+\ell-1]$ and store them in the set implemented by the global variable V. At the beginning of the operation $\text{Gn}(i', v, j', p, t)$, $p = d(v[0 \mathinner{..} j'-1], x[i'-j' \mathinner{..} i'-1]) \leq k$ and we try to extend v with the letter of the pair $L[x[i'], t]$ in the case where $j' < \ell$.

```
GENERATE-NEIGHBORS(ℓ)
V ← ∅
threshold[ℓ − 1] ← k
for i ← 0 to m − ℓ do
    for j ← ℓ − 1 downto 1 do
        threshold[j − 1] ← threshold[j] − cost(L[x[i + j], 0])
    GN(i, ε, 0, 0, 0)
return V
```

```
GN(i′, v, j′, p, t)
if j′ = ℓ then
    V ← V ∪ {v}
elseif t < card A then
    c ← L[x[i′], t]
    if p + cost[c] ≤ threshold[j′] then
        v ← v · letter[c]
        GN(i′ + 1, v[0 . . j′], j′ + 1, p + cost[c], 0)
        GN(i′, v[0 . . j′ − 1], j′, p, t + 1)
```

When the set of all the frequentable neighbors of the ℓ-grams of the string x has been computed, we can build an automaton recognizing the language defined by $V_k(\text{Fact}_\ell(x))$. We can also build it during the production of the frequentable neighbors. The text y is then analyzed with the help of the automaton for finding positions of elements of $V_k(\text{Fact}_\ell(x))$. The method detects the longest sequence of such positions. It then tries to extend, by dynamic programming, to the left or to the right, the found segment of strong similarity. We deduce eventually a local alignment between x and y.

Notes

The techniques described, in this chapter, are overused in molecular biology for comparing sequences of chains of nucleic acids (DNA or RNA) or of amino acids (proteins). The most well-known substitution matrices (Sub_s) are the PAM matrices and BLOSUM matrices (see Attwood and Parry-Smith [55]). These score matrices, empirically computed, witness physicochemical or evolutive properties of the studied molecules. The books of Waterman [68], of Setubal and Meidanis [67], of Pevzner [63], and of Jones and Pevzner [60] constitute excellent introductions to problems of the domain. The book of Sankoff and Kruskal [66] contains applications of alignments to various fields.

The subsequence distance of Section 7.3 is often attributed to Levenshtein [176]. The notion of the longest subsequences common to two strings is used for file comparison. The command `diff` of the UNIX system implements an algorithm based on this notion by considering that the lines of the files are letters of the alphabet. Among the algorithms at the basis of this command are those of Hunt and Szymanski [158] (Exercise 7.7) and of Myers [191]. A general presentation of the algorithms for searching for common subsequences can be found in an article by Apostolico [94]. Wong and Chandra [217] have shown that the algorithm LCS-SIMPLE is optimal in a model where we limit the access to letters to equality tests. Without this condition, Hirschberg [153] gave a (lower) bound $\Omega(n \times \log n)$. On a bounded alphabet, Masek and Paterson [183] gave an algorithm running in time $O(n^2/\log n)$. A sub-quadratic sequence alignment algorithm for unrestricted cost functions has been designed by Crochemore, Landau, and Ziv-Ukelson [124].

The initial algorithm of global alignment, from Needleman and Wunsch [194], runs in cubic time. The algorithm of Wagner and Fischer [215], as well as the algorithm for local alignment of Smith and Waterman [209], run in quadratic time (see [6], page 234). The method of dynamic programming was introduced by Bellman (1957, see [75]). Sankoff [203] discusses the introduction of the dynamic programming in the processing of molecular sequences.

The algorithm LCS is from Hirschberg [152]. The presentation given here refers to the book of Durbin, Eddy, Krogh, and Mitchison [57]. A generalization of this method has been proposed by Myers and Miller [192]. An implementation of the algorithm in the bit-vector model was proposed by Allison and Dix [89], later improved by Crochemore, Iliopoulos, and Pinzon [123].

The algorithm GAP is from Gotoh [146]. A survey of the methods for alignment with gaps was presented by Giancarlo in 1997 (see [1]). The proof of Proposition 7.21 is presented in [67].

The heuristic method of Section 7.6 is the core of the software Blast (see Altschul, Gish, Miller, Myers, and Lipman [90]). The parameters ℓ and k of the section correspond respectively to parameters W (*word size*) and T (*word score threshold*) of the software.

Charras and Lecroq created and maintains the site [52], accessible on the Web, where animations of alignment algorithms are available.

Exercises

7.1 (Distances)

Show that d_{pref}, d_{suff}, d_{fact}, and d_{subs} are distances.

7.2 (Transposition)

Conceive a distance between strings that, in addition to the elementary edit operations, takes into account the transposition of two consecutive letters. Describe a computation algorithm for this distance.

7.3 (One column)

Give a version of the algorithm GENERIC-DP that uses a single table of size $\min\{m, n\}$ in addition to the strings and to constant memory space.

7.4 (Distinguished)

Given two different strings x and y, give an algorithm that finds a shortest subsequence that distinguishes them, that is to say, finds a string z of minimal length that satisfies, either both $z \preceq_{\text{sseq}} x$ and $z \not\preceq_{\text{sseq}} y$, or both $z \not\preceq_{\text{sseq}} x$ and $z \preceq_{\text{sseq}} y$. (*Hint:* see Lothaire [79], Chapter 6.)

7.5 (Automaton)

Give a method for producing the automaton of optimal alignments between two strings x and y from the table T of Section 7.2 using only a linear extra space (in contrast with the algorithm OPT-ALIGN-AUT that utilizes the table E of size $O(|x| \times |y|)$). (*Hint:* memorize a list of current vertices belonging to one or two consecutive antidiagonals.)

7.6 (Alternative)

There exists another method than the one used by the algorithm LCS (Section 7.3) for finding the index k of Equation (7.2). This method consists in computing the values of the last column C_1 of the table T for x and $y[0\,..\,\lfloor n/2\rfloor - 1]$ and in computing the values of the last column C_2 of the table for the reverse of x and the reverse of $y[\lfloor n/2\rfloor\,..\,n-1]$. The index k is then a value such that $-1 \leq k \leq m-1$ and that maximizes the sum $C_1[k] + C_2[m-2-k]$.

Write an algorithm that computes a longest subsequence common to two strings, in linear space, using this method. (*Hint:* see Hirschberg [152].)

7.7 (Abacus)

There exists a method for computing efficiently a longest common subsequence between two strings x and y when they share few letters in common. The letters of y are sequentially processed from the first to the last. Let us consider the situation where $y[0\,..\,j-1]$ has already been processed. The algorithm maintains a partition of the positions on x into classes $I_0, I_1, \ldots, I_k, \ldots$ defined by

$$I_k = \{i : lcs(x[0\,..\,i], y[0\,..\,j-1]) = k\}.$$

In other words, the positions in the class I_k correspond to prefixes of x that have a longest common subsequence of length k with $y[0\,..\,j-1]$.

The analysis of $y[j]$ consists then in considering the positions ℓ on x such that $x[\ell] = y[j]$, positions that are processed in decreasing order. Let ℓ be such a position and I_k be its class. If $\ell - 1$ belongs also to the class I_k, we slide all the positions of I_k greater than or equal to ℓ to the class I_{k+1} (imagine an abacus where each bowl represents a position on x and where each cluster of bowls represents a class).

Implement this method for computing a longest subsequence common to two strings. Show that we can realize it in time $O(m \times n \times \log m)$ and space $O(m)$. Give a condition on x and y that reduces the time to $O(m + n \times \log m)$. (*Hint:* see Hunt and Szymanski [158].)

7.8 (Subsequence automaton)

Give the number of states and of arcs of the automaton $\mathcal{SM}(x)$, minimal automaton recognizing Subs(x), the set of subsequences of x ($x \in A^*$).

Design a sequential algorithm for building $\mathcal{SM}(x)$, then a second algorithm doing it by scanning the string from right to left instead. What are the complexities of the two algorithms?

How and with what complexity can we compute with the help of the automata $\mathcal{SM}(x)$ and $\mathcal{SM}(y)$ ($x, y \in A^*$) a shortest subsequence distinguishing x and y, if it exists, or a longest subsequence common to these two strings?

7.9 (Three strings)

Write an algorithm for aligning three strings in quadratic space.

7.10 (Restricted subsequence)

Let $x \in A^*$ be a string and let $u_0u_1\ldots u_{r-1}$ be a factorization of x with $u_j \in A^*$ for $j = 0, 1, \ldots, r-1$. A string z of length k is a restricted subsequence of x together with its factorization $u_0u_1\ldots u_{r-1}$ if there exists a strictly increasing sequence $\langle p_0, p_1, \ldots, p_{k-1}\rangle$ of positions on x such that

- $x[p_i] = z[i]$ for $i = 0, 1, \ldots, k-1$;
- if two positions p_i and $p_{i'}$ are such that

$$|u_0u_1\ldots u_{j-1}| < p_i, p_{i'} \leq |u_0u_1\ldots u_j|$$

for $j = 1, 2, \ldots, r - 1$, then $z[i] \neq z[i']$. This means that two equal letters of a u_j cannot occur in the restricted subsequence.

A string z is a longest restricted subsequence of a string x factorized into $u_0u_1 \ldots u_{r-1}$ and of a string y factorized into $v_0v_1 \ldots v_{s-1}$ if z is a restricted subsequence of x, z is a restricted subsequence of y, and the length of z is maximum.

Design an algorithm that finds a longest restricted subsequence common to two factorized strings x and y. (*Hint:* see Andrejková [92].)

7.11 (Less frequentable neighbors)

Design an algorithm for the construction of a deterministic automaton recognizing the frequentable neighbors considered in Section 7.6.

Generalize the notion of frequentable neighbors obtained by considering the three edit operations (and not only the substitution). Write up an associated local alignment program.

8
Approximate patterns

In this chapter, we are interested in the approximate search for fixed strings. Several notions of approximation on strings are considered: jokers, differences, and mismatches.

A joker is a symbol meant to represent all the letters of the alphabet. The solutions to the problem of searching a text for a pattern containing jokers use specific methods that are described in Section 8.1.

More generally, approximate pattern matching consists in locating all the occurrences of factors inside a text y that are similar to a string x. It consists in producing the positions of the factors of y that are at distance at most k from x, for a given natural integer k. We assume in the rest that $k < |x| \leq |y|$. We consider two distances for measuring the approximation: the edit distance and the Hamming distance.

The edit distance between two strings u and v, that are not necessarily of the same length, is the minimum cost of a sequence of elementary edit operations between these two strings (see Section 7.1). The method at the basis of approximate pattern matching is a natural extension of the alignment method by dynamic programming of Chapter 7. It can be improved by using a restricted notion of distance obtained by considering the minimum number of edit operations rather than the sum of their costs. With this distance, the problem is known as the approximate pattern matching with k differences. Section 8.2 presents several solutions of it.

The Hamming distance between two strings u and v of the same length is the number of positions where mismatches occur between the two strings. With this distance, the problem is known as the approximate pattern matching with k mismatches. It is treated in Section 8.3.

We examine then (Section 8.4) the case of searching for short patterns for which we extend the bit-vector model of Section 1.5. The solution gives excellent practical results and is very flexible as long as the conditions of its utilization are fulfilled.

We finally tackle (Section 8.5) a heuristic method for finding quickly in a dictionary some occurrences of approximate factors of a fixed string.

8.1 Approximate pattern matching with jokers

In this section, we assume that the string x and the text y can contain occurrences of the letter §, called ***joker***, special letter that does not belong to the alphabet A. The joker[1] matches with itself as well as with all the letters of the alphabet A.

More precisely, we define the notion of ***correspondence*** on $A \cup \{\S\}$ as follows. Two letters a and b of the alphabet $A \cup \{\S\}$ correspond, what we denote by

$$a \approx b,$$

if they are equal or if at least one of them is the joker. We extend this notion of correspondence to strings: two strings u and v on the alphabet $A \cup \{\S\}$ and of the same length m correspond, what we denote by

$$u \approx v,$$

if, at each position, their respective letters correspond, that is to say if, for $i = 0, 1, \ldots, m-1$,

$$u[i] \approx v[i].$$

The search for all the occurrences of a string with jokers x of length m in a text y of length n consists in detecting all the positions j on y for which $x \approx y[j \mathinner{..} j+m-1]$.

Jokers only in the string

When only the string x contains jokers, it is possible to solve the problem by using the same techniques as those developed for the search for a dictionary (see Chapter 2).

Let us assume for the rest that the string x is not empty and that at least one of its letters is in A. It decomposes then in the form

$$x = \S^{i_0} x_0 \S^{i_1} x_1 \ldots \S^{i_{k-1}} x_{k-1} \S^{i_k}$$

[1] Let us add that several distinct jokers can be considered. But the assumption is that, from the point of view of the search, they are not distinguishable.

where $k \geq 1$, $i_0 \geq 0$, $i_q > 0$ for $q = 1, 2, \ldots, k-1$, $i_k \geq 0$, and $x_q \in A^+$ for $q = 0, 1, \ldots, k-1$. Let us denote by X the set of strings $x_0, x_1, \ldots, x_{k-1}$ (these strings are not necessarily all distinct). Then, let $M = \mathcal{D}(X)$ be the dictionary automaton of X (see Section 2.2) whose outputs are defined by: the output of the state u is the set of right positions on x of the occurrences of those strings x_q that are suffixes of u.

The searching algorithm utilizes the automaton M in order to analyze the text y. Moreover, a counter is associated with each position on the text, the initial value of the counter being null. When an occurrence of a factor x_q is discovered at right position j on y, the counters associated with positions $j - p$ for which p is an element of the current output are incremented. When a counter at a position ℓ of the text reaches the value k, it indicates that x occurs at the (left) position ℓ on y. The following code applies this method.

```
JOKER-SEARCH(M, m, k, i_0, i_k, y, n)
1  for j ← −m + 1 to n − 1 do
2        C[j] ← 0
3  r ← initial[M]
4  for j ← i_0 to n − i_k do
5        r ← TARGET(r, y[j])
6        for each p ∈ output[r] do
7              C[j − p] ← C[j − p] + 1
8              OUTPUT-IF(C[j − p] = k)
```

We note that the values $C[\ell]$ with $\ell \leq j - m$ are not useful when the current position on y is j. So, only m counters are necessary for the computation. This allows to state the following result.

Proposition 8.1
The search for the occurrences of a string with jokers, x of length m, of the form $x = \S^{i_0} x_0 \S^{i_1} x_1 \ldots \S^{i_{k-1}} x_{k-1} \S^{i_k}$, in a text of length n can be done in time $O(k \times n)$ and space $O(m)$, with the help of the automaton $\mathcal{D}(\{x_0, x_1, \ldots, x_{k-1}\})$ having the adequate outputs.

Proof After the results of Chapter 2, and if, for the moment, we omit the loop in lines 6–8, the execution time of the algorithm JOKER-SEARCH is $O(k \times n)$ whatever the implementation for the automaton M is. Now, as the number of elements of each output of the automaton is less than k, the loop in lines 6–8 takes a time $O(k)$, whatever the value of j is. We thus get the total time $O(k \times n)$ as announced.

The memory space necessary for the execution of the algorithm is $O(m)$, since it essentially consists in storing m values of the table C after the remark that precedes the statement. ■

The preliminary phase of the execution of the algorithm JOKER-SEARCH consists in producing the automaton $\mathcal{D}(\{x_0, x_1, \ldots, x_{k-1}\})$ with its outputs. And, to be consistent, this computation must be done in time $O(k \times m)$ and space $O(m)$. This is realized by the implementation of the automaton with failure function (see Section 2.3). The outputs of the states are generated as in Section 2.2.

Jokers in the text and in the string

The problem of the search for x in y when the two strings can contain jokers does not solve in the same terms than for a classical string searching. This comes from the fact that the relation $\approx$ is not transitive: for $a, b \in A$, the relations $a \approx §$ and $§ \approx b$ does not necessarily imply $a \approx b$. Moreover, if the comparisons of letters (using the relation $\approx$) constitute the only access to the text, there exists a minimal quadratic bound to the problem, which additionally proves that this problem is different from the other string matching problems.

Theorem 8.2

Let us assume card $A \geq 2$. *If the comparisons of letters constitute the only access to the text y, finding all the occurrences of a string with jokers x of length m in a text with jokers y of length n can require a time $\Omega(m \times n)$.*

Proof The length m being fixed, let us consider the case where $n = 2m$. Let us assume that during its execution, an algorithm does not perform the comparison $x[i]$ vs. $y[j]$ for some $i = 0, 1, \ldots, m-1$ and some $j = i, i+1, \ldots, i+m$. Then the output of this algorithm is the same in the case $x = §^m$ and $y = §^{2m}$, than in the case $x = §^i \mathtt{a} §^{m-i-1}$ and $y = §^j \mathtt{b} §^{2m-j-1}$, though there is one occurrence less in the second case. This shows that such an algorithm is erroneous. It follows that at least $m \times (m+1)$ comparisons must be performed.

When $n > 2m$, we factorize y into factors of length $2m$ (except maybe at the end of y where the factor can be shorter). The previous argument applies to each factor and leads to the bound of $\Omega(m^2 \times \lfloor \frac{n}{2m} \rfloor)$ comparisons. ■

Let us expose now a method that allows to find all the occurrences of a string with jokers in a text with jokers using bit vectors. We assume that $n \geq m \geq 1$.

For any bit vectors p and q of at least one bit, we denote by $p \otimes q$ the product of p and q that is the vector of $|p| + |q| - 1$ bits defined by

$$(p \otimes q)[\ell] = \bigvee_{i+j=\ell} p[i] \wedge q[j],$$

for $\ell = 0, 1, \ldots, |p| + |q| - 2$. For every string u on $A \cup \{\S\}$ and every letter $a \in A$, we denote by $\lambda(u, a)$ the characteristic vector of the positions of a on u defined as the vector of $|u|$ bits satisfying

$$\lambda(u, a)[i] = \begin{cases} 1 & \text{if } u[i] = a, \\ 0 & \text{otherwise,} \end{cases}$$

for $i = 0, 1, \ldots, |u| - 1$.

Now, if r is the vector of $m + n - 1$ bits such that

$$r = \bigvee_{a,b \in A \text{ and } a \neq b} \lambda(y, a) \otimes \lambda(x^{\sim}, b),$$

we have, for $\ell = m - 1, m, \ldots, n - 1$,

$$r[\ell] = 0$$

if and only if

$$x \approx y[\ell - m + 1 \,.\,.\, \ell].$$

An example is shown in Figure 8.1.

The computation time of the bit vector r is $\Theta((\text{card } A)^2 \times m \times n)$ if the computation of the terms $\lambda(y, a) \otimes \lambda(x^{\sim}, b)$ is performed directly on the bit vectors. This time complexity can, however, be sensibly improved if the products $\otimes$ are realized with the help of a fast implementation of integer product. This idea is developed in the proof of the result that follows.

Theorem 8.3

The occurrences of a string with jokers, x of length m, in a text with jokers, y of length n, can be found in time

$$O((\text{card } A)^2 \times n \times (\log m)^2 \times \log \log m).$$

Proof Let first note that if p and q are two bit vectors, their product $p \otimes q$ can be realized as a product of polynomials: it is sufficient to associate $\vee$ with $+$, $\wedge$ with $\times$, the bit 0 with the null value, and the bit 1 with every non-null value. Let us add that the coefficients of the polynomial thus associated with $p \otimes q$ are all smaller than $\min\{|p|, |q|\}$. But the product of the polynomials associated with p and q can itself be realized as the product of two integers if we take care to encode the coefficients on a sufficient number of bits, that is to say on $t = \lceil \log_2(1 + \min\{|p|, |q|\}) \rceil$ bits.

It follows that for realizing the product $s = p \otimes q$, it is sufficient to have three memory cells for storing integer: P of $t \times |p|$ bits, Q of $t \times |q|$ bits, and S of $t \times (|p| + |q| - 1)$ bits. Then to initialize P and Q to zero, to set the bits $P[t \times i]$ to 1 if $p[i] = 1$, to set the bits $Q[t \times i]$ to 1 if $q[i] = 1$, to perform the product $S = P \times Q$, then to set the bits $s[i]$ to 1 if one of the bits of

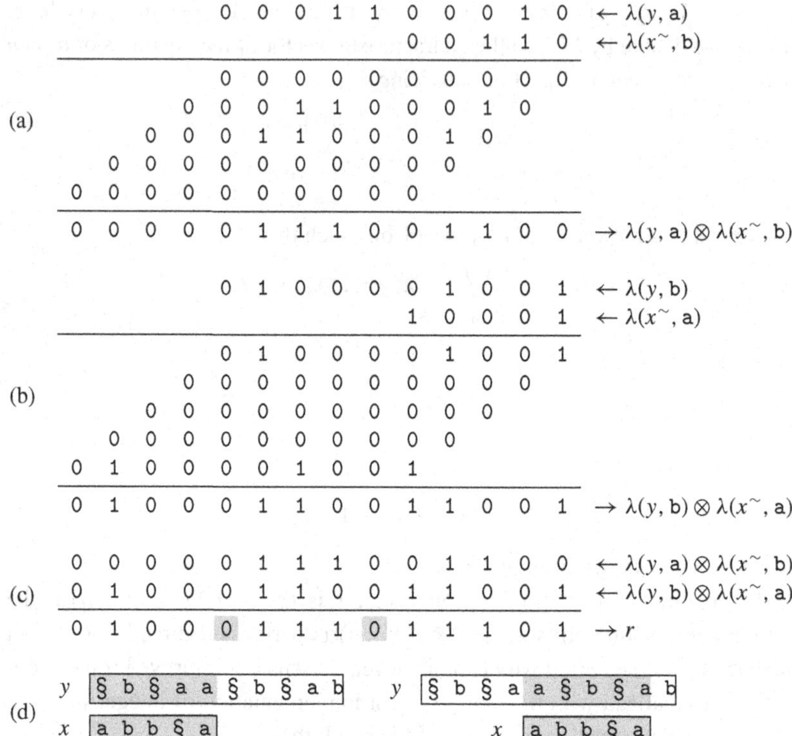

Figure 8.1. Search for the string with jokers $x =$ abb§a of length $m = 5$ in the text with jokers $y =$ §b§aa§b§ab of length $n = 10$. **(a)** Computation of the product $\lambda(y, \texttt{a}) \otimes \lambda(x^{\sim}, \texttt{b})$. **(b)** Computation of the product $\lambda(y, \texttt{b}) \otimes \lambda(x^{\sim}, \texttt{a})$. **(c)** Computation of the bit vector r of length $m + n - 1 = 14$, disjunction of two previous vectors. The positions ℓ on r within $m - 1 = 4$ and $n - 1 = 9$ for which $r[\ell] = 0$, positions 4 and 8 in gray, are the right positions of an occurrence of x in y. **(d)** The two occurrences of x in y, at right positions 4 and 8.

$S[t \times i \,.\,.\, t \times (i + 1) - 1]$ is non-null and to 0 otherwise. The time required to realize the product is thus $O(t \times (|p| + |q|))$ for the initializations and settings, to which we must add the time for performing the product of two numbers of $t \times |p|$ and $t \times |q|$ bits.

We know that it is possible to multiply a number of M digits by a number of N digits in time $O(N \times \log M \times \log\log M)$, for $N \geq M$ (see notes). If we set $p = \lambda(y, a)$ and $q = \lambda(x^{\sim}, b)$, we have $|p| = m$, $|q| = n$, $t = \lceil \log_2(m + 1) \rceil$, $M = t \times m$, and $N = t \times n$. The time necessary for the computation of the product $\lambda(y, a) \otimes \lambda(x^{\sim}, b)$ is thus $O(n \times \log m)$ for the initializations and settings, plus $O(n \times (\log m)^2 \times \log\log m)$ for the multiplication. There are $(\operatorname{card} A - 1)^2$ products of this type to perform. The computation of the bit vector r can be done jointly with those of the products; this requires a time $O((\text{card}\, A)^2 \times n)$. The announced total complexity follows. ■

8.2 Approximate pattern matching with differences

In this section, we consider the approximate pattern matching with differences: locating all the factors of y that are at a given maximal distance k of x. We set $m = |x|$ and $n = |y|$, and we assume $k \in \mathbf{N}$ and $k < m \leq n$. The distance between two strings is defined here as the minimal number of differences between these two strings. A difference can be one of the edit operations: substitution, deletion or insertion (see Section 7.1). The problem corresponds to the utilization of a simplified notion of edit distance. The standard solutions designed to solve the problem consist in using the dynamic programming technique introduced in Chapter 7. We describe three variations around this technique.

Dynamic programming

We first examine a problem a bit more general for which the cost of the edit operations is not necessarily the unit. It consists thus of the ordinary edit distance (see Chapter 7). Aligning x with a factor of y amounts to align x with a prefix of y considering that the insertion of any number of letters of y at the beginning of x is not penalizing. With the table T of Section 7.2 we can check that, in order to solve the problem, it is sufficient then to initialize to zero the values of the first line of the table. The positions of the occurrences are then associated with all the values of the last line of the table that are not greater than k.

To be more formal, to search for approximate factors we utilize the table R defined by

$$R[i, j] = \min\{Lev(x[0\,..\,i], y[\ell\,..\,j]) : \ell = 0, 1, \ldots, j + 1\},$$

for $i = -1, 0, \ldots, m - 1$ and $j = -1, 0, \ldots, n - 1$, where Lev is the edit distance of Section 7.1. The computation of the values of the table R utilizes the recurrence relations of the next proposition.

Proposition 8.4
For $i = 0, 1, \ldots, m - 1$ *and* $j = 0, 1, \ldots, n - 1$, *we have:*

$$R[-1, -1] = 0,$$
$$R[i, -1] = R[i - 1, -1] + Del(x[i]),$$
$$R[-1, j] = 0,$$

$$R[i,j] = \min \begin{cases} R[i-1,j-1] + Sub(x[i],y[j]), \\ R[i-1,j] + Del(x[i]), \\ R[i,j-1] + Ins(y[j]). \end{cases}$$

Proof Analogue to the proof of Proposition 7.3. ∎

The searching algorithm K-DIFF-DP whose code is given thereafter and that translates the recurrence of the previous proposition performs the approximate search. An example is given in Figure 8.2.

```
K-DIFF-DP(x, m, y, n, k)
R[-1, -1] ← 0
for i ← 0 to m - 1 do
        R[i, -1] ← R[i - 1, -1] + Del(x[i])
for j ← 0 to n - 1 do
        R[-1, j] ← 0
        for i ← 0 to m - 1 do
                                     ⎧ R[i - 1, j - 1] + Sub(x[i], y[j])
                R[i, j] ← min ⎨ R[i - 1, j] + Del(x[i])
                                     ⎩ R[i, j - 1] + Ins(y[j])
        OUTPUT-IF(R[m - 1, j] ≤ k)
```

We note that the space used by the algorithm K-DIFF-DP can be reduced to a single column by reproducing the technique of Section 7.3. Besides this technique is implemented further by the algorithm K-DIFF-CUT-OFF. As a conclusion, we get the following result.

Proposition 8.5
The operation K-DIFF-DP(x, m, y, n, k) *finds the factors* u *of* y *for which* $Lev(u, x) \leq k$ *(Lev is the edit distance with general costs) and executes in time* $O(m \times n)$*. It can be implemented to use* $O(m)$ *space.* ∎

Diagonal monotony

In the rest of the section, we consider that the costs of the edit operations are units. This is a simple case for which we can describe more efficient computation strategies than those described above. The restriction allows to state a property of monotony on the diagonals that is at the core of the presented variations.

Since we assume that $Sub(a, b) = Del(a) = Ins(b) = 1$ for $a, b \in A, a \neq b$, the recurrence relation of Proposition 8.4 simplifies and becomes

$$R[-1,-1] = 0,$$

$$R[i,-1] = i+1,$$

$$R[-1,j] = 0,$$

(a)

R	j	-1	0	1	2	3	4	5	6	7	8	9	10	11
i		$y[j]$	C	A	G	A	T	A	A	G	A	G	A	A
-1	$x[i]$	0	0	0	0	0	0	0	0	0	0	0	0	0
0	G	1	1	1	0	1	1	1	1	0	1	0	1	1
1	A	2	2	1	1	0	1	1	1	1	0	1	0	1
2	T	3	3	2	2	1	0	1	2	2	1	1	1	1
3	A	4	4	3	3	2	1	0	1	2	2	2	1	1
4	A	5	5	4	4	3	2	1	0	1	2	3	2	1

(b)

```
(    G A T A A               )
(C A G A T - A A G A G A A   )

(    G A T A A               )
(C A G A T A A G A G A A     )

(    G A T A A               )
(C A G A T A - A G A G A A   )

(  - G A T A A               )
(C A G A T A A G A G A A     )

(      G A T A A             )
(C A G - A T A A G A G A A   )

(    G A T A A -             )
(C A G A T A A G A G A A     )

(              G A T A A     )
(C A G A T A A G A G A A     )
```

Figure 8.2. Search for $x =$ GATAA in $y =$ CAGATAAGAGAA with one difference, considering unit costs for the edit operations. **(a)** Values of table R. **(b)** The seven alignments of x with factors of y ending at positions 5, 6, 7, and 11 on y. We note that the fourth and sixth alignments give no extra information compared to the second alignment.

$$R[i, j] = \min \begin{cases} R[i-1, j-1] & \text{if } x[i] = y[j], \\ R[i-1, j-1] + 1 & \text{if } x[i] \neq y[j], \\ R[i-1, j] + 1, & \\ R[i, j-1] + 1. & \end{cases} \tag{8.1}$$

for $i = 0, 1, \ldots, m-1$ and $j = 0, 1, \ldots, n-1$.

A diagonal d of the table R consists of the positions $[i, j]$ for which $j - i = d$ $(-m \leq d \leq n)$. The property of diagonal monotony expresses that the sequence of values on each diagonal of the table R is increasing and that the difference between two consecutive values is at most one (see Figure 8.2). Before formally stating the property, we show intermediate results. The first result means that two adjacent values on a column of the table R differ by at most one unit. The second result is symmetrical considering the lines of R.

Lemma 8.6
For each position j on the string y, we have

$$-1 \le R[i, j] - R[i-1, j] \le 1$$

for $i = 0, 1, \ldots, m-1$.

Proof From the recurrence on R stated above we deduce, for $i \ge 0$ and $j \ge 0$,

$$R[i, j] \ge \min \begin{cases} R[i-1, j-1] \\ R[i-1, j] + 1 \\ R[i, j-1] + 1 \end{cases} \tag{8.2}$$

and $R[i, j] \le R[i-1, j] + 1$. Thus $R[i, j] - R[i-1, j] \le 1$. This proves one of the inequalities of the statement.

The inequality

$$R[i, j] \le R[i, j-1] + 1, \tag{8.3}$$

that can be obtained by symmetry, is used in the rest.

We show that $R[i, j] - R[i-1, j] \ge -1$ by recurrence on j, for $i \ge 0$ and $j \ge 0$. This property is satisfied for $j = -1$ since $R[i, -1] - R[i-1, -1] = i + 1 - i = 1 \ge -1$.

Let us assume that the inequality is satisfied until $j - 1$, thus

$$R[i, j-1] + 1 \ge R[i-1, j-1]. \tag{8.4}$$

Equation (8.3) gives, after substituting $i - 1$ for i,

$$R[i-1, j-1] \ge R[i-1, j] - 1. \tag{8.5}$$

By combining the Relations (8.2), (8.4), and (8.5), we get

$$R[i, j] \ge \min\{R[i-1, j] + 1, R[i-1, j] - 1\}$$

that is to say $R[i, j] \ge R[i-1, j] - 1$, and thus $R[i, j] - R[i-1, j] \ge -1$. This ends the recurrence and the proof of the inequalities of the statement. ■

Lemma 8.7
For each position i on the string x, we have

$$-1 \le R[i, j] - R[i, j-1] \le 1$$

for $j = 0, 1, \ldots, n-1$.

Proof Symmetrical to the one of Lemma 8.6 by swapping the roles of x and y. ■

We now can state the proposition concerning the property of monotony on the diagonals announced above.

Proposition 8.8 (monotony on the diagonals)
For $i = 0, 1, \ldots, m-1$ *and* $j = 0, 1, \ldots, n-1$, *we have*

$$R[i-1, j-1] \leq R[i, j] \leq R[i-1, j-1] + 1.$$

Proof After Relation (8.1), the inequality $R[i-1, j-1] \leq R[i, j]$ is valid if $R[i-1, j-1] \leq R[i-1, j] + 1$ and $R[i-1, j-1] \leq R[i, j-1] + 1$: this is a consequence of Lemmas 8.6 and 8.7. Moreover, Equation (8.1) gives $R[i, j] \leq R[i-1, j-1] + 1$. The stated result follows. ∎

Partial computation

The property of monotony on diagonals is exploited in the following way in order to avoid to compute some values in the table R that are greater than k, the maximal number of allowed differences. The values are still computed column by column in the increasing order of positions on y, and for each column in the increasing order of positions on x, following the algorithm K-DIFF-DP. When a value equal to $k + 1$ is found in a column, it is useless to compute the next values in the same diagonal since those are all greater than k after Proposition 8.8. For pruning the computation, we keep on each column the lowest position at which is found an admissible value. If q_j is this position, for a given column j, only the values of lines -1 to $q_j + 1$ are computed in the next column (of index $j + 1$).

The algorithm K-DIFF-CUT-OFF below implements this method.

```
K-DIFF-CUT-OFF(x, m, y, n, k)
for i ← −1 to k − 1 do
      C1[i] ← i + 1
p ← k
for j ← 0 to n − 1 do
      C2[−1] ← 0
      for i ← 0 to p do
            if x[i] = y[j] then
                  C2[i] ← C1[i − 1]
            else C2[i] ← min{C1[i − 1], C2[i − 1], C1[i]} + 1
      C1 ← C2
      while C1[p] > k do
            p ← p − 1
      OUTPUT-IF(p = m − 1)
      p ← min{p + 1, m − 1}
```

R	j	-1	0	1	2	3	4	5	6	7	8	9	10	11
i		$y[j]$	C	A	G	A	T	A	A	G	A	G	A	A
-1	$x[i]$	0	0	0	0	0	0	0	0	0	0	0	0	0
0	G	1	1	1	0	1	1	1	1	0	1	0	1	1
1	A		2	1	1	0	1	1	1	1	0	1	0	1
2	T				2	1	0	1	2	2	1	1	1	1
3	A						1	0	1	2	2	2	1	1
4	A							1	0	1	2			1

Figure 8.3. Pruning of the computation of the dynamic programming table when searching for $x =$ GATAA in $y =$ CAGATAAGAGAA with one difference (see Figure 8.2). We notice that 17 values of table R (those that are not shown) are not useful for the computation of occurrences of approximate factors of x in y.

The column -1 is initialized until line $k-1$ that corresponds to the value k. For the next columns of index $j = 0, 1, \ldots, n-1$, the values are computed until line

$$p_j = \min \begin{cases} 1 + \max\{i : 0 \leq i \leq m-1 \text{ and } R[i, j-1] \leq k\}, \\ m-1. \end{cases}$$

The table R is implemented via the two tables C_2 and C_1 that memorize respectively the values of the current column during the computation and of its previous column. The process is the same as the one used in the algorithm LCS-Column of Section 7.3. At each iteration of the loop in lines 6–9, we have

$$\begin{aligned} C_1[i-1] &= R[i-1, j-1], \\ C_2[i-1] &= R[i-1, j], \\ C_1[i] &= R[i, j-1]. \end{aligned}$$

We compute then the value $C_2[i]$ that is also $R[i, j]$. We find thus at this line an implementation of Relation (8.1). An example of computation is given in Figure 8.3.

We note that the memory space used by the algorithm is $O(m)$. Indeed, only two columns are memorized. This is possible since the computation of the values for one column only needs those of the previous column.

Diagonal computation

The variant of the search with differences that we consider now consists in computing the values of the table R according to the diagonals, and in taking into account the monotony property. The interesting positions on diagonals are those where changes happen. These changes are incrementations by one because of the chosen distance.

R	j	-1	0	1	2	3	4	5	6	7	8	9	10	11
i	$y[j]$		C	A	G	A	T	A	A	G	A	G	A	A
-1	$x[i]$						0							
0	G							1						
1	A								1					
2	T									2				
3	A										2			
4	A											3		

Figure 8.4. Values of table R on diagonal 5 for the approximate search for $x =$ GATAA in $y =$ CAGATAAGAGAA. The last occurrences of each value on the diagonal are in gray. The lines where they occur are stored in table L by the algorithm based on diagonal computation. We thus have $L[0, 5] = -1$, $L[1, 5] = 1$, $L[2, 5] = 3$, $L[3, 5] = 4$.

For a number of differences q and a diagonal d, we denote by $L[q, d]$ the index i of the line on which $R[i, j] = q$ for the last time on the diagonal $j - i = d$. The idea of the definition of $L[q, d]$ is shown in Figure 8.4. Formally, for $q = 0, 1, \ldots, k$ and $d = -m, -m + 1, \ldots, n - m$, we have

$$L[q, d] = i$$

if and only if i is the maximal index, $-1 \leq i < m$, for which there exists an index j, $-1 \leq j < n$, with

$$R[i, j] \leq q \text{ and } j - i = d.$$

In other words, for q fixed, the values $L[q, d]$ mark the lowest borderline of the values not greater than q in the table R (gray values in Figure 8.5).

The definition of $L[q, d]$ implies that q is the smallest number of differences between $x[0 \,..\, L[q, d]]$ and a factor of the text ending at position $d + L[q, d]$ on y. It, moreover, implies that the letters $x[L[q, d] + 1]$ and $y[d + L[q, d] + 1]$ are different when they are defined.

The values $L[q, d]$ are computed by iteration on d, for q running from 0 to $k + 1$. The principle of the computation relies on Recurrence (8.1) and the above statements. A simulation of the computation on the table R is presented in Figure 8.5.

For the problem of approximate pattern matching with k differences, only the values $L[q, d]$ for which $q \leq k$ are needed. If $L[q, d] = m - 1$, it means that there is an occurrence of the string x at the diagonal d with at most q differences. The occurrence ending at position $d + m - 1$, this is only valid if $d + m \leq n$. We get other approximate occurrences at the end of y when $L[q, d] = i$ and $d + i = n - 1$; in this case the number of differences is $q + m - 1 - i$.

(a)

R	j	-1	0	1	2	3	4	5	6	7	8	9	10	11
i		$y[j]$	C	A	G	A	T	A	A	G	A	G	A	A
-1	$x[i]$	0	0	0	0	0	0	0	0	0				
0	G				0					0				
1	A					0					0			
2	T						0							
3	A							0						
4	A								0					

(b)

R	j	-1	0	1	2	3	4	5	6	7	8	9	10	11
i		$y[j]$	C	A	G	A	T	A	A	G	A	G	A	A
-1	$x[i]$	0	0	0	0	0	0	0	0	0				
0	G	1	1	1	0	1	1	1	1	0				
1	A			1	1	0	1	1	1	1	0			
2	T					1	0	1			1	1		
3	A						1	0	1				1	
4	A							1	0	1				1

Figure 8.5. Simulation of the diagonal computation for the search for $x =$ GATAA in $y =$ CAGATAAGAGAA with one difference (see Figure 8.2). **(a)** Values computed during the first step (lines 7–11 for $q = 0$ of the algorithm L-DIFF-DIAG); they show an occurrence of x at right position 6 on y (since $R[4, 6] = 0$). **(b)** Values computed during the second step (lines 7–11 for $q = 1$); they indicate the approximate factors of x with one difference at right positions 5, 7, and 11 on y (since $R[4, 5] = R[4, 7] = R[4, 11] = 1$).

d	-2	-1	0	1	2	3	4	5	6	7	8	9
$q = -1$		-2	-2	-2	-2	-2	-2	-2	-2	-2	-2	-2
$q = 0$	-1	-1	-1	-1	4	-1	-1	-1	-1	1	-1	
$q = 1$		0	1	4	4	4	1	1	2	4		

Figure 8.6. Values of the table L of the diagonal computation when $x =$ GATAA, $y =$ CAGATAAGAGAA, and $k = 1$. Lines $q = 0$ and $q = 1$ correspond to a state of the computation simulated on the table R of Figure 8.5. Values $4 = |\text{GATAA}| - 1$ on line $q = 1$ indicate occurrences of x with at most one difference ending at positions $1 + 4 = 5$, $2 + 4 = 6$, $3 + 4 = 7$, and $7 + 4 = 11$ on y.

The algorithm K-DIFF-DIAG performs the approximate search for x in y by computing the values $L[q, d]$. Let us note that the first possible occurrence of an approximate factor of x in y can end at position $m - 1 - k$ on y, which corresponds to diagonal $-k$. The last possible occurrence starts at position $n - m + k$ on y, which corresponds to diagonal $n - m + k$. Thus, only diagonals going from $-k$ to $n - m + k$ are considered during the computation (the initialization is also done on the diagonals $-k - 1$ and $n - m + k + 1$ in order to simplify the writing of the algorithm). Figure 8.6 shows the table L obtained on the example of Figure 8.2.

```
K-DIFF-DIAG(x, m, y, n, k)
 1  for d ← −1 to n − m + k + 1 do
 2      L[−1, d] ← −2
 3  for q ← 0 to k − 1 do
 4      L[q, −q − 1] ← q − 1
 5      L[q, −q − 2] ← q − 1
 6  for q ← 0 to k do
 7      for d ← −q to n − m + k − q do
                   ⎧ L[q − 1, d − 1]
 8          ℓ ← max⎨ L[q − 1, d] + 1
                   ⎩ L[q − 1, d + 1] + 1
 9          ℓ ← min{ℓ, m − 1}
10          L[q, d] ← ℓ
                + |lcp(x[ℓ + 1 . . m − 1], y[d + ℓ + 1 . . n − 1])|
11          OUTPUT-IF(L[q, d] = m − 1 or d + L[q, d] = n − 1)
```

Lemma 8.9

The algorithm K-DIFF-DIAG *computes the table L.*

Proof Let us show that $L[q, d]$ is correctly computed by assuming that all the values of line $q - 1$ of L are exact. Let i be the value of ℓ computed in line 8 of the algorithm, and let $j = d + i$.

It can happen that $i = m$ if $i = L[q - 1, d] + 1$ or $i = L[q - 1, d + 1] + 1$. In the first case, we have $R[i, j] \leq q - 1$ by recurrence hypothesis and thus also $R[i, j] \leq q$, this gives $L[q, d] = i$ as performed by the algorithm after the instruction in line 9. In the second case, we also have $L[q, d] = i$ by Lemma 8.6, and the algorithm correctly performs the computation.

In each of the three cases that happen when $i < m$, we note that $R[i, j] \geq q$ since the maximality of i implies that $R[i, j]$ has not been previously computed. If $i = L[q - 1, d - 1]$, the fact that $R[i, j] = q$ results from Lemma 8.6. If $i = L[q - 1, d + 1] + 1$, the equality comes from Lemma 8.7, and finally if $i = L[q - 1, d] + 1$ it comes from the diagonal monotony. The maximal searched index line is obtained after the instruction in line 10 as a consequence of the recurrence relation (8.1) on R.

We end the recurrence on q by checking that the table L is correctly initialized. ∎

Proposition 8.10

For a string x of length m, a string y of length n, and an integer k such that $k < m \leq n$, the operation K-DIFF-DIAG(x, m, y, n, k) *computes the approximate occurrences of x in y with at most k differences.*

Proof After the previous lemma, the table computed by the algorithm is the table L.

If $L[q,d] = m-1$, by definition of L, $R[m-1, d+m-1] \leq q$. By definition of R, this means that x possesses an approximate occurrence at the diagonal d with at most q differences. The occurrences signaled via this condition in line 11 are thus correct since $q \leq k$. If $d + L[q,d] = n-1$, the algorithm signals an approximate occurrence of x at the diagonal d. The number of differences is no more than $q+m-1-L[q,d]$, that is $q+m-1+d-n+1$, thus $q+m+d-n$. As $d \leq n-m+k-q$ (line 7), we get a number of differences no more than $q+m-n+n-m+k-q = k$ as desired. The occurrences signaled after this second test in line 11 are thus also correct.

Conversely, an approximate occurrence of x in y with k differences can be detected on the table R when one of the conditions $R[m-1, j] \leq k$ or $R[i, n-1] + m - 1 - i \leq k$ is satisfied. The first is equivalent to $L[k, j-m+1] = m-1$, and the algorithm signals it in line 11. For the second, by denoting $q = R[i, n-1]$, we have, by definition of L, $L[q, n-1-i] = i$ and thus $n-1-i+L[q, n-1-i] = n-1$. The occurrence is thus signaled if $q \leq k$, which is immediate after the above inequality, and if the diagonal is examined, that is to say if $n-1-i \leq n-m+k-q$. The inequality is equivalent to $q+m-1-i \leq k$, which shows that the second condition is satisfied. This ends the proof. ■

As the algorithm K-DIFF-DIAG is described, the memory space for its execution is principally used by the table L. We note that it is sufficient to memorize a single line in order to correctly perform the computation, which gives an implementation in space $O(n)$. It is, however, possible to reduce the space to $O(m)$ obtaining a space comparable to that of the algorithm K-DIFF-CUT-OFF (see Exercise 8.5).

Execution time of the diagonal computation

The method of diagonal computation highlights the longest common prefixes. When these prefixes are computed by mere letter comparisons during each call to the function *lcp*, the algorithm is not faster than the previous ones. This is the result stated in the following proposition. But a preprocessing of the strings x and y leads to implement the computation of the longest common prefixes in such a way that each call executes in constant time. We then get the result stated in Theorem 8.12. In a schematically way on the example of Figure 8.5, the first implementation takes a time proportional to the number of values that occur in the second table, while the second implementation takes a time proportional to the number of gray values.

Proposition 8.11
If the computation of lcp(u, v) *is realized in time* $O(|lcp(u, v)|)$, *the algorithm* K-DIFF-DIAG *executes in time* $O(m \times n)$.

Proof The proof relies on the observation that, if the longest common prefix computed in line 10 is of length $p > 0$, the instructions of the loop (lines 8–11) amounts to define $p + 1$ new values in the table R. The cumulated time of these computations of the longest common prefixes is thus $O(m \times n)$. The other instructions of the loop execute in constant time (including the computations of *lcp* that produce the empty string). As the instructions are executed $(k + 1) \times (n - m + k + 1)$ times, they take the global time $O(k \times n)$. As a consequence, the complete computation is done in time $O(m \times n)$. ∎

The previous proof highlights the fact that if the computation of $lcp(u, v)$ can be done in constant time, the algorithm K-DIFF-DIAG executes in time $O(k \times n)$. Actually, it is possible to prepare the strings x and y in such a way to obtain this condition. For this, we utilize the suffix tree, $\mathcal{T}_C(z)$, of the string $z = x\#y\$$ where $\# \notin$ alph(y) and $\$ \notin$ alph(y) (see Chapter 5). The string

$$w = lcp(x[\ell + 1 \mathinner{..} m - 1], y[d + \ell + 1 \mathinner{..} n - 1])$$

is nothing else but $lcp(x[\ell + 1 \mathinner{..} m - 1]\#y\$, y[d + \ell + 1 \mathinner{..} n - 1]\$)$ since $\# \notin$ alph(y). Let f and g be the external nodes of the tree $\mathcal{T}_C(z)$ associated with the suffixes $x[\ell + 1 \mathinner{..} m - 1]\#y\$$ and $y[d + \ell + 1 \mathinner{..} n - 1]\$$ of the string z. Their common prefix of maximal length is then the label of the path leading from the initial state to the lowest node that is a common ancestor to f and g. This reduces the computation of w to the computation of this node.

The problem of the lowest common ancestor that we are interested in here is the one for which the tree is static. A linear-time preprocessing of the tree leads to get constant-time response to the queries (see notes). The consequence of this result is the next theorem.

Theorem 8.12
On a fixed alphabet, after preprocessing the strings x *and* y *in linear time, it is possible to execute the algorithm* K-DIFF-DIAG *in time* $O(k \times n)$.

Proof The preprocessing first consists of the construction of the suffix tree $\mathcal{T}_C(z)$ of the string $z = x\#y\$$, then in the preparation of the tree in order to answer in constant time each query for the lowest common ancestor corresponding to two of its external nodes. We associate also with each node of the tree the length of this node (let us recall that the nodes of the tree are factors of z). The total preparation time is linear since the alphabet is fixed (see Chapter 5 and notes).

The computation of $|lcp(x[\ell+1\,..\,m-1], y[d+\ell+1\,..\,n-1])|$ during the execution of the algorithm K-DIFF-DIAG can then be realized in constant time. It follows, using the proof of the previous proposition, that the global execution time is $O(k \times n)$. ■

8.3 Approximate pattern matching with mismatches

In this section, we restrict the approximate pattern matching to the search for all the occurrences of a string x of length m in a string y of length n with at most k mismatches ($k \in \mathbf{N}$, $k < m \leq n$). We recall from Chapter 7 that the Hamming distance between two strings u and v of the same length is the number of mismatches between u and v, and is defined by

$$Ham(u, v) = \mathrm{card}\{i : u[i] \neq v[i], i = 0, 1, \ldots, |u| - 1\}.$$

The problem can then be expressed as the search for all the positions $j = 0, 1, \ldots, n-m$ on y that satisfy the inequality $Ham(x, y[j\,..\,j+m-1]) \leq k$.

Search automaton

A natural solution to this problem consists in using an automaton that recognizes the language $A^*\{w : Ham(x, w) \leq k\}$. This extends the method developed in Chapter 2. To do this, we can consider the nondeterministic automaton defined as follows:

- each state is a pair (ℓ, i) where ℓ is the level of the state and i is its depth, with $0 \leq \ell \leq k$, $-1 \leq i \leq m-1$, and $\ell \leq i+1$,
- the initial state is $(0, -1)$,
- the terminal states are of the form $(\ell, m-1)$ with $0 \leq \ell \leq k$,
- the arcs are, for $0 \leq \ell \leq k$, $0 \leq i < m-1$, and $a \in A$, either of the form $((0, -1), a, (0, -1))$, or of the form $((\ell, i), x[i+1], (\ell, i+1))$, or finally of the form $((\ell, i), a, (\ell+1, i+1))$ if $a \neq x[i+1]$ and $0 \leq \ell \leq k-1$.

The automaton possesses $k+1$ levels, each level ℓ allowing to recognize the prefixes of x with ℓ mismatches. The arcs of the form $((\ell, i), a, (\ell, i+1))$ correspond to matches while those of the form $((\ell, i), a, (\ell+1, i+1))$

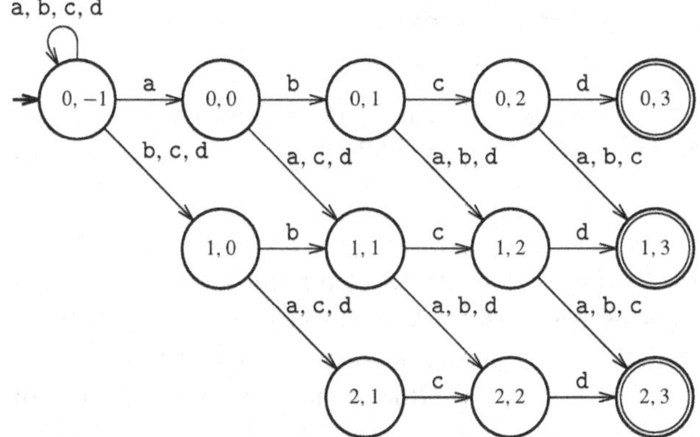

Figure 8.7. The (nondeterministic) automaton for approximate pattern matching with two mismatches corresponding to the string abcd on the alphabet $A = \{a, b, c, d\}$.

correspond to mismatches. The loop on the initial state is for finding all the occurrences of the searched factors. During the analysis of a text with the automaton, if a terminal state $(\ell, m-1)$ is reached, this indicates the presence of an occurrence of x with exactly ℓ mismatches.

It is clear that the automaton possesses $(k+1) \times (m+1-\frac{k}{2})$ states and that it can be build in time $O(k \times m)$. An example is shown in Figure 8.7. Unfortunately, the total number of states of the equivalent deterministic automaton is

$$\Theta(\min\{m^{k+1}, (k+1)!(k+2)^{m-k+1}\})$$

(see notes), and no method indicated in Chapter 2 can reduce simply the size of the representation of the automaton.

We can check that a direct simulation of the automaton produces a search algorithm whose execution time is $O(m \times n)$ using dynamic programming as in the previous chapter. Actually, by using a method adapted to the problem we get, in the rest, an algorithm that performs the search in time $O(k \times n)$. This produces a solution of the same complexity as the one of the algorithm K-DIFF-DIAG that, however, solves a more general problem. But the solution that follows is based on a simple management of lists without using the lowest common ancestor algorithm nor sophisticated processing.

Specific implementation

We show how to reduce the execution time of the simulation of the previous automaton. To obtain the desired time $O(k \times n)$, during the search we make

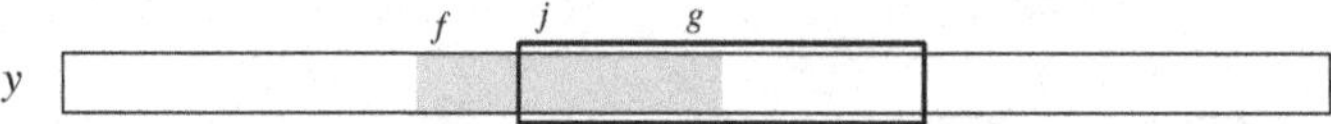

Figure 8.8. Variables of the algorithm K-MISMATCHES. During the attempt at position j, variables f and g spot a previous attempt. The mismatches between $y[f\,..\,g]$ and $x[0\,..\,g-f]$ are stored in the queue F.

use of a queue F of positions that stores detected mismatches. Its update is done by letter comparisons, but also by merging it with queues associated with string x. The sequences that they represent are defined as follows.

For a shift q of x, $1 \leq q \leq m-1$, $G[q]$ is the increasing sequence, of maximal length $2k+1$, of the positions on x of the leftmost mismatches between $x[0\,..\,m-q-1]$ and $x[q\,..\,m-1]$. The sequences are determined during a preprocessing phase that is described at the end of the section.

The searching phase consists in performing attempts at all the positions $j = 0, 1, \ldots, n-m$ on y. During the attempt at position j, we scan the factor $y[j\,..\,j+m-1]$ of the text and the generic situation is the following (see Figure 8.8): the prefix $y[j\,..\,g]$ of the window has already been scanned during a previous attempt at position f, $f < j$, and no comparison happened yet on the suffix $y[g+1\,..\,n-1]$ of the text. The process used here is similar to the one realized by the algorithm PREFIXES of Section 1.6. The difference occurs during the comparison of the already scanned part of the text, $y[j\,..\,g]$, since it is not possible anymore to conclude with the help of a single test. Indeed, around k tests can be necessary to perform the comparison. Figure 8.9 shows a computation example.

The positions of the mismatches detected during the attempt at position f are stored in a queue F. Their computation is done by scanning the positions in increasing order. For the search with k mismatches, we only keep in F at most $k+1$ mismatches (the leftmost ones). Considering a possible $(k+1)$th mismatch amounts to compute the longest prefix of x that possesses exactly k mismatches with the aligned factor of y.

The code of the search algorithm with mismatches, K-MISMATCHES, is given below. The processing at position j proceeds in two steps. It first starts by comparing the factors $x[0\,..\,g-j]$ and $y[j\,..\,g]$ using the queues F and $G[j-f]$. The comparison amounts to perform a merge of these two queues (line 7); this merge is described further. The second step is only applied when the obtained sequence contains less than k positions. It resumes the scanning of the window by simple letter comparisons (lines 10–16). This is during this step that an occurrence of an approximate factor can be detected.

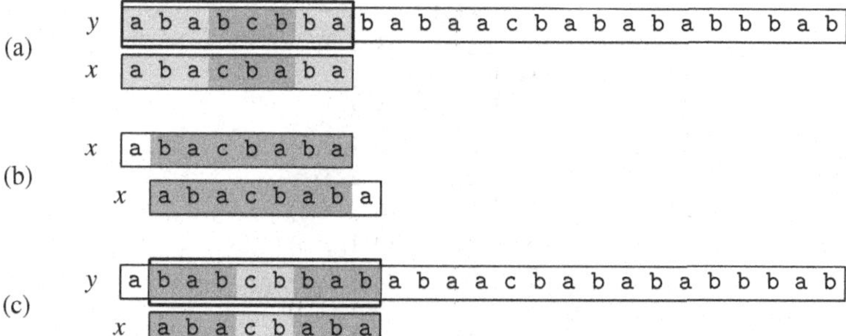

Figure 8.9. Search with mismatches for the string $x =$ abacbaba in the text $y =$ ababcbbababaacbababababbbab. **(a)** Occurrence of the string with exactly three mismatches at position 0 on y. The queue F of mismatches contains positions 3, 4, and 5 on x, $F = \langle 3, 4, 5 \rangle$. **(b)** Shift of length 1. There are seven mismatches between $x[0\,..\,6]$ and $x[1\,..\,7]$, stored in $G[1] = \langle 1, 2, 3, 4, 5, 6, 7 \rangle$ (see Figure 8.10). **(c)** Attempt at position 1: the factor $y[1\,..\,7]$ has already been considered but the letter $y[8] =$ b has never been compared yet. The mismatches at positions 0, 1, 5, and 6 on x can be deduced from the merge of the queues F and $G[1]$. Three letter comparisons are necessary at positions 2, 3, and 4 in order to detect the mismatch at position 2 since these three positions are simultaneously in F and $G[1]$. An extra comparison provides the sixth mismatch at position 7.

```
K-MISMATCHES(x, m, G, y, n, k)
 F ← EMPTY-QUEUE()
 (f, g) ← (−1, −1)
 for j ← 0 to n − m do
     if LENGTH(F) > 0 and HEAD(F) = j − f − 1 then
         DEQUEUE(F)
     if j ≤ g then
         J ← MIS-MERGE(f, j, g, F, G[j − f])
     else J ← EMPTY-QUEUE()
     if LENGTH(J) ≤ k then
         F ← J
         f ← j
         do  g ← g + 1
             if x[g − j] ≠ y[g] then
                 ENQUEUE(F, g − j)
         while LENGTH(F) ≤ k and g < j + m − 1
         OUTPUT-IF(LENGTH(F) ≤ k)
```

An example of table G and of successive values of the queue F of the mismatches is presented in Figure 8.10.

i	$x[i]$	$G[i]$
0	a	$\langle\rangle$
1	b	$\langle 1, 2, 3, 4, 5, 6, 7\rangle$
2	a	$\langle 3, 4, 5\rangle$
3	c	$\langle 3, 6, 7\rangle$
4	b	$\langle 4, 5, 6, 7\rangle$
5	a	$\langle\rangle$
6	b	$\langle 6, 7\rangle$
7	a	$\langle\rangle$

(a)

j	$y[j]$	F
0	a	$\langle 3, 4, 5\rangle$
1	b	$\langle 0, 1, 2, 5\rangle$
2	a	$\langle 2, 3\rangle$
3	b	$\langle 0, 1, 2, 3\rangle$
4	c	$\langle 0, 2, 3\rangle$
5	b	$\langle 0, 3, 4, 5\rangle$
6	b	$\langle 0, 1, 2, 3\rangle$
7	a	$\langle 3, 4, 6, 7\rangle$
8	b	$\langle 0, 1, 2, 3\rangle$
9	a	$\langle 3, 4, 5, 6\rangle$
10	b	$\langle 0, 1\rangle$
11	a	$\langle 1, 2, 3, 4\rangle$
12	a	$\langle 1, 2, 3\rangle$
13	c	$\langle 3, 4, 5, 7\rangle$
14	b	$\langle 0, 1, 2, 3\rangle$
15	a	$\langle 3, 4, 5, 7\rangle$
16	b	$\langle 0, 1, 2, 3\rangle$
17	a	$\langle 3, 5, 6, 7\rangle$

(b)

Figure 8.10. Queues used for the approximate search with three mismatches for $x =$ abacbaba in $y =$ ababcbbababaacbababbbab. **(a)** Values of table G for the string abacbaba. For example, the queue $G[3]$ contains 3, 6, and 7, positions on x of the mismatches between its suffix cbaba and its prefix abacb. **(b)** Successive values of the queue F of mismatches as it is computed by the algorithm K-MISMATCHES. The values at positions 0, 2, 4, 10, and 12 on y have no more than three elements, which reveals occurrences of x with at most three mismatches at these positions. At position 0, for instance, the factor ababcbba of y possesses exactly three mismatches with x: they are at positions 3, 4, and 5 on x.

In the algorithm K-MISMATCHES, the positions stored in the queues F or J are positions on x. They indicate mismatches between x and the factor aligned with it at position f on y. Thus, if p occurs in the queue, we have $x[p] \neq y[f + p]$. When the variable f is updated, the origin of the factor of y is replaced by j, and we should thus translates the positions, that is to say, to decrease the positions by the quantity $j - f$. This is realized in the algorithm MIS-MERGE during the addition of a position in the output queue.

Complexity of the searching phase

Before examining the proof of the algorithm K-MISMATCHES, we discuss the complexity of the searching phase. The running time depends on the function

MIS-MERGE considered further (Lemma 8.14). The preprocessing of the string comes next.

Theorem 8.13

If the merge realized by the algorithm MIS-MERGE *executes in linear time, the execution time of the algorithm* K-MISMATCHES *is* $O(k \times n)$ *in space* $O(k \times m)$.

Proof At each iteration of the loop in lines 3–16, the execution time of the merge instruction in line 7 is $O(k)$ after the assumption since the queue F contains at most $k+1$ elements and $G[j-f]$ contains at most $2k+1$ of them. The contribution to the total time is thus $O(k \times n)$.

The other operations of each of the $n-m+1$ iterations of the loop in lines 3–16, excluding the loop in lines 12–15, execute in constant time, this contributes for $O(n)$ to the global time.

The total number of iterations performed by the loop in lines 12–15 is $O(n)$ since the instructions increase the value of the variable g of one unit at each iteration and this value never decreases.

It follows that the execution time of the algorithm K-MISMATCHES is $O(k \times n)$.

The space occupied by the table G is $O(k \times m)$ and the space occupied by the queues F and J is $O(k)$, this shows that the total space used for the computation is $O(k \times m)$. ■

Merge

The aim of the operation MIS-MERGE$(f, j, g, F, G[j-f])$ (line 7 of the algorithm K-MISMATCHES) is to produce the sequence of positions of the mismatches between the strings $x[0\,..\,g-j]$ and $y[j\,..\,g]$, relying on the knowledge of the mismatches stored in the queues F and $G[j-f]$.

The positions p in F mark the mismatches between $x[0\,..\,g-f]$ and $y[f\,..\,g]$, but only those that satisfy the inequality $f+p \geq j$ (by definition of F we already have $f+p \leq g$) are useful to the computation. The objective of the test in line 4 of the algorithm K-MISMATCHES is precisely to delete from F the useless values. The positions q of $G[j-f]$ denote the mismatches between $x[j-f\,..\,m-1]$ and $x[0\,..\,m-j+f-1]$. Those that are useful must satisfy the inequality $f+q \leq g$ (we already have $f+q \geq j$). The test in line 18 of the algorithm MIS-MERGE takes into account this constraint. Figure 8.11 illustrates the merge (see also Figure 8.9).

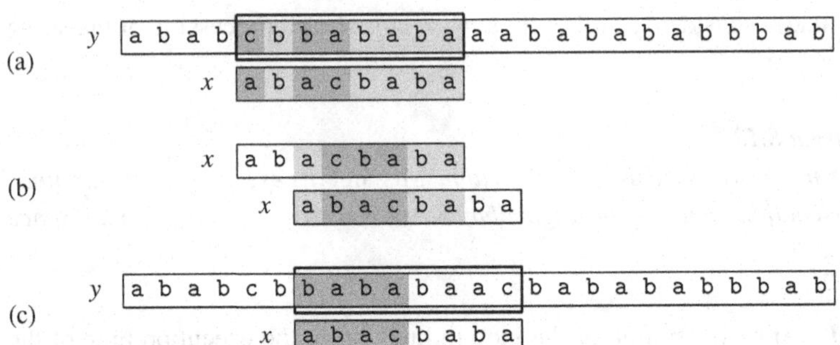

Figure 8.11. Merge during the search with three mismatches for $x =$ abacbaba in $y =$ ababcbbababaacbababababbbab. **(a)** Occurrence of x at position 4 on y with three mismatches at positions 0, 2, and 3 on x; $F = \langle 0, 2, 3\rangle$. **(b)** There are three mismatches between $x[2\,..\,7]$ and $x[0\,..\,5]$; $G[2] = \langle 3, 4, 5\rangle$. **(c)** The sequences conserved for the merge are $\langle 2, 3\rangle$ and $\langle 3, 4, 5\rangle$, and this latter produces the sequence $\langle 2, 3, 4, 5\rangle$ of positions of the first four mismatches between x and $y[6\,..\,13]$. A single letter comparison is necessary at position 3, to detect the mismatch between $x[1]$ and $y[7]$, since the other positions occur in only one of the two sequences.

Let us consider a position p on x such that $j \leq f + p \leq g$. If p occurs in F, this means that $y[f + p] \neq x[p]$. If p is in $G[j - f]$, this means that $x[p] \neq x[p - j + f]$. Four situations can arise for a position p whether it occurs or not in F and $G[j - f]$ (see Figures 8.9 and 8.11):

1. The position p is not in F nor in $G[j - f]$. We have $y[f + p] = x[p]$ and $x[p] = x[p - j + f]$, thus $y[f + p] = x[p - j + f]$.
2. The position p is in F but not in $G[j - f]$. We have $y[f + p] \neq x[p]$ and $x[p] = x[p - j + f]$, thus $y[f + p] \neq x[p - j + f]$.
3. The position p is in $G[j - f]$ but not in F. We have $y[f + p] = x[p]$ and $x[p] \neq x[p - j + f]$, thus $y[f + p] \neq x[p - j + f]$.
4. The position p is in F and in $G[j - f]$. We have $y[f + p] \neq x[p]$ and $x[p] \neq x[p - j + f]$, this does not allow to conclude on the equality between $y[f + p]$ and $x[p - j + f]$.

Among the enumerated cases, only the last three can lead to a mismatch between the letters $y[f + p]$ and $x[p - j + f]$. Only the last case requires an extra comparison of letters. Cases are processed in this respective order in lines 6–7, 9–10, and 11–14 of the merge algorithm.

```
MIS-MERGE(f, j, g, F, G)
1  J ← EMPTY-QUEUE()
2  while LENGTH(J) ≤ k
       and LENGTH(F) > 0 and LENGTH(G) > 0 do
3      p ← HEAD(F)
```

```
        q ← HEAD(G)
        if p < q then
             DEQUEUE(F)
             ENQUEUE(J, p − j + f)
        elseif q < p then
             DEQUEUE(G)
             ENQUEUE(J, q − j + f)
        else DEQUEUE(F)
             DEQUEUE(G)
             if x[p − j + f] ≠ y[f + p] then
                  ENQUEUE(J, p − j + f)
while LENGTH(J) ≤ k and LENGTH(F) > 0 do
        p ← DEQUEUED(F)
        ENQUEUE(J, p − j + f)
while LENGTH(J) ≤ k and LENGTH(G) > 0
    and HEAD(G) ≤ g − f do
        q ← DEQUEUED(G)
        ENQUEUE(J, q − j + f)
return J
```

The next lemma provides the result used as an assumption in Theorem 8.13 for stating the execution time of the algorithm of approximate pattern matching with mismatches.

Lemma 8.14
The algorithm MIS-MERGE *executes in linear time.*

Proof The structure of the algorithm MIS-MERGE is composed of three **while** loops. We notice that the iteration of each of these loops leads to delete one element from the queues F or G (or from both). As the execution time of one iteration is constant, we deduce that the total time required by the algorithm is linear in the sum of the lengths of the two queues F and G. ■

Correctness proof

The proof of correctness of the algorithm K-MISMATCHES relies on the proof of the function MIS-MERGE. One of the main arguments of the proof is a property of the Hamming distance that is stated in the next lemma.

Lemma 8.15
Let u, v, and w be three strings of the same length. Let us set $d = Ham(u, v)$, $d' = Ham(v, w)$, and assume $d' \leq d$. We then have

$$d - d' \leq Ham(u, w) \leq d + d'.$$

Proof The strings being of the same length, they have the same set of positions P. Let us consider the sets $Q = \{p \in P : u[p] \neq v[p]\}$, $R = \{p \in P : v[p] \neq w[p]\}$, and $S = \{p \in P : u[p] \neq w[p]\}$. A position $p \in S$ satisfies the inequality $u[p] \neq w[p]$ and we have thus $u[p] \neq v[p]$ or $v[p] \neq w[p]$ (or both). It follows that $S \subseteq Q \cup R$.

Besides, $p \in Q \setminus R$ implies $p \in S$ since the condition gives $u[p] \neq v[p]$ and $v[p] = w[p]$; thus $u[p] \neq w[p]$. Also, by symmetry, $p \in R \setminus Q$ implies $p \in S$.

As a conclusion, $Ham(u, w) = \text{card}\, S$ is upper bounded by $\text{card}(Q \cup R)$ which is a maximum when Q and R are disjoint; so, $Ham(u, w) \leq d + d'$. Moreover, $Ham(u, w)$ is lower bounded by $\text{card}((Q \cup R) \setminus (Q \cap R))$ which is minimum when $R \subseteq Q$ (since $d' \leq d$). We thus have $Ham(u, w) \geq d - d'$. ■

When the operation MIS-MERGE$(f, j, g, F, G[j - f])$ is executed in the algorithm K-MISMATCHES, the next conditions are satisfied:

1. $f < j \leq g \leq f + m - 1$,
2. $F = \langle p : x[p] \neq y[f + p]$ and $j \leq f + p \leq g)\rangle$,
3. $x[g - f] \neq y[g]$,
4. LENGTH$(F) \leq k + 1$,
5. $G = \langle p : x[p] \neq x[p - j + f]$ and $j \leq f + p \leq g'\rangle$ for an integer g' such that $j \leq g' \leq f + m - 1$.

Moreover, if $g' < f + m - 1$, LENGTH$(G) = 2k + 1$ by definition of G. By taking these conditions as assumptions we get the following result.

Lemma 8.16
Let $J =$ MIS-MERGE$(f, j, g, F, G[j - f])$. *If* LENGTH$(J) \leq k$,

$$J = \langle p : x[p] \neq y[j + p] \text{ and } j \leq j + p \leq g\rangle,$$

and, in the contrary case,

$$Ham(y[j \mathinner{..} g], x[0 \mathinner{..} g - j]) > k.$$

Proof Let us set $u = y[j \mathinner{..} g]$, $v = x[j - f \mathinner{..} g - f]$, and $w = x[0 \mathinner{..} g - j]$. Let us assume $g' < g$ and let us set $v' = x[j - f \mathinner{..} g' - f]$ and $w' = x[0 \mathinner{..} g' - j]$. We have LENGTH$(G) = 2k + 1$, that is to say $Ham(x[j - f \mathinner{..} g' - f], x[0 \mathinner{..} g' - j]) = 2k + 1$. Besides, $Ham(y[j \mathinner{..} g'], x[j - f \mathinner{..} g' - f]) \leq k$ since $g' < g$. After Lemma 8.15, we deduce $Ham(y[j \mathinner{..} g'], x[0 \mathinner{..} g' - j]) \geq k + 1$.

We deduce from this result that if LENGTH$(J) \leq k$, we necessarily have $g \leq g'$, otherwise the merge performed by the algorithm MIS-MERGE would produce at least $k + 1$ elements. A simple verification then shows that the algorithm merges the sequences F and $\langle q : q$ in $G[j - f]$ and $f + q \leq g\rangle$ into a sequence S. And the algorithm produces the sequence $J = \langle q : q + j - f$ in $S\rangle$ that satisfies the equality of the statement.

When LENGTH(J) $> k$, we actually have LENGTH(J) $= k + 1$ since the merge algorithm limits the length of J to $k + 1$. If $g' < g$, we have seen above that the conclusion is satisfied. Otherwise, the algorithm effectively finds $k + 1$ positions q that satisfy $x[q] \neq y[j + q]$ and $j \leq j + q \leq g$. This gives the same conclusion and ends the proof. ■

The proposition that follows is on the correctness of the algorithm K-MISMATCHES. It assumes that the sequences $G[q]$ are computed in accordance with their definition.

Proposition 8.17
If $x, y \in A^*$, $m = |x|$, $n = |y|$, $k \in \mathbf{N}$, and $k < m \leq n$, the algorithm K-MISMATCHES *detects all the positions $j = 0, 1, \ldots, n - m$ on y for which Ham$(x, y[j \mathinner{..} j + m - 1]) \leq k$.*

Proof We start by checking that after each iteration of the main loop (lines 3–16) the queue F contains the longest increasing sequence of positions of mismatches between $y[f \mathinner{..} g]$ and $x[0 \mathinner{..} g - f]$ having a length limited to $k + 1$.

We check it directly for the first iteration with the help of instructions of the loop in lines 12–15, by noting that the initialization of the variable g implies that the test in line 6 is not satisfied, whose consequence is a correct initialization of J then of F.

Let us assume that the condition is satisfied and let us prove that it is still satisfied at the next iteration. We note that the instructions in lines 4–5 have for effect to delete from F the positions less than $j - f$. If the inequality in line 6 is not satisfied, the proof is analogue to the proof of the first iteration. In the contrary case, the queue J is determined by the function MIS-MERGE. If LENGTH(J) $> k$, the variables f, g, and F are unchanged thus the condition remains satisfied. Otherwise, the value of J thus computed initializes the variable F. After Lemma 8.16, the queue contains the increasing sequence of positions of the mismatches between $y[f \mathinner{..} g]$ and $x[0 \mathinner{..} g - f]$. The maximality of its length is obtained after execution of the instructions of the loop in lines 12–15. This ends the induction and the proof of the condition on F.

Let j be a position on y for which an occurrence is reported (line 16). The condition in line 15 indicates that $g = j + m - 1$. The above proof shows that LENGTH(F) $=$ Ham$(x, y[j \mathinner{..} j + m - 1])$, quantity less than k. There is thus one occurrence of an approximate factor at position j.

Conversely, if $Ham(x, y[j \mathinner{..} j+m-1]) \le k$, the instruction in line 16 is executed after Lemma 8.16. The condition on F proved above shows that the occurrence is detected. ∎

Preprocessing

The aim of the preprocessing phase is to compute the values of the table G that is required by the algorithm K-MISMATCHES. Let us recall that for a shift q of x, $1 \le q \le m-1$, $G[q]$ is the increasing sequence of positions on x of the leftmost mismatches between $x[q \mathinner{..} m-1]$ and $x[0 \mathinner{..} m-q-1]$, and that this sequence is limited to $2k+1$ elements.

The computation of the sequences $G[q]$ is realized in an elementary way by the function whose code follows.

```
PRE-K-MISMATCHES(x, m, k)
for q ← 1 to m − 1 do
      G[q] ← EMPTY-QUEUE()
      i ← q
      while LENGTH(G[q]) < 2k + 1 and i < m do
            if x[i] ≠ x[i − q] then
                  ENQUEUE(G[q], i)
            i ← i + 1
return G
```

The execution time of the algorithm is $O(m^2)$, but it is possible to prepare the table in time $O(k \times m \times \log m)$ (see Exercise 8.6).

8.4 Approximate matching for short patterns

The algorithm presented in this section is a method both very fast in practice and very simple to implement for short patterns. The method solves the problems presented in the previous sections in the bit-vector model introduced in Section 1.5. We first describe the method for the exact string searching, then we show how we can adapt it for dealing with the approximate string searching with mismatches and with the approximate string searching with differences. The principal advantage of this method is that it is flexible and so adapts to a large range of problems.

Exact string matching

We first present a technique for solving the problem of the exact search for all the occurrences of a string x in a text y, that is different from the methods already encountered in Chapters 1, 2, and 3.

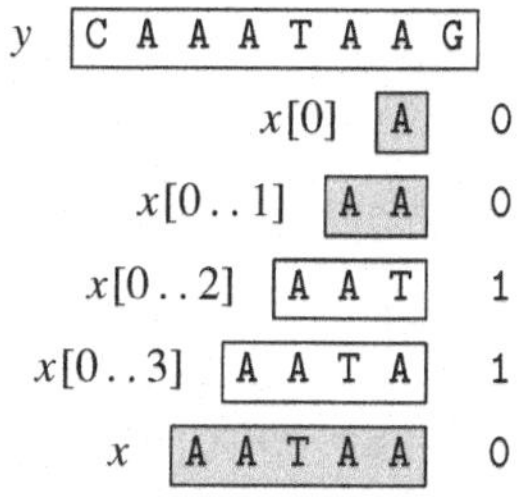

y	C A A A T A A G	
$x[0]$	A	0
$x[0\,.\,.\,1]$	A A	0
$x[0\,.\,.\,2]$	A A T	1
$x[0\,.\,.\,3]$	A A T A	1
x	A A T A A	0

Figure 8.12. Bit vector R^0_6 for the search for $x =$ AATAA in $y =$ CAAATAAG. We have $R^0_6 =$ 00110. The only nonempty prefixes of x that end at position 6 on y are A, AA, and AATAA.

We consider $n + 1$ vectors of m bits, $R^0_{-1}, R^0_0, \ldots, R^0_{n-1}$. The vector R^0_j corresponds to the processing of the letter $y[j]$ of the text. It contains the information relative to the search on all the prefixes of x when their last position is aligned with the position j on the text (see Figure 8.12). It is defined by

$$R^0_j[i] = \begin{cases} 0 & \text{if } x[0\,.\,.\,i] = y[\max\{0, j-i\}\,.\,.\,j], \\ 1 & \text{otherwise,} \end{cases}$$

for $i = 0, 1, \ldots, m-1$. So, $R^0_j[m-1] = 0$ if and only if x occurs at position j. The vector R^0_{-1} corresponds to the prefix of y of null length; consequently, all its components are equal to 1:

$$R^0_{-1}[i] = 1.$$

for $i = 0, 1, \ldots, m-1$.

For $j = 0, 1, \ldots, n-1$, the vector R^0_j is function of the vector R^0_{j-1} in the following way:

$$R^0_j[i] = \begin{cases} 0 & \text{if } R^0_{j-1}[i-1] = 0 \text{ and } x[i] = y[j], \\ 1 & \text{otherwise,} \end{cases}$$

for $i = 1, 2, \ldots, m-1$, and

$$R^0_j[0] = \begin{cases} 0 & \text{if } x[0] = y[j], \\ 1 & \text{otherwise.} \end{cases}$$

The passage from the vector R^0_{j-1} to the vector R^0_j can be computed by the equality given in the next lemma, which amounts to the computation to two operations on bit-vectors. We denote by S_a, for every $a \in A$, the vector of m bits defined by

$$S_a[i] = \begin{cases} 0 & \text{if } x[i] = a, \\ 1 & \text{otherwise.} \end{cases}$$

(a)

i	$x[i]$	$S_{\mathtt{A}}[i]$	$S_{\mathtt{C}}[i]$	$S_{\mathtt{G}}[i]$	$S_{\mathtt{T}}[i]$
0	A	0	1	1	1
1	A	0	1	1	1
2	T	1	1	1	0
3	A	0	1	1	1
4	A	0	1	1	1

(b)

j	0	1	2	3	4	5	6	7	8	9	10	11
$y[j]$	C	A	A	A	T	A	A	T	A	G	A	A
$R_j^0[0]$	1	0	0	0	1	0	0	1	0	1	0	0
$R_j^0[1]$	1	1	0	0	1	1	0	1	1	1	1	0
$R_j^0[2]$	1	1	1	1	0	1	1	0	1	1	1	1
$R_j^0[3]$	1	1	1	1	1	0	1	1	0	1	1	1
$R_j^0[4]$	1	1	1	1	1	1	0	1	1	1	1	1

Figure 8.13. Illustration of the search for string $x = \mathtt{AATAA}$ in text $y = \mathtt{CAAATAATAGAA}$. **(a)** Vectors S. **(b)** Vectors R^0. Each vector R^0 is obtained by shift-or: for example, $R_2^0 = \mathtt{00111}$ produces by shift $\mathtt{00011}$, and then by disjunction with $\mathtt{A} = \mathtt{00100}$ because $y[3] = \mathtt{A}$ the next vector $R_3^0 = \mathtt{00111}$. The string x occurs at position 6 in the text y since $R_6^0[4] = \mathtt{0}$. It only occurs at this position since the other values $R_j^0[4]$ (for $j \neq 6$) are equal to $\mathtt{1}$.

The vector S_a is the characteristic vector[2] of the positions of the letter a on the string x. It can be computed prior to the searching phase.

Lemma 8.18

For $j = 0, 1, \ldots, n-1$, *the computation of* R_j^0 *reduces to two logical operations, a shift and a disjunction:*

$$R_j^0 = (1 \dashv R_{j-1}^0) \vee S_{y[j]}.$$

Proof For $i = 0, 1, \ldots, m-1$, $R_j^0[i] = \mathtt{0}$ means that $x[0\,..\,i]$ is a suffix of $y[0\,..\,j]$, which is true when the two following conditions hold: $x[0\,..\,i-1]$ is a suffix of $y[0\,..\,j-1]$, which is equivalent to $R_{j-1}^0[i-1] = 0$; $x[i]$ is equal to $y[j]$, which is equivalent to $S_{y[j]}[i] = \mathtt{0}$. Moreover, $R_j^0[0] = \mathtt{0}$ when $S_{y[j]}[0] = \mathtt{0}$. This implies $R_j^0 = (1 \dashv R_{j-1}^0) \vee S_{y[j]}$ since the operation $1 \dashv R_{j-1}^0$ introduces one $\mathtt{0}$ in the first position of R_{j-1}^0. ∎

The algorithm SHORT-PATTERN-SEARCH below performs the search for x in y. A single variable, denoted by R^0 in the code, represents the sequence of bit-vectors $R_{-1}^0, R_0^0, \ldots, R_{n-1}^0$. Figure 8.13 shows how the algorithm SHORT-PATTERN-SEARCH works.

[2] The "opposite" characteristic vector has been introduced in Section 8.1.

```
SHORT-PATTERN-SEARCH(x, m, y, n)
1  for each letter a ∈ A do
2      S_a ← 1^m
3  for i ← 0 to m − 1 do
4      S_{x[i]}[i] ← 0
5  R^0 ← 1^m
6  for j ← 0 to n − 1 do
7      R^0 ← (1 ⊣ R^0) ∨ S_{y[j]}
8      OUTPUT-IF(R^0[m − 1] = 0)
```

Proposition 8.19
The algorithm SHORT-PATTERN-SEARCH *finds all the occurrences of a string* x *in a text* y.

Proof The proof is a consequence of Lemma 8.18. ∎

The operations on bit-vectors used in the algorithm SHORT-PATTERN-SEARCH are performed in constant time when the length m of the string x is smaller than the number of bits of a machine word (bit-vector model). Thus the next result follows.

Proposition 8.20
When the length m *of the string* x *is smaller than the number of bits of a machine word, the preprocessing phase of the algorithm* SHORT-PATTERN-SEARCH *executes in time* $\Theta(\text{card } A)$ *in memory space* $\Theta(\text{card } A)$. *The searching phase executes in time* $\Theta(n)$.

Proof The preprocessing phase consists in computing the vectors S_a, which is done by the loops in lines 1–2 and 3–4. The loop in lines 1–2 requires a space $O(\text{card } A)$ and executes in time $O(\text{card } A)$. The loop in lines 3–4 executes in time $O(m)$, thus in constant time after the assumption.

The searching phase performed by the loop in lines 6–8 executes in time $O(n)$ since the scan of each letter of the text y implies only two operations on bit vectors. ∎

One mismatch

The previous algorithm can easily be adapted for solving the approximate pattern matching with k mismatches or substitutions (Section 8.3). To simplify the presentation, we describe the case where at most one substitution is allowed.

We utilize the vectors $R^0_{-1}, R^0_0, \ldots, R^0_{n-1}$, and the vectors S_a with $a \in A$ as done above, and we introduce the m-bit vectors $R^1_{-1}, R^1_0, \ldots, R^1_{n-1}$ for taking

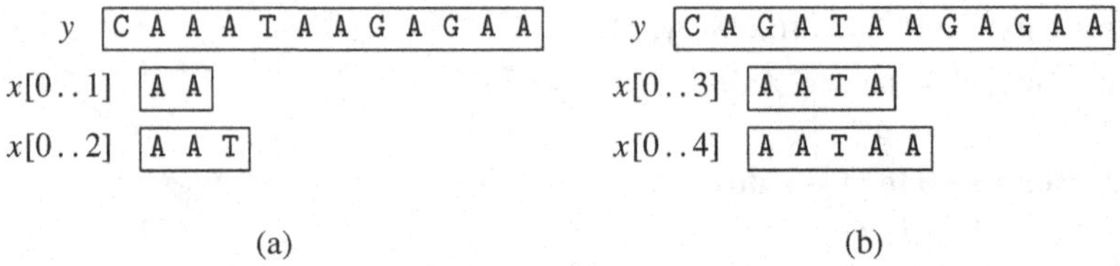

y	C A A A T A A G A G A A
$x[0\,.\,.\,1]$	A A
$x[0\,.\,.\,2]$	A A T

(a)

y	C A G A T A A G A G A A
$x[0\,.\,.\,3]$	A A T A
$x[0\,.\,.\,4]$	A A T A A

(b)

Figure 8.14. Elements of the proof of Lemma 8.21. **(a)** The prefix of length 2 of x is a suffix of $y[0\,.\,.\,2]$, which translates into $R^0_2[1] = 0$. Thus, substituting A for T gives an occurrence with one mismatch of the prefix of length 3 of x when aligned at the end of $y[0\,.\,.\,3]$. Thus $R^1_3[2] = 0$. **(b)** The prefix of length 4 of x occurs with one mismatch when aligned at the end of $y[0\,.\,.\,5]$, this is given by $R^1_5[3] = 0$. Moreover $x[4] = y[6]$: the prefix of length 5 of the string occurs with one mismatch when aligned at the end of $y[0\,.\,.\,6]$, which gives $R^1_6[4] = 0$.

mismatches into account. The aim of vectors R^1_j is to detect all the occurrences of x in y with at most one substitution. They are defined by

$$R^1_j[i] = \begin{cases} 0 & \text{if } \mathit{Ham}(x[0\,.\,.\,i], y[j-i\,.\,.\,j]) \leq 1, \\ 1 & \text{otherwise,} \end{cases}$$

for $i = 0, 1, \ldots, m-1$ (for the sake of simplicity of the expression, we assume that a negative position on y correspond to a letter that is not in the alphabet when $j - i < 0$).

Lemma 8.21

For $j = 0, 1, \ldots, n-1$, the vectors R^1_j corresponding to the approximate pattern matching with one mismatch satisfy the relation

$$R^1_j = ((1 \dashv R^1_{j-1}) \vee S_{y[j]}) \wedge (1 \dashv R^0_{j-1}).$$

Proof Three cases can arise; they are dealt with separately.

Case 1: The first i letters of x match the last i letters of $y[0\,.\,.\,j-1]$ (thus $R^0_{j-1}[i-1] = 0$). In this case, substituting $y[j]$ for $x[i]$ creates an occurrence with at most one substitution between the first $i+1$ letters of x and the last $i+1$ letters of $y[0\,.\,.\,j]$ (see Figure 8.14(a)). Thus, $R^1_j[i] = 0$ when $R^0_{j-1}[i-1] = 0$.

Case 2: There is an occurrence with one substitution between the first i letters of x and the last i letters of $y[0\,.\,.\,j-1]$ (thus $R^1_{j-1}[i-1] = 0$). If $x[i] = y[j]$, then there is one occurrence with one substitution between the first $i+1$ letters of x and the last $i+1$ letters of $y[0\,.\,.\,j]$ (see Figure 8.14(b)). Therefore $R^1_j[i] = 0$ when $R^1_{j-1}[i-1] = 0$ and $y[j] = x[i]$.

Case 3: If neither the condition of Case 1 nor the condition of Case 2 are satisfied, we have $R^1_j[i] = 1$.

It comes from the analysis of the three cases that the expression given in the statement is correct. ∎

The algorithm K-MISMATCHES-SHORT-PATTERN performs the approximate pattern matching with k mismatches using a relation that generalizes that of Lemma 8.21. Its code is given below. The algorithm requires $k+1$ bit-vectors, denoted by $R^0, R^1, \ldots, R^k$. The vectors R^0_j, for $j = -1, 0, \ldots, n-1$, are updated as in the algorithm performing the exact search. The values of the other vectors are computed in accordance with the previous lemma.

```
K-MISMATCHES-SHORT-PATTERN(x, m, y, n, k)
for each letter a ∈ A do
     S_a ← 1^m
for i ← 0 to m − 1 do
     S_x[i][i] ← 0
R^0 ← 1^m
for ℓ ← 1 to k do
     R^ℓ ← (1 ⊣ R^(ℓ−1))
for j ← 0 to n − 1 do
     T ← R^0
     R^0 ← (1 ⊣ R^0) ∨ S_y[j]
     for ℓ ← 1 to k do
          T' ← R^ℓ
          R^ℓ ← ((1 ⊣ R^ℓ) ∨ S_y[j]) ∧ (1 ⊣ T)
          T ← T'
     OUTPUT-IF(R^k[m − 1] = 0)
```

Figure 8.15 shows the vectors R^1 for the example of Figure 8.13, as they are computed by the algorithm K-MISMATCHES-SHORT-PATTERN.

One insertion

We show how to adapt the method of the beginning of the section to the case where only one insertion or only one deletion is allowed. The generalization to k differences and the complete algorithm are given at the end of the section.

We adapt the vectors R^1_j. The vector R^1_{j-1} indicates here all the occurrences with one insertion between a prefix of x and a suffix of $y[0\,..\,j-1]$: $R^1_{j-1}[i-1] = 0$ when the first i letters of x (prefix $x[0\,..\,i-1]$) match at least i of the last $i+1$ letters of $y[0\,..\,j-1]$ (suffix $y[j-i\,..\,j-1]$). The vector R^0

j	0	1	2	3	4	5	6	7	8	9	10	11
$y[j]$	C	A	A	A	T	A	A	T	A	G	A	A
$R^1_j[0]$	0	0	0	0	0	0	0	0	0	0	0	0
$R^1_j[1]$	1	0	0	0	0	0	0	0	0	0	0	0
$R^1_j[2]$	1	1	1	0	0	1	1	0	1	1	1	1
$R^1_j[3]$	1	1	1	1	1	0	1	1	0	1	1	1
$R^1_j[4]$	1	1	1	1	1	1	0	1	1	0	1	1

Figure 8.15. The string $x =$ AATAA occurs twice, at positions 6 and 9, with at most one mismatch in the text $y =$ CAAATAATAGAA. This can be checked on the table R^1 since $R^1_6[4] = R^1_9[4] = 0$.

j	0	1	2	3	4	5	6	7	8	9	10	11
$y[j]$	C	A	A	A	T	A	A	T	A	G	A	A
$R^1_j[0]$	1	0	0	0	0	0	0	0	0	0	0	0
$R^1_j[1]$	1	1	0	0	0	0	0	0	0	1	0	0
$R^1_j[2]$	1	1	1	1	0	0	1	0	0	1	1	1
$R^1_j[3]$	1	1	1	1	1	0	0	1	0	0	1	1
$R^1_j[4]$	1	1	1	1	1	1	0	0	1	1	0	1

Figure 8.16. The factors AAATAA, AATAAT, and AATAGA of $y =$ CAAATAATAGAA match the string $x =$ AATAA with one insertion. They appear at respective positions 6, 7, and 10 on y because $R^1_6[4] = R^1_7[4] = R^1_{10}[4] = 0$.

is updated as previously, and we now show how to update R^1. An example is given in Figure 8.16.

Lemma 8.22

For $j = 0, 1, \ldots, n-1$, the vectors R^1_j corresponding to the approximate pattern matching with one insertion satisfy the relation

$$R^1_j = ((1 \dashv R^1_{j-1}) \vee S_{y[j]}) \wedge R^0_{j-1}.$$

Proof The three cases that can arise are dealt with separately.

Case 1: The strings $x[0\,..\,i]$ and $y[j-i-1\,..\,j-1]$ are identical (thus $R^0_{j-1}[i] = 0$). Then inserting $y[j]$ creates one occurrence with one insertion between $x[0\,..\,i]$ and $y[j-i-1\,..\,j]$ (see Figure 8.17(a)). Thus, $R^1_j[i] = 0$ when $R^0_{j-1}[i] = 0$.

Case 2: There is one occurrence with one insertion between $x[0\,..\,i-1]$ and $y[j-i-1\,..\,j-1]$ (thus $R^1_{j-1}[i-1] = 0$). Then, if $y[j] = x[i]$, there is

y	C A G A T T
$x[0\,..\,2]$	G A T
$x[0\,..\,2]$	G A T -

(a)

y	C A G A T T A A
$x[0\,..\,3]$	G A T - A
$x[0\,..\,4]$	G A T - A A

(b)

Figure 8.17. Elements of the proof of Lemma 8.22. **(a)** The prefix of length 3 of x occurs at the end of $y[0\,..\,4]$, this is given by $R^0_4[2] = 0$. Inserting $y[5]$ gives an occurrence of the prefix of length 3 of x with one insertion at the end of $y[0\,..\,5]$, thus $R^1_5[2] = 0$. **(b)** The prefix of length 4 of x occurs with one insertion at the end of $y[0\,..\,6]$, this is given by $R^1_6[3] = 0$. Moreover, as $x[4] = y[7]$, the prefix of length 5 of x occurs with one insertion at the end of $y[0\,..\,7]$, thus $R^1_7[4] = 0$.

j	0	1	2	3	4	5	6	7	8	9	10	11
$y[j]$	C	A	A	A	T	A	A	T	A	G	A	A
$R^1_j[0]$	0	0	0	0	0	0	0	0	0	0	0	0
$R^1_j[1]$	1	0	0	0	1	0	0	1	0	1	0	0
$R^1_j[2]$	1	1	0	0	0	1	0	0	1	1	1	0
$R^1_j[3]$	1	1	1	0	0	0	1	0	0	1	1	1
$R^1_j[4]$	1	1	1	1	1	0	0	1	0	1	1	1

Figure 8.18. The factors **AATA**, **ATAA**, and **AATA** of $y =$ **CAAATAATAGAA** match the string $x =$ **AATAA** with one deletion. They occur at respective positions 5, 6, and 8 on y because $R^1_5[4] = R^1_6[4] = R^1_8[4] = 0$.

one occurrence with one insertion between $x[0\,..\,i]$ and $y[j-i-1\,..\,j]$ (see Figure 8.17(b)). Thus, $R^1_j[i] = 0$ when $R^1_{j-1}[i-1] = 0$ and $y[j] = x[i]$.

Case 3: If neither the condition of Case 1 nor the condition of Case 2 are satisfied, we have $R^1_j[i] = 1$.

As a conclusion, the expression given in the statement holds. ■

One deletion

We assume now that R^1_j signals all the occurrences with at most one deletion between prefixes of x and suffixes of $y[0\,..\,j]$. An example is given in Figure 8.18.

Lemma 8.23

For $j = 0, 1, \ldots, n-1$, the vectors R^1_j corresponding to the approximate pattern matching with one deletion satisfy the relation

$$R^1_j = ((1 \dashv R^1_{j-1}) \vee S_{y[j]}) \wedge (1 \dashv R^0_j).$$

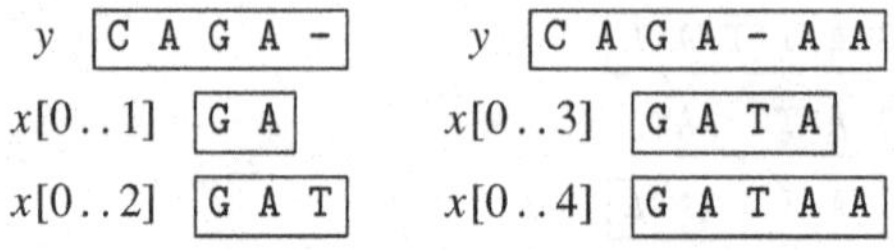

	(a)		(b)
y	C A G A -	y	C A G A - A A
$x[0\,.\,.\,1]$	G A	$x[0\,.\,.\,3]$	G A T A
$x[0\,.\,.\,2]$	G A T	$x[0\,.\,.\,4]$	G A T A A

(a) (b)

Figure 8.19. Elements of the proof of Lemma 8.23. **(a)** The prefix of length 2 of x occurs at the end of $y[0\,.\,.\,3]$, this is given by $R_3^0[1] = 0$. Deleting $x[2]$ gives an occurrence of the prefix of length 3 of x with one deletion at the end of $y[0\,.\,.\,3]$ thus $R_3^1[2] = 0$. **(b)** The prefix of length 4 of x occurs with one deletion at the end of $y[0\,.\,.\,4]$, this is given by $R_4^1[3] = 0$. Moreover, as $x[4] = y[5]$, the prefix of length 5 of x occurs with one deletion at the end of $y[0\,.\,.\,5]$ thus $R_5^1[4] = 0$.

Proof The three cases that can arise are dealt with separately.

Case 1: The strings $x[0\,.\,.\,i-1]$ and $y[j-i-1\,.\,.\,j]$ match (thus $R_j^0[i-1] = 0$). Deleting $x[i]$ creates an occurrence with one deletion between $x[0\,.\,.\,i]$ and $y[j-i-1\,.\,.\,j]$ (see Figure 8.19(a)). Thus, $R_j^1[i] = 0$ when $R_j^0[i-1] = 0$.

Case 2: There is an occurrence with one deletion between $x[0\,.\,.\,i-1]$ and $y[j-i+1\,.\,.\,j-1]$ (thus $R_{j-1}^1[i-1] = 0$). Then, if $y[j] = x[i]$, there is an occurrence with one deletion between $x[0\,.\,.\,i]$ and $y[j-i+1\,.\,.\,j]$ (see Figure 8.19(b)). Thus, $R_j^1[i] = 0$ when $R_{j-1}^1[i-1] = 0$ and $y[j] = x[i]$.

Case 3: If neither the condition of Case 1 nor the condition of Case 2 are satisfied, we have $R_j^1[i] = 1$.

The correctness of the expression given in the statement thus holds. ■

Short patterns with differences

We present now an algorithm for approximate pattern matching of short patterns with at most k differences of the type insertion, deletion, and substitution. This algorithm cumulates the methods described above for each operation taken separately. The algorithm requires $k+1$ bit-vectors $R^0, R^1, \ldots, R^k$. The vectors R_j^0, for $j = -1, 0, \ldots, m-1$, are updated as in the algorithm performing the exact search. The values of the other vectors are computed with the relation of the proposition below. An example of pattern matching with one difference is shown in Figure 8.20.

Proposition 8.24
For $i = 1, 2, \ldots, k$ we have

$$R_j^i = ((1 \dashv R_{j-1}^i) \vee S_{y[j]}) \wedge (1 \dashv (R_j^{i-1} \wedge R_{j-1}^{i-1})) \wedge R_{j-1}^{i-1}.$$

j	0	1	2	3	4	5	6	7	8	9	10	11
$y[j]$	C	A	A	A	T	A	A	T	A	G	A	A
$R_j^1[0]$	0	0	0	0	0	0	0	0	0	0	0	0
$R_j^1[1]$	1	0	0	0	0	0	0	0	0	0	0	0
$R_j^1[2]$	1	1	0	0	0	0	0	0	0	1	1	0
$R_j^1[3]$	1	1	1	0	0	0	0	0	0	0	1	1
$R_j^1[4]$	1	1	1	1	1	0	0	0	0	0	0	1

Figure 8.20. The factors AATA, AATAA, ATAA, AATAAT, AATA, AATAG, and AATAGA of the text $y =$ CAAATAATAGAA match the string $x =$ AATAA with at most one difference. They occur at respective positions 5, 6, 6, 7, 8, 9, and 10 on y because $R_5^1[4] = R_6^1[4] = R_7^1[4] = R_8^1[4] = R_9^1[4] = R_{10}^1[4] = 0$.

Proof The proof of Proposition 8.24 is a direct consequence of Lemmas 8.21, 8.22, and 8.23. The relation

$$R_j^i = ((1 \dashv R_{j-1}^i) \vee S_{y[j]}) \wedge (1 \dashv R_j^{i-1}) \wedge (1 \dashv R_{j-1}^{i-1}) \wedge R_{j-1}^{i-1}$$

can be rewritten in to the one given in the statement. ∎

```
K-DIFF-SHORT-PATTERN(x, m, y, n, k)
for each letter a ∈ A do
    S_a ← 1^m
for i ← 0 to m − 1 do
    S_{x[i]}[i] ← 0
R^0 ← 1^m
for ℓ ← 1 to k do
    R^ℓ ← (1 ⊣ R^{ℓ−1})
for j ← 0 to n − 1 do
    T ← R^0
    R^0 ← (1 ⊣ R^0) ∨ S_{y[j]}
    for ℓ ← 1 to k do
        T' ← R^ℓ
        R^ℓ ← ((1 ⊣ R^ℓ) ∨ S_{y[j]}) ∧ (1 ⊣ (T ∧ R^{ℓ−1})) ∧ T
        T ← T'
    OUTPUT-IF(R^k[m − 1] = 0)
```

Theorem 8.25

When the length m of the string x is smaller than the number of bits of a machine word, the preprocessing phase of the algorithm K-DIFF-SHORT-PATTERN *executes in time* $\Theta(k + \text{card}\,A)$ *within memory space* $\Theta(k + \text{card}\,A)$. *The searching phase executes in time* $\Theta(k \times n)$.

Proof The proof of Theorem 8.25 is similar to that of Proposition 8.20. ∎

8.5 Heuristic for approximate pattern matching with differences

The heuristic method described in this section finds a prefix of x, a suffix of x, or the entire string x in a text y with k differences. It partially uses dynamic programming techniques.

We refer to the diagonals of the set

$$\{0, 1, \ldots, m-1\} \times \{0, 1, \ldots, n-1\}$$

by means of an integer d. The diagonal d is the set of pairs (i, j) for which

$$j - i = d.$$

The pattern matching method is parameterized by two integers $\ell, k > 0$. It proceeds in three phases. In the first phase, all the positions of factors of length ℓ of the string that occur in y are found. This phase is realized with the help of a hashing technique. During the second phase, the diagonal d containing the largest number of factors of length ℓ of the string is selected. The third phase consists in finding an alignment by dynamic programming in a strip of width $2k$ around the diagonal d.

We now describe the details of each phase of the computation.

We define the set Z_ℓ by

$$\begin{aligned} Z_\ell = \{(i, j) : i = 0, 1, \ldots, m - \ell \text{ and } j = 0, 1, \ldots, n - \ell \\ \text{and } x[i \,..\, i + \ell - 1] = y[j \,..\, j + \ell - 1]\}. \end{aligned}$$

In other words, the set Z_ℓ contains all the pairs (i, j) for which the factor of length ℓ starting at position i on x is identical to the factor of length ℓ starting at position j on y. With the notation of Section 4.4, we thus have $\mathit{first}_\ell(x[i \,..\, m-1]) = \mathit{first}_\ell(y[j \,..\, n-1])$.

For each diagonal

$$d = -m + 1, -m, \ldots, n - 1,$$

we consider the number of elements of Z_ℓ located on this diagonal:

$$\mathit{counter}[d] = \text{card}\{(i, j) \in Z_\ell : j - i = d\}.$$

To perform an efficient counting, each factor of length ℓ is encoded by an integer. A factor of length ℓ is considered as the representation in base card A of an integer. Formally, in a bijective way, we associate a rank with each letter a of the alphabet A. The integer $rank(a)$ is within 0 and card $A - 1$. We set

$$code(w[0\,..\,\ell-1]) = \sum_{i=0}^{\ell-1} rank(w[\ell-i-1]) \times (\text{card } A)^i$$

for every string w of length greater or equal to ℓ. Thus, the codes of all the factors of length ℓ of the string and of the text can be computed in linear time using the following relation (for $i \geq 0$):

$$code(w[i+1\,..\,i+\ell]) = (code(w[i\,..\,i+\ell-1]) \bmod (\text{card } A)^{\ell-1}) \times \text{card } A + rank(w[i+\ell]).$$

The codes of the factors of length ℓ of the string x are computed in one pass and we accumulate the positions of the factors in a table *position* of size $(\text{card } A)^\ell$. More precisely, the value of $position[c]$ is the set of right positions of the factor of x of length ℓ whose code is c. The computation of the table is realized by the function Hashing.

```
Hashing(x, m, ℓ)
for c ← 0 to (card A)^ℓ − 1 do
        position[c] ← ∅
(exp, code) ← (1, 0)
for i ← 0 to ℓ − 2 do
        exp ← exp × card A
        code ← code × card A + rank(x[i])
for i ← ℓ − 1 to m − 1 do
        code ← (code mod exp) × card A + rank(x[i])
        position[code] ← position[code] ∪ {i}
return position
```

Second phase: after the initialization of the table *position*, the codes of the factors of the text y are computed. Each time that an equality, between the code of a factor of length ℓ of the string and the code of a factor of length ℓ of the text, is found on a diagonal, the counter of this diagonal is incremented. This is precisely what realizes the function Diagonal.

```
Diagonal(x, m, y, n, ℓ, position)
for d ← −m to n do
        counter[d] ← 0
(exp, code) ← (1, 0)
```

```
for j ← 0 to ℓ − 2 do
    exp ← exp × card A
    code ← code × card A + rank(y[j])
for j ← ℓ − 1 to n − 1 do
    code ← (code mod exp) × card A + rank(y[j])
    for each i ∈ position[code] do
        counter[j − i] ← counter[j − i] + 1
return counter
```

Third phase: for realizing the last phase of the method, it is finally sufficient to detect the diagonal d having the largest counter. We can then produce an alignment between the string x and the text y using a restricted dynamic programming algorithm, called a strip alignment. It considers only paths in the edit graph that are distant from the diagonal d by at most k positions (insertions and deletions are penalized by g). In this final phase also, there is an approximation because other diagonals are discarded during the alignment. The approximation is even stronger when k is small. Figure 8.21 shows how the algorithm works.

```
STRIP-ALIGNMENT(x, m, y, n, d, k)
(i', i'') ← (max{−1, −d − 1 − k}, min{−d − 1 + k, m − 1})
(j', j'') ← (max{−1, d − 1 − k}, min{d − 1 + k, n − 1})
c ← g
for i ← i' to i'' do
    T[i, −1] ← c
    c ← c + g
c ← g
for j ← j' to j'' do
    T[−1, j] ← c
    c ← c + g
for i ← 0 to m − 1 do
    for j ← i + d − k to i + d + k do
        if 0 ≤ j ≤ n − 1 then
            T[i, j] ← T[i − 1, j − 1] + Sub(x[i], y[j])
            if |j − i − 1 − d| ≤ k then
                T[i, j] ← min{T[i, j], T[i, j − 1] + g}
            if |j − i + 1 − d| ≤ k then
                T[i, j] ← min{T[i, j], T[i − 1, j] + g}
return T
```

(a)

T	j	-1	0	1	2	3	4	5	6	7	8	9	10
i		$y[j]$	L	A	W	Y	Q	Q	K	P	G	K	A
-1	$x[i]$		3	6	9	12	15						
0	Y			5	8	9	12	15					
1	W				5	8	11	14	17				
2	C					7	10	13	16	19			
3	Q						7	10	13	16	19		
4	P							9	12	13	16	19	
5	G								11	14	13	16	19
6	K									13	16	13	16

(b)

$$\begin{pmatrix} \mathtt{Y} & \mathtt{W} & \mathtt{C} & \mathtt{Q} & \mathtt{-} & \mathtt{-} & \mathtt{P} & \mathtt{G} & \mathtt{K} \\ \mathtt{A} & \mathtt{W} & \mathtt{Y} & \mathtt{Q} & \mathtt{Q} & \mathtt{K} & \mathtt{P} & \mathtt{G} & \mathtt{K} \end{pmatrix} \quad \begin{pmatrix} \mathtt{Y} & \mathtt{W} & \mathtt{C} & \mathtt{-} & \mathtt{Q} & \mathtt{-} & \mathtt{P} & \mathtt{G} & \mathtt{K} \\ \mathtt{A} & \mathtt{W} & \mathtt{Y} & \mathtt{Q} & \mathtt{Q} & \mathtt{K} & \mathtt{P} & \mathtt{G} & \mathtt{K} \end{pmatrix}$$

$$\begin{pmatrix} \mathtt{Y} & \mathtt{W} & \mathtt{-} & \mathtt{C} & \mathtt{Q} & \mathtt{-} & \mathtt{P} & \mathtt{G} & \mathtt{K} \\ \mathtt{A} & \mathtt{W} & \mathtt{Y} & \mathtt{Q} & \mathtt{Q} & \mathtt{K} & \mathtt{P} & \mathtt{G} & \mathtt{K} \end{pmatrix}$$

Figure 8.21. Illustration of the heuristic method of approximate pattern matching with differences. We consider the case where $x =$ YWCQPGK, $y =$ LAWYQQKPGKA, $\ell = 2$, $k = 2$, card $A = 20$, and where the rank of the letters that occur in x and y is

a	A	C	G	K	L	P	Q	W	Y
$rank(a)$	0	1	5	8	9	12	13	18	19

We get $code(\mathtt{YW}) = 19 \times 20^1 + 18 \times 20^0 = 398$, then, for $i = 2$, $code(\mathtt{WC}) = (code(\mathtt{YW}) \bmod 20) + 1 = 361$, and so on. This gives the following codes for the factors of length ℓ of x:

i	0	2	3	4	5	6
$x[i-1\,.\,.\,i]$	YW	WC	CQ	QP	PG	GK
$code(x[i-1\,.\,.\,i])$	398	361	33	272	245	108

Thus the values of the table *position*, for which we only give those that are distinct from the empty set, are:

code	33	108	245	272	361	398
position[*code*]	{3}	{6}	{5}	{4}	{2}	{1}

The codes associated with the factors of length ℓ of y are:

j	1	2	3	4	5	6	7	8	9	10
$y[j-1\,.\,.\,j]$	LA	AW	WY	YQ	QQ	QK	KP	PG	GK	KA
$code(y[j-1\,.\,.\,j])$	180	18	379	393	273	268	172	245	108	160

The only indices j on *code* corresponding to a nonempty position are 8 and 9. For these two indices, we increment the elements $counter[8-5]$ and $counter[9-6]$, which gives $counter[3] = 2$ after the processing. It follows that the diagonal that possesses the largest counter is diagonal 3. **(a)** Then, with the values $g = 3$, $k = 2$, $Sub(a, a) = 0$, and $Sub(a, b) = 2$ for $a, b \in A$ with $a \neq b$, we compute an alignment far from diagonal 3 by at most two positions. **(b)** The three corresponding alignments.

Let us finally note that the utilization of a divide-and-conquer technique, as in Section 7.3, yields an implementation of the function STRIP-ALIGNMENT that executes in time $O(m \times k)$ and in space $O(n)$.

Notes

Theorem 8.3 is from Fischer and Paterson [138]. The result used in the proof of the theorem stating that it is possible to multiply a number with M digits by a number with N digits in time $O(N \times \log M \times \log\log M)$ for $N \geq M$ is from Schönhage and Strassen [206].

The algorithm K-DIFF-CUT-OFF is from Ukkonen [212]. The algorithm K-DIFF-DIAG together with its implementation with the help of the computation of common ancestors was described by Landau and Vishkin [175]. Harel and Tarjan [150] presented the first algorithm running in constant time that solves the problem of the lowest ancestor common to two nodes of a tree. An improved solution is from Schieber and Vishkin [205].

Landau and Vishkin [174] conceived the algorithm K-MISMATCHES. The size of the automaton of Section 8.3 was established by Melichar [185]. Extension and improvement on the string matching algorithm for k mismatches are by Abrahamson [85] and by Amir, Lewenstein, and Porat [91].

The approximate pattern matching for short strings as reported by the algorithm K-DIFF-SHORT-PATTERN is from Wu and Manber [218] and also from Baeza-Yates and Gonnet [99].

Another method that uses the bit-parallelism technique and is optimal consists actually of a filtration method. It considers sparse q-grams and thus avoids scanning many text positions. It is due to Fredriksson and Grabowski [141].

A notion of seeds for searching genomic sequences speed-up dramatically approximate matching algorithms. It helps filter the data and accelerate their screening. Introduced by Ma, Tromp, and Li [177] for the software Pattern-Hunter, it is an active track of research. The reader can refer to the result of Farach-Colton, Landau, Sahinalp, and Tsur [135], or to the work of Noe and Kucherov [195] on the software YASS.

A synthesis on the approximate pattern matching appears in the book of Navarro and Raffinot [7], with an extensive exposition of techniques based on the bit-vector model. Large experimental results are reported by Navarro [193].

The method of global comparison with insertion and deletion is at the origin of the software FastA (see Pearson and Lipman [197]). The parameter ℓ introduced in Section 8.5 corresponds to parameter *KTup* of the software; its value is commonly set to 6 for processing nucleic acid sequences and to 2 for processing amino acid sequences.

Exercises

8.1 (Action!)

Find all the occurrences of the string with jokers `ab§§b§ab` in the text `bababbaabbaba`.

Find all the occurrences of the string with jokers `ab§§b§a` in the text with jokers `bababb§ab§aba`.

8.2

Find all the occurrences with at most two mismatches of the string `ACGAT` in the text `GACGATATATGATAC`.

8.3 (Costs)

What costs should we attribute to the edit operations for realizing the following operations? For $x, y \in A^+$ and $\gamma \in \mathbf{N}$:

- find the string x in the text y,
- search for the subsequences of y that are equal to x,
- search for the subsequences of y of the form $x_0u_0x_1u_1 \dots u_{k-1}x_{k-1}$ where $x = x_0x_1 \dots x_{k-1}$, and $|u_i| \le \gamma$ for $i = 0, 1, \dots, k-1$.

8.4

Find all the occurrences with at most two differences of the string `ACGAT` in the text `GACGATATATGATAC` using the algorithm K-DIFF-DP.

Solve the same question using the algorithms K-DIFF-CUT-OFF and K-DIFF-DIAG.

8.5 (Savings)

Describe an implementation of the algorithm K-DIFF-DIAG that runs in space $O(m)$. (*Hint:* swap the loops on q and d in the text of the algorithm.)

8.6 (Mismatches)

Design an algorithm for preprocessing the queues of the table G (see Section 8.3) that runs in time $O(k \times m \times \log m)$. (*Hint:* apply the searching phase with mismatches to blocks of indices running from $2^{\ell-1} - 1$ to $2^{\ell} - 2$, for $\ell = 1, 2, \dots, \lceil \log m \rceil$; see Landau and Vishkin [174].)

8.7 (Anagrams)
Write a linear-time algorithm that finds all the permutations of a string x in a text y. (*Hint:* use a counter for each letter of alph(x).)

8.8
Find all the occurrences with at most two differences of the "short string" $x =$ ACGAT in the text $y =$ GACGATATATGATAC.

8.9 (Classy)
Propose an extension of the algorithm K-DIFF-SHORT-PATTERN taking as input a class of strings. A class of strings is an expression of the form $X[0]X[1]\,..\,X[m-1]$ with $X[i] \subseteq A$ for $i = 0, 1, \ldots, m-1$.

8.10 (Gamma-delta)
We consider a distance between letters $d\colon A \times A \to \mathbf{R}$, two positive reals δ and γ, a string x of length m, and a text y of length n.

The string x possesses a δ-approximate occurrence in the text y if there exists a position $j = 0, 1, \ldots, n-m$ on y for which $d(x[i], y[i+j]) \leq \delta$ for $i = 0, 1, \ldots, m-1$. The string x possesses an γ-approximate occurrence in the text y if there exists a position $j = 0, 1, \ldots, n-m$ on y for which

$$\sum_{i=0}^{m-1} d(x[i], y[i+j]) \leq \gamma.$$

The string x possesses an (δ, γ)-approximate occurrence in the text y if x possesses an occurrence that is both δ-approximate and γ-approximate, that is to say, if there exists a position $j = 0, 1, \ldots, n-m$ on y for which $d(x[i], y[i+j]) \leq \delta$ for $i = 0, 1, \ldots, m-1$ and

$$\sum_{i=0}^{m-1} d(x[i], y[i+j]) \leq \gamma.$$

Write an algorithm that finds all the δ-approximate (respectively γ-approximate, (δ, γ)-approximate) occurrences of the string x in the text y. Evaluate its complexity. (*Hint:* see Cambouropoulos, Crochemore, Iliopoulos, Mouchard, and Pinzon [112].)

8.11 (Distributed patterns)
Let X be a list of k strings of length m and Y be a list of ℓ texts of length n. We say that the list X possesses a distributed occurrence in the list Y if for some

position $j = 0, 1, \ldots, n - m$ we have: for each $i = 0, 1, \ldots, m - 1$, there exist p and q for which $0 \leq p \leq k - 1$, $0 \leq q \leq \ell - 1$, and $X_p[i] = Y_q[i + j]$.

Write an algorithm finding all the distributed occurrences of the list X in the list Y. Study the particular cases for which X is reduced to a single string ($k = 1$) and Y is reduced to a single text ($\ell = 1$). (*Hint:* see Holub, Iliopoulos, Melichar, and Mouchard [154].)

9
Local periods

This chapter is devoted to the detection of local periodicities that can occur inside a string.

The method for detecting these periodicities is based on a partitioning of the suffixes that also allows to sort them in lexicographic order. The process is analogue to the one used in Chapter 4 for the preparation of the suffix array of a string and achieves the same time and space complexity, but the information on the string collected during its execution is more directly useful.

In Section 9.1, we introduce a simplified partitioning method that is adapted to different questions in the rest of the chapter. The detection of periods is dealt with immediately after in Section 9.2.

In Section 9.3, we consider squares. Their search in optimal time uses algorithms that require combinatorial properties together with the utilization of the structures of Chapter 5. We discuss also the maximal number of squares that can occur in a string, which gives upper bounds on the number of local periodicities.

Finally, in Section 9.4, we come back to the problem of lexicographically sorting the suffixes of a string and to the computation of their common prefixes. The solution presented there is another adaptation of the partitioning method; it can be used with benefit for the construction of a suffix array (Chapter 4).

9.1 Partitioning factors

The method described in this section is at the basis of algorithms for detecting local periodicities in a string. It consists in partitioning the suffixes of the string with respect to their beginnings of length k. The equivalences used for the partitioning are those of Section 4.4, but the computation method is different.

The adaptation of the method to sorting the suffixes of a string is presented in Section 9.4. The string is denoted by y and its length by n.

We start by recalling some notation introduced in Section 4.4. The beginning of order k, $k > 0$, of a string u is defined by

$$first_k(u) = \begin{cases} u & \text{if } |u| \leq k, \\ u[0\mathinner{\ldotp\ldotp}k-1] & \text{otherwise.} \end{cases}$$

The equivalence relation $\equiv_k$ on the positions on y is defined by

$$i \equiv_k j$$

if and only if

$$first_k(y[i\mathinner{\ldotp\ldotp}n-1]) = first_k(y[j\mathinner{\ldotp\ldotp}n-1]).$$

The equivalence $\equiv_k$ induces a partition of the set of positions in equivalence classes that are numbered from 0. And we denote by $E_k[i]$ the number of the class according to $\equiv_k$ that contains position i.

In Section 4.4, the equivalence $\equiv_{2k}$ is computed from $\equiv_k$ in application of the Doubling Lemma, which induces at most $\lceil \log_2 n \rceil$ steps for the computation of all the considered equivalences, and produces a total time $O(n \log n)$. Here, the computation of the equivalences is incremental on the values of k, but another technique for the computation of the successive equivalences is used. It leads to processing each position at most $\lceil \log_2 n \rceil$ times, which yields the same asymptotic execution time $O(n \log n)$.

We describe now the partitioning technique that works on the partitions associated with the equivalences $\equiv_k$ ($k > 0$). For a class P of the partition we denote by $P - 1$ the set $\{i - 1 : i \in P\}$. Partitioning with respect to a class P consists in replacing each equivalence class C by $C \cap (P - 1)$ and $C \setminus (P - 1)$, and by discarding the empty sets that result from these operations. The algorithm PARTITIONING below computes the equivalences $\equiv_1, \equiv_2, \ldots$ in this order. The central step of the computation consists in partitioning all the classes of the current equivalence with respect to a same class P. The following lemma is used for the correctness of the algorithm and it essentially relies on the remark illustrated by Figure 9.1. Its refinement (Lemma 9.2) is used in the algorithm PARTITIONING.

Lemma 9.1
For every integer $k > 0$, the equivalence classes of $\equiv_{k+1}$ are of the form $G = C \cap (P - 1)$ with $G \neq \emptyset$, where C is a class of $\equiv_k$, and $P = \{n\}$ or P is a class of $\equiv_k$.

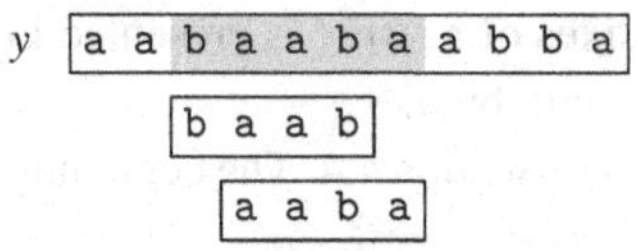

y `a a b a a b a a b b a`

`b a a b`

`a a b a`

Figure 9.1. Element of the proof of Lemma 9.1. In the case where $y =$ aabaabaabba, string baaba is $first_5(y[2\,..\,10])$. It is uniquely identified by its two factors baab, that is $first_4(y[2\,..\,10])$, and aaba, that is $first_4(y[3\,..\,10])$.

Proof First, let i and j be two positions equivalent according to $\equiv_{k+1}$, that is, $i \equiv_{k+1} j$. By definition

$$first_{k+1}(y[i\,..\,n-1]) = first_{k+1}(y[j\,..\,n-1]).$$

We thus have the equality

$$first_k(y[i\,..\,n-1]) = first_k(y[j\,..\,n-1]),$$

which amounts to say that $i, j \in C$ for some class C according to $\equiv_k$. But we have also

$$first_k(y[i+1\,..\,n-1]) = first_k(y[j+1\,..\,n-1])$$

(see Figure 9.1), which means that $i+1, j+1 \in P$ for a class P according to $\equiv_k$, if $i+1 < n$ and $j+1 < n$. We then have $i, j \in (P-1)$. If $i+1 = n$ or $j+1 = n$, we notice that the only possibility is indeed to have $i = j = n-1$. So, a class according to $\equiv_{k+1}$ is of the form $C \cap (P-1)$ as announced.

Conversely, let us consider a nonempty set of the form $C \cap (P-1)$ where C and P satisfy the conditions of the statement, and let $i, j \in C \cap (P-1)$. If $P = \{n\}$, we have $i = j = n-1$ and thus $i \equiv_{k+1} j$. If $P \neq \{n\}$, C and P are classes according to $\equiv_k$ by assumption, and we have $i+1, j+1 < n$. By definition of the equivalence $\equiv_k$, we deduce the equality:

$$first_k(y[i\,..\,n-1]) = first_k(y[j\,..\,n-1]).$$

But we deduce also the equality:

$$first_k(y[i+1\,..\,n-1]) = first_k(y[j+1\,..\,n-1]).$$

This implies

$$first_{k+1}(y[i\,..\,n-1]) = first_{k+1}(y[j\,..\,n-1])$$

(see Figure 9.1), that is to say $i \equiv_{k+1} j$ as expected. This ends the converse part and the whole proof. ∎

The computation of equivalences that directly deduces from the previous lemma can be realized in quadratic time ($O(n^2)$) using a radix sorting as in

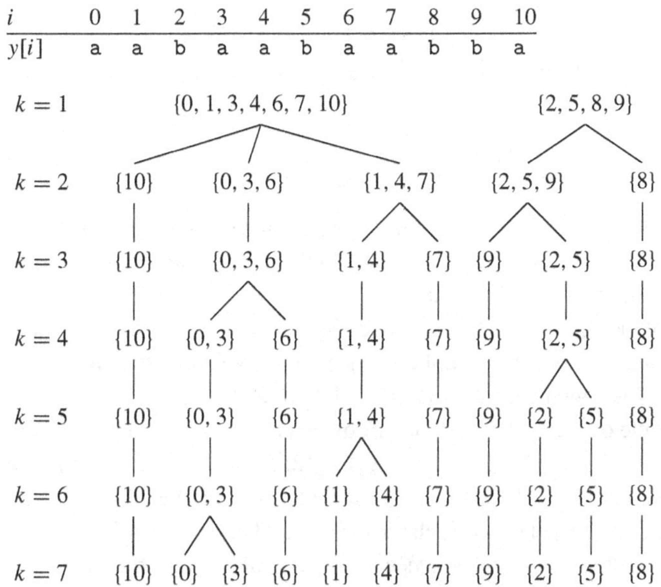

Figure 9.2. Incremental computation of the partitions associated with the equivalences $\equiv_k$ on the string $y =$ aabaabaabba. The classes of positions according to $\equiv_k$ are given from left to right in increasing order of their number. Thus, in line $k = 2$, $E_2[10] = 0$, $E_2[0] = E_2[3] = E_2[6] = 1$, $E_2[1] = E_2[4] = E_2[7] = 2$, $E_2[2] = E_2[5] = E_2[9] = 3$, and $E_2[8] = 4$.

the algorithm SUFFIX-SORT of Section 4.4. Figure 9.2 shows how the algorithm works. We recognize on the schema the structure of the suffix trie of the string. The algorithm for computing the equivalences works, in some sense, by traversing the trie in a width-first manner from its root.

To speed up the partitioning of positions, we consider a notion of difference between the equivalences $\equiv_k$ and $\equiv_{k-1}$ when $k > 1$. For this, we define the small classes of the equivalence $\equiv_k$. The definition is relative to a choice function of subclasses, denoted by c_k, defined on the set of classes according to $\equiv_{k-1}$ and with value in the set of classes according to $\equiv_k$. If C is a class relatively to $\equiv_{k-1}$, $c_k(C)$ is a class according to $\equiv_k$ for which $c_k(C) \subseteq C$, that is to say $c_k(C)$ is a subclass of C. We call ***small class*** of $\equiv_k$ relatively to the choice function c_k of subclasses, every equivalence class according to $\equiv_k$ that is not in the image of the function c_k. For $k = 1$, we consider by convention that all the classes according to $\equiv_1$ are small classes.

Small classes induce a notion of difference between equivalences. Relatively to c_k we denote by $\cong_k$ the equivalence defined on the positions on y by

$$i \cong_k j$$

if and only if

$$i, j \in C \text{ and } C \text{ is a small class according to } \equiv_k$$

or

$$i \in c_k(F) \text{ and } j \in c_k(G) \text{ for } F, G \text{ classes according to } \equiv_{k-1}.$$

The partition of positions induced by $\cong_k$ consists of the small classes of $\equiv_k$, on the one hand, and of the extra class obtained by the union of all classes chosen by the function c_k, on the other hand.

We note that the equivalence $\cong_k$ is coarser than $\equiv_k$ (that is, $\equiv_k$ is a refinement of $\cong_k$), which means that $i \equiv_k j$ implies $i \cong_k j$, or equivalently that every class according to $\equiv_k$ is contained in a class according to $\cong_k$.

In the example of Figure 9.2, defining c_3 by $c_3(\{10\}) = \{10\}$, $c_3(\{0, 3, 6\}) = \{0, 3, 6\}$, $c_3(\{1, 4, 7\}) = \{1, 4\}$, $c_3(\{2, 5, 9\}) = \{2, 5\}$, and $c_3(\{8\}) = \{8\}$, the equivalence $\cong_3$ partitions the set of positions into three classes: $\{7\}$, $\{9\}$, and $\{0, 1, 2, 3, 4, 5, 6, 8, 10\}$. The small classes are $\{7\}$ and $\{9\}$ (see also Figure 9.3).

The next lemma has for consequence that the computation of the partition induced by $\equiv_{k+1}$ can be done from $\equiv_k$ and from its small classes only. This property is used for the correctness of the algorithm PARTITIONING.

Lemma 9.2
For every integer $k > 0$, the equivalence classes $\equiv_{k+1}$ are of the form $G = C \cap (P - 1)$ with $G \neq \emptyset$, where C is a class according to $\equiv_k$, and $P = \{n\}$ or P is a class according to $\cong_k$.

Proof The first part of the proof of Lemma 9.1 also holds for this lemma since $i \equiv_k j$ implies $i \cong_k j$.

Conversely, let us consider a set $C \cap (P - 1)$ for which C and P satisfy to the conditions of the statement, and let $i, j \in C \cap (P - 1)$. If $P = \{n\}$ or if P is a small class, thus a class according to $\equiv_k$, we get the conclusion as in the proof of Lemma 9.1. The remaining case occurs when P is the union of the $c_k(F)$, F class according to $\equiv_{k-1}$. As $i, j \in C$, we have $i \equiv_k j$. And as $i + 1, j + 1 < n$, we deduce $i + 1 \equiv_{k-1} j + 1$. As a result, $i + 1$ and $j + 1$ belong to P and to the same class G according to $\equiv_{k-1}$. By definition of $\cong_k$, they belong thus to $c_k(G)$ that is a class of $\equiv_k$. Finally, from $i \equiv_k j$ and $i + 1 \equiv_k j + 1$, we deduce $i \equiv_{k+1} j$, which ends the converse part and the proof. ■

The code of the algorithm PARTITIONING explicits a large part of the computation method. It is given below. The variable *Small* stores the list of small classes of the current equivalence. This equivalence is represented by the set of its classes, each of them being implemented as a list. During the execution, some positions are transferred to a class called a twin class. Each twin class is empty before the execution of the **for** loop in lines 11–18. It is done similarly for the set of subclasses associated with each class.

The management of equivalence classes as lists is not an essential element of the partitioning. It is used here for allowing a simple description of the algorithm Powers of the next section that really requires such an organization. Figure 9.3 illustrates how the algorithm Partitioning works.

```
Partitioning(y, n)
 1  for r ← 0 to card alph(y) − 1 do
 2        C_r ← ⟨⟩
 3  for i ← 0 to n − 1 do
 4        r ← rank of y[i] in the sorted list of letters of alph(y)
 5        C_r ← C_r · ⟨i⟩
 6  Small ← {C_r : r = 0, 1, . . . , card alph(y) − 1}
 7  k ← 1
 8  while Small ≠ ∅ do
 9        ▷ Invariant: i, j ∈ C_r iff i ≡_k j iff E_k[i] = E_k[j]
10        ▷ Partitioning
11        for each P ∈ Small do
12              for each i ∈ P \ {0}, sequentially do
13                    let C be the class of i − 1
14                    let C_P be the twin class of C
15                    remove i − 1 of C
16                    C_P ← C_P · ⟨i − 1⟩
17              for each considered pair (C, C_P) do
18                    add C_P to the subclasses of C
19        ▷ Choice of the small classes
20        Small ← ∅
21        for each class C considered during the previous step do
22              if C is nonempty then
23                    add C to the subclasses of C
24              replace C by its subclasses
25              G ← one subclass of C of maximal size
26              Small ← Small ∪ ({subclasses of C} \ {G})
27        k ← k + 1
```

The analysis of the execution time, which is $O(n \log n)$, is detailed in the three statements that follow. Lemma 9.3 essentially corresponds to the study of lines 12–18 of the algorithm.

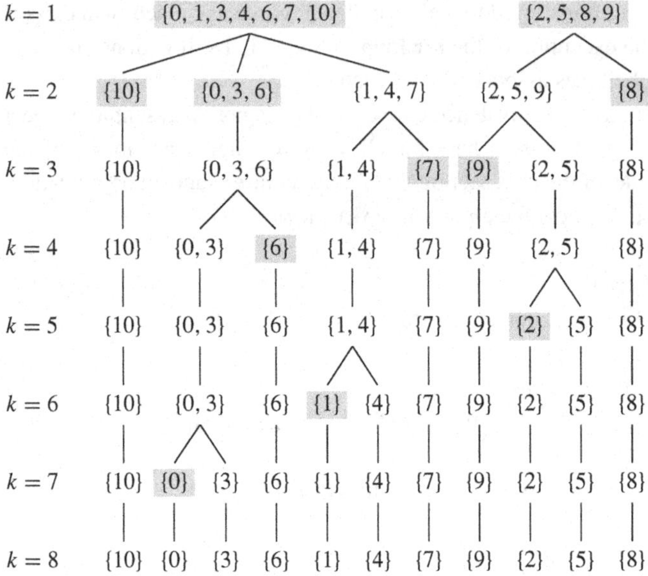

Figure 9.3. Incremental computation of the partitions induced by the equivalences $\equiv_k$ on the string $y =$ aabaabaabba as in Figure 9.2. The small classes are indicated by a gray area. The number of operations executed by the algorithm PARTITIONING is proportional to the total number of elements of the small classes.

An efficient implementation of the manipulated partitions consists in representing each equivalence class by a linked list assigned with a number, and simultaneously to associate with each position the number of its class. In this way, the operations performed on a position for partitioning a class execute in constant time. The operations on a position are composed of access to its class, extraction from its class, and insertion into a class.

Lemma 9.3

The partitioning with respect to a class P can be realized in time $\Omega(\text{card } P)$.

Proof The partitioning of a class C with respect to P consists in computing $C \cap (P-1)$ and $C \setminus C \cap (P-1)$. This is realized by means of an operation of transfer (of position) from one class to another class. With the implementation described before the statement, this operation takes a constant time. The card P transfers take thus a time $\Omega(\text{card } P)$.

All the concerned classes C are processed during the partitioning. The empty sets are eliminated after the scan of all the elements of the class P. As there are at most card P concerned classes C, this step also takes a time $O(\text{card } P)$.

It follows that the total time of the partitioning with respect to P is $\Omega(\text{card } P)$ as announced. ■

Corollary 9.4

For every integer $k > 0$, the computation of $\equiv_{k+1}$ from both the equivalence $\equiv_k$ and its small classes can be realized in time $\Omega(\sum_{P \text{ small class of } \equiv_k} \text{card } P)$.

Proof The result is a direct consequence of Lemma 9.3. ■

Let us consider the example of Figure 9.3 and the computation of $\equiv_4$ (line $k = 4$). The small classes of $\equiv_3$ are $\{7\}$ and $\{9\}$. Thus the computation of $\equiv_4$ consists in simply extracting 6 and 8 from their respective classes. This has for effect to split the class $\{0, 3, 6\}$ into $\{0, 3\}$ and $\{6\}$ (8 being alone in its class), and to produce $\{6\}$ as a small class for the next step.

The algorithm PARTITIONING utilizes a specific choice function. This one selects for each C, class according to the equivalence $\equiv_{k-1}$, a subclass $c_k(C)$ of maximal size among the subclasses of C. This is precisely this particular choice of subclasses that leads to an $O(n \log n)$ running time.

Theorem 9.5

Let $K > 0$ be the smallest integer for which the equivalences $\equiv_K$ and $\equiv_{K+1}$ match. The algorithm PARTITIONING *computes the equivalences $\equiv_1, \equiv_2, \ldots, \equiv_K$, defined on the positions on a string of length n, in time $O(n \log n)$.*

Proof The **for** loops in lines 1–2 and 3–5 compute $\equiv_1$. The instructions in lines 11–27 of the **while** loop compute $\equiv_{k+1}$ from $\equiv_k$ according to Lemma 9.2, after having checked that the small classes are selected correctly. The execution stops as soon as there is no more small class, that is to say when the equivalences $\equiv_k$ and $\equiv_{k+1}$ match for the first time. This happens for $k = K$ by definition of K. The algorithm PARTITIONING computes thus the sequence of equivalences of the statement.

Let us evaluate now its execution time. The running time of the loop in lines 1–2 is $\Omega(\text{card alph}(y))$. The one of the loop in lines 3–5 is $O(n \times \log \text{card alph}(y))$ using an efficient data structure to store the alphabet. The execution time of the loop in lines 8–27 is proportional to the sum of the sizes of all the small classes used during the partitioning after Corollary 9.4.

With the particular choice of small classes, the size of the class of a position that is located in a small class decreases (at least) by half during the partitioning: if $i \in C$, class according to $\equiv_{k-1}$, and $i \in C'$, C' small class of $\equiv_k$ (C' subclass of C), we have $\text{card } C' \leq \text{card } C/2$. As a result, each position belongs to a

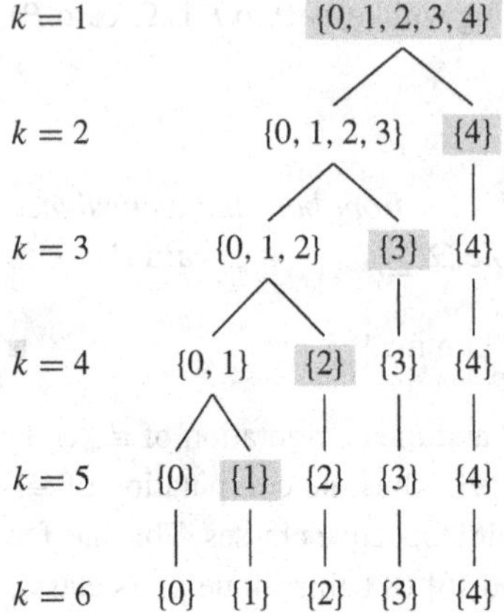

Figure 9.4. Operation PARTITIONING applied to the string $y = \texttt{aaaaa}$. After the initial phase, the computation is done in four steps, each taking a constant time.

small class at most $1 + \lfloor \log_2 n \rfloor$ times. This gives the time $O(n \log n)$ for the execution of the loop in line 8.

The global running time of the algorithm is thus $O(n \log n)$ because $\text{card alph}(y) \leq n$. ■

When the algorithm PARTITIONING is applied to the string $y = a^n$, the execution time is indeed $O(n)$. Figure 9.4 illustrates the computation on the string aaaaa. Each step executes in constant time since, after the initial phase, there is a single small class per step and it is a singleton.

We meet a totally different situation when y is a de Bruijn string (see Section 1.2). The example of the string babbbaaaba is described in Figure 9.5. For these strings, after the initial phase, each step takes a time $O(n)$ since the small classes contain globally around $n/2$ elements. But the number of steps is only $\lfloor \log_2 n \rfloor$. We get thus examples for which the number of operations is $\Omega(n \log n)$.

In a general way, we check that the number K of steps executed by the algorithm PARTITIONING is also $\ell + 1$ where ℓ is the maximal length of factors that possess at least two occurrences in y.

9.2 Detection of powers

In this section, we present a quite direct adaptation of the algorithm PARTITIONING of the previous section. It computes the factors of a string that are powers.

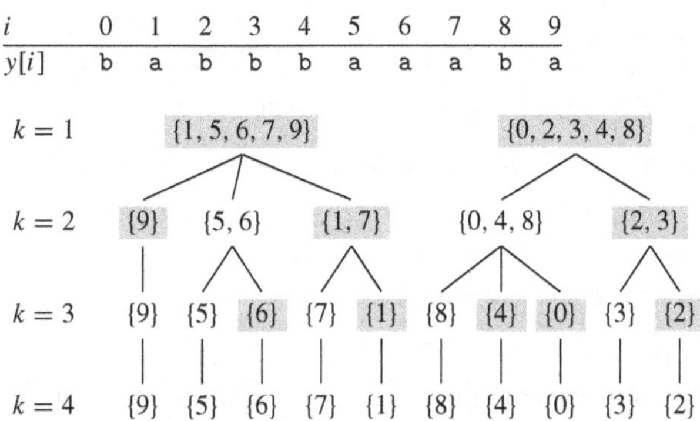

Figure 9.5. Operation PARTITIONING applied to the de Bruijn string $y =$ babbbaaaba. After the initial phase, the computation is done in two steps, each requiring five processings of elements.

We discuss then the number of occurrences of powers that can exist in a string, element that leads to the optimality of the algorithm.

A ***local power*** of a string y of length n is a factor of y of the form u^e. More precisely, u^e is a local power at position i on y if u^e is a prefix of $y[i\,..\,n-1]$ with $u \in A^+$, u primitive, and e integer, $e > 1$. This is a (right) ***maximal local power*** at i if moreover u^{e+1} is not a prefix of $y[i\,..\,n-1]$. We can also consider the left maximal local powers (requiring that u is not a suffix of $y[0\,..\,i-1]$) and the two-sided maximal local powers. Their detection in y is a simple adaptation of the algorithm described for the detection of the right maximal local powers.

An occurrence of a local power u^e is identified by the triplet (i, p, e) where i is its position, $p = |u|$ its period, and e its exponent.

Computation of local powers

The detection of the local powers is done with the help of a notion of distance on positions that is associated with the equivalence $\equiv_k$. For every position i on y, we define this distance by

$$D_k[i] = \begin{cases} \min L & \text{if } L \neq \emptyset, \\ \infty & \text{otherwise,} \end{cases}$$

where

$$L = \{\ell : \ell = 1, 2, \ldots, n-i-1 \text{ and } E_k[i] = E_k[i+\ell]\}.$$

In other words, $D_k[i]$ is the distance from i to the nearest superior position of its class according to $\equiv_k$, when this position exists.

Lemma 9.6
The triplet of integers (i, p, e), *with* $0 \leq i < n$, $p > 0$, *and* $e > 1$, *identifies the occurrence of a maximal local power at position* i *if and only if*

$$D_p[i] = D_p[i + p] = \cdots = D_p[i + (e - 2)p] = p$$

and

$$D_p[i + (e - 1)p] \neq p.$$

Proof We set $u = y[i \,..\, i + p - 1]$.

First, by definition of a maximal local power, the string u occurs at positions $i, i + p, \ldots, i + (e - 1)p$ on y but not at position $i + ep$. We deduce, by definition of D_p, the inequalities $D_p[i] \leq p$, $D_p[i + p] \leq p, \ldots,$ $D_p[i + (e - 2)p] \leq p$, and $D_p[i + (e - 1)p] \neq p$. If some inequality is strict, this implies that u^2 possesses an internal occurrence of u. But this contradicts the primitivity of u after the Primitivity Lemma (see Section 1.2). Therefore, the $e - 1$ inequalities are actually equalities, which proves that the conditions of the statement are satisfied.

Conversely, when the conclusion of the statement holds, by definition of D_p, the string u occurs at positions $i, i + p, \ldots, i + (e - 1)p$ on y since these positions are equivalent relatively to $\equiv_p$, but does not occur at position $i + ep$. It remains thus to check that u is primitive. If this is not the case, y possesses an occurrence of u at a position j, $i < j < i + p$. But this implies $D_p[i] \leq j - i < p$ and contradicts the equality $D_p[i] = p$. Thus, u is primitive and (i, p, e) corresponds to a maximal local power. ■

The detection algorithm for all the occurrences of the maximal local powers occurring in y is called POWERS. It is obtained from the algorithm PARTITIONING by adding extra elements that are described here.

We utilize a table D that implements the table D_k at each step k. We simultaneously maintain the partition of positions associated with the values of the table D. That is to say i and j belong to a same class of this partition if and only if $D[i] = D[j]$. The classes are represented by lists in order to realize transfers in constant time.

The additions to the algorithm PARTITIONING are essentially on the computation of the table D, and also on the simultaneous management of the associated lists, which does not pose any extra difficulty.

The update of D occurs when there is a transfer of a position i to another equivalence class. We strongly utilize the fact that the equivalence classes according to $\equiv_k$ are managed as lists and that the positions are stored in increasing order. If i possesses a predecessor i' in its starting class, the new value of $D[i']$ is $D[i'] + D[i]$. There is no other change for the elements of the class since they are in increasing order. In its target class, i is the last added element, since the partitioning relative to a class P is done in the increasing order of the elements of P (see line 12). We define thus $D[i] = \infty$. Moreover, if i has a predecessor i'' in its new class, we define $D[i''] = i - i''$.

Finally, at each step k, we obtain the powers of exponent k by scanning the list for positions i satisfying $D[i] = k$ in application of Lemma 9.6. The algorithm can then produce the expected triplets (i, p, e). We just have to be sure, during the implementation, that the triplets

$$(i, p, e), (i + p, p, e - 1), \ldots$$

corresponding to maximal local powers at positions

$$i, i + p, \ldots$$

are produced in time proportional to their number, and not in quadratic time.

The above description of Powers shows that the computation of the maximal local powers can be realized in the same time as the partitioning. We also notice that the extra operations that produce the maximal powers have an execution time proportional to this number of powers. Referring to Proposition 9.8 thereafter, we then deduce the next result.

Theorem 9.7
The algorithm Powers *computes all the occurrences of maximal local powers of a string of length n in time $O(n \log n)$.* ■

Let us consider the example $y =$ aabaabaabba of Figure 9.3. When the partition associated with $\equiv_3$ is computed (line $k = 3$), the elements that are at distance 3 from their successors are 0, 1, 2, and 3 ($D[0] = D[1] = D[2] = D[3] = 3$). These elements correspond to the maximal powers $(\texttt{aab})^3$ at 0, $(\texttt{aba})^2$ at 1, $(\texttt{baa})^2$ at 2, and $(\texttt{aab})^2$ at 3.

Number of occurrences of local powers

The execution time of the algorithm Powers depends upon the size of its output, the number of maximal powers. The example of $y = \texttt{a}^n$ shows that a string can contain a quadratic number of local powers. But, with this example, we only get $n - 1$ maximal local powers. Proposition 9.8 gives an upper bound to this quantity, while Proposition 9.9 implies the optimality of the computation time of the algorithm Powers. The optimality also holds for the detection of the two-sided maximal powers.

Proposition 9.8
There are at most $n \log_\Phi n$ occurrences of maximal local powers in a string of length n.

Proof The number of maximal local powers occurring at a given position i on y is equal to the number of squares of primitive strings occurring at position i. As this quantity is bounded by $\log_\Phi n$ after Corollary 9.16 below, we get the result. ■

Proposition 9.9
For every integer $c \geq 6$, the Fibonacci string f_c contains at least $\frac{1}{6}F_c \log_2 F_c$ occurrences of squares (of primitive strings) and of (right) maximal powers, and at least $\frac{1}{12}F_c \log_2 F_c$ occurrences of the two-sided maximal powers.

Proof Let us denote by $\xi(y)$ the number of occurrences of squares of primitive strings that are factors of y. We show by recurrence on c, $c \geq 6$, that $\xi(f_c) \geq \frac{1}{6}F_c \log_2 F_c$.

For $c = 6$, we have $f_6 = \texttt{abaababa}$, $\xi(f_6) = 4$, and $\frac{1}{6} \times 8 \times 3 = 4$. For $c = 7$, we have $f_7 = \texttt{abaababaabaab}$, $\xi(f_7) = 11$, and $\frac{1}{6} \times 13 \times \log_2 13 < 9$.

Let $c \geq 8$. The string f_c is equal to $f_{c-1}f_{c-2}$. We have the equality

$$\xi(f_c) = \xi(f_{c-1}) + \xi(f_{c-2}) + r_c$$

where r_c is the number of occurrences of squares of f_c that are neither counted by $\xi(f_{c-1})$ nor by $\xi(f_{c-2})$, that is to say the occurrences of squares that overlap the separation between the prefix f_{c-1} and the suffix f_{c-2} of f_c. The recurrence hypothesis implies

$$\xi(f_c) \geq \frac{1}{6}F_{c-1}\log_2 F_{c-1} + \frac{1}{6}F_{c-2}\log_2 F_{c-2} + r_c.$$

To obtain the stated result it is sufficient to show

$$\frac{1}{6}F_{c-1}\log_2 F_{c-1} + \frac{1}{6}F_{c-2}\log_2 F_{c-2} + r_c \geq \frac{1}{6}F_c \log_2 F_c,$$

which is equivalent to

$$r_c \geq \frac{1}{6}F_{c-1}\log_2 \frac{F_c}{F_{c-1}} + \frac{1}{6}F_{c-2}\log_2 \frac{F_c}{F_{c-2}},$$

using the equality $F_c = F_{c-1} + F_{c-2}$. As, for $c > 4$,

$$\frac{F_c}{F_{c-1}} \leq \frac{F_5}{F_4} = \frac{5}{3},$$

it is sufficient to show

$$r_c \geq \frac{1}{6}(F_{c-1} + F_{c-2})\log_2 \frac{8}{3}$$

or also

$$r_c \geq \frac{1}{4} F_c.$$

We first show that f_c contains $F_{c-4} + 1$ occurrences of squares of period F_{c-2} that contribute thus to r_c. By rewriting from the definition of Fibonacci strings, we get $f_c = f_{c-2} f_{c-2} f_{c-5} f_{c-4}$, and $f_{c-5} f_{c-4} = f_{c-4} f_{c-7} f_{c-6}$, for $c > 7$. Thus the string $f_{c-2} f_{c-2}$ occurs in f_c. But as f_{c-4} is a prefix of both f_{c-2} and $f_{c-5} f_{c-4}$, we also get F_{c-4} other occurrences of squares of period F_{c-2}.

We show then that f_c contains $F_{c-4} + 1$ occurrences of squares of period F_{c-3} that contribute again to r_c. From the equality $f_c = f_{c-2} f_{c-3} f_{c-3} f_{c-4}$, we see that the occurrence of $f_{c-3} f_{c-3}$ contributes to r_c, as it is for the F_{c-4} other occurrences of squares of period F_{c-3} that can be deduced from the fact that f_{c-4} is a prefix of f_{c-3}.

As a conclusion, for $c > 7$ we get the inequality

$$r_c \geq 2F_{c-4},$$

thus

$$r_c \geq \frac{1}{4} F_c,$$

which ends the recurrence and the proof of the lower bound on the number of occurrences of squares.

There are as many occurrences of right maximal powers as occurrences of squares (a maximal power of exponent e, $e > 1$, contains $e - 1$ occurrences of squares but also $e - 1$ occurrences of right maximal powers that are suffixes of it), which gives the same bound for this quantity.

The second lower bound that refers on the number of occurrences of the two-sided maximal powers is obtained by means of a combinatorial property of the Fibonacci strings: f_c has no factor of the form u^4 with $u \neq \varepsilon$ (see Exercise 9.10). Thus each occurrence of a two-sided maximal power can contain at most two occurrences of squares, which gives the second bound of the statement. ■

9.3 Detection of squares

In this section, we consider powers of exponent 2, namely squares. Locating all the occurrences of squares in a string can be realized with the algorithm of Section 9.2. We cannot hope to find an asymptotically faster algorithm (with the considered representation of powers) because of the result of Proposition 9.9

whose consequence is that the algorithm POWERS is still optimal even if we restrict it to produce squares only. Nevertheless, this does not show its optimality for the detection of all the squares (and not of their occurrences) since a string of length n contains less than $2n$ squares after Lemma 9.17 given further. We start by examining the problem of detecting a square in a string and show that the question can be answered in linear time when the alphabet is fixed. We study then bounds on the number of squares of primitive strings that can occur in a string.

Existence of a square

One of the essential problems in the following is the detection of a square inside the concatenation of two square-free strings. An algorithm for testing the existence of a square by the divide-and-conquer strategy is then deduced. This method is further improved by the utilization of a special factorization of the string to be tested.

We recall from Section 3.3 the definition of the table $suff_u$, for every string $u \in A^*$:

$$suff_u[i] = |lcsuff(u, u[0\,..\,i])| = \max\{|s| : s \preceq_{\text{suff}} u \text{ and } s \preceq_{\text{suff}} u[0\,..\,i]\},$$

for $i = 0, 1, \ldots, |u| - 1$. It gives the maximal length of the suffixes of u that end at each of the positions on u itself. For $u, v \in A^*$, we denote by $p_{v,u}$ the table defined, for $j = 0, 1, \ldots, |u| - 1$, by

$$p_{v,u}[j] = \max\{|t| : t \preceq_{\text{pref}} v \text{ and } t \preceq_{\text{pref}} u[j\,..\,|u| - 1]\}.$$

This second table provides the maximal length of the prefixes of v that start at each position on u. When, for instance, $u =$ `cabacbabcbac` and $v =$ `babcbab` (see Figure 9.6) we get the tables that follow.

i	0	1	2	3	4	5	6	7	8	9	10	11
$u[i]$	c	a	b	a	c	b	a	b	c	b	a	c
$suff_u[i]$	1	0	0	0	3	0	0	0	1	0	0	12
$p_{v,u}[i]$	0	0	2	0	0	6	0	1	0	2	0	0

Considering two strings u and v, we say of a square w^2 occurring at position i on the string $u \cdot v$ that it is a ***square centered*** on u when $i + |w| \le |u|$. In the contrary case, we say that it is centered on v.

Lemma 9.10
Let two strings $u, v \in A^+$. The string $u \cdot v$ contains a square centered on u if and only if for a position i on u we have

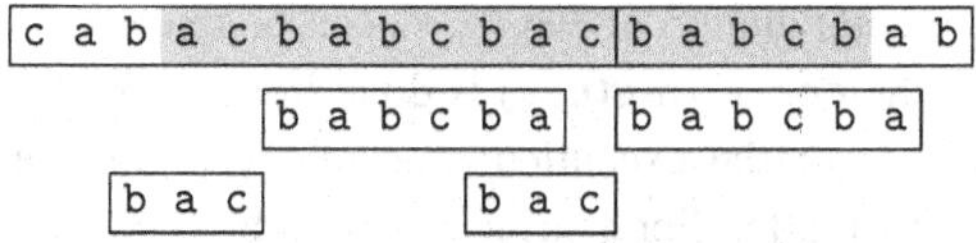

Figure 9.6. Support of the proof of Lemma 9.10. A square in uv whose center is in u is of the form $stst$ with s a suffix of u and t a prefix of v. Here $u =$ cabacbabcbac and $v =$ babcbab. The square (acbabcb)^2 is centered on u. We have $\mathit{suff}_u[4] = |\text{bac}| = 3$, $p_{v,u}[5] = |\text{babcba}| = 6$, $i = 5$, and $|u| - i = 7$. As the inequality $\mathit{suff}_u[i-1] + p_{v,u}[i] \geq |u| - i$ holds, we deduce the squares (bacbabc)^2, (acbabcb)^2, and (cbabcba)^2.

$$\mathit{suff}_u[i-1] + p_{v,u}[i] \geq |u| - i.$$

Proof The proof builds with the help of Figure 9.6. ■

The tables of the above example indicate the existence of at least two squares centered on u in $u \cdot v$ since $\mathit{suff}_u[4] + p_{v,u}[5] \geq 7$ and $\mathit{suff}_u[8] + p_{v,u}[9] = 3$. Actually, there are four squares in this situation: (bacbabc)^2, (acbabcb)^2, (cbabcba)^2, and (cba)^2.

The computation of the table suff_u is described in Section 3.3 and that of the table $p_{v,u}$ comes from an algorithm of Section 2.6. The total time of these two computations is $O(|u|)$ when, for the second, the preprocessing on v is limited to its prefix of length $|u|$ if $|u| < |v|$. Thus the result that follows.

Corollary 9.11
Let $u, v \in A^+$. Testing if $u \cdot v$ contains a square centered on u can be realized in time $O(|u|)$.

Proof Using Lemma 9.10, it is sufficient to compute the table suff_u, and the table $p_{v,u}$ limited to the prefix of v of length $|u|$. The computation of these two tables is done in time $O(|u|)$ as recalled above. The rest of the computation consists in testing the inequality of Lemma 9.10, for each position i on u, this takes again a time $O(|u|)$. The result thus holds. ■

We define the boolean functions *ltest* and *rtest*, that take as arguments the square-free strings u and v, by

$$\mathit{ltest}(u, v) = u \cdot v \text{ contains a square centered on } u,$$

and

$$\mathit{rtest}(u, v) = u \cdot v \text{ contains a square centered on } v.$$

Corollary 9.11 indicates that the computation of *ltest*(u, v) can be realized in time $O(|u|)$, and, by symmetry, the one of *rtest*(u, v) is done in time $O(|v|)$. This result is used in the analysis of the execution time of the algorithm SQUARE-IN whose code is given thereafter. For a string $y \in A^*$, the operation REC-SQUARE-IN(y) returns TRUE if and only if y contains a square. The principle of the computation is a divide-and-conquer strategy based on the utilization of the functions *ltest* and *rtest*. These functions are supposed to be realized by the algorithms LTEST and RTEST respectively.

```
REC-SQUARE-IN(y)
n ← |y|
if n ≤ 1 then
        return FALSE
elseif REC-SQUARE-IN(y[0 . . ⌊n/2⌋]) then
        return TRUE
elseif REC-SQUARE-IN(y[⌊n/2⌋ + 1 . . n − 1]) then
        return TRUE
elseif LTEST(y[0 . . ⌊n/2⌋], y[⌊n/2⌋ + 1 . . n − 1]) then
        return TRUE
elseif RTEST(y[0 . . ⌊n/2⌋], y[⌊n/2⌋ + 1 . . n − 1]) then
        return TRUE
else return FALSE
```

Proposition 9.12

The operation REC-SQUARE-IN(y) *returns* TRUE *if and only if y contains a square. The computation is done in time $O(|y| \times \log |y|)$.*

Proof The correctness of the algorithm comes from a simple recurrence on the length n of y.

Denoting by $T(n)$ the execution time of REC-SQUARE-IN on a string of length n, we get, with the help of Corollary 9.11, the recurrence formulas $T(1) = \alpha$ and, for $n > 1$, $T(n) = T(\lfloor n/2 \rfloor) + T(\lceil n/2 \rceil) + \beta n$, where α and β are constants. The solution of this recurrence gives the announced result (see Exercise 1.13). ∎

It is possible to reduce the execution time of square testing using a more subtle strategy than the previous one. Though the strategy is still of the kind divide-and-conquer, it does not balance the sizes of the subproblems, which is quite nonintuitive. The strategy is based on a factorization of y called its f-factorization.

The ***f-factorization*** of $y \in A^+$ is the sequence of factors $u_0, u_1, \ldots, u_k$ of y defined iteratively as follows. We first have $u_0 = y[0]$. Then we assume that

$u_0, u_1, \ldots, u_{j-1}$ are already defined, with $u_0u_1 \ldots u_{j-1} \prec_{\text{pref}} y$ and $j > 0$. Let $i = |u_0u_1 \ldots u_{j-1}|$ (we have $0 < i < n - 1$) and let w be the longest prefix of $y[i \,..\, n-1]$ that occurs at least twice in $y[0 \,..\, i-1] \cdot w$. Then

$$u_j = \begin{cases} w & \text{if } w \neq \varepsilon, \\ y[i] & \text{otherwise.} \end{cases}$$

We note that the second case of the definition happens when $y[i]$ is a letter that does not occur in $y[0 \,..\, i-1]$. We also note that all the factors of the f-factorization are nonempty strings.

With the string $y =$ abaabbaabbaababa, we obtain for f-factorization the sequence a, b, a, ab, baabbaab, aba, which is a decomposition of y: $y =$ a · b · a · ab · baabbaab · aba.

Lemma 9.13
Let $\langle u_0, u_1, \ldots, u_k\rangle$ be the f-factorization of $y \in A^+$. The string y contains a square if and only if one of the three following conditions is satisfied for some index j, $0 < j \le k$:

1. $|u_0u_1 \ldots u_{j-1}| \le pos_y(u_j) + |u_j| < |u_0u_1 \ldots u_j|$,
2. *$ltest(u_{j-1}, u_j)$ or $rtest(u_{j-1}, u_j)$ is true,*
3. *$j > 1$ and $rtest(u_0u_1 \ldots u_{j-2}, u_{j-1}u_j)$ is true.*

Proof We start by showing that if one of the conditions is satisfied, y contains a square. Let j be the smallest index for which one of the conditions is satisfied. If Condition 1 is satisfied, the current occurrence of u_j and its first occurrence in y overlap or are adjacent without matching. We deduce the existence of a square at position $pos_y(u_j)$.

If Condition 1 is not satisfied, the string u_j does not contain a square since it is of length 1 or is a factor of $u_0u_1 \ldots u_{j-1}$ that does not contain any (which can be shown by recurrence on j using this remark). By definition of the functions *ltest* and *rtest*, and since u_{j-1} and u_j are square-free, if $ltest(u_{j-1}, u_j)$ or $rtest(u_{j-1}, u_j)$ is true, the string $u_{j-1}u_j$ contains a square, which is thus also a square of y. On the other hand, if $ltest(u_{j-1}, u_j)$ and $rtest(u_{j-1}, u_j)$ are false, $u_{j-1}u_j$ does not contain any square; but Condition 3 indicates the existence of a square in y since the arguments of *ltest* are square-free strings.

Conversely, let j be the smallest integer for which $u_0u_1 \ldots u_j$ contains a square, and let ww, $w \neq \varepsilon$, be this square. We have $0 < j < n$ since u_0 is square-free, and the string $u_0u_1 \ldots u_{j-1}$ is square-free by definition of the integer j. If Condition 1 is not satisfied, as in this case u_j is of length 1 or is a factor of $u_0u_1 \ldots u_{j-1}$, it is square-free. If Condition 2 is not satisfied $u_{j-1}u_j$ is also square-free. It remains then to show that the square ww is centered on $u_{j-1}u_j$. In the contrary situation, the occurrence of the second half of the square ww completely covers u_{j-1}, which implies that this string possesses an occurrence that is not a suffix of w. But this contradicts the maximality of the length of u_{j-1} in the definition of the f-factorization. Condition 3 is thus satisfied, which ends the proof. ■

The algorithm SQUARE-IN directly implements the square testing from the conditions stated in Lemma 9.13. The f-factorization can be computed by means of the suffix tree of y (Section 5.2) or of its suffix automaton (Section 5.4). We get thus a linear-time test when the alphabet is fixed.

```
SQUARE-IN(y)
 1  (u_0, u_1, ..., u_k) ← f-factorization of y
 2  for j ← 1 to k do
 3        if |u_0 u_1 ... u_{j-1}| ≤ pos(u_j) + |u_j| < |u_0 u_1 ... u_j| then
 4              return TRUE
 5        elseif LTEST(u_{j-1}, u_j) then
 6              return TRUE
 7        elseif RTEST(u_{j-1}, u_j) then
 8              return TRUE
 9        elseif j > 1 and RTEST(u_0 u_1 ... u_{j-2}, u_{j-1} u_j) then
10              return TRUE
11  return FALSE
```

Theorem 9.14
The operation SQUARE-IN(y) *returns* TRUE *if and only if the string y contains a square. The computation is done in time $O(|y| \times \log \text{card}\, A)$.*

Proof The correctness of the algorithm is a direct consequence of Lemma 9.13.

It can be checked that we can compute the f-factorization of y by means of its suffix automaton, or even during the construction of this structure. Besides, the test in line 3 can be performed during this computation, without changing the asymptotic bound of the construction time. The running time of this step is thus $O(|y| \times \log \text{card}\, A)$ (Section 5.4).

The sum of the execution times of the tests performed in lines 5, 7, and 9 is proportional to $\sum_{j=1}^{k}(|u_{j-1}| + |u_j| + |u_{j-1}u_j|)$ after Corollary 9.11, which is bounded by $2|y|$.

The total time is thus $O(|y| \times \log \text{card}\, A)$. ■

The lemma shows that square testing is linear on a fixed alphabet, result that is also true on a bounded integer alphabet due to the results of Section 4.5 and Exercise 5.4.

Number of prefix or factor squares

We call ***prefix square*** of a string a square that is a prefix of this string.

The lemma that follows presents a combinatorial property that is at the origin of an upper bound on the number of prefix squares (see Corollary 9.16). The upper bound is used in the previous section for bounding the number of occurrences of maximal powers in a string (Proposition 9.8) and for bounding the execution time of the algorithm POWERS.

Lemma 9.15 (Three Prefix Square Lemma)
Let $u, v, w \in A^+$ be three strings such that $u^2 \prec_{\text{pref}} v^2 \prec_{\text{pref}} w^2$ and u is primitive. Then $|u| + |v| \leq |w|$.

Proof We assume by contradiction that $|u| + |v| > |w|$, which, with the assumption, implies $v \prec_{\text{pref}} w \prec_{\text{pref}} vu \prec_{\text{pref}} v^2$. The string $t = v^{-1}w$ satisfies then $t \prec_{\text{pref}} u$, and $|t|$ is a period of v (since v occurs at positions $|v|$ and $|w|$ on w^2 and that $|w| - |v| = |t| \leq |v|$).

We consider two cases, whether u^2 is a prefix of v or not (see Figure 9.7).

Case 1. In this situation, u^2, which is a prefix of v, admits two different periods $|u|$ and $|t|$ that satisfy $|u| + |t| < |u^2|$. The Periodicity Lemma applies and shows that $\gcd(|u|, |t|)$ is also a period of u^2. But, as $\gcd(|u|, |t|) \leq |t| < |u|$, this implies that u is not primitive, in contradiction with the assumptions.

Case 2. In this case, v is a prefix of u^2. The string v possesses two distinct periods: $|u|$ and $|t|$. If $|u| + |t| \leq |v|$, the Periodicity Lemma applies to v and we get the same contradiction as in the previous case. We can thus assume that the converse holds, that is, $|u| + |t| > |v|$.

The string $s = u^{-1}v$ is both a prefix of u and a suffix of v. Its length satisfies $|s| < |t|$ because of the previous inequality, and is a period of u (since u occurs at positions $|u|$ and $|v|$ on w^2 and that $|s| = |v| - |u| \leq |u|$). Let finally $r = t^{-1}u$. We thus have $v = t \cdot r \cdot s$. We get a contradiction by showing again below that u possesses a period that strictly divides its length.

As $|t|$ is a period of v, the string $r \cdot s$ is also a prefix of v (Proposition 1.4). And as $|r \cdot s| < |r| + |t| = |u|$, $r \cdot s$ is even a proper prefix of u. It occurs thus in w^2 at positions $|t|$ and $|u|$. This proves that it has for period $|u| - |t| = |r|$. It also has for period $|s|$ that is a period of u. The Periodicity Lemma applies

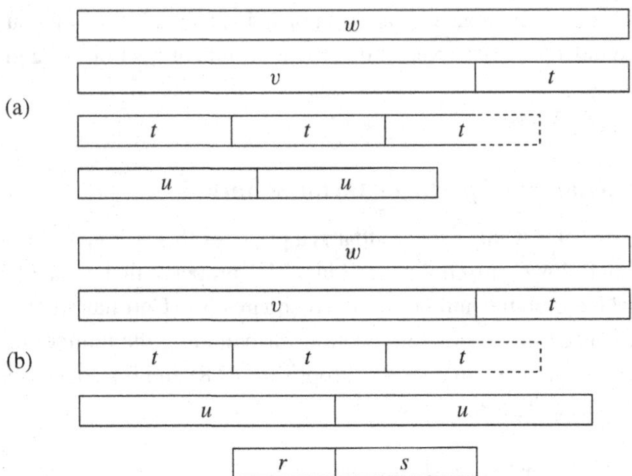

Figure 9.7. Illustration for the two impossible situations considered in the proof of Lemma 9.15. **(a)** Case 1. The string u^2 is a prefix of the string v. **(b)** Case 2. The string v is a prefix of the string u^2.

to $r \cdot s$, which has thus period $p = \gcd(|r|, |s|)$. Indeed, p is also a period of u since p divides $|s|$ that is a period of u.

Let us consider now the string u. It has for periods p and $|t|$ with the inequality $p + |t| \leq |r| + |t| = |u|$. The Periodicity Lemma applies to u, which has thus period $q = \gcd(p, |t|)$. But q divides $|t|$ and $|r|$, thus also their sum $|t| + |r| = |u|$. This contradicts the primitivity of u and ends Case 2.

As Cases 1 and 2 are impossible, the assumption $|u| + |v| > |w|$ leads to a contradiction, which proves the inequality of the statement. ■

Let us consider, for instance, the string aabaabaaabaabaabaaab that has for prefixes the squares $\mathtt{a}^2$, $(\mathtt{aab})^2$, $(\mathtt{aabaaba})^2$, and $(\mathtt{aabaabaaab})^2$. The three strings a, aab, and aabaaba satisfy the assumptions of Lemma 9.15, and their lengths satisfy the inequality: $1 + 3 < 7$. The three strings aab, aabaaba, and aabaabaaab also satisfy the assumptions of Lemma 9.15, and we have the equality: $3 + 7 = 10$. This example shows that the inequality of the statement of the lemma is tight.

Corollary 9.16

Every string y, $|y| > 1$, possesses less than $\log_\Phi |y|$ prefixes that are squares of primitive strings, that is to say

$$\mathrm{card}\{u : u \textit{ primitive and } u^2 \preceq_{\mathrm{pref}} y\} < \log_\Phi |y|.$$

Proof Let us set $\zeta(y) = \text{card}\{u : u \text{ primitive and } u^2 \preceq_{\text{pref}} y\}$. Let us first show by recurrence on c, $c \geq 1$, that

$$\zeta(y) \geq c \text{ implies } |y| \geq 2F_{c+1}.$$

For $c = 1$, we have $|y| \geq 2 = 2F_2$. For $c = 2$, we can check that $|y| \geq 6 > 2F_3 = 4$ (for instance, we have $\zeta(\texttt{aabaab}) = 6$).

Let us assume $\zeta(y) \geq c \geq 3$. Let $u, v, w \in A^+$ be the three longest distinct primitive strings whose squares are prefixes of y. We have $u^2 \prec_{\text{pref}} v^2 \prec_{\text{pref}} w^2$. The strings u^2 and v^2 satisfy thus respectively $\zeta(u^2) \geq c - 2$ and $\zeta(v^2) \geq c - 1$. By recurrence hypothesis, we get $|u^2| \geq 2F_{c-1}$ and $|v^2| \geq 2F_c$.

Lemma 9.15 gives the inequality $|u| + |v| \leq |w|$, which implies $|y| \geq |w^2| \geq |u^2| + |v^2| \geq 2F_{c-1} + 2F_c = 2F_{c+1}$ and ends the recurrence.

As $F_{c+1} \geq \Phi^{c-1}$ and $\Phi < 2$, we get $|y| \geq 2\Phi^{c-1} > \Phi^c$, that is, $c < \log_\Phi |y|$, which means that y possesses less than $\log_\Phi |y|$ prefixes, squares of primitive strings, as announced. ∎

The Fibonacci string $f_7 = \texttt{abaababaabaab}$ has two prefix squares of lengths 3 and 5. We can check, for $i \geq 5$, that f_i has $i - 5$ prefix squares and that $f_{i-2}{}^2$ is the longest one. Exercise 9.11 provides another sequence of strings that have the maximal possible number of prefix squares for a given length.

A direct application of the previous lemma shows that a string of length n cannot contain as factors more than $n \log_\Phi n$ squares of primitive strings. Actually, this bound can be refined as stated in the next proposition.

Proposition 9.17
Any string y, $|y| > 4$, contains at most $2|y| - 6$ factors that are squares of primitive strings, that is,

$$\text{card}\{u : u \textit{ primitive and } u^2 \preceq_{\text{fact}} y\} \leq 2|y| - 6.$$

Proof Let

$$E = \{u^2 : u \text{ primitive and } u^2 \preceq_{\text{fact}} y\}.$$

Let us consider three strings u^2, v^2, and w^2 of E, $u^2 \prec_{\text{pref}} v^2 \prec_{\text{pref}} w^2$. After Lemma 9.15, we have $|u| + |v| \leq |w|$ and thus $2|u| < |w|$, which implies $u^2 \prec_{\text{pref}} w$.

Let us assume that i is a position of u^2, v^2, and w^2 on y. Then i is not the largest position of u^2 on y. Thus, a position i cannot be the largest position of more than two strings of E. This shows that card $E \leq 2|y|$.

We note then that the position $|y| - 1$ is not the position of a string of E, and that each positions $|y| - 2$, $|y| - 3$, $|y| - 4$, $|y| - 5$, can be the largest position of at most one string of E. This reduces the previous upper bound and gives the bound $2|y| - 6$ of the statement. ∎

9.4 Sorting suffixes

An adaptation of the algorithm PARTITIONING (see Section 9.1) yields a lexicographic sorting of the suffixes of the string y. It simultaneously computes the prefixes common to the suffixes of y with the aim of realizing a suffix array (Chapter 4). With this method, the computation requires a linear memory space.

Incremental computation of the ranks of the suffixes

Let us recall, for $k > 0$, that we denote by $R_k[i]$ the rank (counted from position 0) of $\mathit{first}_k(y[i \mathinner{..} n-1])$ in the sorted list of the strings of the set $\{\mathit{first}_k(u) : u \text{ nonempty suffix of } y\}$, and that we set $i \equiv_k j$ if and only if $R_k[i] = R_k[j]$ (see Section 4.4). This equality is also equivalent to $E_k[i] = E_k[j]$ with the notation of Section 9.1.

For sorting the suffixes of y, we transform the algorithm PARTITIONING into the algorithm RANKS. The code of this latter algorithm is given thereafter. The modification consists in maintaining the classes of the current partition in increasing lexicographic order of the beginnings of length k of the suffixes. For this, the classes of the partition are organized as a list and the order of the list is an essential element for obtaining the final order on suffixes. The number of the position i class, denoted by $E_k[i]$ in Section 9.1 and whose value can be chosen relatively freely, is replaced here by the rank of the class in the list of classes, $R_k[i]$, that has a value independent of the implementation of the algorithm.

Another element of the algorithm PARTITIONING is modified in order to get the algorithm RANKS: it concerns the management of the small classes. Among the subclasses of a class C that is split during the partitioning, it is necessary to distinguish the classes that are before the chosen class of maximal size, and those that are after this latter class, in the list of the subclasses of C. They are stored respectively in two lists called *Before* and *After*, their union making the set of small classes, *Small*, considered in the algorithm PARTITIONING.

Finally, as for the algorithm PARTITIONING, the algorithm RANKS is not given in all its details; in particular, it is understood that the lists of subclasses and the twin classes are reset to the empty list after each step.

```
Ranks(y, n)
for r ← 0 to card alph(y) − 1 do
    C_r ← ∅
for i ← 0 to n − 1 do
    r ← rang of y[i] in the sorted list of letters of alph(y)
    C_r ← C_r ∪ {i}
Before ← ⟨⟩
After ← ⟨C_0, C_1, ..., C_{card alph(y)−1}⟩
k ← 1
while Before · After ≠ ⟨⟩ do
    ▷ Invariant: i ∈ C_r if and only if R_k[i] = r
    for each P ∈ Before · After, sequentially do
        for each i ∈ P \ {0} do
            let C be the class of i − 1
            let C_P be the twin class of C
            transfer i − 1 of C in C_P
        for each considered pair (C, C_P) do
            if P ∈ Before then
                SbClBe[C] ← SbClBe[C] · ⟨C_P⟩
            else SbClAf[C] ← SbClAf[C] · ⟨C_P⟩
    Before ← ⟨⟩
    After ← ⟨⟩
    for each class C considered in the previous step,
      in the order of the list of classes do
        if C ≠ ∅ then
            SbCl[C] ← SbClBe[C] · ⟨C⟩ · SbClAf[C]
        else SbCl[C] ← SbClBe[C] · SbClAf[C]
        in the list of classes, replace C by
          the elements of SbCl[C] in the order of this list
        G ← one class of maximal size in SbCl[C]
        Before ← Before · ⟨classes before G in SbCl[C]⟩
        After ← After · ⟨classes after G in SbCl[C]⟩
    k ← k + 1
return permutation of positions associated with the list of classes
```

Theorem 9.18

The algorithm Ranks *sorts the suffixes of* $y \in A^*$ *of length* n *in lexicographic order,* that is, *the permutation* $p = \text{Ranks}(y, n)$ *satisfies the condition*

$$y[p[0]\,..\,n-1] < y[p[1]\,..\,n-1] < \cdots < y[p[n-1]\,..\,n-1].$$

Proof We start by showing that the equivalence

$$i \in C_r \text{ if and only if } R_k[i] = r$$

is an invariant of the **while** loop. This amounts to show that the class of i is before the class of j in the list of classes at step k if and only if $R_k[i] < R_k[j]$, at each step. It is sufficient to show the direct implication since i and j belong to the same class at step k if and only if $i \equiv_k j$ after the proof of the algorithm PARTITIONING that applies here.

We assume the condition is satisfied at the beginning of step k and we examine the effect of the instructions of the **while** loop.

Let i, j be two positions such that $i \in C_r$, $j \in C_s$, and $r < s$ where C_r and C_s are classes according to $\equiv_{k+1}$. If $i \not\equiv_k j$, the relative order of the classes of i and j being conserved because of the instruction in line 26, the class of i precedes the one of j at step k. By assumption, we have thus $R_k[i] < R_k[j]$. This inequality implies $R_{k+1}[i] < R_{k+1}[j]$ by the definition of R.

We assume now $i \equiv_k j$. Let C be the class common to i and j according to the equivalence $\equiv_k$.

Let us assume that C_r and C_s are two before subclasses of C (in $SbClBe[C]$). Then $i+1$ and $j+1$ belong to two classes P' and P'' that are in this order in the list *Before*. By assumption we have thus

$$R_k[i+1] < R_k[j+1]$$

(thus $\mathit{first}_k(y[i+1\mathinner{.\,.}n-1]) < \mathit{first}_k(y[j+1\mathinner{.\,.}n-1])$), and also

$$R_{k+1}[i] < R_{k+1}[j]$$

(thus $\mathit{first}_{k+1}(y[i\mathinner{.\,.}n-1]) < \mathit{first}_{k+1}(y[j\mathinner{.\,.}n-1])$, see Figure 9.1), considering the way in which the list *Before* is made up in line 28. The argument is the same if i is placed in a before subclass of C and j in an after subclass of C, or if both i and j are placed in two after subclasses of C.

Let us assume for finishing that i is not touched and that j is placed in an after class at step k. Then, $i+1 \in G$ where G is a subclass of maximal size of its original class, or $i+1 = n$. The position $j+1$ belongs to an after subclass of the same original class since $i \equiv_{k-1} j$. As the subclass of $j+1$ is located after G due to the constitution of *After* (line 29), we have as previously $R_k[i+1] < R_k[j+1]$, then $R_{k+1}[i] < R_{k+1}[j]$. The argument is analogue when i is placed in a before class and j is untouched.

This ends the proof of the invariant.

For $k = 1$, we notice that the condition is fulfilled after the initialization. The algorithm stops when *Before* · *After* is empty, that is to say when the partition is stabilized, this occurs only when each class is reduced to a singleton. In

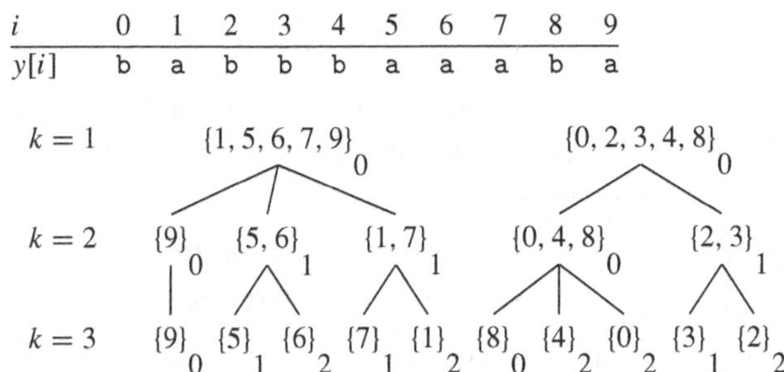

Figure 9.8. Operation Ranks applied to babbbaaaba for sorting its suffixes and computing the longest prefixes common to consecutive suffixes. The final sequence 9, 5, 6, ... gives the suffixes in increasing lexicographic order: a < aaaba < aaba < ⋯. For each class C, the value $LCP[C]$ is denoted by an index of C. Value $LCP[\{1\}] = 2$ indicates, for example, that the longest common prefix to the suffixes at positions 7 and 1, namely aba and abbbaaaba, has length 2.

this situation it comes from the condition that the obtained permutation of positions corresponds to the increasing sequence of values of R, that is to say the increasing sequence of the suffixes in the lexicographic order. Which ends the whole proof. ■

The example of Figure 9.8 follows the example of Figure 9.5. At line $k = 2$ we have one small before class, $\{9\}$, and two small after classes, $\{1, 7\}$ and $\{2, 3\}$. The partitioning at this step is done by taking the small classes in this order. The partitioning according to $\{9\}$ has for effect to extract 8 from its class $\{0, 4, 8\}$ that splits into $\{8\}$ and $\{0, 4\}$ in this order since $\{9\}$ is a before class. With $\{1, 7\}$, 0 is extracted from its class $\{0, 4\}$ that splits into $\{4\}$ and $\{0\}$ in this order since $\{1, 7\}$ is an after class. The positions 7, 2, and 3 are used in the same way. This leads respectively to split $\{5, 6\}$ into $\{5\}$ and $\{6\}$, $\{1, 7\}$ into $\{7\}$ and $\{1\}$, and finally $\{2, 3\}$ into $\{3\}$ and $\{2\}$. We get thus the partition of line $k = 3$ that is the final partition.

Computation of the common prefixes

We indicate how to extend the algorithm Ranks for obtaining a simultaneous computation of the longest common prefixes of the suffixes that are consecutive in the sorted sequence.

For this, we assign to each class C a value denoted by $LCP(C)$ that is the maximal length of the common prefixes between the elements of C and those of the previous class in the list of classes. These values are all initialized to 0.

We know that at step k all the elements of a same class have the same prefix of length k.

The computation of $LCP(C')$ occurs when C' is a new class, subclass of a class C for which $LCP(C)$ is defined. The definition of $LCP(C')$ can be done during the instruction in line 26 using the relation

$$LCP[C'] = \begin{cases} LCP[C] & \text{if } C' \text{ is the first class of } SbCl[C], \\ k & \text{for the other classes of } SbCl[C]. \end{cases}$$

It is easy to see that this rule leads to a correct computation of LCP.

Figure 9.8 illustrates the computation of the common prefixes. At step $k = 2$, the class $\{0, 4, 8\}$ splits into $\{8\}$, $\{4\}$, $\{0\}$. We thus get $LCP[\{8\}] = LCP[\{0, 4, 8\}] = 0$ for the first subclass, then $LCP[\{4\}] = LCP[\{0\}] = k = 2$ for the other two subclasses.

At the end of the execution of the algorithm Ranks, each class contains a single element. If $C = \{i\}$, we have $LCP[C] = LCP[i]$ with the notation of Section 4.3. The rest of the computation of the table LCP, which is the computation of the other components needed for the suffix array, can be done as in Chapter 4.

The analysis of the execution time of the algorithm Partitioning also holds for Ranks. The previous description shows that the computation of the prefixes common to the suffixes does not modify the asymptotic upper bound on the running time of the algorithm. We thus get the next result analogue to the results of Sections 4.4 and 4.6 put together and valid on any alphabet.

Theorem 9.19

The preparation of the suffix array of a string of length n can be performed in time $O(n \log n)$ and linear space by adapting the algorithm Ranks. ■

Notes

The partitioning method described in this chapter finds its origin in an algorithm for minimizing deterministic automata by Hopcroft [155]. The algorithm of Section 9.1 is a variant of it that applies not only to strings but also to graphs (see Cardon and Crochemore [113]). Extensions of the method have been proposed by Paige and Tarjan [196].

The utilization of the partitioning of positions on a string for determining the local powers is from Crochemore [118]. Apostolico and Preparata [97] show that the computation can be performed by means of a suffix tree. Slisenko [208] also proposed a method that relies on a data structure similar to the suffix automaton.

The algorithm SQUARE-IN is from Main and Lorentz [179] who gave a direct algorithm to implement the function *ltest* (see Exercise 9.8). The algorithm is also a basic element of a method for finding all the occurrences of squares proposed by the same authors (see [180]) and whose complexity is the same as the two above methods. They also show that the algorithm is optimal among those that only use letter comparisons of the type $=$ and $\neq$. The algorithm SQUARE-IN (see Crochemore [119]) is also optimal in the class of algorithms that compare letters by means of $<$, $=$, and $>$ assuming an ordering on the alphabet. A method based on naming (see Chapter 4) reaches the same computation time (see Main and Lorentz [181]).

For the utilization of the suffix tree to the detection of squares in a string, we refer to Stoye and Gusfield [210] who designed a linear-time algorithm. The detection of powers in genomic sequences, called tandem repeats, where an approximate notion is necessary was designed by Benson [102] and generated many software implementations.

The Three-Prefix-Square Lemma is from Crochemore and Rytter [129]. Another proof from Diekert can be found in the chapter of Mignosi and Restivo in [80]. This chapter deals in a deeply way on periodicities in strings.

The bound of $2n$ on the number of squares in a string of length n (Proposition 9.17) was established by Fraenkel and Simpson [139]. The exact number of squares in the Fibonacci string, that inspired the previous authors, was evaluated by Iliopoulos, Moore, and Smyth [160]. A simple and direct proof of the result from Dean Hickerson was communicated to us in 2003 by Gusfield. Another simple proof is by Ilie [159]. See also Lothaire [81], Chapter 8.

Kolpakov and Kucherov [172] have extended the previous result by showing that the number of occurrences of the two-sided maximal periodicities, called runs in [160], is still linear. In the meantime they proposed a linear-time algorithm (on a fixed alphabet) to detect these occurrences, improving the result of Main in [178]. They also conjectured that a string of length n has less than n runs. Rytter [201] proved that it is less than $5n$.

The algorithm of Section 9.4 is close to the one described by Manber and Myers [182] for the preparation of a suffix array.

Exercises

9.1 (Tree of squares)

Indicate how to transform the suffix tree of a string y for storing all the factors of y that are squares of a primitive string.

Give a linear-time algorithm that performs the transformation. (*Hint:* see Stoye and Gusfield [210].)

9.2 (Fractional power)

We call fractional exponent of a nonempty string x the quantity

$$\exp(x) = |x|/\text{per}(x).$$

Show, for every integer $k > 1$, that $\exp(x) = k$ if and only if $x = u^k$ for a primitive string u. (In other words the notion of exponent introduced in Chapter 1 and the notion of fractional exponent match in this case.)

Write a linear-time algorithm that computes the fractional exponents of all the prefixes of a string y.

Describe an algorithm running in time $O(n \log n)$ for the computation of the maximal fractional powers of a string of length n. (*Hint:* see Main [178].)

9.3 (Maximal power)

Show that a string of length n contains $O(n)$ occurrences of maximal fractional powers. Give an algorithm that computes them all in time $O(n \times \log \text{card}\, A)$. (*Hint:* see Kolpakov and Kucherov [172].)

9.4 (Thue-Morse morphism)

An ***overlap*** is a string of the form $auaua$ with $a \in A$ and $u \in A^*$. Show that a string x contains (as factor) an overlap if and only if it possesses a nonempty factor v for which $\exp(v) > 2$.

On the alphabet $A = \{\texttt{a}, \texttt{b}\}$, we consider the morphism (see Exercise 1.2) $g: A^* \to A^*$ defined by $g(\texttt{a}) = \texttt{ab}$ and $g(\texttt{b}) = \texttt{ba}$. Show that, for every integer $k \geq 0$, the string $g^k(\texttt{a})$ contains no overlap. (*Hint:* see Lothaire [79].)

9.5 (Overlap-free string)

On the alphabet $A = \{\texttt{a}, \texttt{b}\}$ we consider the substitution g of Exercise 9.4 and the sets:

$$E = \{\texttt{aabb}, \texttt{bbaa}, \texttt{abaa}, \texttt{babb}\},$$
$$F = \{\texttt{aabab}, \texttt{bbaba}\},$$
$$G = \{\texttt{abba}, \texttt{baab}, \texttt{baba}, \texttt{abab}\},$$
$$H = \{\texttt{aabaa}, \texttt{bbabb}\}.$$

Let $x \in A^*$ be an overlap-free string. Show that, if x has a prefix in $E \cup F$, then $x[j] \neq x[j-1]$ for each odd integer j satisfying the condition $3 \leq j \leq |x| - 2$. Show that, if x has a prefix in $G \cup H$, then $x[j] \neq x[j-1]$ for each even integer j satisfying the condition $4 \leq j \leq |x| - 2$.

Show that, if $|x| > 6$, x decomposes in a unique way into $d_x \cdot u \cdot f_x$ with $d_x, f_x \in \{\varepsilon, \texttt{a}, \texttt{b}, \texttt{aa}, \texttt{bb}\}$ and $u \in A^*$.

Show that the string x decomposes in a unique way into

$$d_1 d_2 \ldots d_r \cdot g^{r-1}(u) \cdot f_r \ldots f_2 f_1$$

with $|u| < 7$, $r \in \mathbf{N}$ and

$$d_s, f_s \in \{\varepsilon, g^{s-1}(\mathtt{a}), g^{s-1}(\mathtt{b}), g^{s-1}(\mathtt{aa}), g^{s-1}(\mathtt{bb})\}.$$

Deduce that the number of overlap-free strings of length n grows polynomially according to n. (*Hint:* see Restivo and Salemi [200].)

9.6 (Overlap test)

Deduce from the decomposition of the overlap-free strings of Exercise 9.5 a linear-time algorithm that tests if a string contains an overlap. (*Hint:* see Kfoury [168].)

9.7 (No square)

On the alphabet $A = \{\mathtt{a}, \mathtt{b}, \mathtt{c}\}$, we consider the morphism (see Exercise 1.2) $h\colon A^* \to A^*$ defined by $h(\mathtt{a}) = \mathtt{abc}$, $h(\mathtt{b}) = \mathtt{ac}$, and $h(\mathtt{c}) = \mathtt{b}$. Show, for every integer $k \geq 0$, that the string $h^k(\mathtt{a})$ contains no square. (*Hint:* see Lothaire [79].)

9.8 (Left test)

Detail the proof of Lemma 9.10.

Give an implementation of the function *ltest* that computes *ltest*(u, v) in time $O(|u|)$ using only an extra constant space. (*Hint:* compute sequentially $p_{v,u}[i]$ for well chosen values of i; see Main and Lorentz [179].)

9.9 (Only three squares)

Show that 3 is the smallest integer for which there exist arbitrarily long strings $y \in \{\mathtt{a}, \mathtt{b}\}^*$ satisfying

$$\mathrm{card}\{u : u \neq \varepsilon \text{ and } u^2 \preceq_{\mathrm{fact}} y\} = 3.$$

(*Hint:* see Fraenkel and Simpson [139].)

9.10 (Forth power)

Show that $\mathtt{b}^2$, $\mathtt{a}^3$, babab, and aabaabaa are not factors of Fibonacci strings.

Show that if $u^2 \preceq_{\mathrm{fact}} f_k$, u is a conjugate of a Fibonacci string. (*Hint:* when $|u| > 2$ study the case $u \in \mathtt{a}\{\mathtt{a}, \mathtt{b}\}^+$, and then check that the case $u \in \mathtt{b}\{\mathtt{a}, \mathtt{b}\}^+$ amounts to the previous one.)

Deduce that no Fibonacci string contains forth powers (factor of exponent 4). (*Hint:* see Karhumäki [163].)

9.11 (Prefix squares)

We consider the sequence $\langle g_i : i \in \mathbf{N}\rangle$ of strings of $\{\mathtt{a}, \mathtt{b}\}^*$ defined by $g_0 = \mathtt{a}$, $g_1 = \mathtt{aab}$, $g_2 = \mathtt{aabaaba}$, and, for $i \geq 3$, $g_i = g_{i-1}g_{i-2}$.

Check that ${g_i}^2$ possesses $i + 1$ prefix squares.

Show that if $y \in \{\mathtt{a}, \mathtt{b}\}^*$ possesses $i + 1$ prefixes that are squares of primitive strings, then $|y| \geq 2|g_i|$.

For $i \geq 3$, show that if $y \in \{\mathtt{a}, \mathtt{b}\}^*$ possesses $i + 1$ prefixes that are squares of primitive strings and $|y| = 2|g_i|$, then, up to a permutation of the letters a and b, $y = {g_i}^2$. (*Hint:* see Crochemore and Rytter [129].)

9.12 (Non primitive)

Let $u, v, w \in A^+$ be three strings that satisfy the conditions: $u^2 \prec_{\text{pref}} v^2 \prec_{\text{pref}} w^2$. Show directly, that is, without using the Three Prefix Square Lemma, that u is a suffix of v; deduce Proposition 9.17. Show indeed that u, v, and w are powers of the same string. (*Hint:* see Ilie [159] and Lothaire [80].)

9.13 (Prefix powers)

Let k be an integer, $k \geq 2$, and let $u, v, w \in A^+$ be three strings that satisfy the conditions: $u^k \prec_{\text{pref}} v^k \prec_{\text{pref}} w^k$, and u, v are primitive strings. Show that $|u| + (k-1)|v| \leq |w|$. (*Hint:* for $k \geq 3$ we can use the Primitivity Lemma.)

9.14 (Prefix powers, again)

Let an integer $k \geq 2$. Show that a string y, $|y| > 1$, possesses less than $\log_{\alpha(k)} |y|$ prefixes that are kth powers of primitive strings, that is to say

$$\text{card}\{u : u \text{ primitive and } u^k \preceq_{\text{pref}} y\} < \log_{\alpha(k)} |y|,$$

where

$$\alpha(k) = \frac{k - 1 + \sqrt{(k-1)^2 + 4}}{2}.$$

9.15 (Lot of squares)

Give an infinite family of strings that contain as factor the maximal possible number of squares of primitive strings.

9.16 (Ranks)

Implement the algorithm Ranks.

9.17 (Perfect factorization)

Let $x \in A^+$. Show that there exists a position i on x that satisfies the two properties: $i < 2 \times \text{per}(x)$, and at most one prefix of $x[i \,..\, |x| - 1]$ is of the form u^3, u primitive. (*Hint:* see Galil and Seiferas [144], or [4].)

9.18 (Prefix periodicities)

Let $u, v \in A^+$ be two primitive strings such that $|u| < |v|$.

Show that

$$|lcp(uu, vv)| < |u| + |v| - \gcd(|u|, |v|).$$

Show that there exists a conjugate v' of v for which

$$|lcp(u^\infty, v'v')| \leq \frac{2}{3}(|u| + |v|).$$

Show that each inequality is tight. (*Hint:* use the Periodicity Lemma and see Breslauer, Jiang, and Jiang [111]; see also Mignosi and Restivo in [80].)

Bibliography

Books

Books on string algorithmics.

1. A. Apostolico and Z. Galil, editors. *Pattern Matching Algorithms*. Oxford University Press, Oxford, 1997.
2. C. Charras and T. Lecroq. *Handbook of Exact String Matching Algorithms*. King's College London Publications, London, 2004.
3. M. Crochemore, C. Hancart, and T. Lecroq. *Algorithmique du texte*. Vuibert, Paris, 2001.
4. M. Crochemore and W. Rytter. *Text Algorithms*. Oxford University Press, Oxford, 1994.
5. M. Crochemore and W. Rytter. *Jewels of Stringology*. World Scientific Press, Singapore, 2002.
6. D. Gusfield. *Algorithms on Strings, Trees, and Sequences: Computer Science and Computational Biology*. Cambridge University Press, Cambridge, UK, 1997.
7. G. Navarro and M. Raffinot. *Flexible Pattern Matching in Strings – Practical On-line Search Algorithms for Texts and Biological Sequences*. Cambridge University Press, Cambridge, UK, 2002.
8. W. F. Smyth. *Computing Patterns in Strings*. Addison-Wesley Longman, Reading, MA, 2003.
9. G. A. Stephen. *String Searching Algorithms*. World Scientific Press, Singapore, 1994.

Collections of articles

Collections of articles on string algorithmics that, except the first one, have been edited as special issues of journals or as conference proceedings.

10. J.-I. Aoe, editor. *String Pattern Matching Strategies*. IEEE Computer Society Press, Los Alamitos, CA, 1994.
11. A. Apostolico, editor. String algorithmics and its applications. *Algorithmica*, 12(4/5), 1994.
12. A. Apostolico and Z. Galil, editors. *Combinatorial Algorithms on Words*, Vol. 12. Springer-Verlag, Berlin, 1985.

13. M. Crochemore and L. Gąsieniec, editors. Matching patterns. *J. Discrete Algorithms*, 1(1), 2000.
14. C. S. Iliopoulos and T. Lecroq, editors. *String Algorithmics*. King's College London Publications, London, 2004.
15. W. F. Smyth, editor. Computing patterns in strings. *Fundamenta Informaticae*, 56(1/2), 2003.
16. M. Crochemore, editor. Proceedings of the 1st Annual Symposium on Combinatorial Pattern Matching. *Theoret. Comput. Sci.*, 92(1), 1992.
17. A. Apostolico, M. Crochemore, Z. Galil, and U. Manber, editors. *Proceedings of the 3rd Annual Symposium on Combinatorial Pattern Matching*, Tucson, Arizona. Lecture Notes in Computer Science, Vol. 664. Springer-Verlag, Berlin, 1992.
18. A. Apostolico, M. Crochemore, Z. Galil, and U. Manber, editors. *Proceedings of the 4th Annual Symposium on Combinatorial Pattern Matching*, Padova, Italia. Lecture Notes in Computer Science, Vol. 684. Springer-Verlag, Berlin, 1993.
19. M. Crochemore and D. Gusfield, editors. *Proceedings of the 5th Annual Symposium on Combinatorial Pattern Matching*, Asilomar, California. Lecture Notes in Computer Science, Vol. 807. Springer-Verlag, Berlin, 1994.
20. Z. Galil and E. Ukkonen, editors. *Proceedings of the 6th Annual Symposium on Combinatorial Pattern Matching*, Espoo, Finland. Lecture Notes in Computer Science, Vol. 937. Springer-Verlag, Berlin, 1995.
21. D. S. Hirschberg and E. W. Myers, editors. *Proceedings of the 7th Annual Symposium on Combinatorial Pattern Matching*, Laguna Beach, California. Lecture Notes in Computer Science, Vol. 1075. Springer-Verlag, Berlin, 1996.
22. A. Apostolico and J. Hein, editors. *Proceedings of the 8th Annual Symposium on Combinatorial Pattern Matching*, Aarhus, Denmark. Lecture Notes in Computer Science, Vol. 1264. Springer-Verlag, Berlin, 1997.
23. M. Farach-Colton, editor. *Proceedings of the 9th Annual Symposium on Combinatorial Pattern Matching*, Piscataway, New Jersey. Lecture Notes in Computer Science, Vol. 1448. Springer-Verlag, Berlin, 1998.
24. M. Crochemore and M. Paterson, editors. *Proceedings of the 10th Annual Symposium on Combinatorial Pattern Matching*, Warwick, UK. Lecture Notes in Computer Science, Vol. 1645. Springer-Verlag, Berlin, 1999.
25. R. Giancarlo and D. Sankoff, editors. *Proceedings of the 11th Annual Symposium on Combinatorial Pattern Matching*, Montreal, Canada. Lecture Notes in Computer Science, Vol. 1848. Springer-Verlag, Berlin, 2000.
26. A. Amir and G. M. Landau, editors. *Proceedings of the 12th Annual Symposium on Combinatorial Pattern Matching*, Jerusalem, Israel. Lecture Notes in Computer Science, Vol. 2089. Springer-Verlag, Berlin, 2001.
27. A. Apostolico and M. Takeda, editors. *Proceedings of the 13th Annual Symposium on Combinatorial Pattern Matching* Fukuoka, Japan. Lecture Notes in Computer Science, Vol. 2373. Springer-Verlag, Berlin, 2002.
28. R. A. Baeza-Yates, E. Chávez, and M. Crochemore, editors. *Proceedings of the 14th Annual Symposium on Combinatorial Pattern Matching*, Morelia, Michocán, Mexico. Lecture Notes in Computer Science, Vol. 2676. Springer-Verlag, Berlin, 2003.
29. S. C. Sahinalp, S. Muthukrishnan, and U. Dogrusöz, editors. *Proceedings of the 15th Annual Symposium on Combinatorial Pattern Matching*, Istanbul,

Turkey. Lecture Notes in Computer Science, Vol. 3109. Springer-Verlag, Berlin, 2004.

30. A. Apostolico, M. Crochemore, and K. Park, editors. *Proceedings of the 16th Annual Symposium on Combinatorial Pattern Matching*, Jeju Island, Korea. Lecture Notes in Computer Science, Vol. 3537. Springer-Verlag, Berlin, 2005.
31. M. Lewenstein and G. Valiente, editors. *Proceedings of the 17th Annual Symposium on Combinatorial Pattern Matching*, Barcelona, Spain. Lecture Notes in Computer Science, Vol. 4009. Springer-Verlag, Berlin, 2006.
32. R. Baeza-Yates and N. Ziviani, editors. *Proceedings of the 1st South American Workshop on String Processing*, Minas Gerais, Brazil. Universidade Federal de Minas Gerais, 1993.
33. R. Baeza-Yates and U. Manber, editors. *Proceedings of the 2nd South American Workshop on String Processing*, Valparaiso, Chile. University of Chile, Santiago, 1995.
34. N. Ziviani, R. Baeza-Yates, and K. Guimarães, editors. *Proceedings of the 3rd South American Workshop on String Processing*, Recife, Brazil. Carleton University Press, Montréal, 1996.
35. R. Baeza-Yates, editor. *Proceedings of the 4th South American Workshop on String Processing*, Valparaiso, Chili. Carleton University Press, Montréal, 1997.
36. R. Capocelli, editor. *Sequences, Combinatorics, Compression, Security, and Transmission.* Springer-Verlag, Berlin, 1990.
37. R. Capocelli, A. De Santis, and U. Vaccaro, editors. *Sequences II*. Springer-Verlag, Berlin, 1993.
38. B. Carpentieri, A. De Santis, U. Vaccaro, and J. A. Storer, editors. *Compression and Complexity of Sequences.* IEEE Computer Society, Los Alamitos, CA, 1987.
39. J. Holub, editor. *Proceedings of the Prague Stringology Club Workshop.* Czech Technological University, Prague, 1996.
40. J. Holub, editor. *Proceedings of the Prague Stringology Club Workshop.* Czech Technological University, Prague, 1997.
41. J. Holub and M. Šimánek, editors. *Proceedings of the Prague Stringology Club Workshop.* Czech Technological University, Prague, 1998.
42. J. Holub and M. Šimánek, editors. *Proceedings of the Prague Stringology Club Workshop.* Czech Technological University, Prague, 1999.
43. M. Balík and M. Šimánek, editors. *Proceedings of the Prague Stringology Conference*, Prague. Czech Technological University, Prague, 2000.
44. M. Balík and M. Šimánek, editors. *Proceedings of the Prague Stringology Conference*, Prague. Czech Technological University, Prague, 2001.
45. M. Balík and M. Šimánek, editors. *Proceedings of the Prague Stringology Conference*, Prague. Czech Technological University, Prague, 2002.
46. M. Balík and M. Šimánek, editors. *Proceedings of the Prague Stringology Conference*, Prague. Czech Technological University, Prague, 2003.
47. J. Holub and M. Šimánek, editors. *Proceedings of the Prague Stringology Conference*, Prague. Czech Technological University, Prague, 2004.
48. J. Holub and M. Šimánek, editors. *Proceedings of the Prague Stringology Conference*, Prague. Czech Technological University, Prague, 2005.
49. J. Holub and J. Zdárek, editors. *Proceedings of the Prague Stringology Conference*, Prague. Czech Technological University, Prague, 2006.

Web sites

Some Web sites devoted to string algorithmics. They contain bibliographies, animations of algorithms, pointers to researchers who work on the topics, and different information related to the domain.

50. S. Lonardi. *Pattern Matching Pointers.* `http://www.cs.ucr.edu/~stelo/pattern.html`
51. C. Charras and T. Lecroq. *Exact String Matching Algorithms.* `http://monge.univ-mlv.fr/~lecroq/string/`
52. C. Charras and T. Lecroq. *Sequence Comparison.* `http://monge.univ-mlv.fr/~lecroq/seqcomp/`
53. T. Lecroq. *Bibliography on Stringology.* `http://monge.univ-mlv.fr/~lecroq/tq-en.html`

Applications

Some references on two important domains of application of string algorithmics which are information retrieval, including computational linguistic, and computational biology.

54. S. Aluru, editor. *Handbook of Computational Molecular Biology*, Vol. 9. Chapman and Hall/CRC Computer and Information Science Series, London, 2006.
55. T. K. Attwood and D. J. Parry-Smith. *Introduction to Bioinformatics.* Addison-Wesley Longman Limited, Reading, MA, 1999.
56. R. Baeza-Yates and B. Ribeiro-Neto. *Modern Information Retrieval.* Addison-Wesley, Reading, MA, 1999.
57. R. Durbin, S. Eddy, A. Krogh, and G. Mitchison. *Biological Sequence Analysis Probabilistic Models of Proteins and Nucleic Acids.* Cambridge University Press, Cambridge, UK, 1998.
58. W. B. Frakes and R. Baeza-Yates, editors. *Information Retrieval: Data Structures and Algorithms.* Prentice-Hall, Englewood Cliffs, NJ, 1992.
59. M. Gross and D. Perrin, editors. *Electronic Dictionaries and Automata in Computational Linguistics.* Lecture Notes in Computer Science, Vol. 377. Springer-Verlag, Berlin, 1989.
60. N. C. Jones and P. A. Pevzner. *An Introduction to Bioinformatics Algorithms.* The MIT Press, Cambridge, MA, 2004.
61. A. K. Konopka and M. J. C. Crabbe. *Compact Handbook of Computational Biology.* CRC Press, Boca Raton, FL, 2004.
62. E. W. Myers, editor. Computational molecular biology. *Algorithmica*, 13(1/2), 1995.
63. P. Pevzner. *Computational Molecular Biology: An Algorithmic Approach.* The MIT Press, Cambridge, MA, 2000.
64. É. Roche and Y. Schabes, editors. *Finite State Language Processing.* The MIT Press, Cambridge, MA, 1997.
65. G. Salton. *Automatic Text Processing.* Addison-Wesley, Reading, MA, 1989.

66. D. Sankoff and J. Kruskal, editors. *Time Warps, String Edits, and Macromolecules: The Theory and Practice of Sequence Comparison*, 2nd edition. Cambridge University Press, Cambridge, UK, 1999.
67. J. C. Setubal and J. Meidanis. *Introduction to Computational Molecular Biology*. PWS Publishing Company, 1997.
68. M. S. Waterman. *Introduction to Computational Biology*. Chapman and Hall, London, 1995.

Algorithmics and combinatorics

Textbooks on algorithmics that contain at least one chapter on string algorithmics, and books presenting formal aspects in connection with the subject.

69. A. V. Aho, J. E. Hopcroft, and J. D. Ullman. *Data Structures and Algorithms*. Addison-Wesley, Reading, MA, 1983.
70. A. V. Aho, R. Sethi, and J. D. Ullman. *Compilers – Principles, Techniques, and Tools*. Addison-Wesley, Reading, MA, 1986.
71. M.-P. Béal. *Codage symbolique*. Masson, Paris, 1993.
72. D. Beauquier, J. Berstel, and P. Chrétienne. *Éléments d'algorithmique*. Masson, Paris, 1992.
73. J. Berstel. *Transductions and Context-Free Languages*. Teubner, Leipzig, 1979.
74. J. Berstel and D. Perrin. *Theory of Codes*. Academic Press, New York, 1985.
75. T. H. Cormen, C. E. Leiserson, and R. L. Rivest. *Introduction to Algorithms*. The MIT Press, Cambridge, MA, 1990.
76. G. H. Gonnet and R. Baeza-Yates. *Handbook of Algorithms and Data Structures*. Addison-Wesley, Reading, MA, 1991.
77. M. T. Goodrich and R. Tamassia. *Data Structures and Algorithms in Java*. John Wiley & Sons, New York, 1998.
78. D. E. Knuth. *The Art of Computer Programming: Fundamental Algorithms*. Addison-Wesley, Reading, MA, 1973.
79. M. Lothaire, editor. *Combinatorics on Words*, 2nd edition. Cambridge University Press, Cambridge, UK, 1997.
80. M. Lothaire, editor. *Algebraic Combinatorics on Words*. Cambridge University Press, Cambridge, UK, 2002.
81. M. Lothaire, editor. *Applied Combinatorics on Words*. Cambridge University Press, Cambridge, UK, 2005.
82. J.-É. Pin. *Variétés de langages formels*. Masson, Paris, 1984.
83. R. Sedgewick and P. Flajolet. *An Introduction to the Analysis of Algorithms*. Addison-Wesley Professional, Reading, MA, 1995.
84. W. Szpankowski. *Average Case Analysis of Algorithms on Sequences*. Wiley-Interscience Series in Discrete Mathematics, New York, 2001.

Articles

Articles mentioned in the bibliographic notes.

85. K. R. Abrahamson. Generalized string matching. *SIAM J. Comput.*, 16(6):1039–1051, 1987.

86. A. V. Aho. Algorithms for finding patterns in strings. In J. van Leeuwen, editor, *Handbook of Theoretical Computer Science, Algorithms, and complexity*, Vol. A, pp. 255–300. Elsevier, Amsterdam, 1990.
87. A. V. Aho and M. J. Corasick. Efficient string matching: An aid to bibliographic search. *Comm. ACM*, 18(6):333–340, 1975.
88. C. Allauzen, M. Crochemore, and M. Raffinot. Factor oracle: A new structure for pattern matching. In J. Pavelka, G. Tel, and M. Bartosek, editors, *SOFSEM'99, Theory and Practice of Informatics* (Milovy, Tcheque Republic), pp. 291–306. Lecture Notes in Computer Science, Vol. 1725. Springer-Verlag, Berlin, 1999.
89. L. Allison and T. I. Dix. A bit-string longest-common-subsequence algorithm. *Inform. Process. Lett.*, 23(6):305–310, 1986.
90. S. F. Altschul, W. Gish, W. Miller, E. W. Myers, and D. J. Lipman. A basic local alignment search tool. *J. Mol. Biol.*, 215:403–410, 1990.
91. A. Amir, M. Lewenstein, and E. Porat. Faster algorithms for string matching with k mismatches. *J. Algorithms*, 50(2):257–275, 2004.
92. G. Andrejková. The longest restricted common subsequence problem. In J. Holub and M. Šimánek, editors, *Proceedings of the Prague Stringology Club Workshop*, pp. 14–25. Czech Technological University, Prague, 1998.
93. A. Apostolico. The myriad virtues of subword trees. In A. Apostolico and Z. Galil, editors, *Combinatorial Algorithms on Words*, Vol. 12, pp. 85–96. Springer-Verlag, Berlin, 1985.
94. A. Apostolico. String editing and longest common subsequences. In G. Rozenberg and A. Salomaa, editors, *Handbook of Formal Languages*, pp. 361–398. Springer-Verlag, Berlin, 1997.
95. A. Apostolico and R. Giancarlo. The Boyer–Moore–Galil string searching strategies revisited. *SIAM J. Comput.*, 15(1):98–105, 1986.
96. A. Apostolico and R. Giancarlo. Sequence alignment in molecular biology. *J. Comput. Biol.*, 5(2):173–196, 1998.
97. A. Apostolico and F. P. Preparata. Optimal off-line detection of repetitions in a string. *Theoret. Comput. Sci.*, 22(3):297–315, 1983.
98. R. A. Baeza-Yates. Improved string searching. *Softw. Pract. Exp.*, 19(3):257–271, 1989.
99. R. A. Baeza-Yates and G. H. Gonnet. A new approach to text searching. *Comm. ACM*, 35(10):74–82, 1992.
100. H. Bannai, S. Inenaga, A. Shinohara, and M. Takeda. Inferring strings from graphs and arrays. In *Proceedings of the 28th International Symposium on Mathematical Foundations of Computer Science (MFCS 2003)*, pp. 208–217. Lecture Notes in Computer Science, Vol. 2747. Springer-Verlag, Berlin, 2003.
101. M.-P. Béal, M. Crochemore, and G. Fici. Presentations of constrained systems with unconstrained positions. *IEEE Trans. Inform. Theory*, 51(5):1891–1900, 2005.
102. G. Benson. Tandem repeats finder – a program to analyze DNA sequences. *Nucleic Acids Res.*, 27:573–580, 1999.
103. J. L. Bentley and R. Sedgewick. Fast algorithms for sorting and searching strings. In *Proceedings of the 8th ACM-SIAM Annual Symposium on Discrete Algorithms*, New Orleans, Louisiana, pp. 360–369. ACM Press, New York, 1997.
104. J. L. Bentley and R. Sedgewick. Ternary search trees. *Dr. Dobb's J.*, 1998.

105. A. Blumer, J. Blumer, A. Ehrenfeucht, D. Haussler, M. T. Chen, and J. Seiferas. The smallest automaton recognizing the subwords of a text. *Theoret. Comput. Sci.*, 40(1):31–55, 1985.
106. A. Blumer, J. Blumer, D. Haussler, R. M. McConnell, and A. Ehrenfeucht. Complete inverted files for efficient text retrieval and analysis. *J. ACM*, 34(3):578–595, 1987.
107. A. Blumer, A. Ehrenfeucht, and D. Haussler. Average size of suffix trees and DAWGS. *Discrete. Appl. Math.*, 24:37–45, 1989.
108. K. S. Booth. Lexicographically least circular substrings. *Inform. Process. Lett.*, 10(4):240–242, 1980.
109. R. S. Boyer and J. S. Moore. A fast string searching algorithm. *Comm. ACM*, 20(10):762–772, 1977.
110. D. Breslauer, L. Colussi, and L. Toniolo. On the comparison complexity of the string prefix-matching problem. *J. Algorithms*, 29(1):18–67, 1998.
111. D. Breslauer, T. Jiang, and Z. Jiang. Rotations of periodic strings and short superstrings. *J. Algorithms*, 24(2):340–353, 1997.
112. E. Cambouropoulos, M. Crochemore, C. S. Iliopoulos, L. Mouchard, and Y. J. Pinzon. Algorithms for computing approximate repetitions in musical sequences. In R. Raman and J. Simpson, editors, *Proceedings of the 10th Australasian Workshop on Combinatorial Algorithms*, Perth, Australia, pp. 129–144. Curtin University Press, Perth, 1999.
113. A. Cardon and M. Crochemore. Partitioning a graph in $O(|A| \log_2 |V|)$. *Theoret. Comput. Sci.*, 19(1):85–98, 1982.
114. R. Cole. Tight bounds on the complexity of the Boyer–Moore string matching algorithm. *SIAM J. Comput.*, 23(5):1075–1091, 1994.
115. R. Cole and R. Hariharan. Faster suffix tree construction with missing suffix links. In *32nd Annual ACM Symposium on Theory of Computing*, pp. 407–415. ACM Press, New York, 2000.
116. R. Cole, R. Hariharan, M. Paterson, and U. Zwick. Tighter lower bounds on the exact complexity of string matching. *SIAM J. Comput.*, 24(1):30–45, 1995.
117. S. Constantinescu and L. Ilie. Generalized Fine and Wilf's theorem for arbitrary number of periods. *Theoret. Comput. Sci.*, 339(1):49–60, 2005.
118. M. Crochemore. An optimal algorithm for computing the repetitions in a word. *Inform. Process. Lett.*, 12(5):244–250, 1981.
119. M. Crochemore. Transducers and repetitions. *Theoret. Comput. Sci.*, 45(1):63–86, 1986.
120. M. Crochemore. Longest common factor of two words. In H. Ehrig, R. Kowalski, G. Levi, and U. Montanari, editors, *TAPSOFT*, pp. 26–36. Lecture Notes in Computer Science, Vol. 249. Springer-Verlag, Berlin, 1987.
121. M. Crochemore, A. Czumaj, L. Gąsieniec, S. Jarominek, T. Lecroq, W. Plandowski, and W. Rytter. Speeding up two string matching algorithms. *Algorithmica*, 12(4/5):247–267, 1994.
122. M. Crochemore, A. Czumaj, L. Gąsieniec, T. Lecroq, W. Plandowski, and W. Rytter. Fast practical multi-pattern matching. *Inform. Process. Lett.*, 71(3–4):107–113, 1999.

123. M. Crochemore, C. S. Iliopoulos, and Y. J. Pinzon. Speeding-up Hirschberg and Hunt-Szymanski LCS algorithms. *Fundamenta Informaticae*, 56(1,2):89–103, 2003.
124. M. Crochemore, G. M. Landau, and M. Ziv-Ukelson. A sub-quadratic sequence alignment algorithm for unrestricted cost matrices. *SIAM J. Comput.*, 32(6):1654–1673, 2003.
125. M. Crochemore and T. Lecroq. Tight bounds on the complexity of the Apostolico-Giancarlo algorithm. *Inform. Process. Lett.*, 63(4):195–203, 1997.
126. M. Crochemore, F. Mignosi, and A. Restivo. Automata and forbidden words. *Inform. Process. Lett.*, 67(3):111–117, 1998.
127. M. Crochemore, F. Mignosi, A. Restivo, and S. Salemi. Data compression using antidictionaries. *Proc. IEEE*, 88(11):1756–1768, 2000.
128. M. Crochemore and D. Perrin. Two-way string-matching. *J. Assoc. Comput. Mach.*, 38(3):651–675, 1991.
129. M. Crochemore and W. Rytter. Squares, cubes, and time-space efficient string-searching. *Algorithmica*, 13(5):405–425, 1995.
130. M. Crochemore and R. Vérin. On compact directed acyclic word graphs. In J. Mycielski, G. Rozenberg, and A. Salomaa, editors, *Structures in Logic and Computer Science*, pp. 192–211. Lecture Notes in Computer Science, Vol. 1261. Springer-Verlag, Berlin, 1997.
131. S. Dori and G. M. Landau. Construction of Aho–Corasick automaton in linear time for integer alphabets. *Inform. Process. Lett.*, 98:66–72, 2006.
132. J.-P. Duval, T. Lecroq, and A. Lefebvre. Border array on bounded alphabet. *J. Autom. Lang. Comb.*, 10(1):51–60, 2005.
133. J.-P. Duval, R. Kolpakov, G. Kucherov, T. Lecroq, and A. Lefebvre. Linear-time computation of local periods. *Theoret. Comput. Sci.*, 326(1–3):229–240, 2004.
134. M. Farach-Colton. Optimal suffix tree construction with large alphabets. In *Proceedings of the 38th IEEE Annual Symposium on Foundations of Computer Science*, Miami Beach, Florida, pp. 137–143. IEEE Computer Society Press, Los Alamitos, CA, 1997.
135. M. Farach-Colton, G. Landau, S. C. Sahinalp, and D. Tsur. Optimal spaced seeds for faster approximate string matching. In *Proceedings of the 32th International Colloquium on Automata, Languages, and Programming*, Lisbon, Portugal, pp. 1251–1262. Lecture Notes in Computer Science, Vol. 3580. Springer-Verlag, Berlin, 2005.
136. P. Ferragina and R. Grossi. The string B-tree: A new data structure for string search in external memory and its applications. *J. ACM*, 46:236–280, 1999.
137. P. Ferragina and G. Manzini. Indexing compressed text. *J. ACM*, 52(4):552–581, 2005.
138. M. J. Fischer and M. Paterson. String matching and other products. In R. M. Karp, editor, *Proceedings of the SIAM-AMS Complexity of Computation*, pp. 113–125. 1974.
139. A. S. Fraenkel and R. J. Simpson. How many squares can a string contain? *J. Combin. Theory Ser. A*, 82:112–120, 1998.
140. F. Franěk, S. Gao, W. Lu, P. Ryan, W. Smyth, Y. Sun, and L. Yang. Verifying a border array in linear time. *J. Comb. Math. Comb. Comput.*, 42:223–236, 2002.

141. K. Fredriksson and S. Grabowski. Practical and Optimal String Matching. In *Proceedings of the 12th International Symposium on String Processing and Information Retrieval*, Buenos Aires, Argentina, pp. 374–385. Lecture Notes in Computer Sciences, Vol. 3772. Springer-Verlag, Berlin, 2005.
142. Z. Galil. On improving the worst case running time of the Boyer–Moore string searching algorithm. *Comm. ACM*, 22(9):505–508, 1979.
143. Z. Galil. Open problems in stringology. In A. Apostolico and Z. Galil, editors, *Combinatorial Algorithms on Words*, Vol. 12, pp. 1–8. Springer-Verlag, Berlin, 1985.
144. Z. Galil and J. Seiferas. Time-space optimal string matching. *J. Comput. Syst. Sci.*, 26(3):280–294, 1983.
145. L. Gąsieniec, W. Plandowski, and W. Rytter. Constant-space string matching with smaller number of comparisons: Sequential sampling. In Z. Galil and E. Ukkonen, editors, *Proceedings of the 6th Annual Symposium on Combinatorial Pattern Matching*, Espoo, Finland. Lecture Notes in Computer Science, Vol. 937, pp. 78–89. Springer-Verlag, Berlin, 1995.
146. O. Gotoh. An improved algorithm for matching biological sequences. *J. Mol. Biol.*, 162:705–708, 1982.
147. R. Grossi and J. S. Vitter. Compressed suffix arrays and suffix trees with applications to text indexing and string matching. *SIAM J. Comput.*, 35(2):378–407, 2005.
148. C. Hancart. *Analyse exacte et en moyenne d'algorithmes de recherche d'un motif dans un texte*. Report 93-11, Institut Gaspard-Monge, Université de Marne-la-Vallée, France, 1993.
149. C. Hancart. On Simon's string searching algorithm. *Inform. Process. Lett.*, 47(2):95–99, 1993.
150. D. Harel and R. E. Tarjan. Fast algorithms for finding nearest common ancestors. *SIAM J. Comput.*, 13(2):338–355, 1984.
151. S. Henikoff and J. G. Henikoff. Performance evaluation of amino acid substitution matrices. *Proteins*, 17:49–61, 1993.
152. D. S. Hirschberg. A linear space algorithm for computing maximal common subsequences. *Comm. ACM*, 18(6):341–343, 1975.
153. D. S. Hirschberg. An information-theoretic lower bound for the longest common subsequence problem. *Inform. Process. Lett.*, 7(1):40–41, 1978.
154. J. Holub, C. S. Iliopoulos, B. Melichar, and L. Mouchard. Distributed pattern matching using finite automata. *J. Autom. Lang. Comb.*, 6(2):191–204, 2001.
155. J. E. Hopcroft. An $n \log n$ algorithm for minimizing the states in a finite-automaton. In Z. Kohavi, editor, *Theory of Machines and Computations*, pp. 189–196. Academic Press, New York, 1971.
156. R. N. Horspool. Practical fast searching in strings. *Softw. Pract. Exp.*, 10(6):501–506, 1980.
157. A. Hume and D. M. Sunday. Fast string searching. *Softw. Pract. Exp.*, 21(11):1221–1248, 1991.
158. J. W. Hunt and T. G. Szymanski. A fast algorithm for computing longest common subsequences. *Comm. ACM*, 20(5):350–353, 1977.
159. L. Ilie. A simple proof that a word of length n has at most $2n$ distinct squares. *J. Combin. Theory Ser. A*, 112(1):163–164, 2005.

160. C. S. Iliopoulos, D. Moore, and W. F. Smyth. A characterization of the squares in a Fibonacci string. *Theor. Comput. Sci.*, 172(1–2):281–291, 1997.
161. S. Inenaga, H. Hoshino, A. Shinohara, M. Takeda, S. Arikawa, G. Mauri, and G. Pavesi. On-line construction of compact directed acyclic word graphs. In A. Amir and G. M. Landau, editors, *Proceedings of the 12th Annual Symposium on Combinatorial Pattern Matching*, Jerusalem, Israel. Lecture Notes in Computer Science, Vol. 2089, pp. 169–180. Springer-Verlag, Berlin, 2001.
162. R. W. Irving and L. Love. The suffix binary search tree and suffix AVL tree. *J. Discrete Algorithms*, 1:387–408, 2003.
163. J. Karhumäki. On cube-free ω-words generated by binary morphisms. *Discrete Appl. Math.*, 5:279–297, 1983.
164. J. Kärkkäinen and P. Sanders. Simple linear work suffix array construction. In J. C. M. Baeten, J. K. Lenstra, J. Parrow, and G. J. Woeginger, editors, *Proceedings of the 30th International Colloquium on Automata, Languages, and Programming*, Eindhoven, The Netherlands, pp. 943–955. Lecture Notes in Computer Science, Vol. 2719. Springer-Verlag, Berlin, 2003.
165. R. M. Karp, R. E. Miller, and A. L. Rosenberg. Rapid identification of repeated patterns in strings, trees, and arrays. In *Proceedings of the 4th ACM Symposium on the Theory of Computing*, pp. 125–136. ACM Press, New York, 1972.
166. R. M. Karp and M. O. Rabin. Efficient randomized pattern-matching algorithms. *IBM J. Res. Develop.*, 31(2):249–260, 1987.
167. T. Kasai, G. Lee, H. Arimura, S. Arikawa, and K. Park. Linear-time longest-common-prefix computation in suffix arrays and its applications. In A. Amir and G. M. Landau, editors, *Proceedings of the 12th Annual Symposium on Combinatorial Pattern Matching*, Jerusalem, Israel. Lecture Notes in Computer Science, Vol. 2089, pp. 181–192. Springer-Verlag, Berlin, 2001.
168. A. J. Kfoury. A linear-time algorithm to decide whether a binary word contains an overlap. *Bull. Europ. Assoc. Theoret. Comput. Sci.*, 30:74–80, 1986.
169. D. K. Kim, J. S. Sim, H. Park, and K. Park. Linear-time construction of suffix arrays. In R. A. Baeza-Yates, E. Chávez, and M. Crochemore, editors, *Proceedings of the 14th Annual Symposium on Combinatorial Pattern Matching*, Morelia, Michocán, Mexico. Lecture Notes in Computer Science, Vol. 2676, pp. 186–199. Springer-Verlag, Berlin, 2003.
170. D. E. Knuth, J. H. Morris Jr., and V. R. Pratt. Fast pattern matching in strings. *SIAM J. Comput.*, 6(1):323–350, 1977.
171. P. Ko and S. Aluru. Space Efficient Linear Time Construction of Suffix Arrays. In R. A. Baeza-Yates, E. Chávez, and M. Crochemore, editors, *Proceedings of the 14th Annual Symposium on Combinatorial Pattern Matching*, Morelia, Michocán, Mexico. Lecture Notes in Computer Science, Vol. 2676, pp. 200–210. Springer-Verlag, Berlin, 2003.
172. R. Kolpakov and G. Kucherov. Finding maximal repetitions in a word in linear time. In *Proceedings of the 40th Symposium on Foundations of Computer Science*, New York, pp. 596–604. IEEE Computer Society Press, Los Alamitos, CA, 1999.
173. S. Kurtz. Reducing the space requirement of suffix trees. *Softw. Pract. Exp.*, 29(13):1149–1171, 1999.
174. G. M. Landau and U. Vishkin. Efficient string matching with k mismatches. *Theoret. Comput. Sci.*, 43(2–3):239–249, 1986.

175. G. M. Landau and U. Vishkin. Fast string matching with k differences. *J. Comput. Syst. Sci.*, 37(1):63–78, 1988.
176. V. I. Levenshtein. Binary codes capable of correcting deletions, insertions, and reversals. *Sov. Phys. Dokl.*, 6:707–710, 1966.
177. B. Ma, J. Tromp, and M. Li. PatternHunter: Faster and more sensitive homology search. *Bioinformatics*, 18(3):440–445, 2002.
178. M. G. Main. Detecting leftmost maximal periodicities. *Discrete Appl. Math.*, 25:145–153, 1989.
179. M. G. Main and R. J. Lorentz. An $O(n \log n)$ algorithm for recognizing repetition. Report CS-79-056, Washington State University, Pullman, 1979.
180. M. G. Main and R. J. Lorentz. An $O(n \log n)$ algorithm for finding all repetitions in a string. *J. Algorithms*, 5(3):422–432, 1984.
181. M. G. Main and R. J. Lorentz. Linear time recognition of square-free strings. In A. Apostolico and Z. Galil, editors, *Combinatorial Algorithms on Words*, Vol. 12, pp. 272–278. Springer-Verlag, Berlin, 1985.
182. U. Manber and G. Myers. Suffix arrays: A new method for on-line string searches. *SIAM J. Comput.*, 22(5):935–948, 1993.
183. W. J. Masek and M. S. Paterson. A faster algorithm for computing string edit distances. *J. Comput. Syst. Sci.*, 20(1):18–31, 1980.
184. E. M. McCreight. A space-economical suffix tree construction algorithm. *J. Algorithms*, 23(2):262–272, 1976.
185. B. Melichar. Approximate string matching by finite automata. In V. Hlavác and R. Sára, editors, *Computer Analysis of Images and Patterns*, pp. 342–349. Lecture Notes in Computer Science, Vol. 970. Springer-Verlag, Berlin, 1995.
186. S. Miyamoto, S. Inenaga, M. Takeda, and A. Shinohara. Ternary directed acyclic word graphs. In O. H. Ibarra and Z. Dang, editors, *8th International Conference on Implementation and Application of Automata*, Santa Barbara, California, USA, pp. 120–130. Springer-Verlag, Berlin, 2003.
187. S. Mohanty. Shortest string containing all permutations. *Discrete Math.*, 31:91–95, 1980.
188. J. H. Morris Jr. and V. R. Pratt. *A linear pattern-matching algorithm.* Report 40, University of California, Berkeley, 1970.
189. J. I. Munro, V. Raman, and S. S. Rao. Space efficient suffix trees. *J. Algorithms*, 39(2):205–222, 2001.
190. S. Muthukrishnan. Efficient algorithms for document retrieval problems. In *Proceedings of the 13th ACM-SIAM Annual Symposium on Discrete Algorithms*, San Francisco, California, pp. 657–666. ACM Press, New York, 2002.
191. E. W. Myers. An $O(ND)$ difference algorithm and its variations. *Algorithmica*, 1:251–266, 1986.
192. E. W. Myers and W. Miller. Optimal alignment in linear space. *CABIOS*, 4(1):11–17, 1988.
193. G. Navarro. A guided tour to approximate string matching. *ACM Comp. Surv.*, 33(1):31–88, 2001.
194. S. B. Needleman and C. D. Wunsch. A general method applicable to the search for similarities in the amino acid sequence of two proteins. *J. Mol. Biol.*, 48:443–453, 1970.

195. L. Noe and G. Kucherov. YASS: Enhancing the sensitivity of DNA similarity search. *Nucleic Acids Res.*, 33(2):W540–W543, 2005.
196. R. Paige and R. E. Tarjan. Three partition refinement algorithms. *SIAM J. Comput.*, 16(6):973–989, 1987.
197. W. R. Pearson and D. J. Lipman. Improved tools for biological sequence comparison. *Proc. Natl. Acad. Sci. U.S.A.*, 85:2444–2448, 1988.
198. M. Raffinot. Asymptotic estimation of the average number of terminal states in DAWGs. In R. Baeza-Yates, editor, *Proceedings of the 4th South American Workshop on String Processing*, Valparaiso, Chili, pp. 140–148. Carleton University Press, 1997.
199. M. Raffinot. On the multi backward DAWG matching algorithm (Multi-BDM). In R. Baeza-Yates, editor, *Proceedings of the 4th South American Workshop on String Processing*, Valparaiso, Chili, pp. 149–165. Carleton University Press, 1997.
200. A. Restivo and S. Salemi. Some decision results on non-repetitive words. In A. Apostolico and Z. Galil, editors, *Combinatorial Algorithms on Words*, Vol. 12, pp. 289–295. Springer-Verlag, Berlin, 1985.
201. W. Rytter. The number of runs in a string: Improved analysis of the linear upper bound. In *Proceedings of the 23rd Annual Symposium on Theoretical Aspects of Computer Science*, Marseille, France, pp. 184–195. Lecture Notes in Computer Science, Vol. 3884. Springer-Verlag, Berlin, 2006.
202. K. Sadakane and R. Grossi. Squeezing succinct data structures into entropy bounds. In *Proceedings of the Seventeenth Annual ACM-SIAM Symposium on Discrete Algorithms*, Miami, Florida, USA, pp. 1230–1239. ACM Press, New York, 2006.
203. D. Sankoff. The early introduction of dynamic programming into computational biology. *Bioinformatics*, 16(1):41–47, 2000.
204. A. Sardinas and C. Patterson. A necessary and sufficient condition for the unique decomposition of coded messages. *IRE Intern. Conv. Record*, 8:104–108, 1953.
205. B. Schieber and U. Vishkin. On finding lowest common ancestors: Simplification and parallelization. *SIAM J. Comput.*, 17(6):1253–1262, 1988.
206. A. Schönhage and V. Strassen. Schnelle multiplikation grosser zahlen. *Computing (Arch. Elektron. Rechnen)*, 7:281–292, 1971.
207. I. Simon. String matching algorithms and automata. In R. Baeza-Yates and N. Ziviani, editors, *Proceedings of the 1st South American Workshop on String Processing*, Minas Gerais, Brazil, pp. 151–157. Universidade Federal de Minas Gerais, 1993.
208. A. O. Slisenko. Detection of periodicities and string matching in real time. *J. Soviet Math.*, 22:1316–1386, 1983.
209. T. F. Smith and M. S. Waterman. Identification of common molecular sequences. *J. Mol. Biol.*, 147:195–197, 1981.
210. J. Stoye and D. Gusfield. Simple and flexible detection of contiguous repeats using a suffix tree. In M. Farach-Colton, editor, *Proceedings of the 9th Annual Symposium on Combinatorial Pattern Matching*, Piscataway, New Jersey. Lecture Notes in Computer Science, Vol. 1448, pp.140–152. Springer-Verlag, Berlin, 1998.
211. D. M. Sunday. A very fast substring search algorithm. *Comm. ACM*, 33(8):132–142, 1990.

212. E. Ukkonen. Algorithms for approximate string matching. *Inform. Control*, 64(1–3):100–118, 1985.
213. E. Ukkonen. Finding approximate patterns in strings. *J. Algorithms*, 6(1–3):132–137, 1985.
214. E. Ukkonen. On-line construction of suffix trees. *Algorithmica*, 14(3):249–260, 1995.
215. R. A. Wagner and M. Fischer. The string-to-string correction problem. *J. ACM*, 21(1):168–173, 1974.
216. P. Weiner. Linear pattern matching algorithm. In *Proceedings of the 14th Annual IEEE Symposium on Switching and Automata Theory*, pp. 1–11. Washington, DC, 1973.
217. C. K. Wong and A. K. Chandra. Bounds for the string editing problem. *J. ACM*, 23(1):13–16, 1976.
218. S. Wu and U. Manber. Fast text searching allowing errors. *Comm. ACM*, 35(10):83–91, 1992.
219. A. C. Yao. The complexity of pattern matching for a random string. *SIAM J. Comput.*, 8:368–387, 1979.
220. R. F. Zhu and T. Takaoka. On improving the average case of the Boyer–Moore string matching algorithm. *J. Inform. Process.*, 10(3):173–177, 1987.

Index

This index contains author names, keywords displayed in bold face in the text, algorithm names, notations, and some selected terms of the text.

Printed in the United States
By Bookmasters